NONVERBAL COMMUNICATION IN HUMAN INTERACTION

SIXTH EDITION

MARK L. KNAPP
The University of Texas at Austin

JUDITH A. HALL
Northeastern University

THOMSON
WADSWORTH

Australia • Canada • Mexico • Singapore • Spain • United Kingdom • United States

THOMSON

WADSWORTH

Nonverbal Communication in Human Interaction, Sixth Edition
Mark L. Knapp and Judith A. Hall

Publisher: Holly J. Allen
Acquisitions Editor: Annie Mitchell
Assistant Editor: Aarti Jayaraman
Editorial Assistant: Trina Enriquez
Senior Technology Project Manager:
  Jeanette Wiseman
Senior Marketing Manager: Kimberly Russell
Marketing Assistant: Andrew Keay
Marketing Communications Manager: Shemika Britt
Project Manager, Editorial Production: Christine Sosa
Art Director: Maria Epes

Print Buyer: Karen Hunt
Permissions Editor: Sarah Harkrader
Production Service: Dennis Troutman,
  Stratford Publishing Services, Inc.
Photo Researcher: Kate Gould
Copy Editor: Rebecca Greenberg
Cover Designer: Denise Davidson
Cover Image: Illustration Works
Cover Printer: Webcom
Compositor: Interactive Composition Corporation
Printer: Webcom

Printed in the Canada
1 2 3 4 5 6 7 09 08 07 06 05

For more information about our products, contact us at:
Thomson Learning Academic Resource Center
1-800-423-0563

For permission to use material from this text or product, submit a request online at
http://www.thomsonrights.com.
Any additional questions about permissions can be submitted by email to
thomsonrights@thomson.com.

Library of Congress Control Number: 2004116430

ISBN 0-534-62563-0

Thomson Higher Education
10 Davis Drive
Belmont, CA 94002-3098
USA

Asia (including India)
Thomson Learning
5 Shenton Way
#01-01 UIC Building
Singapore 068808

Australia/New Zealand
Thomson Learning Australia
102 Dodds Street
Southbank, Victoria 3006
Australia

Canada
Thomson Nelson
1120 Birchmount Road
Toronto, Ontario M1K 5G4
Canada

UK/Europe/Middle East/Africa
Thomson Learning
High Holborn House
50–51 Bedford Row
London WC1R 4LR
United Kingdom

CONTENTS

PREFACE

Normally, the final thing authors do in a preface is to thank those who have been instrumental in the development of their book. We'd like to depart from that tradition somewhat by starting with our heartfelt thanks to the thousands of students and instructors who have used and provided feedback during the past 33 years. More than anyone else, you are responsible for the longevity of this book. With this in mind, we undertook this sixth edition by putting what we believe to be instructor and student needs at the forefront of our writing. As with previous editions, we encourage you to let us know whether or not we have succeeded.

The fact that this book is co-authored is worth noting. One of us represents the field of communication and the other social psychology. This collaboration, which requires the blending of two distinct perspectives, is symbolic of the nonverbal literature we report in this volume. The theory and research addressing nonverbal phenomena comes from scholars with a wide variety of academic backgrounds and perspectives—for example, communication, counseling, psychology, psychiatry, linguistics, sociology, management, speech, and others. Understanding the nature of nonverbal communication is truly an interdisciplinary enterprise.

In revising this book, we retained the features that students and instructors valued from the previous edition while changing other things that we expect will improve the book. Chapter 13, Nonverbal Messages in Special Contexts, is new. It is in response to readers who wanted us to increase our emphasis on the role of nonverbal behavior in situations familiar to them. Readers also recognize how important photographs and drawings are in a book like this, so we have continued to use visual representations to aid comprehension of certain nonverbal actions.

In every new edition we incorporate the most recent theory and research while retaining definitive studies from the past. Readers will find that some areas of study have fewer recent references than others. This means that there hasn't been much recent research in that area or that, in our judgment, the recent work does not substantially change the conclusions from earlier studies. Research on a particular topic has an ebb and flow to it. During the 1960s and 1970s, the fear that a worldwide population boom would create terrible problems spawned a lot of research on space, territory, and crowding. In recent years there has been far less research in this area. Gestures, on the other hand, has gone from an area of relatively little research activity during the 1960s and 1970s to an area that is of primary interest to numerous scholars today. To accommodate the explosion of interest in this area, an academic journal, *Gesture*, was first published in 2001.

As in past editions, extensive bibliographies follow each chapter, and we have tried to retain a writing style that is scientifically accurate as well as interesting to the reader. We are honored that our book serves as both a textbook and a reference work. Rhonda Sprague's excellent *Instructor's Manual* for this book provides the information and imagination necessary for effective classroom learning in nonverbal communication.

The book is divided into five parts. Part I introduces the reader to some fundamental ideas and addresses the following questions: What is nonverbal communication? How do verbal and nonverbal communication interrelate? What difference does a knowledge of nonverbal communication make to your everyday life? Are some people more skilled than others at communicating nonverbally? How did they get that way? With this general perspective in mind, Parts II, III, and IV take the reader through the nonverbal elements involved in any interaction: the environment within which the interaction occurs; the physical features of the two interactants themselves; and their behavior (gestures, touching, facial expressions, eye gazing, and vocal sounds). Part V begins with a chapter focused on how all these separate parts of an interaction combine as we seek to accomplish very common goals in daily life—for example, communicating who we are, communicating closeness and distance, and communicating varying degrees of status and/or power; deceiving others; and effectively managing the back-and-forth flow of conversation itself. The last chapter examines nonverbal communication in the context of advertising, therapy, the classroom, politics, and culture. Throughout the book we repeatedly point out how all interactants involved are likely to play a role in whatever behavior is displayed by a single individual—even though this perspective is not always adequately developed in the research we review.

Each of us would like to thank following reviewers for their input during the development of this edition:

Kristen Berkos, Bryant College

Donald Boggs, Anderson University

Narissra Carter, Texas Tech University

Rozell R. Duncan, Kent State University

Michael Howard Eaves, Valdosta State University

Erika Engstrom, University of Nevada, Las Vegas

Sheryl A. Friedley, George Mason University

Ann Herron, Stevens Henager College

Marian L. Houser, Texas State University—San Marcos

Kenneth M. Johnson, Syracuse University

Marc Martin, San Francisco State University

Lisa Miczo, Western Illinois University

Heidi L. Miller, University of Northern Colorado

Christine North, Jamestown College

Clara Popa, Kent State University

Kenna J. Reeves, Emporia State University

Kyra Rothenberg, Kent State University

Shauna Smith, Tallahassee Community College

Mary-Jeanette Smythe, University of Missouri

Doyle Srader, Stephen F. Austin State University

Lesa Stern, Southern Illinois University, Edwardsville

Terry M. Thibodeaux, Sam Houston State University

William R. Todd-Mancillas, California State University, Chico

Michael Weatherson, Southeast Missouri State University

Dennis L. Wignall, Saginaw Valley State University

Richard Wiseman, California State University, Fullerton

Merle Wm. Ziegler, Mississippi College

Both of us would also like to acknowledge the skills exhibited by the publishing staff who helped us develop this edition: Annie Mitchell, acquisitions editor; Aarti Jayaraman, assistant editor; Trina Enriquez, editorial assistant; Maria Epes, executive art director; and Christine Sosa, production project manager.

Part One

AN INTRODUCTION TO THE STUDY OF NONVERBAL COMMUNICATION

What is nonverbal communication? How does nonverbal behavior function in relation to verbal behavior? How does nonverbal communication affect our everyday lives? Do we learn how to perform body language or is it instinctive? Are some people more skilled at communicating with these face, voice, and body signals? The answers to these fundamental questions are the focus of Part One.

Chapter 1

NONVERBAL COMMUNICATION: BASIC PERSPECTIVES

*Those of us who keep our eyes open can read volumes into what we
see going on around us.*

—E. T. HALL

Herr von Osten purchased a horse in Berlin in 1900. When von Osten began training his horse, Hans, to count by tapping his front hoof, he had no idea that Hans would soon become one of the most celebrated horses in history. Hans was a rapid learner and soon progressed from counting to adding, multiplying, dividing, subtracting, and eventually solving problems involving factors and fractions. Even more startling, when von Osten exhibited Hans to public audiences, he counted the size of the crowd or the number wearing eyeglasses. Responding only with taps, Hans could tell time, use a calendar, recall musical pitch, and perform numerous other seemingly fantastic feats. After von Osten taught Hans an alphabet that could be coded into hoofbeats, the horse could answer virtually any question—oral or written. It seemed that Hans, a common horse, had complete comprehension of the German language, the ability to produce the equivalent of words and numerals, and an intelligence beyond that of many human beings.

Even without promotion by the mass media, the word spread quickly, and Hans became known throughout the world. He was soon dubbed "Clever Hans." Because of the profound implications for several scientific fields and because some skeptics thought a gimmick was involved, an investigating committee was established to decide whether deceit tainted Hans's performances. Professors of psychology and physiology, the director of the Berlin Zoological Garden, a director of a circus, veterinarians, and cavalry officers were appointed to this commission. An experiment with Hans from which von Osten was absent demonstrated no change in the apparent intelligence of the horse. This was sufficient proof for the commission to announce that no trickery was involved.

But the appointment of a second commission was the beginning of the end for Clever Hans. Von Osten was asked to whisper a number into the horse's left ear while another experimenter whispered a number into the horse's right ear. Hans was told to add the two numbers—an answer none of the onlookers, von Osten, or the experimenter knew. Hans failed. And with further tests, he continued to fail. The experimenter, Pfungst, had discovered that Hans could answer a question only if someone in his visual field knew the answer and was attentive to the situation (Pfungst, 1911/1965).

When Hans was given the question, onlookers who knew the answer assumed an expectant posture, increased their body tension, and bent their heads slightly forward. When Hans reached the correct number of taps, the onlookers would relax and make a slight upward movement of their heads—which was Hans's signal to stop tapping. Evidence suggests that Hans could detect head movements as slight as one-fifth of a millimeter. Subsequent experiments found that Hans also would cease tapping as a knowledgeable onlooker raised his or her eyebrows or even showed a dilation of the nostrils.

The story of Clever Hans functions as a vivid introduction to the field of nonverbal communication (Sebeok & Rosenthal, 1981; Sebeok & Umiker-Sebeok, 1980). Hans's cleverness was not in his ability to verbalize or understand verbal commands but in his ability to respond to almost imperceptible and unconscious movements by those surrounding him (Spitz, 1997). A French horse named Clever Bertrand may have developed his cleverness from entirely different, but equally subtle, signals—although he was not studied scientifically. It is reported that Bertrand could do everything that Hans could do, but Bertrand was blind! Indeed, some of the experiments with Hans had also shown that when auditory cues were added to the visual, Hans's accuracy increased. So Hans's cleverness was not limited to visual cues.

The story of Clever Hans makes two important points regarding the role of nonverbal behavior in human encounters:

1. While we are in the presence of another person, we are constantly giving signals about our attitudes, feelings, and personality.
2. Others may become particularly adept at sensing and interpreting these signals.

This ability is not unlike the perceptiveness or sensitivity to nonverbal cues exhibited by a Clever Carl, Christine, Frank, or Harriet when closing a business deal, presenting an intelligent and industrious image to a professor, knowing when to leave a party, and acting wisely in many other common situations. We also make interpretations about the *absence* of cues, as well as react to particular cues. For example, when a nephew does not get his usual greeting kiss from his favorite aunt, he wonders what is wrong. (Perhaps he never noticed the kiss nearly as much as he notices its absence.) As another example, when a doctor tries to act professionally neutral by being somewhat blank and unexpressive, the patient is likely to read the lack of cues as aloofness or disinterest, perhaps even suspecting the doctor of withholding important information. This is a good example of how what we *think* we are communicating may be very different from what we are actually communicating.

The purpose of this book is to expand your conscious awareness of the numerous nonverbal stimuli that you produce and confront in your everyday dialogue. Each chapter summarizes behavioral science research in a specific area of nonverbal communication. First, however, let's develop five basic perspectives through which we can view the remaining chapters:

1. Defining nonverbal communication
2. Classifying nonverbal behavior
3. Nonverbal communication in the total communication process

4. The history of nonverbal studies
5. Nonverbal communication in everyday life

PERSPECTIVE 1: DEFINING NONVERBAL COMMUNICATION

To most people, the phrase *nonverbal communication* refers to *communication effected by means other than words* (assuming words are the verbal element). Like most definitions, this one is generally useful, but it does not account adequately for the complexity of this phenomenon. As long as we understand and appreciate the points listed here, this broad definition should serve us well.

First, we need to understand that separating verbal and nonverbal behavior into two separate and distinct categories is virtually impossible. Consider, for example, the hand movements that make up American Sign Language (a language of the deaf). These gesticulations are mostly linguistic (verbal), yet hand gestures are often considered behavior that is "other than words." McNeill (1992) has demonstrated the linguistic qualities of some gestures by noting that different kinds of gestures disappear with different kinds of aphasia, namely, those gestures with linguistic functions similar to the specific verbal loss. Conversely, not all spoken words are clearly or singularly verbal—as, for example, onomatopoeic words such as *buzz* or *murmur* and nonpropositional speech used by auctioneers and some aphasics.

We also need to understand that our definition does not indicate whether the phrase "means other than words" refers to the type of signal *produced* (encoded) or to the perceiver's code for *interpreting* (decoding) the signal. Generally, when people refer to nonverbal behavior, they are talking about the signals to which meaning will be attributed (encoding), not the process of decoding meaning. Let's see what we can learn by examining the encoding and decoding of nonverbal signals in more detail.

ENCODING

Verbal and nonverbal signals can be coded in many different ways. For example, Ekman and Friesen (1969) ask us to consider the following continuum:

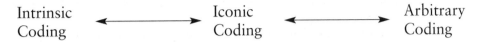

Intrinsic Coding ⟵⟶ Iconic Coding ⟵⟶ Arbitrary Coding

Before these terms are explained, it is important to remember the following:

1. Behavior is a continuum, not discrete categories. A behavior may be identified that seems to fall between two of these points.
2. Although verbal behavior seems suited primarily for the right side of the continuum and nonverbal for the middle and left, there are exceptions.
3. The primary distinguishing feature among these three types of coding is the proximity of the code to its referent, that is, the thing it refers to.

Arbitrary coding puts the greatest distance between the code used and referents for the code. Resemblance to the referent is nonexistent. Most words, for instance, are arbitrarily coded with letters that show no resemblance to the things they refer to. Neither the word *cat* nor any of its letters looks like a cat. Onomatopoeic words, however, such as *buzz* and *murmur,* do take on aspects of the sounds they try to describe. Some nonverbal signals also may be arbitrarily coded; for example, the motions involved in hand waving during the good-bye ritual do not seem to portray the activity of leaving with much fidelity.

Iconic coding preserves some aspects of the referent; that is, there is some resemblance between the code and the referent. Tracing an hourglass shape in the air to symbolize a shapely man or woman is an example of iconic coding, as is holding your hand to mimic a handgun, "slitting" your throat with your finger to indicate that you are "finished," or indicating with your hands how close to someone you would like to stand (with each hand representing a person).

Intrinsic coding puts the least distance between the code used and the referents for the code. At the extreme, it might be said that the manner of coding is the referent itself. Pointing, moving closer to someone, or actually hitting the person are examples of behaviors that do not resemble something else; they *are* the thing they represent. In short, nonverbal behavior can be encoded intrinsically, iconically, or arbitrarily even though arbitrary coding is primarily associated with verbal behavior.

DECODING

Currently, many brain researchers believe that the two hemispheres of the brain specialize in different information processing. Nonverbal messages may be processed by either hemisphere even though the bulk of the work is probably done by the right side. The left hemisphere processes mainly sequentially ordered, digital, verbal, and linguistic information. Nonverbal messages processed by the left hemisphere may involve symbolic gestures and facial expressions that have a closely linked verbal translation—for example, the "speech-independent" gestures noted in chapter 7. The right hemisphere of the brain is normally credited with processing visual/spatial relationships and analogic or Gestalt information. It seems to be the main processing unit for our spontaneous expressive displays, which include facial displays of emotion as well as vocal features that contribute emotion to our voice, for example, stress, rhythm, and pitch (Buck & VanLear, 2002). It is important to remember, though, that few scientists currently believe that either side of the brain deals *exclusively* with a particular kind of information. In fact, the following case illustrates how adaptable the brain can be.

Bruce Lipstadt had the left hemisphere of his brain removed when he was 5.5 years old (Koutlak, 1976). Few doctors had hope for the development of his verbal ability, and most thought the operation would paralyze part of his body. Twenty-six years later, Bruce had an IQ of 126 (better than 9 out of 10 people), swam, rode his bike, and got an A in a statistics course. Because his speech was normal, it was assumed the right side took over many of the functions formerly conducted mainly by the left side. Obviously, this does not always happen as a result of operations of this type, especially after puberty. It does suggest that although the right and left hemispheres seem to specialize in processing certain information, they are by no means limited to one type.

Even when information is being processed primarily by one hemisphere, it is unlikely that the other hemisphere is totally inactive. While someone is reading a story, the right hemisphere may be playing a specialized role in understanding a metaphor or appreciating emotional content while the left side simultaneously works harder at deriving meaning from the complex relations among word concepts and syntax. The different functions of the two brain hemispheres do not seem as clearly differentiated in women as in men, and some left-handed people are known to have hemispheric functions the opposite of those described (Andersen, Garrison, & Andersen, 1979; Iaccino, 1993).

Despite the apparent complexity demonstrated by the brain, much of what is processed by the right hemisphere seems to be what we call *nonverbal phenomena,* and much of what is processed by the brain's left hemisphere is what we categorize as *verbal phenomena.* Obviously, some nonverbal behavior is more closely aligned with verbal behavior than others (e.g., speech-independent gestures as discussed in chapter 7), and we might expect more left hemispheric activity in such cases.

PERSPECTIVE 2: CLASSIFYING NONVERBAL BEHAVIOR

Another way of defining nonverbal communication is to look at the things people study. The theory and research associated with nonverbal communication focus on three primary units: the environmental structures and conditions within which communication takes place, the physical characteristics of the communicators themselves, and the various behaviors manifested by the communicators. A detailed breakdown of these three features follows.

THE COMMUNICATION ENVIRONMENT

Physical Environment

Although most of the emphasis in nonverbal research is on the appearance and behavior of the persons communicating, increasing attention is being given to the influence of nonhuman factors on human transactions. People change environments to help them accomplish their communicative goals; conversely, environments can affect our moods, choices of words, and actions. Thus this category concerns those elements that impinge on the human relationship but are not directly a part of it. Environmental factors include the furniture, architectural style, interior decorating, lighting conditions, colors, temperature, additional noises or music, and the like, amid which the interaction occurs. Variations in arrangements, materials, shapes, or surfaces of objects in the interacting environment can be extremely influential on the outcome of an interpersonal relationship. This category also includes what might be called *traces of action.* For instance, as you observe cigarette butts, orange peels, and wastepaper left by the person you will soon interact with, you form an impression that will eventually influence your meeting. Perceptions of time and timing comprise another important part of the communicative environment. When something occurs, how frequently it occurs, and the tempo or rhythm of actions are clearly a part of the communicative world even though they are not a part of the physical environment per se.

Spatial Environment

Proxemics is the study of the use and perception of social and personal space. Under this heading is a body of work called *small group ecology*, which concerns itself with how people use and respond to spatial relationships in formal and informal group settings. Such studies deal with seating and spatial arrangements as related to leadership, communication flow, and the task at hand. On an even broader level, some attention has been given to spatial relationships in crowds and densely populated situations. Personal space orientation is sometimes studied in the context of conversation distance and how it varies according to sex, status, roles, cultural orientation, and so forth. The term *territoriality* is also used frequently in the study of proxemics to denote the human tendency to stake out personal territory (or untouchable space) much as wild animals and birds do.

The Communicators' Physical Characteristics

This category covers things that remain relatively unchanged during the period of interaction. They are influential nonverbal cues that are not visibly movement bound. Included are physique or body shape, general attractiveness, height, weight, hair, skin color or tone, and so forth. Odors (body or breath) associated with the person are normally considered part of a person's physical appearance. Further, objects associated with the interactants also may affect their physical appearance. These are called *artifacts* and include things such as clothes, lipstick, eyeglasses, wigs and other hairpieces, false eyelashes, jewelry, and accessories such as attaché cases.

Body Movement and Position

Body movement and position typically includes gestures, movements of the body (limbs, hands, head, feet, and legs), facial expressions (smiles), eye behavior (blinking, direction and length of gaze, and pupil dilation), and posture. The furrow of the brow, the slump of a shoulder, and the tilt of a head are all considered body movements and positions. Specifically, the major areas are gestures, posture, touching behavior, facial expressions, and eye behavior.

Gestures

There are many different types of gestures (and variations of these types), but the most frequently studied are the following:

1. **Speech independent.** These gestures are not tied to speech, but they have a direct verbal translation or dictionary definition, usually consisting of a word or two or a phrase. There is high agreement among members of a culture or subculture on the verbal "translation" of these signals. The gestures used to represent "A-OK" or "Peace" (also known as the "V-for-Victory" sign) are examples of speech-independent gestures for large segments of U.S. culture.
2. **Speech related.** These gestures are directly tied to, or accompany, speech—often serving to illustrate what is being said verbally. These movements may accent or

emphasize a word or phrase, sketch a path of thought, point to present objects, depict a spatial relationship, depict the rhythm or pacing of an event, draw a picture of a referent, depict a bodily action, or serve as commentary on the regulation and organization of the interactive process.

Posture

Posture is normally studied in conjunction with other nonverbal signals to determine the degree of attention or involvement, the degree of status relative to the other interactive partner, or the degree of liking for the other interactant. A forward-leaning posture, for example, has been associated with higher involvement, more liking, and lower status in studies where the interactants did not know each other very well. Posture is also a key indicator of the intensity of some emotional states, for example, the drooping posture associated with sadness or the rigid, tense posture associated with anger. The extent to which the communicators mirror each other's posture may also reflect rapport or an attempt to build rapport.

Touching Behavior

Touching may be self-focused or other focused. Self-focused manipulations, not usually made for purposes of communicating, may reflect a person's particular state or a habit. Many are commonly called *nervous mannerisms*. Some of these actions are relics from an earlier time in life—times when we first learn how to manage our emotions, develop social contacts, or perform some instructional task. Sometimes we perform these manipulations as we adapt to such learning experiences, and they stay with us when we face similar situations later in life, often as only part of the original movement. Some refer to these types of self-focused manipulation as *adaptors*. These adaptors may involve various manipulations of one's own body such as licking, picking, holding, pinching, and scratching. Object adaptors are manipulations practiced in conjunction with an object, as when a reformed male cigarette smoker reaches toward his breast pocket for the nonexistent package of cigarettes. Of course, not all behaviors that reflect habitual actions or an anxious disposition can be traced to earlier adaptations, but they do represent a part of the overall pattern of bodily action.

One of the most potent forms of nonverbal communication occurs when two people touch. Touch can be virtually electric, but it also can irritate, condescend, or comfort. Touch is a highly ambiguous form of behavior whose meaning often takes more from the context, the nature of the relationship, and the manner of execution than from the configuration of the touch per se. Some researchers are concerned with touching behavior as an important factor in the child's early development; some are concerned with adult touching behavior. Subcategories include stroking, hitting, greetings and farewells, holding, and guiding another's movements.

Facial Expressions

Most studies of the face are concerned with the configurations that display various emotional states. The six primary affects receiving the most study are anger, sadness, surprise, happiness, fear, and disgust. Facial expressions also can function as regulatory gestures, providing feedback and managing the flow of interaction. In fact, some researchers believe the primary function of the face is to communicate, not to express emotions.

Eye Behavior

Where we look, when we look, and how long we look during interaction are the primary foci for studies of gazing. *Gaze* refers to the eye movement we make in the general direction of another's face. *Mutual gaze* occurs when interactants look into each other's eyes. The dilation and constriction of our pupils also has interest to those who study nonverbal communication because it is sometimes an indicator of interest, attention, or involvement.

Vocal Behavior

Vocal behavior deals with *how* something is said, not what is said. It deals with the range of nonverbal vocal cues surrounding common speech behavior. Generally, a distinction is made between two types of sounds:

1. The sound variations made with the vocal cords during talk that are a function of changes in pitch, duration, loudness, and silence
2. Sounds that result primarily from physiological mechanisms other than the vocal cords, for example, the pharyngeal, oral, or nasal cavities

Most of the research on vocal behavior and its effects on human interaction has focused on pitch level and variability; the duration of sounds (clipped or drawn out); pauses within the speech stream and the latency of response during turn exchanges; loudness level and variability; resonance; precise or slurred articulation; rate; rhythm; and intruding sounds during speech such as "uh" or "um." The study of vocal signals encompasses a broad range of interests, from questions focusing on stereotypes associated with certain voices to questions about the effects of vocal behavior on comprehension and persuasion. Thus even specialized sounds such as laughing, belching, yawning, swallowing, moaning, and the like may be of interest to the extent that they may affect the outcome of interaction.

PERSPECTIVE 3: NONVERBAL COMMUNICATION IN THE TOTAL COMMUNICATION PROCESS

Even though this book emphasizes nonverbal communication, don't forget the inseparable nature of verbal and nonverbal signals. Ray Birdwhistell, a pioneer in nonverbal research, reportedly said that studying only *nonverbal* communication is like studying *noncardiac* physiology. His point is well taken. It is not easy to dissect human interaction and make one diagnosis that concerns only verbal behavior and another that concerns only nonverbal behavior. The verbal dimension is so intimately woven and subtly represented in so much of what has been previously labeled *non*verbal that the term does not always adequately describe the behavior under study. Some of the most noteworthy scholars associated with nonverbal study refuse to segregate words from gestures and hence work under the broader terms of *communication* or *face-to-face interaction* (McNeill, 2000). Kendon (1983, pp. 17, 20) puts it this way:

> It is a common observation that, when a person speaks, muscular systems besides those of the lips, tongue, and jaws often become active . . . . Gesticulation is organized as part of the same overall unit of action by which speech is also organized . . . . Gesture and speech are available as two separate modes of representation and are coordinated because both are being guided by the same overall aim. That aim is to produce a pattern of action that will accomplish the representation of a meaning.

Because verbal and nonverbal systems operate together as part of the larger communication process, efforts to distinguish clearly between the two have not been very successful. One common misconception, for example, assumes nonverbal behavior is used solely to communicate emotional messages, whereas verbal behavior is for conveying ideas. Words can carry much emotion—we can talk explicitly about emotions, and we also communicate emotion between the lines in verbal nuances. Conversely, nonverbal cues are often used for purposes other than showing emotion; as examples, people in conversation use eye movements to help tell each other when it is time to switch speaking turns, and people commonly use hand gestures while talking to help convey their ideas (McNeill, 2000).

Argyle (1988) has identified the following primary functions of nonverbal behavior in human communication:

1. Expressing emotion
2. Conveying interpersonal attitudes (like/dislike, dominance/submission, etc.)
3. Presenting one's personality to others
4. Accompanying speech for the purposes of managing turn taking, feedback, attention, and so on

Argyle also notes that nonverbal behaviors are important in many rituals, such as greeting. Notice that none of these functions of nonverbal behavior is limited to nonverbal behavior alone; that is, we can express emotions and attitudes, present ourselves in a particular light, and manage the interaction using verbal cues too. This does not suggest, however, that in any given situation we might not rely more heavily on verbal behavior for some purposes and on nonverbal for others.

We also need to recognize that the ways we attribute meanings to verbal and nonverbal behavior are not all that different either. Nonverbal actions, like verbal ones, may communicate more than one message at a time—for example, the way you nonverbally make it clear to another person that you want to keep talking may simultaneously express your need for dominance over that person and, perhaps, your emotional state. When you grip a child's shoulder during a reprimand, you may increase comprehension and recall, but you may also elicit such a negative reaction that the child fails to obey. A smile can be a part of an emotional expression, an attitudinal message, part of a self-presentation, or a listener response to manage the interaction. And, like verbal behavior, the meanings attributed to nonverbal behavior may be stereotyped, idiomatic, or ambiguous. Furthermore, the same nonverbal behavior performed in different contexts may, like words, receive different attributions of meaning. For example, looking down at the floor may reflect sadness in one situation and submissiveness or lack of involvement in another.

Finally, in an effort to identify the fundamental categories of meaning associated with nonverbal behavior, Mehrabian (1970, 1981) identified a threefold perspective resulting from his extensive testing:

1. **Immediacy.** Sometimes we react to things by evaluating them—positive or negative, good or bad, like or dislike.
2. **Status.** Sometimes we enact or perceive behaviors that indicate various aspects of status to us—strong or weak, superior or subordinate.
3. **Responsiveness.** This third category refers to our perceptions of activity—slow or fast, active or passive.

In various verbal and nonverbal studies over the past three decades, dimensions similar to Mehrabian's have been reported consistently by investigators from diverse fields studying diverse phenomena. It is reasonable to conclude, therefore, that these three dimensions are basic responses to our environment and are reflected in the way we assign meaning to both verbal and nonverbal behavior. Most of this work, however, depends on subjects translating their reactions to a nonverbal act into one identified by verbal descriptors. This issue has already been addressed in our discussion of the way the brain processes different pieces of information. In general, then, nonverbal signals, like words, can and do have multiple uses and meanings; like words, nonverbal signals have denotative and connotative meanings; and like words, nonverbal signals play an active role in communicating liking, power, and responsiveness. With these in mind, we can now examine some of the important ways verbal and nonverbal behavior interrelate during human interaction. Ekman (1965) identified the following: repeating, conflicting, complementing, substituting, accenting/moderating, and regulating.

REPEATING

Nonverbal communication can simply repeat what was said verbally. For instance, if you told a person he or she had to go north to find a newspaper stand and then pointed in the proper direction, this would be considered repetition.

CONFLICTING

Verbal and nonverbal signals can be at variance with one another in a variety of ways. They may communicate two contradictory messages or two messages that seem incongruous or in conflict with one another (see Figure 1-1). In both instances two messages that do not appear to be consistent with one another are perceived. It is quite common (and probably functional) to have mixed feelings about some things. As a result, incongruous verbal and nonverbal messages may be more common than we realize. But it is the more dramatic contradictions we are more likely to notice. Perhaps it is the parent who yells to his or her child in an angry voice, "Of course I love you!" Or the public speaker, who, with trembling hands and knees and beads of perspiration on the brow, claims, "I'm not nervous."

Why do these conflicting messages occur? In some cases it is a natural response to a situation in which communicators perceive themselves in a bind. They do not want to tell the truth, and they do not want to lie. As a result, their ambivalence and frustration

FIGURE 1-1

(a) Conflicting verbal/nonverbal signals. (b) Is this an aggressive or playful situation? What observations influenced your decision?

a   b

produce a discrepant message (Bavelas, et al., 1990). Suppose you have just given a terrible presentation, and you ask me how you did. I may say you did fine, but my voice, face, and body may not support my words. In other situations, conflicting messages occur because people do an imperfect job of lying. On still other occasions, conflicting messages may be the result of an attempt to communicate sarcasm or irony, saying one thing with words and the opposite with vocal tone and/or facial expression. The term *coy* is used to describe the display of coexisting signals that invite friendly contact with those that signal rejection and withdrawal. We live in a complex world that makes feelings of ambivalence or mixed emotions a much more common experience in everyday life than we sometimes acknowledge (Weigert, 1991).

These displays of incongruous or conflicting signals may occur in a variety of ways. Sometimes two nonverbal signals may manifest the discord (e.g., vocal with visual), but verbal and nonverbal signals can combine in several ways: positive voice/negative words, negative voice/positive words, positive face/negative words, negative face/positive words.

When confronted with conflicting verbal and nonverbal messages that matter to us, how do we react? Leathers (1979) has identified a common three-step process:

1. The first reaction is confusion and uncertainty.
2. Next, we search for additional information that will clarify the situation.
3. If clarification is not forthcoming, we will probably react with displeasure, hostility, or even withdrawal.

Responses to conflicting messages are often ambiguous themselves. Some believe a constant barrage of inconsistent messages can contribute to a psychopathology for the receiver.

This may be particularly true when people have a close relationship and the receiver has no other people he or she can turn to for discussion and possible clarification of the confusion. Some research finds that parents of disturbed children produce more messages with conflicting cues (Bugental, Love, Kaswan, & April, 1971). Other work suggests that the differences are not in conflicting cues but in negative messages; that is, parents with disturbed children send more negative messages (Beakel & Mehrabian, 1969). The combination of negativity, confusion, and punishment can be very harmful if it is a common style of communication directed toward children. Date rape is another situation in which testimony often centers around the extent to which the signals of rejection were unequivocal.

We do not wish to give the impression that all forms of discrepancy are harmful. Our daily conversations are probably peppered with instances where gestures and speech do not exactly match one another—for example, a speaker telling a story about someone climbing up a pipe while simultaneously gesturing like he or she was climbing a ladder (McNeill, Cassell, & McCullough, 1994). Sometimes these discrepancies go unnoticed, and many are cognitively "resolved" without overtly discussing the mismatch. Even contradictions with more important implications for the conversants may not, in some situations, be considered very harmful. Moreover, as stated earlier, discrepancy is *required* for achieving certain effects: Sarcasm occurs when the words are pleasant and the voice quality is unpleasant; when the words are unpleasant but the tone of voice is pleasant, we are likely to communicate the message "just joking."

Finally, some discrepancies may be helpful in certain situations. In an experiment, teachers used mixed messages while teaching a lesson to sixth-grade pupils. When the teachers combined positive words with a negative nonverbal demeanor, pupils learned more than with any other combination (Woolfolk, 1978). Similarly, a study of doctors talking with patients found that the combination of positive words said in a negative voice tone was associated with the highest levels of patient satisfaction with the visit (Hall, Roter, & Rand, 1981). Possibly the positive verbal/negative nonverbal combination is perceived in classrooms and doctors' office as serious and concerned and, therefore, makes a better impression.

Some research has questioned whether we trust and believe nonverbal signals more than verbal when we are confronted with conflicting messages (Bugental, 1974; Mehrabian, 1972; Stiff, Hale, Garlick, & Rogan, 1990). Burgoon (1980, p. 184), after surveying numerous studies in this area, concluded, "the nonverbal channels carry more information and are believed more than the verbal band, and . . . visual cues generally carry more weight than vocal ones."

Burgoon goes on to discuss some important reservations about this general conclusion. It is often assumed that nonverbal signals are more spontaneous, harder to fake, and less likely to be manipulated—hence more believable. It is probably more accurate to say, however, that some nonverbal behaviors are more spontaneous and harder to fake than others and that some people are more proficient than others at nonverbal deception. With two conflicting cues (both of which are nonverbal) we predictably place our reliance on the cues we consider harder to fake. One research team found that people tended to rely primarily on visual cues in visual/auditory discrepancies, but when the discrepancy was great, people tended to rely on the audio signals (DePaulo, Rosenthal, Eisenstat, Rogers, & Finkelstein, 1978).

Credibility of the information presented is also an important factor in determining which cues to believe most in inconsistent messages. If the information being communicated in one channel lacks credibility, we are likely to discount it and look to other channels for the "real" message (Bugental, 1974). Sometimes we are faced with the difficult dilemma of perceiving the meaning communicated by hard-to-fake cues that do not seem credible. If a person says, "This is really great" with a sad tone of voice on receiving a gift you know was long desired, you are likely to search for other explanations—for example, something else may be bothering the person.

Interestingly, young children seem to give less credence to certain nonverbal cues than adults do when confronted with conflicting verbal and nonverbal messages (Bugental, Kaswan, Love, & Fox, 1970; Bugental, Love, & Gianetto, 1971; Volkmar & Siegel, 1982). Conflicting messages in which the speaker smiled while making a critical statement were interpreted more negatively by children than adults, particularly when the speaker was a woman.

Other work casts a further shadow on the "reliance on nonverbal cues in conflicting message situations" theory. Shapiro (1968) found that student judges differed as to whether they relied on linguistic or facial cues when asked to select the affect being communicated by incongruent sketched faces and written messages and to be consistent in their choices. Vande Creek and Watkins (1972) extended Shapiro's work by using real voices and moving pictures. The stimulus persons were portraying inconsistencies in the degree of stress in verbal and nonverbal channels. Again, they found some respondents tended to rely primarily on verbal cues, some tended to rely on nonverbal cues, and some responded to the degree of stress in general regardless of the channels manifesting it. The cross-cultural research of Solomon and Ali (1975) suggests that familiarity with the verbal language may affect our reliance on verbal or nonverbal cues. They found, for instance, that persons who were not as familiar with the language used to construct the contradictory message relied on the content for judgments of affective meaning. Those who knew the language well were more apt to rely on the vocal intonation for the affective meaning. So it appears some people rely more heavily on the verbal message, whereas others rely on the nonverbal.

We do not know all the conditions that affect which signals people look to for valid information. As a general rule, people tend to rely on those signals they perceive harder to fake, but this will most likely vary with the situation; so the ultimate impact of verbal, visual, and vocal signals is best determined by a close examination of the people involved and the communication context.

COMPLEMENTING

Nonverbal behavior can modify, or elaborate on, verbal messages. When the verbal and nonverbal channels are complementary, rather than conflicting, our messages are usually decoded more accurately. Some evidence suggests that complementary nonverbal signals also may be helpful in remembering the verbal message. A student who reflects an attitude of embarrassment when talking to a professor about a poor performance in class assignments is exhibiting nonverbal behavior that complements the verbal. When clarity is of utmost importance (as in a job interview or when making up with a loved one after a fight), we should be especially concerned with making the meanings of verbal and nonverbal behavior complement one another.

SUBSTITUTING

Nonverbal behavior can also substitute for verbal messages. It may indicate more permanent characteristics (sex, age), moderately long-lasting features (personality, attitudes, social group), and relatively short-term states. In the latter case, we may find a dejected and downtrodden executive (or janitor) walk into his or her house after work with a facial expression that substitutes for the statement "I've had a rotten day." With a little practice, people soon learn to identify a wide range of these substitute nonverbal displays—all the way from "It's been a fantastic, great day!" to "Oh, God, am I miserable!" We do not need to ask for verbal confirmation of our perception.

Sometimes, when substitute nonverbal behavior fails, the communicator resorts to the verbal level. Consider the woman who wants her date to stop trying to become physically intimate with her. She may stiffen, stare straight ahead, or act unresponsive and cool. If the suitor still does not stop, she might say something like "Look, Larry, please don't ruin a nice friendship."

ACCENTING/MODERATING

Nonverbal behavior may accent (amplify) or moderate (tone down) parts of the verbal message. Accenting is much like underlining or *italicizing* written words to emphasize them. Movements of the head and hands are frequently used to accent the verbal message. When a father scolds his son about staying out too late, he may accent a particular phrase with a firm grip on the son's shoulder and an accompanying frown. In some instances, one set of nonverbal cues can accent or moderate other nonverbal cues. The intensity of a facial expression of emotion, for example, may be revealed by observing other parts of the body.

REGULATING

Nonverbal behavior is also used to regulate verbal behavior. We do this in two ways:

1. Coordinating our own verbal and nonverbal behavior in the production of our messages
2. Coordinating our verbal and nonverbal message behavior with those of our interaction partner(s)

We regulate the production of our own messages in a variety of ways. Sometimes we use nonverbal signs to segment units of interaction. Posture changes may demarcate a topic change; a gesture may forecast the verbalization of a particular idea; pauses may help in organizing spoken information into units. When we speak of a series of things, we may communicate discreteness by linear, staccato movements of the arm and hand; for example, "We must consider A, B, and C." When we insert one of these chopping gestures after each letter, it may suggest a separate consideration of each letter; a single chop after C might indicate either a consideration of all three (as a group) or just C in particular.

We also regulate the flow of verbal and nonverbal behavior between ourself and an interactant. This may manifest itself in the type of behavior two interactants elicit from one another (e.g., every time one person gets mad and yells, the other behaves in a solicitous manner) or in less obvious ways (e.g., the signals of initiation, continuation, and termination of interaction). The way one person stops talking and another starts in a smooth, synchronized manner may be as important to a satisfactory interaction as the content. After all, we do make judgments about people based on their regulatory skills (for example, "Talking to him is like talking to a wall" or "You can't get a word in edgewise with her"). When another person frequently interrupts or is inattentive, we may feel this person is making a statement about the relationship, perhaps one of disrespect. There are rules for regulating conversations, but they are generally implicit. It is not written down, but we seem to know that two people should not talk at the same time, that each person should get an equal number of turns at talking if he or she desires, that a question should be answered, and so forth. Wiemann's (1977) research found that relatively minute changes in these regulatory behaviors (interruptions, pauses longer than three seconds, unilateral topic changes, etc.) resulted in sizable variations in how competent a communicator was perceived to be. As listeners, we are apparently attending to and evaluating a host of fleeting, subtle, and habitual features of another's conversational behavior. There are probably differences in the actual behaviors used to manage conversational flow across cultures. As children are first learning these rules, they use less subtle cues, for example, tugging on clothing, raising a hand, and the like. Children are also less skilled in accomplishing smooth turn taking, as you will have noticed if you have conversed with a young child on the telephone.

Conversational regulators involve several kinds of nonverbal cues. When we want to indicate we are finished speaking and the other person can start, we may increase our eye contact with the other person. This is often accompanied by the vocal cues associated with ending declarative or interrogative statements. If the other person still does not figuratively pick up the conversational ball, we might extend silence or interject a *trailer,* for example, "you know . . ." or "so, ah . . ." Keeping another from speaking in a conversation means we have to keep long pauses from occurring, decrease eye contact, and perhaps raise the volume if the other tries to speak. When we do not want to take a speaking turn, we might give the other some reinforcing head nods, maintain attentive eye contact, and, of course, refrain from speaking when the other begins to yield. When we do want the floor, we might raise our index finger or enact an audible inspiration of breath with a straightening of the posture as if ready to take over. Rapid nodding may signal the other to hurry up and finish, but, if we have trouble getting in, we may have to talk simultaneously for a few words or engage in stutter starts that, we hope, will be more easily observed cues to signal our desire.

Conversational beginnings and endings also act as regulatory points. When we are greeting others, eye contact indicates that the channels are open. A slight head movement and an *eyebrow flash* of recognition (a barely detectable but distinct up-and-down movement of the eyebrows) may be present. The hands are also used in greetings for salutes, waves, handshakes, handslaps, emblematic signals such as the peace or victory sign, a raised fist, or thumbs-up. Hands may also perform grooming activities (running fingers through one's hair) or be involved in various touching activities such as kissing, embracing, or hitting another on the arm. The mouth may form a smile or an oval shape, as if one were ready to start talking (Krivonos & Knapp, 1975).

Saying good-bye in semiformal interviews was shown, in one study, to elicit many nonverbal behaviors. The most common included the breaking of eye contact more often and for longer periods of time, positioning one's body toward an exit, and leaning forward and nodding. Less frequent, but very noticeable, were accenting behaviors that signaled, "This is the termination of our conversation, and I don't want you to miss it!" These ac-centers included explosive hand and foot movements such as raising the hands and/or feet and bringing them down with enough force to make an audible slap while simultaneously using the hands and feet as leverage to catapult the interactant out of his or her seat. A less direct manifestation was placing hands on thighs or knees in a leveraging position (as if one was preparing to catapult), hoping that the other person picked up the good-bye cue (Knapp, Hart, Friedrich, & Shulman, 1975).

PERSPECTIVE 4: THE HISTORY
OF NONVERBAL STUDIES

The scientific study of nonverbal communication is primarily a post-World War II activity. This does not mean we cannot find important early tributaries of knowledge; even ancient Greek and Roman scholars commented on what we today would call nonverbal behavior. Quintilian's *Institutio Oratoria*, for example, is an important source of information on gesture. It was written in the first century C.E. If we traced the history of fields including animal behavior, anthropology, dance, linguistics, philosophy, psychiatry, psychology, sociology, and speech, we would no doubt find important antecedents for today's work (Asendorpf & Wallbott, 1982; Davis, 1979; DePaulo & Friedman, 1998; Hecht & Ambady, 1999). Nonverbal studies never have been the province of any one particular discipline. In the last half of the 19th century, Delsarte (among others) attempted to codify and set forth rules for managing both "voice culture" and body movements/gestures (Shawn, 1954). Although Delsarte's "science of applied esthetics" and the elocutionary movement gave way to a less formal, less stylized 20th century, it represents one of several early attempts to identify various forms of bodily expression. One of the most influential pre-20th-century works was Darwin's *Expression of the Emotions in Man and Animals* in 1872. This work spawned the modern study of facial expressions, and many of his observations and ideas have been validated by other researchers (Ekman, 1973).

During the first half of the 20th century, there were isolated studies of the voice, physical appearance and dress, and the face. An unsystematic look at the publications during this period suggests that studies of proxemics, the environment, and body movement received even less attention; and the least attention was given to the investigation of eye behavior and touching. Two noteworthy, but very different, events occurred during this period. The first involved some controversial scholarship and a scandal; the second concerns a work of extraordinary influence in the study of nonverbal behavior.

In 1925, Kretschmer authored a book, *Physique and Character*. This was followed in 1940 by Sheldon's book *The Variations of Human Physique*. These works were based on the idea that if we precisely measure and analyze a person's body, we can learn much about his or her intelligence, temperament, moral worth, and future achievement. Sheldon's belief that certain characteristics are associated with certain body types (the thin ecto-morph, the muscular mesomorph, and the fatty endomorph) is still debated (see chapter 6). His work was featured on the cover of the popular magazine *Life* in 1951. To develop a catalogue of body types, Sheldon was permitted to photograph freshman students in the nude at Yale, Wellesley, Vassar, Princeton, Smith, Mt. Holyoke, and other colleges (Rosenbaum, 1995). The students were told it was a project involving posture, and thousands complied—including future president George H. W. Bush and future first lady Hillary Rodham Clinton. The photos have reportedly been destroyed, and Sheldon's personal notes have revealed him as drawing racial conclusions from his work. People continue to associate certain characteristics with different body types, but the validity of these perceptions was not proven by Sheldon or any researchers since.

In contrast, Efron's book *Gesture and Environment* (1941) has become a classic because it made three important contributions. Efron's innovative and detailed methods of studying gesture and body language, along with his framework for classifying nonverbal behavior, influenced future generations of scholars. In addition, Efron's work documented the important role of culture in shaping our gestures and body movement—which, at the time, was contrary to the belief of many (including Adolf Hitler) that people's behavior is not subject to much modification by changing contexts and environments.

The 1950s showed a significant increase in the number of nonverbal research efforts. Some of the milestones of this decade include the following:

1. Birdwhistell's *Introduction to Kinesics* appeared in 1952 and Hall's *Silent Language* in 1959. These anthropologists were responsible for taking some of the principles of linguistics and applying them to nonverbal phenomena, providing new labels for the study of body movement (kinesics) and space (proxemics), and launching a program of research in each area.
2. Trager's 1958 delineation of the components of paralanguage greatly enhanced the precision with which we classify and study vocal cues.
3. Psychiatrist Jurgen Ruesch and photographer Weldon Kees combined their efforts to produce a popular book titled *Nonverbal Communication: Notes on the Visual Perception of Human Relations* in 1956. This was probably the first book to use the term *nonverbal communication* in its title. Therapists, including Freud, had been interested in nonverbal cues prior to the 1950s, but this work provided additional theoretical insights into the origins, usage, and coding of nonverbal behavior and provided extensive visual documentation for the communicative role of environments.
4. Also in 1956, Maslow and Mintz's study of the environmental effects of a "beautiful" room and an "ugly" room was published. This oft-cited study is a highlight in the history of environmental forces impinging on human communication.
5. Frank's comprehensive article "Tactile Communication" appeared in 1957 and suggested a number of testable hypotheses about touching in human interaction.

If the 1950s produced an increase in the number of nonverbal studies, the 1960s must be classified as a nuclear explosion. Specific areas of the body were the subject of extensive programs of research: Exline's work on eye behavior; the Davitz work on vocal expressions of emotion, which culminated in *The Communication of Emotional Meaning* in

1964; Hess's work on pupil dilation; Sommer's continued exploration of personal space and design; Goldman-Eisler's study of pauses and hesitations in spontaneous speech; and the study of a wide range of body activity by Dittmann, Argyle, Kendon, Scheflen, and Mehrabian. During this time, psychologist Robert Rosenthal brought vividly to our attention the potential impact of nonverbal subtleties when he showed how experimenters can affect the outcome of experiments and teachers can affect the intellectual growth of their students through nonverbal behavior (*Experimenter Effects in Behavioral Research*, 1966, and *Pygmalion in the Classroom*, 1968). Perhaps the classic theoretical piece of the 1960s is Ekman and Friesen's article on the origins, usage, and coding of nonverbal behavior (Ekman & Friesen, 1969; Ekman, 1999). This article distinguished five areas of nonverbal study which served as a guide for their own research and ultimately that of many other researchers. These areas were emblems, illustrators, affect display, regulators, and adaptors.

The 1970s began with a journalist's account of nonverbal study from the perspective of a handful of researchers (Fast's *Body Language*, 1970). This best-selling volume was followed by a steady stream of books that attempted to make nonverbal findings understandable and usable to the American public. These books, in the interest of simplification and readability, often misrepresented findings when recounting how to make a sale, detect deception, assert one's dominance, obtain a sexual partner, and the like.

Although such books aroused the public's interest in nonverbal communication, they incurred some anticipated fallout (Koivumaki, 1975). Readers were too often left with the idea that reading nonverbal cues was the key to success in any human encounter; some of these books implied that single cues (legs apart) represent single meanings (sexual invitation). Not only is it important to look at nonverbal *clusters* of behavior but also to recognize that nonverbal cues, like verbal ones, rarely have a single denotative meaning. Some of these popularized accounts do not sufficiently remind us that the meaning of a particular behavior is often understood by looking at the context in which the behavior occurs; for example, looking into someone's eyes may reflect affection in one situation and aggression in another.

Another common reaction to such books was the concern that once the nonverbal code was broken we would be totally transparent; people would know everything about us because we could not control these nonverbal signals. As you will learn from this book, we do have varying degrees of control over our nonverbal behavior. Some behavior is very much under our control; other behavior is not (but may be once awareness is increased). Further, it may be that as soon as someone exhibits an understanding of your body language, you will modify it and make adaptations. We have been studying verbal behavior for more than 2,000 years, and we know much about the impact of certain verbal strategies, but we are still a long way from understanding the totality of verbal behavior.

The 1970s were also a time of summarizing and synthesizing. Ekman's research on the human face (*Emotion in the Human Face*, 1972, with W. V. Friesen and P. Ellsworth); Mehrabian's research on the meaning of nonverbal cues of immediacy, status, and responsiveness (*Nonverbal Communication*, 1972); Scheflen's kinesic research in the framework of general systems theory (*Body Language and Social Order*, 1972); Hess's study of the pupil size (*The Tell-Tale Eye*, 1975); Argyle's study of body movement and eye behavior (*Bodily Communication*, 1975, rev. 1988, and *Gaze and Mutual Gaze*, with M. Cook, 1975); Montagu's *Touching* (1971); and Birdwhistell's *Kinesics and Context* (1970) were all attempts to bring together the growing literature or a particular research program in a single volume.

During the 1980s, some scholars continued to specialize, but others focused on identifying the ways a variety of nonverbal signals work together to accomplish common communicative goals, for example, getting someone to do something for you, showing affection, lying to someone, and so forth (Patterson, 1983). It became clear that we could not fully understand the role of nonverbal behavior in accomplishing these goals unless we also looked at the role of co-occurring verbal behavior and tried to develop theories about how various verbal and nonverbal cues interact in the process (Streeck & Knapp, 1992). Thus we are gradually beginning to learn how to put the pieces back together after several decades of separating them to examine them microscopically. This trend is a manifestation of a larger movement to bring our research efforts more in line with the way we know human communication occurs in life's laboratory (Archer, Akert, & Costanzo, 1993; Knapp, 1984; Patterson, 1984). Therefore, nonverbal research continues to change in the following ways:

- From studying noninteractive situations to studying interactive ones
- From studying one person to studying both interactants
- From studying a single point in time to studying changes over time
- From studying single behaviors to studying multiple behaviors
- From the view that we perceive everything that occurs to acknowledging that we need to know more about how people perceive signals during interaction
- From single-meaning and single-intent perspectives to acknowledging that often multiple meanings occur and multiple goals exist
- From a measurement perspective focused almost exclusively on frequency and duration to one that also includes issues related to when and how a behavior occurs
- From attempting to control context by eliminating important and influential elements to attempting to account for such effects
- From studying only face-to-face interaction to examining the role of nonverbal messages in mediated communication with the new technologies
- From an overemphasis on studying how strangers interact to one equally concerned about how intimates interact
- From studying only culture or only biology as possible explanations of behavior to examining the roles both play

Such a brief historical view inevitably leaves out many important contributions. The preceding discussion is simply our attempt to highlight some important developments and depict a general background for current perspectives.

PERSPECTIVE 5: NONVERBAL COMMUNICATION IN EVERYDAY LIFE

Clearly nonverbal signals are a critical part of all our communicative endeavors. Sometimes nonverbal signals are the most important part of our message. Understanding and effectively using nonverbal behavior is crucial to our success in virtually every social encounter we experience.

First impressions often have a strong impact on any given social interaction and may even affect subsequent interactions. As a result, people try to select the verbal and nonverbal behavior that they feel will give them the best start in accomplishing their communicative goals. Nonverbal cues like attire, eye gaze, smiling, posture, distance, listener responses, and the like are just as important as choosing the right words—sometimes more so as Lt. General David McKiernan found out. In June of 2003, the *Boston Globe* reported that he was taken off the list of possible candidates for the top leadership position of Army Chief of Staff because Pentagon officials observed "bad body language." Apparently, McKiernan was standing with his arms crossed and did not respond in positive ways during "applause lines" while listening to a speech given by Secretary of State Donald Rumsfeld in Iraq (*Austin American Statesman,* 2003). Nonverbal messages are no less important in formal job interviews or in ongoing performance on the job—whether it involves public relations, customer service, marketing, advertising, supervision, or leadership (DePaulo, 1992; Hecker & Stewart, 1988). Diplomats often prefer implicit accommodation rather than explicit, thereby using and relying heavily on nonverbal signals.

Some occupations and leadership positions require establishing or implementing policies involving nonverbal messages. Some schools and businesses have rules about hair length, facial hair, or appropriate clothing; sexual harassment cases may hinge on determining the type of touching that occurred; and some airlines, broadcasters, and others have been involved in lawsuits charging discrimination on the basis of physical appearance. The San Francisco City Council was reportedly discussing a ban on certain nonverbal expressions like a smirk, a raised eyebrow, or a loud guffaw in order to restore civility to council debates (Reuters, 2003).

While the preceding situations may have serious consequences, they are not life-threatening. But in nurse-physician interaction during an operation, effective nonverbal communication can be literally the difference between life and death. One teenager's tragic death was also the result of misreading nonverbal signals. The teen was practicing sign language with his cousin, and some of his gestures were believed by one gang to be signs of a rival gang—so they shot the boy (*Austin American Statesman,* 2000). Other potentially harmful situations involving assault and abuse have been the subject of nonverbal studies.

One study analyzed the appearance and movements of people who walked through one of the highest assault areas in New York City (Grayson & Stein, 1981). Then, prisoners who had knowledge of such matters were asked to view the films of the potential victims and indicate the likelihood of assault. In addition to finding that older people are a prime target, the researchers also found that potential victims tended to move differently. They tended to take long or short strides (not medium); and their body parts did not seem to move in synchrony; that is, they seemed less graceful and fluid in their movement. A related study, using different methods, found similar results and concluded that any cluster of nonverbal signals indicating a person has the energy to defend oneself and/or the ability to escape with ease reduces one's vulnerability to attack (Gunns, Johnston, & Hudson, 2002.) Other studies have tried to identify nonverbal characteristics that rapists use to select their victims. Some rapists look for women who exhibit passivity, a lack of confidence, and vulnerability; others prefer the exact opposite, wishing to "put an uppity woman in her place." The conclusion seems to recommend a public nonverbal demeanor that is confident yet not aggressive (Myers, Templer, & Brown, 1984).

Another study that assessed potentially aggressive acts focused on mothers who abused their children (Givens, 1978). It was noted that even while playing with their children, these mothers communicated their dislike (turning away, not smiling, etc.) by their nonverbal behavior. Just as abusive and nonabusive mothers differ in their behavior, the children of abusive parents and nonabusive parents differ in their nonverbal behavior (Hecht, Foster, Dunn, Williams, Anderson, & Pulbratek, 1986). Facial expressions of children in response to violence on television may also have some predictive value for identifying aggressive behavior (Ekman, Liebert, Friesen, Harrison, Zlatchin, Malmstrom, & Baron, 1972). In short, scientists are examining nonverbal signals of both potential perpetrators of violence and the potential victims of that violence.

Once a person has been charged with a crime and the trial process begins, we can see several important and influential sources of nonverbal cues (Peskin, 1980; Pryor & Buchanan, 1984). One of this text's authors received a letter from an attorney in Florida who was seeking information about nonverbal behavior in order to identify the possible effects of an appellate judge making a decision based on the written record of the trial, without any nonverbal signals. Because of the important implications of decisions made in courtrooms and the desire to maintain impartial communication, almost every facet of the courtroom process is being analyzed. Judges are cautioned to minimize possible signs of partiality in their voice and positioning. Research suggests that judges' attitudes and nonverbal cues may indeed influence the outcome of a trial (Blanck & Rosenthal, 1992). In chapter 6, several studies are reported concerning the effects of physically attractive witnesses and defendants. In some cases, attorneys and witnesses have been videotaped in pretrial practice sessions to determine whether they are conveying nonverbally any messages they want to avoid. The study of nonverbal behavior is also important to the process of jury selection. Although this attention to nonverbal signals emanating from prospective jurors may indicate a degree of sensitivity that did not previously exist, we need not worry that attorneys or social scientists will become so skilled they can rig juries (Saks, 1976).

A list of all the situations in which nonverbal communication plays a significant role would be almost endless and would include such areas as dance, theater, music, film, and photography. The nonverbal symbolism of various ceremonies and rituals (e.g., the trappings of the marriage ceremony, Christmas decorations, religious rituals, funerals, etc.) provide stimuli which guide the responses of those involved. From this broad array of situations in which nonverbal communication plays a central role, we have selected some areas which we feel are particularly meaningful and developed them in chapters 12 and 13. In chapter 12 we examine nonverbal behavior used in communicating intimacy, dominance/status, identity, deception, and interaction management. Chapter 13 is devoted to an analysis of nonverbal signals in advertising, politics, education, culture, and health care.

❖

SUMMARY

The term *nonverbal* is commonly used to describe all human communication events that transcend spoken or written words. At the same time, we should realize that these nonverbal events and behaviors can be interpreted through verbal symbols. We also found that any classification scheme that separates things into two discrete categories (e.g., verbal/nonverbal, left/right brain, vocal/nonvocal, etc.) will not be able to account for factors that do not seem to fit either category. We might more appropriately think of behaviors as existing on a continuum with some behaviors overlapping two continua.

Verbal and nonverbal signals can be coded in different ways. The signals produced can be coded on a continuum of coding behavior ranging from intrinsic (the referent) to iconic (some aspect of the referent preserved) to arbitrary (none or little of the referent preserved). The decoding of nonverbal signals is often done with the right hemisphere of the brain, but there is considerable overlapping of functions between right and left hemispheres—especially if one side has to compensate due to surgery on the other hemisphere. The theoretical writings and research on nonverbal communication can be broken down into the following three areas:

1. The communication environment (physical and spatial)
2. The communicator's physical characteristics
3. Body movement and position (gestures, posture, touching, facial expressions, eye behavior, and vocal behavior)

Nonverbal communication should not be studied as an isolated phenomenon but as an inseparable part of the total communication process. The interrelationships between verbal and nonverbal behavior were illustrated in our discussion of how nonverbal behavior functions in repeating, conflicting with, substituting for, complementing, accenting/moderating, and regulating verbal communication. Nonverbal communication is important because of its role in the total communication system, the tremendous quantity of informational cues it gives in any particular situation, and its use in fundamental areas of our daily life.

This chapter also reviewed some of the historical highlights, noting the current influence of the works of Darwin, Efron, Birdwhistell, Hall, Ruesch and Kees, Mehrabian, Rosenthal, Ekman and Friesen, and others. We reviewed the important role and shortcomings of the popular literature. The chapter concluded with an account of the prevalence and importance of nonverbal signals in selected areas of our daily life.

QUESTIONS FOR DISCUSSION

1. Identify a situation in which you believe verbal behavior was clearly more important to the outcome of an interaction than nonverbal behavior. Explain why.

2. Identify a situation in which you would give more credibility to a person's verbal behavior when their verbal and nonverbal behavior convey different messages.

3. Discuss the most unusual or subtle nonverbal signal or signals you have observed in an interaction partner. What helped you assess their meaning(s)?

4. If you could get an instant and true answer to any question you had about nonverbal communication, what would your question be?

BIBLIOGRAPHY

Andersen, P. A. (1999). *Nonverbal communication: Forms and functions.* Mountain View, CA: Mayfield.

Andersen, P. A., Garrison, J. P., & Andersen, J. F. (1979). Implications of a neurophysiological approach for the study of nonverbal communication. *Human Communication Research, 6,* 74–89.

Archer, D., Akert, R., & Costanzo, M. (1993). The accurate perception of nonverbal behavior: Questions of theory and research design. In Blanck, P. D. (Ed.), *Interpersonal expectations: Theory, research, and applications.* Cambridge: Cambridge University Press.

Argyle, M. (1988). *Bodily communication* (2nd ed.). London: Methuen.

Argyle, M., & Cook, M. (1976). *Gaze and mutual gaze.* New York: Cambridge University Press.

Asendorpf, J., & Wallbott, H. G. (1982). Contributions of the German "Expression Psychology" to nonverbal communication research. *Journal of Nonverbal Behavior, 6,* 135–147, 199–219; and *7,* 20–32.

Austin American Statesman (June 11, 2003). Next Army chief may be retired general.

Austin American Statesman (June 14, 2000). Teen shot while learning to sign.

Bavelas, J. B., Black, A., Chovil, N., & Mullett, J. (1990). *Equivocal communication.* Newbury Park, CA: Sage.

Bavelas, J. B., & Chovil, N. (2000). Visible acts of meaning. An integrated message model of language in face-to-face dialogue. *Journal of Language and Social Psychology, 19,* 163–194.

Beakel, N. G., & Mehrabian, A. (1969). Inconsistent communications and psychopathology. *Journal of Abnormal Psychology, 74,* 126–130.

Benthall, J., & Polhemus, T. (Eds.). (1975). *The body as a medium of expression.* New York: Dutton.

Birdwhistell, R. L. (1952). *Introduction to kinesics: An annotation system for analysis of body motion and gesture.* Washington, DC: Foreign Service Institute, U.S. Department of State/Ann Arbor, MI: University Microfilms.

Birdwhistell, R. L. (1970). *Kinesics and context.* Philadelphia: University of Pennsylvania Press.

Blanck, P. D. (Ed.). (1993). *Interpersonal expectations: Theory, research, and applications.* New York: Cambridge University Press.

Blanck, P. D., & Rosenthal, R. (1992). Nonverbal behavior in the courtroom. In R. S. Feldman (Ed.), *Applications of nonverbal behavioral theories and research.* Hillsdale, NJ: Erlbaum.

Bosmajian, H. (Ed.). (1971). *The rhetoric of nonverbal communication.* Glenview, IL: Scott-Foresman.

Buck, R. (1984). *The communication of emotion.* New York: Guilford.

Buck, R., & VanLear, A. (2002). Verbal and nonverbal communication: Distinguishing symbolic, spontaneous, and pseudo-spontaneous nonverbal behavior. *Journal of Communication, 52,* 522–541.

Bugental, D. E. (1974). Interpretations of naturally occurring discrepancies between words and intonation: Modes of inconsistency resolution. *Journal of Personality and Social Psychology, 30,* 125–133.

Bugental, D. E., Kaswan, J. W., Love, L. R., & Fox, M. N. (1970). Child versus adult perception of evaluative messages in verbal, vocal, and visual channels. *Developmental Psychology, 2,* 367–375.

Bugental, D. E., Love, L. R., & Gianetto, R. M. (1971). Perfidious feminine faces. *Journal of Personality and Social Psychology, 17,* 314–318.

Bugental, D. E., Love, L. R., Kaswan, J. W., & April, C. (1971). Verbal-nonverbal conflict in parental messages to normal and disturbed children. *Journal of Abnormal Psychology, 77,* 6–10.

Bull, P. (1983). *Body movement and interpersonal communication.* New York: Wiley.

Burgoon, J. K. (1980). Nonverbal communication research in the 1970s: An overview. In D. Nimmo (Ed.), *Communication yearbook 4.* New Brunswick, NJ: Transaction.

Burgoon, J. K. (2002). Nonverbal signals. In M. L. Knapp & J. A. Daly (Eds.), *Handbook of interpersonal communication* (3rd ed.). Thousand Oaks, CA: Sage.

Burgoon, J. K., Buller, D. B., & Woodall, W. G. (1996). *Nonverbal communication: The unspoken dialogue.* New York: Harper & Row.

Cappella, J. N. (1981). Mutual influence in expressive behavior: Adult-adult and infant-adult dyadic interaction. *Psychological Bulletin, 89,* 101–132.

Cappella, J. N., & Palmer, M. T. (Eds.). (1989). *Journal of Language and Social Psychology, 8,* 3–4.

Darwin, C. (1872). *The expression of the emotions in man and animals.* London: John Murray.

Davis, F. (1971). *Inside intuition.* New York: McGraw-Hill.

Davis, M. (1979). The state of the art: Past and present trends in body movement research. In A. Wolfgang (Ed.), *Nonverbal behavior: Applications and cultural implications.* New York: Academic Press.

Davitz, J. R. (1964). *The communication of emotional meaning.* New York: McGraw-Hill.

DePaulo, B. M., & Friedman, H. S. (1998). Nonverbal communication. In D. T. Gilbert, S.T. Fiske, & G. Lindzey (Eds.), *The handbook of social psychology* (Vol. 2, 4th ed.). New York: McGraw-Hill.

DePaulo, B. M., Rosenthal, R., Eisenstat, R., Rogers, P. L., & Finkelstein, S. (1978). Decoding discrepant nonverbal cues. *Journal of Personality and Social Psychology, 36,* 313–323.

DePaulo, P. J. (1992). Applications of nonverbal behavior research in marketing and management. In R. S. Feldman (Ed.), *Applications of nonverbal behavioral theories and research.* Hillsdale, NJ: Erlbaum.

Dittmann, A. T. (1977). The role of body movement in communication. In A. W. Siegman & S. Feldstein (Eds.), *Nonverbal behavior and communication.* Potomac, MD: Erlbaum.

Duncan, S., Jr., & Fiske, D. W. (1977). *Face-to-face interaction: Research, methods, and theory.* Hillsdale, NJ: Erlbaum.

Efron, D. (1941). *Gesture and environment.* New York: King's Crown Press (Republished as *Gesture, race and culture* in 1972). The Hague: Mouton.

Ekman, P. (1965). Communication through nonverbal behavior: A source of information about an interpersonal relationship. In S. S. Tomkins & C. E. Izard (Eds.), *Affect, cognition and personality.* New York: Springer.

Ekman, P. (Ed.). (1973). *Darwin and facial expression: A century of research in review.* New York: Academic Press.

Ekman, P. (1977). What's in a name? *Journal of Communication, 27,* 237–239.

Ekman, P. (1999). Emotional and conversational nonverbal signals. In L. S. Messing & R. Campbell (Eds.), *Gesture, speech, and sign* (pp. 45–55). New York: Oxford University Press.

Ekman, P., & Friesen, W. V. (1969). The repertoire of nonverbal behavior: Categories, origins, usage, and coding. *Semiotica, 1,* 49–98.

Ekman, P., Friesen, W. V., & Ellsworth, P. (1972). *Emotion in the human face.* Elmsford, NY: Pergamon Press.

Ekman, P., Liebert, R. M., Friesen, W. V., Harrison, R., Zlatchin, C., Malmstrom, E. J., & Baron, R. A. (Eds.). (1972). Facial expressions of emotion while watching televised violence as predictors of subsequent aggression. In G. A. Comstock, E. A. Rubinstein, & J. P. Murray (Eds.), *Television and social behavior* (Vol. 5). Washington, DC: U.S. Government Printing Office.

Fast, J. (1970). *Body language.* New York: M. Evans.

Feldman, R. S. (Ed.). (1992). *Applications of nonverbal behavioral theories and research.* Hillsdale, NJ: Erlbaum.

Feldman, R. S., & Rimé, B. (Eds.). (1991). *Fundamentals of nonverbal behavior.* New York: Cambridge University Press.

Frank, L. K. (1957). Tactile communication. *Genetic Psychology Monographs, 56,* 209–255.

Givens, D. B. (1978). Contrasting nonverbal styles in mother-child interaction: Examples from a study of child abuse. *Semiotica, 24,* 33–47.

Goffman, E. (1971). *Relations in public.* New York: Basic.

Goldman-Eisler, F. (1968). *Psycholinguistics: Experiments in spontaneous speech.* New York: Academic Press.

Grayson, B., & Stein, M. I. (1981). Attracting assault: Victims' nonverbal cues. *Journal of Communication, 31,* 68–75.

Gunns, R. E., Johnston, L., & Hudson, S. M. (2002). Victim selection and kinematics: A point-light investigation of vulnerability to attack. *Journal of Nonverbal Behavior, 26,* 129–158.

Hall, E. T. (1959). *The silent language.* Garden City, NY: Doubleday.

Hall, J. A. (1984). *Nonverbal sex differences: Communication accuracy and expressive style.* Baltimore: Johns Hopkins University Press.

Hall, J. A., Roter, D. L., & Rand, C. S. (1981). Communication of affect between patient and physician. *Journal of Health and Social Behavior, 22,* 18–30.

Harper, R. G., Wiens, A. N., & Matarazzo, J. D. (1978). *Nonverbal communication: The state of the art.* New York: Wiley.

Harrison, R. P. (1973). Nonverbal communication. In I. deSola Pool, W. Schramm, F. W. Frey, N. Maccoby, & E. B. Parker (Eds.), *Handbook of communication.* Chicago: Rand McNally.

Harrison, R. P., & Knapp, M. L. (1972). Toward an understanding of nonverbal communication systems. *Journal of Communication, 22,* 339–352.

Hecht, M. A., & Ambady, N. (1999). Nonverbal communication and psychology: Past and future. *New Jersey Journal of Communication, 7,* 1–14.

Hecht, M., Foster, S. H., Dunn, D. J., Williams, J. K., Anderson, D. R., & Pulbratek, D. (1986). Nonverbal behavior of young abused and neglected children. *Communication Education, 35,* 134–142.

Hecker, S., & Stewart, D. W. (Eds.). (1988). *Nonverbal communication in advertising.* Lexington, MA: Lexington.

Hess, E. H. (1975). *The tell-tale eye.* New York: Van Nostrand Reinhold.

Hinde, R. A. (Ed.). (1972). *Non-verbal communication.* New York: Cambridge University Press.

Iaccino, J. F. (1993). *Left brain–right brain differences.* Hillsdale, NJ: Erlbaum.

Jones, S., & LeBaron, C. D. (Eds.) (2002). Special issue: Research on the relationship between verbal and nonverbal communication. *Journal of Communication, 52.*

Kendon, A. (1977). *Studies in the behavior of social interaction.* Bloomington: University of Indiana Press.

Kendon, A. (1981). Introduction: Current issues in the study of "nonverbal communication." In A. Kendon (Ed.), *Nonverbal communication, interaction, and gesture.* The Hague: Mouton.

Kendon, A. (1983). Gesture and speech: How they interact. In J. M. Wiemann & R.P. Harrison (Eds.), *Nonverbal interaction.* Beverly Hills, CA: Sage.

Kendon, A. (1989). Nonverbal communication. In E. Barnouw, G. Gerbner, W. Schramm, T. L. Worth, & L. Gross (Eds.). *International encyclopedia of communications* (Vol. 3). New York: Oxford University Press.

Kendon, A., Harris, R. M., & Key, M. R. (Eds.). (1975). *Organization of behavior in face-to-face interaction.* The Hague: Mouton.

Key, M. R. (Ed.). (1980). *The relationship of verbal and nonverbal communication*. The Hague: Mouton.

Knapp, M. L. (1984). The study of nonverbal behavior vis-à-vis human communication theory. In A. Wolfgang (Ed.), *Nonverbal behavior: Perspectives, applications, and intercultural insights*. New York: Hogrefe.

Knapp, M. L., Hart, R. P., Friedrich, G. W., & Shulman, G. M. (1975). The rhetoric of goodbye: Verbal and nonverbal correlates of human leave-taking. *Speech Monographs, 40*, 182–198.

Knapp, M. L., Wiemann, J. M., & Daly, J. A. (1978). Nonverbal communication: Issues and appraisal. *Human Communication Research, 4*, 271–280.

Koivumaki, J. H. (1975). Body language taught here. *Journal of Communication, 25*, 26–30.

Koneya, M. (1977). Nonverbal movements or verbal surrogates? *Journal of Communication, 27*, 235–237.

Koutlak, R. (1976, November 7). With half a brain, his IQ is 126, and doctors are dumbfounded. *Chicago Tribune*, pp. 1–6.

Kretschmer, E. (1925). *Physique and character*. New York: Harcourt Brace Jovanovich.

Krivonos, P. D., & Knapp, M. L. (1975). Initiating communication: What do you say when you say hello? *Central States Speech Journal, 26*, 115–125.

Leathers, D. G. (1979). The impact of multichannel message inconsistency on verbal and nonverbal decoding behaviors. *Communication Monographs, 46*, 88–100.

Leathers, D. G. (1986). *Successful nonverbal communication*. New York: Macmillan.

Marsh, P. (1988). *Eye to eye: How people interact*. Topsfield, MA: Salem House.

Maslow, A. H., & Mintz, N. L. (1956). Effects of esthetic surroundings: I. Initial effects of three esthetic conditions upon perceiving "energy" and "well-being" in faces. *Journal of Psychology, 41*, 247–254.

McNeill, D. (1992). *Hand and mind: What gestures reveal about thought*. Chicago: University of Chicago Press.

McNeill, D. (2000) (Ed.) *Language and gesture*. New York: Cambridge University Press.

McNeill, D., Cassell, J., & McCullough, K. E. (1994). Communicative effects of speech-mismatched gestures. *Research on Language and Social Interaction, 27*, 223–237.

Mehrabian, A. (1970). A semantic space for nonverbal behavior. *Journal of Consulting and Clinical Psychology, 35*, 248–257.

Mehrabian, A. (1972). Inconsistent messages and sarcasm. In A. Mehrabian (Ed.), *Nonverbal communication*. Chicago: Aldine-Atherton.

Mehrabian, A. (1972). *Nonverbal communication*. Chicago: Aldine-Atherton.

Mehrabian, A. (1981). *Silent messages* (2nd ed.). Belmont, CA: Wadsworth.

Melbin, M. (1974). Some issues in nonverbal communication. *Semiotica, 10*, 293–304.

Montagu, M. F. A. (1971). *Touching: The human significance of the skin*. New York: Columbia University Press.

Morris, D. (1977). *Manwatching: A field guide to human behavior*. New York: Abrams.

Morris, D. (1985). *Bodywatching*. New York: Crown.

Myers, M. B., Templer, D. I., & Brown, R. (1984). Coping ability of women who become victims of rape. *Journal of Consulting and Clinical Psychology, 52*, 73–78.

Patterson, M. L. (1983). *Nonverbal behavior: A functional perspective*. New York: Springer-Verlag.

Patterson, M. L. (1984). Nonverbal exchange: Past, present, and future. *Journal of Nonverbal Behavior, 8*, 350–359.

Peskin, S. H. (1980). Nonverbal communication in the courtroom. *Trial Diplomacy Journal, 3*, 8–9 (Spring); 6–7, 55 (Summer).

Pfungst, O. (1965). *Clever Hans (the horse of Mr. Von Osten): A contribution to experimental, animal and human psychology* (C. L. Rahn, Trans.). New York: Holt, Rinehart & Winston. (Original work published 1911)

Polhemus, T. (Ed.). (1978). *The body reader: Social aspects of the human body.* New York: Pantheon.

Poyatos, F. (1980). Interactive functions and limitations of verbal and nonverbal behaviors in natural conversation. *Semiotica, 30,* 211–244.

Poyatos, F. (Ed.). (1992). *Advances in nonverbal communication.* Amsterdam: John Benjamins.

Pryor, B., & Buchanan, R. W. (1984). The effects of a defendant's demeanor on juror perceptions of credibility and guilt. *Journal of Communication, 34,* 92–99.

Quintilian, M. F. (1922). *Quintiliani instituiones* (H. E. Butler, Trans.). London: Heinemann. (Original work published A.D. 100)

Reuters. (April 9, 2003). Proposed smirking ban raises eyebrows.

Rosenbaum, R. (1995, January 15). The posture photo scandal. *New York Times Magazine,* pp. 26–31, 40, 46, 55–56.

Rosenthal, R. (1966). *Experimenter effects in behavioral research.* New York: Appleton-Century-Crofts.

Rosenthal, R. (1985). Nonverbal cues in the mediation of interpersonal expectancy effects. In A. W. Siegman & S. Feldstein (Eds.), *Multichannel integration of nonverbal behavior* (pp. 105–128). Hillsdale, NJ: Erlbaum.

Rosenthal, R., & Jacobson, L. (1968). *Pygmalion in the classroom.* New York: Holt, Rinehart & Winston.

Ruesch, J., & Kees, W. (1956). *Nonverbal communication: Notes on the visual perception of human relations.* Los Angeles: University of California Press.

Saks, M. J. (1976). Social scientists can't rig juries. *Psychology Today, 9,* 48–50, 55–57.

Scheflen, A. E. (1972). *Body language and the social order.* Englewood Cliffs, NJ: Prentice-Hall.

Scherer, K. R., & Ekman, P. (Eds.). (1982). *Handbook of nonverbal behavior research.* New York: Cambridge University Press.

Sebeok, T. A., Hayes, A. S., & Bateson, M. C. (Eds.). (1964). *Approaches to semiotics.* The Hague: Mouton.

Sebeok, T. A., & Rosenthal, R. (Eds.). (1981). The Clever Hans phenomenon. *Annals of the New York Academy of Sciences, 364.*

Sebeok, T. A., & Umiker-Sebeok, J. (1980). *Speaking of apes: Critical anthology of two-way communication with man.* New York: Plenum.

Shapiro, J. G. (1968). Responsivity to facial and linguistic cues. *Journal of Communication, 18,* 11–17.

Shawn, T. (1954). *Every little movement: A book about Francois Delsarte.* Pittsfield, MA: Eagle Print & Binding Co.

Sheldon, W. H. (1940). *The varieties of human physique.* New York: Harper & Row.

Siegman, A. W., & Feldstein, S. (Eds.). (1985). *Multichannel integrations of nonverbal behavior.* Hillsdale, NJ: Erlbaum.

Siegman, A. W., & Feldstein, S. (Eds.). (1987). *Nonverbal behavior and communication* (2nd ed.). Hillsdale, NJ: Erlbaum.

Solomon, D., & Ali, F. A. (1975). Influence of verbal content and intonation on meaning attributions of first-and-second language speakers. *Journal of Social Psychology, 95,* 3–8.

Sommer, R. (1969). *Personal space.* Englewood Cliffs, NJ: Prentice-Hall.

Spiegel, J., & Machotka, P. (1974). *Messages of the body.* New York: Free Press.

Spitz, H. H. (1997). *Nonconscious movements.* Mahwah, NJ: Erlbaum.

Stiff, J. B., Hale, J. L., Garlick, R., & Rogan, R. G. (1990). Effect of cue incongruence and social normative influences on individual judgments of honesty and deceit. *Southern Communication Journal, 55,* 206–229.

Streeck, J., & Knapp, M. L. (1992). The interaction of visual and verbal features in human communication. In F. Poyatos (Ed.), *Advances in nonverbal communication.* Amsterdam: John Benjamins.

Tickle-Degnen, L., Hall, J., & Rosenthal, R. (1994). Nonverbal behavior. In V. S. Ramachandran (Ed.), *Encyclopedia of human behavior* (Vol. 3). New York: Academic Press.

Trager, G. L. (1958). Paralanguage: A first approximation. *Studies in Linguistics, 13,* 1–12.

Vande Creek, L., & Watkins, J. T. (1972). Responses to incongruent verbal and nonverbal emotional cues. *Journal of Communication, 22,* 311–316.

Volkmar, F. R., & Siegel, A. E. (1982). Responses to consistent and discrepant social communications. In R. S. Feldman (Ed.), *Development of nonverbal behavior in children.* New York: Springer-Verlag.

von Cranach, M., & Vine, I. (Eds.). (1973). *Social communication and movement.* New York: Academic Press.

Weigert, A. (1991). Ambivalence as a social reality. In A. J. Weigert (Ed.), *Mixed emotions: Certain steps toward understanding ambivalence* (pp. 33–58). Albany: SUNY Press.

Weitz, S. (Ed.). (1979). *Nonverbal communication: Readings with commentary* (2nd ed.). New York: Oxford University Press.

Wertz, M. D. (1972). *Toward a theory of nonverbal communication: A critical analysis of Albert Scheflen, Edward Hall, George Mahl and Paul Ekman.* Unpublished doctoral dissertation, University of Michigan.

Wiemann, J. M. (1977). Explication and test of a model of communicative competence. *Human Communication Research, 3,* 195–213.

Wiemann, J. M., & Harrison, R. P. (Eds.). (1983). *Nonverbal interaction.* Beverly Hills, CA: Sage.

Wiener, M., Devoe, S., Rubinow, S., & Geller, J. (1972). Nonverbal behavior and nonverbal communication. *Psychological Review, 79,* 185–214.

Wiener, M., & Mehrabian, A. (1968). *Language within language.* New York: Appleton-Century-Crofts.

Wolfgang, A. (Ed.). (1979). *Nonverbal behavior: Applications and cultural implications.* New York: Academic Press.

Woolfolk, A. (1978). Student learning and performance under varying conditions of teacher verbal and nonverbal evaluative communication. *Journal of Educational Psychology, 70,* 87–94.

Chapter 2

THE ROOTS OF NONVERBAL BEHAVIOR

There are no universal gestures. As far as we know, there is no single facial expression, stance, or body position which conveys the same meaning in all societies.

—R. L. BIRDWHISTELL

As we look back on a long phylogenetic history, which has determined our present day anatomical, physiological, and biochemical status, it would be simply astounding if it were found not to affect our behavior also.

—T. K. PITCAIRN AND I. EIBL-EIBESFELDT

In 1967, when David Reimer was eight months old, his genitals were accidentally mutilated when he was being circumcised. Subsequently, on the advice of physicians, David's parents agreed to a surgical sex change and set about raising David as Brenda, a girl. Nurture, it was believed, would triumph over nature. Despite twelve years of social, mental, and hormonal conditioning, however, David never felt he was a girl. His parents gave him dolls, dressed him as a girl, and tried in every way to reinforce his identity as a girl. But his twin brother expressed what others observed as well: "I recognized Brenda as my sister, but she never, ever acted the part . . . when I say there was nothing feminine about Brenda . . . I mean there was *nothing* feminine. She walked like a guy. Sat with her legs apart. She talked about guy things . . . she played with *my* toys" (Colapinto, 2000, p. 57). It wasn't that Brenda didn't learn what others were teaching her about how to behave like a girl. Nurture played its part. But what surprised everyone involved in this real-life nature/nurture experiment was the powerful influence of genetic, or "hard-wired," aspects of one's sexual identity.

During the 20th century, the question about whether human behavior is influenced more by nature or nurture was hotly debated. For many years the behaviorist view that all human behavior was the result of learning prevailed. Behaviorists believed that any differences between individuals could be erased if they experienced the same environmental stimuli, that genetic heritage was malleable. Today, the prevailing view seems to reject the either/or approach to the debate. Instead of trying to argue that all of our behavior is primarily guided by nature or nurture, most scientists believe it is wise to assume that there may be both a nature and a nurture component associated with any given behavior we exhibit. No doubt much of our nonverbal behavior has both innate and learned (including imitative) aspects.

Ekman and Friesen (1969), whose work in this area is detailed later, outline three primary sources of our nonverbal behavior:

1. Inherited neurological programs
2. Experience common to all members of the species (e.g., regardless of culture the hands are used to place food in the mouth)
3. Experience that varies with culture, class, family, or individual

Biological and cultural forces overlap in many important ways. Some common biological processes can be used to communicate—for example, breathing becomes a sigh of relief, grief, or boredom; a hiccup becomes an imitation of a drunk's behavior; audible blowing through one's nose may be interpreted as a snort of scorn; coughing becomes "ahem"; and so on. Later in this chapter, we discuss studies that suggest some aspects of our facial expressions of emotion are inherited and common to members of the human species. These studies, however, do not negate the importance of our cultural learning in manifesting these expressions. The neurological program for any given facial expression can be altered or modified by learned "display rules" specific to our culture (e.g., men should not cry). Different stimuli may trigger a given facial expression, again, depending on one's cultural training. A snake may evoke an expression of fear in one culture and bring out an expression of joy in another (perhaps to those who see it as an important food source). The society we grow up in is also largely responsible for the way we blend two or more emotional expressions (e.g., showing some features of surprise and of anger at the same time).

Studies of birds show clearly the joint impact of biology and environment on behavior. The European male robin attacks strange robins that enter his territory during the breeding season. Research using stuffed models has shown that the red breast alone triggers this attack mechanism. The female robin who shares the nest, however, also has a red breast and is not attacked. Thus this aggressive behavior, which is believed to be innate, is modified by certain conditions in the environment or by the situation that calls forth the response. As another example, some birds instinctively sing a song common to their own species without ever having heard another bird sing the song. These birds may, on hearing the songs of their particular group, develop a variation on the melody that reflects a local dialect. It has also been noted that without exposure to mature songs, the young bird's song remains rudimentary and imperfect. And even when a bird is born with its basic song, it may have to learn to whom the call should be addressed and under what circumstances, and how to recognize signals from other birds. Many of the inherited components of human behavior can be modified similarly. It is like our human predisposition for or capacity to learn verbal language (Lenneberg, 1969). Although we are born with the capacity to learn language, it is not learned without cultural training. Children isolated from human contact do not develop linguistic competence. Some nonverbal signals probably depend primarily on inherited neurological programs; others probably depend primarily on environmental learning; and, of course, many behaviors are influenced by both.

Finally, the answer to the nature/nurture issue concerning nonverbal behavior varies with the behavior under consideration. As we see in chapter 9, there may be multiple origins of facial expressions of emotion. Certain nervous mannerisms or self-touching gestures may be learned primarily as we are also learning to perform certain tasks and cope with various interpersonal experiences. Some behaviors may be primarily the product of imitating others. Some hand gestures, such as the thumbs-up gesture, are primarily culture specific, but certain patterns of eye gaze seem to have a strong genetic component. The stronger the learned component of nonverbal behavior, the more we would expect to find variations across cultural, class, and ethnic lines. Note, however, that a behavior which varies from group to group may still have a common biological base after cultural teachings are stripped away. How can we *ever* know that a single behavior or a pattern of behavior has a common biological base?

THE DEVELOPMENT OF NONVERBAL BEHAVIOR ACROSS EVOLUTIONARY TIME

Human beings, like other species, have evolved through a process of adaptation to changing conditions. Which nonverbal behaviors have ancient roots in human history? On what basis do social scientists conclude that a behavior or behavioral pattern includes an inherited component? It is not an easy task. Some of our current behavioral displays are only fragments of larger patterns no longer enacted in their entirety; some behaviors now embedded in rituals have little to do with their original function; and some behavior that seems to serve one function may be associated with something completely different—for example, self-grooming may be the result of confusion or frustration in achieving a goal rather than enacted for self-preservation, courtship, or cleanliness goals. And studying the fossil record is not much help in understanding the biological roots of behavior. Despite the difficulties inherent in any questions of phylogeny (the roots of behavior in human evolutionary history), researchers have made some important discoveries.

Inferences about whether any given behavior has been inherited and is genetically transmitted to every member of the human species have been made primarily from five research strategies:

1. Evidence from sensory deprivation—noting the manifestation of a behavior in blind and/or deaf people who could not have learned it through visual or auditory channels
2. Evidence from neonates—behaviors displayed within minutes or hours after birth
3. Evidence from identical twins reared in different environments—identifying the behavioral similarities of people whose gene structure is known to be virtually identical and whose learning environment is known to be very different
4. Evidence from nonhuman primates—showing an evolutionary continuity of a behavior up to and including our closest relatives, nonhuman primates

5. Evidence from multicultural studies—observing the manifestation of similar behaviors used for similar purposes in other cultures around the world, both literate and preliterate

Obviously, if we can compile evidence in all five categories, our confidence in a phylogenetic dimension reaches the highest level. At present, no behaviors have been studied with such thoroughness, although the face has received the most attention. The remainder of this chapter is devoted to exploring the innate and learned aspects of facial expressions of emotion, but it should be noted that there is also an important body of research that focuses on the biological and cultural bases of facial attractiveness as well (Rhodes & Zebrowitz, 2002).

Evidence From Sensory Deprivation

Many have observed the early appearance of nonverbal behavior in children. Perhaps the behaviors are just learned quickly. To verify such a hypothesis, we need to examine children who, because of being blind and deaf at birth, could not learn such behaviors from visual or auditory cues. Eibl-Eibesfeldt (1973, 1975; Pitcairn & Eibl-Eibesfeldt, 1976) filmed several blind/deaf children between the ages of two and ten and reached conclusions similar to those of others who have systematically compared the behavior of blind/deaf children with sighted/hearing children. In short, the spontaneous expressions of sadness, crying, laughing, smiling, pouting, anger, surprise, and fear are not significantly different in blind/deaf children. Smiling, crying, and laughing sequences filmed by Eibl-Eibesfeldt are shown in Figures 2-1, 2-2, and 2-3.

Some might argue that such expressions could be learned by touching or a slow reinforcement program. Eibl-Eibesfeldt points out, however, that even so-called "thalidomide babies" (whose mothers were prescribed the drug thalidomide during pregnancy and who suffered severe birth defects as a consequence), who had no arms, and children who could hardly be taught to raise a spoon to their mouths showed similar expressions.

Galati and his colleagues (2003) found similar results with sighted and congenitally blind children between the ages of six months and five years. Spontaneous expressions of sadness, anger, joy, fear, disgust, surprise, and interest were filmed and coded with Ekman and Friesen's Facial Action Coding System (see chapter 9). There were few differences between the expressions of the sighted and blind children, and judges who looked at the faces were able to accurately identify the situations that triggered the expressions for both. Thus, being able to see the facial expressions of others does not seem to provide a significant advantage in being able to make basic facial displays.

In addition to facial expressions, the deaf/blind children studied by Eibl-Eibesfeldt also showed other patterns of movement exhibited by sighted children. They sought contact with others by stretching out one or both hands, wanted to be embraced and caressed when distressed, and, as the pictures in Figure 2-4 reveal, showed a remarkably familiar sequence of refusal gestures.

Eibl-Eibesfeldt also reports some interesting eye patterns of blind children. When he complimented a 10-year-old girl on her piano playing, she looked at him, coyly looked down and away, and then looked at him again. A similar sequence was recorded for an

FIGURE 2-1

Eibl-Eibesfeldt's film of a blind/deaf smiling response. The head is lifted and tilted back as the intensity increases.

11-year-old boy when asked about his girlfriend. This sequence of turning toward and away is also seen in sighted children under similar circumstances.

Naturally, the expressions of blind/deaf children and blind children are different in some ways when compared with those of sighted and hearing children. These differences are particularly evident as the children grow older and learn certain display rules by looking at the way others perform expressions. For example, subtle gradations in the onset and passing of expressions were not observed as often in the blind/deaf children; their expressions seemed to quickly appear and suddenly disappear, leaving the face blank. Display rules about the suitable intensity of expressions is another lesson blind/deaf children appear to be less familiar with—for example, how intense crying and laughing should be in various situations. Sighted children also seemed more likely than blind children to learn a display rule for masking negative emotions (Galati et al., 2001; 2003). The general absence of facial blends among the blind/deaf suggests that this may also depend on learning.

FIGURE 2-2

Blind/deaf crying response filmed by Eibl-Eibesfeldt.

a

b

c

d

e

f

FIGURE 2-3

Laughing response of blind/deaf children filmed by Eibl-Eibesfeldt.

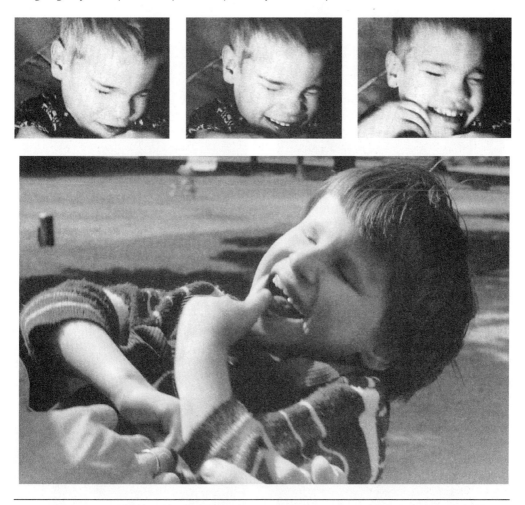

Making voluntary expressions (mimicking facial expressions) is also a learned behavior and young blind/deaf children do not perform this skill very well. But at least one study suggests that congenital blindness does not prevent adults from producing expressions that are as accurately decoded as those of sighted adults (Galati et al., 1997). All of these findings point to a joint role for innate predispositions and social learning.

EVIDENCE FROM INFANTS

Newborn babies (neonates) seem to have the facial muscle actions necessary to express virtually all basic affect displays of adults (Oster & Ekman, 1978). Do newborns show

FIGURE 2-4

A blind/deaf child refusing an offer of a tortoise. The child sniffs at the object and pushes it back while simultaneously lifting her head in a movement of withdrawal. Finally, she puts out her hand in a gesture of warding off.

a   b

c   d

e   f

affect displays resembling those of adults, and if so, do those displays convey the same emotions? Here the evidence is mixed, partly because of intrinsic difficulties in determining what emotion a baby is experiencing.

Researchers disagree: Does an infant's facial repertoire consist of undifferentiated expressions of arousal and distress, which are then shaped by experience, or is a baby instead born with a biologically based predisposition to display the whole repertoire of emotional expressions identified in adults? Much research has been inspired by the latter view, which is embodied in differential emotions theory, or DET (Izard, 1977; Izard & Malatesta, 1987). DET proposes a strong genetic basis for facial expressions, and thus emotions would produce the same distinctive facial patterns in both infants and adults.

Infants only a few months old do display some expressions consistent with prototypical emotional displays in adults—specifically expressions for joy, surprise, and interest (Oster, Hegley, & Nagel, 1992). These expressions are also easily recognizable by untrained observers as representing those emotions. This does not mean, of course, that the infants were actually experiencing those emotions, only that the facial configurations match the adult prototypes (Camras, 1994). For the negative emotions, however, evidence indicates that discrete expressions corresponding to adults' for emotions such as fear, anger, disgust, and sadness do not exist in young infants (Camras, Sullivan, & Michel, 1993; Oster et al., 1992).

Thus there is not complete support for the claim that infant data confirm the biological roots of discrete facial expressions of emotion. Moreover, it has been pointed out that too much emphasis on finding adults' expressions in infants might lead researchers to make several errors, including the following:

1. Reaching erroneous conclusions about what emotions are actually being felt (just because an infant and an adult show the same expression, we do not know they are feeling the same emotion)
2. Failing to observe distinctive infant emotional expressions that do not happen to match up with adult expressions (Barrett, 1993; Oster et al., 1992)

All researchers seem to agree, however, that infants' faces convey information about their states; that more research is needed to uncover exactly what is being conveyed and what regularities exist in the developmental unfolding of emotional expression; and that socialization still plays a crucial role.

The study of pain expression in infants and adults also yields information on the biological basis of expression and seems a less debatable topic than the expression of basic emotions. It is easy to argue that the adaptive advantage of being able to engage adult care from the earliest moments of life would lead to the evolution of an innate program for displaying pain (Prkachin & Craig, 1995). Expressions of pain in infants, even newborns, are highly similar to those observed in adults. These are the five most consistently seen facial movements:

1. A lowered brow
2. Eyes squeezed tightly shut
3. Vertical wrinkles at the side of the nose (the nasolabial furrow)
4. Open lips and mouth
5. A taut cupped tongue (Grunau & Craig, 1990)

Adults routinely recognize these signs of pain, although evidence also indicates that observers tend to underestimate the extent of pain in both infants and adults (Prkachin & Craig, 1995).

Research on imitation highlights the complex intertwining of biology and socialization in the development of expression. The early ability to imitate others' expressions may be inherited and may ultimately play a role in the development of various facial displays. Meltzoff and Moore (1977, 1983a, 1983b) demonstrated that 12- to 21-day-old infants imitated adults who performed four actions: tongue protrusion, mouth opening, lip protrusion (see Figure 2-5), and sequential finger movement. Subsequent research replicated the findings for tongue protrusion and mouth opening for neonates 0.7 to 71 hours old. Their experiments seem to negate explanations for such behavior based on innate releasing mechanisms similar to those found in many animals and the learning processes based on caregiver behavior. Instead, they argue that infants are born with the ability to use what they call "intermodal equivalencies," which means the infant is able to use the "equivalence between the act seen and the act done as the fundamental basis for generating the behavioral match." Perception and production, then, are closely linked and mediated by a common representational system from birth.

Figure 2-5

Sample photographs from videotape recordings of 2- to 3-week-old infants imitating (a) tongue protusion, (b) mouth opening, and (c) lip protrusion demonstrated by an adult experimenter.

Perhaps even more significant for understanding the early processes of learning and socialization is the finding that 9-month-old infants can imitate behavior from memory after a 24-hour delay (Meltzoff, 1985; Meltzoff, 1988a; Meltzoff & Gopnik, 1989), and 14-month-olds can accurately imitate a sequence of acts after a week's delay (Meltzoff, 1988b). The early integration of cognitive, linguistic, and communicative development is also demonstrated by the infant's ability to process visually the connection between mouth shape and sound, for example, that the "ah" sound comes from a mouth with the lips wide open and the "ee" sound comes from a mouth where the corners are pulled back (Kuhl & Meltzoff, 1982).

This research is complemented by other studies (Field, Woodson, Greenberg, & Cohen, 1982) that examined the imitation of specific facial displays of emotion by 2-day-old infants (see Figure 2-6). These findings support those of Meltzoff and Moore and indicate that the ability to discriminate and imitate happy, sad, and surprised facial expressions is one with which children enter their social environment.

EVIDENCE FROM TWIN STUDIES

Monozygotic (identical) twins are sometimes separated at birth and reared in very different environments. Because their genetic similarity is known, it is possible to compare and contrast their abilities and behavior in order to determine how much nature and nurture contribute.

Plomin (1989) provided an extensive review of the research using twins (identical and fraternal) as well as adopted children. This research shows a substantial (usually about 50% for identical twins) hereditary influence on such items as job satisfaction; religious interests, attitudes, and values; IQ; vocational interests; reading disability; mental retardation; extraversion; emotionality; sociability; alcoholism; and delinquency and criminal behavior. The extensive studies of identical twins reared apart at the University of Minnesota indicate the amount of genetic influence on a behavior can be high, but it varies with the behavior in question. General intelligence, for example, has a fairly strong genetic influence (50%–70%) whereas personality traits are at about 50%, occupational interests at 40%, and social attitudes at about 34% (Segal, 1999). The genetic influence on behaviors can be substantial, but nongenetic factors (family and nonfamily environment) are responsible for at least half of the variance in most complex behaviors. Even though genes may account for half of the variance associated with a particular behavior, note that this is almost never a highly deterministic, single-gene influence. And just because we have a genetically based predisposition to behave in a particular way does not mean these behaviors are unalterable or that they will even be displayed.

Despite the intriguing results from a variety of behavioral areas, we have almost no systematic research that bears specifically on nonverbal behavior. In one analysis of identical twins reared apart (Farber, 1981), some statistical evidence showed striking similarities between the twins in pitch, vocal tone, and talkativeness. Other mannerisms such as posture, laughter, style of walking, head turning, and wrist flicking were also observed as "more alike than any quantifiable trait the observers were able to measure." They go on to say, "Possibly the most interesting observation over the years was that many sets had

Figure 2-6

Sample photographs of model's happy, sad, and surprised expressions and infant's corresponding expressions.

FIGURE 2-6   (Continued)

identical 'body languages'—that is, they unconsciously moved and gestured in the same way, even when they had not had an opportunity for mutual identification" (Farber, 1981, p. 90).

Researchers at the University of Minnesota Center for Twin and Adoption Research echo these observations (Bouchard, 1984, 1987; Segal, 1999). For example, Segal says,

> One of my favorite tasks was faithfully capturing hand gestures, head positions, foot tapping and energy level in one-hour videotaped sessions of each twin alone, followed by half-hour videotaped sessions of the twins together. Distinctive physical expressions co-occurring in identical twins reared apart suggest that genetic factors are involved. Jerry Levey and Mark Newman, identical volunteer firemen, held pinky fingers under cans of Budweiser beer long before they met. [See Figure 2-7.] Other pairs were notorious for swaying side-to-side while walking, accenting long slender fingers with abundant jewelry, and belting out warm, rich laughter. (pp. 143–144)

When asked to stand against a wall for a series of photographs, identical twins in the University of Minnesota studies frequently assumed the same posture and hand positions; this happened only occasionally with fraternal twins reared apart. One pair of identical male twins reared apart had grown similar beards, had their hair cut similarly, and wore similar shirts and wire-rimmed glasses. Their photo shows them both with thumbs hooked into their pants tops. Another pair of female twins both started crying at the slightest provocation, and it was later learned that each had behaved in this manner since

FIGURE 2-7

Identical twins Jerry Levey and Mark Newman were reared apart yet both became volunteer firefighters. For a photograph of how they both hold a beer can with a pinky finger underneath, see N. L. Segal (2000), Entwined Lives, *New York: Plume, p. 144.*

childhood. These unsystematic observations do not prove anything about heredity and nonverbal behavior; they only suggest intriguing avenues for research.

Most of the studies comparing twins reared apart have emphasized responses to paper-and-pencil tests. But it seems reasonable to assume detailed observational studies will indicate a hereditary influence associated with behavior as well. For example, studies of twins show an inherited component to the trait of extraversion (Pedersen, Plomin, McClearn, & Friberg, 1988; Viken, Rose, Kaprio, & Koskenvuo, 1994), and we know that certain nonverbal behaviors (e.g., quicker and faster speech) are associated with the trait of extraversion. Therefore, it is possible that these and other nonverbal cues related to extraversion are common between identical twins. Twin studies have also shown a strong hereditary basis for social anxiety (Beatty, Marshall, & Rudd, 2001; Beatty, Heisel, Hall, Levine, & LaFrance, 2002). Nonverbal behavior associated with nervousness and tension are logically linked to social anxiety, but we also know learning can play an important role in controlling such behavior. Other relationship styles such as aggressiveness, in which heredity also seems to play an important part, may eventually reveal more about the extent to which nonverbal behavior has an innate foundation. But until more twin studies are done in which nonverbal behavior is the specific focus, we have to rely on tantalizing, but incomplete, anecdotal observations and reasoned inferences.

EVIDENCE FROM NONHUMAN PRIMATES

Human beings are primates, as are apes and monkeys. If we observe our nonhuman primate relatives manifesting behaviors similar to ours in similar situations, we are more confident that such behavior has phylogenetic origins.

For Charles Darwin, evidence of similarities in expressive behavior across different species constituted important support for his theory of evolution. For Darwin, the increasing use of the face, voice, and body for emotional and communicative purposes demonstrated the process of evolutionary advancement. Darwin (1872/1998) wrote:

> With mankind some expressions, such as the bristling of the hair under the influence of extreme terror, or the uncovering of the teeth under that of furious rage, can hardly be understood, except on the belief that man once existed in a much lower and animal-like condition. The community of certain expressions in distinct, though allied species, as in the movements of the same facial muscles during laughter by man and by various monkeys, is rendered somewhat more intelligible if we believe in their descent from a common progenitor. (p. 19)

Among vertebrates, the functionality of a rich repertoire of expressive and signaling behaviors is clearly related to the complexity of a species' social organization. We need only compare the differing number of facial muscles possessed by a lizard to those of a monkey to understand why Darwin considered expression a critical link in the argument for evolution.

Before we begin emphasizing similarities, we should acknowledge some important differences in human and nonhuman primates. Human beings make little use of changes in body color, but we do have an extensive repertoire of gestures that attend our verbal language. We also seem to have a greater variety of facial blends. Our response repertoire is not nearly as limited to immediate and direct stimuli. And, although other animals are capable of complex acts, the level of complexity, control, and modification shown by the human animal may be hard to match.

Behavioral similarities are often linked to common biological and social problems that confront human and nonhuman primates, for example, mating, grooming, avoiding pain, expressing emotional states, rearing children, cooperating in groups, developing leadership hierarchies, defending, establishing contact, and maintaining relationships. Chimpanzees, like humans, form political alliances to gain power, show empathy for those in distress, do favors for others, and reconcile after a fight with a touch or embrace (de Waal, 2002). Figure 2-8 shows some of these similarities in grooming and bodily contact. Of the many behaviors that might be explored for evolutionary roots (Altmann, 1968; Thorpe, 1972; van Hooff, 1973), we focus on two: (1) facial expressions and (2) eye behavior during greetings.

Studies comparing the facial displays of nonhuman primates and human beings find that the "tense-mouth display" of nonhuman primates (see Figure 2-9) shows social and morphological kinship to anger on human faces. When circumstances trigger a combination of anger and fear, nonhuman primates manifest a threat display (see Figures 2-10 and 2-11). In human beings, this most closely resembles a blend of anger in the mouth (open-mouthed anger expression) and fear in the eye area (Redican, 1982).

Figure 2-8

Upper left: A human couple. Upper right: An approximately 4-year-old female with an older male chimpanzee. Middle left: Rhesus monkey mother with child. Middle right: Sonjo children clasping each other in fright. Lower left: Social grooming of vervet monkeys. Lower right: Social grooming among Bali women.

FIGURE 2-9

A tense-mouth display by an adult female rhesus monkey. Ears are flattened, brows raised, gaze fixed and staring, jaws close together, and lips compressed. Teeth are not prominently exposed, although this animal is highly disposed toward attack. Angry humans display a quite similar configuration.

Table 2-1 provides both written and visual descriptions of probable evolutionary paths for facial displays of anger in three living primates. It shows evolutionary dead ends for some expressions and a continuity for others. Chevalier-Skolnikoff has proposed similar phylogenetic chains for expressions of happiness (smiling and laughter) and sadness (with and without crying) (Chevalier-Skolnikoff, 1973; van Hooff, 1972).

Like human beings, nonhuman primates may accompany their emotional facial displays with complementary cues in other body regions, for example, raised hair, muscle tenseness, and the like. Varying degrees of intensity (and blending) can be produced by nonhuman primates as well (see Figure 2-11).

Extensive studies of different species of macaques also demonstrate a wide variety in the social functions served by particular facial expressions (Preuschoft, 1995). Thus, even within these closely related monkey species, the same facial expression can be used with different overall frequencies and have different meanings. For example, there are "remarkable species differences with respect to the exact social meaning of the silent bared-teeth display" or fear grimace (Preuschoft, 1995, p. 201) shown in Figure 2-12. This "grimace" usually signifies submissiveness and appeasement in species marked by rigid status hierarchies. However, in species in which status differences are weakly expressed, the expression has converged with other expressions (for example, the "play face" shown

Figure 2-10

An adult female rhesus macaque (Macaca mulatta) *displaying a facial threat. Notice that the teeth are not prominently exposed. Ears are flattened against the head, the brow is raised, the gaze is fixed and staring, nostrils are flared, and the upper lip is rounded over the teeth.*

in Figure 2-13 and the "open-mouthed bared-teeth display," a more extreme version of the grimace) to signify genuinely affiliative and reciprocal social interaction—for example, during greeting, grooming, embracing, or huddling—and also to reassure a lower-ranking partner. The likely relation to human smiling has long been noted by primate researchers (van Hooff, 1972). Thus, in species marked by a reduction of power asymmetry and an increased overlap of interests among interactants, there has occurred an "evolutionary emancipation of silent bared-teeth display from its originally fearful motivation" (Preuschoft, 1995, p. 209). Such evidence that the same expression can have a diversity of meanings and functions among macaques should caution researchers of human expressions not to leap to simplistic conclusions about what human expressions mean based on the primate evidence.

Many of our facial expressions have evolved from noncommunicative behaviors such as attacking, moving toward or away from things, self-protective movements, and movements associated with respiration and vision. Chevalier-Skolnikoff argues, for instance, that:

> threat postures of most primates contain elements derived from attack (mouth open and ready for biting) and locomotion toward (body musculature tense and ready to advance), while the submissive postures contain elements derived from protective responses (retraction of lips and ears) and locomotion away from the sender.

FIGURE 2-11

Facial expressions of Macaca arctoides *according to intensity and emotion. Note that on the anger axis (top row, left to right) as the monkey becomes increasingly angry, the stare intensifies, the ears are brought forward, the hair is raised over the head and neck, the lips are tightened and contracted, and the mouth is opened. On the fear axis (left column, top to bottom) as the animal's fear increases, the gaze is averted, the ears are drawn back against the head, where they do not show, and the lips are retracted horizontally and vertically, baring the teeth.*

Reading left to right, and from top to bottom, these are the expressions: (a) Neutral face. (b) "Stare"; mild, confident threat. (c) "Round-mouthed stare"; intense, confident threat. (d) Slight "grimace"; slight fear. (e) No name; a mild fear-anger blend. (f) "Open-mouthed stare"; moderately confident, intense threat. (g) Extreme "grimace"; extreme fear. (h) Mild "bared-teeth stare"; extreme fear blended with anger. (i) "Bared-teeth stare"; intense fear-anger blend.

SOURCE: From Chevalier-Skolnikoff, 1973; p. 27. Drawn by Eric Stoelting.

TABLE 2-1   **A Between-Species Analysis and Probable Evolutionary Paths for Facial Expressions of Anger**

MACAQUES	CHIMPANZEES	HUMAN BEINGS

(a) The closed mouth, Type I Angry Face in humans has an equivalent in both macaques and chimpanzees. In all species, the mouth is closed, eye gaze is direct, and brows are either pulled down and together or raised and lowered as the macaques do. (b) This anger display has no equivalent in human beings. In macaques and chimpanzees, the mouth is partly opened with lips covering teeth. The macaques' mouth is rounded. Gaze is direct and accompanied by a roar or bark. (c) This anger display is found only in macaques. The common elements are direct gaze, jaws slightly to moderately open, and accompanied by a roar or bark. Macaques will raise and lower their brows and sometimes the lips will not cover the lower teeth. (d) An equivalent of this open mouth, Type II Angry Face in humans is found in all the nonhuman primates identified here. Direct gaze, lower eyelids tensed, often producing a squint, brows lowered and pulled together, jaws moderately open in a rectangular form with teeth showing are all part of the human display. Words often accompany this display as do screams and shrieks in other species.

SOURCE: From Chevalier-Skolnikoff, 1973; p. 27. Drawn by Eric Stoelting.

FIGURE 2-12

A grimace by an adult female rhesus macaque. Teeth receive a prominent frontal exposure in this and related compound displays.

Thus a behavior such as flight from an enemy, which was originally critical to survival, may eventually become associated with feelings of fear and/or anger. It is possible, then, that an expression of fear and/or anger may appear even if the original behavior (fleeing) is unnecessary, for example, a monkey that feels fearful when approaching a female to copulate. The facial display has, over time, become associated with a particular feeling state and appears when that feeling state is aroused. It is likely that those animals who substituted facial expressions of threat for actual attack and fighting probably had a higher survival rate and, in turn, passed on this tendency to succeeding generations. Similarly, our dependence on signals received visually (rather than through smell, for instance) may have been especially adaptive as our ancestors moved into open areas and increased in physical size.

To this point, our focus has been on our closest living relatives, nonhuman primates. Although these studies may seem most relevant to us, it is worth noting that nonprimates also show discriminable facial displays. The open-mouth display is seen in reptiles, and the flattening of the ears in situations evoking threat or startle is seen in most mammals. Some discriminable facial displays in greeting, grooming, submission, and threat have been identified in fur seals and walruses (Miller, 1975).

We also can look at entire sequences of behavior that may have some genetic components and evolutionary origins. For instance, many factors may affect the way greetings are handled: place, time, relationship between the greeters, and so forth. With so many

Figure 2-13

A playful chimpanzee (Pan troglodytes) *displaying the primate equivalent to the human laugh and pleasurable smile.*

sources of potential variation, then, it is noteworthy when we find seemingly invariant patterns. Pitcairn and Eibl-Eibesfeldt (1976) observed the eye behavior of adult human beings, human infants and children, blind persons, and nonhuman primates in greeting rituals and found some remarkable similarities. In each case there was a pattern of looking at the anticipated interaction partner from a distance, looking at them during the greeting at a closer distance and as interaction began; then there was a period of looking away prior to reestablishing gaze for interaction. They believe this behavior is a "stream of activity which, once started, must continue to the end" and that there is a strong possibility of a genetic or inherited program behind it.

Eibl-Eibesfeldt's studies of what he calls "basic interaction strategies" in several different cultures led him to conclude that rules related to dominance (and the fear of it) and bonding affiliation (and the fear of it) are at the root of human behavioral displays (nonverbal and verbal), whether in greeting, trying to block aggression, getting the focus of attention, or persuading a partner to give you something. But he acknowledges that cultural teachings and environmental factors may play an enormous role in making these strategies seem very different in one culture and another. Still, his observations of children in various cultures led him to state, "We can assume there exists a system of universal rules that structure social interactions, verbal and nonverbal alike. These rules could be rooted in certain panhuman dispositions that channel the acquisition of norms, and some norms may even be encoded in reference patterns given to us as phylogenetic adaptations" (Eibl-Eibesfeldt, 1987). Although Eibl-Eibesfeldt's view may be perceived as overstated or radically deterministic, given the evidence he provides for behavioral "universality," his observations do open the door for consideration of entire chains or sequences of behavior involved in relating to our fellow human beings that may be rooted in our biological makeup. Cappella (1991) also argues convincingly that there is a biological foundation for certain *patterns* (responses of both interactants) of interaction in humans.

EVIDENCE FROM MULTICULTURAL STUDIES

If we can observe human beings in different environments with different cultural guidelines similarly encoding and/or decoding certain nonverbal behaviors, we develop increasing confidence that inherited components of the species may be responsible. Even though multicultural similarities may be attributable to a common human inheritance, such observations are not absolute proof of innateness. It does mean that the cause of similarities across cultures is due to something we all have in common and makes a genetic explanation a possible one.

Because human beings around the world share certain biological and social functions, it should not be surprising to find areas of similarity. Eibl-Eibesfeldt suggests we might find entire sequences of behavior manifesting cross-cultural similarities, for example, coyness, flirting, embarrassment, open-handed greetings, a lowered posture for communicating submission, and so on. In fact, Schiefenhövel (1997) believes his own work and that of Eibl-Eibesfeldt have "clearly proven the existence of universal facial, proxemic, and to a lesser extent, gestural behaviors" (p. 65). Although others may not share the unequivocality of Schiefenhövel's claim, he reminds us of the extensive body of research ethologists have accumulated around the globe that speaks to our common behavioral heritage. But we should not forget the role of culture, which surely will contribute significantly to differences in nonverbal behavior. The circumstances eliciting the behavior will vary and the cultural norms and rules that govern the management of behavior will differ. Here we detail two behaviors with widespread documentation in a variety of cultures—findings that urge us to look for the possibility of phylogenetic origins: (1) the eyebrow flash and (2) facial expressions of emotion.

Eibl-Eibesfeldt (1972) has identified what he calls the "eyebrow flash." He has observed this rapid raising of the eyebrows (maintained for about one-sixth of a second before lowering) among Europeans, Balinese, Papuans, Samoans, South American Indians, Bushmen, and others (see Figure 2-14). Although the eyebrow flash often can be seen in friendly greeting behavior, it has also been seen when people are giving approval or agreeing, seeking confirmation, flirting, thanking, and when beginning and/or emphasizing a statement. The common denominator seems to be a "yes" to social contact—requesting or approving such contact. Smiles and nods sometimes accompany this gesture. The Japanese, however, are reported to suppress it as an indecent behavior. There are, however, other instances of reported eyebrow raising that seem to indicate disapproval, indignation, or admonishment. These "no" eyebrow signals are often accompanied by a stare and/or head lift with lowering of the eyelids signaling a cutting off of contact. Because Eibl-Eibesfeldt observed eyebrow lifting in some Old World monkeys, he began speculating on the possible evolutionary development. He reasoned that in both the "yes" and "no" displays, a similar purpose was being served: calling attention to someone or letting someone know

FIGURE 2-14

Eyebrow flash during friendly greetings. Filmed by Eibl-Eibesfeldt.

(for sure) they were being looked at. When we display the expression of surprise, for instance, we raise our eyebrows and call attention to the object of our surprise. It may be a friendly surprise or an annoyed surprise. The evolutionary chain hypothesized by Eibl-Eibesfeldt is presented in Figure 2-15.

Perhaps the most conclusive evidence supporting the universality of facial expressions is found in the work of Ekman and his colleagues (Fridlund, Ekman, & Oster, 1987). Photos of 30 faces expressing happiness, fear, surprise, sadness, anger, and disgust/contempt were presented to people in 5 diverse, literate cultures. Faces were selected on the basis of

FIGURE 2-15

Eibl-Eibesfeldt's hypothesized evolution of eyebrow movements.

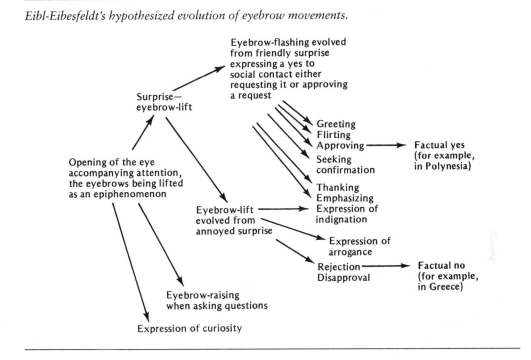

meeting specific criteria for facial musculature associated with such expressions. There was generally high agreement among the respondents regarding which faces fit which emotions. Other studies have found results supporting the accuracy of decoding posed facial expressions of emotion. These studies tested people from 21 different countries ranging from Kirghizistan to Malaysia and from Ethiopia to Estonia (Ekman, 1998; Boucher & Carlson, 1980; Ekman, 1972; Izard, 1971; Niit & Valsiner, 1977; Shimoda, Argyle, & Ricci-Bitti, 1978).

Because these people were exposed to the mass media and travelers, we might argue that they learned to recognize aspects of faces in other cultures from these sources. However, Ekman and Friesen's (1971) research with the South Fore in Papua New Guinea and Heider's (1974) work with the Dani in western New Guinea show that these isolated, nonliterate peoples who were not exposed to the mass media and travelers decoded the posed expressions comparably to the people from literate Eastern and Western cultures. In Ekman's work with the South Fore, stories were told to the subjects who were then asked to select one of three facial photos that reflected the emotion of the story. Distinguishing fear from surprise was the most difficult discrimination to make. Perhaps, as Ekman says, fearful events in this culture are often surprising, too. Interestingly, when Ekman obtained photos of expressions made by these New Guineans and asked Americans to judge them, the Americans accurately decoded all the expressions with high levels of accuracy, with the exception of fear, which was often judged as surprise and vice versa.

Physiological reactions associated with facial expressions have also been established. Ekman, Levenson, and Friesen (1983) found greater heart rate acceleration and increased skin conductance occurred when people in the United States made negative facial expressions (fear, disgust, anger). Levenson, Ekman, Heider, and Friesen (1992) found the same physiological reactions in the Minangkabau of Sumatra.

Although Ekman's program of research is perhaps the most complete, other studies of other cultures support his findings. There does seem to be a universal association between particular facial muscular patterns and discrete emotions. Note that this is only a specific element of universality and does not suggest all aspects of facial affect displays are universal—as Ekman and Friesen (1969) testify:

> . . . we believe that, while the facial muscles which move when a particular affect is aroused are the same across cultures, the evoking stimuli, the linked effects, the display rules and the behavioral consequences all can vary enormously from one culture to another.

Do these cultural display rules follow a pattern too? Matsumoto (1991) believes two important dimensions of culture will help us predict the display rules for facial expressions in any given culture:

1. Power distance, or the extent to which a culture maintains hierarchical, status, and/or power differences among its members
2. Individualism–collectivism, or the degree to which a culture encourages individual needs, wishes, desires, and values versus group and collective ones

Matsumoto hypothesizes that members of high power distance cultures will display more emotions in public that preserve status differences. Cultures that stress individualism, according to this theory, will manifest greater differences in public emotional displays between ingroups and outgroups than in collective cultures.

Although the evidence points toward universal recognition of certain emotions from facial expressions (Ekman, 1994), it is important to acknowledge that recognition is nearly unanimous only for expressions of happiness, as indicated by Table 2-2 (also see Russell, 1994). The smile—surely the most salient feature of the happy expressions—may indeed have nearly universal meaning. But even here, we should note that judgment studies like Ekman's ask people to judge "pure" expressions out of context. The social and

TABLE 2-2   Correct Judgments of Emotion in Five Literate Cultures

	JAPAN	BRAZIL	CHILE	ARGENTINA	UNITED STATES
Happiness	87%	97%	90%	94%	97%
Fear	71	77	78	68	88
Surprise	87	82	88	93	91
Anger	63	82	76	72	69
Disgust/Contempt	82	86	85	79	82
Sadness	74	82	90	85	73
Number of Subjects	29	40	119	168	99

emotional context of a smile, and the exact combination of facial muscles used, can add many new and even contradictory meanings, as we discuss in chapter 9. The claim of universality is not, therefore, that all smiles will always be interpreted as happy, but that the prototypical happy expression, involving movements of certain facial muscles, will have a common meaning universally.

The possibility of great variation in the meanings attributed to facial expressions is made even clearer by the remaining emotions in Table 2-2, for which cross-cultural agreement was noticeably less than was the case for happiness. For these emotions, possibly the biological determinants are weaker or have been more overridden by cultural factors. Russell (1994) demonstrated that recognition scores for people from non-Western cultures are significantly lower than Western subjects for expressions of fear, disgust, and anger. Russell (1994) describes the many problems with assessing universality in emotion recognition and cautions that we should not overlook the degree to which cultures do not agree.

These cross-cultural results suggest that, as with the bird songs mentioned earlier, emotional displays may have a "wired-in," neurologically determined basis that can be modified by local norms, values, and customs (see chapter 9). This notion is consistent with the conclusions of studies, described in chapter 3, showing that even though people may be generally accurate at interpreting others' nonverbal cues, they are *most* accurate when judging cues sent by people from their own culture.

As we see in later chapters, there is also evidence that cultures can differ widely in the overall frequency with which specific gestures or expressions are used, as well as in the meanings attributed to those cues. Thus, again, the debate over universality versus cultural specificity cannot be viewed in an either–or light any more than the nature–versus–nurture debate can be. For illustration, two cultures might engage in different *amounts* of interpersonal touch, but the *meanings attributed to* various kinds of touches—sexual, friendly, dominant, aggressive, and so forth—may be the same in both. Thus, we would see cultural specificity in terms of usage but universality in terms of meaning. Or different cultures might use the very same hand gesture with the same frequency, but use it to convey very different messages. In this case there would be universality of usage but cultural specificity on meaning.

We have ended this chapter by introducing the idea of differences among cultures in emotional displays and recognition. In chapter 3 we expand on the "difference" concept to examine differences among individuals in ability to send and understand nonverbal cues.

❖

SUMMARY

In this chapter, we examined five different ways researchers accumulate data relevant to questions of genetic and learned behavior. If we had data from each area for a particular behavior, the evidence would be strong. Instead, we have fragments and tantalizing possibilities. The evidence that facial expressions of emotion have an inherited component is, to date, the strongest data we have on any nonverbal behavior. Facial expressions of emotion seem to manifest themselves in children deprived of sight and hearing, in infants, in nonhuman primates, and in literate and preliterate cultures around the world. A genetic component passed on to members of the human species seems probable for this behavior. The innate capacity to perceive various kinds of behaviors and imitate them also has important implications for nonverbal study. And even though little detailed and systematic evidence is available, the possibility that entire sequences of behavior may have a link to inheritance is most intriguing.

We take the point of view that neither nature nor nurture is sufficient to explain the origin of many nonverbal behaviors. In many instances, we inherit a neurological program that gives us the capacity to perform a particular act or sequence of acts; the fact that a particular behavior occurs at all may be genetically based. Our environment and cultural training, however, may be responsible for when the behavior appears, the frequency of its appearance, and the display rules accompanying it.

Questions for Discussion

1. What do you think it means to say that nonverbal behavior is universal? State evidence supporting and not supporting such a claim. What exceptions can you think of?

2. Darwin thought there were many similarities between the expressions of humans and those of lower animals. Discuss communication in the animal world. Do you think animals send the same messages via nonverbal behavior that we do?

3. Why, in your opinion, do infants imitate adults' facial movements? Do you think they know what different expressions mean? Why do babies have such expressive faces and voices?

4. The "eyebrow flash" is seen in cultures around the world. Reflect on your own use of this gesture. Do you use it? If so, when do you use it and with what meanings? (You may have to observe your own behavior to answer this question.)

Bibliography

Altmann, S. A. (1968). Primates. In T. A. Sebeok (Ed.), *Animal communication.* Bloomington: Indiana University Press.

Barrett, K. C. (1993). The development of nonverbal communication of emotion: A functionalist perspective. *Journal of Nonverbal Behavior, 17,* 145–169.

Beatty, M. J., Heisel, A. D., Hall, A. E., Levine, T. R., & LaFrance, B. H. (2002). What can we learn from the study of twins about genetic and environmental influences on interpersonal affiliation, aggressiveness, and social anxiety?: A meta-analytic study. *Communication Monographs, 69,* 1–18.

Beatty, M. J., Marshall, L. A., & Rudd, J. E. (2001). A twins study of communicative adaptability: Heritability of individual differences. *Quarterly Journal of Speech, 87,* 366–377.

Bouchard, T. J., Jr. (1984). Twins reared apart and together: What they tell us about human diversity. In S. W. Fox (Ed.), *Individuality and determinism.* New York: Plenum.

Bouchard, T. J., Jr. (1987). Diversity, development and determinism: A report on identical twins reared apart. In M. Amelang (Ed.), *Proceedings of the meetings of the German Psychological Association—1986,* Heidelberg, Germany.

Bouchard, T. J., Jr. (1990). Sources of human psychological differences: The Minnesota Study of Twins Reared Apart. *Science, 250,* 223–228.

Boucher, J. D., & Carlson, G. E. (1980). Recognition of facial expression in three cultures. *Journal of Cross-Cultural Psychology, 11,* 263–280.

Brown, D. (1991). *Human universals.* Philadelphia: Temple University Press.

Cairns, R. B. (1976). The ontogeny and phylogeny of social interactions. In M. E. Hahn & E. C. Simmel (Eds.), *Communicative behavior and evolution.* New York: Academic Press.

Camras, L. A. (1994). Two aspects of emotional development: Expression and elicitation. In P. Ekman & R. J. Davidson (Eds.), *The nature of emotion: Fundamental questions.* New York: Oxford University Press.

Camras, L. A., Sullivan, J., & Michel, G. (1993). Do infants express discrete emotions? Adult judgments of facial, vocal, and body actions. *Journal of Nonverbal Behavior, 17,* 171–186.

Cappella, J. N. (1991). The biological origins of automated patterns of human interaction. *Communication Theory, 1,* 4–35.

Charlesworth, W. R., & Kreutzer, M. A. (1973). Facial expressions of infants and children. In P. Ekman (Ed.), *Darwin and facial expression.* New York: Academic Press.

Chevalier-Skolnikoff, S. (1973). Facial expression of emotion in nonhuman primates. In P. Ekman (Ed.), *Darwin and facial expression.* New York: Academic Press.

Colapinto, J. (2000). *As nature made him: The boy who was raised as a girl.* New York: HarperCollins.

Darwin, C. (1998). *The expression of emotion in man and animals* (3rd ed.). New York: Oxford University Press. (Original work published in 1872)

de Waal, F. B. M. (2002). Evolutionary psychology: The wheat and the chaff. *Current Directions in Psychological Science, 11,* 187–191.

de Waal, F. B. M. (1999). The end of nature versus nurture. *Scientific American, 281,* 94–99.

Eibl-Eibesfeldt, I. (1972). Similarities and differences between cultures in expressive movements. In R. Hinde (Ed.), *Non-verbal communication.* Cambridge: Cambridge University Press.

Eibl-Eibesfeldt, I. (1973). The expressive behavior of the deaf-and-blind born. In M. von Cranach & I. Vine (Eds.), *Social communication and movement.* New York: Academic Press.

Eibl-Eibesfeldt, I. (1975). *Ethology: The biology of behavior* (2nd ed.). New York: Holt, Rinehart & Winston.

Eibl-Eibesfeldt, I. (1987). Social interactions in an ethological, cross-cultural perspective. In F. Poyatos (Ed.), *Cross-cultural perspectives in nonverbal communication.* Toronto: Hogrefe.

Ekman, P. (1972). Universals and cultural differences in facial expressions of emotion. In J. Cole (Ed.), *Nebraska symposium on motivation* (Vol. 19). Lincoln: University of Nebraska Press.

Ekman, P. (1973). Cross-cultural studies of facial expression. In P. Ekman (Ed.), *Darwin and facial expression.* New York: Academic Press.

Ekman, P. (1994). Strong evidence for universals in facial expressions: A reply to Russell's mistaken critique. *Psychological Bulletin, 115,* 268–287.

Ekman, P. (1998). Afterword. Universality of emotional expression? A personal history of the dispute. In C. Darwin, *The expression of emotion in man and animals* (pp. 363–393) (3rd ed.). New York: Oxford University Press.

Ekman, P., & Friesen, W. V. (1969). The repertoire of nonverbal behavior: Categories, origins, usage, and coding. *Semiotica, 1,* 49–98.

Ekman, P., & Friesen, W. V. (1971). Constants across cultures in the face and emotion. *Journal of Personality and Social Psychology, 17,* 124–129.

Ekman, P., Levenson, R. W., & Friesen, W. V. (1983). Autonomic nervous system activity distinguishes between emotions. *Science, 221,* 1208–1210.

Farber, S. L. (1981). *Identical twins reared apart: A reanalysis.* New York: Basic.

Field, T. (1982). Individual differences in the expressivity of neonates and young infants. In R. S. Feldman (Ed.). *Development of nonverbal behavior in children.* New York: Springer-Verlag.

Field, T. M., Woodson, R., Greenberg, R., & Cohen, D. (1982). Discrimination and imitation of facial expressions of neonates. *Science, 218,* 179–181.

Fridlund, A. J., Ekman, P., & Oster, H. (1987). Facial expressions of emotion: Review of literature, 1970–1983. In A. W. Siegman & S. Feldstein (Eds.), *Nonverbal behavior and communication* (2nd ed.). Hillsdale, NJ: Erlbaum.

Galati, D., Miceli, R., & Sini, B. (2001). Judging and coding facial expression of emotions in congenitally blind children. *International Journal of Behavioral Development, 25,* 268–278.

Galati, D., Scherer, K. R., & Ricci-Bitti, P. E. (1997). Voluntary facial expression of emotion: Comparing congenitally blind with normally sighted encoders. *Journal of Personality and Social Psychology, 73,* 1363–1379.

Galati, D., Sini, B., Schmidt, S., & Tinti, C. (2003). Spontaneous facial expressions in congenitally blind and sighted children aged 8–11. *Journal of Visual Impairment & Blindness, 97,* 418–428.

Ghazanfar, A. A., & Logothetis, N. K. (2003). Neuroperception: Facial expressions linked to monkey calls. *Nature, 423,* 937–938.

Grunau, R. V. E., & Craig, K. D. (1990). Facial activity as a measure of neonatal pain perception. In D. C. Tyler & E. J. Krane (Eds.), *Advances in pain research and therapy. Proceedings of the 1st International Symposium on Pediatric Pain.* New York: Raven.

Hahn, M. E., & Simmel, E. C. (Eds.). (1976). *Communicative behavior and evolution.* New York: Academic Press.

Heider, K. (1974). *Affect display rules in the Dani.* Paper presented at the annual meeting of the American Anthropological Association, New Orleans.

Hinde, R. A. (Ed.). (1972). *Non-verbal communication.* Cambridge: Cambridge University Press.

Hinde, R. A. (1974). *Biological bases of human social behavior.* New York: McGraw-Hill.

Izard, C. E. (1971). *The face of emotion.* New York: Appleton-Century-Crofts.

Izard, C. E. (1977). *Human emotions.* New York: Plenum.

Izard, C. E., & Malatesta, C. (1987). Perspectives on emotional development. I: Differential emotions theory of early emotional development. In J. Osofsky (Ed.), *Handbook of infant development.* New York: Wiley.

Kuhl, P. K., & Meltzoff, A. N. (1982). The bimodal perception of speech in infancy. *Science, 218,* 1138–1141.

Lenneberg, E. (1969). *Biological foundations of language.* New York: Wiley.

Levenson, R. W., Ekman, P., Heider, K. & Friesen, W. V. (1992). Emotion and autonomic nervous system activity in the Minangkabau of west Sumatra. *Journal of Personality and Social Psychology, 62,* 972–988.

Matsumoto, D. (1991). Cultural influences on facial expressions of emotion. *Southern Communication Journal, 56,* 128–137.

Meltzoff, A. N. (1985). Immediate and deferred imitation in fourteen- and twenty-four-month-old infants. *Child Development, 56,* 62–72.

Meltzoff, A. N. (1988a). Infant imitation and memory: Nine-month-olds in immediate and deferred tests. *Child Development, 59,* 217–225.

Meltzoff, A. N. (1988b). Infant imitation after a 1-week delay: Long-term memory for novel acts and multiple stimuli. *Developmental Psychology, 24,* 470–476.

Meltzoff, A. N., & Gopnik, A. (1989). On linking nonverbal imitation, representation, and language learning in the first two years of life. In G. E. Speidel & K. E. Nelson (Eds.), *The many faces of imitation in language learning.* New York: Springer-Verlag.

Meltzoff, A. N., & Moore, M. K. (1977). Imitation of facial and manual gestures by human neonates. *Science, 198,* 75–78.

Meltzoff, A. N., & Moore, M. K. (1983a). Newborn infants imitate adult facial gestures. *Child Development, 54,* 702–709.

Meltzoff, A. N., & Moore, M. K. (1983b). The origins of imitation in infancy: Paradigm, phenomena, and theories. In L. P. Lipsitt (Ed.), *Advances in infancy research* (Vol. 2). Norwood, NJ: Ablex.

Meltzoff, A. N., & Moore, M. K. (1989). Imitation in newborn infants: Exploring the range of gestures imitated and the underlying mechanisms. *Developmental Psychology, 25,* 954–962.

Miller, E. H. A. (1975). A comparative study of facial expressions of two species of pinnepeds. *Behavior, 53,* 268–284.

Niit, T., & Valsiner, J. (1977). Recognition of facial expressions: An experimental investigation of Ekman's model. *Tartu Riikliku Ulikooli Toimetised: Trudy po Psikhologii, 429,* 85–107.

Oster, H. & Ekman, P. (1978). Facial behavior in child development. *Minnesota Symposium on Child Psychology, 11,* 231–276.

Oster, H., Hegley, D., & Nagel, L. (1992). Adult judgments and fine-grained analysis of infant facial expressions: Testing the validity of a priori coding formulas. *Developmental Psychology, 28,* 1115–1131.

Pedersen, N. L., Plomin, R., McClearn, G. E., & Friberg, L. (1988). Neuroticism, extraversion, and related traits in adult twins reared apart and reared together. *Journal of Personality and Social Psychology, 55,* 950–957.

Philippot, P., Feldman, R. S., & Coats, E. J. (1999). *The social context of nonverbal behavior.* New York: Cambridge University Press.

Pitcairn, T. K., & Eibl-Eibesfeldt, I. (1976). Concerning the evolution of nonverbal communication in man. In M. E. Hahn & E. C. Simmel (Eds.), *Communicative behavior and evolution.* New York: Academic Press.

Plomin, R. (1989). Environment and genes: Determinants of behavior. *American Psychologist, 44,* 105–111.

Preuschoft, S. (1995). *'Laughter' and 'smiling' in macaques: An evolutionary perspective.* Utrecht, Netherlands: University of Utrecht.

Prkachin, K. M., & Craig, K. D. (1995). Expressing pain: The communication and interpretation of facial pain signals. *Journal of Nonverbal Behavior, 19,* 191–205.

Redican, W. K. (1982). An evolutionary perspective on human facial displays. In P. Ekman (Ed.), *Emotion in the human face* (2nd ed.). Cambridge: Cambridge University Press.

Rhodes, G., & Zebrowitz, L. A. (Eds.). (2002). *Facial attractiveness.* Westport, CT: Ablex.

Russell, J. A. (1994). Is there universal recognition of emotion from facial expression? A review of the cross-cultural studies. *Psychological Bulletin, 115,* 102–141.

Scherer, K. R., & Wallbott, H. G. (1994). Evidence for universality and cultural variation of differential emotion response patterning. *Journal of Personality and Social Psychology, 66,* 329–340.

Schiefenhövel, W. (1997). Universals in interpersonal interactions. In U. Segerstråle & P. Molnár (Eds.), *Nonverbal communication: Where nature meets culture.* Mahwah, NJ: Erlbaum.

Segal, N. L. (1999). *Entwined lives: Twins and what they tell us about human behavior.* New York: Dutton.

Segerstråle, U., & Molnár, P. (1997). *Nonverbal communication: Where nature meets culture.* Mahwah, NJ: Erlbaum.

Shimoda, K., Argyle, M., & Ricci-Bitti, P. (1978). The intercultural recognition of expressions by three national racial groups: English, Italian, and Japanese. *European Journal of Social Psychology, 8,* 169–179.

Smith, W. J. (1969). Displays and messages in intraspecific communication. Semiotica, 1, 357–369.

Spitz, R., & Wolf, K. (1946). The smiling response: A contribution to the ontogenesis of social relations. *Genetic Psychology Monographs, 34,* 57–125.

Thorpe, W. H. (1972). The comparison of vocal communication in animals and man. In R. Hinde (Ed.), *Non-verbal communication.* Cambridge: Cambridge University Press.

van Hooff, J. A. R. A. M. (1972). A comparative approach to the phylogeny of laughter and smiling. In R. Hinde (Ed.), *Non-verbal communication.* Cambridge: Cambridge University Press.

van Hooff, J. A. R. A. M. (1973). A structural analysis of the social behaviour of a semi-captive group of chimpanzees. In M. von Cranach & I. Vine (Eds.), *Social communication and movement.* New York: Academic Press.

Viken, R. J., Rose, R. J., Kaprio, J., & Koskenvuo, M. (1994). A developmental genetic analysis of adult personality: Extraversion and neuroticism from 18 to 59 years of age. *Journal of Personality and Social Psychology, 66,* 722–730.

von Cranach, M., & Vine, I. (Eds.). (1978). *Social communication and movement.* New York: Academic Press.

Wolff, P. H. (1963). Observations of the early development of smiling. In B. M. Foss (Ed.), *Determinants of infant behavior* (Vol. 2). London: Methuen.

Chapter 3

THE ABILITY TO RECEIVE
AND SEND NONVERBAL SIGNALS

The study of nonverbal communication as an interpersonal skill represents a significant shift in the investigation of human social behavior.

—H. S. FRIEDMAN

As we look around, we readily note that some people seem more socially wise than others. Some people can "get along with anybody"; some people we call savvy, tactful, shrewd, or just "with it." In contrast, some people seem insensitive, awkward, or—to use one of our language's great phrases—"out to lunch." All of these qualities fit into the concept of *social competence*. Social competence is not easy to define, but it has long interested researchers, and *social intelligence* is considered a basic intellectual capacity distinct from other cognitive abilities (Riggio, 1992; Rosenthal et al., 1979; Sternberg, 1984). *Emotional intelligence* is a related concept involving our abilities to judge emotional messages, and to regulate our own emotions (Matthews, Zeidner, & Roberts, 2002; Salovey & Mayer, 1989; Salovey & Sluyter, 1997).

We definitely know that skill in nonverbal communication is part of social competence. Some people are comparatively more alert to nonverbal cues and better in tune with what these cues mean; some people are also more proficient at expressing their feelings and attitudes nonverbally. Some people try, using nonverbal as well as verbal cues, to project an image of themselves as cool, reckless, intellectual, sincere, or competent, but they just can't pull it off convincingly—their performances seem fake or flawed. Others do an excellent job of projecting exactly the image they desire. The social competence that comprises such skills is essential in our daily life, whether in the office, the courtroom, the nightclub, or the bedroom, as well as in trying to bridge gaps in social class and/or culture. If we accept the premise that our ability in nonverbal communication is important and that some people are more effective than others, we may legitimately ask how they became effective and whether these abilities can be developed in other people.

In this chapter, we focus on the receiving and sending of nonverbal messages, using the terms nonverbal *skill, ability,* and *accuracy* more or less interchangeably. Although nonverbal communication skills are often talked about with reference to moods and emotions, actually we are called on to perceive (notice, or remember), judge (receive, or decode), or send (express, or encode) many other kinds of nonverbal messages, states, and traits, such as those shown in the following examples. We make such inferences and expressions so often in daily life that we are barely aware of it. Yet each can be appraised for accuracy:

- Interpersonal orientation: "That person was trying to dominate me" or "He didn't seem very threatening"
- Attitudes: "I really like you" or "I could tell that you didn't like that movie"
- Intentions or needs: "She wants to leave" or "She wants attention"
- Physical states: "I'm in pain" or "You look really tired"
- Personality: "She was the most extraverted person I've ever met" or "Matt is so hostile"
- Personal characteristics: "You don't look a day over 30" or "I bet he's gay"
- Intelligence: "I have to seem really smart to get this job" or "He's not as dumb as he looks"
- Deception and insincerity: "I like this present, I really do" or "I thought she was a big phony"
- Appearance and behavior: "Remember Jenny? She's the one who smiles a lot" or "She's worn the same thing three days in a row!"

A person needs to notice nonverbal cues in order to interpret them correctly. Sometimes the noticing by itself is the important thing, as when you notice someone's looks, habits, and attitudes (Horgan et al., 2004). Or sometimes we notice something and don't realize its meaning until later, as in "Oh, you didn't get your promotion. No wonder you were so quiet at dinner."

Social communication skill doesn't rest only on nonverbal cues, however. We also need to grasp verbal meanings (literal, metaphoric, and shades of innuendo) and to integrate verbal and nonverbal cues in order to understand how their meaning is jointly influenced (sarcasm and joking, for example, are expressed through combinations of verbal and nonverbal cues). We also need to understand social contexts and roles—what's expected and unexpected in a given social situation and how people in particular roles (for example, professors and students) are expected to behave (Bernieri, 2001). The ability to associate a name with a face is another skill required in daily life. Psychophysiologists now believe face-recognition ability is located in a particular region of the brain, because injury, such as a stroke, can selectively impair this capacity. Social factors also play an important role in this skill. For example, female faces are easier to recognize than male faces, and it is more difficult to recognize the face of someone from a racial group different from one's own (Bruce, 1988; Hall, 1984).

The notion of nonverbal skill can be used to gain new insight into other long-established concepts. Empathy, rapport, intuition, and charisma, as well as processes such as social comparison and impression formation, can all be construed in terms of accurate sending or receiving of nonverbal cues among people (Friedman, 1979; Rosenthal, 1979). Kurt Danziger (1976) has argued that social interaction is impossible without a subtle and unspoken—in other words, nonverbal—negotiation over the respective roles to be played by the participants. Usually one person lays claim to a particular role or definition of the relationship and the other has to go along or else counter with a different role definition. Until the two people agree, tacitly, on a common understanding, they cannot successfully interact because they cannot effectively enact the roles of "friends," "teacher–student," "salesperson–customer," "doctor–patient," "interrogator–suspect," or "mother–child." Because people generally know how to play these roles very well and do so unconsciously, their negotiating over roles usually slips by unnoticed until one person acts "out of role" or inappropriate to the other's unspoken expectations. Then people are likely to become conscious that the interaction has become problematic, although they still may not know why. Clearly, the ability to read and send the subtle cues required for role negotiation is an important social skill.

Although a large amount of research has been done on nonverbal abilities, there are also many unanswered questions. These include the origins of nonverbal abilities; the role that motivation (trying hard) plays in accurate judgment and expression; whether skill in receiving and sending are part of one larger skill or are separate skills; within the receiving and sending modalities, whether there are many distinct subskills (such as skill in judging emotion, versus skill in judging personality, versus skill in judging deception, and so forth) or whether all can be subsumed within the general concept of "receiving skill"; and whether one's skills are unique to particular circumstances and partners or are a general trait. There are also many methodological issues (Hall, Bernieri, & Carney, in press), some of which we touch upon in the next section.

METHODS FOR IMPROVING NONVERBAL SKILLS

Most of our ability to send and receive nonverbal signals is derived from "on-the-job training"—with the job being the process of daily living. In short, we learn (not always consciously) our nonverbal skills by imitating and modeling ourselves after others and by adapting our responses to the coaching, feedback, and advice of others. This process starts in infancy with babies' mimicry of adult facial expressions. Even within the first few days of life, infants can imitate mouth opening and tongue protrusion; within the first few months imitation extends to lip protrusion, finger movements, brow movements, and even different emotional expressions on the face (see Figures 2-5 and 2-6 in chapter 2). By 9 months, a mother's facial expressions not only are reciprocated but also have a clear influence on the baby's affect and play behavior (Field, 1982; Field, Woodson, Greenberg, & Cohen, 1982; Meltzoff & Moore, 1983; Termine & Izard, 1988). Experts believe that an innate repertoire of facial expressions, innate imitative ability, and selective reinforcement by caretakers combine to produce in a child an understanding of the socially agreed on meanings of different nonverbal cues (Lewis & Rosenblum, 1978). In chapter 9 we discuss nonverbal mimicry further.

That nonverbal and other social skills are strongly rooted in learning seems apparent enough and provides insight into why individuals differ so much in these skills. Among many animals, social interaction is also essential to developing appropriate social behavior later in life. Harlow's famous studies (Harlow & Mears, 1978) of rhesus macaque monkeys showed, for example, that monkeys raised in complete isolation for 6 months and then tested at 2 to 3.5 years of age "displayed aggression even to 1-year-old infants, as no self-respecting socially raised rhesus would" (p. 272). Even specific communication skills in monkeys have been linked to social experience early in life. Miller and his colleagues found that rhesus monkeys reared in isolation were deficient in facial expression and judgment ability. In an experiment, two monkeys could each avoid an electric shock if one could communicate to the other through facial cues that the shock was imminent (indicated to the expressor monkey by a colored light), so that the other monkey could press a bar in time to cancel the shock for both of them. Monkeys reared in isolation were incapable of producing the necessary expressions and, when put in the role of receiver monkey, deficient at reading the fearful facial expressions of the other monkey (Miller, Caul, & Mirsky, 1967).

Feedback from others as we grow up does not have to mention our behavior explicitly; it can be a response *to* our behavior. Feedback, then, may be a person's saying, "Well, you don't look happy" or, even without making such a statement, your partner's responding to you as an unhappy person. Through feedback we increase our awareness of ourselves and others—for example, "Can't you see I don't like you!" We not only learn what behaviors to enact but also how they are performed, with whom, when, where, and with what consequences. You can practice nonverbal sending and receiving frequently, but, without regular, accurate feedback, you may not improve your ability.

Role playing is another popular method for teaching a social skill. Usually a situation is presented and the learner attempts to behave as he or she would if the situation actually occurred. In Stanislavsky's method of teaching acting, for instance, students may improvise various kinds of walks—walking impatiently, walking to pass time, walking to annoy people living in an apartment below them, and so on. Objective data on the effectiveness of role playing in improving nonverbal communication skills are difficult to obtain. Some people undoubtedly learn much from such experiences, although some may convince themselves they learned a lot partly to justify the time and psychological effort expended.

In more rigorous studies using various media for nonverbal skill development, evidence does point to positive effects of training. Studies incorporate a variety of approaches, including teaching the meanings of cues, discussion, practice, and feedback. Studies give encouraging evidence that improvements in decoding nonverbal expressions can result from such training, though the longer term benefits for social functioning are still not clear (Beck & Feldman, 1989; Costanzo, 1992; Davitz, 1964; Ekman & Friesen, 1975; Grinspan, Hemphill, & Nowicki, 2003; Rosenthal et al., 1979). Individuals from one culture have also been successfully trained to understand and enact characteristic nonverbal behaviors of people from a different culture or subculture (Collett, 1971). One study shows an intriguing connection with training in a different modality: Training in keyboard music produced improvements in ability to decode vocal expressions of emotion (Thompson, Schellenberg, & Husain, 2004).

Some kinds of everyday experience may also serve as a form of training. Parents, especially mothers, of toddler-age children were shown to be more accurate in judging nonverbal cues on a standard test than were similar married people without children (Rosenthal et al., 1979). And college students in the United States, Germany, South Africa, and Japan were found to be more skilled in judging the meanings of facial expressions if they had traveled more outside their own countries (Swenson & Casmir, 1998). These studies suggest that the need to decode the feelings and reactions of people who don't speak your language can contribute to enhanced skill.

There have also been efforts to train people's abilities in sending nonverbal cues, especially using the "social skills model" developed by Michael Argyle (1988). According to this model, socially skilled behavior is analogous to skilled motor behavior (such as driving a car). In both kinds of skills, a person makes moves, observes reactions to them (i.e., gets feedback from others from the direct effect of their moves), and takes corrective action, all with the purpose of obtaining a goal. The different elements of social behavior are seen as hierarchical. The finer, lower level elements are automatic and habitual; the higher levels are more strategic in nature and therefore under more direct cognitive control. This kind of training involves more active role playing and practice than the research described previously. Social skills training based on this model has been used to train people of low social competence in the effective use of nonverbal cues to make friends; it is also aimed at helping distressed married couples, psychiatric patients, children with learning disabilities, and professionals who need social skills for their occupations (Argyle, Trower, & Bryant, 1974; Hargie, 1986).

A major category of behavior emphasized in social skills training is *reinforcement*— the provision of encouragement and reward to others in the course of interaction. Reinforcers can be verbal and nonverbal. Verbal reinforcers include acknowledgment, agreement, and praise; nonverbal reinforcers include the positive use of smiles, head nods, looking at the other, touching, body proximity, certain gestures (e.g., thumbs-up), and encouraging voice quality.

Students frequently ask whether attempts to learn about and develop skills in nonverbal communication will have negative consequences. They wonder whether we will know too much about others for their own good and whether those who have this information might use it to manipulate others for self-serving ends. Popular "how-to" books on nonverbal communication often make recommendations for manipulating others. For example, one book says if a man mimics the body positions of a woman to whom he is attracted, she is sure to fall for him. Another suggests that at a business lunch, the client will be put at an unconscious disadvantage if the host gradually moves his or her placemat, plate, and silverware across the table, onto the client's side, thus invading the client's territory and weakening his or her defenses. Another such book says that hiding the palms is a sure sign of deceit. You can be sure that many such recommendations are not based on reputable evidence. Even advice based on sound research would be far from a recipe for success—people are not that predictable.

But assuming that knowledge of nonverbal cues is an asset in everyday life, should we be afraid of this knowledge? We think not. Consider the study of verbal persuasion. People have been studying the art of persuasion for over 2,000 years, yet it does not appear that anyone has become so sophisticated that he or she invariably succeeds in persuading anyone in any situation. Furthermore, it is the nature of human adaptation to change behavior when it becomes unproductive. Whenever people who know more about nonverbal behavior are suspected of using it "against" others, we soon see attempts to expose or counteract the attempted influence. As a general rule, more knowledge is a good thing, for at least it may forewarn a person about others' tactics (a point we also make in chapter 13 in the discussion of advertising). It should also go without saying that each person has the ethical responsibility not to use knowledge for harm.

Interestingly, people seem to be less comfortable with the idea of skilled (conscious) use of nonverbal cues than with the idea of skilled use of words, as in persuasion. People seem to want to believe that nonverbal communication is always a spontaneous (and therefore sincere) reflection of feelings or intentions. As long as people believe all nonverbal cues are spontaneous expressions of feeling, they will be less on guard against nonverbal manipulation and, therefore, more vulnerable to it. But nonverbal communication is much more than a spontaneous "readout" of feelings (see chapter 9). People use nonverbal cues for self-presentation and for a variety of strategic and communicative, sometimes even dishonest, purposes. The trial lawyer must act convinced of her client's innocence; the therapist must appear sincerely interested and accepting of a client's plight, whatever it might be; a manager needs to be able to produce a smile and a cheerful greeting for his subordinates even when his own mood is less than sunny; and a parent uses nonverbal communication constantly and deliberately to reinforce and direct a child's behavior in socially acceptable ways. Each of us has a multitude of roles to play in life, and a skilled understanding of the nonverbal cues relevant to each can only stand us in good stead.

MEASURING ACCURACY OF DECODING AND ENCODING NONVERBAL CUES

Interest in measuring people's decoding and encoding skills goes back to the early decades of the 20th century. Over the years, many researchers have measured these skills in order to answer a variety of scientific questions. Sometimes the purpose has been to study the encoding and decoding process itself. (Can emotions be recognized from nonverbal cues? What cues do people rely on most when making their judgments?) Sometimes the goal is to compare accuracy in different communication channels or among different emotions. (Is it easier to decode the face than the voice? Which are the hardest messages to send via nonverbal cues?) And sometimes the purpose is to compare the accuracy of individuals and groups. It is this last line of research that we emphasize in this chapter.

Even though our working definition of social skill is the accurate receiving (decoding) and sending (encoding) of nonverbal cues, there is still much latitude in how we might measure such skill, as well as in the kinds of things being judged, responded to, or sent as indicated in the list provided earlier. Later in this chapter we will catalogue some of the many correlates of these skills, but first we will give a taste of the variety in method and content of research (Hall & Bernieri, 2001).

Bernieri and his colleagues have studied *rapport* (Bernieri et al., 1996). Rapport is defined as how much positivity, attentiveness, and coordination are experienced by people toward each other when they interact (Tickle-Degnen & Rosenthal, 1990). Bernieri based his explorations of interpersonal sensitivity on observers' accuracy in rating the degree of rapport felt by people interacting on a videotape (by comparing these ratings to the degree of rapport reported by the people on the tape). Ambady, Hallahan, and Conner (1999) measured the accuracy with which people could identify the sexual orientation (gay/lesbian vs. heterosexual) of people shown speaking for only a few seconds. Accuracy was higher than expected by chance, and the less information was provided on which to base a judgment, the more accurate were gay and lesbian observers relative to heterosexual observers. As these examples suggest, decoding (receiving) ability is usually assessed by asking people to identify the emotional or attitudinal state expressed by another person on videotape, in a photograph, or on an audio recording. The stimuli to be judged might show all of the information, as in a full videotape, or the researcher might carve the nonverbal cues up into "channels" such as silent video, face only, voice only, and so on.

For facial encoding, the people who will serve as stimuli are often asked to express a series of emotions or attitudes using the face or to tell about an emotional experience while being videotaped. In the "slide-viewing paradigm" (Buck, Miller, & Caul, 1974), the researcher shows subjects a series of emotionally arousing slides categorized as scenic, sexual, unpleasant, or unusual. Facial reactions to the slides can then be assessed. Such facial expressions are much more spontaneous than in the previously described methods, for subjects do not know they are being videotaped while watching the slides (or films, in some studies). The issue of posed versus spontaneous behavior is discussed later in this chapter and in chapter 9.

For vocal encoding, senders may be asked to recite a standard sentence with emotionally neutral content or the alphabet while expressing different emotional/attitudinal states, or to describe a past emotional experience and thereby re-experience the emotion felt at the time. If, for example, the request is to "talk about a sad experience you have had," the tone of voice you use would reflect how successfully you convey your sadness. If the researcher wants to be sure that verbal cues do not provide the listener with clues as to what message is being conveyed, electronic filtering methods can be applied to make the words unintelligible so that only nonverbal qualities, such as loudness and pitch, remain (see chapter 11).

The accuracy with which the encoders have nonverbally conveyed various emotions or messages is often defined in terms of whether other people (who don't know what the original emotions or messages were) can accurately identify them. Thus, Koerner and Fitzpatrick (2003) had spouses deliberately send emotional messages to one another and scored encoding accuracy by showing the videotapes to a group of naive judges who guessed what emotion was being conveyed. The proportion of these judges whose guesses matched the original affective intention was used as the operational definition of encoding accuracy.

The methods described so far involve presenting a set of nonverbal stimuli to perceivers. Such stimuli are often called *thin slices* because they are short excerpts from the ongoing stream of behavior (Ambady, Bernieri, & Richeson, 2000; Ambady & Rosenthal, 1992; Carney, Colvin, & Hall, 2004; Lippa & Dietz, 2000). The "thin slices" used in research can range in length from a video of people interacting for several minutes to still facial expressions shown for less than one second (Matsumoto et al., 2000). There are many advantages to having the stimuli standardized in a set that can be reused with many different perceivers. However, sometimes a researcher wants to investigate communication between individuals who are actively communicating—for example, the accuracy of communication between subordinates and their bosses (Snodgrass, 1992) or between husbands and their wives (Noller, 1980). Snodgrass (1992) studied communication accuracy in unequal-status dyads in the following manner. After a period of interaction while in assigned boss–employee roles, both dyad members indicated their feelings about each other by making a series of ratings, and then both guessed what the other person's feelings were using the same rating scales. Communication accuracy was defined as the correlation between these two sets of ratings—with accurate communication occurring when one party's pattern of guesses matched the pattern of the other party's ratings. Using this method, it is a challenge to separate the skills of encoder (sender) and decoder (receiver) because high accuracy could result if the encoder sends very clear messages about what he or she thinks and feels, or if the decoder is highly sensitive to the cues conveyed by the encoder, or both. However, by showing videotapes of the interactions to a new group of naive judges, it was possible to disentangle these possibilities (Snodgrass, Hecht, & Ploutz-Snyder, 1998). But most research has taken the simpler approach of showing a standard set of stimuli to all perceivers.

A constant problem for this area of research centers on the question of *criterion:* It is easy to ask decoders to judge what the sender is feeling or communicating, but how do you know whether they are right (Archer & Akert, 1984)? If the communication is posed, the criterion can be simply whatever the encoders were asked to pose. If the sender was asked to look happy, a judge would get a correct answer for saying the person looked happy. Using this system, a judge could get an error through no fault of his or her own if the encoder did a very poor job of showing the intended emotion. Other criteria have been used, but none is perfect. With the slide-viewing technique, a decoder's answer is typically scored as correct if he or she correctly identifies which slide the encoder was viewing when the encoder's face was filmed. This method assumes that encoders' faces show an appropriate response; sometimes they do not. Sometimes experts decide on what emotion is being expressed in a stimulus. Sometimes consensus is used, so a correct answer is based on what the majority of judges say. (See chapter 9 for further discussion of judgment methods.)

STANDARDIZED TESTS OF DECODING ABILITY

Robert Rosenthal and his associates (Rosenthal et al., 1979) developed a multichannel test of nonverbal decoding ability, the Profile of Nonverbal Sensitivity (PONS). The PONS test is a 45-minute videotape that contains 220 auditory and visual segments to which viewers are asked to respond. Each segment is a 2-second excerpt from a scene portrayed by a white American woman. Five scenes portray a positive-dominant affect or attitude (for example, "admiring a baby"); five scenes portray positive-submissive behavior (such as "expressing gratitude"); five scenes portray negative-dominant behavior (such as "criticizing someone for being late"); and five scenes portray negative-submissive behavior (for example, "asking forgiveness"). Each scene is presented to viewers in 11 different ways, representing the single or combined channels of face, body, and 2 different kinds of content-masked speech (see chapter 11 for the description of the methods used to accomplish this). A receiver or viewer obtains a score for particular channels and combinations of channels in addition to a total score. The test has been administered to thousands of people of different ages, occupations, and nationalities.

Figure 3-1 shows three still photos taken from the PONS test. Each item has two choices, for example, "(a) returning faulty item to a store, (b) ordering food in a

FIGURE 3-1

Still photos from the PONS test.

restaurant" or "(a) talking about one's divorce, (b) expressing motherly love." Thus the PONS test measures ability to recognize affective or attitudinal states in a situational context.

In contrast, the DANVA (Diagnostic Analysis of Nonverbal Accuracy; Nowicki & Duke, 1994) is based on recognition of pure emotions—happy, sad, fearful, and angry—shown out of context, and thus it taps into a more unitary kind of knowledge. The DANVA has several versions, including tests of facial expressions of both white and African-American adult expressors, vocal expressions of white American adult expressors, and facial expressions of white American children. The vocal cues were generated by asking expressors to say an ambiguous sentence while trying to convey the four different emotions. The DANVA has been used extensively with children and adults.

A recent addition to these standardized tests is the JACBART (Japanese and Caucasian Brief Affect Recognition Test; Matsumoto et al., 2000). This test shows still photos of facial expressions of white American and Japanese adults *at extremely short exposures*—just fractions of a second. These are "sandwiched" between two neutral expressions of each expressor so that the viewer sees the sequence of neutral–emotion–neutral in very quick succession. The JACBART investigates sensitivity to *micromomentary expressions,* which we discuss further in chapter 9.

In contrast to these tests in which expressors act out different scenes or emotions, the Interpersonal Perception Task (IPT) emphasizes more spontaneous behavior. Its developers reasoned that in "real life" the things we judge about others are often actual events or relationships (Archer & Akert, 1977; Costanzo & Archer, 1989). The test has 2 versions (30 items and 15 items, each item a minute or so long on average). For example, a man and woman are interacting with two children—which one is their own child? Two women discuss a racquetball game they have just played—which was the winner? A man tells his life story, then tells it again quite differently—which story is the truth? Figure 3-2 shows some still frames from a preliminary version of the test. In the final (audiovisual) version of the test, verbal as well as nonverbal information is conveyed by the expressors, but the verbal information is ambiguous enough so the words alone do not "give away" the correct answers.

For each item in the IPT, there is an objectively correct answer; because the scenes are more "ecologically valid" than items on most such tests, it is believed the IPT measures the subtle and complex skills that people use in everyday life. There is, however, a trade-off in using more naturalistic scenes; for example, the test does not isolate cue channels, meaning one cannot separate accuracy for face, body, or voice. The quest for more "real-life" stimuli in nonverbal decoding tasks continues, with two other tests relying on cues generated in highly naturalistic circumstances (Magill-Evans et al., 1995; Trimboli & Walker, 1993). Another method that is based on naturalistic stimuli is called the *empathic accuracy* paradigm, in which a person's ability to "mind read" what another person is thinking and feeling at particular moments in a conversation is measured (by a later review of the videotape by both parties; Ickes, 2001, 2003; Ickes et al., 1990). Accuracy using this method seems to rely largely on information verbally conveyed (Gesn & Ickes, 1999).

FIGURE 3-2

How's your interpersonal perception? In (a), are the two people a couple married two years or strangers posing together? In (b), which woman is the mother of the children? In (c), is the woman waking her husband from a nap, watching an arm wrestling match, or playing with her baby daughter? Answers are given at the end of the chapter.

a

b

(Continued)

Figure 3-2   (Continued)

c

CHARACTERISTICS OF SKILLED NONVERBAL RECEIVERS

People can be extremely sensitive to nonverbal cues. In chapter 1 we showed that students react to very subtle positive and negative expectancy cues from their teachers. Research shows that first impressions of personality, based on superficial observation and no actual interaction, agree impressively among observers and with the targets' own self-descriptions. Thus people agree on others' sociability or extraversion after the barest exposure to each other, and those ratings are more accurate than expected by chance (Albright, Kenny, & Malloy, 1988; Levesque & Kenny, 1993; Marcus & Lehman, 2002). Similarly, observers rating only a few seconds ("thin slices") of behavior can be surprisingly accurate (Ambady, Bernieri, & Richeson, 2000). For example, people who watch brief clips of silent video of teachers' classroom behavior agree remarkably on the teachers' qualities, and their ratings predict performance evaluations by the teachers' own students and principal (Ambady & Rosenthal, 1993). Clips one minute long and shorter produce accuracy above chance levels for a variety of personality traits and intelligence (Carney, Colvin, & Hall, 2004; Murphy, Hall, & Colvin, 2003). The accuracy with which thin slices are judged varies greatly from study to study, and depends both on the method used and the construct being judged. Accuracy of distinguishing truth from lies is typically not much above the guessing level, while accuracy of judging basic emotions and also status differences between people is often very high (Biehl et al., 1997; Malone & DePaulo, 2001; Schmid Mast & Hall, 2004). Comparisons like this must be made with caution, however, because in developing their tests investigators have great latitude in determining how easy or difficult the items are (for example, by varying how much information is made available to perceivers). In order to detect individual variation, test developers often strive to make their tests neither too easy nor too difficult.

SELF-APPRAISALS AND EXPLICIT KNOWLEDGE OF NONVERBAL CUES

Considering the time required to develop, validate, administer, and score nonverbal tests, you might ask whether people could just be asked to appraise their own skills as a short-cut. Unfortunately, this does not work. People high in sensitivity to nonverbal cues are not necessarily those who appraise their own skills highly (Riggio & Riggio, 2001). Evidence from a number of studies shows that the correlation between people's self-evaluations (whether it is a general evaluation or an evaluation of their performance on a test they have just taken) is rather low. This lack of self-awareness of our own skill level is entirely consistent with the view of most experts that our knowledge of nonverbal cues is *tacit*—that is, we process nonverbal cues largely unconsciously, without much awareness of which cues we rely on. Indeed, the cues that people think they use when making nonverbal judgments are often not the ones actually relevant to the judgments they are making (Zuckerman, Koestner, & Driver, 1981).

Recently, however, it has been shown that people do have explicit knowledge of nonverbal communication, that is, knowledge they can articulate on a paper-and-pencil test (Rosip & Hall, 2004). The Test of Nonverbal Cue Knowledge (TONCK) measures knowledge with 81 items that are scored true or false based on findings established through published research. Scores on this test significantly predict accuracy on the PONS and DANVA nonverbal decoding tests, but the correlations are not large enough to permit the TONCK to be used as a substitute for measuring actual decoding of cues. However, a test of nonverbal cue knowledge is a good addition to the instruments available for researchers.

GENDER

One of the most well-established correlates of nonverbal sensitivity is gender. More often than not, girls and women score higher than boys and men on tests of judging the meanings of nonverbal cues (Hall, 1984; McClure, 2000). Women also score higher on the TONCK (just described), and they remember people's appearance and nonverbal cues better than men do (Hall & Murphy, 2004; Horgan et al., 2004). The female advantage in decoding the meanings of nonverbal cues is present from grade school up into adulthood. Although the difference is not great—there is only about a 2% difference in male and female PONS scores, for example—it is extremely consistent. Females scored higher than males in 80% of 133 different groups given the PONS test, including a variety of non-U.S. samples (Hall, 1984; Rosenthal et al., 1979). Reviews of research using many other decoding tests have confirmed that this gender difference exists across ages of participants and regardless of whether the encoders are male or female (Hall, 1978); it also holds up, generally, whether the participants are from the United States or not (Dickey & Knower, 1941; Izard, 1971).

Although these and other studies indicate a superior ability among females to judge nonverbal cues, there are limits and exceptions to a general female advantage. Females are especially good at judging facial cues relative to other channels (Rosenthal & DePaulo, 1979). For the decoding of anger cues, there is some evidence that males may actually have an advantage when the person being judged is male (Rotter & Rotter, 1988; Wagner, MacDonald, & Manstead, 1986). In general, women's advantage over men in decoding nonverbal cues is present whether the persons being judged are male or female (Hall, 1978). Researchers have shown that females do not have an advantage at judging whether another person is lying (Zuckerman, DePaulo, & Rosenthal, 1981), and their advantage is less consistent when the task is Ickes' empathic accuracy paradigm described earlier (ability to guess what another person was thinking and feeling at particular moments in a conversation) (Ickes, Gesn, & Graham, 2000), though women's advantage is sometimes very apparent with that task too (Thomas & Fletcher, 2003). Possibly tasks that show a weaker female advantage are those in which facial expression plays a smaller role. The face is, in fact, a very poor source of valid cues to deception (Zuckerman et al., 1981), and in the empathic accuracy paradigm of Ickes the most important cues appear to be verbal rather than facial (Gesn & Ickes, 1999).

Given how widespread the evidence for females' superiority on nonverbal tasks is, it is no surprise that a common stereotype about women is their interpersonal sensitivity (Briton & Hall, 1995). We think it likely that females' greater skill as interpersonal de-coders has been recognized throughout history and contributes to the layperson's notion of "female intuition." *Intuition* is a fuzzy term that can mean many things, from empathy to extrasensory perception. But we think an important part of the concept is nonverbal sensitivity. The belief that women are more sensitive to nonverbal cues is even present in literature; for example, a passage in George Eliot's *Adam Bede* (1859) describes a scene in which a woman correctly concludes that two young people are in love, based on her observation that the girl trembles in the boy's presence. When asked about this, she replies, "It's on'y the men as have to wait till folks say things afore they find 'em out." Is it a co-incidence, we wonder, that the author was a woman? (George Eliot was the pen name of the English novelist Mary Ann Evans.) More is known about the nature of gender differences in interpersonal sensitivity than about their origins. This is an unresolved question that we return to in chapter 12.

Age

Age also has been studied in relation to decoding skill. Provocative research indicates that infants only a few months old have some ability to discriminate among facial and vocal expressions of emotion (Haviland & Lelwica, 1987; Walker-Andrews, 1997; Walker-Andrews & Lennon, 1991). Of course, it is difficult to assess how much understanding of the cues' *meaning* an infant has; discrimination per se does not demonstrate this kind of understanding. But research did find that 7-month-olds showed increased looking at a face that matched auditory tones on emotional quality; for example, they looked more at a "joyful" face than a "sad" face when the associated tones were ascending, fast oscillating, high, and pulsing (Phillips, Wagner, Fells, & Lynch, 1990). Thus by this age they at least know what emotional cues should go together.

People generally show a gradually increasing decoding skill from kindergarten until ages 20 to 30 (Dimitrovsky, 1964; Harrigan, 1984; Markham & Adams, 1992; Nowicki & Duke, 1994; Rosenthal et al., 1979). More focused investigations have been able to identify the ages when specific skills are gained; for example, children 6 and 7 years old could not tell enjoyment from nonenjoyment smiles (which differ in muscle movements around the eyes), but children 9 and 10 years old could (Gosselin, Perron, Legault, & Campanella, 2002). In a study that compared women averaging 62 years old to women averaging 22, the PONS scores of the older women were significantly lower, suggesting a role for age-related changes in attention, memory, and perception (Lieberman, Rigo, & Campain, 1988).

GENERAL COGNITIVE ABILITY

An important question to examine is whether scores on tests of nonverbal sensitivity reflect a unique ability or, rather, reflect general cognitive skill. If the latter is true, researchers do not need to develop sensitivity tests, but could just administer standard cognitive tests (such as IQ tests). In general, although there is sometimes a correlation between general cognitive ability and tests of nonverbal sensitivity (Davis & Kraus, 1997), the relation is small enough to suggest that the two abilities are separate. In several large groups of high school students there was little relation between the PONS test and IQ scores, SAT scores, class rank, and scores on vocabulary tests (Rosenthal et al., 1979). However, as seen later in this chapter, in children there does seem to be a relation between decoding skill and academic performance, though not one that is large enough to suggest that the skills are interchangeable.

OTHER PERSONAL CORRELATES

Adults who do well on tests of decoding nonverbal cues have been found to exhibit the following personal characteristics (Carney & Harrigan, 2003; Funder & Harris, 1986; Rosenthal et al., 1979; see also review by Hall, 1998): Better adjusted, less hostile and manipulating, more interpersonally democratic and encouraging, more extraverted, less shy, less socially anxious, warmer, more empathic, more cognitively complex and flexible, more popular, seen by others as interpersonally sensitive, able to judge others' interpersonal sensitivity, rated as higher performing by supervisors, and have warmer and more satisfying relationships. In addition, researchers who study the *self-monitoring* construct (Gangestad & Snyder, 2000; Snyder, 1974) would include this trait as a characteristic of accurate decoders of nonverbal information in both face and voice. Self-monitors are sensitive to and exert strong control over their own behavior, but they are also sensitive to the behaviors of others and use these cues as guidelines for monitoring their own self-presentation. Results for the Interpersonal Perception Task support this finding: Higher scorers on this test also scored significantly higher on the Self-Monitoring Scale (Costanzo & Archer, 1989).

Another construct has recently been found to predict nonverbal decoding accuracy as well. The *social monitoring* construct describes the extent to which a person is achieving his or her social inclusion needs and also how strong these needs are. Pickett, Gardner, and Knowles (2004) found that among college students, those higher in self-reported need for social inclusion (irrespective of their sex) scored higher on several different measures of judging the meanings of nonverbal cues. Possibly, such people had more intense and rewarding social lives and this helped their decoding through practice and feedback.

Children in preschool and/or elementary school who score higher at decoding face, posture, gesture, or voice tone have been found to be more popular and more socially competent, less anxious, less emotionally disturbed, less aggressive, less depressed, and higher on internal locus of control (defined as the belief that one's outcomes are controlled by oneself rather than by chance or other people) (Baum & Nowicki, 1998; Izard et al., 2001; Lancelot & Nowicki, 1997; McClure & Nowicki, 2001; Nowicki & Carton, 1997; Nowicki & Duke, 1994; Nowicki & Mitchell, 1998).

A test that consists of African-American facial expressions shows an array of correlates among African-American test-takers (Nowicki, Glanville, & Demertzis, 1998); for example, better decoding scores were associated with higher self-esteem and more internal locus of control in both children and college students. When this test was given along with a corresponding test showing white adult facial expressions to samples of African-American and white college students, the white participants were less accurate than African-Americans when judging African-American expressions, but the two groups did not differ in their accuracy of judging white expressions. These results may be related to the fact that in our society, whites are much less accustomed to judging African-Americans' faces than vice versa. Subsequent research on white and African-American school children showed that popularity with peers was related to success in decoding facial expressions of one's own ethnic group, but not the other (Glanville & Nowicki, 2002).

Children scoring higher on nonverbal decoding tests also score higher on academic achievement (Halberstadt & Hall, 1980; Izard et al., 2001; Nowicki & Duke, 1994). Several studies suggest that although general cognitive ability may contribute to ability to understand nonverbal communication, the nonverbal skills may in turn influence academic achievement, possibly through their impact on the teacher–student relationship. Halberstadt and Hall (1980) found that children scoring higher on the PONS test were *perceived* by their teachers as smarter, even when the pupils' actual academic and IQ scores were controlled statistically, and Izard et al. (2001) found that ability to understand facial expressions at age 5 predicted teachers' ratings of academic competence at age 9, controlling for objectively tested cognitive ability. It is possible that nonverbally sensitive youngsters create such a good impression that adults attribute more cognitive ability to them than they have, which may create a positive self-fulfilling prophecy in which these children are taught more and are encouraged more, leading to actual gains in academic achievement. One study has found that decoding skill also seems to have a direct role in the learning process. Bernieri (1991) found that high school students who scored higher on the PONS learned more from a peer in a brief teaching session than did students who scored lower.

Although it is generally difficult to think of any benefits of a large amount of television viewing, Feldman, Coats, and Spielman (1996) hypothesized that children might actually learn to decode emotional expressions from television (where such expressions tend to be exaggerated). And they were right: Elementary school children who watched over 14 hours of television weekly were more accurate in decoding facial expressions of emotions than children who watched 7 or fewer hours.

Certain groups tend to have greater nonverbal decoding ability. The top three groups on the PONS test were actors, students studying nonverbal behavior, and students studying visual arts. Buck's (1976) research on the interpretation of facial expressions found that students who were fine arts or business majors were better decoders than science majors (students in biology, chemistry, math, and physics). Business executives who took the PONS test did not seem to show the same expertise that Buck's business majors did. Business executives and teachers showed significantly less ability than clinical psychologists and college students, who were significantly lower than the top three groups previously mentioned. (Do not forget that these are group scores. Individual teachers, foreign service officers, and clinicians who were rated excellent at their job also did well on the PONS instrument.)

Mental patients scored considerably lower than a norm group on the PONS (Rosenthal et al., 1979). Other studies concur that schizophrenic patients with both chronic and acute forms of the illness judge facial and vocal expressions less accurately than unimpaired groups, regardless of whether they are medicated (Edwards, Jackson, & Pattison, 2002; Mandal, Pandey, & Prasad, 1998; Mueser et al., 1997). A longitudinal study found that difficulties in judging facial and vocal emotions predicted difficulties with work functioning and independent living a year later in a sample of schizophrenic individuals (Kee et al., 2003).

Specific damaging experiences early in life may also affect accuracy at decoding nonverbal cues. Hodgins and Belch (2000) found that college students who had been exposed to parental violence while growing up were worse at judging happy cues than students who had not, but did not differ when judging other emotional expressions, and Pollak and Sinha (2002) found that abused and maltreated children had a lower threshold for identifying anger in facial expressions.

Deficits in decoding nonverbal cues have been shown across a range of psychological dysfunctions. On the PONS test, decrements in decoding ability were found in boys referred to clinics for various kinds of childhood psychopathology (Russell et al., 1993). Interestingly, boys with problems of self-control and social incompetence made the majority of their decoding errors on PONS items requiring a judgment about the dominant–submissive dimension of behavior, consistent with previous findings that aggressive boys tend to see aggressiveness in neutral stimuli (Dodge & Newman, 1981). Similarly, preschool children rated by their teachers as hostile and dependent were biased in their judgments of their classmates' facial expressions: They were more likely to say the expressions were sad or angry and less likely to say they were happy, compared to children who were not hostile and dependent (Barth & Bastiani, 1997).

A group known for having interpersonal communication difficulties is people with autism (Philippot, Feldman, & McGee, 1992). Autism is a disorder largely defined in terms of deficient verbal, and especially nonverbal, communication and an extreme inability to relate to other human beings. The neurologist Oliver Sacks has written about Temple Grandin, an autistic academician whose insights greatly illuminate our understanding of the psychological experience of autism. Grandin's understanding of others' feelings and intentions comes from "immense intellectual effort" as opposed to the unconscious, intuitive process used by nonautistic people. Commenting on Grandin's childhood experiences, Sacks writes:

> Something was going on between the other kids, something swift, subtle, constantly changing—an exchange of meanings, a negotiation, a swiftness of understanding so remarkable that sometimes she wondered if they were all telepathic. She is now aware of the existence of these social signals. She can infer them, she says, but she herself cannot perceive them, cannot participate in this magical communication directly. . . . This is why she often feels excluded, an alien. (Sacks, 1993, p. 116)

Not surprisingly, individuals with autism (and a milder related condition, Asperger syndrome) consistently perform more poorly than normal-functioning people on tests of decoding facial and vocal expressions (Rutherford, Baron-Cohen, & Wheelwright, 2002).

Alcohol consumption, in its extreme form, can also be considered a psychopathology, and indeed alcoholic patients score lower than a norm group on the PONS test (Rosenthal et al., 1979). An intriguing experiment using photographs of six emotions found that when nonalcoholic participants were given alcohol, their decoding accuracy was impaired, especially men's ability to identify anger, disgust, and contempt (Borrill, Rosen, & Summerfield, 1987). Perhaps some of the antisocial behavior of drinkers is linked to an impairment in their sensitivity to these cues.

The PONS has been administered to people from over 20 nations (Rosenthal et al., 1979). People from countries most similar to the United States in language and culture (modernization, widespread use of communications media) scored highest. The PONS research therefore offers a synthesis of two opposed positions on the universality of emotional expressions: One states that these are universally used and recognized, the other that nonverbal communication is as culture specific as verbal language itself. The universalist position is supported by the fact that all cultures were able to perform at higher than chance levels on the PONS. However, the specificity argument is also supported by the fact that groups more culturally similar to the person shown in the PONS video were able to extract more accurate meaning from the cues. (Chapters 2, 9, and 12 offer further discusson of cultural universality and relativity.)

Finally, specific relationship characteristics have also been examined. A vast amount of research on the topic of attraction suggests that similarity in attitudes or background is a key to selecting and maintaining friends and romantic partners. The nonverbal realm offers supporting evidence. Friends are more similar to each other in their understanding of facial cues of emotion than people who are not friends (Brauer & DePaulo, 1980). When friends are more similar in this kind of skill (Brauer & DePaulo, 1980) or when both have high ability (Hodgins & Zuckerman, 1990), the relationship is marked by deeper emotional sharing. Both Noller (1980) and Koerner and Fitzpatrick (2003) found that higher communication accuracy between spouses was associated with more marital satisfaction.

TASK FACTORS AFFECTING NONVERBAL RECEIVING ACCURACY

You may think the particular channels (face, voice, and the like) that are tested will make a difference in a person's nonverbal receiving accuracy. Generally, judgments of visual channels (especially the face) are more accurate than judgments of the voice, though generalizations like this need to be made with caution because tests of different channels may differ in other methodological ways. Several studies show that emotions and attitudes of liking and disliking are more accurately perceived in the face than in the voice. And, although you may be better able to recognize many emotions and attitudes if you get both audio and visual cues, some messages may be more effectively communicated in one mode than another; for example, vocal cues may be more effective for communicating anxiety and dominance than other communication channels. If you are accurate in recognizing facial signals, you will also be accurate in perceiving vocal ones (Zuckerman et al., 1975). Also, accuracy is usually higher if the expressions are posed than spontaneous, but if you do well in decoding one of these modalities, you'll probably do well in the other (Zuckerman et al., 1976). It is clear that some emotional and attitudinal states are more difficult to judge than others. Negative nonverbal messages, some argue, may be more easily judged than positive ones, although findings are inconsistent on this and also seem to vary with the nonverbal channel in which the cues are conveyed (Zuckerman et al., 1976).

We might also speculate, as did the PONS researchers, that the amount of time a receiver was exposed to a nonverbal signal would affect his or her accuracy in identification. The PONS scenes were presented to people with the exposure time varied, for example, $\frac{1}{24}$ of a second, $\frac{3}{24}$ of a second, and so on up to 2 seconds (Rosenthal et al., 1979). Accuracy did increase as exposure time increased. Research on judgments made of exposures varying between 2 seconds and 5 minutes has found that, often, more information does not yield higher accuracy, and when it does the differences are often not dramatic (Ambady, Bernieri, & Richeson, 2000; Carney, Colvin, & Hall, 2004).

Our moods can influence how we perceive others' behavior. Positive and negative moods produce a bias to see the corresponding emotions in others' faces (Niedenthal et al., 2000; Schiffenbauer, 1974). Sad moods reduce accuracy of judging others, unless the sad person is distracted by being asked to engage in another cognitive activity at the same time (Ambady & Gray, 2002). The latter finding lends support to the argument that sad moods promote a deliberative information-processing style that detracts from accuracy of nonverbal judgments that would otherwise be made in a more automatic and non-analytic manner.

CHARACTERISTICS OF ACCURATE NONVERBAL SENDERS

When broadly conceived, a definition of "nonverbal sending" is even more complex than a definition of nonverbal decoding. In a sense, nonverbal sending is everything we do of an interpersonal nature, minus the words. Indeed, it is inevitable that one's nonverbal cues will be perceived and interpreted by others—even if a person's intention is to appear neutral or unexpressive. Attempts to control nonverbal cues by trying not to express them at all are likely to be interpreted as dullness, withdrawal, uneasiness, aloofness, or even deceptiveness (DePaulo, 1992). It is true, as is sometimes said, that you can't *not* communicate nonverbally.

A person's nonverbal sending is a mixture of spontaneous cues and more deliberate or intentional ones. The latter are used in daily life to convey a host of impressions of ourselves as nice, smart, youthful, honest, dominant, brave, and so forth. We also use nonverbal communication intentionally as part of our effort to act socially appropriate, for example, to be respectful to authorities, dignified in a fancy restaurant, or polite in the face of disappointment.

Children attain these more deliberate self-presentational skills through a long process that combines social experience with their own development of identity; numerous studies testify to developmental trends in these skills (DePaulo, 1992; Harrigan, 1984; Nowicki & Duke, 1994; Rosenthal et al., 1979), although we should not underestimate the skill of young children in simulating and masking expressions of emotion (Halberstadt et al., 1992). According to DePaulo, success at regulating nonverbal behaviors to promote the public presentation of oneself depends on knowledge, skill, practice, experience, confidence, and motivation. The success of nonverbal self-presentation is also limited by the inherent controllability of different nonverbal channels (the face, for example, is believed to be more controllable than voice or body) and the intensity of the reality we might wish to mask (for example, the angrier you are, the harder it will be to act as if everything is fine), as well as individual differences among people.

One individual difference that definitely affects self-presentation is spontaneous expressiveness of the sort we have discussed in relation to the slide-viewing paradigm, for example, how much your face reflects the content of a gruesome or romantic scene you watch on television. These differences are observable in infancy and stable over the course of development. The spontaneously expressive person has many social advantages, as we outline shortly, but may be handicapped whenever self-presentation calls for application of display rules or deception. It is suggested, for example, that a highly expressive person may not make a good poker player (DePaulo, 1992).

Another factor influencing nonverbal self-presentation involves lasting physical and expressive qualities that bestow a particular demeanor on a person. Thus, for example, the man with thick bushy eyebrows may look threatening no matter how gentle he actually is. Research finds that some people's demeanors tend to make them look honest or dishonest or pleasant or unpleasant, no matter what they actually feel or say (Wallbott & Scherer, 1986; Zuckerman et al., 1979). Demeanor can work for or against you, depending on your goals; the socially skilled person may learn to complement demeanor with other expressive cues to enhance self-presentation. For example, the person with a naturally babyish or honest-looking face may develop a repertoire of "innocent" nonverbal cues to enhance the impression of sincerity.

Most research on sending (encoding) accuracy involves emotions. The person who is spontaneously emotionally expressive tends to be female and reports less ability to control his or her emotions (Tucker & Riggio, 1988). It has been suggested that *not* allowing free expression can take a toll on health and cognitive functioning (Berry & Pennebaker, 1993). People who are less expressive experience a higher level of internal physiological arousal (Buck, 1977; Buck, Miller, & Caul, 1974), and experiments in the laboratory show short-term effects of emotional suppression, with negative effects on cardiovascular activity, blood pressure, and memory for stimuli presented during the suppression of emotion (Butler et al., 2003; Richards & Gross, 1999).

The seemingly elusive concept of *charisma* has been operationally defined as expressiveness, including both spontaneous and more intentional sending. Research with the Affective Communication Test (ACT), which measures expressiveness through self-report using statements such as "I show that I like someone by hugging or touching that person," "I dislike being watched by a large group of people" (scored in reverse), "I usually have a neutral facial expression" (scored in reverse), and "I can easily express emotion over the telephone"), documents that the expressive person is socially influential (Friedman et al., 1980; Friedman & Riggio, 1981; Friedman, Riggio, & Casella, 1988). People who scored as more expressive on the ACT were more likely to have given a lecture, to have been elected to office in a political organization, to influence others' moods, and to be perceived as more likable while meeting new people; in a sample of physicians, they were likely to have more patients than their counterparts. High scorers were also more likely to have had acting experience, to have had a job in sales, to desire an occupation that uses social skills (such as counselor, minister, or diplomat), and to be extraverted, affiliative, and dominant. Comparable findings have emerged for a longer self-report instrument designed to measure seven dimensions of social skills (Riggio, 1986).

People can have insight into their spontaneous expressiveness, but research often finds very weak relations between self-reports of posed encoding skill and subjects' ability to act out emotions on purpose (Riggio, Widaman, & Friedman, 1985; Zuckerman & Larrance, 1979). Studies that actually measure people's nonverbal sending abilities (rather than asking for self-reports) have also produced a variety of findings. Females manifest greater encoding skills than males, both in facial expressiveness and posed and spontaneous facial accuracy (Buck, Miller, & Caul, 1974; Friedman, Riggio, & Segall, 1980; Wagner, Buck, & Winterbotham, 1993; Zaidel & Mehrabian, 1969). Possibly contributing to these effects is that females are more successful than males at mimicking facial expressions shown in photographs and on videotape (Berenbaum & Rotter, 1992). However, evidence is mixed on whether there is a gender difference for vocal encoding of emotions. Also, the gender-related difference in sending ability has not been found with children between 4 and 6 years old for spontaneous facial expressions (Buck, 1975). Buck actually found preschool boys to be more accurate senders of spontaneous facial cues than preschool girls, but boys' accuracy declined over the ages 4 through 6, perhaps due to socialization pressure related to the male gender role (Buck, 1977).

Just as boys appear to be learning the expression norms for their gender, girls are learning theirs as well. Aside from becoming more facially expressive, girls learn earlier to use nonverbal cues according to "display rules" (see chapter 9) that dictate what behaviors are socially appropriate. In preschool and elementary ages, girls showed less negativity than boys after receiving a disappointing gift when in the presence of an adult, although control conditions showed they were no less disappointed than the boys (Cole, 1986; Davis, 1995).

Some personality characteristics also have been associated with accurate senders of nonverbal information. As with receivers, high "self-monitors" are better able to send emotional information through facial and vocal channels (Snyder, 1974), and people who are more extraverted are higher on behavioral measures of expressiveness while those who are more neurotic are lower (Riggio & Riggio, 2002). Buck's personality profile for young children shows many of the same characteristics reviewed earlier for decoders (Buck, 1975). Children who were effective senders were extraverted, outgoing, active, popular, and somewhat bossy and impulsive. Ineffective senders tended to play alone and were introverted, passive, shy, controlled, and rated as cooperative. Among adults, highly accurate senders are more dominant and exhibitionistic (Friedman, Riggio, & Segall, 1980); better senders also make an impression of greater expressiveness, confidence, and likability and, among males, use more fluent speech, more fluent body movements, and more smiles (Riggio & Friedman, 1986).

For many years, clinicians and researchers have noticed expression deficits in individuals with schizophrenia. Compared to individuals without the disorder, these patients tend to show reduced facial expressivity, are more likely to show negative than positive expressions, show less congruence between verbal and facial messages, and are less accurate in facial and vocal expressions of affect (Mandal, Pandey, & Prasad, 1998).

Noller (1980; Noller & Gallois, 1986) studied the accuracy of husbands' and wives' nonverbal communication to each other. Women were better encoders than men, both in terms of perceivers' ability to judge them accurately and in terms of correctly using the particular cues associated with a given message (e.g., smiling for a positive message, frowning for a negative message). Marital adjustment was related to encoding skill among men. Men in happier marriages sent clearer messages through the face. High-adjustment husbands were more likely to smile during positive messages than low-adjustment husbands (a correct cue for a positive message), whereas low-adjustment husbands used more eyebrow flashes (a cue not associated with a positive message). This research suggests that marital unhappiness might be partly due to the husband's inadequacy in nonverbal communication. Unhappy husbands were, in fact, more accurate in decoding the nonverbal behavior of an unknown married woman than of their own spouse.

When both spontaneous and posed expressions are obtained from the same people, these two abilities are positively related. That is, if a person's spontaneous facial expression to pleasant stimuli (such as a television comedy scene) and unpleasant stimuli (such as a gory accident scene) was easy to "read," the same person would show skill in performing posed expressions.

Putting Decoding and Encoding Together

There are two ways in which decoding and encoding can be considered together. The first way is to ask whether skilled encoders are also skilled decoders. Interestingly, this question has not been definitively answered despite considerable research. Some research finds that the two kinds of skill are positively related, leading to the hypothesis of a "general communication ability" (Zuckerman et al., 1976). But other researchers have found no, or even *a negative,* relationship between sending and receiving ability. As an example, Lanzetta and Kleck (1970) found that people who were accurate facial senders were poor receivers and vice versa. College-aged males were videotaped as they responded to a series of red and green lights. The red signaled the advent of a shock. These individuals were then asked to discriminate between shock and no-shock trials by viewing the videotaped reactions of the other participants. Those whose faces best revealed which kind of trial they were about to experience were the least able to detect this in the faces of other participants.

Across all the available studies, there is only a weak positive association between encoding and decoding accuracy (DePaulo & Rosenthal, 1979). Researchers do not know what accounts for such variation in results. A negative relation of encoding and decoding skill has been theorized to stem from one's childhood socialization experience, in particular, the communication environment within the family (Izard, 1971; Zuckerman et al., 1975). The reasoning goes like this: In a highly expressive family, expression skills will be well developed; but because emotional cues are so clearly sent by other family members, one never needs to fine-tune one's decoding skill, and, therefore, decoding ability is relatively undeveloped. However, in unexpressive homes, a child's expression skills will be poorly developed, but his or her decoding skill is sharpened because the child is forced to read minimal or ambiguous cues coming from other family members. Using the Family Expressiveness Questionnaire to measure the communication environment in the family, Halberstadt (1983, 1986) found support for the predictions stemming from this theory, namely that encoding skill would be positively related to greater freedom of emotional expression in the family and that decoding skill would be negatively related to freedom of emotional expression.

The second way that we can consider decoding and encoding together is to acknowledge that they occur together in the communication process. Although we have discussed them as separate skills that can be compared, in real interpersonal interaction these skills are used together. A person is required to encode and decode simultaneously—to act out or display feelings, reactions, intentions, and attitudes while at the same time noticing the other's cues, forming impressions, interpreting the meanings of expressions, and evaluating feedback from his or her own behavior. This "parallel processing" aspect of interpersonal communication puts many demands on the cognitive system, insofar as it is difficult to allocate attention or effort to all of these tasks at the same time (Patterson, 1995). The process is made somewhat easier by the fact that a certain amount of nonverbal processing is overlearned and therefore automatic, requiring fewer cognitive resources. The complex sending and receiving of turn-taking cues in conversation is a good example: We know how to do this without much conscious thought. However, when individuals engage in strategic behavior (as in deliberately trying to persuade someone) or suffer from social anxiety, considerable expenditure of cognitive resources is required that can selectively affect either the encoding or decoding process. For example, social anxiety tends to bring a self-focus that would likely detract from one's processing of the other person's cues (Patterson, 1995).

ON BEING AN OBSERVER
OF NONVERBAL COMMUNICATION

The observation of Expression is by no means easy.
—Charles Darwin

As you set out to read the remaining chapters of this book, now seems a good time to reflect on how you can best use the knowledge contained in it. You will learn quite a lot about the meanings and functions of nonverbal behaviors conveyed in all cue channels. You will learn that nonverbal cues are major indicators of emotion and play a crucial role in making social impressions and influencing others. People differ markedly in their skills in judging and using nonverbal cues. Although certain groups such as actors and mental patients fall at the extremes of skill, even in the middle so-called "normal" range there is a great deal of variation from person to person.

The research indicates that there may not be strong general skills; instead, there appear to be distinctive skills in different domains. A person may be skilled at judging emotions in the face but not in the voice; another may have the opposite pattern. Sarah may be good at identifying nonverbal deceptions, whereas Jim specializes in recognizing faces, and Martha can tell who stands where in the pecking order simply from hearing their tone of voice. In short, there are many ways to be accurate in nonverbal communication.

Underlying the various nonverbal abilities are *outlooks* and *attitudes* that profoundly influence what we "see" in the world and what we make of it. At this point let's focus on you as an observer of nonverbal communication in everyday life.

It is not clear why some people seem to make more insightful observations than others, but we can offer a few ideas based on our own experience. The effective observer should be able to maintain a delicate balance between assuming a knowledgeable role as an expert in his or her field and the ignorance and wide-eyed naiveté of a child. When you are feeling very confident about your understanding of what is taking place around you, it is time to shift your perspective to that of the child; when you feel a great deal of chaos and disorder in your observation field, it is time to shift to that of the expert. Just as effective speakers are highly motivated to have their audience understand their ideas, an effective observer probably has a strong interest and drive to understand the behavior of the people being observed. This does not mean, however, that the observer cannot achieve a sense of detachment from those being observed when necessary.

Effective observers probably have had a variety of educational and personal experiences. This experience assists the observer in processing complex and fleeting ongoing stimuli and in putting isolated observations in their proper perspective later. Put another way, the observer should have skills necessary for slow, careful, detailed work *and* the skills necessary to see unifying threads of broad concepts that tie the many isolated observations together. Both suggest a need for patience and perseverance. Finally, if people are going to be effective observers of others, it seems reasonable that they also will show some skill at self-insight—seeing and accepting both positive and negative qualities in themselves.

Another way to view successful observers is to look at the information they seek and obtain. The following list can be useful to observers of any human transaction. At times some of the following information will contribute to observer bias, but the information may be necessary at some point to interpret the observations fully:

1. Find out about the *participants*—age, sex, position, or status; relationship to each other; previous history; and the like.
2. Find out about the *setting* of the interaction—kind of environment, relationship of the participants to the environment, and expected behavior in that environment.
3. Find out about the *purposes* of the interaction—hidden goals, compatibility of goals, and so on.
4. Find out about the *social behavior*—who does what to or with whom, form of the behavior, its intensity, what initiates it, apparent objective of the behavior, effect on the other interactants, and so forth.
5. Find out about the *frequency* and *duration* of such behavior—when it occurs, how long it lasts, whether it recurs, frequency of recurrence, and how typical such behavior is in this situation.

You will also have to decide whether the cues you see are intentional or unintentional. The term *unintentional* may itself have a range of meaning; a behavior may be truly accidental, or it may have significance not recognized by its enactor. Attributions of intention also may vary depending on the nature of the behavior in question. Some people believe that spoken words are generally designed with some goal in mind, but what about situations where you "didn't mean to say that" or ritualistic verbal exchanges such as the following?

"Hi."
"Hi."
"How ya doin'?"
"Fine."
"How 'bout you?"
"Fine."

How much conscious intent is represented here? Even emblems such as the "A-OK" hand gesture are generally planned, but habitual use can almost extinguish a sender's awareness of doing it—even though a receiver might think it consciously enacted. Finally, certain environments cause us to focus or attend to the issue of intention more than others. Take the act of being bumped by another person. At a crowded football stadium, the question of the person's intent may not even be considered, but being bumped while walking down an uncrowded hallway may be another matter entirely. A full understanding of the nuances of intentionality poses many difficult barriers (Stamp & Knapp, 1990).

THE FALLIBILITY OF HUMAN PERCEPTION

It is not unusual for several observers of the same event to see very different things; nor is it unusual for one observer to see very different things in the same event at two different times. Sometimes an observer will perceive a sequence of action as one perceptual unit; another observer may see the same sequence as several units or only part of a unit. The following are some of the factors that may contribute to differences in perception and that successful observers must take into account.

First, we must recognize that our perceptions are structured by our own cultural conditioning, education, and personal experiences. Adults teach children what they think are critical dimensions of others by what they choose to talk about and make note of. Thus we form associations that inevitably enter into our observations. For instance, we may be unable to see what we consider to be contradictory traits or behaviors in others; that is, can you conceive of a person who is both quiet and active? Wealthy and accessible? Short and romantic? Another aspect of this internally consistent worldview that may affect our observations concerns preconceptions about what we will see. For example, "My observations will take place in a nursing home. Therefore, the people I will observe will be noncommunicative, sick, inactive," and so on. Social psychological experimentation has produced many demonstrations that people see what they expect or wish to see, often without any awareness that they are doing so. Expectations and stereotypes can sometimes be helpful, but sometimes they prevent accurate observations.

Sometimes we project our own qualities onto the object of our attention—after all, we think, if these qualities are a part of us, they must be true of others. Sometimes such projection stems less from the desire to flatter ourselves than from a distorted worldview, as in bullies who see others as hostile and threatening. We do reverse the process sometimes when we want to see ourselves as unique; for example, "I am a rational person, but most people aren't." This interaction between our own needs, desires, or even temporary emotional states and what we see in others sometimes causes us to see only what we want to see or miss what may be obvious to others. This process is known as *selective perception*. Because of these perceptual biases, observers must check their observations against the independent reports of others—or check the consistency of their own observations at several different points over an extended period of time.

We must also recognize that our perceptions are influenced by which people we choose to observe. We probably do not use the same criteria for observing our friends, our parents, and strangers. We attribute more positively perceived behaviors to our friend's personality and negatively perceived behaviors to situational constraints. Familiarity can either assist observation or create observational "noise," but it does affect our perceptions. Furthermore, some phenomena will cause us to zero in on one particular kind of behavior, observing it very closely but missing simultaneous behaviors occurring elsewhere. It may be that the behavior receiving the scrutiny is bigger, more active, or just more interesting. It might be that we monitor deviant behavior more closely than normative or expected behavior. When observing a conversation, we cannot possibly attend to everything as it happens. Sometimes we will look for, see, respond to, and interpret a particular set of cues, and at other times the same cues will go unnoticed or disregarded. Sometimes observers will fall prey to the natural tendency to follow the conservational speaking turns, viewing the speaker and missing other nonverbal events associated with the nonspeaker. And, of course, some phenomena are so complex, so minute, or so frequent that observer fatigue becomes a major concern.

Even if two people observe the same event and attach similar meanings to it, they may express their observations differently. Others may suspect, then, that the two observers saw two different things. It is the difference among describing a facial expression as happiness, joy, delight, pleasure, or amusement. Or it might be the difference between saying "She struck him" versus "She pushed him" or between describing a girl as "aggressive" but a boy as "exhibitionistic" when they are engaging in the same behavior. Hence the language we use to express our perceptions can be an important variable in judging the accuracy of those perceptions.

Observers also must be sensitive to the possible influence of order effects. Sometimes we observe some feature of another's behavior that influences our perceptions of what follows. Sometimes a person's last act causes us to reanalyze and reinterpret all the behavior preceding it. Or, we might be so influenced by the person's last act that we forget what went before.

Finally, we must be aware of the difference between factual, nonevaluative descriptions of behavior and the interpretations we give to these descriptions. At the most basic level, we can say that a successful observer is careful not to confuse pure description with inferences or interpretations about the behavior. Failure at the inference stage is aptly illustrated by the familiar story of the scientist who told his frog to jump and, after a few minutes, the frog jumped. The scientist then amputated one of the frog's hind legs. Again he told the frog to jump. He repeated his instruction several times, and, in time, the frog made a feeble attempt to jump with one hind leg. Then the scientist cut off the other hind leg and repeatedly ordered the frog to jump. When no jumping occurred, the scientist recorded in his log, "Upon amputation of one of the frog's hind legs, it begins to lose its hearing; upon severing both hind legs, the frog becomes totally deaf." Clearly, there can be a huge divide between the factual evidence and the interpretations that are made!

When we are judging the meanings of the highly complex behaviors that comprise nonverbal communication, it is quite possible to perceive the behaviors accurately but not know what they mean. Although most people (as well as popular "how-to" books on nonverbal communication) associate certain cues with certain meanings, no "dictionary" of nonverbal cue meanings exists in which we can simply look up a cue and find out its meaning. Thus we must constantly be on guard against simple interpretations and simple cause-and-effect explanations of observed behavior. Only after considering the total context of the event can we even begin to make inferences about why such behavior occurred. Even then, we only speak with varying degrees of probability, never with complete certainty.

Thus, when observers wish to make interpretations of observed behaviors, they must exercise considerable caution. For instance, let's suppose you observed someone from a distance and you saw that person using what you thought was an inordinate number of hand movements. Whether this was just the person's usual communicative style or the result of the situation (for example, talking to a person who didn't speak the language very well) would not be clear until you obtained further information. Sometimes we are faced with the question of whether a behavior is attributable to a person's personality or to something in the immediate situation. We might look for a situational cause for some undesirable behavior, but if we do not find a plausible explanation, we may attribute the behavior to the person's personality with even more confidence. We should, however, recognize that we could have missed the situational cause, being unable to view the situation as the participant does. If we err in any direction, we are more apt to attribute actions to enduring dispositions of others and minimize the situational demands. These perceptual tendencies are only some of the issues that a successful observer must be aware of, adapt to, and account for.

❖

Summary

This chapter dealt with nonverbal skills, how to develop them, and the characteristics of people who have such skills. In the first part of the chapter, we reviewed different definitions of communication skill as well as the major methodologies for measuring sending and receiving skills. We also presented findings on the training of nonverbal skills, using methods such as feedback, observation, and role playing. It appears that nonverbal skill development accrues with a strong desire or motivation to improve, with positive and productive attitudes toward the learning situation, with an adequate understanding of the knowledge related to nonverbal behavior, and with guided experience and practice in a variety of situations.

The second half of the chapter examined traits and conditions associated with effectiveness in nonverbal sending and receiving. Most research in this area has focused on questions of decoding, or receiving ability. We reviewed a large number of different correlates of accuracy in decoding and encoding nonverbal cues, among which one of the most consistent is the tendency for females to be more effective communicators as both decoders and encoders.

We also discussed how our accuracy in decoding may vary with the channel in which the information is presented, what characteristics the expressors had, and how long we saw or heard the behavior. In spite of these possible variations, some evidence suggests that if you are proficient at decoding one channel, you will be proficient in others; and if you are proficient at decoding posed expressions, you will be proficient at decoding spontaneous ones. We also presented problems associated with simultaneously encoding and decoding cues (as we routinely do in conversation). Evidence is extremely mixed on whether being a good decoder implies being a good encoder. It does not necessarily follow that proficiency in one skill (encoding or decoding) makes one proficient in the other, although sometimes this is the case.

Finally, we talked about what is entailed in being a good observer of nonverbal behavior. Knowing the most likely meanings of particular cues and cue combinations is important, but so are other factors relating to our attitudes and the context in which observation is taking place.

Answers to Figure 3-2: *a.* strangers posing together, *b.* woman on the left, *c.* playing with her baby daughter.

QUESTIONS FOR DISCUSSION

1. How much insight do you think people have into the cues they use to make judgments about others' states and traits?

2. It has been suggested that abilities to send and receive nonverbal expressions may be inversely related, in part due to the expression norms within families. Is your own family high or low on expressiveness? How might your family's expression norms have influenced your encoding and decoding skills?

3. Ability to decode other people's nonverbal emotional expressions is only one definition of nonverbal sensitivity. Think of some other definitions of nonverbal sensitivity and analyze why and when they are useful.

4. Are there any moral or ethical issues related to the decoding and encoding of nonverbal cues?

BIBLIOGRAPHY

Albright, L., Kenny, D. A., & Malloy, T. E. (1988). Consensus in personality judgments at zero acquaintance. *Journal of Personality and Social Psychology, 55,* 387–395.

Ambady, N., Bernieri, F., & Richeson, J. A. (2000). Toward a histology of social behavior: Judgmental accuracy from thin slices of the behavioral stream. In M. Zanna (Ed.), *Advances in experimental social psychology,* Vol. 32 (pp. 201–271). San Diego: Academic Press.

Ambady, N., & Gray, H. M. (2002). On being sad and mistaken: Mood effects on the accuracy of thin-slice judgments. *Journal of Personality and Social Psychology, 83,* 947–961.

Ambady, N., Hallahan, M., & Conner, B. (1999). Accuracy of judgments of sexual orientation from thin slices of behavior. *Journal of Personality and Social Psychology, 77,* 538–547.

Ambady, N., & Rosenthal, R. (1992). Thin slices of expressive behavior as predictors of interpersonal consequences: A meta-analysis. *Psychological Bulletin, 111,* 256–274.

Ambady, N., & Rosenthal, R. (1993). Half a minute: Predicting teacher evaluations from thin slices of nonverbal behavior and physical attractiveness. *Journal of Personality and Social Psychology, 64,* 431–441.

Archer, D., & Akert, R. (1977). Words and everything else: Verbal and nonverbal cues in social interaction. *Journal of Personality and Social Psychology, 35,* 443–449.

Archer, D., & Akert, R. M. (1984). Problems of context and criterion in nonverbal communication: A new look at the accuracy issue. In M. Cook (Ed.), *Issues in person perception.* New York: Methuen.

Argyle, M. (1988). *Bodily communication* (2nd ed.). London: Methuen.

Argyle, M., Trower, P., & Bryant, B. (1974). Explorations in the treatment of personality disorders and neuroses by social skills training. *British Journal of Medical Psychology, 47,* 63–72.

Bales, R. F. (1970). *Personality and interpersonal behavior.* New York: Holt, Rinehart & Winston.

Barth, J. M., & Bastiani, A. (1997). A longitudinal study of emotion recognition and preschool children's social behavior. *Merrill-Palmer Quarterly, 43,* 107–128.

Baum, K. M., & Nowicki, S., Jr. (1998). Perception of emotion: Measuring decoding accuracy of adult prosodic cues varying in intensity. *Journal of Nonverbal Behavior, 22,* 89–107.

Beck, L., & Feldman, R. S. (1989). Enhancing children's decoding of facial expression. *Journal of Nonverbal Behavior, 13,* 269–278.

Beldoch, M. (1964). Sensitivity to expression of emotional meaning in three modes of communication. In J. R. Davitz (Ed.), *The communication of emotional meaning.* New York: McGraw-Hill.

Berenbaum, H., & Rotter, A. (1992). The relationship between spontaneous facial expressions of emotion and voluntary control of facial muscles. *Journal of Nonverbal Behavior, 16,* 179–190.

Bernieri, F. J. (1991). Interpersonal sensitivity in teaching interactions. *Personality and Social Psychology Bulletin, 17,* 98–103.

Bernieri, F. J. (2001. Toward a taxonomy of interpersonal sensitivity. In J. A. Hall & F. J. Bernieri (Eds.), *Interpersonal sensitivity: Theory and measurement.* Mahwah, NJ: Erlbaum.

Bernieri, F. J., Gillis, J. S., Davis, J. M., & Grahe, J. E. (1996). Dyad rapport and the accuracy of its judgment across situations: A lens model analysis. *Journal of Personality and Social Psychology, 71,* 110–129.

Berry, D. S., & Pennebaker, J. W. (1993). Nonverbal and verbal emotional expression and health. *Psychotherapy and Psychosomatics, 59,* 11–19.

Biehl, M., Matsumoto, D., Ekman, P., Hearn, V., Heider, K., Kudoh, T., & Ton, V. (1997). Matsumoto and Ekman's Japanese and Caucasian Facial Expressions of Emotion (JACFEE): Reliability data and cross-national differences. *Journal of Nonverbal Behavior, 21,* 3–21.

Borrill, J., Rosen, B. K., & Summerfield, A. B. (1987). The influence of alcohol on judgment of facial expressions of emotion. *British Journal of Medical Psychology, 60,* 71–77.

Boyatzis, C. J., & Satyaprasad, C. (1994). Children's facial and gestural decoding and encoding: Relations between skills and with popularity. *Journal of Nonverbal Behavior, 18,* 37–55.

Brauer, D. V., & DePaulo, B. M. (1980). Similarities between friends in their understanding of nonverbal cues. *Journal of Nonverbal Behavior, 5,* 64–68.

Briton, N. B., & Hall, J. A. (1995). Beliefs about female and male nonverbal communication. *Sex Roles, 32,* 79–80.

Bruce, V. (1988). *Recognising faces.* Hillsdale, NJ: Erlbaum.

Brunswik, E. (1956). *Perception and the representative design of psychological experiments.* Berkeley, CA: University of California Press.

Buck, R. (1975). Nonverbal communication of affect in children. *Journal of Personality and Social Psychology, 31,* 644–653.

Buck, R. (1976). A test of nonverbal receiving ability: Preliminary studies. *Human Communication Research, 2,* 162–171.

Buck, R. (1977). Nonverbal communication of affect in preschool children: Relationships with personality and skin conductance. *Journal of Personality and Social Psychology, 35,* 225–236.

Buck, R., Miller, R. E., & Caul, W. F. (1974). Sex, personality and physiological variables in the communication of affect via facial expression. *Journal of Personality and Social Psychology, 30,* 587–596.

Buck, R., Savin, V., Miller, R., & Caul, W. (1972). Communication of affect through facial expressions in humans. *Journal of Personality and Social Psychology, 23,* 362–371.

Butler, E. A., Egloff, B., Wilhelm, F. H., Smith, N. C., Erickson, E. A., & Gross, J. J. (2003). The social consequences of expressive suppression. *Emotion, 3,* 48–67.

Camras, L. A., Ribordy, S., Hill, J., Martino, S., Spaccarelli, S., & Stefani, R. (1988). Recognition and posing of emotional expressions by abused children and their mothers. *Developmental Psychology, 24,* 776–781.

Carli, L. (1982). *Are women more social and men more task-oriented? A meta-analytic review of sex differences in group interaction, reward allocation, coalition formation, and cooperation in the Prisoner's Dilemma Game.* Unpublished manuscript, University of Massachusetts at Amherst.

Carney, D. R., Colvin, C. R., & Hall, J. A. (2004). *What, when, and for how long? A look at judgmental accuracy from thin slices of social behavior.* Manuscript submitted for publication.

Carney, D. R., & Harrigan, J. A. (2003). It takes one to know one: Interpersonal sensitivity is related to accurate assessments of others' interpersonal sensitivity. *Emotion, 3,* 194–200.

Carton, J. S., Kessler, E. A., & Pape, C. L. (1999). Nonverbal decoding skills and relationship well-being in adults. *Journal of Nonverbal Behavior, 23,* 91–100.

Coats, E. J., & Feldman, R. S. (1995). The role of television in the socialization of nonverbal behavioral skills. *Basic and Applied Social Psychology, 17,* 327–341.

Cole, P. M. (1986). Children's spontaneous control of facial expression. *Child Development, 57,* 1309–1321.

Collett, P. (1971). On training Englishmen in the non-verbal behaviour of Arabs: An experiment in intercultural communication. *International Journal of Psychology, 6,* 209–215.

Colvin, C. R., & Bundick, M. J. (2001). In search of the good judge of personality: Some methodological and theoretical concerns. In J. A. Hall & F. J. Bernieri (Eds.), *Interpersonal sensitivity: Theory and measurement.* Mahwah, NJ: Erlbaum.

Costanzo, M. (1992). Training students to decode verbal and nonverbal cues: Effects on confidence and performance. *Journal of Educational Psychology, 84,* 308–313.

Costanzo, M., & Archer, D. (1989). Interpreting the expressive behavior of others: The Interpersonal Perception Task. *Journal of Nonverbal Behavior, 13,* 225–245.

Danziger, K. (1976). *Interpersonal communication.* New York: Pergamon.

Davis, M. H., & Kraus, L. A. (1997). Personality and empathic accuracy. In W. Ickes (Ed.), *Empathic accuracy* (pp. 144–168). New York: Guilford.

Davis, T. L. (1995). Gender differences in masking negative emotions: Ability or motivation? *Developmental Psychology, 31,* 660–667.

Davitz, J. R. (1964). *The communication of emotional meaning.* New York: McGraw-Hill.

DePaulo, B. M. (1992). Nonverbal behavior and self-presentation. *Psychological Bulletin, 111,* 203–243.

DePaulo, B. M., & Rosenthal, R. (1979). Ambivalence, discrepancy, and deception in nonverbal communication. In R. Rosenthal (Ed.), *Skill in nonverbal communication: Individual differences.* Cambridge, MA: Oelgeschlager, Gunn & Hain.

Dickey, E. C., & Knower, F. H. (1941). A note on some ethnological differences in recognition of simulated expressions of emotions. *American Journal of Sociology, 47,* 190–193.

DiMatteo, M. R. (1979). Nonverbal skill and the physician–patient relationship. In R. Rosenthal (Ed.), *Skill in nonverbal communication: Individual differences.* Cambridge, MA: Oelgeschlager, Gunn & Hain.

Dimitrovsky, L. (1964). The ability to identify the emotional meaning of vocal expressions at successive age levels. In J. R. Davitz (Ed.), *The communication of emotional meaning.* New York: McGraw-Hill.

Dodge, K. A., & Newman, J. P. (1981). Biased decision-making process in aggressive boys. *Journal of Abnormal Psychology, 60,* 375–379.

Edwards, J., Jackson, H. J., & Pattison, P. E. (2002). Emotion recognition via facial expression and affective prosody in schizophrenia: A methodological review. *Clinical Psychology Review, 22,* 789–832.

Ekman, P., & Friesen, W. V. (1975). *Unmasking the face.* Englewood Cliffs, NJ: Prentice-Hall.

Eliot, G. (1859). *Adam Bede.* New York: Harper & Brothers.

Feldman, R. S., Coats, E. J., & Spielman, D. A. (1996). Television exposure and children's decoding of nonverbal behavior. *Journal of Applied Social Psychology, 26,* 1718–1733.

Field, T. (1982). Individual differences in the expressivity of neonates and young infants. In R. S. Feldman (Ed.), *Development of nonverbal behavior in children.* New York: Springer-Verlag.

Field, T. M., Woodson, R., Greenberg, R., & Cohen, D. (1982). Discrimination and imitation of facial expressions of neonates. *Science, 218,* 179–181.

Friedman, H. S. (1979). The concept of skill in nonverbal communication: Implications for understanding social interaction. In R. Rosenthal (Ed.), *Skill in nonverbal communication: Individual differences.* Cambridge, MA: Oelgeschlager, Gunn & Hain.

Friedman, H. S., Prince, L. M., Riggio, R. E., & DiMatteo, M. R. (1980). Understanding and assessing nonverbal expressiveness: The Affective Communication Test. *Journal of Personality and Social Psychology, 39,* 333–351.

Friedman, H. S., & Riggio, R. E. (1981). Effect of individual differences in nonverbal expressiveness on transmission of emotion. *Journal of Nonverbal Behavior, 6,* 96–104.

Friedman, H. S., Riggio, R. E., & Cassella, D. F. (1988). Nonverbal skills, personal charisma, and initial attraction. *Personality and Social Psychology Bulletin, 14,* 203–211.

Friedman, H. S., Riggio, R. E., & Segall, D. O. (1980). Personality and the enactment of emotion. *Journal of Nonverbal Behavior, 5,* 35–48.

Fujita, B. N., Harper, R. G., & Wiens, A. N. (1980). Encoding–decoding of nonverbal emotional messages: Sex differences in spontaneous and enacted expressions. *Journal of Nonverbal Behavior, 4,* 131–145.

Funder, D. C., & Harris, M. J. (1986). On the several facets of personality assessment: The case of social acuity. *Journal of Personality, 54,* 528–550.

Gangestad, S. W., & Snyder, M. (2000). Self-monitoring: Appraisal and reappraisal. *Psychological Bulletin, 126,* 530–555.

Gesn, P. R., & Ickes, W. (1999). The development of meaning contexts for empathic accuracy: Channel and sequence effects. *Journal of Personality and Social Psychology, 77,* 746–761.

Glanville, D. N., & Nowicki, S. (2002). Facial expression recognition and social competence among African American elementary school children: An examination of ethnic differences. *Journal of Black Psychology, 28,* 318–329.

Gosselin, P., Perron, M., Legault, M., & Campanella, P. (2002). Children's and adults' knowledge of the distinction between enjoyment and nonenjoyment smiles. *Journal of Nonverbal Behavior, 26,* 83–108.

Grinspan, D., Hemphill, A., & Nowicki, S., Jr. (2003). Improving the ability of elementary school-age children to identify emotion in facial expression. *Journal of Genetic Psychology, 164,* 88–100.

Halberstadt, A. G. (1983). Family expressiveness styles and nonverbal communication skills. *Journal of Nonverbal Behavior, 8,* 14–26.

Halberstadt, A. G. (1986). Family socialization of emotional expression and nonverbal communication styles and skills. *Journal of Personality and Social Psychology, 51,* 827–836.

Halberstadt, A. G., Grotjohn, D. K., Johnson, C. A., Furth, M. S., & Greig, M. M. (1992). Children's abilities and strategies in managing the facial display of affect. *Journal of Nonverbal Behavior, 16,* 215–230.

Halberstadt, A. G., & Hall, J. A. (1980). Who's getting the message? Children's nonverbal skill and their evaluation by teachers. *Developmental Psychology, 16,* 564–573.

Hall, J. A. (1978). Gender effects in decoding nonverbal cues. *Psychological Bulletin, 85,* 845–857.

Hall, J. A. (1984). *Nonverbal sex differences: Communication accuracy and expressive style.* Baltimore: Johns Hopkins University Press.

Hall, J. A. (1998). How big are nonverbal sex differences? The case of smiling and sensitivity to nonverbal cues. In D. J. Canary & K. Dindia (Eds.), *Sex differences and similarities in communication: Critical essays and empirical investigations of sex and gender in interaction.* Mahwah, NJ: Erlbaum.

Hall, J. A., & Bernieri, F. J. (Eds.) (2001). *Interpersonal sensitivity: Theory and measurement.* Mahwah, NJ: Erlbaum.

Hall, J. A., Bernieri, F. J., & Carney, D. R. (in press). Interpersonal sensitivity and nonverbal accuracy. In J. A. Harrigan, K. R. Scherer, & R. Rosenthal (Eds.), *Handbook of methods for the affective sciences.* Cambridge, UK: Cambridge University Press.

Hall, J. A., Carter, J. D., & Horgan, T. G. (2001). Status roles and recall of nonverbal cues. *Journal of Nonverbal Behavior, 25,* 79–100.

Hall, J. A., & Halberstadt, A. G. (1997). Subordination and nonverbal sensitivity: A hypothesis in search of support. In M. R. Walsh (Ed.), *Women, men, and gender: Ongoing debates.* New Haven: Yale University Press.

Hall, J. A., & Murphy, N. A. (2004). *Recall of nonverbal and verbal cues: Exploring a new definition of interpersonal sensitivity.* Manuscript submitted for publication.

Hargie, O. (Ed.). (1986). *A handbook of communication skills.* New York: New York University Press.

Hargie, O., Saunders, C., & Dickson, D. (1987). *Social skills in interpersonal communication,* 2nd ed. Cambridge, MA: Brookline Books.

Harlow, H. F., & Mears, C. (1978). The nature of complex, unlearned responses. In M. Lewis & L. A. Rosenblum (Eds.), *The development of affect.* New York: Plenum.

Harrigan, J. A. (1984). The effects of task order on children's identification of facial expressions. *Motivation and Emotion, 8,* 157–169.

Haviland, J. M., & Lelwica, M. (1987). The induced affect response: 10-week-old infants' responses to three emotion expressions. *Developmental Psychology, 23,* 97–104.

Henley, N. M. (1977). *Body politics: Power, sex, and nonverbal communication.* Englewood Cliffs, NJ: Prentice-Hall.

Hodgins, H. S., & Belch, C. (2000). Interparental violence and nonverbal abilities. *Journal of Nonverbal Behavior, 24,* 3–24.

Hodgins, H. S., & Zuckerman, M. (1990). The effect of nonverbal sensitivity on social interaction. *Journal of Nonverbal Behavior, 14,* 155–170.

Horgan, T. G., Schmid Mast, M., Hall, J. A., & Carter, J. D. (2004). Gender differences in memory for the appearance of others. *Personality and Social Psychology Bulletin, 30,* 185–196.

Ickes, W. (2001). Measuring empathic accuracy. In J. A. Hall & F. J. Bernieri (Eds.), *Interpersonal sensitivity: Theory and measurement.* Mahwah, NJ: Erlbaum.

Ickes, W. (2003). *Everyday mind reading: Understanding what other people think and feel.* Amherst, NY: Prometheus Books.

Ickes, W., Gesn, P. R., & Graham, T. (2000). Gender differences in empathic accuracy: Differential ability or differential motivation? *Personal Relationships, 7,* 95–109.

Ickes, W., Stinson, L., Bissonnette, V., & Garcia, S. (1990). Naturalistic social cognition: Empathic accuracy in mixed-sex dyads. *Journal of Personality and Social Psychology, 59,* 730–742.

Izard, C. E. (1971). *The face of emotion.* New York: Appleton-Century-Crofts.

Izard, C. E., Fine, S., Schultz, D., Mostow, A., Ackerman, B., & Youngstrom, E. (2001). Emotion knowledge as a predictor of social behavior and academic competence in children at risk. *Psychological Science, 12,* 18–23.

Kee, K. S., Green, M. F., Mintz, J., & Brekke, J. S. (2003). Is emotion processing a predictor of functional outcome in schizophrenia? *Schizophrenia Bulletin, 29,* 487–497.

Keeley-Dyreson, M., Burgoon, J. K., & Bailey, W. (1991). The effects of stress and gender on nonverbal decoding accuracy in kinesic and vocalic channels. *Human Communication Research, 17,* 584–605.

Kellogg, W. N., & Eagleson, B. M. (1931). The growth of social perception in different racial groups. *Journal of Educational Psychology, 22,* 374–375.

Knower, F. H. (1945). Studies in the symbolism of voice and action: V. The use of behavioral and tonal symbols as tests of speaking achievement. *Journal of Applied Psychology, 29,* 229–235.

Koerner, A. F., & Fitzpatrick, M. A. (2003). Nonverbal communication and marital adjustment and satisfaction: The role of decoding relationship relevant and relationship irrelevant affect. *Communication Monographs, 69,* 33–51.

Lancelot, C., & Nowicki, S., Jr. (1997). The association between receptive nonverbal processing abilities and internalizing/externalizing problems in girls and boys. *Journal of Genetic Psychology, 158,* 297–302.

Lanzetta, J. T., & Kleck, R. E. (1970). Encoding and decoding nonverbal affect in humans. *Journal of Personality and Social Psychology, 16,* 12–19.

Levesque, M. J., & Kenny, D. A. (1993). Accuracy of behavioral predictions at zero acquaintance. A social relations analysis. *Journal of Personality and Social Psychology, 65,* 1178–1187.

Levy, P. K. (1964). The ability to express and perceive vocal communication of feelings. In J. R. Davitz (Ed.), *The communication of emotional meaning.* New York: McGraw-Hill.

Lewis, M., & Rosenblum, L. A. (Eds.). (1978). *The development of affect.* New York: Plenum.

Lieberman, D. A., Rigo, T. G., & Campain, R. F. (1988). Age-related differences in nonverbal decoding ability. *Communication Quarterly, 36,* 290–297.

Lippa, R. A., & Dietz, J. K. (2000). The relation of gender, personality, and intelligence to judges' accuracy in judging strangers' personality from brief video segments. *Journal of Nonverbal Behavior, 24,* 25–43.

Magill-Evans, J., Koning, C., Cameron-Sadava, A., & Manyk, K. (1995). The Child and Adolescent Social Perception Measure. *Journal of Nonverbal Behavior, 19,* 151–169.

Malone, B. E., & DePaulo, B. M. (2001). Measuring sensibility to deception. In J. A. Hall & F. J. Bernieri (Eds.), *Interpersonal sensitivity: Theory and measurement.* Mahwah, NJ: Erlbaum.

Mandal, M. K., Pandey, R., & Prasad, A. B. (1998). Facial expressions of emotions and schizophrenia: A review. *Schizophrenia Bulletin, 24,* 399–412.

Marangoni, C., Garcia, S., Ickes, W., & Teng, G. (1995). Empathic accuracy in a clinically relevant setting. *Journal of Personality and Social Psychology, 68,* 854–869.

Marcus, D. K., & Lehman, S. J. (2002). Are there sex differences in interpersonal perception at zero acquaintance? A social relations analysis. *Journal of Research in Personality, 36,* 190–207.

Markham, R., & Adams, K. (1992). The effect of type of task on children's identification of facial expressions. *Journal of Nonverbal Behavior, 16,* 21–39.

Matsumoto, D., LeRoux, J., Wilson-Cohn, C., Raroque, J., Kooken, K., Ekman, P., Yrizarry, N., Loewinger, S., Uchida, H., Yee, A., Amo, L., & Goh, A. (2000). A new test to measure emotion recognition ability: Matsumoto and Ekman's Japanese and Caucasian Brief Affect Recognition Test (JACBART). *Journal of Nonverbal Behavior, 24,* 179–209.

Matthews, G., Zeidner, M., & Roberts, R. D. (Eds.). (2002). *Emotional intelligence: Science & myth.* Cambridge, MA: MIT Press.

McClure, E. B. (2000). A meta-analytic review of sex differences in facial expression processing and their development in infants, children, and adolescents. *Psychological Bulletin, 126,* 424–453.

McClure, E. B., & Nowicki, S., Jr. (2001). Associations between social anxiety and nonverbal processing skill in preadolescent boys and girls. *Journal of Nonverbal Behavior, 25,* 3–19.

Meltzoff, A. N., & Moore, M. K. (1983). Newborn infants imitate adult facial gestures. *Child Development, 54,* 702–709.

Miller, R. E., Caul, W. F., & Mirsky, I. A. (1967). Communication of affects between feral and socially isolated monkeys. *Journal of Personality and Social Psychology, 7,* 231–239.

Mueser, K. T., Penn, D. L., Blanchard, J. J., & Bellack, A. S. (1997). Affect recognition in schizophrenia: A synthesis of findings across three studies. *Psychiatry, 60,* 301–308.

Murphy, N. A., Hall, J. A., & Colvin, C. R. (2003). Accurate intelligence assessments in social interaction: Mediators and gender effects. *Journal of Personality, 71,* 465–493.

Niedenthal, P., Halberstadt, J. B., Margolin, J., & Innes-Ker, A. H. (2000). Emotional state and the detection of change in facial expression of emotion. *European Journal of Social Psychology, 30,* 211–222.

Noller, P. (1980). Misunderstandings in marital communication: A study of couples' nonverbal communication. *Journal of Personality and Social Psychology, 39,* 1135–1148.

Noller, P., & Gallois, C. (1986). Sending emotional messages in marriage: Non-verbal behaviour, sex and communication clarity. *British Journal of Social Psychology, 25,* 287–297.

Nowicki, S., Jr., & Carton, E. (1997). The relation of nonverbal processing ability of faces and voices and children's feelings of depression and competence. *Journal of Genetic Psychology, 158,* 357–363.

Nowicki, S., Jr., & Duke, M. P. (1994). Individual differences in the nonverbal communication of affect: The Diagnostic Analysis of Nonverbal Accuracy Scale. *Journal of Nonverbal Behavior, 18,* 9–35.

Nowicki, S., Jr., Glanville, D., & Demertzis, A. (1998). A test of the ability to recognize emotion in the facial expressions of African American adults. *Journal of Black Psychology, 24,* 335–350.

Nowicki, S., Jr., & Mitchell, J. (1998). Accuracy in identifying affect in child and adult faces and voices and social competence in preschool children. *Genetic, Social, and General Psychology Monographs, 124,* 39–59.

Odom, R. D., & Lemond, C. M. (1972). Developmental differences in the perception and production of facial expressions. *Child Development, 43,* 359–369.

Patterson, M. L. (1995). A parallel process model of nonverbal communication. *Journal of Nonverbal Behavior, 19,* 3–29.

Philippot, P., Feldman, R. S., & McGee, G. (1992). Nonverbal behavioral skills in an educational context: Typical and atypical populations. In R. S. Feldman (Ed.), *Applications of nonverbal behavioral theories and research.* Hillsdale, NJ: Erlbaum.

Phillips, R. D., Wagner, S. H., Fells, C. A., & Lynch, M. (1990). Do infants recognize emotion in facial expressions?: Categorical and "metaphorical" evidence. *Infant Behavior and Development, 13,* 71–84.

Pickett, C. L., Gardner, W. L., & Knowles, M. (2004). Getting a cue: The need to belong and enhanced sensitivity to social cues. *Personality and Social Psychology Bulletin, 30,* 1095–1107.

Pollak, S. D., & Sinha, P. (2002). Effects of early experience on children's recognition of facial displays of emotion. *Developmental Psychology, 38,* 784–791.

Reynolds, D. J., & Gifford, R. (2001). The sounds and sights of intelligence: A lens model channel analysis. *Personality and Social Psychology Bulletin, 27,* 187–200.

Richards, J. M., & Gross, J. J. (1999). Composure at any cost? The cognitive consequences of emotional suppression. *Personality and Social Psychology Bulletin, 25,* 1033–1044.

Riggio, R. E. (1986). Assessment of basic social skills. *Journal of Personality and Social Psychology, 51,* 649–660.

Riggio, R. E. (1992). Social interaction skills and nonverbal behavior. In R. S. Feldman (Ed.), *Applications of nonverbal behavioral theories and research.* Hillsdale, NJ: Erlbaum.

Riggio, R. E., & Friedman, H. S. (1986). Impression formation: The role of expressive behavior. *Journal of Personality and Social Psychology, 50,* 421–427.

Riggio, H. R., & Riggio, R. E. (2002). Emotional expressiveness, extraversion, and neuroticism: A meta-analysis. *Journal of Nonverbal Behavior, 26,* 195–218.

Riggio, R. E., & Riggio, H. R. (2001). Self-report measurement of interpersonal sensitivity. In J. A. Hall & F. J. Bernieri (Eds.), *Interpersonal sensitivity: Theory and measurement.* Mahwah, NJ: Erlbaum.

Riggio, R. E., Widaman, K. F., & Friedman, H. S. (1985). Actual and perceived emotional sending and personality correlates. *Journal of Nonverbal Behavior, 9,* 69–83.

Rosenthal, R. (Ed.). (1979). *Skill in nonverbal communication: Individual differences.* Cambridge, MA: Oelgeschlager, Gunn & Hain.

Rosenthal, R., & DePaulo, B. M. (1979). Sex differences in accommodation in nonverbal communication. In R. Rosenthal (Ed.), *Skill in nonverbal communication: Individual differences.* Cambridge, MA: Oelgeschlager, Gunn & Hain.

Rosenthal, R., Hall, J. A., DiMatteo, M. R., Rogers, P. L., & Archer, D. (1979). *Sensitivity to nonverbal communication: The PONS test.* Baltimore: Johns Hopkins University Press.

Rosip, J. C., & Hall, J. A. (2004). Knowledge of nonverbal cues, gender, and nonverbal decoding accuracy. *Journal of Nonverbal Behavior, 28,* 267–286.

Rotter, N. G., & Rotter, G. S. (1988). Sex differences in the encoding and decoding of negative facial emotions. *Journal of Nonverbal Behavior, 12,* 139–148.

Russell, R. L., Stokes, J., Jones, M. E., Czogalik, D., & Rohleder, L. (1993). The role of nonverbal sensitivity in childhood psychopathology. *Journal of Nonverbal Behavior, 17,* 69–83.

Rutherford, M. D., Baron-Cohen, S., & Wheelwright, S. (2002). Reading the mind in the voice: A study with normal adults and adults with Asperger syndrome and high functioning autism. *Journal of Autism & Developmental Disorders, 32,* 189–194.

Sacks, O. (1993, December 27/1994, January 3). An anthropologist on Mars. *The New Yorker,* pp. 106–125.

Salovey, P., & Mayer, J. D. (1989). Emotional intelligence. *Imagination, Cognition, and Personality, 9,* 185–211.

Salovey, P., & Sluyter, D. J. (Eds.). (1997). *Emotional development and emotional intelligence: Educational implications.* New York: Basic.

Schiffenbauer, A. (1974). Effect of observer's emotional state on judgments of the emotional state of others. *Journal of Personality and Social Psychology, 30,* 31–35.

Schmid Mast, M., & Hall, J. A. (2004). Who is the boss and who is not? Accuracy of judging status. *Journal of Nonverbal Behavior, 28,* 145–165.

Shapiro, P. N., & Penrod, S. (1986). Meta-analysis of facial identification studies. *Psychological Bulletin, 100,* 139–156.

Snodgrass, S. E. (1992). Further effects of role versus gender on interpersonal sensitivity. *Journal of Personality and Social Psychology, 62,* 154–158.

Snodgrass, S. E., Hecht, M. A., & Ploutz-Snyder, R. (1998). Interpersonal sensitivity: Expressivity or perceptivity? *Journal of Personality and Social Psychology, 74,* 238–249.

Snyder, M. (1974). Self-monitoring of expressive behavior. *Journal of Personality and Social Psychology, 30,* 526–537.

Stamp, G., & Knapp, M. L. (1990). The construct of intent in interpersonal communication. *Quarterly Journal of Speech, 76,* 282–299.

Sternberg, R. (1984). *Beyond I.Q.: A triarchic theory of human intelligence.* Cambridge, UK: Cambridge University Press.

Swenson, J., & Casmir, F. L. (1998). The impact of culture-sameness, gender, foreign travel, and academic background on the ability to interpret facial expression of emotion in others. *Communication Quarterly, 46,* 214–230.

Termine, N. T., & Izard, C. E. (1988). Infants' responses to their mothers' expressions of joy and sadness. *Developmental Psychology, 24,* 223–229.

Thomas, G., & Fletcher, G. J. O. (2003). Mind-reading accuracy in intimate relationships: Assessing the roles of the relationship, the target, and the judge. *Journal of Personality and Social Psychology, 85,* 1079–1094.

Thompson, D. F., & Meltzer, L. (1964). Communication of emotional intent by facial expression. *Journal of Abnormal and Social Psychology, 68,* 129–135.

Thompson, W. F., Schellenberg, E. G., & Husain, G. (2004). Decoding speech prosody: Do music lessons help? *Emotion, 4,* 46–64.

Tickle-Degnen, L., & Rosenthal, R. (1990). The nature of rapport and its nonverbal correlates. *Psychological Inquiry, 1,* 285–293.

Trimboli, A., & Walker, M. (1993). The CAST test of nonverbal sensitivity. *Journal of Language and Social Psychology, 12,* 49–65.

Tucker, J. S., & Riggio, R. E. (1988). The role of social skills in encoding posed and spontaneous facial expressions. *Journal of Nonverbal Behavior, 12,* 87–97.

Wagner, H. L. (1993). On measuring performance in category judgment studies of nonverbal behavior. *Journal of Nonverbal Behavior, 17,* 3–28.

Wagner, H. L., Buck, R., & Winterbotham, M. (1993). Communication of specific emotions: Gender differences in sending accuracy and communication measures. *Journal of Nonverbal Behavior, 17,* 29–53.

Wagner, H. L., MacDonald, C. J., & Manstead, A. S. R. (1986). Communication of individual emotions by spontaneous facial expressions. *Journal of Personality and Social Psychology, 50,* 737–743.

Walker-Andrews, A. S., (1997). Infants' perception of expressive behaviors: Differentiation of multimodal information. *Psychological Bulletin, 121,* 437–456.

Walker-Andrews, A. S., & Lennon, E. (1991). Infants' discrimination of vocal expressions: Contributions of auditory and visual information. *Infant Behavior and Development, 14,* 131–142.

Wallbott, H. G., & Scherer, K. R. (1986). Cues and channels in emotion recognition. *Journal of Personality and Social Psychology, 51,* 690–699.

Zaidel, S., & Mehrabian, A. (1969). The ability to communicate and infer positive and negative attitudes facially and vocally. *Journal of Experimental Research in Personality, 3,* 233–241.

Zuckerman, M., DeFrank, R. S., Hall. J. A., Larrance, D. T., & Rosenthal, R. (1979). Facial and vocal cues of deception and honesty. *Journal of Experimental Social Psychology, 15,* 378–396.

Zuckerman, M., DePaulo, B. M., & Rosenthal, R. (1981). Verbal and nonverbal communication of deception. In L. Berkowitz (Ed.), *Advances in experimental social psychology* (Vol. 14). New York: Academic Press.

Zuckerman, M., Hall, J. A., DeFrank, R. S., & Rosenthal, R. (1976). Encoding and decoding of spontaneous and posed facial expressions. *Journal of Personality and Social Psychology, 34,* 966–977.

Zuckerman, M., Koestner, R., & Driver, R. (1981). Beliefs about cues associated with deception. *Journal of Nonverbal Behavior, 6,* 105–114.

Zuckerman, M., & Larrance, D. T. (1979). Individual differences in perceived encoding and decoding abilities. In R. Rosenthal (Ed.), *Skill in nonverbal communication: Individual differences.* Cambridge, MA: Oelgeschlager, Gunn & Hain.

Zuckerman, M., Lipets, M. S., Koivumaki, J. H., & Rosenthal, R. (1975). Encoding and decoding nonverbal cues of emotion. *Journal of Personality and Social Psychology, 32,* 1068–1076.

Part Two

THE COMMUNICATION ENVIRONMENT

The features of the environment within which our interactions take place can exert a powerful influence on human interaction. Lighting, color schemes, furniture, and architecture, among other features, affect what we say and even how often we say it; sometimes we deliberately structure these same features in order to obtain certain responses from others. Part Two explores the way we affect and are affected by interaction distance and territorial claims to these environments as a preface to discussing the people who do the communicating and their behavior.

Chapter 4

THE EFFECTS OF THE ENVIRONMENT ON HUMAN COMMUNICATION

Every interior betrays the nonverbal skills of its inhabitants. The choice of materials, the distribution of space, the kind of objects that command attention or demand to be touched—as compared to those that intimidate or repel—have much to say about the preferred sensory modalities of their owners.

—J. RUESCH AND W. KEES

When people communicate with one another, there are always features of the surrounding environment that exert an influence on their interaction. What are these environmental features, and how do they affect us?

First, let's look at a familiar communication environment—the classroom. Most often, it is a rectangular room with straight rows of chairs for student seating. A row of windows along one side of the room may determine the direction students face (and, consequently, the "front" of the room). It is not uncommon for classroom seats to be permanently attached to the floor for ease of maintenance and tidiness. Classrooms typically have some type of partition (a desk or lectern) separating the teacher from students. Most students and teachers can provide a long list of problems encountered in environments designed for learning: poor lighting and acoustics; inadequate climate control; external construction noises; banging radiators; inoperative electrical outlets; immovable seats; gloomy, dull, or distracting color schemes; unpleasant odors; and so forth. Both students and teachers recognize that such problems impede the purpose for gathering in these rectangular rooms—to increase knowledge through effective student/teacher communication. The influence of the classroom environment on student and teacher behavior remained relatively unexplored until Sommer (1967, 1969, 1974) took a closer look. He focused his attention on the influence of classroom design on student participation.

Sommer selected several different types of classrooms for his study. He wanted to compare the amount of student participation in these classrooms and to analyze aspects of participatory behavior in each type. He selected seminar rooms with movable chairs, usually arranged in a horseshoe shape; laboratories (complete with Bunsen burners, bottles, and gas valves), which represented an extreme in straight-row seating; a windowless room; and one with an entire wall of windows. Among other things, Sommer concluded the following from his studies:

1. Students and teachers who dislike their learning environment will try to avoid it or change it.
2. In general, the amount of student participation decreases as the number of students in the class increases. The length of a student's participation is also longer in smaller classes.
3. The content of student participation in large classes is more likely to be devoted to questions of clarification or requests to repeat an idea rather than participation focused on the ideas themselves.
4. Participation was most frequent among those students within range of the instructor's eye gaze. In a seminar room, the students sitting directly across from the instructor participated more. A follow-up study by Adams and Biddle (1970) found a zone of participation in the center of the room (see Figure 4-1). This center zone is most likely to occur when the instructor stands in the middle of the room. The students in close proximity to the instructor and in the center of the room are most affected by the instructor's visual contact. But there is more to this story. Koneya (1973) found that when high, moderate, and low participating students were given a chance to select any seat they desired, high participators were the most likely to select seats in the zone of participation. We can conclude from this that student participation can be facilitated by visual contact from the instructor, but that students who are likely to participate tend to position

FIGURE 4-1

The zone of class participation.

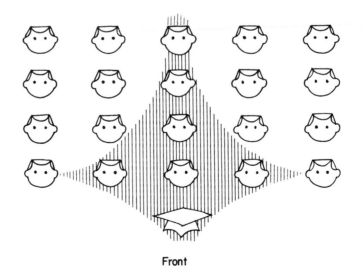

Front

themselves in seats apt to receive the instructor's gaze. Also note that an instructor's eye gaze can be used to inhibit communication as well as facilitate it. When students feel they will be punished (or at least not rewarded) for participating, the zone of participation is inoperative.

5. What happens when you take moderate and low participating students and deliberately seat them in the zone of participation? Koneya (1973) found that moderate participators increased their participation, but low participators remained low. This suggests that where students sit may affect their classroom participation, but this effect is less likely with low participators. Haber (1982) found that ethnic, racial, and religious minorities at five colleges tended to select seating peripheral to the zone of participation—even when they were a majority at a particular college.

From these studies, we can conclude that classroom seating is not random, certain types of people gravitate to central and noncentral areas, and the zone of participation (heavily influenced by teacher/student visibility) promotes participation for everyone except initially low participators. Even then, we might find increased participation at some point if a teacher rewards and supports participation.

The preceding discussion of the classroom is an example of a specific context in which spatial relationships, architecture, and objects surrounding the participants influence the amount and type of interaction that occurs. We will examine other environmental factors that impinge on human communication behavior, but we should remember that the environment is only one element in structuring such behavior. If students, administrators, teachers, secretaries, and custodians want to run a school or university like a prison or a dehumanized bureaucracy, changes in the classroom structure may have very little impact.

Throughout this chapter, we discuss a number of characteristics of environments, but let's initiate our exploration of environments by examining the way we perceive our surroundings. The way we perceive our surroundings can be very influential in the way we feel and the way we choose to communicate.

PERCEPTIONS OF OUR SURROUNDINGS

The number of places in which we communicate with others is limitless—buses, homes, apartments, restaurants, offices, parks, hotels, sports arenas, factories, libraries, movie theaters, museums. Despite their diversity, we probably evaluate these environments along similar dimensions. Once we perceive our environment in a certain way, we may incorporate such perceptions in the development of the messages we send. And, once these messages have been sent, the environmental perceptions of the other person have been altered. Thus we influence and are influenced by our environments.

How do we see our environments? We believe the following six dimensions are central to our perceptions and consequently to how we send and receive messages.

PERCEPTIONS OF FORMALITY

One familiar dimension along which we can classify environments is a formal/informal continuum. Reactions may be based on the objects present, the people present, the functions performed, or any number of other variables. Individual offices may be more formal than a lounge in the same building; a year-end banquet takes on more formality than a "come as you are" party; an evening at home with one other couple may be more informal than an evening with 10 other couples. The greater the formality, the greater the chances that the communication behavior will be less relaxed and more superficial, hesitant, and stylized.

PERCEPTIONS OF WARMTH

Environments that make us feel psychologically warm encourage us to linger, to relax and feel comfortable. It may be some combination of the color of the drapes or walls, paneling, carpeting, texture of the furniture, softness of the chairs, soundproofing, and so on. Fast-food chains try to exhibit enough warmth in their decor to seem inviting but enough coldness to encourage rapid turnover. Interestingly, environments that make us feel psychologically warm may also make us feel physically warmer. Students were asked to spend 2 hours studying or reading in a room with a neutral decor, similar to that of a classroom. Then they were asked to read or study in a room that resembled a walk-in meat cooler. Nearly all the students felt the second room was cooler, even though the temperature was actually the same in both rooms. Then the meat cooler room was paneled, carpeted, and equipped with subdued lighting and other appointments. Another group of students was asked to read or study in each room. This time, the redesigned meat cooler room was judged to have a higher temperature than the classroom. Again, actual temperatures were the same (Rohles, 1980).

PERCEPTIONS OF PRIVACY

Enclosed environments usually suggest greater privacy, particularly if they accommodate only a few people. If the possibility of other people's entering and/or overhearing our conversation is small (even if we are outdoors), there is a greater feeling of privacy. Personal items such as toilet articles, low or focused lighting, high-density situations, partitions, noise, and other environmental factors can affect perceptions of privacy (Buslig, 1999). With greater privacy, we will probably find close speaking distances and more personal messages, designed and adapted for the specific other person rather than people in general.

PERCEPTIONS OF FAMILIARITY

When we meet a new person or encounter an unfamiliar environment, our responses typically are cautious, deliberate, and conventional. Unfamiliar environments are laden with ritual and norms we do not yet know, so we are hesitant to move too quickly. We will probably go slowly until we can associate this unfamiliar environment with one we know. One interpretation for the stereotyped structures of quick-food stops is that they allow us (a mobile society) to readily find a familiar and predictable place that will guarantee minimal demands for active contact with strangers. In unfamiliar environments, the most likely initial topic of conversation will be the environment itself—for example, "Have you ever been here before? What is it like? Who comes here?"

PERCEPTIONS OF CONSTRAINT

Part of our total reaction to our environment is based on our perception of whether (and how easily) we can leave it. Some students feel confined in their own homes during the school Christmas break. But consider the differences between this 2-week constraint and a permanent live-at-home arrangement. The intensity of these perceptions of constraint is closely related to the space available to us (and the privacy of this space) during the time we are in the environment. Some environments seem to be only temporarily confining, such as a long trip in an automobile; other environments seem more permanently confining, such as prisons, spacecrafts, or nursing homes.

PERCEPTIONS OF DISTANCE

Sometimes our responses within a given environment are influenced by how close or far away we must conduct our communication with another. This may reflect actual physical distance (an office on a different floor, a house in another part of the city), or it may reflect psychological distance (barriers clearly separating people who are fairly close physically). You may be seated close to someone and still not perceive it as a close environment, for example, interlocking chairs facing the same direction in an airport. When the setting forces us into close quarters (elevators, crowded buses) with other people not well known to us, we try to increase distance psychologically to reduce threatening feelings of intimacy. We can do this through less eye contact, body tenseness and immobility, cold silence, nervous laughter, jokes about the intimacy, and public conversation directed at all present.

The perceptions just described represent only some of the dimensions along which we can view communication settings. Generally, more intimate communication is associated with informal, unconstrained, private, familiar, close, and warm environments. In everyday situations, however, these dimensions combine in complex ways. The mixture of intimate and nonintimate factors can be seen in an elevator if it is perceived as close, familiar, and temporarily confining but also public, formal, and cold.

REACTING TO ENVIRONMENTS

Once these perceptions are made, how do they affect our reactions? Mehrabian (1976) argued that we react emotionally to our surroundings. These emotional reactions can be accounted for in terms of (1) how *aroused* the environment makes us feel, (2) how *pleasurable* we feel, and (3) how *dominant* we feel. *Arousal* refers to how active, stimulated, frenzied, or alert we are. *Dominance* refers to feelings of being in control, importance, and freedom to act in a variety of ways. *Pleasure* refers to feelings of joy, satisfaction, and happiness.

Novel, surprising, and complex environments probably produce higher arousal. Those people less able to screen out unwanted information from the environment inevitably have to respond to more stimuli and, in turn, become more aroused. Although we all probably respond as "screeners" and "nonscreeners" on occasions, some people tend to respond habitually as either screeners or nonscreeners. *Nonscreeners* are less selective in what they respond to in any environment. They see, hear, smell, and otherwise sense more stimuli. *Screeners*, in contrast, are selective in what they respond to. They impose a hierarchy of importance on various components in a complex situation. Nonscreeners not only become more aroused than screeners in novel, changing, and sudden situations, but they remain aroused longer—even after leaving the arousing environment. That is why nonscreeners are most attracted to environments that are both arousing and pleasurable.

PERCEPTIONS OF TIME

Time is also a part of the communicative environment. At first, it may seem strange to include something as seemingly intangible as time in the same environmental package as chairs, walls, noise, or even weather conditions. However, people in the United States do treat time as something tangible, a commodity that can be divided up, saved, spent, and made. Furthermore, we often project temporal qualities onto objects within our environment, for example, a chair that looks like it has been there "forever" or an elevator that "never seems to be on time."

Time is important to us. It governs when we eat and sleep; it often determines how much we get paid at work; and it sets limits on how much material students can learn in a given class period. Time plays a key role in social interaction as well. It influences our perceptions of people; for example, responsible people are "on time," boring people talk "too long," or a good romantic partner gives us some "time to ourself" (Leonard, 1978; Werner & Baxter, 1994). A course in "time management" is a staple for anyone expecting to climb the corporate ladder in U.S. organizations. Time plays such an important role in our lives that we often carry the date and time around with us on our wrist. Most cars have clocks, and some of them even have devices for computing the time it will take to drive from one location to another. We are very much aware of the stress time can create in our lives. We think of a vacation as a retreat to a place where time matters less. Ironically, though, vacations themselves are usually thought of as a set period of time. Ballard and Seibold (2000) succinctly capture the reciprocal relationship between communication and time when they say, "Communication creates persons' views and understanding of time, yet our sense of time enables and constrains communication in important ways" (p. 219).

Time is perceived very differently in other cultures (Hall, 1959). These varying orientations to time are often a central factor in misunderstandings among members of different cultures. Psychology professor Robert Levine gives this account of his teaching experience in Brazil:

> As I left home for my first day of class, I asked someone the time. It was 9:05 a.m., which allowed me time to relax and look around the campus before my 10 o'clock lecture. After what I judged to be half an hour, I glanced at the clock I was passing. It said 10:20! In a panic, I broke for the classroom, followed by gentle calls of "Hola, professor" and "Tudo bem, professor?" from unhurried students, many of whom, I later realized, were my own. I arrived breathless to find an empty room. Frantically, I asked a passerby the time. "Nine forty-five" was the answer. No, that couldn't be. I asked someone else. "Nine fifty-five." Another said: "Exactly 9:43." The clock in a nearby office read 3:15. I had learned my first lesson about Brazilians: Their timepieces are consistently inaccurate. And nobody minds. My class was scheduled from 10 until noon. Many students came late, some very late . . . none seemed terribly concerned about lateness . . . . The real surprise came at noon . . . only a few students left immediately. Others drifted out during the next fifteen minutes, and some continued asking me questions long after that. (Levine & Wolff, 1985, p. 30)

To understand cultural variations in perceiving time, we must first understand our own culture. We know that our responses are influenced by our experiences with time at several different levels (Cottle, 1976; Friedman, 1990; Hall, 1983; McGrath & Kelly, 1986). Biologically, our bodies seem to be programmed so that "internal clocks" regulate our physical, emotional, and intellectual functioning (Luce, 1971). We also know that people have differing psychological orientations to time. There are important differences among people within this culture regarding their orientations to the past, present, and future. These orientations may represent a long-term style or be subject to change; for example, a person who "lives for the moment" at one point in his or her life might later adapt to a future-oriented style that involves evaluating today's "moments" in terms of the "long-range picture" (Gonzalez & Zimbardo, 1985). Different orientations toward time not only affect the way people interact in specific encounters, but they are also used to evaluate more enduring qualities. For example, some people think that being punctual and meeting deadlines are signs of not only successful people, but "good" people.

In social encounters, the following perceptions of time are fundamental. As we understand more about the environmental stimuli and conditions that trigger the following perceptions, we can use this knowledge to construct environments that give off the temporal messages we desire.

1. As the location of events
2. As the duration of events
3. As the interval between events
4. As the patterning of intervals

TIME AS LOCATION

Some of our perceptions of time have to do with when something happens, the timing of an event. The onsets of some events are evaluated as well timed, for example, "You hugged me at the exact moment I needed it most"; some are viewed as ill timed, for example, "I don't like eating dinner at 10 p.m." Sometimes our perceptions of when something happens are precise, and sometimes they represent a general time frame. For some, the time to eat lunch is precisely noon; for others it can be anytime between 11 a.m. and 2 p.m. Just as we attribute many different meanings to the timing of events in our lives, we also can communicate multiple meanings as we set deadlines for the occurrence of events in the future. For example, if something is due much sooner than expected, it may mean it is a form of punishment, a reward, very important, or very unimportant.

TIME AS DURATION

Our temporal perceptions also include how long some event lasts. We develop expectations for the proper and improper length of events, but perceptions of duration are not always a reflection of actual duration. An environment with little activity can be perceived as so boring that we feel we have been there "forever."

TIME AS INTERVALS

The periods between events also constitute a way of perceiving time. The rate at which something happens is really a perception of the time since it last occurred. The perceived tempo of our lives is likely to be a reflection of how much or how little time separates each of our activities. We learn to expect certain intervals with certain activities. The phrase "It's been too long since I've seen you" suggests a contact-interval norm associated with close relationships that has been exceeded for this person. Similarly, we may not object to a person's using obscene language, but we may object to the brevity of the intervals between usage.

TIME AS PATTERNS OF INTERVALS

As we observe recurrent sequences of intervals, we begin to sense social rhythm—the regularity/irregularity, order/disorder comprising the cycles of our behavior and routines. Of all our time-bound perceptions, the pattern of intervals is the most complex and the most difficult to articulate to others. Understanding the patterning of intervals is, however, crucial to understanding ourselves as well as understanding our interaction with another person. When we feel in tune with another person, we are focusing on a pleasing perception of interactional synchrony, and when we feel awkward with someone, it may be because their patterning of nonverbal gestures or pauses is very different from ours. The understanding of patterns of intervals in our environment, whether it is a talk/silence pattern or a sunny/cloudy atmospheric pattern, is fundamental to making daily predictions about our lives.

We devote the remainder of this chapter to the characteristics of environments that form the bases of the perceptions just outlined (perceptions of our surroundings and perceptions of time). Each environment has three major components:

1. The natural environment—geography, location, atmospheric conditions
2. The presence or absence of other people
3. Architectural and design features, including movable objects

THE NATURAL ENVIRONMENT

Some of us live in densely populated urban areas, some in smaller towns, some in suburban areas on the outskirts of these cities and towns, and others in rural areas. Within these broad areas, we find other environmental features that affect the nature of human interaction, for example, apartment complexes, neighborhoods, high-rise buildings, and so forth. The places we live, play, and work are bound to have an impact on our behavior. The number of people we communicate with can influence our interaction style, but perhaps more important is the number of different people for whom we have to adapt our messages. Some environments are very homogeneous and provide inhabitants with fewer experiences and examples of diverse styles, behavior, and values. The pace of life and the time devoted to developing social and personal relationships may also vary as a function of where we live. In slums or ghettos in urban areas, we often find a social climate that encourages or fosters unconventional and deviant behavior—or at least tolerates it. Thus slum areas show a high incidence of juvenile delinquency, prostitution, alcohol and drug addiction, physical and mental disability, and crimes of violence (Krupat, 1985).

Behavioral scientists have also been interested in the effects of barometric pressure. For example, high or rising barometric pressure has been associated with feelings of good health; low or falling barometric pressure is more likely to be linked to feelings of pain or depression. Optimum student behavior and performance have been observed when the barometer was high or rising and on cool days with little wind and precipitation. Increase in positive air ions also seems to increase a person's irritability and tension.

The changing seasons seem to have an impact on behavior, too. Even in areas of the United States with minimal seasonal variations in temperature, national routines associated with changing seasons are still followed, for example, taking summer vacations and starting school in the fall. Some of the ways in which our behavior varies with the seasons include the following:

1. Suicide rates and admissions to public mental hospitals rise dramatically in the spring and peak in the summer.
2. College students tend to break up with their dating partners at the beginnings and endings of semesters (May/June, September, or December/January).
3. During the summer, people tend to see their friends more often.
4. During the summer, crimes of assault and rape increase.
5. From July to November, people tend to report less happiness but more activity and less boredom.
6. One study found people using the phone less in the summer than winter.

Temperature and the way it affects human responses is the climatic factor that has received the most scientific attention—specifically, the extent to which hot temperatures increase aggressive motivation and aggressive behavior.

Lengthy periods of extreme heat are often associated with discomfort, irritability, reduced work output, and unfavorable evaluations of strangers. Hot temperatures increased aggressive horn honking for drivers without air conditioning (Kendrick & MacFarlane, 1984). Vrij, van der Steen, & Koppelaar (1994) studied the reactions of police officers to a simulated burglary in which the temperature varied from comfortably cool to hot. When the temperature was hot, officers reported more aggressive and threatening impressions of the suspect and were more likely to draw their weapon. As Anderson (2001) observes, uncomfortably warm temperatures seem to increase the likelihood that ambiguous social interactions will be viewed as aggressive. A simple question like "Is it really necessary that I do that?" may be taken as an aggressive challenge to one's authority that demands some form of retaliation.

An analysis of riots in India over a 22-year period found that most took place during the months when the temperature was between 80 and 90 degrees Fahrenheit (Berke & Wilson, 1951). The National Advisory Commission on Civil Disorders, reporting on riots in the United States, said that hot summer nights added to an already explosive situation that eventually resulted in widespread rioting in ghetto areas: "In most instances, the temperature during the day on which the violence erupted was quite high" (Report of the National Advisory Commission on Civil Disorders, 1968, p. 71; also see Goranson & King, 1970). An analysis of 102 riots in the United States between 1967 and 1971 concluded that the most likely temperature/riot sequence was one in which the temperature rose to between 81 and 85 degrees Fahrenheit and remained within that range for about

7 days preceding the riot. Riots tended not to occur as temperatures rose into the high 80s and 90s. If extremely hot temperatures tend to minimize rioting, this effect is not likely to occur until mid-90 degree temperatures and above (Baron & Ransberger, 1978; Carlsmith & Anderson, 1979).

Obviously, the relationship between temperature and aggression is not simple. Probably a number of factors interact with the temperature to increase the chance of aggression, for example, prior provocation, the presence of aggressive models, negative affect experienced from sources other than temperature, perceived ability to leave the environment, and so on. A thorough review of the literature, however, concludes the following:

> Clearly, hot temperatures produce increases in aggressive motives and tendencies. Hotter regions of the world yield more aggression; this is especially apparent when analyses are done within countries. Hotter years, quarters of years, seasons, months, and days all yield relatively more aggressive behaviors such as murders, rapes, assaults, riots, and wife beatings, among others. Finally, those concomitant temperature–aggression studies done in the field also yielded clear evidence that uncomfortably hot temperatures produce increases in aggressive motives and behaviors. (Anderson, 1989, p. 93)

The heat–aggression relationship seems to carry over to our sporting activities as well. An analysis of all major league baseball games between 1986 and 1988 showed a strong correlation between higher temperatures and the number of batters hit by pitched balls (Reifman, Larrick, & Fein, 1991).

Griffitt varied heat and humidity under controlled laboratory conditions for students and confirmed a relationship to interpersonal responses. As temperature and humidity increased, evaluative responses for interpersonal attraction to another student decreased (Griffitt, 1970; Griffitt & Veitch, 1971). There may be more truth than fiction in the familiar explanation for a particularly unpleasant encounter, "Oh, he was just hot and irritable." Note, however, that sometimes unpleasant environmental factors such as heat or noise can increase attraction for others. In such cases, the aversive stimulus may function as "something we both have in common" (Kenrick & Johnson, 1979; Schneider, Lesko, & Garrett, 1980). The extent to which heat and other environmental variables increase or decrease attraction for others depends on how these interact with many other factors—the interactants' personalities and the presence or absence of simultaneously occurring rewarding stimuli, for example.

The effects of the moon and sunspots on human behavior also have been studied scientifically. Psychiatrist Arnold Lieber reasoned that human beings, like the earth, are subject to gravitational forces created by different positions of the moon. (Human beings are, like the planet itself, about 80% water and 20% solids.) He then plotted the number of murders in relation to the position of the moon and concluded a strong relationship between the two (Lieber, 1978). There is considerable skepticism about Lieber's theory and similar work because research of this type shows how two things vary together, *not* that a particular moon position actually *causes* certain behaviors. Several other factors likely are interacting and affecting the two. Two separate analyses of over 37 studies that purportedly linked moon positions and the frequency of psychiatric hospital admissions, suicides, homicides, traffic accidents, and changes in the stock market concluded that there is a spurious relationship between moon phases and these acts of human behavior (Campbell & Beets, 1978; Rotton & Kelly, 1985).

Aside from the influence of high temperatures on aggressive tendencies, we don't have a lot of reliable and valid information on how the natural environment affects our communication behavior. It seems reasonable to believe that various aspects of the natural environment will have an influence, but the exact nature and degree of this influence is still unknown. Most people seem to believe the weather has less impact on their own behavior than it does on others' behavior; that it has less impact on behavior than it does on emotional states; and that it has more impact on positive states than negative ones (Jorgenson, 1981). Kraut and Johnston (1979) found that people walking on the sidewalk smiled more when the weather was sunny and pleasant than when it was rainy and overcast. This difference was much smaller than the effect of being with others; people smiled much more when in interaction than when alone. Thus, compared to more social factors, climatic and other environmental variables may have weak influences on our behavior.

OTHER PEOPLE IN THE ENVIRONMENT

Chapter 5 examines the reactions of people to overpopulated environments. For now, we point out that people can be perceived as part of the environment and have an effect on the behavior of others. These people may be perceived as active or passive participants, depending on the degree to which they are perceived as "involved" (speaking or listening) in conversations. In many situations, these people are seen as active, especially if they are able to overhear what is being said. In some situations, we grant another person or persons the dubious status of "nonperson" and behave accordingly. This may occur in high-density situations, but it is also common with just one other person. Cab drivers, janitors, and children achieve nonperson status with regularity. The presence of nonpersons, of course, allows the uninhibited flow of interaction because, as far as the active participants are concerned, they are the only human interactants present. Parents sometimes talk to others about very personal aspects of their child while the child is playing nearby. For the interactants, the child is perceived as "not here." Any relevant verbal or nonverbal responses on the part of the nonperson that are picked up by the interactants immediately strip the person of the nonperson role.

When others are perceived as an active ingredient in the environment, certain kinds of communication may be facilitated or inhibited. The chief difference in communication with active others is that messages must be adapted to multiple audiences rather than to a single one. Even telephone conversations in which the third party can hear only one of the interactants are altered to account for the uninvited listener. Sometimes the existence of these additional audiences presents such a strain or threat that one or both communicators leave the scene. However, the appearance of a third party can provide an opportunity to ease out of a conversation with an undesirable other by "dumping" the focus of the interaction onto this third party and making a polite exit.

The presence of others may increase our motivation to look good in what we say and do, which may be either detrimental (distorting information) or beneficial. The benefits of looking good in the presence of others is exemplified by constructive approaches to conflict. For instance, the presence of others may prohibit overt fighting, albeit temporarily. Others in the environment have ensured a delay, which may act as a cooling-off period or may further frustrate and/or aggravate the person who had to repress such feelings.

When researchers observed that the home team was usually the winner in sporting events (53% of the time in professional baseball, 58% in professional football, 60% in college football, 67% in professional basketball, and 64% in professional hockey), it was attributed primarily to the home team's familiarity with the home field or to the visiting team's travel fatigue. Further analysis showed, however, that the primary factor contributing to the home team's victories was the spectators, who seemed to provide psychological support that improved performance. In contrast, unfriendly home crowds may increase performance errors (Schwartz & Barsky, 1977; Thirer & Rampey, 1979). Some analyses of home team performances before supportive fans suggested a tendency for the home team to "choke" in championship games, but some studies do not show this to be true for baseball or basketball (Schlenker et al., 1995). Within the framework of these generalizations, we also may observe that sometimes friendly support is taken for granted, and performance lags or performers may excel in response to negative feedback from others. The point to remember, though, is that friendly or unfriendly "hometown" supporters in the communication environment, just as in sporting events, are likely to have a profound effect on performance.

The ways in which groups influence individual performance are too numerous and too large a topic to discuss here. Two examples illustrate the subtlety of some of these effects:

1. In one of social psychology's first experiments, boys wound line on fishing reels faster when others were present performing the same activity, even though there was no competition and no emphasis on speed. Many studies have since found this "*social facilitation*" effect whereby performance (on simple and well-learned tasks, at least) is enhanced by the mere presence of others.
2. If people feel others are working with them on a joint task, they often slack off without realizing it. "*Social loafing*" is strongest when people feel their own contributions cannot be tallied or evaluated (Harkins & Szymanski, 1987).

ARCHITECTURAL DESIGN AND MOVABLE OBJECTS

Hall (1966) has labeled the architecture and objects in our environment as either fixed-feature space or semifixed-feature space. *Fixed feature* refers to space organized by unmoving boundaries (rooms of houses); *semifixed feature* refers to the arrangement of movable objects such as tables or chairs. Both can have a strong impact on our communication behavior.

At one time in U.S. history, banks were deliberately designed to project an image of strength and security. The design frequently featured large marble pillars, an abundance of metal bars and doors, uncovered floors, and bare walls. This style generally projected a cold, impersonal image to visitors. Later, bankers perceived the need to change their environment, to create a friendly, warm, "homey" place where people would enjoy sitting down and discussing their financial needs and problems. Bank interiors began to change. Carpeting was added; wood replaced metal; cushioned chairs were added; potted plants and art were brought in for additional warmth. This is only one example of the recognition that many times the interior in which interaction occurs can significantly influence the nature of the interaction. Nightclub owners and restaurateurs are aware that dim lighting and sound-absorbing surfaces such as carpets, drapes, and padded ceilings provide greater intimacy and cause patrons to linger longer than they would in an interior with high illumination and no soundproofing.

One of the earliest studies to focus on the influence of interior decoration on human responses was conducted by Maslow and Mintz (1956) and Mintz (1956). They selected three rooms for study: One was an "ugly" room (designed to give the impression of a janitor's storeroom in disheveled condition); one was a "beautiful" room (complete with carpeting, drapes, and the like); and one was an "average" room (a professor's office). Subjects sitting in these rooms were asked to rate a series of negative print photographs (to control for color, shading, and so forth) of faces. The experimenters tried to keep all factors, such as time of day, odor, noise, type of seating, and experimenter, constant from room to room so results could be attributed to the type of room.

Results showed that people in the beautiful room gave significantly higher ratings on "energy" and "well-being" to the faces than did participants in the ugly room. Experimenters and subjects alike engaged in various escape behaviors to avoid the ugly room. The ugly room was variously described as producing monotony, fatigue, headache, discontent, sleep, irritability, and hostility. The beautiful room, however, produced feelings of pleasure, comfort, enjoyment, importance, energy, and desire to continue the activity. In this instance, we have a well-controlled study that offers some evidence of the impact of visual-aesthetic surroundings on the nature of human interaction. Similar studies found that students do better on tests, rate teachers higher, and solve problems more effectively in "beautiful" rooms than in "ugly" ones (Campbell, 1979; Wollin & Montagre, 1981).

Because at least one study did not find mood or evaluations of others to change with drastic changes in appointments and decor (Kasmar, Griffin, & Mauritzen, 1968), we are reminded that the impact of the environment is only one source of influence on our perceptions. Sometimes it is a powerful force, but sometimes the close relationship between the two parties, an understanding of or tolerance for clutter, positive behavior on the part of the other person, and other factors offset any negative effects emanating from an "ugly" environment.

Sometimes we get very definite person- or couple-related messages from home environments (see Figure 4-2). The designation of places in the home for certain activities (and not for others); the symbolism attached to various objects in the home; and ways of decorating the home may tell us a lot about the nature of a couple's relationship (Altman et al., 1992). Sometimes the way a home is decorated will tell us whether the inhabitants decorated their home for themselves, for others, for conformity, for comfort, and so on (Sandalla, 1987). Lohmann, Arriaga, & Goodfriend (2003) were able to use decorative objects in a home to determine the closeness of the inhabitant's relationship. They asked couples who were either married or living together in a romantic relationship to identify objects in their homes they most wanted visitors to notice and to specify their favorite objects. Each object was also identified as either individually acquired or jointly acquired. Couples completed questionnaires that measured their relationship commitment and closeness. The couples who had greater commitment and closer relationships were also couples who had a higher proportion of jointly acquired objects that they wanted visitors to notice and more jointly acquired favorite objects.

FIGURE 4-2

Environmental Perception Test: (a) Describe the person or persons who live here. (b) Tell why you would or would not like to meet the person(s) who lives here. (c) How much communication takes place here? (d) What topics are mostly likely discussed? (e) Which dimensions listed on pp. 105–107 influenced your perceptions most? (f) Compare your answers with others.

Gosling et al. (2002) were interested in whether personality characteristics could accurately be predicted from a person's office or bedroom. Observers who experienced various offices and bedrooms firsthand indicated the extent to which the environment they saw reflected the person's extraversion, agreeableness, emotional stability, openness to experience, and conscientiousness. The personality profile of the people who worked in the offices and slept in the bedrooms were obtained from their own responses to personality measures. These environments seem to have enough signals associated with conscientiousness and openness to experience to enable the observers to effectively judge inhabitants with those characteristics, but they were not as successful judging the other personality characteristics.

The way people decorate their rooms may also forecast future behavior. In one study, researchers took photographs of 83 college freshman students' rooms. When the photos of the rooms of students who had dropped out of school a year and a half later were analyzed, it was noted that the dropouts had more decorations reflecting high school and home and fewer related to the university community. Dropouts also seemed to have fewer ways to protect their privacy. Their favorite way to combat unwanted noise was to override it with more noise of their own (Vinsel et al., 1980).

COLOR

People believe colors can affect behavior. In fact, some believe "prisoner mischief" will vary as a function of the colors surrounding them. For example, the walls of the San Diego city jail were at one time reportedly painted pink, baby blue, and peach on the assumption that pastel colors would have a calming effect on the inmates. In Salem, Oregon, the cell bars of Oregon's correctional institution were painted soft greens, blues, and buffs; some cell doors were painted bright yellow, orange, green, and blue. In addition, the superintendent of the institution said the color schemes would be continually changed to keep it "an exciting place to work and live in." Initial studies of people exposed to environments painted "Baker-Miller pink" found decreasing heart rates, pulse, and respiration. Subsequent studies in adult and juvenile correctional facilities, psychiatric hospitals, and controlled laboratory studies with undergraduate students supported the belief that this pink color aided in suppressing violent and aggressive behaviors (Pelligrini & Schauss, 1980; Schauss, 1985).

But not all experiences with pink have been so positive. The county jail in San Jose, California, reportedly painted two holding cells "shocking pink" in the belief that prisoner hostility would be reduced. Prisoners seemed less hostile for about 15 minutes, but soon the hostility reached a peak, and after 3 hours some prisoners were tearing the paint off the wall. This result is consistent with the research of Smith, Bell, & Fusco (1986) who found pink to be arousing rather than weakening. In fact, any color that is highly saturated and bright is likely to be more arousing and garner more attention than paler colors (Camgoz, Yener, & Guvenc, 2004; Garber & Hyatt, 2003). When prisoners are allowed to paint their cells with colors they choose, it may have an aggression-reducing effect, but the effect may have more to do with the prisoner's control over the choice of color than the colors themselves. Nevertheless, the preceding reports show how various institutions have tried (with mixed results) to apply the findings from color research in order to affect the nature of human interaction in certain environments.

Colors are also believed to influence student learning. Colors which will facilitate, or at least not impede, learning are always a concern during classroom construction. In Munich, Germany, a group of researchers studied the impact of colors on mental growth and social relations ("Blue Is Beautiful," 1973). Children who were tested in rooms they thought beautiful scored about 12 points higher on an IQ test than those in rooms they thought ugly. Blue, yellow, yellow-green, and orange were considered beautiful; white, black, and brown were considered ugly. The beautifully colored rooms also seemed to stimulate alertness and creativity. In the orange room, these psychologists found that positive social reactions (friendly words, smiles) increased 53%, whereas negative reactions (irritability, hostility) decreased 12%.

Ball's (1965) summary of the color research prior to 1965 found what others have found since then—that people associate serenity and calm with the colors blue and green, while red and orange are perceived to be arousing and stimulating. The research of Wexner (1954) and Murray & Deabler (1957) is representative of this tradition. Wexner

Table 4-1   Colors Associated with Moods

Mood-Tone	Color	Frequency of Times Chosen
Exciting/Stimulating	Red	61
Secure/Comfortable	Blue	41
Distressed/Disturbed/Upset	Orange	34
Tender/Soothing	Blue	41
Protective/Defending	Red	21
	Brown	17
	Blue	15
	Black	15
	Purple	14
Despondent/Dejected/Unhappy/Melancholy	Black	25
	Brown	25
Calm/Peaceful/Serene	Blue	38
	Green	31
Dignified/Stately	Purple	45
Cheerful/Jovial/Joyful	Yellow	40
Defiant/Contrary/Hostile	Red	23
	Orange	21
	Black	18
Powerful/Strong/Masterful	Black	48

(see Table 4-1) presented 8 colors and 11 mood tones to 94 research participants. The results show that for some mood tones a single color is significantly related; for others there may be two or more colors.

It is difficult to know how to interpret this research. First, research participants are normally asked to judge colors outside of any context even though the colors we respond to in daily life are perceived within a particular context. Separating color from the objects and forms which give it shape, the surrounding colors, and other contextual features may elicit some learned stereotypes about the relationship of mood and color, but this stereotype may or may not be relevant when given a context. Pink may be your favorite color, but you may still dislike pink hair. Hines (1996) found the residents of four American cities believed red meant danger, warmth, love, strength, and safety, but when these same people were asked to think about red in terms of products, they said red meant Coca-Cola.

We can't make any final judgments about the impact of color on human interaction from the research to date, but common sense tells us that colors in our environment will affect the way we respond. We just don't know how and how much. A series of studies on the color of uniforms worn by football and hockey players pinpointed the complex ways colors may affect behavior. Frank and Gilovich (1988) began by demonstrating that students rated black uniforms as connoting meanness and aggression more than other colors.

Then they examined statistics from actual professional games and found that football and hockey teams wearing black uniforms were penalized more than teams wearing other colors. And when a team changed its color to black from some other color, it began getting more penalties! The researchers then asked whether the effect was caused by the players themselves (maybe they acted meaner and rougher wearing black) or by the stereotyped perceptions of referees. The researchers made experimental films in which they varied the uniforms of players engaging in identical moves and then showed these to subjects acting as "referees." These "referees" did find more instances of penalizable behavior among those suited in black, even though there actually were no differences. However, when the researchers put black uniforms on students, they found evidence that wearing a black uniform produced more aggressive behavior in the wearer. Thus both processes seem to be at work: Players wearing black may be rougher, but people also *perceive* the play of those in black uniforms as rougher. This perception could, of course, make black-suited players even rougher, because of the ways people treat them.

SOUND

Types of sounds and their intensity also seem to affect interpersonal behavior. We may have very different reactions to the drone of several people's voices, the overpowering sound of a nearby jackhammer, or the soothing or stimulating sounds of music. Music can be arousing or soothing.

Most of us are aware of how music can affect our moods. Our selection of music may be designed to match or even change our mood. Depressing music can add to the intensity of an already gloomy mood; uplifting music can enhance a joyful feeling. Beginning with ideas like this, Honeycutt and Eidenmuller (2001) conducted an exploratory study in which they asked couples to work at resolving a source of conflict in their relationship while background music was playing. Some couples experienced music rated as more positive and/or uplifting while others experienced negative and/or dreary music. Their results suggest not only that the type of music will affect the verbal and nonverbal behavior of the interactants (i.e., agitating music was more likely to be linked to argument), but the intensity of the music can affect the intensity of the interaction.

Music can also unwittingly affect our consumer behavior. Scientists at the University of Leicester in England displayed four French and four German wines in a local supermarket. The wines from the two countries were similar in price, sweetness, and dryness. For 2 weeks, a tape deck on a nearby shelf alternated each day with either French accordian music or German beer hall music. Placement on the shelves was alternated midway through the experiment. Sales were clearly linked to the type of music being played. When French music was played, French wines outsold German wines, but when German music was played, German wines outsold French wines. Only about 7% of those purchasing wines were willing to acknowledge that the music may have influenced their decision (North, Hargreaves, & McKendrick, 1997).

Glass and Singer (1973) conducted a series of studies on the impact of noise on performance. People were asked to perform a variety of tasks, varying in complexity, while noises were manipulated by the experimenters. Noise levels were varied; some noise was predictable (following a pattern) and some was not. Various noise sources were tested (for example, typewriters, machinery, people speaking a foreign language). Although noise alone did not seem to have a substantial effect on performance, deterioration was observed when noise interacted with other factors. For instance, performance decreased when the workload was high and the noise uncontrollable and unpredictable. Other factors determining whether noise is a problem or a pleasure include the type of noise (e.g., music versus people talking), the volume, the length of time it lasts, and whether the listener is accustomed to it or not. Obviously, some individuals may be more influenced by noise than others. Noise-sensitive incoming college students perceived more noise than other students, and these perceptions increased after seven months into the school year. The noise-sensitive students also received lower grades, felt less secure in their social interactions, and had a greater desire for privacy than did their peers who were less sensitive to noise (Weinstein, 1978).

LIGHTING

Lighting also helps structure our perceptions of an environment, and these perceptions may influence the type of messages we send. If we enter a dimly lit or candlelit room, we may talk more softly, sit closer together, and presume that more personal communication will take place (Meer, 1985). When the dim lights are brightened, however, the environment tends to invite less intimate interaction. When dimly lit nightclubs flash on bright lights, it is often a signal that closing time is near and allows patrons some time to make the transition from one mood to another. Carr and Dabbs found that the communication of intimate questions in dim lighting with nonintimates caused a significant hesitancy in responding, a significant decrease in eye gaze, and a decrease in the average length of gaze (Carr & Dabbs, 1974). All of these nonverbal behaviors appear to be efforts to create more psychological distance and decrease the perceived inappropriateness of the intimacy created by the lighting and the questions.

The absence of light seems to be a central problem for people who suffer from "seasonal affective disorder (SAD)," a form of depression particularly acute in winter months (Rosenthal, 1993). Therapists have successfully treated these people by exposing them to extremely bright lighting for several hours each morning. Artificial lighting that provides a full-range light spectrum like that of the sun is most effective in this therapy (Lewy et al., 1998). In view of this need for sunlight, some researchers wondered whether cities that had the lowest amount of annual sunlight also had the highest suicide rates. Their findings do not provide support for this hypothesis (Lester, 1988).

MOVABLE OBJECTS

If we know that the arrangement of certain objects in our environment can help structure communication, it is not surprising that we often try to manipulate objects to elicit certain types of response. This was what Attorney General John Ashcroft had in mind when he arranged for the "Spirit of Justice" statue to be covered up with a blue curtain. The statue, which has been in the Department of Justice since it was built in the 1930s, is a 12-foot-high female who represents the spirit of justice. Her arms are raised and a toga is draped over part of her body. However, one of her breasts is completely exposed (see Figure 4-3)

FIGURE 4-3

Attorney General John Ashcroft and the Spirit of Justice statue.

and photographs of Ashcroft at press briefings invariably include this statue in the background. The $8,000 curtain provides a neutral background, but the same effect might have been achieved by moving the lectern to the side. Photographers are not unaware that the statue can add meaning to a photograph. In the 1980s, an image of Attorney General Edwin Meese, holding up a report on pornography, was captured with the partially nude female statue standing in the background.

Manipulating objects in the environment to communicate particular messages also occurs in personal living spaces. In preparation for an intimate evening at home, a person may light candles; play soft, romantic music; fluff the pillows on the couch; and hide the dirty dishes, clothes, and other unpleasant reminders of daily living.

Employees often use objects to personalize their offices. These signs of personal identity make them feel more satisfied with their work life and provide visitors with information to initiate a conversation. Because the company also wants to communicate its identity, the amount and kind of personal objects employees display must also be consistent with the image the company wants to display. Objects in our work environment also can be arranged to reflect certain role relationships—to demarcate boundaries or to encourage greater affiliation. The interior of an executive suite clearly may indicate the perceived status of the inhabitant, for example, expensive paintings, large desk, plush sofa and chairs, drapes, and so forth (Monk, 1994). Such an atmosphere may be inappropriate for a personal counseling situation, but it can be rearranged to make it more conducive to such a purpose. Of course, we sometimes are able to communicate well in seemingly inappropriate settings, as when lovers say good-bye in relatively cold and public airport terminals.

Desks seem to be important objects in the conduct of interpersonal communication. An early experiment in this area set in a doctor's office suggests that the presence or absence of a desk may significantly alter the patient's "at ease" state (White, 1953). With the desk separating doctor and patient, only 10% of the patients were perceived "at ease," whereas removal of the desk increased the percentage of "at ease" patients to 55%. Student/student interaction in classrooms can be constrained by eliminating any possible movement of the student desks/seats (see Figure 4-4). And student/teacher relationships can also be affected by desk placement (Zweigenhaft, 1976). Faculty members were asked to sketch the furniture arrangement of their offices. These sketches were collected and analyzed with other information obtained from the professors and a schoolwide teacher evaluation. Twenty-four of 33 senior faculty members put their desks between themselves and their students, but only 14 of 30 junior faculty members did so. Furthermore, students rated the "unbarricaded" professors as more willing to "encourage the development of different viewpoints by students," ready to give "individual attention to students who need it," and less likely to show "undue favoritism." Because another study did not find the desk barrier related to undesirable experiences in student/professor interactions, we are reminded that other factors may neutralize or override the potentially troublesome effects of the desk barrier (Campbell & Herren, 1978). For example, students expect greater formality in student/teacher relationships in some situations than others, or the basis for

FIGURE 4-4

A classroom design with immovable chairs discourages student-to-student interactions.

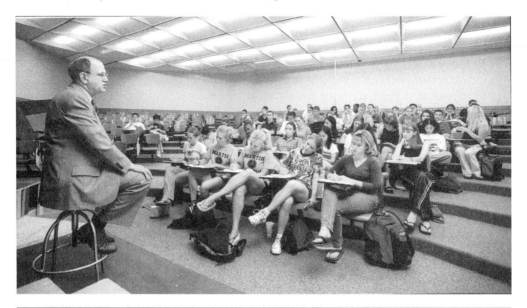

an effective working relationship may have been established outside the professor's office, so the "barrier" is not perceived as such. The podium separating the president's press secretary from the press during White House press briefings also has been perceived both as appropriate and as a barrier to effective communication. During the Nixon administration, press briefings were formal, and the press secretary stood behind a podium. Ron Nessen, President Ford's press secretary, felt the podium contributed to an unproductive "us and them" feeling, which prompted him to conduct briefings without the obstacle.

Less obvious barriers also exist. For instance, if you find a delicate objet d'art placed in front of some books in a bookcase, you likely will feel hesitant about using the books. Keep in mind that desks and other "barriers" are not inherently good or bad. Should you want to keep a distant, formal relationship, the desk can help create that feeling.

The arrangement of other items of furniture can facilitate or inhibit communication. The location of the television set in a room very likely will affect the placement of chairs and, in turn, the pattern of conversations in that room. Sommer and Ross found that some residents in a geriatric ward were "apathetic" and had few friends, in spite of a generally cheerful and bright environment. They were able to double the frequency of resident conversations by rearranging the chairs so more of them faced each other (Sommer & Ross, 1958). Even when conversational possibilities have been maximized, not everyone will talk to everyone else. Consider the arrangement of Figure 4-5. We would predict exchanges marked by the arrows to be most frequent, but the 4 people seated on the couch as well as persons F and G will probably talk to each other infrequently. The 4 people on one end are not likely to communicate very often with the 4 people on the other end. If the participants are periodically rearranged, the conversational groupings can be altered.

In some environments, people are not expected to linger, so chairs are deliberately designed without comfort in mind. Hotel owners and airport designers are well aware of the "too comfortable" phenomenon. You may have noticed the slightly uncomfortable nature of the 10 degree forward angle of chairs in some fast-food restaurants. This feature encourages customers to eat and move along quickly to provide seats for others. The Port Authority Bus Terminal in New York replaced its old wooden seats with folding plastic seats, only 8 inches deep, that "require so much concentration to balance that sleeping or

FIGURE 4-5

Conversation flow and furniture arrangement.

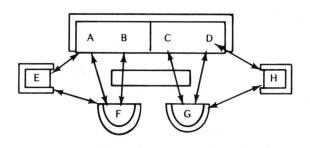

SOURCE: From *Public Places and Private Spaces* by Albert Mehrabian. Copyright © 1976 by Basic Books, Inc. Reprinted by permission of Basic Books, a member of Perseus Books, L.L.C.

even sitting for long is impossible." This was done to keep homeless people from sleeping in the terminal ("For Homeless," 1989).

Some environments seem to have an unwritten code that virtually prohibits interaction. Lone men entering, sitting through, and leaving XXX-rated movies without uttering a word are a case in point.

STRUCTURE AND DESIGN

We pass much of our time in buildings. Most of us spend the day in a dwelling supposedly designed for effective performance of our work; in the evening, we enter another structure supposedly designed for the effective conduct of our personal and family life. The architecture of these buildings can go a long way toward determining who meets whom, where, and perhaps for how long.

The life of domestic animals is controlled through, among other things, the erection of fences, flap doors, or the placement of food and water in particular locations. Although verbal and nonverbal actions help control human situations, manipulation of barriers, openings, and other physical arrangements is also helpful. Meeting places can be appropriately arranged to regulate human traffic and, to a certain extent, the network of communication.

U.S. office buildings often are constructed from a standard plan that reflects a pyramidal organization. A large number of people are supervised by a few executives at the upper levels. These executives generally have the most space, the most privacy, and the most desirable office locations, namely, on the highest floor of the structure. Achieving a height above the "masses" and occupying a significant amount of space are only two indications of power. Corner offices, large picture windows, and private elevators also are associated with status and power (Monk, 1994). An office next to an important executive also may be a formidable power base. A similar pattern seems to exist in academic settings as well, with the higher ranking professors normally having more space, windows, privacy, and choice of office location (Farrenkopf & Roth, 1980). The offices of top-level executives are often hard to reach, the assumption being that the more complicated the path to get to the executive, the more powerful he or she seems. Figure 4-6 is a hypothetical, but not far-fetched, example of the long and circuitous route to a president's office. To get to the office, the visitor must be screened by a receptionist and a private secretary and in either or both places may be asked to sit and wait. So, although the status and power of an executive may be related to his or her inaccessibility, secretaries and receptionists may value open views that allow them to act as lookouts and defenders against unwanted intrusions. It is common for people on the lowest rungs of the organizational ladder to find themselves in a large open "pit." These so-called "offices" (really desks) have little or no privacy, and complaints are common. Although privacy is minimal, communication opportunities are plentiful.

Some dormitories are built from floor plans that resemble many office buildings and old hotels. It has been speculated that these corridor-type dorms tend to encourage bureaucratic management, which seems to fit the orderly and uniform structure. Rigid rules are easier to enforce in these structures, and interaction among the residents is discouraged. Compared with suite-type dorms, corridor types are perceived by residents as more

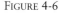

FIGURE 4-6

Getting to the president's office. A = receptionist. B = private secretary. C = president. D = private room with rear exit.

crowded, less private, and conducive to avoiding others (Baum & Valins, 1979). The sense of community and the resulting responsibility for the living space are difficult to achieve. Lounges are sometimes intended to facilitate such interaction, but their usefulness has been questioned by architects and behavioral scientists. Lounges, like other design features, must be integrated into the entire architectural plan developed from an analysis of *human needs*—not inserted in places where they fit nicely or look good for parents and visitors.

If you look carefully, you can see many environmental structures that inhibit or prohibit communication. Fences separating yards create obvious barriers, even if they are only waist high; locating laundry rooms in dark, isolated areas of apartment buildings and public housing discourages their use, particularly at night; providing access to patios only through a bedroom probably discourages use; and so on.

Other environmental situations seem to facilitate interaction. Homes located in the middle of a block seem to draw more interpersonal exchanges than those located in other positions. Houses with adjacent driveways seem to have a built-in structure, drawing the neighbors together and inviting communication. The likelihood of interaction between strangers at a bar varies directly with the distance between them. As a rule, a span of three bar stools is the maximum distance over which patrons will attempt to initiate an encounter. Most bars are not designed for optimum interaction. Note that the three bar designs in Figure 4-7 provide very different opportunities for facing an interaction partner, for mutual eye gaze, and for getting physically close. Most bars are similar to type B, which seems to discourage interaction the most.

Some recent designs for housing elderly people have taken into consideration the need for social contact. In these apartment dwellings, the doors of the apartments on each floor

FIGURE 4-7

Designs for drinking.

open onto a common entranceway. This greatly increases the probabilities for social exchange as compared to buildings in which apartment doors are staggered on either side of a long hallway with no facing doorways. If you want a structure that encourages social interaction, you must have human paths crossing; but if you want people to interact, there must be something that will encourage them to linger. Differences in interaction frequency are often related to the distances people must travel between activities. For example, consider this comparison made between two high schools: One was "centralized" with classrooms in one or two buildings; one was "campus style" with classrooms spread among several buildings. The campus design prompted 5% to 10% more interactions in the halls, stairs, and lobbies but 7% to 10% fewer in the classrooms than the centralized design. There were 20% fewer interactions between students and teachers before and after class in the campus-style high school (Myrick & Marx, 1968). It is no secret that the architecture of a school can affect a student's motivation to learn, a teacher's motivation to teach, how much students and teachers talk to each other, how long they talk, and to a certain extent what they talk about. But older school designs were often based on how to maintain strict discipline, emphasize status differences between students and teachers, and minimize informal talking.

Fast-food restaurants also seem to vary regarding how much they contribute to the interactive involvement of their customers. In one study, for example, the behavior of customers at McDonald's showed more involvement than those at Burger King (Eaves & Leathers, 1991). The shorter distance across the tables and the generally less comfortable surroundings seemed to be factors in the greater involvement of the patrons at McDonald's.

Architects and social scientists have even been experimenting with new prison designs. The older structures, which had linear tiers of steel cages, are being replaced with modular units that have fewer inmates and fewer barriers between them and their guards. These new designs, coupled with new ways of managing the prisoners, seem to result in more positive behavior on the part of both guards and prisoners, reduce costs, and provide more opportunities for rehabilitation (Cronin, 1992).

Furthermore, the nature of the design may encourage or discourage certain *types* of communication—that is, the structure may determine how much interaction takes place and the general content of that interaction. Drew (1971) reports a study of three different designs for nursing stations within a mental hospital. In one, interaction had to take place by opening a door; in another, interaction was conducted through a glass-enclosed counter;

and in the third, interaction took place over an open counter. Although substantially more patients entered the nursing station with the door, interactions occurred less frequently than in the other two stations. An average of only 1 interaction per each 15-minute observation period occurred with the door; 5.3 interactions per period occurred in the glass-enclosed counter; and 8.7 occurred with the open counter. Although interaction was higher for the open counter, the author noted a preponderance of social conversation here; the door design seemed to encourage more item requests and permission interactions. In short, the more inaccessible setting decreased interaction frequency and increased task-oriented messages; the more accessible setting increased interaction frequency and increased the amount of "small talk."

A more complete analysis of physical proximity and spatial distance appears in chapter 5, but it is clearly relevant to this discussion on the environment as well. Over 60 years ago, Stouffer (1940) made this observation that holds true today:

> Whether one is seeking to explain why persons go to a particular place to get jobs, why they go to trade at a particular store, why they go to a particular neighborhood to commit a crime, or why they marry a particular spouse they choose, the factor of spatial distance is of obvious significance. (p. 845)

Many studies have confirmed Stouffer's remark. Students tend to develop stronger friendships with students who share their classes, dormitory, or apartment building, or who sit near them, than with others who are geographically distant. Workers tend to develop closer friendships with those who work near them. The effect of proximity seems to be stronger for employees with less status in the organization. Managers are more likely to choose their business friends according to their status rather than their proximity (Schutte & Light, 1978). Some believe that increased proximity of ethnic groups will assist in reducing prejudice. Although close proximity may bring about positive attitude changes, we must exercise caution in generalizing such an idea. If the two groups are extremely polarized, or perceive no mutual problems or projects requiring cooperation, proximity may only magnify the hostilities.

Several studies show an inverse relationship between the distance separating potential marriage partners and the number of marriages. Proximity allows us to obtain more information about the other person. The inescapable conclusion is that as proximity increases, attraction is likely to increase. We might also posit that as attraction increases, proximity will tend to increase.

A number of studies have shown how proximity influences friendships. In one study conducted in a townhouse development, most friendships occurred between people who lived within 100 feet of each other. Next-door neighbors became close friends 46% of the time; neighbors who lived two or three doors away became close friends 24% of the time; and people who lived three or four doors away became friends 13% of the time (Athanasiou & Yoshioka, 1973). Historically, the most famous study of proximity, friendship choice, and interpersonal contact was conducted by Festinger, Schachter, and Back (1950) in a housing development for married students. Concern for what the authors called "functional distance" led to data clearly demonstrating that architects can have a tremendous influence on the social life of residents in these housing projects. Functional distance is determined by the number of contacts that position and design encourage, for

FIGURE 4-8

Design influences the social lives of residents in apartment buildings.

example, factors such as which way apartments face, where exits and entranceways are located, and location of stairways, mailboxes, and the like. Figure 4-8 shows the basic design of one type of building studied.

The researchers asked the residents of 17 buildings (with the design of Figure 4-8) which people they saw most often socially and what friendship choices they made. Among the findings from this study, the following are noteworthy:

1. There seemed to be a greater number of friendship choices for those physically close to one another (on the same floor or in the same building). It was rare to find a friendship between people separated by more than four or five houses.
2. People living in apartments 1 and 5 gave and received from the upper-floor residents more friendship choices than the people living in any other apartments on the lower floor.
3. Apartments 1 and 6 exchanged more choices than apartments 2 and 7. Similarly, apartments 5 and 10 exchanged more choices than apartments 4 and 9. Although this represents the same physical distance, functional distance differed.
4. Because of the mailboxes, apartment 5 chose more upper-level friends, more of those choices being apartments 9 and 10.

Making friends takes many forms, but functional distance seems to be highly influential, and it is sometimes the result of architectural design.

REGULATING ENVIRONMENTS AND COMMUNICATION

It should be clear by now that our communication is affected by the social and physical environment. We have some control over our environment. We can paint our walls a different color, substitute candles for electric lights, and so on. But our communication environments are influenced by others, too. Earlier in this chapter we noted how architects and furniture designers affect our social interaction, but government laws and regulations (local and federal) also play an important role in creating the environments that affect our communicative behavior. It is important to conclude the chapter with this reminder because gaining control over the environment that affects our communication may mean becoming a community activist or leader.

Zoning laws, for example, determine whether a part of our environment will be used for industrial, commercial, or residential activity. Zoning laws also determine the density of an area (how many units per acre). Laws prohibiting adult bookstores from operating too close to churches are essentially saying the two environments generate very different forms of communication that are not likely to happily share the same territory. When business hours of operation are regulated, it affects when streets are empty, when they are crowded, or what segment of the population occupies the street. Some communities have specific laws governing their signs and billboards (where they can be placed, materials and colors that can be used, etc.). Obviously these and similar regulations governing parking areas, parks, display windows, and vending machines impact our social lives.

In addition, there are penal codes that punish loitering, smoking, and drinking alcoholic beverages (among other behaviors). Smoking regulations have changed where smokers congregate, how long they spend talking after a dinner in a nonsmoking restaurant (and whether they go to such restaurants), who they talk to, and the friendships they develop. The many factors leading to the demise of the neighborhood tavern as a social gathering place prompted Drucker and Gumpert (1996) to say this:

> Public bars, taverns, and pubs have historically provided social centers, supported social and political webs, and provided the site where revolutions were planned, artistic movements launched, friendships formed, and community ties forged. The institution of the English and Irish pub is alive and well, but the American tavern is a dying institution. (p. 289)

❖

SUMMARY

The environment in which people communicate frequently contributes to the overall outcome of their encounters. We have seen that both the frequency and the content of our messages are influenced by various aspects of the setting in which we communicate. We have seen how the environment influences our behavior, but we also know that we can alter environments in order to elicit certain types of responses. As our knowledge of environments increases, we may deliberately use them to help us obtain desired responses. In many respects, we are products of our environment, and if we want to change behavior, we need to learn to control the environment in which we interact.

Throughout this chapter, we referred to a number of different types of environments— the classroom, dormitories, offices, prisons, fast-food restaurants, homes, and bars. We suggested several different ways of looking at environments. Mehrabian, following research in other areas of human perception, commented that all environments could profitably be examined by looking at emotional reactions to them. These emotions, or feelings, says Mehrabian, can be plotted on three dimensions: arousing/nonarousing, pleasant/unpleasant, and dominant/submissive. We suggested six perceptual bases for examining environments: formal/informal, warm/cold, private/public, familiar/unfamiliar, constraining/ free, and distant/close. We also pointed out that people perceive temporal aspects of their environments: when things happen, how long they last, how much time exists between events, and the pattern or rhythm of events.

Each environment seems to have three major characteristics:

1. The natural environment
2. The presence of or absence of other people
3. Architectural design and movable objects, including lighting, sound, color, and general visual-aesthetic appeal

The quantity and quality of the research in each of these areas vary considerably, but clearly any analysis of human behavior must account for the influence of environmental features.

QUESTIONS FOR DISCUSSION

1. Select a familiar environment that effectively encourages or discourages human interaction. Now indicate all the changes you would make so this environment would have the exact opposite effect.

2. Assume the role of a stranger entering your own apartment or your family's home. What messages does the environment communicate?

3. Identify an environment that is clearly designed to accomplish certain goals or effects—but does not. What explanation helps us understand this situation?

4. How do people communicate time-related messages by their behavior?

BIBLIOGRAPHY

Adams, R. S. (1969). Location as a feature of instructional interaction. *Merrill-Palmer Quarterly, 15,* 309–321.

Adams, R. S., & Biddle, B. (1970). *Realities of teaching: Explorations with video tape.* New York: Holt, Rinehart & Winston.

Altman, I., Brown, B. B., Staples, B., & Werner, C. M. (1992). A transactional approach to close relationships: Courtship, weddings, and placemaking. In B. Walsh, K. Craik, & R. Price (Eds.), *Person-environment psychology: Contemporary models and perspectives.* Hillsdale, NJ: Erlbaum.

Altman, I., & Chemers, M. M. (1988). *Culture and environment.* New York: Cambridge University Press.

Altman, I., & Gauvain, M. (1981). A cross-cultural and dialectic analysis of homes. In L. S. Liben, A. H. Patterson, & N. Newcombe (Eds.), *Special representation and behavior across the life span.* New York: Academic Press.

Altman, I., & Low, S. M. (Eds.). (1992). *Place attachment. Human behavior and environment: Advances in theory and research* (Vol. 12). New York: Plenum.

Anderson, C. A. (2001). Heat and violence. *Current Directions in Psychological Science, 10,* 33–38.

Anderson, C. A. (1989). Temperature and aggression: Ubiquitous effects of heat on occurrence of human violence. *Psychological Bulletin, 106,* 74–96.

Anderson, C. A., & Anderson, D. C. (1984). Ambient temperature and violent crime: Tests of the linear and curvilinear hypotheses. *Journal of Personality and Social Psychology, 46,* 91–97.

Anderson, C. A., Anderson, K. B., Dorr, N., DeNeve, K. M., & Flanagan, M. (2000). Temperature and aggression. In M. Zanna (Ed.), *Advances in experimental social psychology* (Vol. 32, pp. 63–133). New York: Academic Press.

Athanasiou, R., & Yoshioka, G. A. (1973). The spatial character of friendship formation. *Environment and Behavior, 5,* 43–65.

Ball, V. K. (1965). The aesthetics of color: A review of fifty years of experimentation. *Journal of Aesthetics and Art Criticism, 23,* 441–452.

Ballard, D. I., & Seibold, D. R. (2000). Time orientation and temporal variation across work groups: Implications for group and organizational communication. *Western Journal of Communication, 64,* 218–242.

Barker, R. (1968). *Ecological psychology.* Palo Alto, CA: Stanford University Press.

Barker, R., & Wright, H. (1957). *Midwest and its children.* Lawrence: University of Kansas Press.

Baron, R. A. (1972). Aggression as a function of ambient temperature and prior anger arousal. *Journal of Personality and Social Psychology, 21,* 183–189.

Baron, R. A., & Bell, P. A. (1975). Aggression and heat: Mediating effects of prior provocation and exposure to an aggressive model. *Journal of Personality and Social Psychology, 31,* 825–832.

Baron, R. A., & Bell, P. A. (1976). Aggression and heat: The influence of ambient temperature, negative affect, and a cooling drink on physical aggression. *Journal of Personality and Social Psychology, 33,* 245–255.

Baron, R. A., & Lawton, S. F. (1972). Environmental influences on aggression: The facilitation of modeling effects by high ambient temperatures. *Psychonomic Science, 26,* 80–82.

Baron, R. A., & Ransberger, V. M. (1978). Ambient temperature and the occurrence of collective violence: The "long hot summer" revisited. *Journal of Personality and Social Psychology, 36,* 351–360.

Baum, A., & Davis, G. E. (1980). Reducing the stress of high density living: An architectural intervention. *Journal of Personality and Social Psychology, 38,* 471–481.

Baum, A., & Valins, S. (1979). Architectural mediation of residential density and control: Crowding and regulation of social contact. In L. Berkowitz (Ed.), *Advances in experimental social psychology* (Vol. 12). New York: Academic Press.

Baumeister, R. F. (1995). Disputing the effects of championship pressures and home audiences. *Journal of Personality and Social Psychology, 68,* 649–652.

Berke, J., & Wilson, V. (1951). *Watch out for the weather.* New York: Viking.

Birren, F. (1969). *Light, color, and environment.* New York: Van Nostrand Reinhold.

Blake, R. R., Rhead, C. C., Wedge, B., & Mouton, J. S. (1956). Housing architecture and social interaction. *Sociometry, 19,* 133–139.

Blue is beautiful. (1973, September 17). *Time,* p. 66.

Breed, G., & Colaiuta, V. (1974). Looking, blinking, and sitting: Nonverbal dynamics in the classroom. *Journal of Communication, 24,* 75–81.

Bruneau, T. (1985). Silencing and stilling processes: The creative and temporal bases of signs. *Semiotica, 56*(3/4), 279–290.

Buslig, A. L. S. (1999). "Stop" signs regulating privacy with environmental features. In L. Guerrero, J. A. DeVito, & M. L. Hecht (Eds.) *The nonverbal communication reader* (2nd Ed., pp. 241–249). Prospect Heights, IL: Waveland Press.

Byrne, D. (1961). The influence of propinquity and opportunities for interaction on classroom relationships. *Human Relations, 14,* 63–70.

Camgoz, N., Yener, C., & Guvenc, D. (2004). Effects of hue, saturation, and brightness: Part 2: Attention. *Color Research and Application, 29,* 20–28.

Campbell, D. E. (1979). Interior office design and visitor response. *Journal of Applied Psychology, 64*, 648–653.

Campbell, D. E., & Beets, J. L. (1978). Lunacy and the moon. *Psychological Bulletin, 85*, 1123–1129.

Campbell, D. E., & Herren, K. A. (1978). Interior arrangement of the faculty office. *Psychological Reports, 43*, 234.

Canter, D. (1977). *The psychology of place.* London: Architectural Press.

Carlsmith, J. M., & Anderson, C. A. (1979). Ambient temperature and the occurrence of collective violence: A new analysis. *Journal of Personality and Social Psychology, 37*, 337–344.

Carr, S. J., & Dabbs, J. M. (1974). The effect of lighting, distance, and intimacy of topic on verbal and visual behavior. *Sociometry, 37*, 592–600.

Cheek, F. E., Maxwell, R., & Weisman, R. (1971). Carpeting the ward: An exploratory study in environmental psychiatry. *Mental Hygiene, 55*, 109–118.

Cottle, T. J. (1976). *Perceiving time.* New York: Wiley.

Craik, K. (1981). Environmental assessment and situational analysis. In D. Magnusson (Ed.), *Toward a psychology of situations: An interactional perspective.* New York: Erlbaum.

Cronin, M. (May 1992). Gilded cages. *Time,* pp. 52–54.

Csikszentmihalyi, M., & Rochberg-Halton, E. (1981). *The meaning of things: Domestic symbols and the self.* New York: Cambridge University Press.

Deutsch, M., & Collins, M. (1951). *Interracial housing: A psychological evaluation of a social experiment.* Minneapolis: University of Minnesota Press.

Doob, L. (1964). *Patterning of time.* New Haven, CT: Yale University Press.

Drew, C. J. (1971). Research on the psychological–behavioral effects of the physical environment. *Review of Educational Research, 41*, 447–463.

Drucker, S. J., & Gumpert, G. (1996). The regulation of public social life: Communication law revisited. *Communication Quarterly, 44*, 280–296.

Duncan, F. (1981). Dormitory architecture influences patterns of student social relations over time. *Environment and Behavior, 13*, 23–41.

Eaves, M. H., & Leathers, D. G. (1991). Context as communication: McDonald's vs. Burger King. *Journal of Applied Communication Research, 19*, 263–289.

Falender, C. A., & Mehrabian, A. (1978). Environmental effects on parent–infant interaction. *Genetic Psychology Monographs, 97*(Pt. 1), 3–41.

Farrenkopf, T., & Roth, V. (1980). The university faculty office as an environment. *Environment and Behavior, 12*, 467–477.

Festinger, L. (1951). Architecture and group membership. *Journal of Social Issues, 1*, 152–163.

Festinger, L., Schachter, S., & Back, K. (1950). *Social pressures in informal groups: A study of human factors in housing.* New York: Harper & Row.

For homeless, no welcome in public places. (1989, November 18). *New York Times.*

Fraisse, Paul. (1963). *The psychology of time.* New York: Harper & Row.

Frank, M. S., & Gilovich, T. (1988). The dark side of self- and social perception: Black uniforms and aggression in professional sports. *Journal of Personality and Social Psychology, 54*, 74–85.

Fraser, J. T. (1981). A report on the literature of time, 1900–1980. In J. T. Fraser, N. Lawrence, & D. Park (Eds.), *The study of time IV.* New York: Springer-Verlag.

Friedman, W. J. (1990). *About time.* Cambridge, MA: MIT Press.

Gans, H. J. (1961). Planning and social life: Friendship and neighbor relations in suburban communities. *Journal of the American Institute of Planners, 27*, 134–140.

Garber, L. L., Jr., & Hyatt, E. M. (2003). Color as a tool for visual persuasion. In L. M. Scott and R. Batra (Eds.), *Persuasive imagery: A consumer response perspective* (pp. 313–336). Mahwah, NJ: Erlbaum.

Gifford, R. (1987). *Environmental psychology: Principles and practice.* Boston: Allyn & Bacon.

Glass, D., & Singer, J. E. (1973). Experimental studies of uncontrollable and unpredictable noise. *Representative Research in Social Psychology, 4,* 165.

Gonzalez, A., & Zimbardo, P. G. (1985). Time in perspective. *Psychology Today, 19,* 21–26.

Goranson, R. E., & King, D. (1970). *Rioting and daily temperature: Analysis of the U.S. riots in 1967.* Unpublished manuscript, York University, Ontario, Canada.

Gosling, S. D., Ko, S. J., Mannarelli, T., & Morris, M. E. (2002). A room with a cue: Personality judgments based on offices and bedrooms. *Journal of Personality and Social Psychology, 82,* 379–398.

Griffin, W. V., Mauritzen, J. H., & Kasmar, J. V. (1969). The psychological aspects of the architectural environment: A review. *American Journal of Psychiatry, 125,* 1057–1062.

Griffitt, W. (1970). Environmental effects of interpersonal affective behavior. Ambient effective temperature and attraction. *Journal of Personality and Social Psychology, 15,* 240–244.

Griffitt, W., & Veitch, R. (1971). Hot and crowded: Influence of population density and temperature on interpersonal affective behavior. *Journal of Personality and Social Psychology, 17,* 92–98.

Haber, G. M. (1982). Spatial relations between dominants and marginals. *Social Psychology Quarterly, 45,* 221–228.

Hall, E. T. (1959). *The silent language.* Garden City, NY: Doubleday.

Hall, E. T. (1966). *The hidden dimension.* Garden City, NY: Doubleday.

Hall, E. T. (1983). *The dance of life.* Garden City, NY: Anchor.

Hambrick-Dixon, P. J. (1986). Effects of experimentally imposed noise on task performance of black children attending day care centers near elevated subway trains. *Developmental Psychology, 22,* 259–264.

Harkins, S., & Szymanksi, K. (1987). Social facilitation and social loafing: New wine in old bottles. In C. Hendrick (Ed.), *Review of personality and social psychology* (Vol. 9). Beverly Hills, CA: Sage.

Hazard, J. N. (1962). Furniture arrangement as a symbol of judicial roles. *ETC, 19,* 181–188.

Heilweil, M. (Ed.). (1973). Student housing, architecture, and social behavior [Special issue]. *Environment and Behavior, 5.*

Hines, T. (1996). *The total package.* New York: Little, Brown.

Holahan, C. J. (1972). Seating patterns and patient behavior in an experimental dayroom. *Journal of Abnormal Psychology, 80,* 115–124.

Holahan, C. J., Wilcox, B. L., Burnam, M. A., & Culler, R. E. (1978). Social satisfaction and friendship formation as a function of floor level in high-rise student housing. *Journal of Applied Psychology, 63,* 527–529.

Honeycutt, J. M. & Eidenmuller, M. E. (2001). Communication and attribution: An exploration of the effects of music and mood on intimate couples' verbal and nonverbal conflict resolution behaviors. In V. Manusov and J. H. Harvey (Eds.), *Attribution, Communication Behavior, and Close Relationships* (pp. 21–37). New York: Cambridge University Press.

Infante, D. A., & Berg, C. M. (1979). The impact of music modality on the perception of communication situations in video sequences. *Communication Monographs, 46,* 135–141.

Jackson, P. W. (1968). *Life in classrooms.* New York: Holt, Rinehart & Winston.

Johnson, J. D. (1987). Development of the communication and physical environment scale. *Central States Speech Journal, 38,* 35–43.

Jorgenson, D. O. (1981). Perceived causal influence of weather: Rating the weather's influence on affective states and behaviors. *Environment and Behavior, 13,* 239–256.

Kasmar, J. V., Griffin, W. V., & Mauritzen, J. H. (1968). The effect of environmental surroundings on outpatients' mood and perception of psychiatrists. *Journal of Consulting and Clinical Psychology, 32,* 223–226.

Katz, A. M., & Hill, R. (1958). Residential propinquity and marital selection: A review of theory, method, and fact. *Marriage and Family Living, 20,* 327–335.

Kennedy, R. (1943). Premarital residential propinquity. *American Journal of Sociology, 48,* 580–584.

Kenrick, D. T., & Johnson, G. A. (1979). Interpersonal attraction in aversive environments: A problem for the classical conditioning paradigm? *Journal of Personality and Social Psychology, 37,* 572–579.

Kenrick, D. T., & MacFarlane, W. W. (1984). Ambient temperature and horn-honking: A field study of the heat/aggression relationship. *Environment and Behavior, 18,* 179–191.

Koneya, M. (1973). *The relationship between verbal interaction and seat location of members of large groups.* Unpublished doctoral dissertation, Denver University.

Korda, M. (1975, January 13). Office power—You are where you sit. *New York Times,* pp. 36–44.

Kraut, R. E., & Johnston, R. E. (1979). Social and emotional messages of smiling: An ethological approach. *Journal of Personality and Social Psychology, 37,* 1539–1553.

Krupat, E. (1985). *People in cities: The urban environment and its effects.* New York: Cambridge University Press.

Krupat, E., & Kubzansky, P. E. (1987). Designing to deter crime. *Psychology Today, 21,* 58–61.

Lawton, M. P., & Cohen, J. (1974). Environments and the well-being of elderly inner-city residents. *Environment and Behavior, 6,* 194–211.

Leonard, G. (1978). The rhythms of relationships. In G. Leonard (Ed.), *The silent pulse.* New York: Elsevier-Dutton.

Lester, D. (1988). Geographical variables and behavior: XLVIII. Climate and personal violence (suicide and homicide): A cross-cultural study. *Perceptual and Motor Skills, 66,* 602.

Levine, D. W., O'Neal, E. C., Garwood, S. G., & McDonald, P. J. (1980). Classroom ecology: The effects of seating position on grades and participation. *Personality and Social Psychology Bulletin, 6,* 409–412.

Levine, R. (1997). *A geography of time: The temporal misadventures of a social psychologist or how every culture keeps time just a little bit differently.* New York: Basic.

Levine, R., & Wolff, E. (1985). Social time: The heartbeat of a culture. *Psychology Today, 19,* 30.

Lewy, A. J., Bauer, V. K., Cutler, N. L., Sack, R. L., Ahmed, S., Thomas, K. H., Blood, M. L., & Jackson, J. M. L. (1998). Morning vs. evening light treatment of patients with winter depression. *Archives of General Psychiatry, 55,* 890–896.

Lewy, A. J., Sack, R. L., Miller, L. S., & Hoban, T. M. (1987). Anti-depressant and circadian phase shifting effects of light. *Science, 235,* 352–353.

Lieber, A. L. (1978). *The lunar effect: Biological tides and human emotions.* New York: Anchor/Doubleday.

Lipman, A. (1968). Building design and social interaction. *The Architect's Journal, 147,* 23–30.

Lohmann, A., Arriaga, X. B., & Goodfriend, W. (2003). Close relationships and placemaking: Do objects in a couple's home reflect couplehood? *Personal Relationships, 10,* 437–449.

Luce, G. G. (1971). *Biological rhythms in human and animal physiology.* New York: Dover.

Maines, David R. (1987). The significance of temporality for the development of sociological theory [Special issue]. *The Sociological Quarterly, 28*(3), 303–311.

Maslow, A. H., & Mintz, N. L. (1956). Effects of esthetic surroundings: I. Initial effects of three esthetic conditions upon perceiving "energy" and "well-being" in faces. *Journal of Psychology, 41,* 247–254.

McClanahan, L. E., & Risly, T. R. (1975). Design of living environments for nursing home residents: Increasing participation in recreation activities. *Journal of Applied Behavior Analysis, 8,* 261–268.

McCroskey, J. C., & McVetta, W. R. (1978). Classroom seating arrangements: Instructional communication theory versus student preferences. *Communication Education, 27,* 99–110.

McGrath, J. E., & Kelly, J. R. (1986). *Time and human interaction.* New York: Guilford Press.

McLuhan, M. (1976). Inside on the outside or the spaced-out American. *Journal of Communication, 26,* 46–53.

Meer, J. (1985, September). The light touch. *Psychology Today, 19,* 60–67.

Mehrabian, A. (1976). *Public places and private spaces.* New York: Basic.

Mehrabian, A., & Diamond, S. G. (1971). The effects of furniture arrangement, props, and personality on social interaction. *Journal of Personality and Social Psychology, 20,* 18–30.

Mehrabian, A., & Russell, J. A. (1974). The basic emotional impact of environments. *Perceptual and Motor Skills, 38,* 283–301.

Mehrabian, A., & Russell, J. A. (1975). Environmental effects on affiliation among strangers. *Humanitas, 11,* 219–230.

Merton, R. (1948). The social psychology of housing. In W. Dennis (Ed.), *Current trends in social psychology.* Pittsburgh: University of Pittsburgh Press.

Michael, R. P., & Zumpe, D. (1983). Sexual violence in the United States and the role of season. *American Journal of Psychiatry, 140,* 883–886.

Michelson, W. (1971). Some like it hot: Social participation and environmental use as functions of the season. *American Journal of Sociology, 76,* 1072–1083.

Mintz, N. L. (1956). Effects of esthetic surroundings: II. Prolonged and repeated experience in a "beautiful" and "ugly" room. *Journal of Psychology, 41,* 459–466.

Monk, R. (1994). *The employment of corporate non-verbal status communicators in Western organisations.* Unpublished doctoral dissertation, The Fielding Institute, Santa Barbara, CA.

Moos, R. H. (1976). *The human context: Environmental determinants of behavior.* New York: Wiley.

Moos, R. H., Harris, R., & Schonborn, K. (1969). Psychiatric patients and staff reaction to their physical environment. *Journal of Clinical Psychology, 25,* 322–324.

Moriarty, B. M. (1974). Socioeconomic status and residential location choice. *Environment and Behavior, 6,* 448–469.

Murray, D. C., & Deabler, H. L. (1957). Colors and mood-tones. *Journal of Applied Psychology, 41,* 279–283.

Myrick, R., & Marx, B. S. (1968). *An exploratory study of the relationship between high school building design and student learning.* Washington, D.C.: U.S. Department of Health, Education and Welfare, Office of Education, Bureau of Research.

Newman, O. (1973). *Defensible space.* New York: Macmillan.

North, A. C., Hargreaves, D. J., & McKendrick, J. (1997, November 13). In store music affects product choice. *Nature,* p. 132.

Oldenburg, R. (1989). *The great good place: Cafes, coffee shops, community centers, beauty parlors, general stores, bars, hangouts, and how they get you through the day.* New York: Pergamon Press.

Osmond, H. (1957). Function as the basis of psychiatric ward design. *Mental Hospitals, 8,* 23–29.

Pelligrini, R. F., & Schauss, A. G. (1980). Muscle strength as a function of exposure to hue differences in visual stimuli: An experiential test of Kinesoid theory. *Journal of Orthomolecular Psychiatry, 2,* 144–147.

Rapoport, A. (1982). *The meaning of the built environment.* Beverly Hills, CA: Sage.

Reifman, A. S., Larrick, R. P., & Fein, S. (1991). Temper & temperature on the diamond: The heat–aggression relationship in major league baseball. *Personality and Social Psychology Bulletin, 17,* 580–585.

Report of the National Advisory Commission on Civil Disorders (1968). Washington, D.C.: U.S. Government Printing Office.

Rieber, M. (1965). The effect of music on the activity level of children. *Psychonomic Science, 3,* 325–326.

Roethlisberger, F. J., & Dickson, W. J. (1939). *Management and the worker.* Cambridge, MA: Harvard University Press.

Rohles, F. H., Jr. (1967). Environmental psychology: A bucket of worms. *Psychology Today, 1,* 54–62.

Rohles, F. H., Jr. (1980). Temperature or temperament: A psychologist looks at thermal comfort. *ASHRAE Transactions, 86*(1), 541–551.

Rosenfield, P., Lambert, N. M., & Black, A. (1985). Desk arrangement effects on pupil classroom behavior. *Journal of Educational Psychology, 77,* 101–108.

Rosenthal, N. E. (1993). *Winter blues.* New York: Guilford.

Rotton, J., & Cohn, E. G. (2002). Climate, weather, and crime. In R. B. Bechtel & A. Churchman (Eds.), *Handbook of environmental psychology* (pp. 481–498). New York: Wiley.

Rotton, J., & Kelly, I. W. (1985). Much ado about the full moon: A meta-analysis of lunar-lunacy research. *Psychological Bulletin, 97,* 286–306.

Rubin, Z. (1979). Seasonal rhythms in behavior. *Psychology Today, 12,* 12–16.

Ruesch, J., & Kees, W. (1956). *Nonverbal communication.* Berkeley and Los Angeles: University of California Press.

Russell, J. A., & Mehrabian, A. (1976). Environmental variables in consumer research. *Journal of Consumer Research, 3,* 62–63.

Sandalla, E. (1987). Identity symbolism in housing. *Environment and Behavior, 19,* 569–587.

Schauss, A. G. (1985). The physiological effect of color on the suppression of human aggression: Research on Baker-Miller Pink. *International Journal of Biosocial Research, 7,* 55–64.

Schlenker, B. R., Phillips, S. T., Boniecki, K. A., and Schlenker, D. R. (1995). Championship pressures: Choking or triumphing in one's own territory? *Journal of Personality and Social Psychology, 68,* 632–643.

Schneider, F. W., Lesko, W. A., & Garrett, W. A. (1980). Helping behavior in hot, comfortable, and cold temperatures: A field study. *Environment and Behavior, 12,* 231–240.

Schutte, J. G., & Light, N. M. (1978). The relative importance of proximity and status for friend-ship choices in social hierarchies. *Social Psychology, 41,* 260–264.

Schwartz, B., & Barsky, S. (1977). The home advantage. *Social Forces, 55,* 641–661.

Schwebel, A. I., & Cherlin, D. L. (1972). Physical and social distancing in teacher–pupil relation-ships. *Journal of Educational Psychology, 63,* 543–550.

Smith, E., Bell, P. A., & Fusco, M. E. (1986). The influence of color and demand characteristics on muscle strength and affective ratings of the environment. *Journal of General Psychology, 113,* 289–297.

Smith, R. H., Downer, D. B., Lynch, M. T., & Winter, M. (1969). Privacy and interaction within the family as related to dwelling space. *Journal of Marriage and the Family, 31,* 559–566.

Sommer, R. (1967). Classroom ecology. *Journal of Applied Behavioral Science, 3,* 487–503.

Sommer, R. (1969). *Personal space.* Englewood Cliffs, NJ: Prentice-Hall.

Sommer, R. (1972). *Design awareness.* San Francisco: Rinehart Press.

Sommer, R. (1974). *Tight spaces: Hard architecture and how to humanize it.* Englewood Cliffs, NJ: Prentice-Hall.

Sommer, R., & Gilliland, G. W. (1961). Design for friendship. *Canadian Architect, 6,* 59–61.

Sommer, R., & Ross, H. (1958). Social interaction in a geriatric ward. *International Journal of Social Psychiatry, 4,* 128–133.

Stires, L. (1980). Classroom seating location, student grades, and attitudes: Environment or self selection? *Environment and Behavior, 12,* 241–254.

Stokois, D. (1981). Group x place transactions: Some neglected issues in psychological research on settings. In D. Magnusson (Ed.), *Toward a psychology of situations: An interactional perspec-tive.* New York: Erlbaum.

Stouffer, S. A. (1940). Intervening opportunities: A theory relating mobility and distance. *American Sociological Review, 5,* 845–867.

Sundstrom, E. (1986). *Workplaces: The psychology of the physical environment in offices and factories.* New York: Cambridge University Press.

Tars, S., & Appleby, L. (1974). The same child in home and institution. *Environment and Behavior, 5,* 3.

Thirer, J., & Rampey, M. S. (1979). Effects of abusive spectators' behavior on performance of home and visiting intercollegiate basketball teams. *Perceptual and Motor Skills, 48,* 1047–1053.

Todd-Mancillas, W. R. (1982). Classroom environments and nonverbal behavior. In L. L. Barker (Ed.), *Communication in the classroom.* Englewood Cliffs, NJ: Prentice-Hall.

Vinsel, A., Brown, B. B., Altman, I., & Foss, C. (1980). Privacy regulation, territorial displays, and effectiveness of individual functioning. *Journal of Personality and Social Psychology, 39,* 1104–1115.

Vrij, A., van der Steen, J., & Koppelaar, L. (1994). Aggression of police officers as a function of temperature: An experiment with the Fire Arms Training System. *Journal of Community and Applied Social Psychology, 4,* 365–370.

Weinstein, C. S. (1979). The physical environment of the school: A review of research. *Review of Educational Research, 49,* 577–610.

Weinstein, N. D. (1978). Individual differences in reactions to noise: A longitudinal study in a college dormitory. *Journal of Applied Psychology, 63,* 458–466.

Wells, B. W. P. (1965). The psycho-social influence of building environment: Sociometric findings in large and small office spaces. *Building Spaces, 1,* 153–165.

Werner, C. M., & Baxter, L. A. (1994). Temporal qualities of relationships: Organismic, transactional, and dialectical views. In M. L. Knapp & J. R. Miller (Eds.), *Handbook of interpersonal communication* (2nd ed.). Thousand Oaks, CA: Sage.

Werner, C. M., Irwin, A., & Brown, B. B. (1992). A transactional approach to interpersonal relations: Physical environment, social context, and temporal qualities. *Journal of Social and Personal Relationships, 9,* 297–323.

Wexner, L. B. (1954). The degree to which colors (hues) are associated with mood-tones. *Journal of Applied Psychology, 38,* 432–435.

White, A. G. (1953). The patient sits down: A clinical note. *Psychosomatic Medicine, 15,* 256–257.

Whyte, W. (1949). The social structure of a restaurant. *American Journal of Sociology, 54,* 302–310.

Wilner, D., Walkley, R. P., & Cook, S. W. (1952). Residential proximity and intergroup relations in public housing projects. *Journal of Social Issues, 8,* 45–69.

Wollin, D. D., & Montagre, M. (1981). College classroom environment: Effects of sterility versus amiability on student and teacher performance. *Environment and Behavior, 13,* 707–716.

Wong, H., & Brown, W. (1923). Effects of surroundings upon mental work as measured by Yerkes' multiple choice method. *Journal of Comparative Psychology, 3,* 319–331.

Zerubavel, E. (1981). *Hidden rhythms: Schedules and calendars in social life.* Chicago: University of Chicago Press.

Zweigenhaft, R. (1976). Personal space in the faculty office: Desk placement and the student–faculty interaction. *Journal of Applied Psychology, 61,* 529–532.

Chapter 5

THE EFFECTS OF TERRITORY
AND PERSONAL SPACE
ON HUMAN COMMUNICATION

Spatial changes give a tone to a communication, accent it, and at times even override the spoken word.

—E. T. HALL

"If you can read this, you're too close," announces a familiar automobile bumper sticker. It is an attempt to regulate the amount of space between vehicles for traffic safety. Signs reading "Keep Out" and "Authorized Personnel Only" are also attempts to regulate the amount of space among human beings. We do not put up signs in daily conversation, but we use other signals to avoid uncomfortable crowding and other perceived invasions of our personal space. Our use of space (our own and others') can affect dramatically our ability to achieve certain desired communication goals, whether they involve romance, diplomacy, or aggression. A fundamental concept in any discussion of human spatial behavior is the notion of territoriality. An understanding of this concept provides a useful perspective for our later examination of conversational space.

THE CONCEPT OF TERRITORIALITY

The term *territoriality* has been used for years in the study of animal and bird behavior. Generally, it means behavior characterized by identification with a geographic area in a way that indicates ownership and defense of this territory against perceived "invaders." Some territorial indicators around the home are particularly strong—Dad's chair, Mom's study, Billy's closet, or Barbara's phone. There are many kinds of territorial behavior, and, frequently, they perform useful functions for a given species. For instance, territorial behaviors may help coordinate activities, regulate density, ensure propagation of the species, hold the group together, provide a sense of well-being, and offer hiding places.

Most behavioral scientists agree that territoriality exists in human behavior, too. It helps regulate social interaction, but it also can be the source of social conflict. Like other animals, the more powerful, dominant humans seem to have control over more territory—as long as the group or societal structure is stable.

Altman (1975) identified three types of territories: (1) *primary,* (2) *secondary,* and (3) *public.* The key distinction is the extent of ownership felt or warranted. *Primary territories* are clearly the exclusive domain of the owner. They are central to the daily functioning of the owner, and they are guarded carefully against uninvited intruders. For this reason, we believe that the invisible buffer zone surrounding our body also qualifies as a primary territory. It is not stationary and visible like other territories, but the degree of ownership is extremely high, the access to others is very limited, and the defense against unwanted intrusions can be particularly fierce.

Homes or bedrooms often qualify as primary territory. Goffman's (1971) description of possessional territories also seems to fit the requirements of primary territory. Possessional territories include personal effects such as jackets, purses, and even dependent children. In this same category, Goffman discusses objects that can be claimed temporarily by people, for example, a magazine, a television set, or eating utensils. These, however, seem to be more representative of what Altman calls *secondary territories,* which are not as central to the daily life of the owner, nor are they perceived as clearly exclusive to the owner. The neighborhood bar or the objects cited earlier are examples of secondary territories. More frequent conflicts are apt to develop over these territories because the public/private boundary is blurred—for example, "Let me watch my program on TV. You don't own it." *Public territories* are available to almost anyone for temporary ownership, for example, parks, beaches, streets, seats on public transportation, telephone booths, a place in line, or an unobstructed line of vision to see a particular object of interest. The words *temporary occupancy* are important. Most of us would not consider it a territorial violation if a cleaning person entered our office to clean without our permission. It would be a different story, however, if this person occupied the office all day or used it for noncleaning activities such as eating lunch.

Territorial behavior seems to be a standard part of our daily contact with others, and it also is evident when sufficient social contact is denied. Altman and Haythorn (1967) analyzed the territorial behavior of socially isolated and nonisolated pairs of men. For 10 days, two individuals lived in a small room with no outside contact while a matched group received outside contacts. The men in the isolated groups showed a gradual increase in territorial behavior and a general pattern of social withdrawal. They desired more time alone. Their territorial behavior first evidenced itself with fixed objects (areas of the room) and personal objects (beds). Later they began to claim more mobile and less personal objects. Incompatibility of the two men living together with respect to dominance and affiliation resulted in greater territorial behavior.

TERRITORIALITY: INVASION AND DEFENSE

Instructions to police interrogators sometimes suggest sitting close to the suspect without the intervention of a desk that might provide protection or comfort. This theory of interrogation assumes that invasion of the suspect's personal territory (with little opportunity for defense) will give the officer a psychological advantage. Other examples of human territorial invasion and defense include members of adolescent gangs and ethnic groups who stake out territory in urban areas and defend it against intruders. Preserving national boundaries often underlies international disputes. What happens when somebody invades your territory? For instance, how do you feel when the car behind you is tailgating? When you have to stand in an overpopulated theater lobby or bus? When somebody sits in *your* seat? What do you do? Researchers have asked similar questions, and their answers help us understand further how we treat the objects and space around us.

Obviously, not all territorial encroachments are the same. Lyman and Scott (1967) identify three types:

1. *Violation* involves the unwarranted use of another's territory. This may be done with the eyes (staring at somebody eating in a public restaurant); with the voice or other sounds (somebody talking loudly nearby on their cell phone or construction noise next to a classroom); or with the body (taking up two subway seats).
2. *Invasion* is more all-encompassing and permanent. It is an attempt to take over another's territory. This may be an armed invasion of another country or the act of a wife who has turned her husband's den into her computer room.
3. *Contamination* is defiling another's territory, not by our presence but by what we leave behind. When we take temporary occupancy of a hotel room, for instance, we do not want to find the previous "owner's" toilet articles and soiled sheets. Similarly, we are frequently upset when someone else's dog leaves feces in our yard or when we find food particles on "our" silverware in restaurants.

Encroachments on our territory do not always produce defensive maneuvers. The intensity of our reaction to territorial encroachment varies depending on a number of factors including the following:

1. Who violated our territory? We may have very different reactions to friends as opposed to strangers; males as opposed to females; high-status individuals as opposed to low-status ones; objects as opposed to people; and peers as opposed to people of very different ages.
2. Why did they violate our territory? If we feel that the violator "knew better," we might react more strongly than if we felt he or she "couldn't help it" or was naive.
3. What type of territory was it? We may perceive a violation of our primary territory as far more serious than a violation of a public territory.
4. How was the violation accomplished? If our body was touched, we may be more aroused than if someone walked across our grass.
5. How long did the encroachment last? If the violation is perceived as temporary, reactions may be less severe.
6. Do we expect further violations in the future? If so, the initial territorial defense may be more intense.
7. Where did the violation occur? The population density and opportunities for negotiating new territorial boundaries will surely affect our reaction.

The two primary methods for territorial defense are prevention and reaction. *Prevention* is a means of staking out our territory so others recognize it as ours and go elsewhere.

FIGURE 5-1

Marking public territory.

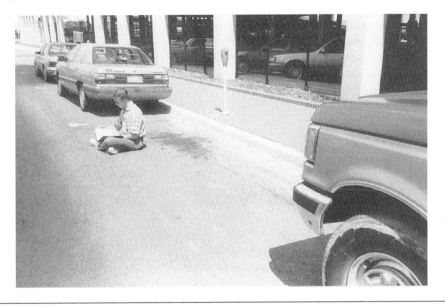

A person's mere presence in a place can keep others from entering it. If we stay in a place long enough or often enough, others think we "own" it, for example, a seat in a classroom. Sometimes we ask others to assist us in staking out and defending territory—for example, "Would you hold my seat while I go get some popcorn?" (see Figure 5-1). Neighbors' help will vary, of course, depending on how urgently their aid is requested, for how long, how important the territory appears, and so on. Objects are also used as territorial *markers* to designate "your" spatial area. In places with relatively low density, markers such as umbrellas, coats, notebooks, and so on, are often effective; indeed, sometimes these markers will reserve not only a seat in a public area but also an entire table. Markers that appear more personal probably are more effective in preventing violations. If the marked territory is highly desirable to many others in the immediate area, markers probably will maintain their effectiveness for shorter periods of time. In public territories, it may be more effective to leave several markers, as these areas are open to nearly everyone. Sometimes uniforms help identify the territory that can be legitimately used by a particular person. Often we construct fences and grow hedges to demarcate territory. And sometimes we stake out territory simply by the way we conduct our verbal interaction; for example, a special jargon or dialect can warn others that a particular space is reserved for those who "know the language."

If the prevention of territorial violations does not work, how do people *react?* When people come close to us in face-to-face encounters, we are physiologically aroused; heart rate and galvanic skin responses increase (Finando, 1973; McBride, King, & James, 1965). Arousal varies with eye gaze and touch as well as distance. Once aroused, we need to label our state as "positive" (liking, love, relief) or "negative" (dislike, embarrassment, stress, anxiety). If the aroused state is labeled positively, Patterson (1976) predicts, we will reciprocate the behavior; if it is labeled negatively, we will take measures to compensate. If someone is aroused by another person's approach and identifies it as undesirable, we would predict behavior designed to restore the "proper" distance between the interactants: looking away, changing the topic to a less personal one, crossing one's arms to form a frontal barrier to the invasion, covering body parts, rubbing one's neck (making the elbow protrude sharply toward the invader), and so on.

Russo conducted a 2-year study of invading the territory of female college students seated in a college library (Sommer, 1969). The study compared the responses of those invaded and a similar group that was not invaded. Several different invasion techniques were used—sitting next to subjects, across from them, and so on. The quickest departure or flight was triggered when the researcher sat next to a subject and moved her chair closer (approximately a foot). Other researchers have suggested that when strangers are involved, males feel more stress from frontal invasions, whereas women react more unfavorably to adjacent invasions (Hall, 1984). After approximately 30 minutes, about 70% of the people Russo approached at the 1-foot distance moved. From Russo's study, a whole vocabulary of defense was developed. For instance, defensive and offensive displays included the use of position, posture, and gesture. *Position* refers to location in the room; a newcomer to the room will interpret the situation differently if the other person has selected a corner position rather than one in the middle of the room. *Posture* refers to such indicators as whether a person has materials spread out "like he or she owned the place" or whether they are tightly organized. *Gestures* can be used to indicate receptivity or rejection of communication, for example, hostile glances, turning or leaning away, blocking with hands or arms, and so on. Although verbal defense is not a common first reaction, requests or even profanity can be effectively used. Russo's work is summarized by Sommer (1969):

> There were wide individual differences in the ways victims reacted—there is no single reaction to someone's sitting too close; there are defensive gestures, shifts in posture, and attempts to move away. If these fail or are ignored by the invader, or he shifts position too, the victim eventually takes to flight. . . . There was a dearth of direct verbal responses to the invasions. . . . Only one of the eighty students asked the invader to move over. (pp. 35–36)

It is worth remembering that the norm of politeness is strong enough to inhibit such direct verbal responses. This demonstrates one important feature of nonverbal communication: It is often "*off the record*" and can convey messages subtly, without provoking confrontation. The person who glares, shuffles papers, or leans away does not have to acknowledge publicly his or her irritation. Barash (1973) conducted a study similar to Russo's, but the library invaders' status was manipulated. Students fled more quickly from the more formally dressed, "high-status" invaders. Knowles (1973) also experimented with a familiar type of invasion—talking to somebody in a hallway while other people decide whether to walk through the conversants or around them. Only 25% of the people in this study walked through, but when the conversants were replaced with barrels, 75% of the passersby walked through. The fewest intrusions occurred with 4-person groups (rather than a dyad) and "high-status" conversants (older and more formally dressed). This study illustrates that, besides not wanting others to violate our territory, we generally do not want to violate others' territory either—as the mumbled apologies and bowed heads of some of Knowles's invaders testified.

Increasing population density also results in territorial violations. What happens when the population becomes so dense that we cannot exercise usual territorial behavior? The possibility of human overpopulation makes this a particularly important concern.

DENSITY AND CROWDING

During the 1960s, many people were alarmed about the rapidly increasing world population. The first edition of Erlich's (1971) best-selling book, *The Population Bomb,* was published in 1968. It pointed to a rapidly increasing birth rate and predicted the death of hundreds of millions of people due to the effects of an overpopulated world. The growth of urban areas and increasing violence in inner-city areas also fueled concern for the effects of population growth. If the worldwide population increased dramatically, would there be dire consequences? Some highly publicized research with rats seemed to fully support the fear that in highly dense populations, bad things are going to happen (Calhoun, 1962).

Calhoun noted that with plenty of food and no danger from predators, Norway rats in a quarter-acre outdoor pen stabilized their population at about 150. His observations, covering 28 months, indicated that spatial relationships are extremely important. He then designed an experiment in which he could maintain a stressful situation through overpopulation while three generations of rats were reared. He labeled this experiment a *behavioral sink,* an area or receptacle where most of the rats exhibited gross distortions of behavior. Some of Calhoun's observations are worth noting:

1. Some rats withdrew from social and sexual intercourse completely; others began to mount anything in sight; courtship patterns were totally disrupted, and females were frequently pursued by several males.
2. Nest-building patterns, ordinarily neat, became sloppy or nonexistent.
3. Litters of young rats became mixed; newborn and young rats were stepped on or eaten by invading hyperactive males.
4. Unable to establish spatial territories, dominant males fought over positions near the eating bins; classes of rats shared territories and exhibited similar behaviors; the hyperactive males violated all territorial rights by running around in packs and disregarding any boundaries except those backed by force.
5. Pregnant rats frequently had miscarriages; disorders of the sex organs were numerous; only a fourth of the 558 newborns in the sink survived to be weaned.
6. Aggressive behavior increased significantly.

Can we generalize from rats to people? Some early studies that found moderate correlations between various socially undesirable outcomes, such as crime, delinquency, mental and physical disorders, and high population density seemed to say yes. Others facetiously contend that the only generalization we can make from Calhoun's work is "Don't crowd a rat!" But even this injunction is an overstatement. Judge (2000), who analyzed numerous studies of high density among animal populations, would probably say, "Don't crowd rats with aggressive tendencies." In his own words:

> The individual characteristics and aggressive tendencies of animals that compose popula-
> tions can influence aggression more so than increasing population density. Even the results
> of Calhoun's (1962) influential rat studies were dictated by the unique behavior of a few
> individuals. The infamous "behavioral sinks" developed when a few dominant adult males
> established breeding territories in quarter sections of the compartmentalized pens used in
> the experiments. The remainder of the colony became restricted to single compartments. In
> colonies in which males did not establish territories or did so in a manner that did not
> restrict the rest of the colony, no "behavioral sinks" developed (Calhoun, 1962). This
> outcome of increased density is rarely cited. (p. 144)

Furthermore, nonhuman animals do not always respond to high density in negative or
aggressive ways (Freedman, 1979; Judge & de Waal, 1993). In one study, the number of
aggressive acts performed by monkeys living in environments of differing densities (from
cages to free-ranging activity on an island) were compared (Judge & de Waal, 1997).
Aggression was not significantly more prevalent in high-density environments, but *coping
behavior* was. As density increased, the following types of coping behavior also increased:
mutual grooming, rapid reconciliation after a fight, and the use of specific facial expressions to indicate the desire to avoid trouble. This tendency to develop ways to cope with
high-density life in ways other than aggression is much like the human adaptations reported in the next two sections. Behavioral sinks are not a natural result of unchecked
population growth. Stress and aggression among those in high-density situations may also
be affected by the amount of space available, the duration of the high-density experience,
the ability to enact coping behavior, the extent to which key relationships can be maintained, and other factors. In other words, the widely publicized results of Calhoun's work,
which suggested unequivocally harmful consequences of increasing density, are incorrect.
Based on the human density and crowding research conducted thus far, the results are also
complex and do not lend themselves to a simple "crowding is good or bad" answer.

To understand the effects of population density on human beings, we must first distinguish between the terms *density* and *crowding*. *Density* refers to the number of people
per unit of space; *crowding* is a feeling state that may develop in high- or low-density situations. What determines whether we are likely to feel crowded? Perceptions of being
crowded may be increased by the following factors:

1. *Environmental factors*, such as reduced space; unwanted noise; the lack of
   needed resources or the ability to obtain them; and the absence of territorial
   markers such as screens and partitions.
2. *Personal factors*, such as gender (males tend to feel the effects of density more
   acutely than females); personality characteristics reflecting low self-esteem,
   dominance, or control; a low desire for social contact; and prior unpleasant
   experiences with high density.
3. *Social factors*, such as a high frequency of unwanted social contact from many
   people at close quarters (and the inability to change such patterns); inescapable
   interactions with people from an unfamiliar group; and unpleasant interactions
   (hostile or competitive).
4. *Goal-related factors*, such as the inability to accomplish what is desired.

The central theme characterizing most of the research in this area is that perceptions of crowding tend to increase as we perceive a decrease in our ability to control and influence our physical and social surroundings. Although the factors in the preceding list may contribute to perceptions of crowding, most high-density situations are characterized by some factors that decrease control and some that do not. Given these conditions, what can we say about the effects of high density and human reactions to it?

THE EFFECTS OF HIGH DENSITY ON HUMAN BEINGS

Definitions of density are complex and varied. Correlational studies have used number of people per city, per census tract, per dwelling unit; number of rooms per dwelling unit; number of buildings per neighborhood; and so on. Experimental studies sometimes put the same-sized group into different-sized rooms; others vary the number of people in the same room. Laboratory studies that vary density in order to analyze its effects on perceptions of crowding may have relevance only to those situations in which high density is a temporary condition, for example, elevators, buses, and so forth. Few studies have considered the rate at which high density evolves or whether participants feel they had any control over the development of a high-density situation. In order to sort through these variations in measurement, the following conclusions seem warranted.

First, it seems clear that increased density does not automatically increase stress or antisocial behavior for human beings. Sometimes we even seek the pleasures of density (see Figure 5-2). Football games and rock concerts are familiar examples. If we take responsibility for our presence in a highly populated situation, and if we know the condition will terminate in a matter of hours, the chances of negative effects seem to be minimal. Although some studies have found results that might fit well into a "behavioral sink" theory (e.g., aggression, stress, criminal activity, hostility toward others, and a deterioration of mental and physical health), in most every case, we find other studies that do not confirm these effects. Usually, the difference lies in the fact that one of the factors mentioned earlier (environmental, personal, social, goal oriented) provided a form of control that was influential in offsetting undesirable influences. For example, Altman (1975) cites a study by Rohe and Patterson (1974), which found that if children were provided with enough of the toys they wanted, increased density would not produce the withdrawal and aggression suggested by previous studies. Some high-density neighborhoods that are highly cohesive actually have a lower incidence of mental and physical health problems.

Second, we sometimes blame high density for undesirable effects either because it is an obvious feature of the situation and has a reputation for causing problems or because the real causes are things we do not wish to face. Students who took a long time to complete their college registration tended to perceive the large number of students trying to register as the cause for their delays. They did not attribute their delays to forgetting needed forms, filling out forms incorrectly, and not preparing alternative course selections prior to registration (Gochman & Keating, 1980). High density *can* produce a host of problems, but human beings do not stand by passively in situations that demand a long-term commitment to high density. Instead, they try various methods to cope with or offset potentially harmful effects. What are some of the methods of coping?

FIGURE 5-2

A high-density beach.

COPING WITH HIGH DENSITY

City dwellers are often exposed to an overload of information, people, things, problems, and so forth. As a result, they engage in behavior designed to reduce this overload, which sometimes causes outsiders to see them as distant and emotionally detached from others. Here are some of these methods for coping in populated cities:

1. Spending less time with each input, for example, having shorter conversations with people
2. Disregarding low-priority inputs, for example, ignoring the drunk on the sidewalk or not talking to people seen on a commuter train every day
3. Shifting the responsibility for some transactions to others, for example, relieving bus drivers of the responsibility for making change
4. Blocking inputs, for example, using attendants to guard apartment buildings

Now let's shift our attention from spatial relationships in overpopulated conditions to those involved in a two-person conversation.

CONVERSATIONAL DISTANCE

As children, we are exposed to gradually increasing distances for various communication situations. The first few years of life provide a familiarity with what is known as intimate distance; the child then learns appropriate conversational distances for an increasing number of acquaintances obtained from family, neighborhood, and school; and by about age 7 the child may have incorporated the concept of public distance into his or her behavioral repertoire. So by the time children reach about the third grade, they have learned that conversational distance has meaning. As they age, they will gradually reflect adult norms for their culture as they make spatial adjustments to interactants who are known or unknown, tall or short, higher status or lower status, and so on. What are these adult norms? What are comfortable conversational distances (see Figure 5-3)?

To answer these questions, first we need to acknowledge the astute observations about human spatial behavior made by anthropologist Edward T. Hall as published in his books *The Silent Language* (1959) and *The Hidden Dimension* (1966). Hall identified several types of space, but our concern here is with what he called *informal space*. Others have referred to this as "personal space," but because the space between people is the result of negotiating their personal preferences, it is more appropriately labeled *interpersonal* space. The informal space for each individual expands and contracts under varying circumstances, depending on the type of encounter, the relationship of the communicating persons, their personalities, and many other factors. Hall further classified informal space into four subcategories: (1) intimate, (2) casual–personal, (3) social–consultative, and (4) public. According to Hall, *intimate* distances range from actual physical contact to about 18 inches; *casual–personal* extends from 1.5 feet to 4 feet; *social–consultative* (for impersonal business) ranges from 4 to 12 feet; and *public* distance covers the area from 12 feet to the limits of visibility or hearing. Hall was quick to note that these distances are based on his observations of a particular sample of adults from business and professional occupations, primarily white middle-class males native to the northeastern United States, and any generalization to other ethnic and racial groups in the United States should be made with considerable caution.

Robert Sommer (1961) also sought answers to questions about comfortable conversational distance. He studied people who were brought into a room and told to discuss various impersonal topics. Two sofas were placed in this room at various distances, and subjects were observed to see whether they sat opposite or beside one another. It was hypothesized that when they began to sit side by side, it would mean the conversational distance was too far to sit opposite one another on the two couches. From 1 to 3 feet, the subjects sat on different couches facing one another. After 3.5 feet, people sat side by side. If we measure distance "nose to nose," this would make the participants 5.5 feet apart when they started to sit side by side. In a follow-up study, Sommer used chairs and hence was able to vary side-by-side distance as well as distance across. Here he found that people chose to sit across from one another until the distance across exceeded the side-by-side distance; they then sat side by side.

How generalizable are these findings? A critical look at this study immediately leads us to question what other variables may affect the distance relationship. For instance, this study was conducted with people who knew each other slightly, were discussing impersonal

Figure 5-3

Variations in conversational distance and position.

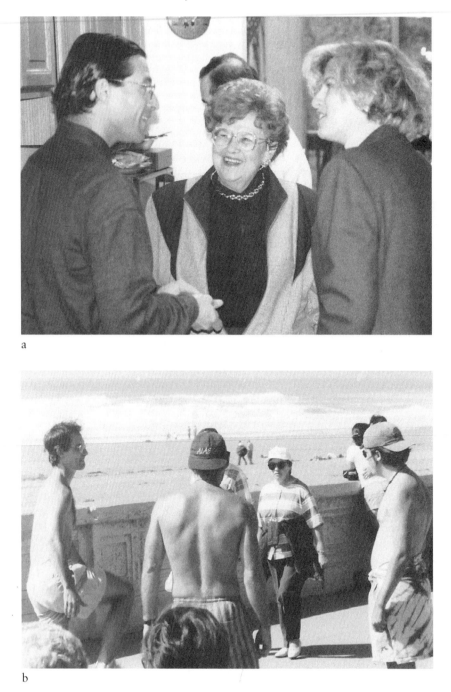

a

b

topics, and were in a large lounge. How would other factors affect the distance relationship? For a long time, researchers have theorized that distance is based on the balance of approach and avoidance forces. What are some of these forces? Burgoon (1978) and Burgoon and Jones (1976) say that the distance we choose in a given conversation is a function of our cultural and personal expectations for an appropriate distance. When someone violates that distance (too close or too far), we assess the rewards associated with the violator. Space violations by communicators perceived as rewarding to us will, according to this theory, cause us to evaluate the violator more favorably. What are some of these expectations for conversational distance, and how do they develop? What factors modify the distances we choose?

Answering these questions is the focus for the remainder of this chapter. Again, however, we must sort through conflicting results due to variations in research methodology and conceptualization of personal space. Logically, we know that conversational distance is the product of both interactants' negotiations. But some research is based on the behavior of a single person; some research does not distinguish between actual physical distance and perceptions of distance; some research measures distance by floor tiles or space between chair legs and totally ignores the ability of the communicators to vary the "psychological distance" by changes in topic, eye gaze, and body lean; and most research does not distinguish between initial distance and changes that take place over the course of a conversation. Because the methods of measuring personal space vary, we even have to be cautious about results that agree with other studies. Sometimes people complete questionnaires about preferred distances; sometimes they are asked to approach nonhuman objects, for example, coat racks and life-sized photographs; sometimes people are unknowingly approached at various distances by others; and sometimes they are asked to arrange miniature dolls, photographs, or silhouettes as if they were in various communication situations. With these factors in mind, we selected the following important sources of variation in conversational distance. They encompass much of what Sommer (2002) called the "best substantiated" findings about personal space.

1. Sex
2. Age
3. Cultural and ethnic background
4. Topic or subject matter
5. Setting for the interaction
6. Physical characteristics
7. Attitudinal and emotional orientation
8. Characteristics of the interpersonal relationship
9. Personality characteristics

SEX

Many studies have looked at sex differences in interpersonal space, using all the methodologies listed earlier. Hall (1984) has summarized this research. In naturalistic interaction—that is, settings where people are interacting more or less naturally and are not aware of being observed—females predominantly choose to interact with others (of either sex) more closely than males do.

Not all ways of measuring distance preferences find such compelling evidence for females' closer distances. For example, in some studies, people are asked outright by the experimenter to stand at a comfortable distance from a confederate; in others, they manipulate or position stick figures or cutouts of people. Research using these non-naturalistic methods finds very weak evidence that females prefer closer distances. Why should this be? Hall (1984) suggests that the answer may be in the emotional tone of the encounters being studied. In naturalistic studies, the encounters are almost always friendly, or at least neutral, in emotional tone. In the more artificial studies, the experimeter often varies who the other person is—for example, a threatening or angry other as opposed to a liked or friendly other. When this is done, the sex differences tend to diverge, with females now establishing smaller distances than males with the friendly others (which is consistent with the naturalistic studies) but *larger* distances with the alienating others. This divergence could make the overall sex difference for these kinds of studies disappear. Thus, it appears, females prefer closer distances as long as they are neutral or friendly interactions (Bell, Kline, & Barnard, 1988).

Another way of understanding sex differences in interpersonal distance is to examine how the *other person's sex* influences the distance one sets. (The preceding discussion applies only to the influence of one's own sex on that distance.) The research shows very convincingly that people approach females closer than they approach males, and this remains true no matter what kind of methodology is used. When the effects for one's own sex and those for the other's sex are combined, they yield a pattern of interaction such that female–female pairs interact most closely and male–male pairs interact most distantly, with mixed-sex pairs setting intermediate distances. This pattern shows up frequently in the research, especially in Anglo-American samples.

Several theories have been put forth to explain these sex differences in preferred conversational distances. One popular notion is rooted in the different amounts of space children experience. It has been noted, for example, that the same stimuli may cause parents to put male infants on the floor or in a playpen but to hug the females or put them in a nearby high chair. Boys are frequently given toys that seem to encourage activities demanding more space, often away from the confines of the home itself—for example, footballs, cars, trains, and so forth. Girls, in contrast, may receive dolls, dollhouses, and other toys that require less space. Some observational studies have confirmed that young boys at play utilize more space than young girls, but this does not explain those instances in which women want greater interaction distance. The "oppression hypothesis" says women choose a closer interaction distance because people with less status in society are accorded less space, but Atsuko (2003) did not find evidence to support this theory. Using social orientation as the basis for explaining the interaction distances chosen by women has the advantage of explaining both closer and more distant interaction preferences. Women, these theorists argue, are more socially oriented than males so they should prefer distances that connote warmth, trust, and friendship. Eagly (1987), using social role theory, believes women play a more person-oriented and prosocial role in society which manifests itself in various kinds of behavior—including interaction distances that are consistent with that role.

Age

If distance reflects our general comfort with a person, it seems reasonable to predict that we would interact closer to people in our own general age range. The exceptions, of course, are the very old and very young who, for various reasons, often elicit interaction at closer quarters. Generally, interaction distance seems to expand gradually from about age 6 to early adolescence, when adult norms seem to be reflected (Aiello & Aiello, 1974). Adults are more likely to hold older children responsible for an understanding of adult norms, too. When 5-year-olds invaded the personal space of people waiting in line to see a movie, they were received positively, but when 10-year-olds were the invaders, they were met with negative responses (Fry & Willis, 1971). Obviously, these reactions are modified by the communicative context, but these studies do suggest that adults expect the norms for conversational distance to be learned before the child is 10. Children are able to decode proxemic meanings before they encode them in their daily interactions, as is true of many behaviors.

CULTURAL AND ETHNIC BACKGROUND

Volumes of folklore and isolated personal observations suggest that spatial relationships in other cultures with different needs and norms may produce very different distances for interacting.

Infants reared in different cultures learn different proxemic patterns. Japanese mothers tend to spend more time than a comparable group of mothers in the United States in close contact with their infants. Mother, father, and infant in Japan usually sleep in the same room. In the Nyansongo culture of Kenya, infants are always in close proximity to a family member, and the infant sleeps in the mother's arms at night (Caudill & Weinstein, 1972). It is not hard to see how such patterns provide a different sense of distance when compared to those of children who are put into a separate room to sleep several times during the day as well as at night.

Hall (1966) used the terms *contact* and *noncontact* to distinguish the behavior of people from different cultural groups. Compared to noncontact cultures, interactants in contact cultures are expected to face one another more directly, interact closer to one another, touch one another more, look one another in the eye more, and speak in a louder voice. In a study by Watson (1970), contact cultures were Arabs, Latin Americans, and southern Europeans. Noncontact cultures were Asians, Indians and Pakistanis, northern Europeans, and people living in the United States. Studies by Watson and others have found support for these predicted differences. But it is important to remember that these broad cultural norms may or may not manifest themselves in any particular conversation within a culture (Remland, Jones, & Brinkman, 1991). Whether interactants know each other, whether they are arguing or not, whether they are talking to a person of their same sex or not, and a host of other factors may sometimes offset these broad cultural tendencies. For example, Sanders, Hakky, and Brizzolara (1985) found few differences between the comfortable conversational space of Egyptian and American males, but Egyptian females were not like their American counterparts. Comfortable interaction distance for male friends of the Egyptian women was nearly as distant as for male strangers. In another study, close seating of two brothers was more comfortable to Saudi students than to American students, but when the interactants were a brother and sister, it was the American students who found a comfort zone in closer interaction distances (Hewitt & Alqahtani, 2003).

Shuter's systematic field observations (1976, 1977) in contact and noncontact cultures reminds us that there may be somewhat different proxemic norms for groups within the larger culture. He found, for instance, significant differences within the so-called Latin

American cultural group. Costa Ricans interacted more closely than did Panamanians or Colombians. And, contrary to predictions, he found no significant differences in interaction distance and touching for women in Milwaukee, Wisconsin, and Venice, Italy. Italian men did not manifest closer interaction positions or face their interaction partners more directly than German men, but they did engage in more touching.

Variations in proxemic patterns in the United States have been the subject of several research projects. For example, the question of whether black Americans interact at closer distances than white Americans has been studied. Developmental studies show that when entering elementary school, black children may exhibit closer interaction distances than white children, but by the fifth grade these differences are minimized, and by age 16 black Americans tend to maintain greater conversational distances (Aiello & Thompson, 1980; Halberstadt, 1985). Obviously, the racial composition of the schools attended and the socioeconomic class of the students are also going to play an important role in determining comfortable interaction distance. Most studies reveal that interactions involving black and white communicators occur at greater distances than those involving persons of the same race. Another large cultural group in the United States, Hispanic Americans, has also been observed. These studies generally support the prediction that Hispanic Americans interact at closer distances than do Anglo Americans.

Scherer (1974) contended that any differences between blacks and whites (and presumably Hispanic Americans) may be confounded by socioeconomic factors not attributable to ethnic background. This study found middle-class children maintained greater conversational distance than lower-class children, but there were no differences between middle-class blacks and whites or lower-class blacks and whites. Because proxemic norms are learned, it is reasonable to assume that people (no matter what their skin color or ethnic heritage) who grow up in the same neighborhood will share more expectations for comfortable conversational distance than those raised in different parts of a city, state, or country.

TOPIC OR SUBJECT MATTER

Erickson (1975) wanted to find out if proxemic shifts (forward or backward) were associated with any other events in a conversation. By coding co-occurring behavior, he determined that proxemic shifts may mark important segments of the encounter (e.g., beginnings, endings, and topic changes).

Earlier we noted that Sommer, in his efforts to examine the limits of conversational distance, tried to use impersonal topics that would not obviously influence the distances chosen. Personal topics, for intimates, may demand less conversational distance unless other factors, such as an impersonal setting, neutralize such inclinations.

Leipold's (1963) work demonstrates how anticipated treatment of the same general topic can influence conversational distance. Students entered a room and were given either a negative comment ("Your grade is poor, and you have not done your best"); praise ("You are doing very well, and Mr. Leipold wants to talk to you further"); or a neutral comment ("Mr. Leipold is interested in your feelings about the introductory course"). Students given the negative comment sat farthest from the experimenter; those who were praised sat closest. Following insults, people may want to assume a greater distance than they normally would with that person, particularly if the person giving the insult was perceived as a higher status person (O'Neal et al., 1980). Regardless of topic, close distances may result in less talking generally (Schulz & Barefoot, 1974).

SETTING FOR THE INTERACTION

Obviously, the social setting makes a great deal of difference in how far we stand from others in conversation. A crowded cocktail party demands a different distance than a comfortable evening in the living room with one's spouse or significant other. Lighting, temperature, noise, and available space affect interaction distance. Some authors have hypothesized that as room size increases, people tend to sit closer together. Noisy, urban street locations outside an office building may prompt people to stand closer to one another than they do when conversing inside the building. And, if the setting is perceived as a formal and/or unfamiliar one, we would predict greater distances from unknown others and closer distances to known others.

PHYSICAL CHARACTERISTICS

Height seems to make a difference in the distance people select for interacting. Irrespective of sex, shorter individuals seem to invite smaller interpersonal distances than taller individuals (Caplan & Goldman, 1981). When the two communicators are vastly different in height, the distance has to be adjusted so faces can be seen. Evidence also indicates that obese people are accorded greater interaction distances (Lerner, Venning, & Knapp, 1975).

A series of studies conducted by Kleck (1969; Kleck & Strenta, 1985) shows that persons interacting with stigmatized individuals (a left-leg amputation was simulated with a special wheelchair) choose greater *initial* speaking distances than with nonstigmatized persons, but that this distance decreases as the length of the interaction increases. Similar results have been found for perceived epileptics and people with facial disfigurations (scars and port-wine stains). Kleck points out that when people with physical disabilities expect others to behave in a distant manner, they may prepare themselves for such reactions and thereby increase the chances it will happen.

ATTITUDINAL AND EMOTIONAL ORIENTATION

Some experiments have been conducted by telling a person he or she was going to interact with a person who was either "warm and friendly" or "unfriendly." Not surprisingly, greater distances were chosen when interacting with a person perceived to be unfriendly. Similarly, when told to enter into conversation with another person and to behave in a friendly way, people chose closer distances than when told to "let him/her know you aren't friendly." This friendly/unfriendly relationship to distance seems to manifest itself even with preschool children (King, 1966). The number of unfriendly acts was directly related to the distance maintained by the recipient of such acts during free-play situations. The distance could be reduced, however, by putting a prized toy near the aggressive child. In some instances, our anger will cause us to withdraw from others, but if we seek retaliation, we may of course reduce our distance (Meisels & Dosey, 1971). Changes in our emotional state can sometimes make vast differences in how close or far away we want to be from others, for example, states of depression or fatigue versus states of extreme excitement or joy.

A study reported by Patterson (1968) reveals we may make a whole host of interpersonal judgments about another person based on distance. Subjects were told to interview others and secretly rate them on traits of friendliness, aggressiveness, dominance, extraversion, and intelligence. The interviewees were actually confederates who approached the interviewers at different distances and gave standard answers to the questions asked. The mean ratings for all the traits at four different distances were tabulated and revealed that the most distant position yielded significantly lower (less favorable) ratings. So, barring any contradictory information, people choosing closer distances are often seen as warmer, liking one another more, more empathic, and more understanding.

When we seek to win another's approval, we reduce conversational distance as opposed to instances when we are deliberately trying to avoid approval. Females seeking approval maintained a mean distance of 57 inches; those trying to avoid approval averaged 94 inches. When the distance was held constant at 5 feet, approval seekers compensated by smiling more and engaging in more gestural activity (Rosenfeld, 1965, 1966). Mehrabian (1969) concluded his review of attitude/distance research by saying,

> . . . the findings from a large number of studies corroborate one another and indicate that communicator–addressee distance is correlated with the degree of negative attitude communicated to and inferred by the addressee. In addition, studies carried out by sociologists and anthropologists indicate that distances which are too close, that is, inappropriate for a given interpersonal situation, can elicit negative attitudes when the communicator–addressee relationship is not an intimate one. (p. 363)

Characteristics of the Interpersonal Relationship

A number of studies also show that conversational distance varies as a function of our relationship with the other person. Strangers begin conversations at a greater distance than acquaintances, and acquaintances are a bit more distant than friends. In a study of 108 married couples, husbands were asked to walk toward their wives and stop when they got to a comfortable conversation distance. The more dissatisfied the husbands were with their marriage, the greater the distance they chose (Crane et al., 1987). Preschoolers seem to be able to use distance as a criterion for determining liking and disliking, too. Like adults, children seem to maintain greater distances with unknown adults, unfriendly and/or threatening persons, teachers, and endomorphs.

These and other studies suggest that closer relationships are likely to be associated with closer interaction distance. Obviously, there is a point at which we would not expect interactants to get any closer, no matter how close their relationship. And even people who are very close will not always interact at close distances due to the ebb and flow of their relationship as well as the influence of other distance-altering factors.

Personality Characteristics

Much has been written about the influence of introversion and extraversion on spatial relationships. It is difficult to draw any firm conclusions, but the bulk of the evidence seems to indicate that introverts tend to stand farther away than extraverts and to generally prefer greater interpersonal distances. Other studies suggest that anxiety-prone individuals maintain greater distances, but closer distances are seen when people have a high self-concept, have affiliative needs, are low on authoritarianism, high on interdependence, and are "self-directed." People with various personality abnormalities can probably be counted on to show greater non-normative spatial behavior, both too far away and too close.

In addition to studying human spatial behavior in high-density situations and in conversation, some researchers have examined such questions in the context of the small group, particularly in regard to seating patterns.

SEATING BEHAVIOR AND SPATIAL ARRANGEMENTS IN SMALL GROUPS

The body of work on seating behavior and spatial arrangements in small groups is known as *small group ecology*. Results of these studies show that our seating behavior is not generally accidental or random. Explanations are available for much of it, whether we are fully conscious of them or not. The particular position chosen in relation to the other person or persons varies with the task at hand, the degree of relationship between the interactants, the personalities of the two parties, and the amount and kind of available space. We can summarize the findings about seating behavior and spatial positioning under the following categories:

- Leadership
- Dominance
- Task
- Sex and acquaintance
- Introversion–extraversion

LEADERSHIP

It seems to be a norm, in the United States at least, that leaders are expected to be found at the head or foot of the table. In households in which the husband is considered the "head of the household," he is likely to be found sitting at the end of a rectangular dinner table. Elected group leaders generally put themselves in the head positions at rectangular tables, and the other group members try to position themselves so they can see the leader. In mock jury deliberations, the man seated on the end position is more likely to be chosen as the leader. The reaction to women who are positioned at the head of a table of men and women

has, in the past, been less consistently linked to the leadership role (Porter & Geis, 1981). As long as the group consisted of all women, the one at the head of the table was perceived as the leader. With the recent growth of women in positions of leadership in business and government, we would expect women seated at the end position in groups of men and women to be more consistently chosen as the leader, too.

Howells and Becker (1962) added further support to the idea that one's position in a group is an important factor in leadership emergence. They reasoned that spatial position determines the flow of communication, which, in turn, determines leadership emergence. Five-person decision-making groups were examined. Three people sat on one side of a rectangular table and two sat on the other side. Because previous work suggested that communication usually flows across the table rather than around it, the researchers predicted that the side with two people would be able to influence the most people (or at least talk more) and therefore emerge more often as group leaders. This hypothesis was confirmed.

An experiment by Ward (1968) helps unravel how seating position can create leaders. College males were assigned at random to sit in particular seats at a round table. The experimenters arranged it so more people were seated around one half of the table than in the other; only two people sat at the less populated end, and these two seats were considered visually central because their occupants would receive more undivided gaze from people at the other, more densely occupied, end. As predicted, occupants of these visually central seats received higher ratings of leadership after discussions had taken place. But were they really leaders or just perceived to be? Other research (Taylor & Fiske, 1975) does indicate that the person on whom attention is centered will appear to be an initiator (causally responsible for the course of the conversation), but in Ward's study evidence indicated that those who were visually central actually behaved differently: They talked more. It would be interesting to unravel further the complex routes by which seating position might affect leadership. For example, does the visually central person think, "I'm in a central position; I'd better start acting like a leader"? Or do the attention and subtle cues of the other members of the group trigger leaderlike behavior, perhaps without the visually central person even realizing it?

People seem well aware of these different perceptions and communicative potential associated with different seating positions. When people were asked to select seats to convey different impressions, they chose end positions to convey leadership or dominance, positions with the closest distances to convey interpersonal attraction, and seats that afforded the greatest interpersonal distance and least visual accessibility vis-à-vis the end positions to indicate they did not wish to participate (Reiss & Rosenfeld, 1980).

DOMINANCE

The end positions also seem to carry a status or dominance factor. Russo (1967) found that people rating various seating arrangements on an "equality" dimension stated that one person seated at the head and one on the side indicated more unequal status than if they were seated side by side or both on the ends. In an analysis of talking frequency in small groups, Hare and Bales (1963) noted that people in positions 1, 3, and 5 (at left) were frequent talkers. Subsequent studies revealed that these people were likely to be dominant personalities, whereas those who avoided the central or focal positions (by choosing seats 2 and 4) were more anxious and actually stated they wanted to stay out of the discussion. These self-

selection effects demonstrate the importance of conducting randomized studies such as Ward's, mentioned earlier. We don't know whether the communication of nondominant persons placed in focal positions would radically change their behavior.

Positions 1, 3, and 5 also were considered positions of leadership, but leadership of different types depending on the position. The two end positions (1 and 5) attracted the *task-oriented leader,* whereas the middle position attracted a *socioemotional leader*—one concerned about group relationships, getting everyone to participate, and so forth.

TASK

Sommer's observations of seating behavior in student cafeterias and libraries led him to study how students would sit in different task situations. The same study was conducted by Cook in the United Kingdom with Oxford University students and a sample of nonstudents—civil servants, schoolteachers, and secretaries. In each case, persons were asked to imagine themselves sitting at a table with a friend of the same sex in each of the following four situations:

1. **Conversation.** Sitting and chatting for a few minutes before class ("before work" for nonstudents)
2. **Cooperation.** Sitting and studying together for the same exam ("sitting doing a crossword or the like together" for nonstudents)
3. **Coaction.** Sitting studying for different exams ("sitting at the same table reading" for nonstudents)
4. **Competition.** Competing to see who will be the first to solve a series of puzzles

Each subject was shown a round table and a rectangular table. Each had six chairs. The combined results for all the groups surveyed in these two studies are presented in Table 5-1 for rectangular tables and Table 5-2 for circular tables.

There are many similarities between the different groups concerning order of preference. Conversations before class (or work) involved primarily corner or "short" opposite seating at rectangular tables and side-by-side seating at round tables. Cooperation seems to elicit a preponderance of side-by-side choices. Coaction, studying for different exams,

TABLE 5-1   Seating Preferences at Rectangular Tables

	X¦X□	□X	XX□	X□X	X□X	□X
Conversation	45%	36%	12%	1%	4%	2%
Cooperation	23	13	42	8	10	4
Coaction	8	8	10	21	34	19
Competition	6	22	7	40	19	6

TABLE 5-2   Seating Preferences at Round Tables

	X X○	X○X	X○X
Conversation	60%	27%	13%
Cooperation	68	13	19
Coaction	18	32	50
Competition	12	23	65

SOURCE: (Table 5-1 and 5-2) From "Experiments in orientation and proxemics" by M. Cook, *Human Relations* Vol. 23, p. 61–76. Copyright © 1970 The Tavistock Institute. Reprinted by permission of Sage Publications.

or reading at the same table necessitated plenty of room between the participants, and the most distant seating positions were generally selected. Most persons wanted to compete in an opposite seating arrangement. However, the U.S. students wanted to establish a closer opposite relationship. Apparently this would afford them an opportunity not only to see how the other person was progressing but would also allow them to use various gestures, body movements, and eye contact to upset their opponents. The more distant opposite position chosen by the United Kingdom samples would, in contrast, prevent spying.

SEX AND ACQUAINTANCE

The nature of the relationship may make a difference in spatial orientation and hence in seating selection. Cook (1970) conducted a questionnaire study and obtained some observational data of persons interacting in a restaurant and several bars. People in the questionnaire study were asked to select seating arrangements in the following situations:

- Sitting with a casual friend of the same sex
- Sitting with a casual friend of the opposite sex
- Sitting with a boyfriend or girlfriend

The results for the "public house," or bar, are found in Table 5-3 and results for the restaurant in Table 5-4.

The predominant seating pattern, as stated by questionnaire respondents using a bar as a referent, was corner seating for the same-sex friends and casual friends of the opposite sex. Intimate friends appear to require side-by-side seating, however. In a restaurant, both nonintimate relationship categories selected predominantly opposite seating, but as intimacy increased, other types of seating became more acceptable. There may be some very practical

TABLE 5-3   Seating Preferences for a Bar or "Public House"

	X / X□	X / □ / X	X X / □	OTHER
Same-sex friend	70	25	45	2
Casual friend of opposite sex	63	37	29	7
Intimate friend of opposite sex	43	11	82	4

TABLE 5-4   Seating Preferences for a Restaurant

	X / X□	X / □ / X	X X / □	OTHER
Same-sex friend	30	73	34	4
Casual friend of opposite sex	43	64	28	4
Intimate friend of opposite sex	40	53	46	2

SOURCE: (Table 5-3 and 5-4) From "Experiments in orientation and proxemics" by M. Cook, *Human Relations* Vol. 23, p. 61–76. Copyright © 1970 The Tavistock Institute. Reprinted by permission of Sage Publications.

reasons for opposite seating in restaurants. For instance, other patrons will not have to sit opposite you, which might create some uncomfortable situations with respect to eye contact and overheard conversation. In addition, you will not poke the other person with your elbow while eating. Actual observations of seating in a restaurant, presented in Table 5-5, seem to validate the questionnaire responses. Most people do select opposite seating in restaurants. However, the observations of people sitting in bars do not agree with the questionnaire study of seating preferences in bars (see Table 5-6). Although questionnaire preferences favored corner seating, observations show a marked preference for side-by-side seating. Cook suggests this may have been because the bars were equipped with many seats located against the

TABLE 5-5 Observations of Seating Behavior in a Restaurant

	X / □ / X	X X / □	X / □ / X
Two males	6	0	0
Two females	6	0	1
Male with female	36	7	1
Total	48	7	2

TABLE 5-6 Observations of Seating Behavior in Three Bars

	X X / □	X / □ / X	X X / □
Bar A			
Two males	7	8	13
Male with female	6	4	21
Total	13	12	34
Bar B			
Two males	1	0	9
Male with female	4	3	20
Total	5	3	29
Bar C			
Two males	0	11	7
Male with female	1	4	10
Total	1	15	17
Overall			
Two males	8	19	29
Male with female	11	11	51
Total	19	30	80

SOURCE: (Table 5-5 and 5-6) From "Experiments in orientation and proxemics" by M. Cook, *Human Relations* Vol. 23, p. 61–76. Copyright © 1970 The Tavistock Institute. Reprinted by permission of Sage Publications.

wall. Supposedly this allowed persons to sit side by side, not have their backs to anyone, and have a good view of the other patrons. Thus paper-and-pencil preferences were overruled by environmental factors. From this study, we must conclude that sex and acquaintance with the other person do have an effect on one's actual and preferred seating positions.

INTROVERSION–EXTRAVERSION

We have already discussed the possible influence of introversion and extraversion on conversational distance. Some evidence indicates that this personality variable also affects seating preferences. Extraverts are likely to choose to sit opposite (either across the table or down the length of it) and disregard positions that would put them at an angle. Extraverts also tend to choose positions that would put them in close physical proximity to the other person. Introverts generally choose positions that would keep them more at a distance, visually and physically.

A discussion of the shape of the negotiating table at the 1968 Paris peace talks (attempting to end the Vietnam War) is a most appropriate way to conclude this chapter.

FIGURE 5-4

Proposals for a table to be used at the Paris peace talks, 1968.

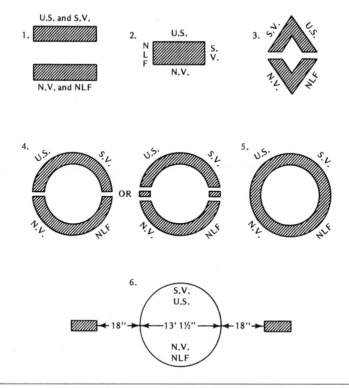

SOURCE: From McCroskey, Larson, Knapp, *An Introduction to Interpersonal Communication,* published by Allyn and Bacon, Boston, MA. Copyright © 1971 by Pearson Education. Reprinted by permission of the publisher.

It incorporates elements of territoriality and seating arrangements that are influenced by culture, attitudes, leadership perceptions, and the type of task undertaken. It took negotiators 8 months just to reach an agreement on the shape of the table! The diagrams in Figure 5-4 mark the chronology of the seating proposals.

> The United States (U.S.) and South Vietnam (S.V.) wanted a seating arrangement in which only two sides were identified. They did not want to recognize the National Liberation Front (NLF) as an equal party in the negotiations. North Vietnam (N.V.) and the NLF wanted equal status given to all parties, represented by a four-sided table. The final arrangement was such that both parties could claim "victory." The round table minus the dividing lines allowed North Vietnam and NLF to claim all four delegations were equal. The existence of the two secretarial tables (interpreted as dividers), the lack of identifying symbols on the table, and an AA, BB speaking rotation permitted the United States and South Vietnam to claim victory for the two-sided approach. Considering the lives lost during the 8 months needed to arrive at the seating arrangement, we must certainly conclude that proximity and territoriality are far from trivial concerns in some human encounters. (McCroskey, Larson, & Knapp, 1971, p. 98)

❖

SUMMARY

Our perceptions and use of space contribute extensively to various communication outcomes we seek. Some of our spatial behavior is related to a need to stake out and maintain territory. Our territorial behavior can be helpful in regulating social interaction and controlling density; it also can be the source of conflict when territory is disputed or encroached on. We identified three different types of territories (primary, secondary, and public) and several different levels at which territorial behavior exists (individual, group, community, and nation). Although we often think people vigorously defend their territory, the type of defense depends very much on who the intruder is, why the intrusion is taking place, what type of territory is being encroached on, what type of encroachment is used (violation, invasion, or contamination), how long the encroachment takes, and where it occurs. We often try to prevent people from moving into our territory by marking it as "ours." This can be done by our physical presence or the presence of a friend who agrees to "watch" our territory. Territorial invasion also can be prevented by using markers (fences, coats, and the like) or a special kind of language. When someone does invade another's territory, we sometimes find the "owner's" physiological arousal increased. In addition, various defensive maneuvers are used, for example, flight, hostile looks, turning or leaning away, blocking advances with objects or hands and arms, or even verbal defenses. Just as people do not like others to invade their territory, we also find they are reluctant to invade the territory of others, often apologizing when it cannot be prevented.

We examined density and crowding in both animal and human interaction. Some animal studies showed undesirable effects from overpopulation. High-density human situations, however, are not always disruptive. Sometimes we want the company of many people. The best predictor of individually stressful and socially undesirable outcomes seems to be the number of people per room rather than other density measures. When people do feel the stress of a crowded situation, they seek ways to cope with it. We also distinguished between density (number of people per unit of space) and crowding (a feeling brought on by the environment, personal, or social factors).

Our examination of spatial behavior in conversations revealed many ways of conceptualizing and measuring this behavior. As a result, firm conclusions are difficult to reach. We do know that each of us seeks a comfortable conversational distance that varies depending on age, sex, cultural and ethnic background, setting, attitudes, emotions, topics, physical characteristics, personality, and our relationship with the other person. We also know conversational distance changes during the course of a conversation.

Finally, we discussed seating arrangements in small groups. Distances and seats chosen do not seem to be accidental. Leaders and dominant personalities tend to choose specific seats, but seating position also can determine one's role in a group. Seating also varies with the topic at hand, the nature of the relationships among the parties, and certain personality variables.

QUESTIONS FOR DISCUSSION

1. Identify a secondary territory you have experienced. Discuss what happened.

2. What cultural differences within the United States would you expect to find in comfortable conversational distances?

3. When is a woman's purse a primary territory? When can it become a secondary territory?

4. Think of a time when you did not experience a comfortable conversational distance with someone. What were the major factors influencing this situation? How did you deal with it?

BIBLIOGRAPHY

Aiello, J. R. (1987). Human spatial behavior. In D. Stokols & I. Altman (Eds.), *Handbook of environmental psychology*, (Vol. I, pp. 389–504). New York: Wiley.

Aiello, J. R., & Aiello, T. C. (1974). The development of personal space: Proxemic behavior of children 6 through 16. *Human Ecology, 2*, 177–189.

Aiello, J. R., & Jones, S. E. (1971). Field study of the proxemic behavior of young school children in three subcultural groups. *Journal of Personality and Social Psychology, 19*, 351–356.

Aiello, J. R., & Thompson, D. E. (1980). Personal space, crowding, and spatial behavior in a cultural context. In I. Altman, A. Rapoport, & J. F. Wohlwill (Eds.), *Human behavior and environment* (Vol. 4). New York: Plenum.

Albert, S., & Dabbs, J. M., Jr. (1970). Physical distance and persuasion. *Journal of Personality and Social Psychology, 15*, 265–270.

Allekian, C. I. (1973). Intrusions of territory and personal space: An anxiety-inducing factor for hospitalized persons. *Nursing Research, 22*, 236–241.

Allgeier, A. R., & Byrne, D. (1973). Attraction toward the opposite sex as a determinant of physical proximity. *Journal of Social Psychology, 90*, 213–219.

Altman, I. (1975). *The environment and social behavior*. Monterey, CA: Brooks/Cole.

Altman, I., & Chemers, M. M. (1988). *Culture and environment*. New York: Cambridge University Press.

Altman, I., & Haythorn, W. W. (1967). The ecology of isolated groups. *Behavioral Science, 12*, 169–182.

Ardrey, R. (1966). *The territorial imperative*. New York: Atheneum Press.

Argyle, M., & Dean, J. (1965). Eye contact, distance and affiliation. *Sociometry, 28*, 289–304.

Atsuko, A. (2003). Gender differences in interpersonal distance: From the viewpoint of oppression hypothesis. *Japanese Journal of Experimental Social Psychology, 42*, 201–218.

Barash, D. P. (1973). Human ethology: Personal space reiterated. *Environment and Behavior, 5*, 67–73.

Baum, A., & Greenberg, C. I. (1975). Waiting for a crowd: The behavioral and perceptual effects of anticipated crowding. *Journal of Personality and Social Psychology, 32*, 671–679.

Baum, A. & Paulus, P. B. (1987). Crowding. In D. Stokols & I. Altman (Eds.), *Handbook of environmental psychology*, (Vol. I, pp. 533–570). New York: Wiley.

Baum, A., Riess, M., & O'Hara, J. (1974). Architectural variants of reaction to spatial invasion. *Environment and Behavior, 6*, 91–100.

Baxter, J. C. (1970). Interpersonal spacing in natural settings. *Sociometry, 33*, 444–456.

Bechtel, R. B. (1997). *Environment and behavior*. Thousand Oaks, CA: Sage.

Becker, F. D. (1973). Study of spatial markers. *Journal of Personality and Social Psychology, 26*, 439–445.

Bell, P. A., Greene, T. C., Fisher, J. D., & Baum, A. (1996). *Environmental psychology* (4th ed.). Fort Worth, TX: Harcourt Brace.

Bell, P. A., Kline, L. M., & Barnard, W. A. (1988). Friendship and freedom of movement as moderators of sex differences in interpersonal spacing. *Journal of Social Psychology, 128*, 305–310.

Brown, B. B. (1987). Territoriality. In D. Stokols & I. Altman (Eds.), *Handbook of environmental psychology*, (Vol. I, pp. 505–532). New York: Wiley.

Bull, R. (1985). The general public's reactions to facial disfigurement. In J. A. Graham & A. M. Kligman (Eds.), *The psychology of cosmetic treatments*. New York: Praeger.

Buller, D. B. (1987). Communication apprehension and reactions to proxemic violations. *Journal of Nonverbal Behavior, 11*, 13–25.

Burgoon, J. K. (1978). A communication model of personal space violations: Explication and an initial test. *Human Communication Research, 4*, 129–142.

Burgoon, J. K. (1982). Privacy and communication. In M. Burgoon (Ed.), *Communication yearbook 6*. Beverly Hills, CA: Sage.

Burgoon, J. K. (1983). Nonverbal violations of expectations. In J. M. Wiemann & R. P. Harrison (Eds.), *Nonverbal interaction*. Beverly Hills, CA: Sage.

Burgoon, J. K., & Jones, S. B. (1976). Toward a theory of personal space expectations and their violations. *Human Communication Research, 2*, 131–146.

Calhoun, J. B. (1962). Population density and social pathology. *Scientific American, 206*, 139–148.

Caplan, M. E., & Goldman, M. (1981). Personal space violations as a function of height. *Journal of Social Psychology, 114*, 167–171.

Cappella, J. N. (1986). Violations of distance norms: Reciprocal and compensatory reactions for high and low self-monitors. In M. L. McLaughlin (Ed.), *Communication yearbook 9*. Beverly Hills, CA: Sage.

Carpenter, C. R. (1958). Territoriality: A review of concepts and problems. In A. Roe & G. G. Simpson (Eds.), *Behavior and evolution*. New Haven: Yale University Press.

Caudill, W., & Weinstein, H. (1972). Maternal care and infant behavior in Japan and America. In C. Lavatelli & F. Stendler (Eds.), *Readings in child behavior and development*. New York: Harcourt.

Christian, J. J., & Davis, D. E. (1964). Social and endocrine factors are integrated in the regulation of mammalian populations. *Science, 146,* 1550–1560.

Ciolek, T. M., & Kendon, A. (1980). Environment and the spatial arrangement of conversational encounters. *Sociological Inquiry, 50,* 237–276.

Connolly, P. R. (1975). The perception of personal space among black and white Americans. *Central States Speech Journal, 26,* 21–28.

Cook, M. (1970). Experiments on orientation and proxemics. *Human Relations, 23,* 61–76.

Crane, D. R., Dollahite, D. C., Griffin, W., & Taylor, V. L. (1987). Diagnosing relationships with spatial distance: An empirical test of a clinical principle. *Journal of Marital and Family Therapy, 13,* 307–310.

DeLong, A. J. (1970). Dominance–territorial relations in a small group. *Environment and Behavior, 2,* 190–191.

DiPietro, J. A. (1981). Rough and tumble play: A function of gender. *Developmental Psychology, 17,* 50–58.

Drucker, S. J., & Gumpert, G. (1991). Public space and communication: The zoning of public interaction. *Communication Theory, 1,* 294–310.

Eagly, A. H. (1987). *Sex differences in social behavior: A social-role interpretation.* Hillsdale, NJ: Erlbaum.

Edney, J. J. (1974). Human territoriality. *Psychological Bulletin, 31,* 959–975.

Efran, M. G., & Cheyne, J. A. (1974). Affective concomitants of the invasion of shared space: Behavioral, physiological and verbal indicators. *Journal of Personality and Social Psychology, 29,* 219–226.

Erickson, F. (1975). One function of proxemic shifts in face-to-face interaction. In A. Kendon, R. M. Harris, & M. R. Key (Eds.), *Organization of behavior in face-to-face interaction.* Chicago: Aldine.

Erlich, P. R. (1971). *The population bomb.* Ballantine Books: New York.

Esser, A. H. (1971). *Environment and behavior: The use of space by animals and men.* New York: Plenum.

Evans, G. W. (1979). Behavioral and physiological consequences of crowding in humans. *Journal of Applied Social Psychology, 9,* 27–46.

Evans, G. W., & Howard, R. B. (1973). Personal space. *Psychological Bulletin, 80,* 334–344.

Evans, G. W., Lepore, S. J., & Allen, K. M. (2000). Cross-cultural differences in tolerance for crowding: Fact or fiction? *Journal of Personality and Social Psychology, 79,* 204–210.

Felipe, N. J., & Sommer, R. (1966). Invasions of personal space. *Social Problems, 14,* 206–214.

Finando, S. J. (1973). *The effects of distance norm violation on heart rate and length of verbal response.* Unpublished doctoral dissertation, Florida State University.

Fisher, J. D., & Byrne, D. (1975). Too close for comfort: Sex differences in response to invasions of personal space. *Journal of Personality and Social Psychology, 32,* 15–21.

Freedman, J. L. (1975). *Crowding and behavior.* New York: Viking.

Freedman, J. L. (1979). Reconciling apparent differences between the responses of humans and other animals to crowding. *Psychological Review, 86,* 80–85.

Fry, A. M., & Willis, F. N. (1971). Invasion of personal space as a function of the age of the invader. *Psychological Record, 21,* 385–389.

Galle, O. R., Gove, W. R., & McPherson, J. M. (1972). Population density and pathology: What are the relationships for man? *Science, 176,* 23–30.

Gifford, R. (1982). Projected interpersonal distance and orientation choices: Personality, sex, and social situation. *Social Psychology Quarterly, 45,* 145–152.

Gifford, R. (1987). *Environmental psychology: Principles and practice.* Boston: Allyn & Bacon.

Gifford, R., & O'Connor, B. (1986). Nonverbal intimacy: Clarifying the role of seating distance and orientation. *Journal of Nonverbal Behavior, 10,* 207–214.

Gochman, I. R., & Keating, J. P. (1980). Misattributions to crowding: Blaming crowding for non-density caused events. *Journal of Nonverbal Behavior, 4,* 157–175.

Goffman, E. (1971). *Relations in public.* New York: Basic Books.

Greenberg, C. I., & Firestone, I. J. (1977). Compensatory responses to crowding: Effects of personal space intrusion and privacy reduction. *Journal of Personality and Social Psychology, 35,* 637–644.

Guardo, C. J., & Meisels, M. (1971). Child–parent spatial patterns under praise and reproof. *Developmental Psychology, 5,* 365.

Halberstadt, A. G. (1985). Race, socioeconomic status and nonverbal behavior. In A. W. Siegman & S. Feldstein (Eds.), *Multichannel integrations of nonverbal behavior.* Hillsdale, NJ: Erlbaum.

Hall, E. T. (1959). *The silent language.* Garden City, NY: Doubleday.

Hall, E. T. (1966). *The hidden dimension.* Garden City, NY: Doubleday.

Hall, J. A. (1984). *Nonverbal sex differences: Communication accuracy and expressive style.* Baltimore: Johns Hopkins University Press.

Hansen, J. F. (1976). Proxemics and the interpretive processes in human communication. *Semiotica, 17,* 165–179.

Hare, A., & Bales, R. (1963). Seating position and small group interaction. *Sociometry, 26,* 480–486.

Harper, L., & Sanders, K. M. (1975). Preschool children's use of space: Sex differences in outdoor play. *Developmental Psychology, 11,* 119.

Hartnett, J. J., Bailey, K. G., & Hartley, C. S. (1974). Body height, position, and sex as determinants of personal space. *Journal of Psychology, 87,* 129–136.

Hayduk, L. A. (1978). Personal space: An evaluative and orienting overview. *Psychological Bulletin, 85,* 117–134.

Hayduk, L. A. (1994). Personal space: Understanding the simplex model. *Journal of Nonverbal Behavior, 18,* 245–260.

Hearn, G. (1957). Leadership and the spatial factor in small groups. *Journal of Abnormal and Social Psychology, 104,* 269–272.

Hediger, H. P. (1961). The evolution of territorial behavior. In S. L. Washburn (Ed.), *Social life of early man* (pp. 34–57). Chicago: Aldine.

Hewitt, J., & Algahtani, M. A. (2003). Differences between Saudi and U.S. students in reaction to same- and mixed-sex intimacy shown by others. *Journal of Social Psychology, 143,* 233–242.

Hildreth, A. M., Derogatis, L. R., & McCusker, K. (1971). Body buffer zone and violence: A reassessment and confirmation. *American Journal of Psychiatry, 127,* 1641–1645.

Holland, R. W., Roeder, U-R., van Baaren, R. B., Brandt, A. C., & Hannover, B. (2004). Don't stand so close to me: The effects of self-construal on interpersonal closeness. *Psychological Science, 15,* 237–242.

Hoppe, R. A., Greene, M. S., & Kenney, J. W. (1972). Territorial markers: Additional findings. *Journal of Social Psychology, 88,* 305–306.

Horowitz, M. J. (1965). Human spatial behavior. *American Journal of Psychotherapy, 19,* 20–28.

Horowitz, M. J. (1968). Spatial behavior and psychopathology. *The Journal of Nervous and Mental Disease, 146,* 24–35.

Howells, L. T., & Becker, S. W. (1962). Seating arrangement and leadership emergence. *Journal of Abnormal and Social Psychology, 64,* 148–150.

Hutt, C., & Vaizey, M. J. (1966). Differential effects of group density on social behavior. *Nature, 209,* 1371–1372.

Jones, S. E., & Aiello, J. R. (1973). Proxemic behavior of black and white first, third, and fifth grade children. *Journal of Personality and Social Psychology, 25,* 21–27.

Judge, P. G. (2000). Coping with crowded conditions. In F. Aureli & F. B. M. de Waal (Eds.), *Natural conflict resolution* (pp. 129–154). Berkeley, CA: University of California Press.

Judge, P. G., & de Waal, F. B. M. (1993). Conflict avoidance among rhesus monkeys: Coping with short-term crowding. *Animal Behaviour, 46,* 221–232.

Judge, P. G., & de Waal, F. B. M. (1997). Rhesus monkey behaviour under diverse population densities: Coping with long-term crowding. *Animal Behaviour, 54,* 643–662.

King, M. J. (1966). Interpersonal relations in preschool children and average approach distance. *Journal of Genetic Psychology, 109,* 109–116.

Kinzel, A. S. (1970). Body buffer zone in violent prisoners. *American Journal of Psychiatry, 127,* 59–64.

Kleck, R. E. (1969). Physical stigma and task oriented interaction. *Human Relations, 22,* 51–60.

Kleck, R. E., Buck, P. L., Goller, W. L., London, R. S., Pfeiffer, J. R., & Vukcevic, D. P. (1968). The effect of stigmatizing conditions on the use of personal space. *Psychological Reports, 23,* 111–118.

Kleck, R. E., & Strenta, A. C. (1985). Physical deviance and the perception of social outcomes. In J. A. Graham & A. M. Kligman (Eds.), *The psychology of cosmetic treatments.* New York: Praeger.

Klopfer, P. M. (1969). *Habitats and territories: A study of the use of space by animals.* New York: Basic.

Knowles, E. S. (1973). Boundaries around group interaction: The effect of group size and member status on boundary permeability. *Journal of Personality and Social Psychology, 26,* 327–332.

Knowles, E. S. (1979). An affiliative conflict theory of personal and group spatial behavior. In P. B. Paulus (Ed.), *Psychology of group influence.* Hillsdale, NJ: Erlbaum.

Latta, R. M. (1978). Relation of status incongruence to personal space. *Personality and Social Psychology Bulletin, 4,* 143–146.

Leibman, M. (1970). The effects of sex and race norms on personal space. *Environment and Behavior, 2,* 208–246.

Leipold, W. E. (1963). *Psychological distance in a dyadic interview.* Unpublished doctoral dissertation, University of North Dakota.

LePoire, B. A., Burgoon, J. K., & Parrott, R. (1992). Status and privacy restoring communication in the workplace. *Journal of Applied Communication Research, 20,* 419–436.

Lerner, R. M., Venning, J., & Knapp, J. R. (1975). Age and sex effects on personal space schemata toward body build in late childhood. *Developmental Psychology, 11,* 855–856.

Little, K. B. (1965). Personal space. *Journal of Experimental Social Psychology, 1,* 237–247.

Little, K. B. (1968). Cultural variations in social schemata. *Journal of Personality and Social Psychology, 10,* 1–7.

Loo, C. M. (1973). The effect of spatial density on the social behavior of children. *Journal of Applied Social Psychology, 2,* 372–381.

Lott, D. F., & Sommer, R. (1967). Seating arrangements and status. *Journal of Personality and Social Psychology, 7,* 90–94.

Lyman, S. M., & Scott, M. B. (1967). Territoriality: A neglected sociological dimension. *Social Problems, 15,* 236–249.

Malmberg, T. (1980). *Human territoriality.* Mouton: The Hague.

McBride, G., King, M. G., & James, J. W. (1965). Social proximity effects on galvanic skin responses in adult humans. *Journal of Psychology, 61,* 153–157.

McCallum, R., Rusbult, C. E., Hong, G. K., Walden, T. A., & Schopler, J. (1979). Effects of resource availability and importance of behavior on the experience of crowding. *Journal of Personality and Social Psychology, 37,* 1304–1313.

McCroskey, J. C., Larson, C. E., & Knapp, M. L. (1971). *An introduction to interpersonal communication.* Englewood Cliffs, NJ: Prentice-Hall.

McDowell, K. V. (1972). Violations of personal space. *Canadian Journal of Behavioral Science, 4,* 210–217.

Mehrabian, A. (1969). Significance of posture and position in the communication of attitude and status relationships. *Psychological Bulletin, 71,* 363.

Mehrabian, A., & Diamond, S. G. (1971). Seating arrangement and conversation. *Sociometry, 34,* 281–289.

Meisels, M., & Dosey, M. (1971). Personal space, anger arousal, and psychological defense. *Journal of Personality, 39,* 333–334.

Meisels, M., & Guardo, C. (1969). Development of personal space schemata. *Child Development, 40,* 1167–1178.

Milgram, S. (1970). The experience of living in cities. *Science, 167,* 1461–1468.

Mitchell, R. (1971). Some social implications of higher density housing. *American Sociological Review, 36,* 18–29.

Moos, R. H., & Kulik, J. (1976). Population density, crowding and the use of space. In R. H. Moos (Ed.), *The human context.* New York: Wiley.

Newman, O. (1972). *Defensible space.* New York: Macmillan.

O'Neal, E. C., Brunalt, M. A., Carifio, M. S., Troutwine, R., & Epstein, J. (1980). Effect of insult upon personal space preferences. *Journal of Nonverbal Behavior, 5,* 56–62.

Pagan, G., & Aiello, J. R. (1982). Development of personal space among Puerto Ricans. *Journal of Nonverbal Behavior, 7,* 59–68.

Pastalan, L., & Carson, D. H. (Eds.). (1970). *Spatial behavior of older people.* Ann Arbor: University of Michigan/Wayne State University Press.

Patterson, M. L. (1968). Spatial factors in social interaction. *Human Relations, 21,* 351–361.

Patterson, M. L. (1975). Personal space—time to burst the bubble? *Man–Environment Systems, 5,* 67.

Patterson, M. L. (1976). An arousal model of interpersonal intimacy. *Psychological Review, 83,* 235–245.

Patterson, M. L. (1978). The role of space in social interaction. In A. W. Siegman & S. Feldstein (Eds.), *Nonverbal behavior and communication.* Hillsdale, NJ: Erlbaum.

Patterson, M. L., & Edinger, J. A. (1987). A functional analysis of space in social interaction. In A. W. Siegman & S. Feldstein (Eds.), *Nonverbal behavior and communication* (2nd ed.). Hillsdale, NJ: Erlbaum.

Patterson, M. L., Mullens, S., & Romano, J. (1971). Compensatory reactions to spatial intrusion. *Sociometry, 34,* 114–121.

Pedersen, D. M., & Shears, L. M. (1973). A review of personal space research in the framework of general system theory. *Psychological Bulletin, 80,* 367–388.

Petschauer, P. W. (1997). *Human space.* New York: Praeger.

Porter, E., Argyle, M., & Salter, V. (1970). What is signalled by proximity? *Perceptual and Motor Skills, 30,* 39–42.

Porter, N., & Geis, F. (1981). Women and nonverbal leadership cues: When seeing is not believing. In C. Mayo & N. M. Henley (Eds.), *Gender and nonverbal behavior.* New York: Springer-Verlag.

Reiss, M., & Rosenfeld, P. (1980). Seating preferences as nonverbal communication: A self-presentational analysis. *Journal of Applied Communication Research, 8,* 22–30.

Remland, M. S., Jones, T. S., and Brinkman, H. (1991). Proxemic and haptic behavior in three European countries. *Journal of Nonverbal Behavior, 15,* 215–232.

Rohe, W., & Patterson, A. H. (1974). *The effects of varied levels of resources and density on behavior in a day care center.* Paper presented at Environmental Design and Research Association, Milwaukee, WI.

Rosenfeld, H. (1965). Effect of approval-seeking induction on interpersonal proximity. *Psychological Reports, 17,* 120–122.

Rosenfeld, H. (1966). Instrumental and affiliative functions of facial and gestural expressions. *Journal of Personality and Social Psychology, 4,* 65–72.

Russo, N. (1967). Connotation of seating arrangement. *Cornell Journal of Social Relations, 2,* 37–44.

Sanders, J. L., Hakky, U. M., & Brizizzolara, M. M. (1985). Personal space amongst Arabs and Americans. *International Journal of Psychology, 20,* 13–17.

Scheflen, A. E. (1975). Micro-territories in human interaction. In A. Kendon, R. M. Harris, & M. R. Key (Eds.), *Organization of behavior in face-to-face interaction.* Chicago: Aldine.

Scheflen, A. E., & Ashcraft, N. (1976). *Human territories: How we behave in space–time.* Englewood Cliffs, NJ: Prentice-Hall.

Scherer, S. E. (1974). Proxemic behavior of primary school children as a function of their socioeconomic class and subculture. *Journal of Personality and Social Psychology, 29,* 800–805.

Schmidt, D. E., & Keating, J. P. (1979). Human crowding and personal control: An integration of the research. *Psychological Bulletin, 86,* 680–700.

Schulz, R., & Barefoot, J. (1974). Non-verbal responses and affiliative conflict theory. *British Journal of Social and Clinical Psychology, 13,* 237–243.

Shuter, R. (1976). Proxemics and tactility in Latin America. *Journal of Communication, 26,* 46–52.

Shuter, R. (1977). A field study of non-verbal communication in Germany, Italy and the United States. *Communication Monographs, 44,* 298–305.

Smith, D. E. (1986). The influence of contextual variables on interpersonal spacing. *Journal of Communication, 29* (Autumn), 34–39.

Smith, M. J., Reinheimer, R. E., & Gabbard-Alley, A. (1981). Crowding, task performance, and communicative interaction in youth and old age. *Human Communication Research, 7,* 259–272.

Sobel, R. S., & Lillith, N. (1975). Determinants of nonstationary personal space invasion. *Journal of Social Psychology, 97,* 39–45.

Sommer, R. (1959). Studies in personal space. *Sociometry, 22,* 247–260.

Sommer, R. (1961). Leadership and group geography. *Sociometry, 24,* 99–110.

Sommer, R. (1962). The distance for comfortable conversation: A further study. *Sociometry, 25,* 111–116.

Sommer, R. (1965). Further studies of small group ecology. *Sociometry, 28,* 337–348.

Sommer, R. (1967). Small group ecology. *Psychological Bulletin, 67,* 145–152.

Sommer, R. (1969). *Personal space.* Englewood Cliffs, NJ: Prentice-Hall.

Sommer, R. (2002). Personal space in a digital age. In R. B. Bechtel and A. Churchman (Eds.), *Handbook of environmental psychology* (pp. 647–660). New York: Wiley.

Sommer, R., & Becker, F. D. (1969). Territorial defense and the good neighbor. *Journal of Personality and Social Psychology, 11,* 85–92.

Sommer, R., & Ross, H. (1958). Social interaction on a geriatrics ward. *International Journal of Social Psychiatry, 4,* 128–133.

Stockdale, J. E. (1978). Crowding: Determinants and effects. In L. Berkowitz (Ed.), *Advances in experimental social psychology* (Vol. 11). New York: Academic Press.

Stokols, D. (1972). On the distinction between density and crowding: Some implications for future research. *Psychological Review, 79,* 275–278.

Stokols, D., Rall, M., Pinner, B., & Schopler, J. (1973). Physical, social, and personal determinants of the perception of crowding. *Environment and Behavior, 5,* 87–117.

Stratton, L. O., Tekippe, D. J., & Flick, G. L. (1973). Personal space and self-concept. *Sociometry, 36,* 424–429.

Strodtbeck, F., & Hook, L. (1961). The social dimensions of a twelve man jury table. *Sociometry, 24,* 397–415.

Strube, M. J., & Werner, C. (1984). Personal space claims as a function of interpersonal threat: The mediating role of need for control. *Journal of Nonverbal Behavior, 8,* 195–209.

Sundstrom, E. (1978). Crowding as a sequential process: Review of research on the effects of population density on humans. In A. Baum & Y. M. Epstein (Eds.), *Human responses to crowding.* Hillsdale, NJ: Erlbaum.

Sundstrom, E., & Altman, I. (1976). Interpersonal relationships and personal space: Research review and theoretical model. *Human Ecology, 4,* 47–67.

Sundstrom, E., & Sundstrom, M. G. (1977). Personal space invasions: What happens when the invader asks permission? *Environmental Psychology and Nonverbal Behavior, 2,* 76–82.

Sussman, N. M., & Rosenfeld, H. M. (1982). Influence of culture, language, and sex on conversational distance. *Journal of Personality and Social Psychology, 42,* 66–74.

Taylor, R. B. (1988). *Human territorial functioning.* New York: Cambridge University Press.

Taylor, S. E., & Fiske, S. T. (1975). Point of view and perceptions of causality. *Journal of Personality and Social Psychology, 32,* 429–445.

Vine, I. (1975). Territoriality and the spatial regulation of interaction. In A. Kendon, R. M. Harris, & M. R. Key (Eds.), *Organization of behavior in face to face interaction.* Chicago: Aldine.

Ward, C. (1968). Seating arrangement and leadership emergence in small discussion groups. *Journal of Social Psychology, 74,* 83–90.

Watson, O. M. (1970). *Proxemic behavior: A cross-cultural study.* The Hague: Mouton.

Watson, O. M. (1972). *Symbolic and expressive uses of space: An introduction to proxemic behavior. Module No. 20.* Reading, MA: Addison-Wesley.

Watson, O. M. (1973). Proxemics. In T. A. Sebeok (Ed.), *Current trends in linguistics.* The Hague: Mouton Press.

Watson, O. M., & Graves, T. D. (1966). Quantitative research in proxemic behavior. *American Anthropologist, 68,* 971–985.

Williams, J. L. (1971). Personal space and its relation to extroversion–introversion. *Canadian Journal of Behavioral Science, 3,* 156–160.

Willis, F. N. (1966). Initial speaking distance as a function of the speaker's relationship. *Psychonomic Science, 5,* 221–222.

Willis, F. N., Jr., Gier, J. A., & Smith, D. E. (1979). Stepping aside: Correlates of displacement in pedestrians. *Journal of Communication, 29,* 34–39.

Worchel, S. (1986). The influence of contextual variables on interpersonal spacing. *Journal of Nonverbal Behavior, 10,* 230–254.

Part Three

THE COMMUNICATORS

Much of our nonverbal behavior is characterized by change and movement during a conversation. But some of the nonverbal signals we bring to each interaction remain relatively unchanged during the course of the interaction. These are the individual features of each communicator—skin color, hairstyle, facial features, height, weight, clothes, and so forth. These features affect how others perceive us and how they communicate with us.

Chapter 6

THE EFFECTS OF PHYSICAL CHARACTERISTICS ON HUMAN COMMUNICATION

By a man's finger-nails, by his coat-sleeve, by his boots, by his trouser-knees, by the callosities of his forefinger and thumb, by his expression, by his shirt-cuffs—by each of these things a man's calling is plainly revealed. That all united should fail to enlighten the competent inquirer in any case is almost unconceivable.

—SHERLOCK HOLMES

Picture the following scene: Mr. and Mrs. American wake and prepare to start the day. Mrs. American takes off her nighttime bra and replaces it with a "slightly padded uplift" bra. After removing her chin strap, she further pulls herself together with her girdle. Then she begins to "put on her face." This may involve eye shadow, eyeliner, mascara, false eyelashes, lipstick, and blush. She has removed the hair under her arms and on her legs. She takes a curling iron to her hair. False fingernails, nail polish, and tinted contact lenses precede the deodorant, perfume, and numerous decisions concerning clothes. Mr. American shaves the hair on his face and puts a toupee on his head. He removes his false teeth from a solution used to whiten them, gargles with a breath sweetener, selects his aftershave lotion, puts on his elevator shoes, and begins making his clothing decisions. This hypothetical example represents an extreme, but without a doubt people do go to great lengths, even surgery, to make themselves attractive. Surgery may reconstruct a nose; change breast size; eliminate bags, wrinkles, or birthmarks; flatten ears; "tuck" thighs or tummies; vacuum fat from the body (liposuction) or insert fat (lipofilling); or even remove the upper layer of skin if it is perceived as too blotchy or rough (a "chemical peel"). Over a million Americans have cosmetic surgery each year, and between 10 and 15% of them are men. Thousands are adolescents. Why do men and women expend so much effort and invest so much money trying to improve their physical attractiveness? Does it influence human interaction?

OUR BODY: ITS GENERAL ATTRACTIVENESS

People care a great deal about each other's appearance. If a friend tells you about someone you have not met, you are likely to ask what the person looks like—you want a face to associate with the information you are receiving. Why? Novelists present intricately detailed descriptions of their characters' appearance. Publishers put photos of book authors on book jackets and in book ads. Why? Even the austere *Wall Street Journal,* which does not print news photos, includes line drawings of the faces of the main persons featured in its front-page stories. Why must readers *see* the person being discussed in an article on airline deregulation, stock fraud, or the manufacture of computer chips? Because people think they learn things from appearance. We take looks as indicators of a person's background, character, personality, talents, and likely future behavior.

Although it is not uncommon to hear people muse about inner beauty being the only thing that really counts, research suggests that outer beauty, or physical attractiveness, plays an influential role in determining responses for a broad range of interpersonal encounters. The evidence from our culture overwhelmingly supports the notion that *initially* we respond much more favorably to those we perceive as physically attractive than to those we see as unattractive. Numerous studies reveal that physically attractive persons exceed unattractive ones on a wide range of socially desirable evaluations, such as success, personality, popularity, sociability, sexuality, persuasiveness, and often happiness (Hatfield & Sprecher, 1986; Herman, Zanna, & Higgins, 1986). Even when positive personality traits are not attributed to physically attractive people, such people still seem to have a positive appeal (Timmerman & Hewitt, 1980). Our behavior toward unattractive people seems to be largely negative, however. For example, unattractive patients in hospitals are reportedly visited less, remain hospitalized longer, are judged less pleasant, and are less involved with others.

Judgments linked to a person's attractiveness begin early in life. One study found children as young as 2 to 3 months looking significantly longer at an attractive face (as judged by adults) than at an unattractive one. This tendency occurred regardless of whether the infant's mother was considered attractive or unattractive (Langlois et al., 1987; Slater et al., 1998). Cultural guidelines for physical attractiveness are well established by age 6 (Cavior & Lombardi, 1973; Dion & Berscheid, 1972). It is not surprising, then, to find peer popularity and physical attractiveness highly correlated in a number of elementary and secondary schools. The perceptions of attractiveness in a child's world are not limited to his or her peers. Teachers tend to see attractive children as more intelligent, more socially adept, higher in educational potential, and more positive in their attitudes toward school—even when the unattractive children had similar academic performance records. As children develop, they are exposed to these attitudes and evaluations made by teachers and parents. Teachers interact less (and less positively) with the so-called unattractive elementary school child. There are many occasions in a child's life when adults ask in a punitive tone of voice, "Who did this?!" If an unattractive child is available, the chances are stronger that he or she will be pointed out as the culprit. As unattractive children grow older, they probably are not discriminated against if their task performance is impressive; but as soon as performance declines, less attractive people receive more sanctions than unattractive ones. Antisocial behavior, such as throwing a brick through a window, was seen differently for attractive and unattractive children (Dion, 1972). The transgression was seen as an enduring trait of the unattractive child but only a temporary problem for the attractive one. The act was evaluated more negatively for the unattractive child, too. It does not surprise us, then, to find that juvenile delinquents were also rated as lower on attractiveness. In a study of 9- to 14-year-old boys, differences in perceived physical attractiveness were systematically related to social acceptance (Kleck, Richardson, & Ronald, 1974).

Although much evidence testifies to the existence of a norm that says, "what is beautiful is good," physical attractiveness also may be associated with undesirable traits, for example, vanity, egotism, snobbishness, unsympathetic attitudes toward oppressed people, and a greater likelihood to have marital problems (Dermer & Thiel, 1975). These negative attributions and the knowledge that beautiful people sometimes experience appearance-related problems suggest all is not perfect for these people. The research to date, however, still suggests it is far better to be attractive than unattractive. In fact, women who were average in looks were rated higher when viewed in a photograph in which they were posed alongside other women who were attractive. Subsequently, these average-looking women were viewed with other average-looking women and perceived as more attractive by those who had seen them with the attractive women. So it appears that women can boost their attractiveness ratings by being seen with more attractive women, and this linkage does not seem to decrease the attractive women's ratings (Geiselman, Haight, & Kimata, 1984).

Although there are some who would like us to believe that "everything is beautiful in its own way," there are many reasons to believe that things are often beautiful in the same way to many people. Within the United States, people are constantly exposed to standards for male and female beauty through the mass media, so it is not surprising to find a great deal of agreement on standards for beauty within this culture. But there is also evidence that there may be some inherent standards for physical attractiveness that cut across cultures. Studies involving people from Australia, Austria, China, England, India, Japan, Korea, and Scotland have found significant agreement on facial attractiveness (Etcoff, 1999; Langlois et al., 2000). Dion (2002) points out, however, that agreement is higher when the judges are students from other countries who are studying in the United States and when comparisons are made among different ethnocultural groups within a culture. Agreement is not as high with more geographically isolated groups. Even if there is a universal and biologically based standard for human beauty, cultures may impose certain variations. Nevertheless, participation in global activities like the Miss World contest may affect local standards. Miss World 2001 was Miss Nigeria, but in her home country she was far too skinny to be considered attractive, even though many young Nigerians reportedly favor the new look.

Common standards for physical attractiveness permeate our culture and are particularly evident in the areas discussed next.

DATING AND MARRIAGE

Physical attractiveness is probably more important to dating partners than it is to friends or married couples, although perceptions of physical attractiveness still may play an important role in such relationships. Physical attraction may be most important when dating involves short-term goals and more public, rather than private, activities. Certainly there

TABLE 6-1   Is Attractiveness a Crucial Quality in the Ideal Man
or Woman?

	MALE RESPONDENTS	FEMALE RESPONDENTS
In the ideal man	26%	29%
In the ideal woman	47	32

is no shortage of testimony from unmarried men and women that physical attractiveness also is a valued feature in mate selection. Based on the responses of 28,000 readers of *Psychology Today*, Table 6-1 also shows an emphasis on female attractiveness primarily by men, but generally supported by women. The percentages indicate the number of respondents who said attractiveness was "essential" or "very important" to the ideal man or woman (Tavris, 1977). Even though physical attractiveness may be valued by both men and women, it seems to have greater importance to men. Buss (1994, pp. 57–58) found this gender difference reflected in every one of the 37 different cultures he studied. Women may desire physical characteristics like strength or facial attractiveness, but often rank characteristics like ambition, social and economic status, and dependability/stability above physical features—particularly for mate selection. Nevertheless, more masculine faces with thicker eyebrows, smaller eyes, thinner lips, and squarer jaws (see Figure 6-1) may be perceived as markers of "good genes" and gain importance for women seeking a short-term relationship or during periods when conception is most likely (Little et al., 2002).

In recent years males have become increasingly concerned about their own physical appearance. Another survey of the *Psychology Today* readership indicated a heightened concern on the part of males regarding the impact of their physical appearance. Men, in fact, thought physical appearance was more influential in women's preferences for them than women openly indicated. One group of women did, however, place a high value on male physical appearance—those women who were attractive and financially independent (Pertschuk, Trisdorfer, & Allison, 1994).

We might suspect that actual dating patterns would reflect the preference for a physically attractive partner. This hypothesis was confirmed by a series of "computer dance" studies at the universities of Texas, Illinois, and Minnesota, in which physical attractiveness superseded a host of other variables in determining liking for one's partner and desire to date in the future. For example, Walster and her colleagues randomly paired 752 college students for a freshman dance (Walster et al., 1966). A great deal of information was gathered from each student, including self-reports about popularity, religious preference, height, race, expectations for the date, self-esteem, high school academic percentile rank, scholastic aptitude score, and personality test scores. In addition, each student was rated by several judges for attractiveness. Physical attractiveness was by far the most important determinant of how much a date would be liked by his or her partner. It appears that physical attractiveness was just as important an asset for a man as for a woman because it was a reliable predictor for both groups. Brislin and Lewis (1968) replicated this study with 58 unacquainted men and women and again found a strong correlation (.89) between "desire to date again" and "physical attractiveness." In addition, this study asked each person

FIGURE 6-1

Left: 50% feminized male composite; right; 50% masculinized male composite.

whether he or she would like to date anyone else at the dance. Of the 13 other people named, all had previously, and independently, been rated as very attractive.

In light of the many findings that seem to favor the physically attractive, note that there are times when the very physically attractive do not enjoy all the benefits. For example, women who had more variable attractiveness ratings (not uniformly judged as very attractive or unattractive) were the group most satisfied with their socializing in general with both men and women. They also had as many dates as the most attractive women. Some men did not seek dates with the extremely attractive women because they felt the chances of rejection were high and that the women may perceive their interest as limited to their physical attractiveness (Reis, Nezlek, & Wheeler, 1980; Reis et al., 1982). When less attractive women are in the company of attractive women, this also seems to increase the chances they will be seen as a good choice for a date.

So it seems that although there is a strong preference for people who are physically attractive, other forces enable those who fall short of the ideal in physical attractiveness to date, marry, and have satisfying relationships. One of these forces that exerts a powerful influence is called the "matching hypothesis." Since this hypothesis was presented, other studies have confirmed its validity, including a study of middle-aged married couples. Essentially, the *matching hypothesis* argues that each person may be attracted to only the best-looking partners, but reality sets in when actual dates are made. You may face an unwanted rejection if you select only the best-looking person available, so the tendency is to select a person similar to yourself in physical attractiveness (Hinsz, 1989). Or, alternatively, the least good-looking people must settle for each other after all the most good-looking people choose each other (Kalick & Hamilton, 1986). In fact, one study found evidence to suggest that the greater the match on physical attractiveness for romantic couples at low levels of intimacy, the greater the chances that this couple would develop a more intimate relationship (White, 1980). Even same-sex friends have been rated similarly on physical attractiveness (Cash & Derlega, 1978). Thus we seem to try to maximize the attractiveness of our choice while simultaneously minimizing the possibilities of rejection. If you have high self-esteem, you might seek out highly attractive partners in spite of a considerable gap between your looks and theirs (Berscheid & Walster, 1969). Self-esteem, in this case, will affect the perception of and possible reaction to rejection.

Sometimes we observe couples whose physical attractiveness seems to be "mis-matched." One study suggests that evaluations of males may change dramatically if they are viewed as "married" to someone very different in general attractiveness (Bar-Tal & Saxe, 1976). Unattractive men who were seen with attractive women were judged, among other things, as making more money, as being more successful in their occupations, and as being more intelligent than attractive men with attractive partners. Judges must have rea-soned that for an unattractive man to marry an attractive women, he must have to offset this imbalance by succeeding in other areas, such as making money. Unattractive women seen with attractive men, however, did not receive compensating attributions. This study raises the question of what "other resources" unattractive women are perceived to have to offset deficits in physical attractiveness.

The importance of physical attractiveness also varies with the goals of the relation-ship. Male college students said they were interested in different characteristics in a woman depending on whether it was a purely sexual relationship or one expected to be long term. A wide range of features associated with physical attractiveness were chosen for the sexual partner, but such features played a far less important role for long-term partners. Female students wanted virtually the same qualities in a long-term relationship as the men (honesty, fidelity, sensitivity, warmth, personality, kindness, character, tender-ness, patience, and gentleness), but, unlike the men, they also wanted more than mere physical attractiveness for the sexual relationship (Nevid, 1984).

ON THE JOB

Several studies suggest that physical attractiveness may be an advantage in obtaining a job, obtaining a more prestigious job, and being hired at a higher salary (Cash, Gillen, & Burns, 1977; Dipboye, Arvey, & Terpstra, 1977; Hamermesh & Biddle, 1994). Unless the job is deemed inappropriate or irrelevant to the applicant's level of attractiveness, the more attractive applicants are more likely to get the job, assuming all other qualifications are equal. Sometimes attractiveness provides an edge even when the less attractive com-petitor is more qualified for the position. Once a position has been obtained, less attrac-tive workers may be discriminated against on performance appraisals unless they maintain a consistently high level of productivity.

Even though both men and women can profit from their physical attractiveness in the workplace, it is not always beneficial. The higher the level of advancement, the more im-portant it is for one's physical attractiveness to be viewed as "task attractiveness" and not as "social attractiveness." Because physically attractive women are more likely than men to have their physical attractiveness viewed in a social context by men in corporate environments, physically attractive women may want to dress so their physical beauty is not the immediate focus of attention (Heilman & Saruwatari, 1979). And even though sexual harassment charges brought by unattractive women may garner less credibility with a jury (Seiter & Dunn, 2000), the attractiveness of both parties involved and the gender of jury members are factors which may work against advantages normally associated with physical attractiveness (Wuensch & Moore, 2004).

PERSUADING OTHERS

Getting others to agree with you or do something for you is often based on the extent to which you can demonstrate your knowledge or expertise as well as your ability to marshal effective supporting arguments (Maddux & Rogers, 1980). But, as several research projects show, being physically attractive also may help (Chaiken, 1986). This is especially true when the persuader seeks compliance on relatively low ego-involving topics; when the persuasion involves a relatively short, perhaps one-time, request; and when the effects of initial impressions are crucial to achieving influence. Although most of this research has been done with college students, the association of persuasive effectiveness with physical attractiveness has been documented in the behavior of 10- and 11-year-old children (Dion & Stein, 1978).

The following research on persuasiveness focused on the attractiveness of female communicators (Mills & Aronson, 1965). Actually, one woman was made up to look different under two conditions. In the unattractive condition, she was rated "repulsive" by independent observers; she wore loose-fitting clothing, her hair was messy, makeup was conspicuously absent, a trace of a mustache was etched on her upper lip, and her complexion was oily and "unwholesome looking." The experimenter suggested to a group of students that they would complete some questionnaires more quickly if a volunteer would read the questions aloud and indicate what they meant. The "volunteer" was either the attractive or unattractive woman. The attractive woman, especially when she stated her desire to influence the audience, was far more effective in modifying the opinions of college students toward issues dealing with higher education. Other studies also support the influence of attractiveness in persuasive situations (Horai, Naccari, & Faloultah, 1974; Widgery, 1974).

The preceding research focused primarily on female communicators, but attractiveness also seems to help male persuaders. Independent assessments of their verbal performance as well as their ability to obtain signatures on a campus petition showed attractive men and women outperforming those who were rated as unattractive. In another study, physically attractive men and women were judged to have better sales skills, treated more cordially, and elicited more willingness by people to contribute to a charitable organization (Reingen & Kernan, 1993). Is the persuasiveness of attractive communicators due solely to their looks, or do they actually have persuasive skills? An examination of previous tests showed attractive students to have higher grades, SAT scores, self-concepts, and communication skills (Chaiken, 1979). In summary, then, physically attractive persuaders (as compared with unattractive ones) *initially* elicit higher credibility and expectations for a skilled performance. Some evidence indicates that physically attractive people seem to have these skills. The advantages derived from one's physical attractiveness is probably strongest during the initial stages of a persuasive effort.

SELF-ESTEEM

Does physical attractiveness increase self-esteem? The answer seems to be yes, particularly for women. Women who perceive themselves as physically attractive seem also to perceive greater happiness, self-esteem, and less neuroticism than those who perceive themselves as unattractive (Mathes & Kahn, 1975). As noted earlier, physical attractiveness is playing a more important role in a man's life today, so men, too, probably think better of themselves when they feel more attractive. Women aged 18 to 60 who used cosmetics to improve their appearance also reported psychological benefits from doing so. Greater attractiveness for those between the ages of 40 and 60 was perceived as most beneficial for masking the aging process and improving one's physical and mental health (Graham & Jouhar, 1982). Training in the use of cosmetics for elderly women has reportedly had a positive effect on self-image, too.

Because physical attractiveness seems to have its greatest impact during the initial stages of a relationship, it is reasonable to assume that attractive men and women whose occupational demands or lifestyles necessitate meeting people in short-term encounters may obtain more self-esteem from their physical attractiveness than an equally attractive person who has a few long-term relationships. Although the self-esteem derived from appearance is important, it is only one factor that makes people feel good about themselves. Sometimes looking good is very important; sometimes it is not. But the knowledge that we can achieve attractiveness when we want to should make us feel much better than the person who isn't sure he or she can. Hatfield and Sprecher (1986) point out that there are people who are more likely to give us a boost in self-esteem by positively evaluating our looks, for example, people who have a great deal of self-esteem themselves, people who are sexually aroused, people who look like us, people who know us, and people who are not likely to compare our looks with media idols.

ANTISOCIAL BEHAVIOR

What happens when attractive and unattractive people are charged with committing a criminal act? Are judges and juries influenced by a person's looks? As expected, a number of studies show that attractive defendants are less likely to be judged guilty and, if convicted, more likely to receive a shorter sentence (Downs & Lyons, 1991; Efran, 1974; Kulka & Kessler, 1978; Weiten, 1980). The evidence for attractive defendants receiving lighter sentences is stronger than the evidence linking attractiveness to guilt or innocence. Although much of the research is based on the results of simulated juries and cases, Stewart (1980) had the attractiveness of 67 actual defendants rated. The less attractive defendants were charged with more serious crimes and given longer sentences, but attractiveness did not significantly affect judgments of conviction or acquittal.

Obviously, a defendant's attractiveness is rarely assessed in isolation in the courtroom, and other factors interact with attractiveness, for example, the extent to which the defendant expresses repentance, the degree of commitment jurors have toward impartiality, the extent to which jurors discuss the case, the perceived similarity of jurors and defendant, defendant verbalizations, and the nature of the crime being examined. For some crimes, attractiveness may be a liability for the defendant, as when it is used to commit a crime such as a swindle. For the crime of rape, the relative attractiveness of the victim and the defendant may influence the jury. Attractive rape victims may be perceived as more likely to have provoked the attack (Jacobson, 1981; Seligman, Brickman, & Koulack, 1977).

Once a person has been convicted and sent to prison, some feel that antisocial behavior can sometimes be reduced by radical changes in appearance. It is reported, for instance, that a 19-year-old woman with a face "so deformed that little kids ran away crying" threw a brick through a bank window and waited for police to arrest her. "I was willing to die to get a better face," she said. The judge ordered extensive plastic surgery ("Deformed Brick-Thrower," 1975). The same reasoning launched a massive plastic surgery program for reshaping noses, removing tattoos, tightening sagging skin, disguising ugly scars, reducing extensive ear protrusion, and removing other deformities of convicts at the Kentucky State Reformatory (Watson, 1975). Authorities at this institution reasoned that everyday social ridicule and potential discrimination in hiring may lead to a feeling of rejection and frustration that can manifest itself in antisocial behavior. Similar programs by doctors at the University of Virginia and Johns Hopkins have not shown significant changes in postinstitutionalized behavior for convicts with changes in their appearance. Obviously, appearance is only one factor that might contribute to antisocial behavior.

THE POWER OF PHYSICAL ATTRACTIVENESS: SOME IMPORTANT QUALIFICATIONS

As the preceding sections attest, no shortage of research supports the benefits and power of physical attractiveness. And even though we have tried to point out instances in the research when physical attractiveness was not an asset, there have not been many. As a result, if you do not see yourself as physically attractive or you wish it wasn't such an influential factor, you may be discouraged. The goal of this section is not to say that physical attractiveness isn't capable of having a powerful effect in human interaction, but to show how an understanding of various factors associated with much of the research can make the results seem less overwhelming.

THE EFFECTS OF INTERACTION

Methodological issues may provide some comfort to those who perceive themselves as less attractive. Although it is not true of all studies of physical attractiveness, most use frontal facial photographs that, prior to the study, are judged by a panel of "experts" to fall into the "beautiful" or "ugly" category. Hence, in most cases, we are not reporting results from living, moving, talking human beings in a particular environment, nor are we generally dealing with subtle differences in physical attractiveness that lie between the extremes of beautiful and ugly.

We know little about the socially skilled but homely person, and we know little about what constitutes communicative beauty. We do know that talk can significantly affect perceptions. When we talk to others we become a part of the object we are evaluating and this involvement has the potential to change the way we see the appearance of our partner. Berg (2004) found that even a six minute get-acquainted conversation can significantly affect perceptions of physical attractiveness of moderately attractive people—positively or negatively. College student photos were rated prior to a brief interaction and again later, after interacting with the person. This brief interaction significantly changed perceptions of physical attractiveness and for most of them (75%) the change was positive. An examination of the verbal and nonverbal behavior indicated a variety of behaviors which may have been influential change agents—for example, giving agreement and support, showing interest in the other person, sharing information, and showing a sense of humor.

Many romantic partners tell stories about how their initial perception of their partner's physical attractiveness was not particularly high when compared with their ideal. But they report that continued positive interaction changed this perception. A man who had been married for 20 years told this story about his courtship:

> Initially, I saw her as pretty average in physical attractiveness. I remember telling a friend soon after I met her that she was kind of chunky. But after we dated and I fully appreciated how well we related to each other, I saw her as much more physically attractive. I actually saw her differently. Now I can't see her as any less physically attractive.

We also know that people who want to divorce each other find it hard to see their partner as physically attractive in the face of so much negative verbal behavior. Exactly how verbal behavior affects our perceptions of physical attractiveness is not clear at this time, but there are indications that it plays an important role in how we see another person's beauty (Albada, Knapp, & Theune, 2002).

THE EFFECTS OF OTHER FACTORS

Judgments of one's appearance interact with other factors in everyday life. Kniffin & Wilson (2004) have demonstrated that nonphysical traits such as liking, respect, familiarity, and contribution to shared goals can be powerful factors that influence our judgments of physical attractiveness. In addition, one's appearance may be relative to the context in which it is judged. For example, we may perceive a popular singer on stage or television as sexy, but the same person in our living room may seem much less glamorous. Similarly, a person who looks good in an isolated rural setting may not look as good in a city environment where he or she is compared with a far greater variety of potential partners.

Some researchers wanted to find out if the song about how "all the girls get prettier at closing time" had any validity to it. Pennebaker et al. (1979) obtained information about the general attractiveness of bar patrons at several different bars at different times leading up to closing time. True to the lyrics of the song, both men and women perceived a significant increase in the attractiveness of others as closing time drew near. Although the gradually dwindling pool of potential partners may have had some effect, research also shows that even moderate alcohol consumption tends to increase the ratings of physical attractiveness of the opposite sex (Jones et al., 2003).

Men who rated the attractiveness of middle-aged women tended to give lower ratings when they were in the presence of other men and their rating was made public than they did when in the company of women or when their ratings were kept private (Berman,

O'Nan, & Floyd, 1981). Attraction ratings also may vary as a function of the rater's gender. Often the highest evaluations of attractiveness come from the opposite sex. These are only a few of many factors that can affect the way someone perceives physical attractiveness.

CHANGING STANDARDS OVER TIME

Judgments of attractiveness may change over the course of a lifetime. Ratings of facial attractiveness (not body) appear to be somewhat stable from about ages 16 to 50, but the overall ratings of attractiveness for both men and women tend to decline as we reach middle and old age. The decline is more severe for women.

In one study of the effects of time on attractiveness, the high school pictures of 1,300 males and females were rated for attractiveness. The lives of these people were examined 15 years later. Attractive females in high school had husbands with more education and higher salaries, but their own occupational status and income were not significantly different from their less attractive counterparts. The least attractive males in high school had more prestigious occupations and more education, and they married women with more education than the men who were judged attractive in high school. Income levels did not differ. The authors speculate that the social ostracism of the less attractive men in high school may have turned their attention to educational achievements that paid off later in life (Udry & Eckland, 1984). Aging also may reveal changes associated with self-esteem and attractiveness. Middle-aged women who had been identified as attractive college students seemed to be less happy, less satisfied with their lives, and less well adjusted than their plainer counterparts (Berscheid & Walster, 1974, pp. 200–201).

Because appearance can be changed, people judged unattractive are not necessarily doomed to a long list of pitfalls or problems. Changes in makeup and hairstyle have been shown to increase ratings of general attractiveness as well as ratings of desired personality characteristics (Graham & Jouhar, 1981). Cosmetics have even been used to aid recovery and adjustment of people recuperating from illnesses.

Now that we have examined the global concept of attractiveness, we can ask, What *specific* aspects of another's appearance do we respond to? Does it make any difference how we perceive our own body and appearance? We focus on the answers to these questions in the remainder of this chapter.

OUR BODY: ITS SPECIFIC FEATURES

THE FACE

Even though the face has long been the specific body feature most commonly examined in studies of physical attractiveness, a basic question remained unanswered: What is facial beauty? Most researchers believed this question could not be answered by measuring facial features and depended instead on people's judgments of general attractiveness. The research by Langlois and Roggman (1990), however, not only pointed the way toward a measure of facial attractiveness but also made a surprising discovery. Contrary to popular belief, Langlois and Roggman found that physically attractive faces approximate the mathematical average of all faces in a particular population. For example, this research would predict that a physically attractive man or woman in a school is one who comes closest to the school average for male or female facial features.

Langlois and Roggman took photographs of 96 college males and 96 college females. These photos were scanned by a video lens connected to a computer that converted each picture into a matrix of tiny digital units with numerical values. The authors divided the male and female faces into 3 subsets of 32 faces each. From each subset, the computer randomly chose 2 faces and mathematically averaged their digitized values. It then transformed this information into a composite face of the 2 individuals. Composite faces then were generated for 4, 8, 16, and 32 members of each set. Ratings by students showed that composite faces were more attractive than virtually any of the individual faces, and the most attractive faces were composites of 16 and 32 faces (see Figure 6-2). Rhodes et al. (2002) found that the averaged faces of persons within their own culture were also appealing to Chinese and Japanese students.

Langlois and her colleagues acknowledge that in some cases people are perceived as attractive by large numbers of people even though their features obviously are not the population average. In fact, the most attractive faces are not likely to be average at all. The most attractive faces tend to emphasize those features associated with physically attractive faces. A woman, for example, would have a higher than average forehead, fuller than average lips, shorter than average jaw, and a smaller than average chin and nose. Other female facial features often associated with physical attractiveness are clear skin, high cheekbones, lustrous hair, and big eyes. A woman of any age who has small eyes, a relatively large nose, and wide thin lips will look older, more masculine, and be seen as less attractive. Powerful jaws and facial hair, although indicators of male facial attractiveness, may need large eyes and a wide smile to avoid being seen as too masculine. This means that extremes of masculinity may not be a good predictor of a dependable and loving relationship partner (Cunningham, Barbee, & Pike, 1990). One study found that during the time of the month when women were more likely to conceive, they were more receptive to men with more rugged, masculine features. During the other 3 weeks of the month, including the menstrual period, women chose faces that were smoother and more feminine (Penton-Voak et al., 1999).

Another promising approach for identifying facial attractiveness is based on the principle of symmetry (Grammer & Thornhill, 1994). Photographs of male and female students are precisely measured at numerous points to determine whether features on one side of the face are equidistant to a midpoint as the same features on the other side of the face. For example, to what extent does the midpoint between the corners of your mouth match up to the midpoint between the corners of your eyes? On perfectly symmetrical faces, all the midpoints meet and roughly form a vertical line. Movie actor Denzel Washington has a very symmetrical face, whereas singer Lyle Lovett does not. Some asymmetry is desirable; otherwise, the face may not look real. Horizontal symmetry is also calculated. The most symmetrical faces were also those chosen as the most attractive. The researchers believe these results are consistent with findings that show symmetry is also a powerful attractant for other animal and insect species. Symmetry, like averageness, is likely to garner high ratings of facial attractiveness, but neither is a guarantee of the most attractive faces (Cunningham, Barbee, & Philhower, 2002).

FIGURE 6-2

Progression of mathematically averaged faces from 2 faces to 32 faces.

2-face composite

4-face composite

8-face composite

16-face composite

32-face composite

Because the face is so central in judgments of attractiveness, it is no surprise that it is the source of stereotyping. People long have believed that the face reveals important information about character and personality. The most famous promoter of the idea that facial features indicate personality was J. C. Lavater, the Swiss physiognomist born in 1741. Lavater's book (1783) promoting his so-called science was extremely popular, published in over a dozen editions in many languages. Although today we look skeptically on the idea that brows, nose, or shape of mouth reveal whether someone is mean, smart, or benevolent, Lavater was a sincere believer who saw his work as scientific.

We should credit Lavater with his attempts to be scientific. However, Lavater confused facial *stereotypes* with *actual* associations between features and behavior; he chronicled what he (and others, no doubt) believed were these associations, without recognizing the need to test the validity of this initial premise. Apparently his many readers, as well as readers of similar books published in the next century, also failed to make this distinction. In the 1970s, such books were still being written: *Face Reading* by Timothy T. Mar was published by a major U.S. paperback company in 1974. Among the innumerable claims in this book are these:

- A dark mole just above the eyebrows is an obstacle to official promotion and a sign of repeated career changing.
- Three vertical lines below the eyes predict an unhappy marriage ending in divorce or death.
- Full, firm, large ears indicate nobility and prosperity while ears with the middle overgrown signify an inability to save money.

We do not report these claims simply to amuse you. Students of human behavior find two serious lessons here. First, people's willingness over the centuries to believe in physiognomy tells us something important about human nature: People latch on to such bogus principles because they help reduce uncertainty in their own minds and provide a sense of control and understanding in daily life. And, once the stereotype is planted in the mind, every confirmation is remembered and serves to strengthen the stereotype ("That man who held me up had thick bushy eyebrows just like a criminal!"), and every disconfirmation (the handsome serial killer Ted Bundy) is conveniently forgotten.

The other lesson is that, in spite of their falseness, facial stereotypes surely influence the behavior of the stereotype holder. If people believe a drooping nose is a sign of treachery, then an unfortunate neighbor with such a nose is at a considerable disadvantage in interpersonal relations. Moreover, the way people are treated can bring about self-fulfilling prophecies, so that facial stereotypes can, conceivably, have potent effects on the subsequent behavior of the target.

Behavioral scientists have long been interested in facial stereotypes and their possible effects on behavior. Laser and Mathie (1982), for example, engaged an artist to prepare nine charcoal drawings of a male face, varying thickness of the eyebrows and lips and the shape of the face. Subjects rated these faces with adjectives. The features had marked effects on these ratings: The face with thick eyebrows was seen as less warm, angrier, sterner, less cheerful, and less at ease than those with thin or normal brows; thicker lips connoted warmth and less tension than thinner lips; and narrow faces were seen as more tense and suspicious than the others.

McArthur and her colleagues have gone beyond simply describing facial stereotypes to develop a theory for why they exist. Their work focuses on facial features associated with age and the kinds of interpretations people make of faces that have more or less "youthful" features; in particular, they focus on the adult with "baby-faced" features such as large forehead, short chin, and big eyes. McArthur and Baron (1983) proposed that people correctly differentiate traits which accompany younger age but then incorrectly ascribe these traits (overgeneralize them) to people with younger-looking faces, even though they are not necessarily young. McArthur and her colleagues found, in support of this, that people rated babyish adult faces as weaker, more submissive, and more intellectually naive than mature-looking faces (Berry & McArthur, 1986).

These investigators also simulated a courtroom trial in which a defendant was charged with an offense that was marked either by negligence or by deliberate deception; the defendant's appearance was manipulated to be either baby faced or mature faced. Subjects, acting as jurors, more often convicted the baby-faced man for crimes of negligence and the mature-faced man for intentional crimes. This result was predicted based on the earlier finding that adults with babyish features were perceived as more naive and more honest.

Facial babyishness has also been found to affect judgments of attractiveness (Berry, 1991). Facially attractive people are rated higher on characteristics such as honesty, warmth, and sincerity when facial babyishness is high—and lower on those same traits when facial babyishness is low. Because all the faces were perceived as attractive, this suggests the possibility of different types of facial attractiveness.

So it seems that a number of social outcomes are consistent with the principle that baby-faced people are more likely to acquire influence, jobs, and judicial convictions when the influence strategies, job descriptions, or alleged crimes fit the characteristics they are expected to have (Zebrowitz, 1997).

In sum, there is no doubt that the way one's face is structured and contoured creates strong impressions on others. Facial endowment may harm or benefit a person, depending on the stereotypes associated with the features. Future research may be able to tell us to what extent actual personality and ways of expressing ourselves will override initial impressions based on facial stereotype; we suspect such initial impressions are easily overturned by behavioral evidence. As one example, baby-faced soldiers are not expected to be very brave. As a consequence, when mature-faced and baby-faced soldiers exhibit valor, the baby-faced soldier is more likely to be decorated.

BODY SHAPE

To add a personal dimension to some of the theory and research in this section, a short Self-Description Test follows. By taking this test, you can gather some data on yourself, which can be compared with that of others who have taken it.

Instructions: Fill in each blank with a word from the suggested list following each statement. For each blank, 3 in each statement, you may select any word from the list of 12 immediately below. An exact word to fit you may not be in the list, but select the words that seem to fit *most closely* the way you are.

1. I feel most of the time _____, _____, and _____.

calm	relaxed	complacent
anxious	confident	reticent
cheerful	tense	energetic
contented	impetuous	self-conscious

2. When I study or work, I seem to be ——————, ——————, and ——————.

efficient	sluggish	precise
enthusiastic	competitive	determined
reflective	leisurely	thoughtful
placid	meticulous	cooperative

3. Socially, I am ——————, ——————, and ——————.

outgoing	considerate	argumentative
affable	awkward	shy
tolerant	affected	talkative
gentle-tempered	soft-tempered	hot-tempered

4. I am rather ——————, ——————, and ——————.

active	forgiving	sympathetic
warm	courageous	serious
domineering	suspicious	soft-hearted
introspective	cool	enterprising

5. Other people consider me rather ——————, ——————, and ——————.

generous	optimistic	sensitive
adventurous	affectionate	kind
withdrawn	reckless	cautious
dominant	detached	dependent

6. Underline *one* word out of the three in each of the following lines that most closely describes the way you are:
   (a) assertive, relaxed, tense
   (b) hot-tempered, cool, warm
   (c) withdrawn, sociable, active
   (d) confident, tactful, kind
   (e) dependent, dominant, detached
   (f) enterprising, affable, anxious

This test has been given to numerous individuals in studies on the relationship between certain personality and temperament characteristics and certain body types or builds. Generally, these studies are concerned with a person's physical similarity to three extreme varieties of human physique, shown in Figure 6-3.

Because most people do not fit these extremes exactly, a system has been developed for specifying body type based on the assumption that they may have some features of all three types. Let's assume a person's physical characteristics are rated on a scale from 1 to 7, with 7 representing the highest correspondence with one of the three body types. The first number refers to the degree of *endomorphy*, the second to the degree of *mesomorphy*, and the third to the degree of *ectomorphy*. A grossly fat person, then, would be 7/1/1; a broad shouldered, athletic person would be 1/7/1; and a very skinny person would be a 1/1/7. Reportedly, Jackie Gleason was roughly 6/4/1, Muhammad Ali 2/7/1 (in his prime), and Abraham Lincoln 1/5/6.

Now look at the test you took earlier. The test has shown a high correspondence between self-reported temperament characteristics and measures of physique (Cortes & Gotti, 1965). To calculate your score on the Self-Description Test, simply add the number

FIGURE 6-3

(a) The endomorph: soft, round, fat. (b) The mesomorph: bony, muscular, athletic. (c) The ectomorph: tall, thin, fragile.

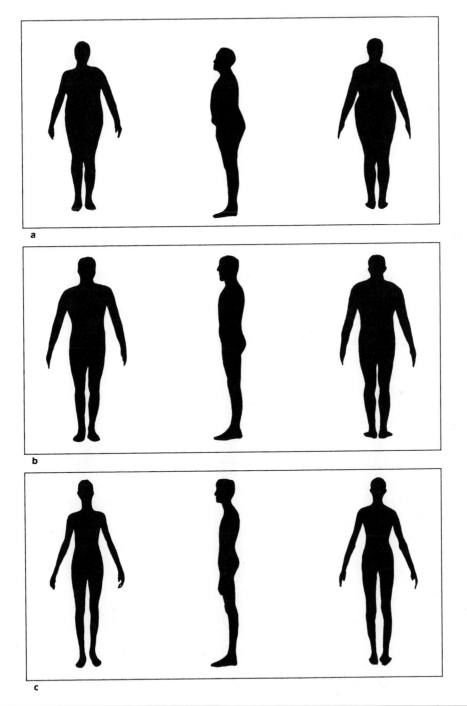

TABLE 6-2   **Three Physique Categories and Temperament Stereotypes**

ENDOMORPHIC	MESOMORPHIC	ECTOMORPHIC
dependent	dominant	detached
calm	cheerful	tense
relaxed	confident	anxious
complacent	energetic	reticent
contented	impetuous	self-conscious
sluggish	efficient	meticulous
placid	enthusiastic	reflective
leisurely	competitive	precise
cooperative	determined	thoughtful
affable	outgoing	considerate
tolerant	argumentative	shy
affected	talkative	awkward
warm	active	cool
forgiving	domineering	suspicious
sympathetic	courageous	introspective
soft-hearted	enterprising	serious
generous	adventurous	cautious
affectionate	reckless	tactful
kind	assertive	sensitive
sociable	optimistic	withdrawn
soft-tempered	hot-tempered	gentle-tempered

of adjectives you chose from each of the endomorph, mesomorph, and ectomorph categories listed in Table 6-2. If you chose 6 adjectives from the endomorph list, 12 from the mesomorph, and 3 from the ectomorph, your temperament score would be 6/12/3. If we assume a high correlation with body features, we would assume you are primarily mesomorphic with a leaning toward endomorphism. The first author of this text was 5/11/5 in 1978, 8/10/3 in 1982, 8/9/4 in 1988, 10/7/4 in 1996, 8/10/3 in 2001, and 6/12/3 in 2004. Although this test is able to make some reasonably accurate predictions about physique for some people, it is, like all predictive tests, based on probabilities and hence less accurate for others.

We should not assume from this work that the body causes temperament traits. The high correspondence between certain temperament traits and body builds may be due to life experiences, environmental factors, self-concept, and a host of other variables, including other people's expectations. If there are clearly defined and generally accepted physique–temperament stereotypes, we can reason that they will have much to do with the way people are perceived and responded to by others and with the personality traits expected of people by others. Wells and Siegel (1961) uncovered some data supporting the existence of such stereotypes. One hundred twenty adult subjects were shown silhouette drawings of the endomorph, ectomorph, and mesomorph and asked to rate them on a set of 24 bipolar adjective scales such as lazy/energetic, fat/thin, intelligent/unintelligent, dependent/self-reliant, and so forth. The investigators deliberately chose people who had not attended college, assuming these people would not be contaminated with information from previous studies that might structure their answers. Their results show the following:

1. The *endomorph* was rated fatter, older, shorter (silhouettes were the same height), more old-fashioned, less strong physically, less good looking, more talkative, more warmhearted and sympathetic, more good natured and agreeable, more dependent on others, and more trusting of others.
2. The *mesomorph* was rated stronger, more masculine, better looking, more adventurous, younger, taller, more mature in behavior, and more self-reliant.
3. The *ectomorph* was rated thinner, younger, more ambitious, taller, more suspicious of others, more tense and nervous, less masculine, more stubborn and inclined to be difficult, more pessimistic, and quieter.

Clearly, the evidence shows we do associate certain personality and temperament traits with certain body builds. These expectations may or may not be accurate, but they do exist; they are a part of the psychological mortar in interpersonal communication. We must recognize these stereotypes as potential stimuli for communication responses so we can deal with them effectively.

As early as kindergarten, children seem to prefer the more muscular mesomorphs to either the thin or fat body types (Johnson & Staffieri, 1971; Lerner & Gellert, 1969; Lerner & Korn, 1972; Lerner & Schroeder, 1971; Staffieri, 1972). Youngsters seem to have a particular aversion to the fat physiques. Older children who select descriptive adjectives for these body types tend to see the mesomorph as "all things good," with ectomorphs and endomorphs attracting a host of unfavorable descriptors. In fact, 10- and 11-year-olds seemed to consider body build as a more important characteristic in judging physical appearance than deformities, disfigurements, and handicaps (Richardson et al., 1961). The psychological aversion to chubby figures results in children maintaining a greater physical distance from them (Lerner, Karabenick, & Meisels, 1975; Lerner, Venning, & Knapp, 1975). In turn, we find that chubby children often tend to have a negative perception of their own bodies, which may later generalize to a negative self-image (Walker, 1963). Even the elderly rate the endomorph as a less desirable communication partner—both socially as well as for working on tasks together (Portnoy, 1993).

Negative reactions to overweight individuals are frequently reported. Such individuals report being discriminated against when seeking to obtain life insurance, adopt children, get jobs, and gain entrance to college (Channing & Mayer, 1966). Although only a small amount of empirical evidence supports the bases of these claims (DeJong & Kleck, 1986), it is safe to say that being excessively overweight in our culture is often a handicap. Researchers who followed 10,000 people between the ages of 16 and 24 for 7 years found obesity meant you were less likely to marry, more likely to have a lower income, and more likely to receive less schooling (Gortmaker et al., 1993). People often believe that the inability to lose weight reflects a character flaw. During the past three decades, the cultural ideal for U.S. women has tended toward thinness. As a result, women have tended to be more conscious of their weight than have men. In recent years, though, there seem to be more media portrayals (and a generally greater acceptance) of female bodies that are not extremely slender. And men are increasingly concerned about their weight. Another trend in recent years has been toward the development of healthy bodies—"eating right," exercising, and developing muscle strength. These body standards apply to both men and women and will probably constitute some of the features comprising the next cultural standard for the ideal body shape.

Earlier we noted that the mesomorph physique was often rated as "better looking" or more physically attractive. Women say their favorite male physique has a medium-wide upper trunk, a medium-thin lower trunk, and thin legs (a "V" look). The most disliked physique has either a thin upper trunk or a wide lower trunk (pear-shaped look). Women who see themselves as traditionally feminine and conservative in their lifestyle seem to favor "muscle men"; more "liberated" women liked thinner, more linear bodies; big women tend to go for big men. The best clue to a woman's favorite male physique, however, is the type of physique belonging to the man who is "most important to her at the present time" (Beck, Ward-Hull, & McLear, 1976; Lavrakas, 1975; Pertschuk, Trisdorfer, & Allison, 1994; Wiggins & Wiggins, 1969). The fact that women tend to like the physique of the man who is currently most important to them suggests (1) romantic partners are selected for many reasons besides physical attractiveness; and (2) people can favor an ideal body type but still be happy with a person who does not match that ideal.

Another feature of body shape that seems to play an important role in judgments of a woman's physical attractiveness is the *waist–hip ratio* (Singh, 1993, 1995; Streeter & McBurney, 2003). A waist–hip ratio of .70 means the waist is 70% the size of the hips, which is considered the ideal. Singh says early Greek paintings, ancient Indian sculptures, Miss America winners, and *Playboy* centerfolds all show waist–hip ratios very close to .70. He has surveyed people of many age groups, cultures, and ethnic groups, and their preferences are for the .70 waist–hip ratio. Others argue from their research that the preferred waist–hip ratio will increase as body size (weight) increases even though "small and medium" waists and hips are preferred regardless of weight (Tassinary & Hansen, 1998; Forestell, Humphrey, & Stewart, 2004). There is no doubt that the waist–hip ratio is one of several features that affect perceptions of female attractiveness, but one study found that the perceived age of a woman's face had a greater overall impact on judgments of physical attractiveness than the waist–hip ratio (Furnham, Disha, & McClelland, 2004). What about men? Singh's research indicates that the ideal waist–hip ratio for men is between .80 and .95.

HEIGHT

Height also influences interpersonal responses. People seem to know height can be important to their social and work lives. Pediatricians report that parents are often concerned their child is not as tall as he or she should be at a certain age. Children themselves are asked to focus on height when their teachers tell them to line up by height. Adults seem to overestimate their height. Advertisements for romantic partners often give height as one critical piece of information (Cameron, Oskamp, & Sparks, 1978; Harrison & Saeed, 1977). In some areas of the country, police officers and firefighters are required to meet minimum height requirements. Some applicants, according to newspaper accounts, have actually bludgeoned their heads in the hope that the swelling would make up the difference between their height and the required height!

Height derives its importance from a widespread belief that major deviations from median heights (about 5 feet, 4 inches for women and 5 feet, 9 inches for men) will incur negative judgments from others. Although it is possible to be "too tall," most negative judgments are thought to be associated with shortness. As Stabler and his colleagues (1980) noted, "There is a pervasive social attitude which associates tallness with positive characteristics and assigns negative attributes to shortness." Is there any truth to this? The anecdotal evidence is far more plentiful than the empirical research. In addition, most of the research focuses on men only (Roberts & Herman, 1986). Still, it seems we tend to favor tallness in our culture. The research examines three dominant perceptions associated with height: status, attractiveness, and competence.

Height and Status

Height has long been a metaphor for power and prestige. The taller of the two U.S. presidential candidates has usually won since 1900, with Jimmy Carter and George W. Bush notable exceptions. When Carter debated President Ford, his campaign advisers did not want him to be seen standing next to the 6-foot, 1-inch president. Consequently, they asked that the debates be conducted from a sitting position. Ford's advisers refused. The compromise involved placing the lecterns far apart. Further testimony to the stigma associated with shorter people and power is that behavior labeled "competitive" for a taller man is labeled a "Napoleonic complex" for a shorter one. If status and power inhere in taller people, are they also more persuasive? One study indicates they are not (Baker & Redding, 1962). Photographs were taken of the same person (a male) from two different angles: one designed to make him look short, one to make him look tall. These pictures, plus a tape-recorded persuasive speech, were the stimuli for various student groups. Attitude measures indicated no statistically significant difference between the "tall" and "short" speakers.

It is more likely that tallness interacts with other factors, such as general body size, girth, and facial features. In your own experience, you probably can recall some tall individuals who seemed almost frighteningly "overpowering," whereas others of the same height did not have this quality. Science has not yet established a clear-cut relationship between a person's actual height and his or her social status. Nevertheless, the connection is often made when, without any other information, people are asked to make a judgment about height and status. We know of a woman who earned her doctoral degree under a famous psychologist and believed, while she was his student, that he was a tall, imposing figure. Later, she was genuinely surprised to realize he was actually a short man! He had merely *seemed* tall to her.

Height and Attractiveness

Taller men are frequently perceived as more attractive than shorter men. The ideal male lover is not described as "short, dark, and handsome." Male romantic leads in movies are usually either tall or made to look tall by camera angles. Numerous sources attest to the important role of height in perceptions of attractiveness, but obviously we do not make judgments of another's attractiveness based on height alone. Therefore, we can conclude that height is one important feature involved in judgments of attractiveness, but we cannot say that tallness is always associated with the highest judgments of attractiveness. We do know that moviegoers are often taken aback when they learn that a male icon of physical attractiveness is much shorter than he is portrayed in his movies.

Height and Competence

Several reports indicate tall males are perceived as more competent on the job and rewarded with higher salaries. For example, an analysis of studies in this area led Judge and Cable (2004) to conclude that taller people have higher self-esteem, are more likely to be in leadership positions, make more money, and get better performance evaluations at work than shorter people. This was more likely to be the case with men, but there was a strong relationship to women as well. In another study, actual performance records showed few differences between shorter and taller police officers, but their supervisors felt shorter police officers were more aggressive law enforcers and more likely to be a source of discontent in the police department (Lester & Sheehan, 1980). Another study indicated that men who were selected to advance in corporate training programs were significantly taller than average (Farb, 1978). Further evidence of discrimination against the short man comes from a study of 140 sales recruiters who were asked to choose between two men just by reading their applications for employment. The applications were exactly the same except that one listed a height of 6 feet, 1 inch and the other 5 feet, 5 inches. Only 1% favored the shorter man (Kurtz, 1969).

BODY IMAGE

So far we have discussed our perceptions of others. An equally important dimension of interpersonal communication is what we think of ourselves—our self-image. The self-image is the root system from which our overt communication behavior grows. Our overt communication behavior is an extension of the accumulated experiences that have made up our understanding of self. In short, what you are, or think you are, organizes what you say and do. An important part of your self-image is body image, perhaps the first part formed in young children. Adult males seem to be most satisfied with their bodies when they are somewhat larger than normal; females are most satisfied when their bodies are smaller than normal but when their busts are larger than average. In an effort to test the belief that larger bust sizes were more desirable to others, photographs were taken of three women who artificially altered their bust size. The smallest (about 34 inches) received the highest ratings on competence, ambition, intelligence, morality, and modesty (Kleinke & Staneski, 1980). Sex researchers have frequently noted emotional problems in males stemming from a perceived incongruence between their genital size and the supposed masculine ideal perpetuated by our literary and folklore heritage. More than 71% of the women in one survey agreed or strongly agreed that "men seem too concerned with the size and shape of their genitals" (Pertschuk, Trisdorfer, & Allison, 1994).

As we develop, we learn the cultural ideal of what the body should be like. This results in varying degrees of satisfaction with the body, particularly during adolescence. Wolf (1991) and others believe the standards of beauty promulgated in the mass media are oppressive and create an undesirable yearning for often unreasonable goals. A national survey of several thousand adults indicated that between 1972 and 1986 both men and women's dissatisfaction with their bodies rose sharply. Weight was a major factor of dissatisfaction for both men and women (Cash, Winstead, & Janda, 1986). Given the fact that about 30% (roughly 59 million people) of the U.S. population were considered obese in 2000, dissatisfaction with weight is probably still a concern (Flegal et al., 2002). A number of studies show, however, that we are not always very accurate in our perceptions of our own body size and weight. In some cases, constant exposure to ideal body images on television contribute to misperceptions of body shape and size (Myers & Biocca, 1992; Bissell & Zhou, 2004). In addition to misjudgments of our own body size and weight, we may also misjudge the body type that is most appealing to the opposite sex. Women seem to think men prefer a thinner person than men actually report; men seem to think women want a heavier man than women actually report. Men thought that having an attractive face and body build was more important to women than women said it was (Fallon & Rozin, 1985; Pertschuk, Trisdorfer, & Allison, 1994).

BODY COLOR

We do make some judgments about temporary color changes that show up on people's bodies. On light-skinned people, for example, a pale color may indicate a person is ill; a rosy flush may indicate embarrassment; or a red neck can appear with anger. But in many respects, permanent skin colors have been the most potent body stimulus for determining interpersonal responses in our culture. There is no need to review the abuses heaped on black persons in America on the basis of skin color alone. The words of a white man who changed his skin pigmentation and experienced the dramatic and unforgettable life of a black man in America is sufficient reminder:

> When all the talk, all the propaganda has been cut away, the criterion is nothing but the color of skin. My experience proved that. They judged me by no other quality. My skin was dark. That was sufficient reason for them to deny me those rights and freedoms without which life loses its significance and becomes a matter of little more than animal survival.
>
> I searched for some other answer and found none. I had spent a day without food and water and for no other reason than that my skin was black. I was sitting on a tub in the swamp for no other reason. (Griffin, 1960, pp. 121–122)

As U.S. demographics change, the variety of skin colors manifested by the people in our work and leisure activities will continue to increase, and sharp distinctions among peoples' skin colors will become increasingly difficult to make. Still, there will always be those who want a simple method of classifying their social world, and skin color is easily observed. We can only hope that the number of people who believe skin color is an accurate gauge for identifying friend and foe will continue to decrease.

The standards for beauty are usually set by the economically dominant group within a society. People in less dominant groups are judged by the standards of the dominant group and, seeing the reward value, may try to mimic the standards of the dominant group. The standards in the United States have traditionally been those associated with the features of the people whose ancestors immigrated here from northern and western Europe. Among other features, they had "white" skin. There is nothing inherently more attractive about "white" skin or the features shared by these Americans who had a northern and/or western European heritage. In fact, pale skin is more likely to have freckles and more prone to skin cancer and wrinkles earlier than the skin of many Asians and Africans. In time, the dominant group will change and no doubt some of the standards for physical attractiveness will change with it.

BODY SMELL

It is obvious that vision and hearing are the most important sensors for social situations in Western societies, but the sense of smell also may influence responses. The scientific study of the human olfactory system is in its infancy, but we know other animals obtain a great deal of information from their sense of smell: the presence of an enemy, territorial markers, finding members of the same species or herd, sexual stimulation, and emotional states. Dogs are well known for their ability to sense fear, hate, or friendship in human beings and to track them by only the scent from clothing. The difficulty dogs seem to have in distinguishing between the smells of identical twins prompted Davis (1971) to suggest that we each have an "olfactory signature."

Americans do not seem to rely consciously on their sense of smell for much interpersonal information unless perspiration odor, breath, or some other smell is unusually strong or inappropriate to the situation. It is believed that all of us could enhance our olfactory sensitivity if we learned the words needed to differentiate among various odors. We have a rather limited vocabulary for discussing subtle differences in smells, which, in turn, may hinder their identification. If it is true that we tend to neglect our olfactory skills, it seems ironic that we spend so much time and money on artificial scents. Each year American men and women spend millions of dollars on deodorant containers and soaps, mouthwashes, breath mints, perfumes, aftershave lotions, and other products used to add to or cover up natural body scents. Publicly, the so-called natural scent seems to have a low priority in our cultural development, but we are not at all reluctant to buy a commercial product that will purportedly make us smell "*natural* and sexy."

Artificial scents are not always designed for pleasant reactions. During World War II, scientists developed a noxious-smelling compound they called "Who Me?" This product was put into collapsible plastic tubes and distributed to Chinese children in cities occupied by the Japanese. The children squirted "Who Me?" onto the trouser seats of Japanese officers. The foul-smelling result was more than just a temporary irritant—it was nearly impossible to wash out (Russell, 1981). Odors which are so foul smelling that they are capable of emptying buildings and even incapacitating people may have contemporary applications in law enforcement and the military. The Monell Chemical Senses Center in Philadelphia is reportedly working on just such a product.

What is the role of human odors in daily interaction? Our reactions may be consciously or unconsciously processed, but the message can be quite strong. During heightened emotional arousal, chemical-olfactory signals may even assume an importance that rivals the normally dominant visual/auditory channels. Human odors are primarily emitted through glands found in the anal/genital region and secretory glands in the face, hands, feet, and sometimes across the chest. Odors collect in the mouth and regions of the body with hair. Several experiments attest to the fact that people are usually able to identify the odors of specific other human beings. These "dirty T-shirt" studies instructed people to wear a cotton T-shirt for periods ranging from 1 day to 1 week and to avoid using any perfumes and deodorants. Seventy-five percent of the people tested were able to sniff out their own T-shirt and those of a male and female stranger; 50% of the spouses were able to identify their mate's T-shirt. Parents can identify their children (some only 2 hours old) with accuracy rates sometimes over 90%; and children are generally able to identify their siblings (Lord & Kasprzak, 1989; Porter, Cernoch, & Balogh, 1985; Porter, Cernoch, & McLaughlin, 1983; Porter & Moore, 1981; Russell, 1976). By the age of 6 weeks, infants respond to the odor on a breast pad from their mother and not from a stranger. One study even found people able to identify gender from hand odors. An important qualification is in order: Although we do seem to be able to identify others by smell, the accuracy rate depends a great deal on how many competing stimuli we have to judge from. It may be much easier to choose a spouse's T-shirt from one other than from 20.

Smells not only help us identify people, but smells may also play a role in relationship development. When unmarried women were asked to select a male's T-shirt that had an odor that they'd like to smell if they had to smell it all the time, they selected T-shirts from males who were genetically similar, but not too similar, to their fathers (Jacob et al., 2002).

Odor also seems to play a role in synchronizing female menstrual cycles. It was discovered that friends and college roommates moved from an average of 8.5 days apart in their menstrual cycle to less than 5 during the school year. Another experimenter attempted to explain why, by taking odor samples from the underarm of a female colleague, which was called "Essence of Genevieve." This odor was dabbed on the upper lips of female volunteers three times a week for 4 months. Another group of women were dabbed with alcohol. The alcohol group showed no change, but the group receiving "Essence of Genevieve" tended to synchronize their cycle with Genevieve's. This group went from an average of 9.3 days apart in their cycle to 3.4, with 4 women moving to within 1 day of Genevieve's cycle. Subsequent work has examined the role of a man's perspiration odor on women's menstrual cycles. The procedures used in the "Essence of Genevieve" study were replicated using women whose cycles were longer than normal and shorter than normal. Those whose upper lips were dabbed with the male odor developed cycles closer to normal; the control group did not (Cutler et al., 1986; McClintock, 1971; Russell, 1976; Stern & McClintock, 1998).

In addition to affecting the menstrual cycle, male perspiration also seems to have a positive effect on women's moods in the form of stress reduction and relaxation (Preti et al., 2003). The preceding studies are important reminders of the linkage between physiological processes and odor. Physicians have long known that people with certain illnesses tend to give off certain odors, but now we are finding that certain physiological processes can be modified by odor. It does not surprise us that such effects take place in the animal or insect worlds, but until recently we have not thought of human behavior in this way. Now there are people who practice aromatherapy, using odors to alleviate anxiety, headaches, and hypertension, for example.

Another source of odor is flatulent air, generally adding a negative or insulting aura to an interpersonal encounter in our culture (Lippman, 1980). In fact, anticipation of expelling flatus may lead to rapid termination of an interpersonal contact. Under certain conditions, however, emission of flatulent air may be used deliberately to draw attention to oneself. The extent to which odors attributed to flatus or unpleasant body odors are evaluated negatively is probably related to the extent to which others believe people are aware of it and whether it is controllable.

The role of odors in human interaction varies considerably from culture to culture. Asians are reported to manifest underarm odor only rarely. But odor seems to play a prominent role in some Arab countries:

> Olfaction occupies a prominent place in Arab life. Not only is it one of the distance-setting mechanisms, but it is a vital part of a complex system of behavior. Arabs consistently breathe on people when they talk. However, this habit is more than a matter of different manners. To the Arab good smells are pleasing and a way of being involved with each other. To smell one's friend is not only nice but desirable, for to deny him your breath is to act ashamed. Americans, on the other hand, trained as they are not to breathe in people's faces, automatically communicate shame in trying to be polite. (Hall, 1966, pp. 159–160)

In addition to human odors, environmental odors also may affect human encounters by setting the mood or bringing back memories associated with the smell. For the first author of this book, a distinct smell is associated with high schools; each time he enters one it triggers a chain of memories from his own history.

BODY HAIR

The length of a person's hair can dramatically affect perceptions and human interaction. In 1902 the U.S. Commissioner of Indian Affairs sent out an order to forcibly, if necessary, cut all male Indians' hair so they would look "civilized." Similar behavior has occurred from the 1960s to the present.

During the 1960s, white males who allowed the hair on their head to grow over their ears and foreheads and sometimes to their shoulders found they frequently attracted abuse similar to that leveled at black-skinned individuals. Cases of discrimination in housing, school admittance, jobs, and commercial establishments, to mention a few, were numerous.

The media regularly report stories involving reactions to, or regulations directed toward, human hair, mostly male hair. A small sampling from 1972 to 2004 illustrates this is a recurring issue—and not limited to the United States:

West Germany (1972)

Fifteen months before, a defense minister said members of the German army could have beards and long hair as long as they were clean and well groomed. The hoopla created by this order—including complaints by longtime soldiers that long hair interfered with discipline and troop readiness—caused the defense minister to revise his order so that no soldier's hair falls below his collar.

Austin, Texas (1973)

Long hair on boys and men is the sign of a sissy and should be banned from American athletic fields, according to the lead article in the May issue of the Texas High School Coaches Association's magazine. A head football coach at a junior high school in Houston said God made man to dominate woman and, therefore, meant for man to wear short hair. Simpson told his fellow coaches in the article that "a good hair code will get abnormals out of athletics before they become coaches and bring their 'losers' standards into the coaching profession."

New Jersey (1973)

The headmaster of a well-known preparatory school (who sports a beard and a mustache) said about 60 seniors will be suspended if they don't cut their hair to meet regulations on hair grooming. One student reported he was told by the headmaster, "I hold your diploma. Either you get a haircut or don't get your diploma."

Connecticut (1975)

A woman was fired from her waitress job because she refused to shave her legs.

Seoul, Korea (1980)

The national police were ordered to refrain from arresting males because of their long hair. During the first 8 months of the year 14,911 men were arrested on such a charge.

Lubbock, Texas (1990)

A mother in Texas did not see how the rat-tail hairdo her 11-year-old son had been wearing for 3 years was suddenly in violation of the Lubbock Independent School District's dress code. LISD officials were enforcing a policy that prohibits boys from having longer than shoulder-length hair, ponytails, rat tails, patterns shaved into their hair, and braids. Her son, a Boy Scout and honor student before his withdrawal, was being tutored at home because he refused to conform to the new policy.

Washington, D.C. (1994)

A woman with a mustache alleged that her facial hair was the reason she was fired.

Columbia, South Carolina (1995)

Prisoners at a correctional institution stabbed five guards and took three hostages to protest a policy that would require them to cut their hair.

Bastrop, Texas (1996)

A state appeals court ruled school officials were out of bounds when they sent a ponytailed 8-year-old to the equivalent of solitary confinement. The school district's claims that its hair rule was needed to prevent gangs, teach gender identity, and maintain discipline were sheer nonsense, the Third Court of Appeals said. "[The boy] wore the same hairstyle during the previous school year without causing any disruption," the court said. The school district's lawyer said he would recommend the district take the case to the Texas Supreme Court.

Harlingen, Texas (2004)

A 16-year-old student who had several cases of cancer in his family wanted to grow his hair long and then donate it to Locks of Love, a nonprofit organization that uses donated hair to create custom-fitted hairpieces for children suffering from medical hair loss. School officials say this would violate the policy which forbids males to grow hair that hangs below their shoulders. The school superintendent said that the school district's success is rooted in not making exceptions to the policies in place.

Most of the negative reactions against long hair are directed at males; negative reactions against hair that is too short ("microbuzzes") are more likely to be directed against females. Men are often concerned about baldness as detracting from their attractiveness. Just as often, women report male baldness does not significantly detract from a male's attractiveness. The motivation for negative responses to these extreme hairstyles by some members of our culture is an interesting question but not our major concern here. The fact that hair length, in and of itself, elicits feelings either of appreciation or repugnance is the important point (see Figure 6-4).

Other body hair also seems to be important in judgments of attractiveness as well. One study that looked at male facial hair from an historical perspective suggests that men sport more facial hair when they want to be more attractive to women—during times when marriage is valued and the competition for brides is intense (Barber, 2001). But another study indicates that male beards may not be much of an asset in obtaining a management trainee job (Shannon & Stark, 2003). "Hairy" men—men with a lot of hair on their bodies—are attractive to some women and repulsive to others. What about the hair on women's bodies? For years, *Playboy* magazine neatly airbrushed or did not display pubic hair on its models. Even magazines depicting figures in nudist colonies were so well known for such alterations of pubic hair that many subsequently advertised their magazines as "unretouched." But when nude photographs of the pop singer Madonna appeared in two national magazines, many people commented more about the hair under her arms than about her lack of clothing. Some liked it; some did not. Many people in the United States do not find underarm hair attractive on women even though this perception is not shared in other countries. It is reported that the Cacobo Indians of the Amazon rain forest carefully trim and groom their head hair but feel other body hair is not attractive; they methodically eliminate eyebrows by plucking them. The lack of eyebrows on the Mona Lisa is some evidence that at one time it may have been desirable to pluck them for beauty's sake.

The shape of our body, our skin color, our smell, and the hair on our body are probably the major factors affecting our responses to a person's appearance. Still, many other

FIGURE 6-4

How do hair length and style influence your perceptions?

body features, in any given situation, may play an important role—for example, freckles, moles, acne, and so-called beauty marks. The numerous individuals who have had surgery, popularly dubbed "nose jobs," must have felt their nose created a sufficiently undesirable impression in face-to-face interaction to have it changed. We now turn to how we alter our body's appearance with clothing and artifacts such as cosmetics, eyeglasses, jewelry, and so forth.

OUR BODY: CLOTHES AND OTHER ARTIFACTS

Examine the clothing types shown in Figure 6-5. What are your first impressions?

Below is a list of 20 characteristics that may be associated with one or more of these clothing types. Check the spaces you think apply to specific clothing types, and compare your impressions with those of your friends, family, or associates.

Did you find any similarities in your responses and those of your peers? Were there any major differences between your responses and the responses of people with distinctly different backgrounds? Later in this chapter we focus on what specific messages and impressions clothes communicate, but first let's consider the fundamental question: Is clothing, in and of itself, an important factor in communicating?

MALES				FEMALES				
1	2	3	4	1	2	3	4	
___	___	___	___	___	___	___	___	1. Has smoked marijuana.
___	___	___	___	___	___	___	___	2. Is shy, doesn't talk much.
___	___	___	___	___	___	___	___	3. Is a fraternity or sorority member.
___	___	___	___	___	___	___	___	4. Is a Democrat.
___	___	___	___	___	___	___	___	5. Is involved in athletics.
___	___	___	___	___	___	___	___	6. Is married.
___	___	___	___	___	___	___	___	7. Is generous.
___	___	___	___	___	___	___	___	8. Drives a sports car.
___	___	___	___	___	___	___	___	9. Is a Republican.
___	___	___	___	___	___	___	___	10. Is vocationally oriented.
___	___	___	___	___	___	___	___	11. Is active politically.
___	___	___	___	___	___	___	___	12. Is dependable.
___	___	___	___	___	___	___	___	13. Listens most to classical music.
___	___	___	___	___	___	___	___	14. Lives with parents.
___	___	___	___	___	___	___	___	15. Has long hair.
___	___	___	___	___	___	___	___	16. Has many friends.
___	___	___	___	___	___	___	___	17. Is intelligent.
___	___	___	___	___	___	___	___	18. Is religious.
___	___	___	___	___	___	___	___	19. Is open-minded.
___	___	___	___	___	___	___	___	20. Is older.

FIGURE 6-5

Four clothing styles.

a

b

CLOTHING AND COMMUNICATION

As early as 1954, Hoult's experiments verified what we take to be common sense today— You can change perceptions of a person by changing his or her clothing. Today many people are willing to confirm Hoult's findings. For instance, the Associated Press once reported that the Lutheran Church believed the attire worn by clergy in the pulpit was responsible for some churchgoers' switching denominations. Many tailors, manufacturers, and sellers of clothes claim to be "wardrobe engineers"—engineering their clients' outward appearance to increase their sales, assert their authority, or win more court cases.

Career specialists tell us that a job applicant's attire and grooming are an important indicator of his or her attitude toward the company and that appropriate dress aids career advancement.

Some research supports the belief that clothes are an important factor in first impressions. Males and females were asked what they notice about people when they first meet them. They were given 10 characteristics of appearance from which to choose. Females noticed clothes first for both same- and opposite-sexed partners; males also looked at clothes first for same-sexed partners, but for members of the opposite sex, clothes took third place behind figure and face ("First Impressions," August/September 1983). Positive first impressions of a person's clothing style are also more likely if the style of the person being judged and the person doing the judging are similar (Reid, Lancuba, & Morrow, 1997).

School dress codes also provide clear testimony that people believe clothes communicate important messages. The Associated Press reported in 1994 that several Houston-area school districts outlawed what they called the "grunge look." Students were prohibited from wearing baggy pants; untucked shirts; pierced rings in the lips, nose, or eyebrows; torn or ripped clothing; duster-type coats; or trench coats. Earrings were prohibited for boys, and girls could not wear miniskirts, tank tops, cutoffs, halter tops, strapless garments, casual pants, dress slacks, or skirts worn on hips. Administrators reportedly wanted to ban clothing that could hide weapons, ban clothing that might convey gang-related messages, and encourage clothing that would convey dignity and respect.

We can make two important conclusions from the preceding examples: (1) right or wrong, many people believe clothes communicate important messages; and (2) clothing communicates most effectively when it is adapted to the wearer's role and the attendant surroundings. This second conclusion relates to the earlier testimony about how to dress for job interviews and positive first impressions, but it is also supported by the following research. People who were dressed well (as opposed to sloppily) asked others for money to make a phone call. When well dressed, those requesting aid received more cooperation in a clean, neatly appointed airport where most of the people were also well dressed; when they were poorly dressed, the greatest cooperation was obtained from those in a bus station where the people and surroundings more closely resembled their poorly dressed outfits (Hensley, 1981). Sometimes we're very much aware of what attire fits the situation. Most people know, for example, that the business outfits of working women on television programs are sexier and often not appropriate for women who do not work "on camera" (White, 1995). Other situations aren't so clear as Victoria Clark, Assistant Secretary of Defense for Public Affairs, found out in 2003. She was criticized by some for wearing bright colors while answering questions about the war in Iraq. As one person put it, "pink is not an appropriate color in a time of war."

FUNCTIONS OF CLOTHING

To understand the relationship between clothes and communication, we must be familiar with the various functions clothes may fulfill: decoration, protection (both physical and psychological), sexual attraction, self-assertion, self-denial, concealment, group identification; persuasion; attitude, ideology, or mood reflection/creation; authority; and status or role display (Barnard, 2001). Because there are some widely accepted cultural rules for combining certain colors and styles of dress, clothes also may function to inform the observer of one's knowledge of such rules. When romantic couples wear similar or matching clothing, the clothing serves as a visible bonding agent for the relationship. Clothing that functions as a means of persuasion has been the subject of numerous studies.

An old but classic study tested the ability of people dressed in "high-status" clothing to get unsuspecting bystanders to violate a traffic signal light. Lefkowitz, Blake, and Mouton (1955) found pedestrians much more likely to violate a traffic signal light at an intersection if another person violated it ahead of them—but especially if that other person's attire represented a person with social status. Other studies find that a variety of requests (making change, accepting leaflets, giving detailed street directions, returning money left in a phone booth, and so on) are more easily accomplished if one is dressed to fit the situation or is dressed in what would be considered higher status clothing (Fortenberry et al., 1978; Levine, Bluni, & Hochman, 1998). Bickman (1974a, 1974b), for example, had 4 men stop 153 adults on the streets of Brooklyn and make various requests. The men's clothing varied and included civilian (sports jacket and tie), milkman (uniform, white pants, milk bottles), and guard (uniform, badge, insignia, no gun). The men asked pedestrians to pick up a bag, to put a dime in a parking meter for someone else, or to stand on the opposite side of a bus-stop sign. In each case, when dressed in the guard uniform, the men received greater compliance. In fact, 83% of those who were asked to put a dime in the parking meter obeyed even after the person in the guard uniform had left the scene. Uniforms do help people identify the wearer's probable areas of expertise. And this knowledge may be persuasive. In public service announcements, the same woman dressed as a nurse and as a businesswoman asked for contributions to fight leukemia. The nurse was judged to be more knowledgeable and received more pledged contributions (Lawrence & Watson, 1991). Uniformed police officers want their uniform to be persuasive, but it is sometimes difficult because of the different goals their job requires. Can the same uniform communicate approachability and friendliness as well as authoritativeness in enforcing the law? (Young, 1999). Lawyers have long known that their client's manner of dress may have a persuasive impact on the judgments made by the judge and/or jury. Some defendants have even been encouraged to put on a simulated wedding ring to offset any prejudice against single persons.

CLOTHING AS INFORMATION ABOUT THE PERSON

To make a list of the things invariably communicated by clothes would be impossible; such a list would vary with the demand of each particular situation, ethnic group, time (of day and era), region of the country, and so forth. Making the task even harder is the fact that any given item of clothing can be worn in such a way as to convey multiple meanings. The design of a tie may convey sophistication and status, but the way it is knotted (tight or loose) and worn (thrown over shoulder) may send other messages.

Some of the personal attributes that may be communicated by dress include sex, age, nationality, relation to a companion (e.g., matching sweaters), socioeconomic status, identification with a specific group, occupational or official status, mood, personality, attitudes, interests, and values. Clothes also set our expectations for the behavior of the wearer. When the target of our observations is a person well known to us, that knowledge will guide our interpretations of clothing. We may, for example, see radical clothing changes as representing temporary moods rather than lasting personality changes. Obviously, the accuracy of such judgments varies considerably; *the more concrete items such as age, sex, and socioeconomic status are signaled with greater accuracy than more abstract qualities such as attitudes, values, and personality.* In recent years, the "message" T-shirt has become a vehicle for communicating some attitudes that might otherwise be more difficult to assess.

EFFECTS OF CLOTHING ON THE WEARER

Up to this point, we have established that clothing communicates a variety of messages and the people we interact with respond in various ways to those messages. But what about the effect of clothing on the self-image of the wearer? Some authors feel clothes help satisfy a personal image of one's ideal self. Gibbins, in his work with 15- and 16-year-old girls, for instance, found a definite relationship between clothes that were liked and ratings of ideal self. Clothing was a means of communicating messages about the wearer, and liking for a particular outfit was "related to the extent to which this message is similar to the subject's ideal self-image" (Gibbins, 1969). In another fascinating discovery, we see a potential link between clothing and self-concept. High school boys who had higher achievement test scores but who wore clothing deemed "unacceptable" by their peers were found to have lower grade point averages than those who wore "acceptable" clothing (Hamilton & Warden, 1966). This latter group also found themselves in less conflict and in more school activities. Clothes, then, may encourage or discourage certain patterns of communication. A new outfit may promote feelings of gaiety and happiness; people may feel less efficient in shoes that hurt; self-consciousness may result from wearing an "inappropriate" outfit—a common feeling for adolescents trying to understand their own self-image. Some graduate teaching assistants wear suits to class to distinguish themselves from their students who frequently are almost age-mates. Some report that such attire gives them added confidence or assurance in dealing with their students, but their attire seems to have relatively little effect on the perceptions of their students when compared with their behavior (Gorham, Cohen, & Morris, 1999; Roach, 1997).

The mutual effects of clothing on wearer and on perceiver were amply demonstrated in a study of the uniforms worn by teams in the National Hockey League and National Football League. In this study, teams with black uniforms ranked near the top of their leagues in penalties, and those teams who switched from nonblack to black uniforms incurred more penalties after the switch. The authors suggest that wearers of the black uniforms perceive themselves as more aggressive and that this, coupled with similar perceptions by referees, leads to more penalties (Frank & Gilovich, 1988).

The issue of wearing uniforms to school has gained a great deal of notoriety in recent years. One of the prominent arguments for adopting school uniforms is that the style of dress changes how wearers feel about themselves and, in turn, changes behavior. One large-scale study of 10th-grade students did not find any direct effects of uniforms on substance use, behavioral problems, or attendance and found a negative effect on achievement (Brunsma & Rockquemore, 1998). For some students, uniforms provide a needed form of structure and control and they are a symbol of school unity, but it is not realistic to expect uniforms to eliminate most of the offensive behaviors manifested by troubled teens. School uniforms by themselves, without the support of both students and parents, are not likely to accomplish much.

CLOTHING AND PERSONALITY

Rosenfeld and Plax (1977) wanted to determine whether attitudes toward clothing are related to certain personality characteristics. This study obtained responses from both males and females on a questionnaire about clothing attitudes. A massive battery of personality tests also was given to this group of 371 men and women. The results of these personality tests were then matched with the scores on four dimensions of the clothing questionnaire. These results are listed as follows according to the males and females who scored high or low on each dimension:

1. Clothing consciousness ("The people I know always notice what I wear.")
   - High males were deliberate; guarded; deferential to authority, custom, and tradition. They did not value beauty, form, and unity very highly, and they believed people were easily manipulated.
   - High females were inhibited, anxious, compliant before authority, kind, sympathetic, loyal to friends.
   - Low males were aggressive, independent, and did not believe people could be easily manipulated.
   - Low females were forceful, independent, dominant, clear thinking, and had low motivation for heterosexual relationships or for manipulating others.
2. Exhibitionism ("I approve of skimpy bathing suits and wouldn't mind wearing one myself.")
   - High males were aggressive, confident, outgoing, unsympathetic, unaffectionate, moody, impulsive, and had a low self-concept regarding their familial interactions.
   - High females were radical, detached from interpersonal relationships, and had a high opinion of their own self-worth and moral/ethical beliefs.
   - Low males were guarded about self-revelations. They had a low self-concept regarding their familial interactions, and they believed people could be easily manipulated.
   - Low females were timid, sincere, accepting of others, patient, and had a low motivation for heterosexual relationships. They also had feelings of inferiority.
3. Practicality ("When buying clothes, I am more interested in practicality than beauty.")
   - High males were inhibited, cautious, rebellious, dissatisfied, and had a low motivation to make friends, sustain relationships, or gain recognition from authorities.
   - High females were clever, enthusiastic, confident, outgoing, and guarded about personal self-revelations. They had feelings of superiority but did not wish to lead.
   - Low males were success oriented, mature, forceful, serious, and analytical and tried to predict responses of others in various situations.
   - Low females were self-centered, independent, detached.

4. Designer ("I should love to be a clothes designer.")
   - High males were cooperative, sympathetic, warm, helpful, impulsive, irritable, demanding, and conforming. They worried about their behavior and sought encouragement from others.
   - High females were irrational, uncritical, stereotyped in thinking, quick, expressive, and ebullient.
   - Low males were adventurous, egotistic, dissatisfied, and anxious. They had feelings of superiority and were not highly motivated to form friendships.
   - Low females were efficient, clear thinking, resourceful, persistent, and easily disorganized under pressure. They believed people were easily manipulated, and they were pessimistic about their occupational future.

ARTIFACTS AND BODY DECORATIONS

People adorn themselves with a number of *artifacts* such as badges, tattoos, masks, earrings, and jewelry (see Figure 6-6). We must take these artifacts into consideration in any discussion of clothing because they are also potential communicative stimuli. A ring worn

FIGURE 6-6

People around the world use tattoos to decorate their bodies.

on a particular finger, a fraternity or sorority pin worn in a particular configuration, and a single earring worn on a particular ear all may communicate something about the nature of one's relationships and self-image.

We know that people around the world choose to decorate and alter their bodies in a variety of ways. Sometimes the body is scarred, mutilated, or painted. In the case of binding infant feet, bone structure is reshaped. In our society, we circumcise many male children, and the piercing of various body parts with rings has become increasingly popular with young adults in recent years. The use of tattoos to decorate the body is also widely practiced (Sanders, 1989).

In addition, we know people sometimes react strongly to a particular artifact or decoration—for example, eyeglasses or lipstick. And although the initial effect of such features may be strong, co-occurring features and verbal behavior soon blend together to form an overall impression—thereby minimizing the effect of any single feature.

❖

SUMMARY

Appearance and dress are part of the total nonverbal stimuli that influence interpersonal responses, and under some conditions they are the primary determinants of such responses. Physical attractiveness may be influential in determining whether a person is sought out; it may have a bearing on whether a person is able to persuade or manipulate others. It is often an important factor in the selection of dates and marriage partners; it may determine whether a defendant is deemed guilty or innocent; it may even have an effect on whether the prisoner is able to decrease the antisocial behavior responsible for his or her imprisonment. It may be a major factor contributing to how others judge personality, sexuality, popularity, success, and often happiness. Fortunately for some and unfortunately for others, such judgments begin early in life. Not all children are conventionally beautiful. There are indications that teachers not only make attractiveness judgments about young children but also treat the unattractive ones with fewer and less positive communications. A sizable proportion of the American public still thinks of the ideal man or woman in terms of physical attractiveness.

In spite of the overwhelming evidence that physical attractiveness is a highly desirable quality in interpersonal situations, other factors temper these general findings. For instance, all positive findings for attractiveness are based on probabilities, not certainty. Many less-attractive persons are not evaluated unfavorably. For example, judgments can be tempered by the persons they are seen with, the environment in which they are judged, other communicative behavior they engage in, and/or the time of life at which they are evaluated. In addition, many of the attractiveness studies have used photographs rather than live, interacting human beings.

In addition to the importance of general physical attractiveness in influencing the responses of others, we have some information on stereotyped responses to specific features—general body build, skin color, odor, hair, and clothes. These specific features may have a profound influence on one's self-image and hence on patterns of communication with others.

The way we clothe our bodies may also communicate important messages in our work and social lives. It is one of the first things people perceive about us. We can judge age, sex, and socioeconomic status from clothing with more accuracy than we can a person's attitudes or beliefs. Wearing attire that others perceive as similar to theirs, appropriate to the situation, or representative of an expert or authority figure makes clothing an instrument of persuasion. We also know that clothing and the other ways we decorate our bodies (jewelry, colors, tatoos, etc.) affect how we feel about ourselves, which, in turn, affects how we communicate.

QUESTIONS FOR DISCUSSION

1. Can our verbal behavior affect the way people perceive our physical attractiveness? What verbal behavior might cause people to perceive us as less physically attractive? What verbal behavior might make us appear more physically attractive?

2. Throughout this chapter you have read about a number of stereotypes people have about physical appearance. In your opinion, is there any truth to these stereotypes? Which ones?

3. If you wanted to change stereotypes about physical appearance, how would you do it? Take one stereotype as an example, and show what you would do to change it.

4. People have been refused employment or fired from their job because of perceived problems with their height, weight, odor, skin color, clothing, hairstyle, or general attractiveness. Under what conditions (if any) do you think such characteristics are legitimate reasons for not hiring a person or for firing an employee?

BIBLIOGRAPHY

Adams, G. R. (1977). Physical attractiveness research: Toward a developmental social psychology of beauty. *Human Development, 20,* 217–239.

Addison, W. E. (1989). Beardedness as a factor in perceived masculinity. *Perceptual and Motor Skills, 68,* 921–922.

Aiken, L. (1963). Relationship of dress to selected measures of personality in undergraduate women. *Journal of Social Psychology, 59,* 119–128.

Albada, K. F., Knapp, M. L., & Theune, K. E. (2002). Interaction appearance theory: Changing perceptions of physical attractiveness through social interaction. *Communication Theory, 12,* 8–40.

Aronson, E., & Golden, B. W. (1962). The effect of relevant and irrelevant aspects of communicator credibility on opinion change. *Journal of Personality, 30,* 135–146.

Baber, R. E. (1939). *Marriage and family.* New York: McGraw-Hill.

Baker, E. E., & Redding, W. C. (1962). The effects of perceived tallness in persuasive speaking: An experiment. *Journal of Communication, 12,* 51–53.

Banner, I. (1986). *American beauty.* Chicago: University of Chicago Press.

Bar-Tal, D., & Saxe, L. (1976). Perceptions of similarly and dissimilarly attractive couples and individuals. *Journal of Personality and Social Psychology, 33,* 772–781.

Barber, N. (2001). Mustache fashion covaries with a good marriage market for women. *Journal of Nonverbal Behavior, 25*, 261–272.

Barnard, M. (2001). *Fashion as communication* (2nd ed.). New York: Routledge.

Bassett, R. E. (1979). Effects of source attire on judgments of credibility. *Central States Speech Journal, 30*, 282–285.

Beck, S. B., Ward-Hull, C. I., & McLear, P. M. (1976). Variables related to women's somatic preferences of the male and female body. *Journal of Personality and Social Psychology, 34*, 1200–1210.

Berg, R. C. (2004). *Interaction appearance theory and initial interactions*. Unpublished master's thesis, University of Texas.

Berman, P. W., O'Nan, B. A., & Floyd, W. (1981). The double standard of aging and the social situation: Judgments of attractiveness of the middle-aged woman. *Sex Roles, 7*, 87–96.

Berry, D. S. (1991). Attractive faces are not all created equal: Joint effects of facial babyishness and attractiveness on social perception. *Personality and Social Psychology Bulletin, 17*, 523–531.

Berry, D. S., & McArthur, L. Z. (1986). Perceiving character in faces: The impact of age-related craniofacial changes on social perception. *Psychological Bulletin, 100*, 3–18.

Berscheid, E., & Walster, E. H. (1969). *Interpersonal attraction*. Reading, MA: Addison-Wesley.

Berscheid, E., & Walster, E. H. (1974). Physical attractiveness. In L. Berkowitz (Ed.), *Advances in experimental social psychology* (Vol. 7). New York: Academic Press.

Bickman, L. (1971). The effects of social status on the honesty of others. *Journal of Social Psychology, 85*, 87–92.

Bickman, L. (1974a). The social power of a uniform. *Journal of Applied Social Psychology, 4*, 47–61.

Bickman, L. (1974b). Social roles and uniforms: Clothes make the person. *Psychology Today, 7*, 48–51.

Bissell, K. L., & Zhou, P. (2004). Must-see TV or ESPN: Entertainment and sports media exposure and body-image distortion in college women. *Journal of Communication, 54*, 5–21.

Brain, R. (1979). *The decorated body*. New York: Harper & Row.

Brislin, R. W., & Lewis, S. A. (1968). Dating and physical attractiveness: Replication. *Psychological Reports, 22*, 976.

Brunsma, D. L., & Rockquemore, K. A. (1998). Effects of student uniforms on attendance, behavior problems, substance use, and academic achievement. *Journal of Educational Research, 92*, 53–62.

Buss, D. M. (1989). Sex differences in human mate preferences: Evolutionary hypotheses tested in 37 cultures. *Behavioral and Brain Sciences, 12*, 1–14.

Buss, D. M. (1994). *The evolution of desire*. New York: Basic Books.

Byrne, D., Ervin, C. R., & Lamberth, J. (1970). Contiguity between the experimental study of attraction and real-life computer dating. *Journal of Personality and Social Psychology, 16*, 157–165.

Cahnman, W. J. (1968). The stigma of obesity. *Sociological Quarterly, 9*, 283–299.

Cameron, C., Oskamp, S., & Sparks, W. (1978). Courtship American style: Newspaper advertisements. *The Family Coordinator, 26*, 27–30.

Cash, T. F., & Derlega, V. J. (1978). The matching hypothesis: Physical attractiveness among same-sexed friends. *Personality and Social Psychology Bulletin, 4*, 240–243.

Cash, T. F., Gillen, B., & Burns, S. (1977). Sexism and "beautism" in personnel consultant decision making. *Journal of Applied Psychology, 62*, 301–310.

Cash, T. F., & Pruzinsky, T. (1990). *Body images: Development, deviance, and change*. New York: Guilford.

Cash, T. F., Winstead, B. A., & Janda, L. H. (1986). The great American shape-up. *Psychology Today, 20*, 30–37.

Cavior, N., & Lombardi, D. H. (1973). Developmental aspects of judgment of physical attractiveness in children. *Developmental Psychology, 8,* 67–71.

Chaiken, S. (1979). Communicator physical attractiveness and persuasion. *Journal of Personality and Social Psychology, 37,* 1387–1397.

Chaiken, S. (1986). Physical appearance and social influence. In C. P. Herman, M. P. Zanna, & E. T. Higgins (Eds.), *Physical appearance, stigma, and social behavior: The Ontario Symposium* (Vol. 3). Hillsdale, NJ: Erlbaum.

Chaikin, A. L., Derlega, V. J., Yoder, J., & Phillips, D. (1974). The effects of appearance on compliance. *Journal of Social Psychology, 92,* 199–200.

Channing, H., & Mayer, J. (1966). Obesity—Its possible effect on college acceptance. *New England Journal of Medicine, 275,* 1172–1174.

Cortes, J. B., & Gatti, F. M. (1965). Physique and self-description of temperament. *Journal of Consulting Psychology, 29,* 432–439.

Cortes, J. B., & Gatti, F. M. (1966). Physique and motivation. *Journal of Consulting Psychology, 30,* 408–414.

Cunningham, M. R., Barbee, A. P., & Philhower, C. L. (2002). Dimensions of facial physical attractiveness: The intersection of biology and culture (pp. 193–238). In G. Rhodes & L. A. Zebrowitz (Eds.), *Facial attractiveness.* Westport, CT: Ablex.

Cunningham, M. R., Barbee, A. R., & Pike, C. L. (1990). What do women want? Facialmetric assessment of multiple motives in the perception of male facial physical attractiveness. *Journal of Personality and Social Psychology, 59,* 61–72.

Cunningham, M. R., Roberts, A. R., Barbee, A. P., Druen, P. B., & Wu, C. H. (1995). "Their ideas of beauty are, on the whole, the same as ours": Consistency and variability in the cross-cultural perception of female physical attractiveness. *Journal of Personality and Social Psychology, 68,* 261–279.

Curran, J. P. (1973). Correlates of physical attractiveness and interpersonal attraction in the dating situation. *Social Behavior and Personality, 1,* 153–157.

Curran, J. P., & Lippold, S. (1975). The effects of physical attraction and attitude similarity on dating dyads. *Journal of Personality, 43,* 528–539.

Cutler, W. B., Preti, G., Krieger, A., Huggins, G. R., Garcia, C. R., & Lawley, H. J. (1986). Human axillary secretions influence women's menstrual cycles: The role of donor extract from men. *Hormones and Behavior, 20,* 463–473.

Dannenmaier, W., & Thumin, F. (1964). Authority status as a factor in perceptual distortion of size. *Journal of Social Psychology, 63,* 361–365.

Darley, J. M., & Cooper, J. (1972). The "Clean Gene" phenomenon: The effect of students' appearance on political campaigning. *Journal of Applied Social Psychology, 2,* 24–33.

Davis, F. (1971). *Inside intuition.* New York: McGraw-Hill.

Davis, F. (1992). *Fashion, culture, and identity.* Chicago: University of Chicago Press.

Deformed brick-thrower eyes future with new face. (1975, December 15). *Lafayette Journal and Courier,* p. A-6.

DeJong, W., & Kleck, R. E. (1986). The social psychological effects of overweight. In C. P. Herman, M. P. Zanna, & E. T. Higgins (Eds.), *Physical appearance, stigma, and social behavior: The Ontario Symposium* (Vol. 3). Hillsdale, NJ: Erlbaum.

DeLong, R. R. (1978). Dimensions of visual perceptions of clothing. *Perceptual and Motor Skills, 47,* 907–910.

Dermer, M., & Thiel, D. L. (1975). When beauty may fail. *Journal of Personality and Social Psychology, 31,* 1168–1176.

Dion, K. K. (1972). Physical attractiveness and evaluation of children's transgressions. *Journal of Personality and Social Psychology, 24,* 207–213.

Dion, K. K. (1973). Young children's stereotyping of facial attractiveness. *Developmental Psychology,* 9, 183–188.

Dion, K. K. (2002). Cultural perspectives on facial attractiveness (pp. 239–259). In G. Rhodes & L. A. Zebrowitz (Eds.), *Facial attractiveness.* Westport, CT: Ablex.

Dion, K. K., & Berscheid, E. (1972). Physical attractiveness and peer perception among children. *Sociometry, 37,* 1–12.

Dion, K. K., Berscheid, E., & Walster, E. (1972). What is beautiful is good. *Journal of Personality and Social Psychology, 24,* 285–290.

Dion, K. K., & Stein, S. (1978). Physical attractiveness and interpersonal influence. *Journal of Experimental Social Psychology, 14,* 97–108.

Dipboye, R. L., Arvey, R. D., & Terpstra, D. E. (1977). Sex and physical attractiveness of raters and applicants as determinants of resume evaluations. *Journal of Applied Psychology, 62,* 288–294.

Doty, R. L. (1981). Olfactory communication in humans. *Chemical Senses, 6,* 351–376.

Doty, R. L., Orndorff, M. M., Leyden, J., & Kligman, A. (1978). Communication of gender from human axillary odors: Relationship to perceived intensity and dedonicity. *Behavioral Biology, 23,* 373–380.

Douty, H. I. (1963). Influence of clothing on perception of persons. *Journal of Home Economics, 55,* 197–202.

Downs, A. C., & Lyons, P. M. (1991). Natural observations of the links between attractiveness and initial legal judgments. *Personality and Social Psychology Bulletin, 17,* 541–547.

Efran, M. G. (1974). The effect of physical appearance on the judgment of guilt, interpersonal attraction, and severity of recommended punishment in a simulated jury task. *Journal of Experimental Research in Personality, 8,* 45–54.

Etcoff, N. (1999). *Survival of the prettiest.* New York: Random House.

Fallon, A., & Rozin, P. (1985). Sex differences in perceptions of desirable body shape. *Journal of Abnormal Psychology, 94,* 102–105.

Farb, B. (1978). *Humankind.* Boston: Houghton-Mifflin.

Farina, A., Fischer, E., Sherman, S., Smith, W., Groh, T., & Mermin, P. (1977). Physical attractiveness and mental illness. *Journal of Abnormal Psychology, 86,* 510–517.

First impressions. (1983, August/September). *Public Opinion,* p. 6.

Flegal, K. M., Carroll, M. D., Ogden, C. L., & Johnson, C. L. (2002). Prevalence and trends in obesity among U.S. adults, 1999–2000. *JAMA, 288,* 1772–1773.

Flugel, J. (1930). *The psychology of clothes.* London: Hogarth Press.

Forestell, C. A., Humphrey, T. M., & Stewart, S. H. (2004). Involvement of body weight and shape factors in ratings of attractiveness by women: A replication and extension of Tassinary and Hansen (1998). *Personality & Individual Differences, 36,* 295–305.

Fortenberry, J. H., MacLean, J., Morris, P., & O'Connell, M. (1978). Modes of dress as a perceptual cue to deference. *Journal of Personality and Social Psychology, 104,* 139–140.

Frank, M. G., & Gilovich, T. (1988). The dark side of self- and social perception: Black uniforms and aggression in professional sports. *Journal of Personality and Social Psychology, 54,* 74–85.

Freedman, R. (1986). *Beauty bound.* Lexington, MA: Lexington.

Friday, N. (1996). *The power of beauty.* New York: HarperCollins.

Friend, R. M., & Vinson, M. (1974). Leaning over backwards: Jurors' responses to defendants' attractiveness. *Journal of Communication, 24,* 124–129.

Furnham, A., Disha, M., & McClelland, A. (2004). The influence of age of the face and the waist-to-hip ratio on judgments of female attractiveness and traits. *Personality & Individual Differences, 36,* 1171–1185.

Garner, D. M., Garfinkel, P. E., Schwartz, D., & Thompson, M. (1980). Cultural expectations of thinness in women. *Psychological Reports, 47,* 483–491.

Geiselman, R. E., Haight, N., & Kimata, L. (1984). Context effects of the perceived physical attractiveness of faces. *Journal of Experimental Social Psychology, 20,* 409–424.

Gibbins, K. (1969). Communication aspects of women's clothes and their relation to fashionability. *British Journal of Social and Clinical Psychology, 8,* 301–312.

Giles, H., & Chavasse, W. (1975). Communication length as a function of dress style and social status. *Perceptual and Motor Skills, 40,* 961–962.

Gillis, J. S., & Avis. W. E. (1980). The male-taller norm in mate selection. *Personality and Social Psychology Bulletin, 6,* 396–401.

Goldberg, P. A., Gottesdiener, N., & Abramson, P. R. (1975). Another put-down of women?: Perceived attractiveness as a function of support for the feminist movement. *Journal of Personality and Social Psychology, 32,* 113–115.

Gorden, W. I., Tengler, C. D., & Infante, D. A. (1982). Women's clothing predispositions as predictors of dress at work, job satisfaction, and career advancement. *Southern Speech Communication Journal, 17,* 422–434.

Gorham, J., Cohen, S. H., & Morris, T. L. (1999). Fashion in the classroom: III. Effects of instructor attire and immediacy in natural classroom interactions. *Communication Quarterly, 47,* 281–299.

Gortmaker, S. L., Must, A., Perrin, J. N., Sobol, A. M., & Dietz, W. H. (1993). Social and economic consequences of overweight in adolescence and young adulthood. *New England Journal of Medicine, 329,* 1008–1012.

Graham, J. A., & Jouhar, A. J. (1980). Cosmetics considered in the context of physical attractiveness: A review. *International Journal of Cosmetic Science, 2,* 77–101.

Graham, J. A., & Jouhar, A. J. (1981). The effects of cosmetics on person perception. *International Journal of Cosmetic Science, 3,* 199–210.

Graham, J. A., & Jouhar, A. J. (1982). *The effects of cosmetics on self perception: How we see ourselves.* Unpublished manuscript, University of Pennsylvania.

Graham, J. A., & Kligman, A. M. (Eds.). (1985). *The psychology of cosmetic treatments.* New York: Praeger.

Grammer, K., & Thornhill, R. (1994). Human (homo sapiens) facial attractiveness and sexual selection: The role of symmetry and averageness. *Journal of Comparative Psychology, 108,* 233–242.

Graziano, W. G., Jensen-Campbell, L. A., Shebilske, L. J., & Lundgren, S. R. (1993). Social influence, sex differences, and judgments of beauty: Putting the interpersonal back into interpersonal attraction. *Journal of Personality and Social Psychology, 65,* 522–531.

Griffin, J. H. (1960). *Black like me.* Boston: Houghton Mifflin.

Gurel, L., Wilbur, J. C., & Gurel, L. (1972). Personality correlates of adolescent clothing styles. *Journal of Home Economics, 64,* 42–47.

Halberstadt, J., & Rhodes, G. (2003). It's not just average faces that are attractive: Computer-manipulated averageness makes birds, fish, and automobiles attractive. *Psychonomic Bulletin & Review, 10,* 149–156.

Hall, E. T. (1966). *The hidden dimension.* Garden City, NY: Doubleday.

Hallpike, C. R. (1969). Social hair. *Man, 4,* 256–264.

Hamermesh, D. S., & Biddle, J. E. (1994). Beauty and the labor market. *American Economic Review, 84,* 1174–1194.

Hamid, P. (1972). Some effects of dress cues on observational accuracy: A perceptual estimate, and impression formation. *Journal of Social Psychology, 86,* 279–289.

Hamilton, J., & Warden, J. (1966). Student's role in a high school community and his clothing behavior. *Journal of Home Economics, 58,* 789–791.

Harrison, A. A., & Saeed, L. (1977). Let's make a deal: An analysis of revelations and stipulations in Lonely Hearts advertisements. *Journal of Personality and Social Psychology, 35,* 257–274.

Hartmann, G. W. (1949). Clothing: Personal problem and social issue. *Journal of Home Economics, 41,* 295–298.

Hatfield, E., & Sprecher, S. (1986). *Mirror, mirror . . . : The importance of looks in everyday life.* Albany: SUNY Press.

Heilman, M. E., & Saruwatari, L. F. (1979). When beauty is beastly: The effects of appearance and sex on evaluations of job applicants for managerial and nonmanagerial jobs. *Organizational Behavior and Human Performance, 22,* 360–372.

Hendricks, S. H., Kelley, E. A., & Eicher, J. B. (1968). Senior girls' appearance and social acceptance. *Journal of Home Economics, 60,* 167–172.

Hensley, W. E. (1981). The effects of attire, location, and sex on aiding behavior: A similarity explanation. *Journal of Nonverbal Behavior, 6,* 3–11.

Herman, C. P., Zanna, M. P., & Higgins, E. T. (Eds.). (1986). *Physical appearance, stigma, and social behavior: The Ontario Symposium* (Vol. 3). Hillsdale, NJ: Erlbaum.

Hinsz, V. B. (1989). Facial resemblance in engaged and married couples. *Journal of Social and Personal Relationships, 6,* 223–229.

Holman, R. H. (1980). A transcription and analysis system for the study of women's clothing. *Semiotica, 32,* 11–34.

Hopson, J. L. (1979). *Scent signals.* New York: William Morrow.

Horai, J., Naccari, N., & Fatoultah, E. (1974). The effects of expertise and physical attractiveness upon opinion agreement and liking. *Sociometry, 37,* 601–606.

Hoult, R. (1954). Experimental measurement of clothing as a factor in some social ratings of selected American men. *American Sociological Review, 19,* 324–328.

Hubble, M. A., & Gelso, C. J. (1978). Effect of counselor attire in an initial interview. *Journal of Counseling Psychology, 25,* 581–584.

Iliffe, A. M. (1960). A study of preferences in feminine beauty. *British Journal of Psychology, 51,* 267–273.

Jackson, L. A. (1992). *Physical appearance and gender: Sociobiological and sociocultural perspectives.* Albany: SUNY Press.

Jacob, S., McClintock, M. K., Zelano, B., & Ober, C. (2002). Paternally inherited HLA alleles are associated with women's choice of male odor. *Nature Genetics, 30,* 175–179.

Jacobson, M. B. (1981). Effects of victim's and defendant's physical attractiveness on subjects' judgments in a rape case. *Sex Roles, 7,* 247–255.

Jacobson, S. K., & Berger, C. R. (1974). Communication and justice: Defendant attributes and their effects on the severity of his sentence. *Speech Monographs, 41,* 282–286.

Jensen-Campbell, L. A., Graziano, W. G., & West, S. G. (1995). Dominance, prosocial orientation, and female preferences: Do nice guys really finish last? *Journal of Personality and Social Psychology, 68,* 427–440.

Johnson, B. H., Nagasawa, R. H., & Peters, K. (1977). Clothing style differences: Their effect on the impression of sociability. *Home Economics Research Journal, 6,* 58–63.

Johnson, K. K. P., & Lennon, S. (Eds.). (1999). *Appearance and power.* Oxford University Press: New York.

Johnson, P. A., & Staffieri, J. R. (1971). Stereotypic affective properties of personal names and somatypes in children. *Developmental Psychology, 5,* 176.

Jones, B. T., Jones, B. C., Thomas, A. P., & Piper, J. (2003). Alcohol consumption increases attractiveness ratings of opposite-sex faces: A possible third route to risky sex. *Addiction, 98,* 1069–1075.

Joseph, N., & Alex, N. (1972). The uniform: A sociological perspective. *American Journal of Sociology, 77,* 719–730.

Joseph, W. B. (1982). The credibility of physically attractive communicators: A review. *Journal of Advertising, 11,* 15–24.

Judge, T. A., & Cable, D. M. (2004). The effects of physical height on workplace success and income: Preliminary test of a theoretical model. *Journal of Applied Psychology, 89,* 428–441.

Kaiser, S. B. (1985). *The social psychology of clothing.* New York: Macmillan.

Kalick, S. M., & Hamilton, T. E. (1986). The matching hypothesis reexamined. *Journal of Personality and Social Psychology, 51,* 673–682.

Kanazawa, S., & Kovar, J. L. (2004). Why beautiful people are more intelligent. *Intelligence, 32,* 227–243.

Keating, C. F. (1985). Gender and the physiognomy of dominance and attractiveness. *Social Psychology Quarterly, 48,* 61–70.

Keating, C. F., Mazur, A., & Segall, M. H. (1977). Facial features which influence the perception of status. *Sociometry, 40,* 374–378.

Keating, C. F, Mazur, A., & Segall, M. H. (1981). A cross-cultural exploration of physiognomic traits of dominance and happiness. *Ethology and Sociobiology, 2,* 41–48.

Kenny, C., & Fletcher, D. (1973). Effects of beardedness on person perception. *Perceptual and Motor Skills, 37,* 413–414.

Kenrick, D. T., & Gutierres, S. E. (1980). Contrast effects and judgments of physical attractiveness: When beauty becomes a social problem. *Journal of Personality and Social Psychology, 38,* 131–140.

Keyes, R. (1980). *The height of your life.* New York: Warner.

Kiesler, S. B., & Baral, R. L. (1970). The search for a romantic partner: The effects of self-esteem and physical attractiveness on romantic behavior. In K. J. Gergen & D. Marlowe (Eds.), *Personality and social behavior.* Reading, MA: Addison-Wesley.

Kitson, H. D. (1922). Height and weight as factors in salesmanship. *Journal of Personnel Research, 1.*

Kleck, R. E., Richardson, S. A., & Ronald, L. (1974). Physical appearance cues and interpersonal attraction in children. *Child Development, 45,* 305–310.

Kleinke, C. L., & Staneski, R. A. (1980). First impression of female bust size. *Journal of Social Psychology, 110,* 123–124.

Knapp, M. L. (1985). The study of physical appearance and cosmetics in Western culture. In J. A. Graham & A. M. Kligman (Eds.), *The psychology of cosmetic treatments.* New York: Praeger.

Kniffin, K. M., & Wilson, D. S. (2004). The effect of nonphysical traits on the perception of physical attractiveness: Three naturalistic studies. *Evolution & Human Behavior, 25,* 88–101.

Krebs, D., & Adinolfi, A. A. (1975). Physical attractiveness, social relations, and personality style. *Journal of Personality and Social Psychology, 31,* 107–114.

Kretschmer, E. (1925). *Physique and character.* New York: Harcourt Brace.

Kulka, R. A., & Kessler, J. B. (1978). Is justice really blind?—The influence of litigant physical attractiveness on juridical judgment. *Journal of Applied Social Psychology, 8,* 366–381.

Kurtz, D. L. (1969, December). Physical appearance and stature: Important variables in sales recruiting. *Personnel Journal,* pp. 981–983.

Lakoff, R. T., & Scherr, R. L. (1985). *Face value: The politics of beauty.* London: Routledge & Kegan Paul.

Lambert, S. (1972). Reactions to a stranger as a function of style of dress. *Perceptual and Motor Skills, 35,* 711–712.

Landy, D., & Sigall, H. (1974). Beauty is talent: Task evaluation as a function of the performer's physical attractiveness. *Journal of Personality and Social Psychology, 29,* 299–304.

Langlois, J. H., & Downs, A. C. (1979). Peer relations as a function of physical attractiveness: The eye of the beholder or behavioral reality? *Child Development, 50,* 409–418.

Langlois, J. H., Kalakanis, L. E., Rubenstein, A. J., Larson, A. D., Hallam, M. J., & Smoot, M. T. (2000). Maxims or myths of beauty: A meta-analysis and theoretical review. *Psychological Bulletin, 126,* 390–423.

Langlois, J. H., & Roggman, L. A. (1990). Attractive faces are only average. *Psychological Science, 1,* 115–121.

Langlois, J. H., Roggman, L. A., Casey, R. J., Ritter, J. M., Rieser-Danner, L. A., & Jenkins, V. Y. (1987). Infant preferences for attractive faces: Rudiments of a stereotype? *Developmental Psychology, 23,* 363–369.

Langlois, J. H., Roggman, L. A., & Musselman, L. (1994). What is average and what is not average about attractive faces? *Psychological Science, 5,* 214–220.

Largey, G. P., & Watson, D. R. (1972). The sociology of odors. *American Journal of Sociology, 77,* 1021–1034.

Laser, P. S., & Mathie, V. A. (1982). Face facts: An unbidden role for features in communication. *Journal of Nonverbal Behavior, 7,* 3–19.

Lavater, J. C. (1783). *Essays on physiognomy.* London: Ward, Lock.

Lavrakas, P. J. (1975). Female preferences for male physiques. *Journal of Research in Personality, 9,* 324–334.

Lawrence, S. G., & Watson, M. (1991). Getting others to help: The effectiveness of professional uniforms in charitable fund-raising. *Journal of Applied Communication Research, 19,* 170–185.

Lefkowitz, M., Blake, R., & Mouton, J. (1955). Status factors in pedestrian violation of traffic signals. *Journal of Abnormal and Social Psychology, 51,* 704–706.

Lerner, R. M., & Gellert, E. (1969). Body build identification, preference, and aversion in children. *Developmental Psychology, 1,* 456–462.

Lerner, R. M., Karabenick, S. A., & Meisels, M. (1975). Effects of age and sex on the development of personal space schemata toward body build. *Journal of Genetic Psychology, 127,* 91–101.

Lerner, R. M., Karabenick, S. A., & Stuart, J. L. (1973). Relations among physical attractiveness, body attitudes, and self-concept in male and female college students. *Journal of Psychology, 85,* 119–129.

Lerner, R. M., & Korn, S. J. (1972). The development of body build stereotypes in males. *Child Development, 43,* 908–920.

Lerner, R. M., & Schroeder, C. (1971). Physique identification, preference, and aversion in kindergarten children. *Developmental Psychology, 5,* 538.

Lerner, R. M., Venning, J., & Knapp, J. R. (1975). Age and sex effects on personal space schemata toward body build in late childhood. *Developmental Psychology, 11,* 855–856.

Lester, D., & Sheehan, D. (1980). Attitudes of supervisors toward short police officers. *Psychological Reports, 47,* 462.

Levine, J. M., & McBurney, D. H. (1977). Causes and consequences of effluvia: Body odor awareness and controllability as determinants of interpersonal evaluation. *Personality and Social Psychology Bulletin, 3,* 442–445.

Levine, L. R., Bluni, T. D., & Hochman, S. H. (1998). Attire and charitable behavior. *Psychological Reports, 83,* 15–18.

Lippman, L. G. (1980). Toward a social psychology of flatulence: The interpersonal regulation of natural gas. *Psychology: A Quarterly Journal of Human Behavior, 17,* 41–50.

Little, A. C., Penton-Voak, I. S., Burt, D. M., & Perrett, D. I. (2002). Evolution and individual differences in the perception of attractiveness: How cyclic hormonal changes in self-perceived attractiveness influence female preferences for male faces (pp. 59–90). In G. Rhodes & L. A. Zebrowitz (Eds.), *Facial attractiveness.* Westport, CT: Ablex.

Long, T. J. (1978). Influence of uniform and religious status on interviewees. *Journal of Counseling Psychology, 25,* 405–409.

Lord, T., & Kasprzak, M. (1989). Identification of self through olfaction. *Perceptual and Motor Skills, 69,* 219–224.

Lurie, A. (1981). *The language of clothes.* New York: Random House.

Maddux, J. E., & Rogers, R. W. (1980). Effects of source expertness, physical attractiveness, and supporting arguments on persuasion: A case of brains over beauty. *Journal of Personality and Social Psychology, 39,* 235–244.

Malloy, J. T. (1975). *Dress for success.* New York: P. H. Wyden.

Malloy, J. T. (1977). *The women's dress for success book.* Chicago: Follet.

Mar, T. T. (1974). *Face reading.* New York: New American Library (Signet Book).

Martin, J. G. (1964). Racial ethnocentrism and judgment of beauty. *Journal of Social Psychology, 63,* 59–63.

Mathes, E. W., & Kahn, A. (1975). Physical attractiveness, happiness, neuroticism, and self esteem. *Journal of Psychology, 90,* 27–30.

McArthur, L. Z., & Baron, R. M. (1983). Toward an ecological theory of social perception. *Psychological Review, 90,* 215–238.

McBurney, D. H., Levine, J. N., & Cavanaugh, P. H. (1977). Psychophysical and social ratings of human body odor. *Personality and Social Psychology Bulletin, 3,* 135–138.

McClintock, M. K. (1971). Menstrual synchrony and suppression. *Nature, 229,* 244–245.

Mills, J., & Aronson, E. (1965). Opinion change as a function of the communicators' attractiveness and desire to influence. *Journal of Personality and Social Psychology, 1,* 173–177.

Monetmayor, R. (1978). Men and their bodies: The relationship between body type and behavior. *Journal of Social Issues, 34,* 48–64.

Morris, T. L., Gorham, J., Cohen, S. H., & Huffman, D. (1996). Fashion in the classroom: Effects of attire on student perceptions of instructors in college classes. *Communication Education, 45,* 135–148.

Murstein, B. I. (1972). Physical attractiveness and marital choice. *Journal of Personality and Social Psychology, 23,* 8–12.

Murstein, B. I., & Christy, P. (1976). Physical attractiveness and marriage adjustment in middle-aged couples. *Journal of Personality and Social Psychology, 34,* 537–542.

Murstein, B. I., Gadpaille, W. J., & Byrne, D. (1971). What makes people sexually appealing? *Sexual Behavior, 1,* 75–77.

Myers, P. N., Jr., & Biocca, F. A. (1992). The elastic body image: The effect of television advertising and programming on body image distortions in young women. *Journal of Communication, 42,* 108–133.

Nemmeth, C., & Hyland, R. (1973). A simulated jury study: Characteristics of the defendant and the jurors. *Journal of Social Psychology, 90,* 223–229.

Nevid, J. S. (1984). Sex differences in factors of romantic attraction. *Sex Roles, 2,* 401–411.

Parnell, R. W. (1958). *Behavior and physique: An introduction to practical and applied somatometry.* London: Edward Arnold.

Pellegrini, R. J. (1973). The virtue of hairiness. *Psychology Today, 6,* 14.

Pellegrini, R. J. (1989). Beardedness as a stimulus variable: Note on methodology and metaanalysis of impression-formation data. *Perceptual and Motor Skills, 69,* 161–162.

Pennebaker, J. W., Dyer, M. A., Caulkins, R. S., Litowitz, D. L., Ackerman, P. L., Anderson, D. B., & McGraw, K. M. (1979). Don't the girls get prettier at closing time: A country and western application to psychology. *Personality and Social Psychology Bulletin, 5,* 122–125.

Penton-Voak, I. S., Perrett, D. I., Castles, D. L., Kobayashi, T., Burt, D. M., Murray, L. K., & Minamisawa, R. (1999). Menstrual cycle alters face preference. *Nature, 399,* 741–742.

Pertschuk, M., Trisdorfer, A., & Allison, P. D. (1994). Men's bodies—the survey. *Psychology Today,* 35–36, 39, 72.

Polhemus, T., & Proctor, L. (1978). *Fashion and anti-fashion: An anthropology of clothing and adornment.* London: Thames & Hudson.

Polivy, J., Garner, D. M., & Garfinkel, P. E. (1986). Causes and consequences of the current preference for thin female physiques. In C. P. Herman, M. P. Zanna, & E. T. Higgins (Eds.), *Physical appearance, stigma, and social behavior: The Ontario Symposium* (Vol. 3). Hillsdale, NJ: Erlbaum.

Porter, R. H., Cernoch, J. M., & Balogh, R. D. (1985). Odor signatures and kin recognition. *Physiology and Behavior, 34,* 445–448.

Porter, R. H., Cernoch, J. M., & McLaughlin, F. J. (1983). Maternal recognition of neonates through olfactory cues. *Physiology and Behavior, 30,* 151–154.

Porter, R. H., & Moore, J. D. (1981). Human kin recognition by olfactory cues. *Physiology and Behavior, 27,* 493–495.

Portnoy, E. J. (1993). The impact of body type on perceptions of attractiveness by older individuals. *Communication Reports, 6,* 101–108.

Preti, G., Wysocki, C. J., Barnhart, K. T., Sondheimer, S. J., & Leyden, J. J. (2003). Male axillary extracts contain hormones that affect pulsatile secretion of luteinizing hormone and mood in women recipients. *Biology of Reproduction, 68,* 2107–2113.

Raymond, B., & Unger, R. (1972). The apparel oft proclaims the man. *Journal of Social Psychology, 87,* 75–82.

Reed, J. A. P. (1973). *Clothing: A symbolic indicator of the self.* Unpublished doctoral dissertation, Purdue University.

Reid, A., Lancuba, V., & Morrow, B. (1997). Clothing style and formation of first impressions. *Perceptual and Motor Skills, 84,* 237–238.

Reingen, P. H., & Kernan, J. B. (1993). Social perception and interpersonal influence: Some consequences of the physical attractiveness stereotype in a personal selling setting. *Journal of Consumer Psychology, 2,* 25–38.

Reis, H. T., Nezlek, J., & Wheeler, L. (1980). Physical attractiveness in social interaction. *Journal of Personality and Social Psychology, 38,* 604–617.

Reis, H. T., Wheeler, L., Spiegel, N., Kernis, M. H., Nezlek, J., & Perri, M. (1982). Physical attractiveness in social interaction: II. Why does appearance affect social experience? *Journal of Personality and Social Psychology, 43,* 979–996.

Rhodes, G., Harwood, K., Sakiko, Y., Nishitani, M., & McLean, I. (2002). The attractiveness of average faces: Cross-cultural evidence and possible biological basis (pp. 35–58). In G. Rhodes & L. A. Zebrowitz (Eds.), *Facial attractiveness.* Westport, CT: Ablex.

Rhodes, G., & Zebrowitz, L. A. (Eds.). (2002). *Facial attractiveness.* Westport, CT: Ablex.

Richardson, S. A., Goodman, N., Hastorf, A., & Dornbusch, S. (1961). Cultural uniformities in relation to physical disabilities. *American Sociological Review, 26,* 241–247.

Roach, K. D. (1997). Effects of graduate teaching assistant attire on student learning, misbehaviors, and ratings of instruction. *Communication Quarterly, 45,* 125–141.

Roach, M. E., & Eicher, J. B. (Eds.). (1965). *Dress, adornment, and the social order.* New York: Wiley.

Roberts, J. V., & Herman, C. P. (1986). The psychology of height: An empirical review. In C. P. Herman, M. P. Zanna, & E. T. Higgins (Eds.), *Physical appearance, stigma, and social behavior: The Ontario Symposium* (Vol. 3). Hillsdale, NJ: Erlbaum.

Rosenfeld, L. B., & Plax, T. G. (1977). Clothing as communication. *Journal of Communication, 27,* 24–31.

Rosenthal, T. L., & White, G. M. (1972). On the importance of hair in students' clinical inferences. *Journal of Clinical Psychology, 28,* 43–47.

Rubenstein, A. J., Langlois, J. H., & Roggman, L. A. (2002). What makes a face attractive and why: The role of averageness in defining facial beauty (pp. 1–33). In G. Rhodes & L. A. Zebrowitz (Eds.), *Facial attractiveness.* Westport, CT: Ablex.

Rudofsky, B. (1971). *The unfashionable human body*. Garden City, NY: Doubleday.

Rump, E. E., & Delin, P. S. (1973). Differential accuracy in the status–height phenomenon and an experimenter effect. *Journal of Personality and Social Psychology, 28*, 343–347.

Russell, F. (1981). *The secret war*. Chicago: Time Life.

Russell, M. J. (1976). Human olfactory communication. *Nature, 260*, 520–522.

Ryan, M. S. (1966). *Clothing: A study in human behavior*. New York: Holt, Rinehart & Winston.

Ryckman, R. M., Robbins, M. A., Thornton, B., Kaczor, L. M., Gayton, S. L., & Anderson, C. V. (1991). Public self-consciousness and physique stereotyping. *Personality and Social Psychology Bulletin, 17*, 400–405.

Sanders, C. (1989). *The body: The art and culture of tattooing*. Philadelphia: Temple University Press.

Secord, P. F., Dukes, W. F., & Bevan, W. W. (1954). Personalities in faces: I. An experiment in social perceiving. *Genetic Psychology Monographs, 49*, 231–279.

Seiter, J. S., & Dunn, D. (2000). Beauty and believability in sexual harassment cases: Does physical attractiveness affect perceptions of veracity and the likelihood of being harassed? *Communication Research Reports, 17*, 203–209.

Seligman, C., Brickman, J., & Koulack, D. (1977). Rape and physical attractiveness: Assigning responsibility to victims. *Journal of Personality, 45*, 554–563.

Shannon, M. L., & Stark, C. P. (2003). The influence of physical appearance on personnel selection. *Social Behavior and Personality, 31*, 613–624.

Sheldon, W. H. (1940). *The varieties of human physique*. New York: Harper & Row.

Sheldon, W. H. (1942). *The varieties of temperament*. New York: Harper & Row.

Sheldon, W. H. (1954). *Atlas of man: A guide for somatyping the adult male at all ages*. New York: Harper & Row.

Shontz, F. C. (1969). *Perceptual and cognitive aspects of body experience*. New York: Academic Press.

Sigall, H., & Landy, D. (1973). Radiating beauty: Effects of having a physically attractive partner on person perception. *Journal of Personality and Social Psychology, 26*, 218–223.

Sigall, H., & Ostrove, N. (1975). Beautiful but dangerous: Effects of offender attractiveness and nature of the crime of juridic judgment. *Journal of Personality and Social Psychology, 31*, 410–414.

Singer, J. E. (1964). The use of manipulative strategies: Machiavellianism and attractiveness. *Sociometry, 27*, 128–151.

Singh, D. (1993). Adaptive significance of female physical attractiveness: Role of waist-to-hip ratio. *Journal of Personality and Social Psychology, 65*, 293–307.

Singh, D. (1995). Female judgment of male attractiveness and desirability for relationships: Role of waist-to-hip ratio and financial status. *Journal of Personality and Social Psychology, 69*, 1089–1101.

Slater, A., Von der Schulennurg, C., Brown, E., Badenoch, M., Butterworth, G., Parsons, S., & Samuels, C. (1998). Newborn infants prefer attractive faces. *Infant Behavior and Development, 21*, 345–354.

Smith, K., & Sines, J. O. (1960). Demonstration of a peculiar odor in the sweat of schizophrenic patients. *Archives of General Psychiatry, 2*, 184–188.

Sobal, J., & Stunkard, A. J. (1989). Socioeconomic status and obesity: A review of the literature. *Psychological Bulletin, 105*, 260–275.

Solender, E. K., & Solender, E. (1976). Minimizing the effect of the unattractive client on the jury: A study of the interaction of physical appearance with assertions and self-experience references. *Human Rights, 5*, 201–214.

Solomon, M. R. (Ed.). (1985). *The psychology of fashion*. New York: Lexington.

Stabler, B., Whitt, K., Moreault, D., D'Ercole, A., & Underwood, L. (1980). Social judgments by children of short stature. *Psychological Reports, 46,* 743–746.

Staffieri, J. R. (1972). Body build and behavioral expectancies in young females. *Developmental Psychology, 6,* 125–127.

Stern, K., & McClintock, M. K. (1998). Regulation of ovulation by human pheromones. *Nature, 392,* 177–179.

Stewart, J. E. (1980). Defendant's attractiveness as a factor in the outcome of criminal trials: An observational study. *Journal of Applied Social Psychology, 10,* 348–361.

Stewart, R. A., Tufton, S. J., & Steel, R. E. (1973). Stereotyping and personality: Sex differences in perception of female physiques. *Perceptual and Motor Skills, 36,* 811–814.

Streeter, S. A., & McBurney, D. H. (2003). Waist-hip ratio and attractiveness: New evidence and a critique of a "critical test" *Evolution and Human Behavior, 24,* 88–98.

Stroebe, W., Insko, C. A., Thompson, V. D., & Layton, B. D. (1971). Effects of physical attractiveness, attitudes similarity, and sex on various aspects of interpersonal attraction. *Journal of Personality and Social Psychology, 79,* 79–91.

Strongman, K. T., & Hart, C. J. (1968). Stereotyped reactions to body build. *Psychological Reports, 23,* 1175–1178.

Suedfeld, P., Bochner, S., & Matas, C. (1971). Petitioner's attire and petition signing by peace demonstrators: A field experiment. *Journal of Applied Social Psychology, 1,* 278–283.

Tassinary, L. G., & Hansen, K. A. (1998). A critical test of the waits-to-hip ratio hypothesis of female physical attractiveness. *Psychological Science, 9,* 150–155.

Tavris, C. (1977). Men and women report their views on masculinity. *Psychology Today, 10,* 34–42, 82.

Thornhill, R., & Gangestad, S. W. (1993). Human facial beauty: Averageness, symmetry, and parasite resistance. *Human Nature, 4,* 237–269.

Timmerman, K., & Hewitt, J. (1980). Examining the halo effect of physical attractiveness. *Perceptual and Motor Skills, 51,* 607–612.

Udry, J. R., & Eckland, B. K. (1984). Benefits of being attractive: Differential payoffs for men and women. *Psychological Reports, 54,* 47–56.

Urbaniak, G. C., & Kilmann, P. R. (2003). Physical attractiveness and the "nice guy paradox": Do nice guys really finish last? *Sex Roles, 49,* 413–426.

Walker, R. N. (1963). Body build and behavior in young children: II. Body build and parents' ratings. *Child Development, 34,* 1–23.

Wallace, P. (1977). Individual discrimination of human by odor. *Physiology and Behavior, 19,* 577–579.

Walster, E., Aronson, V., Abrahams, D., & Rottmann, L. (1966). Importance of physical attractiveness in dating behavior. *Journal of Personality and Social Psychology, 4,* 508–516.

Watson, B. (1975, May 16). Cons get cosmetic surgery. *Lafayette Journal and Courier,* p. A–8.

Weiten, W. (1980). The attraction–leniency effect in jury research: An examination of external validity. *Journal of Applied Social Psychology, 10,* 340–347.

Wells, W., & Siegel, B. (1961). Stereotyped somatypes. *Psychological Reports, 8,* 77–78.

White, G. L. (1980). Physical attractiveness and courtship progress. *Journal of Personality and Social Psychology, 39,* 660–668.

White, S. E. (1995). A content analytic technique for measuring the sexiness of women's business attire in media presentations. *Communication Research Reports, 12,* 178–185.

Widgery, R. N. (1974). Sex of receiver and physical attractiveness of source as determinants of initial credibility perceptions. *Western Speech, 38,* 13–17.

Wiener, H. (1966). External chemical messengers: I. Emission and reception in man. *New York State Journal of Medicine, 66,* 3153.

Wiggins, J. S., Wiggins, N., & Conger, J. C. (1968). Correlates of heterosexual somatic preference. *Journal of Personality and Social Psychology, 10,* 82–90.

Wiggins, N., & Wiggins, J. S. (1969). A topological analysis of male preferences for female body types. *Multivariate Behavioral Research, 4,* 89–102.

Wilson, P. R. (1968). Perceptual distortion of height as a function of ascribed academic status. *Journal of Social Psychology, 10,* 97–102.

Wolf, N. (1991). *The beauty myth.* New York: Morrow.

Wuensch, K. L., & Moore, C. H. (2004). Effects of physical attractiveness on evaluations of a male employee's allegation of sexual harassment by his female employer. *Journal of Social Psychology, 144,* 207–217.

Yates, J., & Taylor, J. (1978). Stereotypes for somatypes: Shared beliefs about Sheldon's physiques. *Psychological Reports, 43,* 777–778.

Young, M. (1999). Dressed to commune, dressed to kill: Changing police imagery in England and Wales. In K. K. P. Johnson and S. J. Lennon (Eds.), *Appearance and power.* New York: Oxford University Press.

Zebrowitz, L. A. (1997). *Reading faces.* Boulder, CO: Westview Press.

Part Four

THE COMMUNICATORS' BEHAVIOR

M ost of our nonverbal behavior involves change or movement. We exhibit different gestures and postures during an encounter; sometimes we touch others and sometimes we do not; our face, eyes, and voice also are displayed in various patterns. Part Four examines these behaviors individually, but in everyday conversation the combination of such signals working in concert characterizes our communication behavior.

Chapter 7

THE EFFECTS OF GESTURE AND POSTURE ON HUMAN COMMUNICATION

We respond to gestures with an extreme alertness and, one might say, in accordance with an elaborate and secret code that is written nowhere, known by none, and understood by all.

—EDWARD SAPIR

Sapir's view (quoted here) aptly characterized the prevailing view of gestures during the *first* part of the 20th century. If he were alive today, his assessment would no doubt be somewhat different. Spoken language and gestures are commonly acknowledged as building blocks of human interaction (informal conversation as well as more formal public discourse), but, unlike language, gestures received relatively little scholarly attention until the last part of the 20th century. Kendon (1981a) identified only six scholarly books on gesture published between 1900 and 1979 in the English language. Now, however, gestures are carefully scrutinized by scholars from around the world, and an academic journal specifically devoted to gesture research, *Gesture*, was launched in 2001. As a result, our knowledge of how people use and respond to gestures has greatly increased.

What exactly is a gesture? *Gestures* are movements made by the body or some part of it. Typically, gestures are thought of as arm and hand movements, but head gestures are also well known. Normally gestures are produced without bodily touch, but it does happen. For example, a pointing gesture may touch the speaker's own body or that of the listener. The movements involved while actually performing tasks such as grooming, smoking, eating, drawing, or hammering a nail are not considered gestures, but arm and hand movements that allude to and represent the performance of such behaviors are definitely considered gestures. In fact, people whose daily work involves a variety of manual manipulations, like the work of a car mechanic, may develop a gestural repertoire that emanates from this work (Streeck, 2002).

Gestures perform many functions. They may replace speech (during dialogue or when speech is not used at all), regulate the flow and rhythm of interaction, maintain attention, add emphasis and/or clarity to speech, help characterize and make memorable the content of speech, act as forecasters of forthcoming speech, and help speakers access and formulate speech.

What types of gestures are commonly employed in everyday interaction? Gestures may be categorized in many ways (McNeill, 2000; Morris, 1977, 1994). This chapter uses a classification system based on the extent to which a gesture is dependent on speech for its meaning. This is a useful distinction and we can learn a lot about gestures as either *speech-independent* or *speech-dependent*. At the same time, however, it is also important to recognize the difficulties in neatly categorizing a behavior which, on the surface, may seem relatively uncomplicated. Take, for example, the head shake (Kendon, 2002). Sometimes we use the head shake as a speech-independent gesture meaning "no" (even though a side-to-side head wobble in parts of India and Bulgaria means just the opposite). And while a "no" meaning can be communicated without speech, sometimes people will say "no" during the shake. The meaning of the shake has a greater dependence on the accompanying speech when it is used to signal disapproval or doubt which may occur while saying, "Well, I guess I could talk to him . . ." In addition, the head shake also accompanies statements to underscore intensity or impossibility, as in "You just wouldn't believe how beautiful she was." The head shake, like all the gestures discussed in this chapter, can be used and interpreted in different ways, depending on the way it is enacted and the context in which it occurs. With this in mind, let's examine those gestures that are less dependent on speech for their meaning.

SPEECH-INDEPENDENT GESTURES

Speech-independent gestures are also known as *emblems* (Ekman, 1976, 1977) or *autonomous gestures* (Kendon, 1984, 1989). They are nonverbal acts that have a direct verbal translation or dictionary definition, usually consisting of a word or two or a phrase. There is high agreement among members of a culture or subculture on the verbal translation of these signals. These gestures are the least dependent on speech for their meaning and most commonly occur as a single gesture. The "ring gesture" in Figure 7-1 is an example of a speech-independent gesture found in several cultures.

Children are able to decode some of these speech-independent gestures by the time they are 3 years old, and this ability increases dramatically by age 5 (Kumin & Lazar, 1974; Michael & Willis, 1968, 1969). In one study, 4-year-olds of both sexes accurately decoded the emblems for "yes," "no," "come here," "quiet," "good-bye," "two," "I won't listen," "blowing a kiss," "I'm going to sleep," and "I won't do it." None of the 4-year-olds was able to accurately decode "crazy." Generally, children at this age understand and decode accurately more speech-independent gestures than they actually use in their own interactions. However, with prompting and support by caregivers, babies who have not learned to talk can effectively use between 10 and 60 signs to communicate (Acredolo & Goodwyn, 1996).

Adult awareness of speech-independent gestures is about the same as of word choice. It is a behavior we are usually very conscious of enacting. These gestures often are produced with the hand, but not exclusively. A nose wrinkle may say "I'm disgusted!" or

FIGURE 7-1

The ring gesture signifies "A-OK" or "good" in the United States as a speech-independent gesture. It may stand for "zero" or "worthless" in certain conversational/cultural contexts.

"Phew! It stinks!" To say "I don't know" or "I'm helpless" or "I'm uncertain," we might turn both palms up, shrug the shoulders, or do both simultaneously. Ekman believes that facial emblems differ from facial expressions of emotion by being more stylized and presented for longer or shorter duration. Facial emblems also may emphasize particular parts of the face, for example, smiling to indicate happiness or mechanically dropping the jaw or dramatically raising the eyebrows to indicate surprise.

In some cultures, speech-independent gestures are strung together to form a sequential message, but this is unusual in the United States. Although it could happen if you were on the phone when a visitor enters your office and you need to indicate "wait a minute," "come in," and "sit down" in succession. Sometimes an entire system of speech-independent gestures develops as with underwater divers, umpires, and television directors. Even though these gestures form a system of signals related to performing a specific task, such systems can grow beyond the boundaries of those tasks. In the sawmills of British Columbia, for example, the noise level made spoken communication very difficult. A system of task-related gestures developed but eventually came to include messages not associated with the tasks of the sawmill (Meissner & Philpott, 1975). Gesture systems not limited to a specific task are known as *sign languages*. Sign language is commonly thought of as a form of communication for the hearing impaired, but sign languages also develop in other contexts. Examples are in religious orders where vows of silence are taken and in social situations where some participants are forbidden to speak, as has been reported for Armenian wives in the presence of their husbands (Kendon, 1983).

Speech-independent gestures may be used when verbal channels are blocked or fail, but they also are used during verbal interaction. A person may be telling the story of another person's strange behavior and may conclude by making a gesture that communicates "He's crazy." In this case, the circular gesture at the side of the head substitutes for the entire sentence. This gesture also could be used to complete an utterance: "If you ask me, I think . . ." In this case, the verbalizations are redundant and unnecessary for understanding the message being communicated. In this example, the speech-independent gesture occurred at the end of a speaker's turn, but others may occur at the beginning. Ekman's study of the "shrug" emblem finds it occurs most often at the beginning of a speaker's turn (see Figure 7-2).

In an interview observed by Ekman, he noted an emblem that was used for a long time during the interaction and served as the interviewee's commentary on the episode. This "emblematic slip" (analogous to a slip of the tongue) occurred when a woman was subjected to a stressful interview by a person whose status forbade free expressions of dislike. The woman, unknown to herself or the interviewer during the interview, displayed "the finger" on one hand as it rested on the arm of the chair. Listeners may also use speech-independent

FIGURE 7-2

The shrug gesture.

gestures to comment on or qualify what the speaker is saying. "Yes" and "no" gestures are common listener responses during another's speech.

Thus, even though speech-independent gestures can communicate messages without attendant speech, their meanings are still influenced by context. Giving someone "the finger" can be humorous or insulting, depending on who is performing it, who is the target, and what other behaviors accompany it. Facial expressions and eye movement accompanying speech-independent gestures are likely to expand the range of possible meanings associated with a hand gesture. And it is always possible that the meaning associated with a gesture in the absence of speech will be modified if it is accompanied by speech, including those occasions when the accompanying speech is seemingly redundant. Some of these emblematic gestures are specifically adapted to particular subgroups within a given culture. In the United States, for example, the finger-wag gesture indicating "no-no" is used primarily when adults are addressing children; the "shame on you" gesture seems limited to usage by children (see Figure 7-3).

Sherzer's (1974, 1982) detailed work of the pointed lip gesture used by the San Blas Cuna of Panama and the thumbs-up gesture used by urban Brazilians illustrates how gestures may have a general meaning that is modified by context. For example, the thumbs-up gesture has a general meaning of "good" or "positive" (see Figure 7-4). Context, however, expands the range of meanings. It can be used to indicate understanding the point of what someone said or did; to acknowledge a favor granted; to greet someone; to indicate knowledge of the next move in an interactional sequence and who is going to perform it; and to request permission to carry out an action, as when a customer signals a waiter about the availability of a table.

Sometimes the context does not affect the meaning so much as the slight changes in the way the gesture is performed. When the forefinger extended (with the rest of the hand

FIGURE 7-3

Finger emblems used in the United States for "no" (left) and "shame on you" (right).

FIGURE 7-4

The thumbs-up gesture by 2004 vice presidential candidate John Edwards.

in a fist) is held motionless about 12 inches in front of one's chest, the meaning is "wait a minute"; when the finger repeatedly moves up and down, the meaning shifts to one of emphasis or reprimand; when the same finger and hand are put perpendicularly in front of the lips, it means "be quiet."

There are published lists of emblematic gestures for cultures around the world (Armstrong & Wagner, 2003; Axtell, 1991; Barakat, 1973; Creider, 1977; Johnson, Ekman, & Friesen, 1975; Morris et al., 1979; Poggi, 2002; Saitz & Cervenka, 1972; Sparhawk, 1978; Trupin, 1976; Wylie, 1977). Kendon's (1981b) analysis of over 800 emblematic gestures contained in some of these lists revealed three broad categories of meaning that accounted for 80% of the speech-independent gestures observed in the United States, Colombia, France, southern Italy, and Kenya and 66% of those found in Iran. These categories were *interpersonal control, announcement of one's current state or condition,* and *an evaluative response to the actions or appearance of another.* Ekman's studies of five cultures indicate each had emblematic gestures for greeting and departing, replying, directing locomotion (all forms of interpersonal control); for insults as evaluation of another's actions or appearance; and for referring to one's physical and affective state or announcing one's current condition or state. Some cultures have many emblems in a particular category (e.g., evaluations of another's behavior), whereas the emblems in another culture may emphasize other messages (e.g., interpersonal control).

As yet, no speech-independent gestures have been found that are made the same and have the same meaning in every culture studied. Future research may identify some, however. The most likely candidates are gestures having to do with affirmation, negation, stop, don't know, and sleeping, eating, and drinking (functions all human beings share).

Far more common are examples of gestures of similar form that differ in meaning from culture to culture. In 1877–1878, Bulgaria and Russia combined forces to fight Turkey. The alliance discovered a real problem in that the Russian way of saying "no" was to shake the head from side to side, and a very similar Bulgarian gesture (a head sway or wobble) meant "yes" (Jacobson, 1972). The ring gesture (thumb and forefinger in a circle) pictured in Figure 7-1 indicates "you're worth zero" in France and Belgium; "money" in Japan; "asshole" in parts of southern Italy; and in Greece and Turkey it is an insulting or vulgar sexual invitation. Of course, to many U.S. residents it is simply "A-OK." Things certainly would not be "A-OK" if the ring gesture was used in cultures that attach other meanings to it.

The thumbs-up gesture pictured in Figure 7-4 is usually decoded as "good," "positive," or "OK" in the United States, but in the Middle East it is an obscene gesture. The thumb inserted between the index and third finger (fig gesture) is an invitation to have sex in Germany, Holland, and Denmark but is a wish for good luck or protection in Portugal and Brazil (see Figure 7-5). The "V" gesture with the palm toward the performer is a sexual insult in Great Britain but means "victory" if the palm is facing away from the body. During World War II, Winston Churchill made the "V for victory" gesture world famous. In the United States, there does not seem to be the British meaning of sexual insult associated with the "V" sign, nor is there any distinction in the form of the "V" for victory and the "V" for peace—a meaning that gained popularity in the anti–Vietnam War protests of the 1960s (Figure 7-6 shows Persian Gulf War demonstrators making the "V" sign for peace).

The vertical horn sign pictured in Figure 7-7 is normally decoded "cuckold" in Portugal, Spain, Italy, and places in Central and South America. Students from cultures in which this gesture indicates that "your wife has been unfaithful to you, and you are either too stupid to know it or not man enough to satisfy her" would indeed be surprised if they were to attend the University of Texas. Here, and throughout Texas, the horns hand is used to show identification with the university and represents school spirit. It is modeled

FIGURE 7-5

The fig gesture.

FIGURE 7-6

(a) "V" gesture used as an insult in Britain. (b) Richard Nixon makes the "V for victory" gesture at the 1968 Republican Convention in Miami.

a

b

FIGURE 7-6   (Continued)

(c) People at an anti–Persian Gulf War demonstration in Washington, D.C., using the "V" gesture to signify "peace."

c

after longhorn cattle and literally represents the University of Texas Longhorns. Consider the reaction of people who associate the horns hand with "cuckold" viewing a University of Texas football game with 75,000 fans making the sign vigorously, repeatedly, and in unison. In addition, another sign that is similar, but has the thumb thrust out instead of tucked in, is decoded by many people around the world as "I love you." The origin of this sign is in the finger spelling of deaf communicators.

Many autonomous gestures have no equivalent in other cultures. In France, for example, one can signal "drunk" by making a fist around the nose and twisting. Some messages have different gestural forms from culture to culture. Notice how the gestures for suicide in Figure 7-8 reflect the most common methods of suicide in each culture. The number of speech-independent gestures used within a given culture may vary considerably, from fewer than 100 in the United States to more than 250 identified with Israeli students.

One of the problems in comparing studies of speech-independent gestures across cultures is the lack of a uniform method for identifying them. Johnson, Ekman, and Friesen's study (1975) of American emblematic gestures proposes a systematic procedure that future studies may want to use. The authors ask members of a particular group or culture to produce emblems associated with a list of verbal statements and phrases. They

FIGURE 7-7

(a) The vertical horn gesture. (b) The "I love you" sign.

(c) Hank Aaron ends a short speech before a game between the Texas Rangers and the Colorado Rockies with the University of Texas "Hook 'em Horns" salute in Arlington, Texas.

FIGURE 7-7   (Continued)

(d) Miss America 1995, Heather Whitestore, a former Miss Alabama, walks down the runway and signs "I love you" to the crowd after she won the 74th annual pageant in Atlantic City. (e) The double horn gesture in Naples means "cuckolded."

d   e

report that after about 10 or 15 informants have been tested, a great majority of the emblems have been identified. To qualify as a "verified" emblem, at least 70% of the encoders must perform the action in a similar way. The emblems similarly encoded are then presented to a group of decoders who are asked to identify the meaning of the gestures and the extent to which they reflect natural usage in everyday situations. Gestures used primarily for games like charades normally are not considered "natural." Inventions and performances that require speech are also eliminated. At least 70% of the decoders also have to match the encoder's meaning and judge the gesture to be used naturally in everyday communication situations. The index finger pointed at the head can mean "smart" or "stupid" depending on context, but if 70% of those in a given community say it means "stupid" (without accompanying contextual information), then this is considered a verified emblem for "stupid" among this group. It does not prevent context from changing the meaning, however.

Figure 7-8

Cultural variations in suicide gestures: Top left: *the South Fore, Papua New Guinea;* Bottom: *Japan;* Top right: *the United States.*

SPEECH-RELATED GESTURES

Speech-related gestures, sometimes called *illustrators,* are directly tied to, or accompany, speech. The meanings and functions of these gestures are revealed as we examine how they relate to the attendant spoken language. Attempts to classify the various types of speech-related gestures have used different terminology (Efron, 1941/1972; Ekman, 1977; Kendon, 1989; McNeill, 1992, 2000; Streeck & Knapp, 1992) but four common types emerge:

1. Gestures related to the speaker's referent—concrete or abstract
2. Gestures indicating the speaker's relationship to the referent
3. Gestures that act as visual punctuation for the speaker's discourse
4. Gestures that assist in the regulation and organization of the spoken dialogue between two interactants

REFERENT-RELATED GESTURES

As we talk, we use gestures to characterize the content of our speech. Sometimes these are movements depicting fairly concrete referents; sometimes vague, abstract ideas are the referent for gestural depiction.

Pointing movements, for instance, can help indicate a specific person, place, or thing being discussed. The referent may be in the immediate conversational environment or something more distant, as is the case when you say, "And where did you come from before that?" while pointing your finger in the direction of the referred-to place. Gestures that draw the referent's shape or movement and gestures that depict spatial relationships can be used to help a listener visualize features associated with concrete referents. When you say, "I had to bend the branch way back" while illustrating how you did this, the gesture bears a close relationship to the concrete semantic content of your speech. When referent-related gestures outline the referent by drawing a picture in space (e.g., an hourglass figure signifying "shapely woman"), it may be asked whether this is truly speech related. The test for determining whether such a picture may be speech independent is if 70% of the members of the usage community respond with the "shapely woman" meaning when confronted with the gestural portrayal without any speech context.

More abstract referents are characterized when we sketch the path or direction of an idea in the air; when we make a series of circular movements with the hand and/or arm suggesting, "I mean more than the specific words I've used"; and when we use expansion and contraction gestures, like those of an accordion player, to indicate the breadth of the subject being discussed. Sometimes we represent abstract content via gestural metaphors. For example, cup-shaped gestures in the following sample of discourse (McNeill, 1985) represent containers of what could be supposed. When they spread apart, they seem to convey the idea that "anything is possible," and their sudden disappearance suggests that what might have been did not happen:

> "Even though one might *(both hands form cups and spread wide apart)* have supposed *(cups vanish abruptly)* ..."

SPEAKER'S-RELATIONSHIP-TO-THE-REFERENT GESTURES

These gestures, rather than characterizing the nature of the thing being talked about, comment on the speaker's orientation to the referent. The positioning of the palms can show very different orientations toward one's own message (see Figure 7-9). For example, palms up for more uncertainty ("I think" or "I'm not sure"); palms down for certainty ("clearly" or "absolutely"); palms out and facing the listener for assertions ("Let me say this ..." or "Calm down"); and palms facing the speaker for embracing a concept ("I've got this great idea ..."). Palm positions can have other speech-related associations, such as a speaker's palms up when pleading, begging, or even anticipating closeness in greetings.

Oscillating hand movements suggest a speaker "isn't sure" or "could go either way." Charles de Gaulle, former president of France, was noted for his grasping gesture, which many felt signified his desire to control the subject under discussion (see Figure 7-10).

Figure 7-9

Palm gestures.

Figure 7-10

General Charles de Gaulle's characteristic gesture, perceived by many as "grasping for control of an idea."

1950   1964

Punctuation Gestures

Punctuation gestures accent, emphasize, and organize important segments of the discourse. Such a segment may be a single word or a larger utterance unit (e.g., a summary or a new theme). When these gestures are used to emphasize a particular word or phrase, they often coincide with the primary voice stress. Punctuation gestures can also organize the stream of speech into units. When we speak of a series of things, we may communicate discreteness by rhythmic chopping hand gestures, for example, "We must consider A (gesture), B (gesture), and C (gesture)." Sometimes a single chopping hand gesture after C indicates C will be considered separately, or A, B, and C will be considered as a group. A slight downward movement of the head may accompany the hand gestures. Pounding the

FIGURE 7-11

Punctuation gestures.

hand or fist in the air or on another object also acts as a device for adding emphasis and visually underlining a particular point being made (see Figure 7-11).

Punctuation can, of course, be accomplished with body movements other than the hands. The "eye flash" (not the "eye*brow*" flash" discussed in chapters 2 and 10) is one such display (Bull & Connelly, 1985; Walker & Trimboli, 1983). The momentary widening of a speaker's eyelids, without involving the eyebrows, has been found to occur most often in conjunction with spoken adjectives and used for emphasis.

INTERACTIVE GESTURES

Thus far, the gesture categories discussed have focused on the content of the speaker's monologue. *Interactive gestures* acknowledge the other interactant relative to the speaker and help regulate and organize the dialogue itself. Because they are directed at the ongoing involvement and shared roles of the interactants, these gestures occur only in the presence of others. The main function of interactive gestures, then, is to include the interaction partner in the dialogue. This is usually done through some form of pointing gesture in the partner's direction. Such gestures probably constitute about 10% to 20% of the gestures observed in conversation.

Bavelas (1994) and her colleagues (1992, 1995) have identified four primary functions served by these gestures:

1. Delivering information
2. Citing a previous contribution by your partner
3. Seeking to solicit a specific response from your partner
4. Referring to issues associated with the exchange of speaking turns

These functions and certain variations associated with them are identified in Table 7-1 and illustrated in Figure 7-12. Others have found that the "thinking face" facial gesture also elicits audience coparticipation in word searches and thereby serves the overall inclusion function. The Goodwins (1986) have pointed out that self-touching contributes to a state of conversational disengagement, the opposite of inclusion.

TABLE 7-1   **Functions of Interactive Gestures**

1. **Delivery Gestures**   As a group, these gestures refer to the delivery of information by the speaker to the addressee.

   General delivery gestures mark the standard relation of speaker to addressee; the speaker "hands over" to the addressee new information relevant to his or her main point. A verbal paraphrase is often "Here's my point."

   Shared information gestures mark material that the addressee probably already knows—information that is part of their common ground (Clark & Brennan, 1991). They mean, essentially, "As you know."

   Digression gestures mark information that should be treated by the addressee as an aside from the main point. Analogous to "By the way" or "Back to the main point."

   Elliptical gestures mark information that the addressee should elaborate for himself or herself; the speaker will not provide further details. Analogous to "or whatever."

2. **Citing Gestures**   As a group, these gestures refer to a previous contribution by the addressee.

   General citing indicates "as you said earlier," that is, that the point the speaker is now making had been contributed by the addressee.

   Acknowledgment of the addressee's response indicates that the speaker saw or heard that the addressee understood what had been said. Paraphrased, "I see that you understood me."

3. **Seeking Gestures**   As a group, these gestures aim to elicit a specific response from the addressee.

   Seeking help requests a word or phrase that the speaker cannot find at the moment. A verbal paraphrase would be "Can you give me the word for . . . ?"

   Seeking agreement asks whether the addressee agrees or disagrees with the point being made. Analogous to "Do you agree?"

   Seeking following asks whether the addressee understands what is being said. Verbal equivalents include "you know?" or "eh?" at the end of a phrase.

4. **Turn Gestures**   As a group, these gestures refer to issues around the speaking turn.

   Giving turn hands it over to the other person. As if to say, "Your turn."

   Taking turn accepts the turn from the other person. Paraphrased as "OK, I'll take over."

   Turn open indicates that it is anyone's turn, as if to say "Who's going to talk next?"

SOURCE: From Bavelas, *Research on Language and Social Interaction* 27(3): 213, 1994. Reprinted with permission of Lawrence Erlbaum Associates, Inc.

Although the preceding fourfold classification of speech-related gestures is useful for understanding how gestures and speech work together, some gestures may not be limited to a single function. For example, a speaker's relationship with the referent may be highly intense. Some of the gestural displays illuminating this relationship, however, may also emphasize (punctuate) certain specific message units. Nevertheless, we must recognize that there are different types of speech-related gestures and they may serve different functions for the parties involved. Efron's (1941/1972) cross-cultural comparison shows how helpful gestural distinctions can be. He found that as southern Italians talked, they made extensive use of gestures that had a close resemblance to their referent (e.g., pictorial), whereas eastern European Jews made very little use of such gestures. It seems reasonable that different cultures value different kinds of information, and gestures vary accordingly. Even the number of gestures in all categories may vary from culture to culture.

FIGURE 7-12

Interactive gestures.

a. General delivery: "Here's my point."

b. Citing: "As you said earlier . . ."

c. Seeking help: "What's the word . . . ?"

d. Giving turn: "You go ahead."

GESTURE FREQUENCY

The frequency of gesturing can be influenced by several key factors: (1) First, we would expect to find more gestures in face-to-face communication and when the speaker expects the recipient will see his or her message (Alibali & Don, 2001; Bavelas et al., 2002; Cohen, 1977; Cohen & Harrison, 1973). We do, of course, use some gestures when our listeners cannot see us, for example, when talking on the telephone (see Figure 7-13). Continued

FIGURE 7-13

Gesture made while speaking on the telephone.

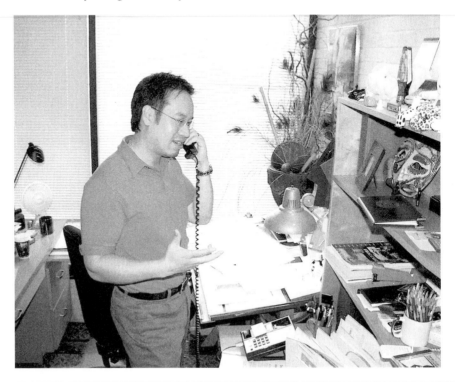

communication without visible contact, however, is likely to reduce the number of gestures used. It is curious why we use any gestures when our audience cannot see them. It
may be habit, but because some gestures are knowingly used to help communicate ideas,
we may continue to use them in order to maximize the effectiveness of the only channel
being used—the voice. In this sense, gestures act as a priming mechanism that activates the
entire communicative system and thereby gets the most out of the vocal signals. (2) Gestures are also likely to increase when a speaker is enthusiastic and involved in the topic
being discussed. (3) We would expect speakers concerned about their listeners' comprehension of their messages to use more gestures, too—especially in difficult or complex
communicative situations, as when the listener is perceived as not paying attention, is not
comprehending, or the speaker cannot find the right words to express an idea (Bavelas
et al., 2002; Holler & Beattie, 2003). Even though exposure to gestures that accompany
speech may sometimes facilitate more accurate decoding on the part of the listener, there
are other occasions when the contribution is negligible (Krauss et al., 1995). (4) Speakers
trying to dominate conversations also would be expected to use more speech-related gestures. (5) The speech content plays a role in the number of gestures used. When answering
questions about manual activities ("Explain how to change a car or bicycle tire" or "Explain

how to wrap a box for a present"), we would expect more gestures than when answering questions about visual or abstract images (Feyereisen & Havard, 1999).

As we note in the next section, speech and gesture are intimately linked, and it would be hard for anyone to abstain completely from gesturing while speaking for very long. Even if it were possible, it would be ill advised because gestures play an important role in communicating. An experiment reported in a 1931 Soviet publication asked subjects to talk while inhibiting all gestures of the head, hands, face, and body. It is reported that no one was able to carry out the instructions completely, and "the speech . . . lost its intonation, stress and expressiveness; even the very selection of words needed for the expression of content became labored; there was a jerkiness to the speech, and a reduction of the number of words used" (Dobrogaev, 1931). Without gestures, speakers also would have to increase the number of phrases and words used to describe spatial relations and would probably pause more often (Graham & Heywood, 1976). Rimé (1982) found speakers' fluency to be adversely affected when their gestures were restricted. Listeners are also likely to experience a serious loss: Gestures often facilitate comprehension and help listeners access linguistic cues in their memory (Berger & Popelka, 1971; Rogers, 1978; Woodall & Folger, 1981). Actually, a more accurate statement is that gestures synchronized with and supporting the vocal/verbal stream increase comprehension. This is accomplished through the functions we have outlined: by vivifying ideas, by intensifying points, by maintaining listener attention and focus, and by marking the organizational structure of the discourse. Gestures out of synchrony with the vocal/verbal stream are distracting and interfere with listener comprehension (Woodall & Burgoon, 1981). Experiments conducted by Krauss and his colleagues (1995, 1996) indicate that gestures may not be aiding listener comprehension by contributing *semantic* information. Instead, they argue, speech-related gestures are more likely to aid listener comprehension by getting attention, activating images or motoric representations in the listener's mind, and aiding recall.

THE COORDINATION OF GESTURE, POSTURE, AND SPEECH

Earlier we said that speech-related gestures are tied to, or accompany, speech. That they are connected to speech is easily understood, but the exact nature of that connection is more difficult to understand. Most scholars agree that body movements and gestures are not randomly produced during the stream of speech; they are inextricably linked as parts of the same system. The disagreements among scholars in this area focus on how to define coordination or synchrony of speech and movement. Must two things happen at exactly the same time to be in sync? For the same length of time? If speech and gesture are closely coordinated, does the same part of the brain control both systems? Is there a synchrony of speech and movement between two speakers as well as within the behavior of a single speaker? This section focuses on the research on these issues. The first part addresses the coordination of a single speaker's speech and movement; the second examines the coordination of two speakers' behavior.

SELF-SYNCHRONY

In the early 1960s William S. Condon began a microscopic analysis of the coordination between movement and speech. By examining individual frames of a 16 mm film, he was able to match body movements with a speech transcript. This allowed him to observe speech–body orientation accurate to $\frac{1}{24}$th of a second. Condon (1976; Condon & Ogston, 1966) showed that even at the most microscopic levels (e.g., spoken syllables and smaller), speech and movement are rhythmically coordinated. This means a change in one behavior (a body part, for instance) will coincide or be coordinated with the onset of change in another behavior (phonological segment or some other body part). Just as speech units can be grouped together to form larger units, so can movement units. A sweep of the arm or a turn of the head may occur over an entire phrase of several words, but we may see movements of the face and fingers coordinated with smaller units of speech. At every level, however, the phrases of speech production and the phrases of movement seem closely coordinated.

The smallest idea unit in spoken language is called the *phonemic clause*. This group of words, averaging about five in length, has only one primary stress, which is indicated by changes in pitch, rhythm, or loudness, and it is terminated by a juncture. This unit commonly has shown systematic relationships to body movements. Slight jerks of the head or hand often accompany the primary stress points in the speech of American English speakers. Gestures also seem to peak at the most salient part of the idea unit as well. At the junctures or boundaries, we also find movements of the head or hands indicating completion or initiation.

Birdwhistell's (1966) analysis of nonverbal activity that accompanies verbal behavior led him to postulate what he calls *kinesic markers*. These nonverbal behaviors mark a specific oral language behavior. Markers seem to operate at several different levels. For instance, we might see an eye blink at the beginning and end of some words; a microlateral head sweep may be seen during the expression of a compound word we would hyphenate in the written form. Figure 7-14 shows head, hand, and eyelid markers occurring at the end of statements and questions. Similarly, after making a point, speakers may turn the head to one side, or tilt, or flex or extend the neck, signaling the transition to another point.

Another level of markers is characterized by gross shifts in postural behavior (involving half the body) indicating or marking a sequence of points or point of view expressed by the speaker. One marker on this level is simply the shift from leaning back when listening to leaning forward when talking. The observation that postural shifts mark new stages of interaction or topic shifts, particularly at the beginning or ending of speech segments, has been made by several researchers (Bull & Brown, 1977; Erickson, 1975; Scheflen, 1973). Markers on the next level are frequently complete changes in location, following the presentation of one's total position during an interaction.

Kendon's (1972b, 1980, 1987, 1988) detailed analyses of speech and body movement confirm the notion of self-synchrony. He also supports the idea of a hierarchy of body movements that acts in conjunction with our speech behavior. Kendon found that the wrist and fingers tended to change positions most often, followed by the forearm, then the upper arm; elements of the face generally changed more often than the head; trunk and lower limb movements were rare. The larger units of body movement were related to the larger units of speech; the smaller body units were related to the smaller verbal units.

FIGURE 7-14

Some postural-kinesic markers of syntactic sentences in the United States.

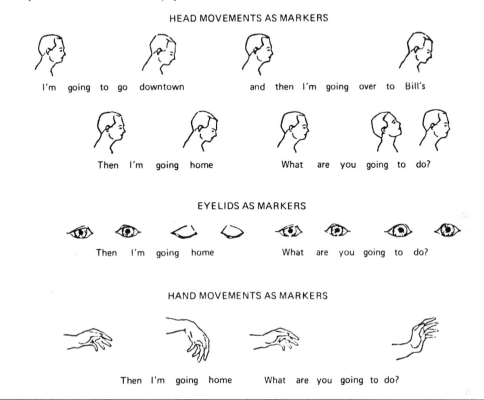

HEAD MOVEMENTS AS MARKERS

I'm going to go downtown   and then I'm going over to Bill's

Then I'm going home   What are you going to do?

EYELIDS AS MARKERS

Then I'm going home   What are you going to do?

HAND MOVEMENTS AS MARKERS

Then I'm going home   What are you going to do?

Kendon also made some important observations of when movements occur in relation to the speech stream. Some movements accompany speech, but many precede speech units. The time between the speech preparatory body movement and the onset of speech is apparently related to the size of the impending speech unit, with earlier and more extensive behavior (more body parts involved) for larger speech units. A change in body posture, for instance, may precede a long utterance and be held for the duration of the utterance. Like other researchers in this area, Kendon believes the hierarchically structured body movements probably convey information about verbal structure and communicative involvement. The positions of the head, limb, and body sometimes forecast information to a listener, such as length of utterance, change in argument strategy or viewpoint, and the like. The act of forecasting upcoming components of talk through gesture is a crucial function in social interaction. Speakers often shift their gaze to their hands during the production of iconic gestures, thereby calling them to the attention of the listener. Speaker gaze returns to the listener as the speech unit projected by the gesture is completed. In this process, gaze acts like a pointer (Streeck, 1993; Streeck & Knapp, 1992).

The linkage of gestures to speech has also been demonstrated in studies that show how gestures help speakers access and retrieve words from their mental lexicon (Hadar, 1989;

Krauss & Hadar, 1999; Krauss, Chen, & Chawla, 1996; Morrel-Samuels & Krauss, 1992). Hanlon, Brown & Gerstman (1990) showed that they could improve word retrieval in a picture naming task by training aphasics to perform gestures just prior to the naming task. This important role of gestures in lexical retrieval and speech production is often overlooked and underemphasized, but it is clear that gestures facilitate both the invention of messages as well as their organization and delivery.

The preceding research leads us to conclude that speech and gesture are coordinated. But why? Most likely because they are two components used in the expression of a single unit of content. Both systems are being guided by the same overall purpose, and both systems seem to be under the governance of the same parts of the brain (Cicone et al., 1979; Kimura, 1976). As Kendon (2000, p. 61) said, "[A]lthough each expresses somewhat different dimensions of the meaning, speech and gesture are co-expressive of a single inclusive ideational complex, and it is this that is the meaning of the utterance." It is not unreasonable, then, to assume a pathological state for people manifesting out-of-sync behavior (Condon, 1980). Nor should it surprise us that gestures and speech both break down in aphasia (McNeill, 1992).

Gesture and speech also appear to grow up together. In one remarkable study, Petitto and Marentette (1991) argue that *manual* infant babbling (rather than oral) may serve as a precursor to language learning. Several other studies indicate that children use more gestures as they develop, just as they use more words, and the nature of that gesticulation varies with the changing nature of the speech production (McNeill, 1992). Kendon (1983, p. 25) put it this way:

> There appears to be a shift away from elaborate enactments or pantomimes, which serve instead of speech, toward a more precise coordination, as if gesture is coming to be used more selectively. Gesture is used much less to depict whole scenes. It is brought in only at certain points along the way. There is also an increasing use of abstract, discourse-making gesture; iconic gesture becomes more symbolic and more restricted in the aspects of meaning it is called upon to display.

INTERACTION SYNCHRONY

The preceding section revealed a speech–body movement coordination within the actions of a single speaker. This section provides information about a speech–body movement coordination between two speakers—a kind of social rhythm (Bernieri & Rosenthal, 1991). This behavior has been studied in two ways, which we call *matching* and *meshing*.

Matching

Without always being very aware of it, human beings commonly tend to mimic the mannerisms, facial expressions, postures, and other behavior of the people they interact with. This has been called the "chameleon effect" (Chartrand & Bargh, 1999)—not because people, like chameleons, change colors to match their environment, but because people change their postures, gestures, and mannerisms to match those of their interaction partners. This kind of mimicry can occur completely outside of our conscious awareness even though matching behavior may also be used intentionally when a person is trying to communicate affiliation. Matching the behavior of our fellow interactant may occur in several different ways. Sometimes a speaker's behavior is followed in kind by the listener when he or she becomes the speaker (Cappella, 1981). Here the matched behavior occurs not simultaneously but in sequence. Chapter 11 reports research that shows how we tend to match our partner's utterance duration, loudness, precision of articulation, latency of response, silence duration, and speech rate. In some instances, the speaker's behavior elicits an offsetting or compensatory behavior from the other interaction partner. For example, if a speaker is leaning toward a listener and the listener perceives the interaction distance to be too close, the listener is likely to lean back or in other ways increase the interaction distance (see chapter 5).

Other researchers have been interested in those occasions when both interaction partners exhibit the same behavior at the same time. Postural congruence is one of those frequently matched behaviors. It may involve crossing the legs and/or arms, leaning, head propping, or any number of other positions. Notice the variety of postural congruence in Figures 7-15, 7-16, and 7-17. When the listener's behavior is a mirror image of the speaker's, this form of matching is called *mirroring*.

FIGURE 7-15

Postural congruence. The pair facing each other in the foreground are showing matching postures; the pair facing each other in the background are showing mirror-image postures.

FIGURE 7-16

Examples of postural congruence through head-propping and leaning.

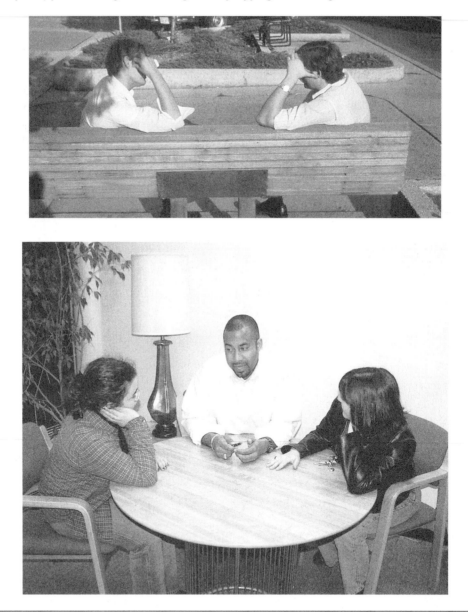

FIGURE 7-17

Notice the postural congruence exhibited by cabinet official Joseph Califano and former President Jimmy Carter, 1977.

Postural congruence has been observed to occur during periods of more positive speech; rated by observers as an indicator of rapport and cooperation; and established as an act that is influential in creating rapport (Charney, 1966; LaFrance, 1979, 1985; LaFrance & Broadbent, 1976; Trout & Rosenfeld, 1980). Nonconscious mimicry has also been found to occur more often with people who enter an interaction with the goal to affiliate or establish rapport (Lakin & Chartrand, 2003). In one study, a trained actor selectively mimicked postures and gestures of only some students in an interview situation. In a postinterview assessment of their partner (the actor), students who had been mimicked evaluated their partner significantly more favorably and indicated they "identified" with him or that he "thought like me" (Dabbs, 1969). None of the students reported an awareness of the mimicry. Chartrand & Bargh (1999) also found mimicry to increase the degree of liking on the part of an interaction partner. In short, mimicry seems to occur more often when we are other-oriented—for example, wanting to be liked by others, feeling concerned about others, seeking a closer relationship with others, showing dependence on others, and so on.

Bavelas and her colleagues would agree that postural mimicry is most likely to occur when we are other-oriented, but they did not find that it was a sign of rapport or cooperation. Instead, they found that postural mimicry occurred during periods of conversational involvement rather than during cooperation or periods of rapport. Bavelas maintains it is a signal that the participants are talking *with* each other rather than *at* each other—performing symmetrical roles rather than complementary ones. Thus, from this perspective, the matching of an interaction partner's nonverbal behavior reflects the moment-to-moment aspects of conversational involvement.

Bavelas has also studied a related phenomenon she calls *motor mimicry*. A common example of motor mimicry is when a person you are near drops a heavy weight on his or her foot. As the injured party reacts in pain, your wincing facial expression seems to register an empathic response (see Figure 7-18). Sometimes we lean in the direction of another person's efforts; sometimes we smile at another's joy. For many years, scholars believed this was a purely empathic reaction based on a vicarious experience. The work of Bavelas et al. does not deny this inner experience, but their research also shows motor mimicry is primarily a communicative phenomenon. Wincing in reaction to another's injury, for example, depended strongly on the visual accessibility of the injured party in Bavelas's experiments. Furthermore, the pattern and timing of the wincer's reaction was determined by eye contact with the victim (Bavelas et al., 1988; Bavelas et al., 1986).

This tendency to match and mimic the behavior of others (posturally, facially, vocally, and so forth) sometimes leads to a condition known as *emotional contagion*, which occurs when an emotional experience is triggered as a result of mimicking someone else's behavior. Two of the essential conditions for this process to occur include strongly felt emotions and communicators who are skilled encoders and decoders (Hatfield, Cacioppo, & Rapson, 1994).

Meshing

Another way of examining the phenomenon of interaction synchrony has been to observe the ongoing co-occurrence of changes in movement and speech by each of the two interactants. Changes, in this type of research, refer to the initiation, termination, speed, and/or

FIGURE 7-18

(a) Former President Ronald Reagan and former defense secretary Casper Weinberger exchange similar facial expressions. (b) An onlooker winces in pain as another experiences it.

a

b

direction of the behaviors under study. Like matching behavior, meshing has also been linked to conversational satisfaction and liking for one's interaction partner (Cappella, 1997).

The study of meshing behavior arose out of Condon's earlier work on self-synchrony. He observed how both interactants seemed to coordinate their actions. One person (Davis, 1971) who viewed his films reported this:

> The third film clip Condon showed me was an example of heightened synchrony. A man and a woman—employer and job applicant—sat facing each other in a sequence that at normal speed seemed merely to involve rather a lot of shifting around, as the man first uncrossed and then recrossed his legs and the woman stirred in her chair. But when the film was run through a few frames at a time, their synchrony became clear. In the same frame, the two began to lean toward each other. They stopped at the same split second, both raised their heads, and then they swept backwards together into their chairs, stopping in the same frame. It was very like the elaborate courtship dances of some birds, or—in Condon's favorite analogy—they were like puppets moved by the same set of strings. Condon told me that this kind of heightened synchrony happens often between male and female. During courtship, it's one of the ways in which vast statements can be made between a man and a woman without a word being said. (p. 103)

As Condon suggests, this kind of interaction synchrony may reflect the nature of the ongoing relationship, whether it is the extent of involvement, rapport, or the degree of intimate, interpersonal knowledge about the other. In some instances, this relationship is dramatically visible by the kind of synchrony taking place; at other times, the coordination may only be seen in the microscopic analysis of individual film frames. Out-of-sync partners are not likely to value the experience. The fact that out-of-sync experiences tend to stand out for us reminds us how often we operate in synchrony with others. Out-of-sync behavior may reflect decreased listening, a lack of knowledge of one's partner, and so forth. Interaction synchrony may also be a precursor of language learning. Condon and Sander (1974) found babies 12 hours old whose head, hands, elbows, hips, and leg movements tended to correspond to the rhythms of human speech. When the babies were exposed to disconnected speech or to plain tapping sounds, however, the rhythmic pattern was not observed. If this finding is validated by other researchers, it may mean an infant has participated in and laid the groundwork for various linguistic forms and structures long before formal language learning begins (see Bernieri, Reznick, & Rosenthal, 1988).

Sometimes our responses as listeners and the feedback we provide in the form of facial expressions or head movements appear at specific junctures in the speech of our partner. Vocalizations ("mmm-hmm," "I see," and the like), head nods, and movements of hands and feet tend to occur at the ends of rhythmical units of the talker's speech, that is, at pauses within phonemic clauses but mainly at junctures between these clauses. Vocally stressed words also tend to be accompanied by movements. Listener gestures and movements are often indications that the listener understands, appreciates, or anticipates speaker behavior.

Dittmann (1972) noticed that adults sometimes believe children are not listening to them and badger them with questions like "Did you hear me?" Dittmann reasoned that this common adult–child perception may be associated with what he calls "listener responses," for example, head nods, some eyebrow raises, some types of smiles, "yeah," "I see," and so on. His study of children in grades 1, 3, and 5 found these listener responses were nearly absent except under "the strongest social pull" by the other interactant. Subsequent studies indicated the major deficiencies were in "mmm-hmm" and head-nod responses. By eighth grade, a dramatic increase in these listener responses is found. Now the early adolescent's peers are beginning to lengthen their response duration (providing more opportunity for such listener responses); the "response pull" from adult interactants is increasing; and there is a continuing movement away from a purely self-orientation and toward imagining what others are experiencing.

The detailed observations of researchers like Condon, Dittmann, and Kendon offer clear evidence that human interactants do exhibit a speech–body movement interaction synchrony. It is also clear that this synchrony may take place on very microscopic levels. Still, there are questions. How much of this synchrony is due to an ordered relationship between speech and body movements, and how much is due to coincidence? Are there social contexts that intensify the degree of synchrony? How much synchrony is desirable? At least one study suggests that *moderately* rhythmic social interactions are evaluated most positively (Warner et al., 1987). Is it possible to predict which behaviors will synchronize with which other behaviors at which times? What is the best method of measuring these minute behavioral changes (Gatewood & Rosenwein, 1981; McDowall, 1978a, 1978b; Rosenfeld, 1981)?

❖

SUMMARY

Although gestures are difficult to define, we often seem to know what movements a person is using to communicate and what movements are merely nervous mannerisms, expressions associated with emotion, and task-related movements. Gestures help us communicate in many ways: They replace speech when we cannot or do not want to talk, help us regulate the back-and-forth flow of interaction, establish and maintain attention, add emphasis to our speech, and assist in making memorable the content of our speech. Although we do gesture when interaction partners are not visible (over the telephone), gestures are more frequent when both interactants are visible to one another. We seem to use more gestures when we are knowledgeable about the topic being discussed, highly motivated to have our listener(s) understand our message, trying to dominate a conversation, excited and enthusiastic about the topic being discussed, and speaking about manual activities. Gestures also play an important role in word retrieval and speech production. So the absence of gestures may negatively affect the speaker's message as well as a listener's comprehension.

Two major types of gestures were discussed: speech independent and speech related. Speech-independent gestures are operationally defined as gestures that 70% of the usage community decodes in a similar way. They have an almost direct verbal definition. We are normally very aware of using this type of gesture. Culture affects the number, frequency, and meanings associated with speech-independent gestures. Although no universal gestures of this type have been found (that is, having the same meaning and form in every culture studied), the most likely candidates would be "affirmation," "negation," "stop," "don't know," "sleeping," "eating," and "drinking." Some speech-independent gestures are culture specific (not found in the same form in other cultures); many gestures have basically the same form but different meanings from culture to culture. These different meanings are often the source of cross-cultural misunderstandings.

The other major category of gestures is called speech-related gestures. Some of these gestures characterize the content of speech; some show the speaker's relationship to the referent by indicating whether the speaker is certain or uncertain, embracing an idea or distancing herself or himself from it, and the like; some are used to accent or emphasize speech units. Interactive gestures, unlike the other speech-related gestures, focus on the dialogue rather than the speaker's monologue. Interactive gestures focus on the ongoing involvement of the interactants and their shared roles.

The last part of this chapter examined the coordination and synchrony of speech and body movements. This synchrony between the larger and smaller units of speech and body is called self-synchrony. Gesture and speech, then, seem to be different outward manifestations of a process controlled and guided by the same part of the brain. Gesture and speech both play a role in communicating the same content. In addition to a self-synchrony, interactants also seem to display coordinated exchanges of behavior in many ways that suggest the existence of an interaction synchrony as well. Interaction synchrony can manifest itself through matching behavior—similar behavior occurring at the same time (postural congruence or motor mimicry) or similar behavior occurring in sequence (one speaker raises his or her voice, followed by the next speaker raising his or her voice). Interaction synchrony can also manifest itself in the moment-to-moment coordination of changes in the direction and timing of speech and movement—even though we do not yet know exactly what behaviors will change and how they will change.

QUESTIONS FOR DISCUSSION

1. Spend some time during the day interacting without using hand gestures. What does your experience tell you about the relationship of gestures and speech?

2. Some researchers have found matching behavior to be associated with rapport between the interactants. Can you think of a situation in which rapport would not involve matching behavior?

3. Can you think of any instance in which gestures might pose a challenge to the doctrine of freedom of speech?

4. Select a speech-independent gesture. Discuss the meaning of this gesture when accompanied by different facial expressions and speech.

BIBLIOGRAPHY

Acredolo, L. P., & Goodwyn, S. (1996). *Baby signs*. Chicago: Contemporary.
Alibali, M. W., & Don, L. S. (2001). Children's gestures are meant to be seen. *Gesture, 1*, 113–127.
Allport, G. W., & Vernon, P. E. (1933). *Studies in expressive movement*. Boston: Houghton Mifflin.
Archer, D. (1997). Unspoken diversity: Cultural differences in gestures. *Qualitative Sociology, 20*, 79–105.

Armstrong, N., & Wagner, M. (2003). *Field guide to gestures*. Philadelphia: Quirk Books.

Axtell, R. (1991). *Gestures*. New York: Wiley.

Barakat, R. (1973). Arabic gestures. *Journal of Popular Culture, 6,* 749–792.

Barroso, F., Freedman, N., Grand, S., & van Meel, J. (1978). Evocation of two types of hand movements in information processing. *Journal of Experimental Psychology: Human Perception and Performance, 4,* 321–329.

Barten, S. S. (1979). Development of gesture. In N. R. Smith & M. Franklin (Eds.), *Symbolic functioning in childhood*. Hillsdale, NJ: Erlbaum.

Bavelas, J. B. (1994). Gestures as part of speech: Methodological implications. *Research on Language and Social Interaction, 27,* 201–221.

Bavelas, J. B., Black, A., Chovil, N., Lemery, C. R., & Mullett, J. (1988). Form and function in motor mimicry: Topographic evidence that the primary function is communicative. *Human Communication Research, 14,* 275–299.

Bavelas, J. B., Black, A., Lemery, C. R., & Mullett, J. (1986). "I show you how I feel": Motor mimicry as a communicative act. *Journal of Personality and Social Psychology, 50,* 322–329.

Bavelas, J. B., Chovil, N., Coates, L., & Roe, L. (1995). Gestures specialized for dialogue. *Personality and Social Psychology Bulletin, 21,* 394–405.

Bavelas, J. B., Chovil, N., Lawrie, D. A., & Wade, A. (1992). Interactive gestures. *Discourse Processes, 15,* 469–489.

Bavelas, J., Kenwood, C., Johnson, T., & Phillips, B. (2002). An experimental study of when and how speakers use gestures to communicate. *Gesture, 2,* 1–17.

Baxter, J. C., Winters, E. P., & Hammer, R. E. (1968). Gestural behavior during a brief interview as a function of cognitive variables. *Journal of Personality and Social Psychology, 8,* 303–307.

Beattie, G. W., & Beattie, C. A. (1981). Postural congruence in a naturalistic setting. *Semiotica, 35,* 41–55.

Berger, K. W., & Popelka, G. R. (1971). Extra-facial gestures in relation to speech reading. *Journal of Communication Disorders, 3,* 302–308.

Bernieri, F. J., Reznick, J. S., & Rosenthal, R. (1988). Synchrony, pseudosynchrony, and dissynchrony: Measuring the entrainment process in mother–infant interactions. *Journal of Personality and Social Psychology, 54,* 243–253.

Bernieri, F. J., & Rosenthal, R. (1991). Interpersonal coordination: Behavior matching and interactional synchrony. In R. S. Feldman & B. Rimé (Eds.), *Fundamentals of nonverbal behavior*. New York: Cambridge University Press.

Birdwhistell, R. L. (1952). *Introduction to kinesics*. Louisville: University of Louisville Press. (Now available on microfilm only. Ann Arbor, MI: University Microfilms.)

Birdwhistell, R. L. (1955). Background to kinesics. *ETC, 13,* 10–18.

Birdwhistell, R. L. (1960). Kinesics and communication. In E. Carpenter & M. McLuhan (Eds.), *Explorations in communication*. New York: Beacon.

Birdwhistell, R. L. (1963). Kinesic analysis in the investigation of emotions. In P. Knapp (Ed.), *Expression of the emotions in man*. New York: International Universities Press.

Birdwhistell, R. L. (1966). Some relations between American kinesics and spoken American English. In A. G. Smith (Ed.), *Communication and culture*. New York: Holt, Rinehart & Winston.

Birdwhistell, R. L. (1967). Some body motion elements accompanying spoken American English. In L. Thayer (Ed.), *Communication: Concepts and perspectives* (pp. 53–76). Washington, DC: Spartan.

Birdwhistell, R. L. (1970). *Kinesics and context*. Philadelphia: University of Pennsylvania Press.

Blake, J., & Dolgoy, S. J. (1993). Gestural development and its relation to cognition during the transition to language. *Journal of Nonverbal Behavior, 17,* 87–102.

Blass, T., Freedman, N., & Steingart, I. (1974). Body movement and verbal encoding in the congenitally blind. *Perceptual and Motor Skills, 39,* 279–293.

Boomer, D. S. (1978). The phonemic clause: Speech unit in human communication. In A. W. Siegman & S. Feldstein (Eds.), *Nonverbal behavior and communication*. Hillsdale, NJ: Erlbaum.

Bremmer, J., & Roodenburg, H. (Eds.). (1991). *A cultural history of gesture*. Ithaca, NY: Cornell University Press.

Brewer, W. D. (1951). Patterns of gesture among the Levantine Arabs. *American Anthropologist, 53*, 232–237.

Bull, P. E. (1987). *Posture and gesture*. New York: Pergamon Press.

Bull, P. E., & Brown, R. (1977). The role of postural change in dyadic conversation. *British Journal of Social and Clinical Psychology, 16*, 29–33.

Bull, P., & Connelly, G. (1985). Body movements and emphasis in speech. *Journal of Nonverbal Behavior, 9*, 169–187.

Burgoon, J. K., Stern, L. A., & Dillman, L. (1995). Interpersonal adaptation: *Dyadic interaction patterns*. New York: Cambridge University Press.

Butterworth, B., & Beattie, G. W. (1978). Gesture and silence as indicators of planning in speech. In R. Campbell & P. Smith (Eds.), *Recent advances in psychology of language: Formal and experimental approaches*. New York: Plenum.

Butterworth, B., & Hadar, U. (1989). Gesture, speech and computational stage: A reply to McNeill. *Psychological Review, 96*, 168–174.

Cappella, J. N. (1981). Mutual influence in expressive behavior: Adult–adult and infant–adult dyadic interaction. *Psychological Bulletin, 89*, 101–132.

Cappella, J. N. (1997). Behavioral and judged coordination in adult informal social interactions: Vocal and kinesic indicators. *Journal of Personality and Social Psychology, 72*, 119–131.

Carmichael, L., Roberts, S., & Wessell, N. (1937). A study of the judgment of manual expression as presented in still and motion pictures. *Journal of Social Psychology, 8*, 115–142.

Charney, E. J. (1966). Postural configurations in psychotherapy. *Psychosomatic Medicine, 28*, 305–315.

Chartrand, T. L., and Bargh, J. A. (1999). The chameleon effect: The perception–behavior link and social interaction. *Journal of Personality and Social Psychology, 76*, 893–910.

Cicone, M., Wapner, W., Foldi, N., Zurif, E., & Gardner, H. (1979). The relation between gesture and language in aphasic communication. *Brain and Language, 8*, 324–349.

Clark, H. H., & Brennan, S. A. (1991). Grounding in communication. In L. B. Resnick, J. M. Levine, & S. D. Teasely (Eds.), *Perspectives on socially shared cognition*. Washington, DC: APA.

Cohen, A. A. (1977). The communicative functions of hand illustrators. *Journal of Communication, 27*, 54–63.

Cohen, A. A., & Harrison, R. P. (1973). Intentionality in the use of hand illustrators in face-to-face communication situations. *Journal of Personality and Social Psychology, 28*, 276–279.

Condon, W. S. (1976). An analysis of behavioral organization. *Sign Language Studies, 13*, 285–318.

Condon, W. S. (1980). The relation of interaction synchrony to cognitive and emotional processes. In M. R. Key (Ed.), *The relationship of verbal and nonverbal communication*. The Hague: Mouton.

Condon, W. S., & Ogston, W. D. (1966). Soundfilm analysis of normal and pathological behavior patterns. *Journal of Nervous and Mental Disease, 143*, 338–347.

Condon, W. S., & Ogston, W. D. (1967). A segmentation of behavior. *Journal of Psychiatric Research, 5*, 221–235.

Condon, W. S., & Ogston, W. D. (1971). Speech and body motion synchrony of the speaker–hearer. In D. L. Horton & J. J. Jenkins (Eds.), *Perception of language*. Columbus, OH: Merrill.

Condon, W. S., & Sander, L. W. (1974). Neonate movement is synchronized with adult speech: Interaction participation in language acquisition. *Science, 183*, 99–101.

Creider, C. (1977). Toward a description of East African gestures. *Sign Language Studies, 14*, 1–20.

Critchley, M. (1939). *The language of gesture*. London: Arnold.

Dabbs, J. M. (1969). Similarity of gestures and interpersonal influence. *Proceedings of the 77th annual convention of the American Psychological Association, 4,* 337–338.

Davis, F. (1971). *Inside intuition.* New York: McGraw-Hill.

de Jorio, A. (2000). *Gesture in Naples and gesture in classical antiquity.* (Translation and Introduction by Adam Kendon. First published in 1832). Bloomington, IN: Indiana University Press.

Delis, D., Foldi, N. S., Hamby, S., Gardner, H., & Zurif, E. A. (1979). Note on temporal relations between language and gestures. *Brain and Language, 8,* 350–354.

Deutsch, F. (1947). Analysis of postural behavior. *Psychoanalytic Quarterly, 16,* 195–213.

Dittmann, A. T. (1962). The relationship between body movements and moods in interviews. *Journal of Consulting Psychology, 26,* 480.

Dittmann, A. T. (1971). Review of kinesics in context. *Psychiatry, 34,* 334–342.

Dittmann, A. T. (1972). The body movement–speech rhythm relationship as a cue to speech encoding. In A. W. Siegman & B. Pope (Eds.), *Studies in dyadic communication.* New York: Pergamon Press.

Dittmann, A. T. (1987). The role of body movement in communication. In A. W. Siegman & S. Feldstein (Eds.), *Nonverbal behavior and communication* (2nd ed.). Hillsdale, NJ: Erlbaum.

Dittmann, A. T., & Llewellyn, L. G. (1967). The phonemic clause as a unit of speech decoding. *Journal of Personality and Social Psychology, 6,* 341–349.

Dittmann, A. T., & Llewellyn, L. G. (1968). Relationships between vocalizations and head nods as listener responses. *Journal of Personality and Social Psychology, 11,* 98–106.

Dittmann, A. T., & Llewellyn, L. G. (1969). Body movement and speech rhythm in social conversation. *Journal of Personality and Social Psychology, 11,* 98–106.

Dobrogaev, S. M. (1931). The study of reflex in problems of linguistics (M. Kendon, Trans.). In E. A. Marr (Ed.), *Lazykovedenie i materializm* (Vol. 2). Moscow and Leningrad: State Social Economic Publishing House.

Duffy, R. J., & Duffy, J. R. (1981). Three studies of deficits in pantomimic expression and pantomimic recognition in aphasia. *Journal of Speech and Hearing Research, 46,* 70–84.

Efron, D. (1972). *Gesture, race and culture.* The Hague: Mouton. (Original work published 1941 as *Gesture and environment.* New York: Kings Crown Press).

Ekman, P. (1964). Body position, facial expression, and verbal behavior during interviews. *Journal of Abnormal and Social Psychology, 48,* 295–301.

Ekman, P. (1976). Movements with precise meanings. *Journal of Communication, 26,* 14–26.

Ekman, P. (1977). Biological and cultural contribution to bodily and facial movement. In J. Blacking (Ed.), *The anthropology of the body.* London: Academic Press.

Ekman, P. (1979). About brows. In M. von Cranach, K. Foppa, W. Lepenier, & D. Ploog (Eds.), *Human ethology: Claims and limits of a new discipline.* Cambridge: Cambridge University Press.

Ekman, P. (1999). Emotional and conversational nonverbal signals. In L. S. Messing & R. Campbell (Eds.), *Gesture, speech, and sign* (pp. 45–55). New York: Oxford University Press.

Ekman, P., & Friesen, W. (1969). The repertoire of non-verbal behavior: Categories, origins, usage, and coding. *Semiotica, 1,* 49–98.

Ekman, P., & Friesen, W. V. (1972). Hand movements. *Journal of Communication, 22,* 353–374.

Emmorey, K., & Casey, S. (2001). Gesture, thought and spatial language. *Gesture, 1,* 35–50.

Emmorey, K., & Reilly, J. S. (1995). *Language, gesture, and space.* Mahwah, NJ: Erlbaum.

Erickson, F. (1975). One function of proxemic shifts in face-to-face interaction. In A. Kendon, R. M. Harris, & M. R. Key (Eds.), *Organization of behavior in face-to-face interaction.* The Hague: Mouton.

Evans, M. A., & Rubin, K. H. (1979). Hand gestures as a communicative mode in school-aged children. *Journal of Genetic Psychology, 135,* 189–196.

Feyereisen, P. (1987). Gestures and speech, interactions and separations: A reply to McNeill. *Psychological Review, 94,* 493–498.

Feyereisen, P., & Havard, I. (1999). Mental imagery and production of hand gestures while speaking in younger and older adults. *Journal of Nonverbal Behavior, 23,* 153–171.

Feyereisen, P., & Lannoy, J. D. (1991). *Gestures and speech: Psychological investigations.* New York: Cambridge University Press.

Freedman, N. (1972). The analysis of movement behavior during clinical interviews. In A. Siegman & B. Pope (Eds.), *Studies in dyadic communication.* New York: Pergamon Press.

Freedman, N., Blass, T., Rifkin, A., & Quitkin, F. (1973). Body movements and the verbal encoding of aggressive affect. *Journal of Personality and Social Psychology, 26,* 72–85.

Frey, S. (1975). Tonic aspects of behavior in interaction. In A. Kendon, R. M. Harris, & M. R. Key (Eds.), *Organization of behavior in face-to-face interaction.* Chicago: Aldine.

Gatewood, J. B., & Rosenwein, R. (1981). Interactional synchrony: Genuine or spurious? A critique of recent research. *Journal of Nonverbal Behavior, 6,* 12–29.

Givens, D. B. (1977). Shoulder shrugging: A densely communicative expressive behavior. *Semiotica, 19,* 13–28.

Goffman, E. (1979). Footing. *Semiotica, 25,* 1–29.

Goodglass, H., & Kaplan, E. (1963). Disturbance of gesture and pantomime in aphasia. *Brain, 86,* 702–712.

Goodwin, C. (1981). *Conversational organization.* New York: Academic Press.

Goodwin, C. (1986). Gestures as a resource for the organization of mutual orientation. *Semiotica, 62,* 29–49.

Goodwin, C., & Goodwin, M. H. (1986). Gesture and coparticipation in the activity of searching for a word. *Semiotica, 62,* 51–75.

Graham, J. A., & Argyle, M. A. (1975). A cross-cultural study of the communication of extra verbal meaning by gestures. *International Journal of Psychology, 10,* 56–67.

Graham, J. A., & Heywood, S. (1976). The effects of elimination of hand gestures and of verbal codability on speech performance. *European Journal of Social Psychology, 5,* 189–195.

Hadar, U. (1989). Two types of gesture and their role in speech production. *Journal of Language and Social Psychology, 8,* 221–228.

Hamalian, L. (1965). Communication by gesture in the Middle East. *ETC, 22,* 43–49.

Hanlon, R. E., Brown, J. W., & Gerstman, L. J. (1990). Enhancement of naming in non-fluent aphasia through gesture. *Brain and Language, 38,* 298–314.

Hatfield, E., Cacioppo, J. T., & Rapson, R. L. (1994). *Emotional contagion.* New York: Cambridge University Press.

Hayes, F. C. (1957). Gestures: A working bibliography. *Southern Folklore Quarterly, 21,* 218–317.

Hess, U., Philippot, P., & Blairy, S. (1999). Mimicry: Facts and fiction. In P. Philippot, R. S. Feldman, & E. J. Coats (Eds.), *The social context of nonverbal behavior* (pp. 213–241). New York: Cambridge University Press.

Hewes, G. W. (1957). The anthropology of posture. *Scientific American, 196,* 123–132.

Hewes, G. W. (1973). Primate communication and the gestural origin of language. *Current Anthropology, 14,* 1–2, 5–12.

Hewes, G. W. (1974). Gesture language in culture contact. *Sign Language Studies, 4,* 1–34.

Hewes, G. W. (1976). The current status of the gestural theory of language origin. *Annals of the New York Academy of Sciences, 280,* 482–504.

Hinsz, V. B., & Tomhave, J. A. (1991). Smile and (half) the world smiles with you, frown and you frown alone. *Personality and Social Psychology Bulletin, 17,* 586–592.

Holler, J., & Beattie, G. (2003). Pragmatic aspects of representational gestures: Do speakers use them to clarify verbal ambiguity for the listener? *Gesture, 3,* 127–154.

Iverson, J. M., Tencer, J. L., & Goldin-Meadow, S. (2000). The relation between gesture and speech in congenitally blind and sighted language-learners. *Journal of Nonverbal Behavior, 24,* 105–130.

Jacobson, R. (1972). Motor signs for yes and no. *Language in Society, 1,* 91–96.

Jaffe, J., & Feldstein, S. (1970). *Rhythms of dialogue.* New York: Academic Press.

James, W. (1932). A study of the expression of bodily posture. *Journal of General Psychology, 7,* 405–436.

Jancovic, M. A., Devoe, S., & Wiener, M. (1975). Age related changes in hand and arm movements as non-verbal communication: Some conceptualizations and an empirical exploration. *Child Development, 46,* 922–928.

Johnson, D. R. (1972). Black kinesics: Some nonverbal communication patterns in the black culture. In L. A. Samovar & R. E. Porter (Eds.), *Intercultural communication: A reader.* Belmont, CA: Wadsworth.

Johnson, H. G., Ekman, P., & Friesen, W. V. (1975). Communicative body movements: American emblems. *Semiotica, 15,* 335–353.

Kempton, W. (1980). The rhythmic basis of interactional micro-synchrony. In M. R. Key (Ed.), *The relationship of verbal and nonverbal communication.* The Hague: Mouton.

Kendon, A. (1970). Movement coordination in social interaction: Some examples described. *Acta Psychologica, 32,* 101–125.

Kendon, A. (1972a). Review of *Kinesics and context. American Journal of Psychology, 85,* 447–455.

Kendon, A. (1972b). Some relationships between body motion and speech: An analysis of an example. In A. Siegman & B. Pope (Eds.), *Studies in dyadic communication.* New York: Pergamon Press.

Kendon, A. (1975). Gesticulation, speech, and the gesture theory of language origins. *Sign Language Studies, 9,* 349–373.

Kendon, A. (1980). Gesticulation and speech: Two aspects of the process of utterance. In M. R. Key (Ed.), *The relationship of verbal and nonverbal communication.* The Hague: Mouton.

Kendon, A. (1981a). Current issues in 'nonverbal communication.' In A. Kendon (Ed.), *Nonverbal communication, interaction and gesture.* The Hague: Mouton.

Kendon, A. (1981b). Geography of gesture. *Semiotica, 37,* 129–163.

Kendon, A. (1983). Gesture and speech: How they interact. In J. M. Wiemann & R. P. Harrison (Eds.), *Nonverbal interaction.* Beverly Hills, CA: Sage.

Kendon, A. (1984). Did gesture have the happiness to escape the curse at the confusion of Babel? In A. Wolfgang (Ed.), *Nonverbal behavior: Perspectives, applications, intercultural insights.* Toronto: Hogrefe.

Kendon, A. (1987). On gesture: Its complementary relationship with speech. In A. W. Siegman & S. Feldstein (Eds.), *Nonverbal behavior and communication* (2nd ed.). Hillsdale, NJ: Erlbaum.

Kendon, A. (1988). How gestures can become like words. In F. Poyatos (Ed.), *Cross-cultural perspectives in nonverbal communication.* Toronto: Hogrefe.

Kendon, A. (1989). Gesture. *International encyclopedia of communications* (Vol. 2). New York: Oxford University Press.

Kendon, A. (1992). Some recent work from Italy on quotable gestures ("emblems"). *Journal of Linguistic Anthropology, 2,* 72–93.

Kendon, A. (1993). Human gesture. In K. R. Gibson & T. Ingold (Eds.), *Tools, language and cognition in human evolution.* New York: Cambridge University Press.

Kendon, A. (1994). Do gestures communicate?: A review. *Research on Language and Social Interaction, 27,* 175–200.

Kendon, A. (2000). Language and gesture: Unity or duality? In D. McNeill (Ed.), *Language and gesture.* New York: Cambridge University Press.

Kendon, A. (2002). Some uses of the head shake. *Gesture, 2,* 147–182.

Kendon, A. (2004). *Gesture: visible action as utterance.* New York: Cambridge University Press.

Kimura, D. (1976). The neural basis of language via gesture. In H. Whitaker & H. A. Whitaker (Eds.), *Studies in neurolinguistics* (Vol. 2). New York: Academic Press.

Kirk, L., & Burton, M. (1976). Physical versus semantic classification of nonverbal forms: A cross-cultural experiment. *Semiotica, 17,* 315–338.

Knapp, R. H. (1965). The language of postural interpretation. *Journal of Social Psychology, 67,* 371–377.

Krauss, R. M., & Hadar, U. (1999). The role of speech-related arm/hand gestures in word retrieval. In L. S. Messing & R. Campbell (Eds.), *Gesture, speech, and sign* (pp. 93–116). New York: Oxford University Press.

Krauss, R. M., Chen, Y., & Chawla, P. (1996). Nonverbal behavior and nonverbal communication: What do conversational hand gestures tell us? In M. Zanna (Ed.), *Advances in experimental social psychology* (Vol. 28). San Diego, CA: Academic Press.

Krauss, R. M., Dushay, R. A., Chen, Y., & Rauscher, F. (1995). The communicative value of conversational hand gestures. *Journal of Experimental Social Psychology, 31,* 533–552.

Krauss, R. M., Morrel-Samuels, P., & Colasante, C. (1991). Do conversational gestures communicate? *Journal of Personality and Social Psychology, 61,* 743–754.

Krout, M. (1954a). An experimental attempt to determine the significance of unconscious manual symbolic movements. *Journal of General Psychology, 51,* 296–308.

Krout, M. (1954b). An experimental attempt to produce unconscious manual symbolic movements. *Journal of General Psychology, 51,* 121–152.

Kumin, L., & Lazar, M. (1974). Gestural communication in preschool children. *Perceptual and Motor Skills, 38,* 708–710.

LaBarre, W. (1964). Paralinguistics, kinesics, and cultural anthropology. In T. A. Sebeok, A. S. Hayes, & M. C. Bateson (Eds.), *Approaches to semiotics.* The Hague: Mouton.

LaFrance, M. (1979). Non-verbal synchrony and rapport: Analysis by the cross-lag panel technique. *Social Psychology Quarterly, 42,* 66–70.

LaFrance, M. (1985). Postural mirroring and intergroup relations. *Personality and Social Psychology Bulletin, 11,* 207–217.

LaFrance, M., & Broadbent, M. (1976). Group rapport: Posture sharing as a non-verbal indicator. *Group and Organization Studies, 1,* 328–333.

LaFrance, M., & Ickes, W. (1981). Posture mirroring and interactional involvement: Sex and sex typing effects. *Journal of Nonverbal Behavior, 5,* 139–154.

Lakin, J. L., & Chartrand, T. L. (2003). Using nonconscious behavioral mimicry to create affiliation and rapport. *Psychological Science, 14,* 334–339.

Lakin, J. L., Jefferis, V. E., Cheng, C. M., & Chartrand, T. L. (2003). The chameleon effect as social glue: Evidence for the evolutionary significance of nonconscious mimicry. *Journal of Nonverbal Behavior, 27,* 145–162.

Lindenfeld, J. (1971). Verbal and non-verbal elements in discourse. *Semiotica, 3,* 223–233.

Mahl, G. F. (1987). *Explorations in nonverbal and vocal behavior.* Hillsdale, NJ: Erlbaum.

Mallery, G. (1972). *Sign language among North American Indians compared with that among other peoples and deaf-mutes.* The Hague: Mouton Press. (Original work published Washington, DC: Smithsonian Institution Bureau of Ethnology, 1880).

Markel, N. N. (1975). Coverbal behavior associated with conversation turns. In A. Kendon, R. M. Harris, & M. R. Key (Eds.), *Organization of behavior in face-to-face interaction.* Chicago: Aldine.

Matsumoto, D., & Kudoh, T. (1987). Cultural similarities and differences in the semantic dimensions of body postures. *Journal of Nonverbal Behavior, 11,* 166–179.

Maurer, R. E., & Tindall, J. H. (1983). Effect of postural congruence on client's perception of counselor empathy. *Journal of Counseling Psychology, 30,* 158–163.

McDowall, J. J. (1978a). Interactional synchrony: A reappraisal. *Journal of Personality and Social Psychology, 36,* 963–975.

McDowall, J. J. (1978b). Microanalysis of filmed movement: The reliability of boundary detection by observers. *Environmental Psychology and Nonverbal Behavior, 3,* 77–88.

McNeil, N. M., Alibali, M. W., & Evans, J. L. (2000). The role of gesture in children's comprehension of spoken language: Now they need it, now they don't. *Journal of Nonverbal Behavior, 24,* 131–150.

McNeill, D. (1985). So you think gestures are nonverbal? *Psychological Review, 92,* 350–371.

McNeill, D. (1986). Iconic gestures of children and adults. *Semiotica, 62,* 107–128.

McNeill, D. (1992). *Hand and mind.* Chicago: Chicago University Press.

McNeill, D. (2000). *Language and gesture.* New York: Cambridge University Press.

McNeill, D., Cassell, J., & McCullough, K. (1994). Communicative effects of speech-mismatched gestures. *Research on Language and Social Interaction, 27,* 223–237.

McNeill, D., & Levy, E. (1982). Conceptual representations in language activity and gesture. In R. J. Jarvella & W. Klein (Eds.), *Speech, place and action: Studies in deixis and related topics.* Chichester: Wiley.

Meissner, M., & Philpott, S. B. (1975). The sign language of sawmill workers in British Columbia. *Sign Language Studies, 9,* 291–308.

Meltzoff, A. N., & Moore, M. K. (1989). Imitation in newborn infants: Exploring the range of gestures imitated and the underlying mechanisms. *Developmental Psychology, 25,* 954–962.

Messing, L. S., & Campbell, R. (Eds.). (1999). *Gesture, speech, and sign.* New York: Oxford University Press.

Michael, G., & Willis, F. N. (1968). The development of gestures as a function of social class, education and sex. *Psychological Record, 18,* 515–519.

Michael, G., & Willis, F. N. (1969). The development of gestures in three subcultural groups. *Journal of Social Psychology, 79,* 35–41.

Morrel-Samuels, P., & Krauss, R. M. (1992). Word familiarity predicts temporal asynchrony of hand gestures and speech. *Journal of Experimental Psychology: Learning, Memory and Cognition, 18,* 615–662.

Morris, D. (1977). *Manwatching: A field guide to human behavior.* New York: Abrams.

Morris, D. (1994). *Bodytalk: The meaning of human gestures.* New York: Crown.

Morris, D., Collett, P., Marsh, P., & O'Shaughnessy, M. (1979). *Gestures: Their origins and distribution.* London: Jonathon Cape.

Morsbach, H. (1988). Nonverbal communication and hierarchical relationships: The case of bowing in Japan. In F. Poyatos (Ed.), *Cross-cultural perspectives in nonverbal communication.* Toronto: Hogrefe.

Nicoladis, E. (2002). Some gestures develop in conjunction with spoken language development and others don't: Evidence from bilingual preschoolers. *Journal of Nonverbal Behavior, 26,* 241–266.

Pelose, G. C. (1987). The functions of behavioral synchrony and speech rhythm in conversation. In S. J. Sigman (Ed.), *Research on language and social interaction* (Vol. 20). Edmonton, Alberta: Boreal.

Peterson, L. N., & Kirshner, H. S. (1981). Gestural impairment and gestural ability in aphasia: A review. *Brain and Language, 14,* 333–348.

Petitto, L. A., & Marentette, P. F. (1991, March 22). Babbling in the manual mode: Evidence for the ontogeny of language. *Science, 251,* 1493–1496.

Pickett, L. (1974). An assessment of gestural and pantomimic deficit in aphasic patients. *Acta Symbolica, 65,* 69–86.

Poggi, I. (2002). Symbolic gestures: The case of the Italian gestionary. *Gesture, 2,* 71–98.

Poyatos, F. (1975). Gesture inventories: Fieldwork methodology and problems. *Semiotica, 13,* 199–227.

Rimé, B. (1982). The elimination of visible behaviour from social interactions: Effects on verbal, nonverbal and interpersonal behaviour. *European Journal of Social Psychology, 12,* 113–129.

Rimé, B., & Schiaratura, L. (1991). Gesture and speech. In R. Feldman & B. Rimé (Eds.), *Fundamentals of nonverbal behavior.* New York: Cambridge University Press.

Riseborough, M. G. (1985). Physiographic gestures as decoding facilitators: Three experiments exploring a neglected facet of communication. *Journal of Nonverbal Behavior, 5,* 172–183.

Rogers, W. T. (1978). The contribution of kinesic illustrators toward the comprehension of verbal behavior within utterances. *Human Communication Research, 5,* 54–62.

Rosenberg, B. G., & Langer, J. (1965). A study of postural-gestural communication. *Journal of Personality and Social Psychology, 2,* 593–597.

Rosenfeld, H. M. (1967). Nonverbal reciprocation of approval: An experimental analysis. *Journal of Experimental Social Psychology, 3,* 102–111.

Rosenfeld, H. M. (1981). Whither interactional synchrony? In K. Bloom (Ed.), *Prospective issues in infant research.* Hillsdale, NJ: Erlbaum.

Rosenfeld, H. M. (1987). Conversational control functions of nonverbal behavior. In A. W. Siegman & S. Feldstein (Eds.), *Nonverbal behavior and communication* (2nd ed.). Hillsdale, NJ: Erlbaum.

Rosenfeld, H. M., & Hancks, M. (1980). The nonverbal context of verbal listener responses. In M. R. Key (Ed.), *The relationship of verbal and nonverbal communication.* The Hague: Mouton.

Saitz, R. L., & Cervenka, E. J. (1972). *Handbook of gestures: Colombia and the United States.* The Hague: Mouton.

Sapir, E. (1949). The unconscious patterning of behavior in society. In D. G. Mandelbaum (Ed.), *Selected writings of Edward Sapir in language, culture and personality.* Berkeley: University of California Press.

Scheflen, A. (1973). *Communicational structure: Analysis of a psychotherapy transaction.* Bloomington: University of Indiana Press.

Scheflen, A. E. (1964). The significance of posture in communication systems. *Psychiatry, 27,* 316–331.

Scheflen, A. E., & Scheflen, A. (1972). *Body language and the social order.* Englewood Cliffs, NJ: Prentice-Hall.

Schegloff, E. A. (1984). On some gestures' relation to talk. In J. M. Anderson & J. Heritage (Eds.), *Structures of social action: Studies in conversational analyses.* Cambridge: Cambridge University Press.

Sherzer, J. (1974). Verbal and nonverbal deixis: The pointed lip gesture among the San Blas Cuna. *Language in Society, 2,* 117–131.

Sherzer, J. (1982). *Levels of analysis in sociolinguistics and discourse analysis: Two illustrative examples.* Paper presented at the meeting of the American Sociological Association, Los Angeles.

Slama-Cazacu, T. (1976). Nonverbal components in message sequence: "Mixed syntax." In W. C. McCormack & S. A. Wurm (Eds.), *Language and man: Anthropological issues.* The Hague: Mouton.

Sousa-Poza, J. F., Rohrberg, R., & Mercure, A. (1979). Effects of type of information (abstract–concrete) and field dependence on asymmetry of hand movements during speech. *Perceptual and Motor Skills, 48,* 1323–1330.

Sparhawk, C. M. (1978). Contrastive identificational features of Persian gesture. *Semiotica, 24,* 49–86.

Stokoe, W. C. (1980). Sign language and sign languages. *Annual Review of Anthropology, 9,* 365–390.

Streeck, J. (1988). The significance of gesture: How it is established. *Papers in Pragmatics, 2,* 25–59.

Streeck, J. (1993). Gesture as communication: I. Its coordination with gaze and speech. *Communication Monographs, 60,* 275–299.

Streeck, J. (1994). Gesture as communication: II. The audience as co-author. *Research on Language and Social Interaction, 27,* 239–267.

Streeck, J. (2002). A body and its gestures. *Gesture, 2,* 19–44.

Streeck, J., & Knapp, M. L. (1992). The interaction of visual and verbal features in human communication. In F. Poyatos (Ed.), *Advances in nonverbal communication.* Amsterdam: Benjamins.

Tabensky, A. (2001). Gesture and speech rephrasings in conversation. *Gesture, 1,* 213–235.

Taylor, A. (1975). Nonverbal communication systems in native North America. *Semiotica, 13,* 329–374.

Teodorrson, S. T. (1980). Autonomy and linguistic status of non-speech language forms. *Journal of Psycholinguistic Research, 9,* 121–145.

Trout, D. L., & Rosenfeld, H. M. (1980). The effect of postural lean and body congruence on the judgment of psychotherapeutic rapport. *Journal of Nonverbal Behavior, 4,* 176–190.

Trupin, C. M. (1976). *Linguistics and gesture: An application of linguistic theory to the study of emblems.* Unpublished doctoral dissertation, University of Michigan.

van de Koppel, J. M. H., de Bok-Huurman, J. F. H., & Moezelaar, M. J. M. (1988). Understanding gestures in another culture: A study with children from the Dutch Antilles and the Netherlands. In F. Poyatos (Ed.), *Cross-cultural perspectives in nonverbal communication.* Toronto: Hogrefe.

Varney, N. R. (1978). Linguistic correlates of pantomime recognition in asphasic patients. *Journal of Neurology, Neurosurgery and Psychiatry, 41,* 546–568.

Walker, M. B., & Trimboli, C. (1983). The expressive functions of the eye flash. *Journal of Nonverbal Behavior, 8,* 3–13.

Warner, R. M., Malloy, D., Schneider, K., Knoth, R., & Wilder, B. (1987). Rhythmic organization of social interaction and observer ratings of positive affect and involvement. *Journal of Nonverbal Behavior, 11,* 57–74.

Washabaugh, W., Woodward, J., & DeSantis, S. (1978). Providence Island sign language: A context dependent language. *Anthropological Linguistics, 20,* 95–109.

Webb, J. T. (1972). Interview synchrony: An investigation of two speech rate measures. In A. W. Siegman & B. Pope (Eds.), *Studies in dyadic communication.* New York: Pergamon Press.

Wilkinson, L. C., & Rembold, K. L. (1981). The form and function of children's gestures accompanying verbal directives. In P. S. Dale & D. Ingram (Eds.), *Child language: An international perspective.* Baltimore: University Park Press.

Wolff, C. (1945). *A psychology of gesture.* London: Methuen.

Wolff, P., & Gustein, J. (1972). Effects of induced motor gestures on vocal output. *Journal of Communication, 22,* 277–288.

Woodall, W. G., & Burgoon, J. K. (1981). The effects of nonverbal synchrony on message comprehension and persuasiveness. *Journal of Nonverbal Behavior, 5,* 207–223.

Woodall, W. G., & Folger, J. P. (1981). Encoding specificity and nonverbal cue content: An expansion of episodic memory research. *Communication Monographs, 48,* 39–53.

Wundt, W. (1973). *The language of gestures.* The Hague: Mouton. (Original work published 1900).

Wylie, L. (1977). *Beaux gestes: A guide to French body talk.* Cambridge, MA: The Undergraduate Press.

Chapter 8

THE EFFECTS OF TOUCH ON HUMAN COMMUNICATION

We often talk about the way we talk, and we frequently try to see the way we see, but for some reason we have rarely touched on the way we touch.

—D. MORRIS

The scene is a university library, but it could just as easily be the local supermarket, bank, or restaurant. What happens takes about half a second, and it is not noticed by those experiencing it. Remarkably, however, this event affects their evaluation of their experience in the library. What could be so mysterious and so powerful?

The answer begins with researchers at Purdue University (Fisher, Rytting, & Heslin, 1976), who wanted to investigate systematically the effects of a brief, seemingly accidental touch in a nonintimate context. They had male and female clerks return library cards to some students by placing their hand directly over the student's palm, making physical contact; other students were not touched. Outside the library, a researcher approached the students and asked questions about their feelings toward the library clerk and the library in general. Students who were touched, especially the females, evaluated the clerk and the library significantly more favorably than those not touched. This was true for both students who were aware of being touched and those who were not.

Other studies of fleeting and seemingly insignificant touches find similar results. Waitresses who touched diners got bigger tips (Crusco & Wetzel, 1984), customers who were touched briefly by their waitress drank more alcohol compared to their partners than customers who were not touched (Kaufman & Mahoney, 1999), and psychologists who touched students on the shoulder when requesting help found greater compliance (Patterson, Powell, & Lenihan, 1986). Maybe this is why politicians are so eager to shake hands ("press the flesh") with as many voters as possible. Thus we know brief touch can be functionally influential; now we must find out how touch works in conjunction with other aspects of the setting, the relationship to the other, past experiences with touch, other behaviors, and so on.

Touching behavior is sometimes an important part of health care, as we demonstrate later. Positive effects of massage have been found, as well as positive effects of touching by physicians and nurses on hospitalized patients, although the physiological, behavioral, and attitudinal effects are not *always* positive. Counselors use touch to reassure clients and to develop a relationship in which their clients trust them and feel free to talk. However, it is the type, timing, and location of the touch, as well as the counselor's comfort in giving the touch, that are the keys to success, not the act of touching by itself.

Touch is a crucial aspect of most human relationships. It plays a part in giving encouragement, expressing tenderness, and showing emotional support. Body awareness and personal growth workshops enroll many Americans who feel a need to rediscover communication through touch. These workshops encourage physical contact as a way to break through some psychological barriers. People try to become more aware of themselves, other people, and the world around them through physical experiences rather than through words or sight. Some say it reflects a yearning for human contact and a desire to restore some unfilled tactile needs. As Montagu (1971) said,

> When affection and involvement are conveyed through touch, it is those meanings as well as the security-giving satisfactions, with which touch will become associated. Inadequate tactile experience will result in a lack of such associations and a consequent inability to relate to others in many fundamental human ways. (p. 292)

The act of touching is like any other message we communicate—it may elicit negative reactions as well as positive ones depending on the configuration of the touch, the people, and the circumstances. We know that sometimes people get tense, anxious, and/or uncomfortable when touched; we know that touching perceived as inappropriate for the relationship can be met with aggressive reactions—touching back in the form of slapping or hitting. Some people seem to evaluate almost all touching negatively. In some cases, this dislike for touching may be related to early experiences with touch. What do we know about touching as it occurs throughout the life span?

TOUCHING AND HUMAN DEVELOPMENT

Tactile communication is probably the most basic or primitive form of communication. In fact, tactile sensitivity may be the first sensory process to become functional. In fetal life, the child begins to respond to vibrations of the mother's pulsating heartbeat, which impinge on the child's entire body and are magnified by the amniotic fluid. Researchers have documented that a living fetus aborted during the third month of gestation, when only 3 inches long, will respond reflexively to the touch of a hair around its mouth (Maurer & Maurer, 1988). In one sense, our first input about what life itself will be like comes from the sense of touch.

Research shows that touch is critical to normal physiological growth in newborns. Maternal licking of rat pups stimulates growth hormone production, and massage with pressure stimulates weight gain in preterm infants and continues to be associated with mental and motor development 1 year later (Field, 1998).

Infants gain knowledge of themselves and the world around them through tactile explorations with their mouths and hands. Some common touch experiences include the obstetrician's hands and the parental (or caregiver) hands that change diapers, feed, bathe, rock, and give comfort. During early childhood, words accompany touch until the child associates the two; then words may replace touch entirely. For example, a mother may gently stroke or pat an infant to console him or her. As the child grows older, she strokes and pats while murmuring encouraging words. Eventually, the mother may call from another room, "It's all right, dear—Mommy's here." As words replace touch, an intimate closeness is replaced by distance.

Gender differences show up early. After 6 months of age, girls are not only allowed but also encouraged to spend more time touching and staying near their parents than boys. Harrison-Speake and Willis (1995) gathered adults' views on the appropriateness of different kinds of parental touch with children of different ages. Rather clear norms were evident. Touch was seen as increasingly inappropriate as children grew from toddlers to young teenagers, especially for fathers and for boys. White respondents were more approving of parental touch than were African-American respondents, regardless of the kind of touch, the child's age, or the gender of the child or parent. However, because the interviewer was always white in this study, it is necessary to replicate the ethnic group differences using African-American interviewers.

Several observations of touching behavior have been made in the context of the developing child's school experiences. In one study, preschool boys tended to touch their male teachers more than their female teachers; preschool girls touched teachers of both sexes about equally. The teachers themselves usually touched children of their own sex more (Perdue & Connor, 1978). Willis and his colleagues (Willis & Hoffman, 1975; Willis & Reeves, 1976) observed children in elementary school and junior high school. From kindergarten through sixth grade the amount of touching steadily declined but still surpassed most reports of adult touching. This same trend occurred in junior high, with about half as much touching as in the primary grades. The most touching occurred between same-sex dyads. African-American children, especially African-American females, tended to exhibit more touching behavior. Although touching in the primary grades is more often initiated with the hands, the junior high students showed much more shoulder-to-shoulder and elbow-to-elbow touching. Junior high females began to show more aggressive touching, and junior high boys were touched in more places, primarily because of the play fighting so common at that age. During adolescence, tactile experiences with members of the same sex, and then the opposite sex, become increasingly important.

The use of touch to communicate emotional and relational messages to the elderly may be crucial, particularly as the reliance on verbal/cognitive message wanes. Although we seem to give the aged in the United States a greater license to touch others, it is not clear how much others touch them. No doubt the infirmities of age require more touching, but it may make a big difference whether this increased touching is merely functional and professional or expresses affection. Observations of touching in four homes for the elderly revealed that this is a context in which females tend to initiate more touching than do males. And, as in childhood, same-sex touch is more likely than touch between members of the opposite sex (Rinck, Willis, & Dean, 1980).

Early tactile experiences seem crucial to later mental and emotional adjustment. Youngsters who have little physical contact during infancy may be slower to learn to walk and talk, and some instances of difficulties and retardation in reading and speech are also associated with early deprivation of, and confusion in, tactile communication. Physical violence in adults may also be related to deprivation of touch during infancy.

Ashley Montagu (1971) cited many animal and human studies to support the theory that tactile satisfaction during infancy and childhood is of fundamental importance to subsequent healthy behavioral development. He maintains that we cannot handle a child too much, as "there is every reason to believe that, just as the salamander's brain and nervous system develops more fully in response to peripheral stimulation, so does the brain and nervous system of the human being" (p. 188). Harlow's (1958) famous "surrogate mother" experiments offer some supporting evidence from the animal world for the importance of touch to infants. Harlow constructed a monkey mother figure out of wire that could provide milk and protection; then he constructed another one out of sponge rubber and terry cloth that did not provide milk. Because infant monkeys consistently chose the terry cloth mother, Harlow concluded that contact comfort was a more important part of the mother–child relationship for monkeys than was sustenance per se. Psychologically, nursing was less important as a food source and more important as a source of reassuring touch.

WHO TOUCHES WHOM, WHERE, WHEN, AND HOW MUCH?

The amount and kind of contact in adulthood vary considerably with the age, personality, sex, situation, culture, and relationship of the parties involved. We explore these factors briefly here (see chapter 12 for more discussion of gender, dominance, and culture). There are reports of married couples who either have so little to say to each other, or who find it so difficult to establish closeness through verbal contact, that physical contact during sexual encounters becomes a primary mode of communication for establishing closeness. Many factors in the development of American society have led to a common expectation that touching is conducted only in extremely personal and intimate relationships, which leads to the belief that all touching is somehow sensuous in nature. The irony is that long-term intimates probably touch each other less, and less intimately, than those who are either working to establish a romantic relationship or working to restore one that is losing intimacy (Emmers & Dindia, 1995; Guerrero & Andersen, 1991; McDaniel & Andersen, 1998). For intimates in long-established romantic relationships, the quality of touch has likely replaced the quantity needed to initially establish the relationship as an intimate one. In married relations also, people are more likely to *reciprocate* touch than in dating relationships (Guerrero & Andersen, 1994).

For some individuals, the contact occurring in a crowded commuter train or theater lobby is very discomforting, especially opposite-sex contacts for women and same-sex contacts for men. Explanations for such feelings are numerous. Some children grow up learning not to touch a multitude of animate and inanimate objects. They are told not to touch their own body and later not to touch the body of their dating partner. Care is taken so children do not see their parents touch one another intimately; some parents demonstrate a noncontact norm through the use of twin beds. Touching is associated with admonitions of "not nice" or "bad" and punished accordingly, and frequent touching between father and son is thought to be less than masculine. Because of such experiences, some people become nontouchers in any situation. Several studies have tried to identify the personality characteristics of people who enjoy touching and those who do not (Andersen, Andersen, & Lustig, 1987; Deethardt & Hines, 1983). Nontouchers, when compared with touchers, report more anxiety and tension in their lives, less satisfaction with their bodies, and more suspicion of others; they are also more socially withdrawn and more likely to be rigid or authoritarian in their beliefs. Men are also more likely to describe themselves as touch avoidant than women are.

Certain situations have a facilitating or inhibiting effect on touching behavior. Several studies have demonstrated that in public places, where most observational research is done, touching can be quite infrequent. As an example, Hall and Veccia (1990) observed 4,500 pairs of people in public places and found that only 15% were already touching or touched during the observation period. Similarly, Remland, Jones, and Brinkman (1991) observed dyads in public places in several European locations and found that people touched in only 9% of the interactions observed. Some researchers, frustrated at the infrequency of touches in many settings, have designed clever ways to increase the likelihood that a touch will occur. Juni and Brannon (1981) disguised a confederate as a blind person, who then went out on the street and asked directions from passersby. The investigators reasoned that people would be less inhibited about touching a blind person while giving directions than about touching a sighted person.

Henley (1977) gathered people's opinions on touch patterns and concluded that people think that the likelihood of touch is increased in the following situations, which imply underlying themes of power, intimacy, and emotion:

1. Giving information or advice rather than asking for it
2. Giving an order rather than responding to it
3. Asking a favor rather than agreeing to do one
4. Trying to persuade rather than being persuaded
5. Participating in a deep rather than casual conversation
6. Interacting at a party rather than at work
7. Communicating excitement rather than receiving it from another
8. Receiving messages of worry from another rather than sending such messages

Greetings and departures at airport terminals are communicative situations that reflect a higher incidence of touching than would normally be expected. In one study, 60% of the people observed in greetings touched; another study reported that 83% of the participants touched (Greenbaum & Rosenfeld, 1980; Heslin & Boss, 1980). Heslin and Boss (1980) found that extended embraces and greater intimacy of touch were more likely to occur during departures than greetings. The greater the emotion (as reflected in facial expressions) and the closer the perceived relationship, the greater the chances of increased touching. Actual relationship closeness (e.g., romantic vs. friends) has in fact been shown to predict the amount of interpersonal touching in public (Afifi & Johnson, 1999; Guerrero, 1997).

Another situation likely to show a higher incidence of touch than normally found in public settings involves team sports. In one study, the touching behavior of bowlers during league play was observed and found to be far more frequent than observations during normal social interaction (Smith, Willis, & Gier, 1980). Similarly, Kneidinger, Maple, and Tross (2001) counted touches made on-field during college baseball and softball games and found a high touching rate—averaging more than 20 touches per inning.

Anthropologists and travelers, as well as researchers, have noted that touch patterns differ according to culture and nationality. Some cultures seem very tactile, and others are more "hands off" (DiBiase & Gunnoe, 2004; McDaniel & Andersen, 1998). We explore this topic further in chapter 13, but here let us note that cultures can differ in overall quantity of touch, the contextual rules that determine when and how people touch, and in the meanings expressed by touch. Research has not progressed far in mapping out these sources of variation. A strong likelihood is that most touches have common meanings in different cultures but the norms for who can touch whom, and when, follow local customs. Most of our knowledge about the psychology of touch (and other nonverbal behaviors) is based on the study of white Americans.

Gender and relationships influence touching patterns. In his classic study, Jourard (1966) asked what parts of the body people think are touched most often. He administered a questionnaire to students, who indicated which of 24 body parts they had seen or touched on others or that others had seen or touched on them within the past 12 months. The other persons were specified as mother, father, same-sex friend, and opposite-sex friend. Among other findings, Jourard's study found females were perceived as considerably more accessible to touch by all persons than males were. Opposite-sex friends and mothers were reported as doing the most touching. Many fathers were recalled as touching not much more than the hands of the subjects. The likelihood of opposite-sex touching of course depends greatly on the relationship between the parties; this kind of touch is more likely when intimacy and familiarity are high (Stier & Hall, 1984).

Jourard's data were gathered nearly 40 years ago. A replication of this study more than a decade later revealed about the same results—with one exception (Rosenfeld, Kartus, & Ray, 1976). It seems that both males and females are perceived as even more accessible to opposite-sex friends than they were in the preceding decade, with increased touching reported for body parts normally considered more intimate, such as chest, stomach, hips, and thigh.[1] When people are asked to recall where they are touched and/or how often, there is always the possibility that these recollections will not be accurate. Jones (1991), using Jourard's methods, found that the number of body parts actually contacted was consistently lower than those anticipated or recalled by students filling out a questionnaire. In the area of touching, expectations about which touches *should* occur seem to exert an important influence on questionnaire responses.

We pursue the topic of gender differences in touch further in chapter 12. Suffice it to say here that the topic of gender differences in nonverbal behavior raises many interesting questions about determinants. Henley (1977) proposed the hypothesis that gender differences in touch as well as several other nonverbal behaviors are closely tied to gender

---

[1] A third study using Jourard's method was conducted in the 1980s, but the respondents were students attending a small Catholic liberal arts college. Although the results show less touch reported by these students, it is not clear how much of this finding is attributable to cultural changes associated with the 1980s and how much is related to the nature of the respondents (Hutchinson & Davidson, 1990).

differences in dominance and power, with the general hypothesis being that differences between men and women parallel differences between powerful and weak people in society at large. The evidence supporting Henley's hypothesis is extremely mixed and is undermined by the very inconsistent evidence of systematic differences in nonverbal behavior (including touching) according to the dominance–power dimension (Hall, Coats, & Smith LeBeau, 2004).

DIFFERENT TYPES OF TOUCHING BEHAVIOR

Argyle (1975) listed the following kinds of bodily contact as most common in Western culture*:

TYPE OF TOUCH	BODILY AREAS TYPICALLY INVOLVED
Patting	Head, back
Slapping	Face, hand, buttocks
Punching	Face, chest
Pinching	Cheek
Stroking	Hair, face, upper body, knee, genitals
Shaking	Hands, shoulders
Kissing	Mouth, cheek, breasts, hand, foot, genitals
Licking	Face, genitals
Holding	Hand, arm, knee, genitals
Guiding	Hand, arm
Embracing	Shoulder, body
Linking	Arms
Laying on	Hands
Kicking	Legs, buttocks
Grooming	Hair, face
Tickling	Almost anywhere

* We made the following alterations to the original list: (1) changed *bottom* to *buttocks*; (2) added *genitals* to four categories; (3) added *shoulders* to the "shaking" category.

Desmond Morris (1977) distinguished between touching others and touching the self. He reported that field observations led to the naming of 457 types of body contact falling into 14 major types of public body contact occurring between 2 people. These are called *tie signs* because they signal that some type of relationship exists between the two participants. Sometimes the specific nature of that relationship can be deduced by observing the way the touching is enacted. Morris's major categories of nonaggressive touching include the following:

1. **The Handshake.** The strength of the tie or desired tie between the participants can often be observed by watching the nonshaking hand.

2. **The Body-Guide.** Here, touching is a substitute for pointing. The person guiding the other's body is frequently the person in charge during that encounter.
3. **The Pat.** Morris says when adults pat other adults it is often a condescending gesture or a sexual one. The well-known exception is the congratulatory pat (often on the buttocks) following a successful performance in men's team sports.
4. **The Arm-Link.** This may be used for support when one person is infirm, but it is also frequently used to indicate a close relationship. The person in charge, says Morris, is less likely to be the person grasping the other's arm.
5. **The Shoulder Embrace.** This half-embrace is used in male–female romantic relationships as well as to signify "buddies" in male–male relationships.
6. **The Full Embrace.** This gesture, sometimes called a hug, frequently occurs during moments of intense emotion, sporting events, romance, greetings, and farewells. It is also used ritualistically to show a relationship closer than a handshake would indicate.
7. **The Hand-in-Hand.** When adults hold hands with children, it is designed for support, to keep the child close, or to protect the child. As adults, hand holding (because both parties are performing the same act) suggests an equality within the relationship. It is often thought of in opposite-sex relationships, but same-sex hand holding is not uncommon, particularly in groups.
8. **The Waist Embrace.** According to Morris, the waist embrace is frequently substituted for the full embrace when the participants wish to signal more intimacy than hand holding or a shoulder embrace yet still remain mobile.
9. **The Kiss.** The location, pressure, duration, and openness of a kiss help signal the closeness or desired closeness of a particular moment.
10. **The Hand-to-Head.** Given the highly vulnerable nature of the head area, letting someone touch us on the head shows a trusting, often intimate, relationship.
11. **The Head-to-Head.** Two people touching heads renders them incapable of regarding other ongoing activities in a normal manner, so this is usually thought of as an agreement by both parties to shut out the rest of the world—a condition especially common to young lovers.
12. **The Caress.** Signal associated with romantic feelings for one's partner, although, like any signal, it can be used by nonintimates who are trying to deceive others about the depth of their relationship.
13. **The Body Support.** Parents often support children by carrying, lifting, or letting them sit in their laps. Such support may be sought among adults in playful situations or when one person feels physically helpless.
14. **The Mock Attack.** Aggressive-looking behaviors performed in a nonaggressive manner, for example, arm punches, hair rufflings, pushes, pinches, ear nibbles, and so forth. We sometimes allow or even encourage such gestures with friends to show the range of behavioral understanding between us. And sometimes these mock-attack touches are substitutes for more loving touches that, in the case of some fathers wishing to show love for their sons, may be too embarrassing.

Some of these forms of touch can be seen in Figure 8-1.

FIGURE 8-1

Some common forms of touch. (a) Full embrace. (b) Shoulder embrace. (c) Arm-link.

a

b

c

Another method of categorizing the various types of touching was undertaken by Heslin (Heslin & Alper, 1983). This taxonomy is based on the functions of the messages communicated and ranges from less personal to more personal types of touch. Accidental touches and aggressive touches seem to be a part of the intimacy continuum but are not presented in this list.

1. **Functional/Professional.** The communicative intent of this impersonal, often cold and businesslike, touching is to accomplish some task or to perform some

FIGURE 8-1   (Continued)

(d) Kiss. (e) Head-to-head.

d   e

service. The other person is considered as an object or nonperson to keep any intimate or sexual messages from interfering with the task at hand. Examples of such situations may include a golf pro with a student, a tailor with a customer, or a physician with a patient.

2. **Social/Polite.** This type of touching affirms the other person's identity as a member of the same species, operating by essentially the same rules of conduct. Although the other is treated as a person, there is still very little perceived involvement between the interactants. The handshake is the best example of this type of touching. Although the handshake is only about 150 years old, it was preceded by a handclasp, which goes back at least as far as ancient Rome.

3. **Friendship/Warmth.** This kind of touching behavior begins to recognize more of the other person's uniqueness and expresses a liking for that person. It is oriented toward the other person as a friend. However, this type of touch may engender uneasiness because it can be misunderstood as intimate or sexual touching. Private situations may exacerbate this problem, so it probably will take place in public if the toucher anticipates the possibility of misinterpretation.

4. **Love/Intimacy.** When we lay a hand on the cheek of a person or when we fully embrace another person, we are probably expressing an emotional attachment or attraction through touch. The other person is the object of feelings of intimacy or love. The various kinds of touching at this point are probably the least stereotyped and the most adapted to the specific other person.

5. **Sexual Arousal.** Although sexual arousal is sometimes an integral part of love and intimacy, it also may have characteristics distinct from that category. Here we are primarily looking at touch as an experience of physical attraction only. The other person is, in common parlance, a sex object.

Morris (1971) proposed that heterosexual couples in Western culture normally go through a sequence of steps (like courtship patterns in other animal species) on the road to sexual intimacy. Notice that each step, aside from the first three, involves some kind of touching.

1. Eye to body
2. Eye to eye
3. Voice to voice
4. Hand to hand
5. Arm to shoulder
6. Arm to waist
7. Mouth to mouth
8. Hand to head
9. Hand to body
10. Mouth to breast
11. Hand to genitals
12. Genitals to genitals (and/or mouth to genitals)

According to Morris, these steps generally follow the same order, although with variations. One form of skipping steps or moving to a level of intimacy beyond what would be expected is found in socially formalized types of bodily contact, for example, a good-night kiss or hand-to-hand introduction. Although mouth-to-mouth touching frequently may reflect an advancing stage of intimacy, it also may occur in the most nonintimate settings with the most nonintimate meaning attached to it, for example, when a host of a television quiz show dutifully "pecks" the contestants as they are greeted or as they depart.

THE MEANINGS AND IMPACT OF INTERPERSONAL TOUCH

The meanings of nonaccidental touch have been assessed in several different ways. One approach simply tries to determine whether touching is perceived as a positive or negative experience. However, without further knowledge of the participants and how, when, where, and why the touch was performed, statements about the positive or negative reactions to touch are of questionable value.

Data gathered by Jones and Yarbrough (1985) indicate a wide range of meanings associated with touch. They had 39 male and female university students record the details of each touch experience over a 3-day period. Over 1,500 acts of social touching were analyzed. The following meanings incorporate their findings.

TOUCH AS POSITIVE AFFECT

The touching in this category is very similar to what Heslin called warmth/intimacy and sexual arousal. It may involve support, reassurance, appreciation, affection, sexual attraction, or, if the touch is sustained, it may indicate inclusion ("we're together"). Some kinds of touching behavior from nurses, if it is perceived as comforting and relaxing, would fit in this category. Back rubs and massages may also express positive affect from a friend but be perceived as task related when performed by a professional massage therapist. Mental health therapists, too, recognize the importance of performing touch in such a way that it communicates positive regard but not too much intimacy. If touch is perceived as an indication of interpersonal warmth, it may bring forth other related behaviors, for example, increased verbal output of patients and improved patient attitudes toward nurses (Aguilera, 1967; Pattison, 1973). The enhanced positive affect that can be produced by even fleeting and innocuous touches may generalize to the entire local environment, as found in the library study described at the beginning of this chapter and in the consumer studies of Hornik (1991, 1992). Shoppers touched by student greeters spent more time shopping, bought more, and evaluated the store more favorably.[2]

TOUCH AS NEGATIVE AFFECT

The students in Jones and Yarbrough's study did not report very many touches in this category, but we clearly perceive some touches as an expression of negative attitudes and emotions. It may be an expression of anger or frustration suggested by hitting, slapping, or tightly squeezing another's arm so the person cannot escape. Generally, negative touch is much more likely among young children than among adults.

TOUCH AS PLAY

Sometimes we interpret the touching we give and receive as attempts to reduce the seriousness of a message—whether it is affection or aggression. When one person goes through the motions of landing a knockout punch on the other person, then stops the forward movement of the fist just as it makes contact with the other person's skin, the message is "I'm not fighting; I'm playing." An accompanying smile or laugh may further reinforce this message. The ultimate in playful touch is tickling, a phenomenon first addressed by psychologists nearly a century ago and discussed even by Charles Darwin. One question is why we cannot tickle ourselves, and whether the "other" who does the tickling must be human or could as easily be a mechanical device. According to Harris and Christenfeld (1997, 1999), a machine can tickle as well as a person provided there is an element of unpredictability to it.

TOUCH AS INFLUENCE

When the goal of the touch is to persuade the other to do something, touch is associated with influence. Jones and Yarbrough called these "compliance touches." Several independent

---

[2] To demonstrate effects of touch (or any nonverbal behavior), experimenters often train confederates to deliberately engage in the behavior, or not, as in the library and shoppers studies mentioned here. Such experiments are an important way of studying the impact of specific behaviors. Lewis et al. (1997) offer a valuable caution about such experiments, however. Despite training, confederates may have difficulty controlling one behavior, such as touch, without simultaneous changes in other behaviors, such as smiling and gazing. It is sometimes hard, therefore, to know which behavioral cue was crucial in influencing the recipient of the cues. A critical reader is wise to consider possible confounding effects of unintended cues when evaluating research with these designs.

studies show that touch increased the rate of getting signatures on petitions, increased the chances people would return money found in a phone booth, and helped in obtaining favors. People who were touched after agreeing to fill out a survey answered a significantly larger number of items than people who agreed but were not touched (Nannberg & Hansen, 1994). Being touched on the arm for 1 second or less increased willingness to hold onto a very active, large dog for 10 minutes while the requester went to the pharmacy (Guéguen & Fischer-Lokou, 2002). Even without a direct request, being touched can increase helpfulness (as when the toucher leaves and then drops his possessions; Guéguen & Fischer-Lokou, 2003) and other positive acts, such as leaving a bigger tip for a waitperson (Crusco & Wetzel, 1984). In all likelihood, the psychological mechanism accounting for such effects is positive affect and the personal bonding that may be implied by even a fleeting and seemingly insignificant touch between strangers. These findings suggest that one could try to use touch manipulatively—for example, waitpersons might deliberately touch their customers in order to get bigger tips.

TOUCH AS INTERACTION MANAGEMENT

We try to structure or control conversations or elements of conversations in many ways. These management touches may guide someone without interrupting verbal conversation; get someone's attention by touching or tugging at that person's arm or tapping him or her on the shoulder; indicate or mark the beginning (greeting) or end (good-bye) of a conversation; or fulfill some ritualistic function such as touching a baby's head at a baptism.

TOUCH AS PHYSIOLOGICAL STIMULUS

Obviously, touch is preeminently important at all stages of sexual interaction. Touch is also a strong, but complex, stimulus in more mundane interactions. When people are in experiments in which they are forewarned they will be touched in a professional, innocuous manner, researchers find predictable heart rate decreases (Drescher, Gantt, & Whitehead, 1980), which is said to demonstrate that touch is intrinsically calming and relates to the evolutionary importance of mother–infant bonding. However, when touch is unexpected and/or unexplained, heart rate increases have been found; for example, when females were touched unexpectedly on the wrist for 10 seconds by a male experimenter, a significant increase in heart rate was found, and, moreover, all subjects showed increases in blood pressure in this condition compared to a no-touch condition and a condition in which touch was expected (taking their pulse) (Nilsen & Vrana, 1998). Such research underscores that the impact of touch depends on social–contextual factors and on the interpretations given to the touch.

TOUCH AS INTERPERSONAL RESPONSIVENESS

Sometimes the meanings attributed to touch concern the level of involvement, responsiveness, or activity of the communicator(s) (Afifi & Johnson, 1999). Sometimes touch simply means that the intensity of the interaction or the interactants' level of involvement in the conversation is high. Interpersonal responsiveness may be perceived as positive affect when it is mutually felt or when one person feels he or she contributed to the other's behavior.

Touch as Task Related

There are times when we need to help someone get out of a car or our hands touch as the result of passing something back and forth. These touches, associated with the performance of the task, are similar to what Heslin called functional/professional touch. As with any other message, the two communicators may not share a similar meaning for the touch—or one person may deliberately try to mislead another. A not unfamiliar example of the latter deception is when one person touches another in a joking context but intends the touch to be a step toward intimacy. Such a blending of functions also occurred in studies such as the library touch study described earlier: The touch occurred during task performance (handing the library card to the patron) but the effect was positive–emotional.

Touch as Healing

A miraculous cure is one that cannot be explained by recognized medical or physiological therapy. Throughout recorded history, wondrous healings of the sick and infirm by religious workers, royalty, and other charismatic persons have had interpersonal touch as a major ingredient. Jesus was said to heal many by touch, and he was often described as being surrounded by crowds who pressed around him hoping for his touch. The French and English kings were widely believed to be able to accomplish healing by the laying on of hands. Edward I of England is documented to have touched 938 of his subjects suffering from scrofula in the 28th year of his reign and over 1,000 subjects 4 years later (Older, 1982). In later centuries, including our own, healing touch became the province of ministers and others who attribute the healing touch to the power of God. The physical healing power of touch in such miraculous cases has not been studied in a controlled way that could establish its effectiveness and the mechanisms by which it may work. Although it may be difficult to rule out God's love or unknown physical forces, Older (1982) attributes the inexplicable cures to psychological factors:

- The patient feels a great need for improvement.
- The patient has profound trust in the healer's powers.
- The patient is part of a group that increases pressure and adds encouragement.
- There is a shared, irrational belief system, usually of a religious nature.
- Emotions are at a high pitch in the patient and any onlookers.

Currently, the medical and nursing professions have renewed interest in touching as a form of therapy (Borelli & Heidt, 1981; Krieger, 1987). Moreover, the physiological mechanisms for some kinds of touch are being studied as well. Massage, long known for its relaxing and pleasurable properties, has now received extensive scientific scrutiny for its effects on brain activity, attentiveness and alertness, pain relief, anxiety and depression, stress hormones, sleep, appetite, pulmonary function in asthmatic children, immune function, weight gain in preterm infants, and other clinical indicators of health. Field (1995, 1998, 2001) reports positive effects for all of these outcomes, suggesting among other possibilities that parasympathetic nervous system activity is the mechanism underlying massage's favorable impact (the pressure stimulates the vagal nerve, which lowers physiological arousal and stress hormones). Even a single massage therapy session has beneficial effects on anxiety, blood pressure, and heart rate (Moyer, Rounds, & Hannum, 2004). It is possible also that the experience of touch is beneficial even when it is not received as massage. One reason why having pets has been shown in controlled studies to have beneficial physiological and psychological effects may be that relationships with pets entail high levels of touching (Allen, 2003).

Mental health professionals debate whether touch should be incorporated into the therapeutic process (Hetherington, 1998; Smith, Clance, & Imes, 1998). Risk of sexual involvement, or simply risk that clients will take offense, is weighed against the potential value of human physical contact during stressful moments in therapy. Certainly therapists need to be highly sensitive to the responses that clients may have to being touched.

TOUCH AS SYMBOLISM

Perhaps because touch outside of intimate relationships is so infrequent, it is highly salient when it occurs. Touch can be so fraught with meaning that the act of touch itself comes to represent the significance of the relationship, ritual, or occasion. The touch shown in Figure 8-2 between Israeli leader Yitzhak Rabin and Palestinian leader Yasir Arafat on the day they announced an Israeli–Palestinian reconciliation says more than words could. Ironically, that same handshake apparently sparked Rabin's assassin to plan the prime minister's death ("With a Handshake," 1995).

Sometimes, the symbolism is experienced at a very personal level through one's own experience of touch. We are all familiar with photographs of screaming fans reaching

FIGURE 8-2

Rabin and Arafat shaking hands.

out to touch a famous rock star. Even in everyday situations people often find value in touching someone who is important to them. They might say proudly, "I shook so-and-so's hand!" The vicarious–symbolic power of touch is sometimes evident even when the actual touch is one step removed, as when one can touch or possess a remnant or souvenir of the important person. Even an autograph fits this description because the important person has touched the pen and paper. Certainly, throughout the history of Christianity it has been very meaningful to claim to own a piece of a saint's body or clothing.

Figure 8-3 vividly portrays members of Congress reaching out to touch President Bush after his State of the Union address. One study of touch patterns in a state legislature noted that though the governor was touched by many, he was not seen to touch anyone during the observation period (Goldstein & Jeffords, 1981). The daughter of the Buddhist

FIGURE 8-3

The audience is eager to touch President Bush after his State of the Union address.

(Continued)

Figure 8-3   (Continued)

Panchen Lama (a holy man second in importance to the Dalai Lama) recollected a trip to Tibet when she was seven years old: "They told me that there were people lining the road for fifty miles. Thousands and thousands of people, all wanting to touch me" (Hilton, 2004). On another trip, at age 17, she told of being exhausted by the crowds surrounding her. But, she said, "I can't complain, because it makes them so happy to see me and to touch me." But she had to ask her bodyguards to stop them from lifting up her skirt to get to her legs. As she explained, devotees wish to touch the feet of an important figure.

   Touching in these scenarios gives the toucher the feeling of acquiring something important; something has "rubbed off" onto the toucher. It does not always seem to matter whether the significant other person is the toucher or the recipient. What is rubbed off can vary, too. Sometimes it is vicarious power—one is suddenly more important among one's friends after touching a famous person. Other times, what is gained is less definable though no less important: We might say that one feels one has acquired some piece of the other's essence through touch. Whatever the valuable quality possessed by the other, people feel they have gained a bit of it through initiating touch. This somewhat magical way of thinking has its reverse side, too, when we feel contaminated by touching or being touched by undesirable people. It is surely no coincidence that the lowest caste in traditional Indian society was called the Untouchables.

CONTEXTUAL FACTORS IN THE MEANING
OF INTERPERSONAL TOUCH

The meanings of touch depend on many environmental, personal, and contextual variables, as the previous section made clear. Indeed, it is likely that much of the time, the meaning of touch derives from such qualifying variables and not from the nature of the touch *per se*. Often, touch intensifies ongoing emotional experiences rather than conveying specific meanings in itself. The relationship between the interactants provides important context for interpreting the meaning of touch. A touch on the arm, which might be interpreted as a social/polite or merely friendly gesture between strangers, may acquire sexual overtones if a friendly relationship already exists. An embrace may take on different intimacy connotations if displayed by two men versus two women (Floyd, 1999), or if two men embrace on the sports field versus in a bar (Kneidinger, Maple, & Tross, 2001). Interpretations of touch are also related to other contextual variables such as duration, the specific form of the touch, other cues, and other contextual features, singly and in combination—for example, a touch might seem more intimate if it is accompanied by other signals such as prolonged gaze, if the touch is held an instant too long, if the environment is private, and so forth. A brief shoulder touch by waitpersons to their customers resulted in bigger tips, but especially if it was opposite-gender touching in a bar (Hubbard et al., 2003). Friendship/warmth touching may be more likely to occur (between people who are not intimate) in public settings because the same kind of contact in private is more likely to take on connotations of love or sexual intimacy. Certain parts of the body connote greater intimacy than other parts, but intimacy is also linked to the manner of touch. For instance, a touch and release on any part of the body is likely to be perceived as less intimate than a touch and hold. Both of the preceding ways of touching are likely to be perceived as less intimate than a touch and stroke. Touch meaning also may vary as a result of the sequencing. Jones and Yarbrough found a number of instances in which positive affect touching was repeated, either by one person or in a reciprocal pattern (1985). They speculate that this increases the intensity of the feeling being expressed. Other sequences begin with one type of touch and then change to another, for example, affectionate touching that precedes influence touching.

Like other forms of nonverbal behavior, touching may support or contradict information communicated by other systems. A doctor may explain that you need not worry about your pending operation, and his or her touch may add confirmation; but it may contradict the verbalization if the doctor's touch seems nervous or lacking in confidence. Men and women may also attribute different meanings to similar types of touch. In Whitcher and Fisher (1979), female nurses touched patients during the explanation of procedures prior to surgery. Females reacted positively, showing lower anxiety, more positive preoperative behavior, and more favorable postoperative physiological responses. But men touched in the same way reacted less positively. A similar result was obtained by Lewis et al. (1995), who obtained ratings of photographic representations of nurses touching or not touching patients at the bedside. Male subjects rated the nurses (both male and female) as more supportive if they did not touch the patient, whereas female subjects thought the nurses were more supportive if they did touch the patient.

Recognizing the many variables that can affect the meanings that people attribute to touch, Heslin and his colleagues (Heslin, Nguyen, & Nguyen, 1983; Nguyen, Heslin, &

Nguyen, 1975, 1976) undertook a series of studies that examined the combined effects of type and location of touch, the gender of the communicators, and their relationship. In the first two studies, the researchers asked married and unmarried people to examine diagrams showing different regions of the body. Each person was asked to indicate what it meant to him or her to be touched in each of the 11 areas—that is, patted, squeezed, stroked, or brushed. To focus reactions, subjects were asked to respond only in the context of touching by an opposite-sex friend (not parents, siblings, or relatives). The method of responding was limited to scales representing various degrees of playfulness, warmth/love, friendship/fellowship, pleasantness, and sexual desire.

Generally, married persons reported a more positive reaction toward touch and tended to associate it with sex more often than did unmarried respondents. Unless the touch was in the genital region, sexual desire was not a common response for the unmarrieds. Although unmarried women did not perceive sexual touching to be as pleasant and as warm as unmarried men, married women did. Married men attributed less warmth/love and pleasantness to sexual touching than either single men or married women.

The type of touch seemed to be closely linked to judgments of playfulness and warmth/love; for example, patting was associated with play, but stroking was associated with warmth/love and sexual desire. On the other hand (no pun intended), friendliness and sexuality seemed most closely linked to the location of the touch. For example, hands, no matter how they were touched, were seen as pleasant, warm, and friendly; the genital area was not seen as playful regardless of what kind of touching was being evaluated.

Heslin's third study used the same methodology and focused on same-sex touching and touching from strangers. Overall, the touches from opposite-sex friends were perceived as more pleasant and less of an invasion of privacy than the same touching from same-sex friends or strangers of either sex. This was true for both men and women. However, men and women revealed important differences regarding the persons from whom touching would be the greatest invasion of privacy. Women indicated that touch from a stranger would be the greatest invasion of privacy, whereas men felt that touch from a same-sex person would be the greatest invasion of privacy. Men reported themselves to be as comfortable with touch from women strangers as they were with touch from women friends! Both men and women agreed that the most pleasant type of touch was stroking in sexual areas by an opposite-sex friend. But the second most pleasant type of touch reported by women was for a male friend to stroke nonsexual areas, and the second most pleasant type of touch by men was for a female stranger to stroke sexual areas.

TOUCH—A POWERFUL UNCONSCIOUS FORCE IN INTERACTION

As several studies cited earlier indicate, touch can influence our perceptions, moods, and behaviors even when it is fleeting, subtle, and possibly even unnoticed—as when library clerks touched the library patrons' hands, store greeters touched the shoppers, waitpersons in restaurants touched their customers, or survey takers touched the people they were interviewing. In these cases, the recipient of the touch is likely to be barely aware of the touch, and highly unlikely to associate the touch with his or her own subsequent reactions.

But just as the influence of touch can be unconscious on the part of the person being touched, so too can it be unconscious on the part of the *toucher*. A most vivid demonstration of this point can be found in the phenomenon called "facilitated communication," a technique developed for improving the communication of individuals with autism, mental retardation, and physical diseases that impair motor abilities (e.g., cerebral palsy). Facilitated communication was hailed on several continents as a breakthrough in the ability of speech-impaired individuals to communicate, and it became widely practiced and taught in the 1980s and 1990s (Jacobson, Mulick, & Schwartz, 1995; Spitz, 1997). The technique is based on close tactile contact between the facilitator and the communicator, as well as a close psychological relationship in which trust is established. The key feature of facilitated communication is that the facilitator holds the communicator's hands while the communicator types words or sentences on a keyboard as part of creating a focused and physically steady environment for the communicator. Using facilitated communication, many communication-impaired clients typed out highly revealing, often eloquent, accounts of their feelings and thoughts. Some even told of abuse they experienced at the hands of parents or caretakers. At last, they could overcome their isolation; they could break out of their terrible enforced silence. Or so it seemed.

Unfortunately for the many parents and teachers whose hopes were raised, skepticism set in. Communicators were able to answer questions only when their facilitator knew the question and its answer, and communicators' responses often seemed much too verbally advanced for their intellectual level. In fact, communicators could even type out answers to questions when they were not looking at the keyboard (Kezuka, 1997; Spitz, 1997). Proceeding despite strong objections by those who believed in the system, researchers persisted in conducting controlled experiments which ultimately revealed that, possibly without exception, facilitated communication effects were due to the facilitator's *unconsciously guiding the communicator's hand to type out what was in the facilitator's mind*. Research showed that when facilitators were fed incorrect information about the communicator's background and then had to ask the communicator about those same facts, the "answers" given reflected the misinformation, not the true answers (Burgess et al., 1998). Kezuka (1997), using mechanical methods of determining physical force exerted by the facilitators, demonstrated that facilitators did indeed use tiny muscle movements of their hand (and sometimes facial and other cues) to influence the position of the communicator's hand. Thus, the facilitators were the real communicators.

What makes the case of facilitated communication important for behavioral scientists is the fact that, in all likelihood, the great majority of facilitators were not frauds or charlatans, but were sincere believers (Spitz, 1997). Needless to say, the exposure of the true nature of facilitated communication was a great disappointment to those who believed in it. However, the actual—that is, unconscious—mechanism of its effect is no less astonishing than were the original claims. How could the facilitators be expressing their own thoughts without being aware of it?

But this is not the first phenomenon involving unconscious movements that has been documented. In the 19th century, there was great interest in pendulums that swing in response to mysterious forces. There was the stick called a dousing rod that suddenly seems to point downward when the holder walks over a place where there is underground water. And there was furniture that suddenly moved or turned, supposedly under the influence of spirits (Spitz, 1997). But in all of these cases, there were no supernatural forces, only strong expectancies that produced motor responses that were out of awareness, which in turn produced physical effects in the environment. We can also include on this list Clever Hans, the brilliant horse described in chapter 1. The horse's brilliance was not that he could read and do math (he could not, of course), but that he noticed and acted on the minute movements of the eyes and heads made by the people asking him the questions—who, like the facilitated communicators, were completely unaware that their movements were producing the wonderful behaviors they were observing. All of these phenomena rest on what Wegner, Fuller, and Sparrow (2003) call "authorship confusion"—attributing the source of action to the wrong person or agent.

SELF-TOUCHING

We also engage in self-touching. Self-touching includes any touching of the self including holding, stroking, nail chewing, picking on one's skin, twirling one's hair, wringing one's hands, biting one's lips, and self-grooming activities. This category of behavior has not been well studied. It is not clear what psychological functions are served by self-touching, though researchers generally agree that they are more an out of awareness expression of personal needs than reflective of intentional communication—more "signs" than "signals." However, intentional communication sometimes involves self-touching. Various kinds of self-touching, or self-touching used in different circumstances, may serve different functions. Figure 8-4 shows several kinds of self-touching.

Desmond Morris (1971) offered a list of different kinds of self-touching:

1. **Shielding Actions.** These behaviors usually involve reducing input or output, for example, putting one's hand over one's mouth or ears.
2. **Cleaning Actions.** Sometimes we bring our hands up to our head to scratch, rub, pick, wipe—for literal cleaning. But sometimes similar self-touching is used for attending to one's appearance, for example, hair grooming, clothes straightening, and other types of preening. Observations and subsequent interviews with people in public restrooms found women engaging in more of this behavior than men. People in the process of building an intimate relationship did more preening than those whose intimate relationship had been established for some time (Daly et al., 1983).
3. **Specialized Signals.** These gestures are used to communicate specific messages such as cupping the ear with one's hand to signal the inability to hear or holding a hand under one's chin to signal "I'm fed up to here."
4. **Self-Intimacies.** Self-intimacies, according to Morris, are comforting actions that represent unconsciously reproduced acts of being touched by someone else. They may involve holding one's own hands, arm folding, leg crossing, masturbation, and so on. Some, he maintains, are more likely to be performed by women than men, for example, the head-lowered-on-to-the-shoulder posture and leg hugging. Thus self-touching can be a substitute for comfort that might otherwise be provided by others.

Some self-touching behaviors are what Ekman and Friesen called *adaptors*. As the term implies, they are behavioral adaptations we make in response to certain learning situations,

FIGURE 8-4

Self-touching.

for example, performing some bodily or instrumental action, managing our emotions, satisfying our needs, or getting along with other people. These behaviors (or some residue of them) seem to appear in situations that we feel approximate the conditions of the early learning experiences. Generally, we are not aware of performing these behaviors, but frequent feedback may heighten our sensitivity—for example, "Stop picking your nose!" Although the research on adaptors is not extensive, there seems to be some consensus that adaptors are generally associated with negative feelings for oneself or another person. There are also some useful classifications of different types of adaptors, which include both the probable referent for the behavior (self, other, object) and the type of behavior (scratching, rubbing).

Research on psychiatric patients has found that self-adaptors increase as a person's psychological discomfort, anxiety, or depression increase (Ekman & Friesen, 1972; Freedman, 1972; Freedman et al., 1973; Freedman & Hoffman, 1967; Waxer, 1977). If, however, the anxiety level is too high, a person may freeze, engaging in little movement at all. The finding that self-adaptors also were associated with guilt feelings in the patients studied illuminates one aspect of the deception research we review in chapter 12. Ekman and Friesen also discovered picking and scratching self-adaptors to be related to a person's hostility and suspiciousness. Theoretically, this picking and scratching is a manifestation of aggression against oneself or aggression felt for another person, which is projected to oneself. Other speculations and hypotheses about self-adaptors include the possibility that rubbing is used to give self-assurance, that covering one's eyes is associated with shame and/or guilt, that self-grooming shows concern for one's self-presentation, and that self-touching is an outlet for nervous energy.

A number of studies have indicated that self-touching is associated with situational anxiety or stress. This is the case in baboons as well as in people (Castles, Whitens, & Aureli, 1999). Ekman and Friesen (1974) asked people to watch one of two films, one highly stressful and the other quite pleasant. Viewers were then instructed to describe the film as pleasant to an interviewer; thus those watching the stressful film were trying to deceive, which in itself can be considered stressful. Participants in this group engaged in more self-touch than those simply describing the pleasant film as pleasant. Self-touching is also greater in people who are chronically more anxious, for example, among people who are shy but also have a desire to be sociable (Cheek & Buss, 1981). In a study of physician–patient communication, patients were more likely to touch their bodies when talking about their more conflictual hidden agendas than when talking about the primary complaint (Shreve et al., 1988). An interesting question is whether the self-touching associated with anxiety is simply a sign or indicator that anxiety is occurring or whether touching oneself actually relieves stress.

Another source of body-focused movements is cognitive (information-processing) demand. When engaged in a monologue, people touched themselves more than when simply sitting still, and in Heaven and McBrayer (2000), they touched themselves more when answering questions about a passage they heard than when just listening to it. When asked to read the names of colors that were printed in contradictory colors (e.g., the word *red* printed in blue), people touched themselves more than if they were given color-consistent color names to read (Kenner, 1993). These results suggest that mental concentration and/or stress can be a cause of self-touching.

The concept of adaptors can be extended to behaviors other than self-touching. Such behaviors are theorized to have been learned in conjunction with our early experiences with interpersonal relations: giving and taking from another, attacking or protecting, establishing closeness or withdrawing, and so forth. Ekman believes that many of the restless movements of the hands and feet, which have typically been considered indicators of anxiety, may be residues of adaptors necessary for flight from the interaction. An example from the interaction behavior of baboons helps illustrate the nature of these "other-adaptors." When a young baboon is learning the fundamentals of attack and aggression, the mother baboon is watching from close by. The young baboon enacts aggressive behavior but also turns its head laterally to check whether its mother is still there. As an adult, the baboon may still perform this lateral head movement in threatening conditions even though the mother is no longer there and the movement seems to serve no functional purpose.

Object-adaptors involve the manipulation of objects for no obvious purpose and may be derived from the performance of some instrumental task (for example, smoking, or writing with a pencil). Some people engage in these mannerisms more than others. Although people are typically unaware of performing self-adaptor behaviors, they are probably more aware of the object-adaptors. Such movements are often learned later in life, and fewer social taboos seem to be associated with them. Anxiety, stress, or cognitive load may play a part in object-adaptors, as with self-adaptors.

Because there seem to be social constraints on displaying some self-adaptors, they are more often seen when a person is alone. At any rate, we would expect to see the full act rather than just a fragment of it. Alone you might pick your nose without inhibition; with other people, you may just touch your nose or rub it casually. Although adaptors are typically not intended for use in communication, they may be triggered by verbal behavior in a situation associated with conditions occurring when the adaptive habit was first learned.

Individual and group differences in self-touching have been found. In a study of children from four countries, those speaking English (England and Australia) engaged in significantly less self-touching during experimental tasks than did Italian children and French-speaking children in Belgium. Possibly, touching of other people may parallel these self-touching differences across these cultures. Also in those samples, significant individual variation was revealed, meaning that some children were consistently more likely to touch themselves across a variety of experimental tasks (Kenner, 1993). Another group difference relates to gender, in that females touch themselves in interpersonal interaction somewhat more than males do (Hall, 1984). It is not clear to what extent this may reflect greater social anxiety or arousal on the part of females, a heightened self-consciousness about appearance, or the simple fact that women's clothes and hair often demand readjustment.

❖

SUMMARY

Our first information about ourselves, others, and our environment probably comes from touching. The act of touching or being touched can have a powerful impact on our response to a situation, even if that touch was unintentional. In some cases, touching is the most effective method for communicating; in others, it can elicit negative or hostile reactions. The meanings we attach to touching behavior vary according to what body part is touched, how long the touch lasts, the strength of the touch, the method of the touch (for example, open or closed fist), and the frequency of the touch. Touch also means different things in different environments (institutions, airports, and so on) and varies with communicators' age, gender, culture, personality, and relationship.

The common types of interpersonal touching and self-touching may communicate a variety of messages, including influence, positive affect, negative affect, play, interpersonal responsiveness, unintentional contact, interaction management, and task requirements. Touching can also intensify whatever emotional experience is ongoing. Heslin classified the various types of touching behavior on an intimacy continuum:

1. Functional/Professional
2. Social/Polite
3. Friendship/Warmth
4. Love/Intimacy
5. Sexual Arousal

Indications are that children in U.S. culture touch more than adults; there seems to be a decreasing amount of touch from kindergarten through junior high school. Investigators agree that early experiences with touch are crucial for later adjustment. Touch can be a powerful source of behavioral influence, and both the toucher and the recipient of touch may be unaware of its occurrence and effects.

QUESTIONS FOR DISCUSSION

1. Think of a person whom you know who does not like touching or being touched. What analysis can you offer for this person's characteristic? How much do you think it reflects personal history and personality versus social and cultural norms?

2. What do you think about the ethics of using touch in order to achieve compliance or a favor from someone? Is it different from using persuasive language or using other forms of nonverbal communication, such as smiling or generally being "nice"?

3. Most studies find that touch is a rather infrequent event. Do you think this is correct? Discuss exceptions to this generalization. Why do you think touch might seem to be not very common?

4. Sometimes people are eager to touch others because they gain something of psychological value by doing so. Yet, people often feel violated by being touched. Discuss these different perspectives on the phenomenon of touch.

BIBLIOGRAPHY

Afifi, W. A., & Johnson, M. L. (1999). The use and interpretation of tie signs in a public setting: Relationship and sex differences. *Journal of Social and Personal Relationships, 16,* 9–38.

Aguilera, D. C. (1967). Relationships between physical contact and verbal interaction between nurses and patients. *Journal of Psychiatric Nursing, 5,* 5–21.

Alagna, F. J., Whitcher, S. J., Fisher, J. D., & Wicas, E. A. (1969). Evaluative reaction to interpersonal touch in a counseling interview. *Journal of Counseling Psychology, 26,* 465–472.

Allen, K. (2003). Are pets a healthy pleasure? The influence of pets on blood pressure. *Current Directions in Psychological Science, 12,* 236–239.

Andersen, J. F., Andersen, P. A., & Lustig, M. W. (1987). Opposite sex touch avoidance: A national replication and extension. *Journal of Nonverbal Behavior, 11,* 89–109.

Andersen, P. A., & Leibowitz, K. (1978). The development and nature of the construct touch avoidance. *Environmental Psychology and Nonverbal Behavior, 3,* 89–106.

Argyle, M. (1975). *Bodily communication.* New York: International Universities Press.

Barnlund, D. C. (1975). Communicative styles in two cultures: Japan and the United States. In A. Kendon, R. M. Harris, & M. R. Key (Eds.), *Organization of behavior in face-to-face interaction.* The Hague: Mouton.

Barroso, F., & Feld, J. K. (1986). Self-touching and attentional processes: The role of task difficulty, selection stage, and sex differences. *Journal of Nonverbal Behavior, 10,* 51–64.

Blondis, M., & Barbara, J. (1982). *Nonverbal communication in nursing: Back to the human touch.* New York: Wiley-Medical.

Borelli, M., & Heidt, P. (1981). *Therapeutic touch: A book of readings.* New York: Springer.

Brownlee, J., & Bakeman, R. (1981). Hitting in toddler–peer interaction. *Child Development, 52,* 1076–1079.

Burgess, C. A., Kirsch, I., Shane, H., Niederauer, K. L., Graham, S. M., & Bacon, A. (1998). Facilitated communication as an ideomotor response. *Psychological Science, 9,* 71–74.

Burgoon, J. K. (1991). Relational message interpretations of touch, conversational distance, and posture. *Journal of Nonverbal Behavior, 15,* 233–259.

Casler, L. (1965). The effects of extra tactile stimulation on a group of institutionalized infants. *Genetic Psychology Monographs, 71,* 137–175.

Castles, D. L., Whitens, A., & Aureli, F. (1999). Social anxiety, relationships and self-directed behaviour among wild female olive baboons. *Animal Behavior, 58,* 1207–1215.

Cheek, J. M., & Buss, A. H. (1981). Shyness and sociability. *Journal of Personality and Social Psychology, 41,* 330–339.

Cooper, C. L., & Bowles, D. (1973). Physical encounter and self-disclosure. *Psychological Reports, 33,* 451–454.

Cooper, V. W. (1987). The tactile communication system: State of the art and research perspectives. In B. Dervin & M. J. Voigt (Eds.), *Progress in communication sciences* (Vol. 8). Norwood, NJ: Ablex.

Crusco, A. H., & Wetzel, C. G. (1984). The Midas touch: The effects of interpersonal touch on restaurant tipping. *Personality and Social Psychology Bulletin, 10,* 512–517.

Daly, J. A., Hogg, E., Sacks, D., Smith, M., & Zimring, L. (1983). Sex and relationship affect social self-grooming. *Journal of Nonverbal Behavior, 7,* 183–189.

Deethardt, J. F., & Hines, D. G. (1983). Tactile communication and personality differences. *Journal of Nonverbal Behavior, 8,* 143–156.

DiBiase, R., & Gunnoe, J. (2004). Gender and culture differences in touching behavior. *Journal of Social Psychology, 144,* 49–62.

Drescher, V. M., Gantt, W. H., & Whitehead, W. E. (1980). Heart rate response to touch. *Psychosomatic Medicine, 42,* 559–565.

Dresslar, F. B. (1984). Studies in the psychology of touch. *American Journal of Psychology, 6,* 313–368.

Ekman, P., & Friesen, W. V. (1972). Hand movements. *Journal of Communication, 22,* 353–374.

Ekman, P., & Friesen, W. V. (1974). Detecting deception from the body or face. *Journal of Personality and Social Psychology, 29,* 288–298.

Emmers, T. M., & Dindia, K. (1995). The effect of relational stage and intimacy on touch: An extension of Guerrero and Andersen. *Personal Relationships, 2,* 225–236.

Field, T. (1995). Massage therapy for infants and children. *Developmental and Behavioral Pediatrics, 16,* 105–111.

Field, T (1998). Touch therapy effects on development. *International Journal of Behavioral Development, 22,* 779–797.

Field, T. (1999). American adolescents touch each other less and are more aggressive toward their peers as compared with French adolescents. *Adolescence, 34,* 753–758.

Field, T. (2001). *Touch.* Cambridge, MA: MIT Press.

Fisher, J. D., Rytting, M., & Heslin, R. (1976). Hands touching hands: Affective and evaluative effects of an interpersonal touch. *Sociometry, 39,* 416–421.

Floyd, K. (1999). All touches are not created equal: Effects of form and duration on observers' interpretations of an embrace. *Journal of Nonverbal Behavior, 23,* 283–299.

Forden, C. (1981). The influence of sex-role expectations on the perception of touch. *Sex Roles, 7,* 889–894.

Frank, L. K. (1957). Tactile communication. *Genetic Psychology Monographs, 56,* 209–255.

Freedman, N. (1972). The analysis of movement behavior during the clinical interview. In A. W. Siegman & B. Pope (Eds.), *Studies in dyadic communication.* New York: Pergamon Press.

Freedman, N., Blass, T., Rifkin, A., & Quitkin, F. (1973). Body movements and the verbal encoding of aggressive affect. *Journal of Personality and Social Psychology, 26,* 72–85.

Freedman, N., & Hoffman, S. P. (1967). Kinetic behavior in altered clinical states: Approach to objective analysis of motor behavior during clinical interviews. *Perceptual and Motor Skills, 24,* 527–539.

Goldberg, M. A., & Katz, B. (1990). The effect of nonreciprocated and reciprocated touch on power/dominance perception. *Journal of Social Behavior and Personality, 5,* 379–386.

Goldberg, S., & Rosenthal, R. (1986). Self-touching behavior in the job interview: Antecedents and consequences. *Journal of Nonverbal Behavior, 10,* 65–80.

Goldstein, A. G., & Jeffords, J. (1981). Status and touching behavior. *Bulletin of the Psychonomic Society, 17,* 79–81.

Greenbaum, P. E., & Rosenfeld, H. M. (1980). Varieties of touching in greetings: Sequential structure and sex-related differences. *Journal of Nonverbal Behavior, 5,* 13–25.

Gúeguen, N., & Fischer-Lokou, J. (2002). An evaluation of touch on a large request: A field setting. *Psychological Reports, 90,* 267–269.

Gúeguen, N., & Fischer-Lokou, J. (2003). Tactile contact and spontaneous help: An evaluation in a natural setting. *Journal of Social Psychology, 143,* 785–787.

Guerrero, L. K. (1997). Nonverbal involvement across interactions with same-sex friends, opposite-sex friends and romantic partners: Consistency or change? *Journal of Social and Personal Relationships, 14,* 31–58.

Guerrero, L. K., & Andersen, P. A. (1991). The waxing and waning of relational intimacy: Touch as a function of relational stage, gender and touch avoidance. *Journal of Social and Personal Relationships, 8,* 147–165.

Guerrero, L. K., & Andersen, P. A. (1994). Patterns of matching and initiation: Touch behavior and touch avoidance across romantic relationship stages. *Journal of Nonverbal Behavior, 18,* 137–153.

Halberstadt, A. G. (1985). Race, socioeconomic status, and nonverbal behavior. In A. W. Siegman and S. Feldstein (Eds.), *Multichannel integrations of nonverbal behavior.* Hillsdale, NJ: Erlbaum.

Hall, E. T. (1966). *The hidden dimension.* New York: Doubleday Anchor.

Hall, J. A. (1984). *Nonverbal sex differences: Communication accuracy and expressive style.* Baltimore: Johns Hopkins University Press.

Hall, J. A. (1996). Touch, status, and gender at professional meetings. *Journal of Nonverbal Behavior, 20,* 23–44.

Hall, J. A., Coats, E. J., & Smith LeBeau, L. (2004). *Nonverbal behavior and the vertical dimension of social relations: A meta-analysis.* Manuscript submitted for publication.

Hall, J. A., & Veccia, E. M. (1990). More "touching" observations: New insights on men, women, and interpersonal touch. *Journal of Personality and Social Psychology, 59,* 1155–1162.

Harlow, H. F. (1958). The nature of love. *American Psychologist, 13,* 678–685.

Harrigan, J. A., Lucic, K. S., Kay, D., McLaney, A., & Rosenthal, R. (1991). Effect of expresser role and type of self-touching on observers' perceptions. *Journal of Applied Social Psychology, 21,* 585–609.

Harris, C. R., & Christenfeld, N. (1997). Humour, tickle, and the Darwin-Hecker hypothesis. *Cognition & Emotion, 11,* 103–110.

Harris, C. R., & Christenfeld, N. (1999). Can a machine tickle? *Psychonomic Bulletin & Review, 6,* 504–510.

Harrison-Speake, K., & Willis, F. N. (1995). Ratings of the appropriateness of touch among family members. *Journal of Nonverbal Behavior, 19,* 85–100.

Heaven, L., & McBrayer, D. (2000). External motivators of self-touching behavior. *Perceptual & Motor Skills, 90,* 338–342.

Heller, M. A., & Schiff, W. (Eds.). (1991). *The psychology of touch.* Hillsdale, NJ: Erlbaum.

Henley, N. (1973a). Status and sex: Some touching observations. *Bulletin of the Psychonomic Society, 2,* 91–93.

Henley, N. (1973–1974). Power, sex and non-verbal communication. *Berkeley Journal of Sociology, 18,* 1–26.

Henley, N. (1977). *Body politics: Power, sex, and nonverbal communication.* Englewood Cliffs, NJ: Prentice-Hall.

Heslin, R., & Alper, T. (1983). Touch: A bonding gesture. In J. M. Wiemann & R. P. Harrison (Eds.), *Nonverbal interaction.* Beverly Hills, CA: Sage.

Heslin, R., & Boss, D. (1980). Nonverbal intimacy in airport arrival and departure. *Personality and Social Psychology Bulletin, 6,* 248–252.

Heslin, R., Nguyen, T. D., & Nguyen, M. L. (1983). Meaning of touch: The case of touch from a stranger or same sex person. *Journal of Nonverbal Behavior, 7,* 147–157.

Hetherington, A. (1998). The use and abuse of touch in therapy and counselling. *Counselling Psychology Quarterly, 11,* 361–364.

Hilton, I. (2004). The Buddha's daughter. *The New Yorker,* March 29, pp. 42–50.

Hollender, M. H., & Mercer, A. J. (1976). Wish to be held and wish to hold in men and women. *Archives of General Psychiatry, 33,* 49–51.

Hornik, J. (1991). Shopping time and purchasing behavior as a result of in-store tactile stimulation. *Perceptual and Motor Skills, 73,* 969–970.

Hornik, J. (1992). Tactile stimulation and consumer response. *Journal of Consumer Research, 19,* 449–458.

Hubbard, A. S. E, Tsuji, A. A., Williams, C., & Seatriz, V., Jr. (2003). Effects of touch on gratuities received in same-gender and cross-gender dyads. *Journal of Applied Social Psychology, 33,* 2427–2438.

Hutchinson, K. L., & Davidson, C. A. (1990). Body accessibility re-revisited: The 60s, 70s, and 80s. *Journal of Social Behavior and Personality, 5,* 341–352.

Jacobson, J. W., Mulick, J. A., & Schwartz, A. A. (1995). A history of facilitated communication: Science, pseudoscience, and antiscience. *American Psychologist, 50,* 750–765.

Jones, S. (1991). Problems of validity in questionnaire studies of nonverbal behavior: Jourard's tactile body-accessibility scale. *Southern Communication Journal, 56,* 83–95.

Jones, S. E. (1986). Sex differences in touch communication. *Western Journal of Speech Communication, 50,* 227–241.

Jones, S. E. (1994). *The right touch: Understanding and using the language of physical contact.* Cresskill, NJ: Hampton Press.

Jones, S. E., & Yarbrough, A. E. (1985). A naturalistic study of the meanings of touch. *Communication Monographs, 52*, 19–56.

Jourard, S. M. (1966). An exploratory study of body-accessibility. *British Journal of Social and Clinical Psychology, 26*, 235–242.

Jourard, S. M. (1968). *Disclosing man to himself.* New York: Van Nostrand Reinhold.

Jourard, S. M., & Rubin, J. E. (1968). Self-disclosure and touching: A study of two modes of interpersonal encounter and their interrelation. *Journal of Humanistic Psychology, 8*, 39–48.

Juni, S., & Brannon, R. (1981). Interpersonal touching as a function of status and sex. *Journal of Social Psychology, 114*, 135–136.

Kauffman, L. E. (1971). Tacesics, the study of touch: A model for proxemic analysis. *Semiotica, 14*, 149–161.

Kaufman, D., & Mahoney, J. M. (1999). The effect of waitresses' touch on alcohol consumption in dyads. *Journal of Social Psychology, 139*, 261–267.

Kenner, A. N. (1984). The effect of task differences, attention and personality on the frequency of body-focused hand movements. *Journal of Nonverbal Behavior, 8*, 159–171.

Kenner, A. N. (1993). A cross-cultural study of body-focused hand movement. *Journal of Nonverbal Behavior, 17*, 263–279.

Kezuka, E. (1997). The role of touch in facilitated communication. *Journal of Autism and Developmental Disorders, 27*, 571–593.

Kneidinger, L. M., Maple, T. L., & Tross, S. A. (2001). Touching behavior in sport: Functional components, analysis of sex differences, and ethological considerations. *Journal of Nonverbal Behavior, 25*, 43–62.

Krieger, D. (1987). *Living the therapeutic touch: Healing as a lifestyle.* New York: Dodd, Mead.

Krout, M. (1954a). An experimental attempt to determine the significance of unconscious manual symbolic movements. *Journal of General Psychology, 51*, 296–308.

Krout, M. (1954b). An experimental attempt to produce unconscious manual symbolic movements. *Journal of General Psychology, 51*, 121–152.

Lewis, R. J., Derlega, V. J., Nichols, B., Shankar, A., Drury, K. K., & Hawkins, L. (1995). Sex differences in observers' reactions to a nurse's use of touch. *Journal of Nonverbal Behavior, 19*, 101–113.

Lewis, R. J., Derlega, V. J., Shankar, A., Cochard, E., & Finkel, L. (1997). Nonverbal correlates of confederates' touch: Confounds in touch research. *Journal of Social Behavior and Personality, 12*, 821–830.

Lockard, J. S., & Adams, R. M. (1980). Courtship behaviors in public: Different age/sex roles. *Ethology and Sociobiology, 1*, 245–253.

Lomranz, J., & Shapira, A. (1974). Communicative patterns of self-disclosure and touching behavior. *Journal of Psychology, 88*, 223–227.

Maier, R. A., & Ernest, R. C. (1978). Sex differences in the perception of touching. *Perceptual and Motor Skills, 46*, 577–578.

Maines, D. R. (1977). Tactile relationships in the subway as affected by racial, sexual, and crowded seating situations. *Environmental Psychology and Nonverbal Behavior, 2*, 100–108.

Major, B. (1981). Gender patterns in touching behavior. In C. Mayo & N. M. Henley (Eds.), *Gender and nonverbal behavior.* New York: Springer-Verlag.

Major, B., & Heslin, R. (1982). Perceptions of same-sex and cross-sex touching: It's better to give than to receive. *Journal of Nonverbal Behavior, 6*, 148–162.

Major, B., Schmidlin, A. M., & Williams, L. (1990). Gender patterns in touch: The impact of age and setting. *Journal of Personality and Social Psychology, 58*, 634–643.

Maurer, D., & Maurer, C. (1988). *The world of the newborn.* New York: Basic.

McCorkle, R. (1974). Effects of touch on seriously ill patients. *Nursing Research, 23*, 125–132.

McCormick, N. B., & Jones, A. J. (1989). Gender differences in nonverbal flirtation. *Journal of Sex Education & Therapy, 15*, 271–282.

McDaniel, E., & Andersen, P. A. (1998). International patterns of interpersonal tactile communication: A field study. *Journal of Nonverbal Behavior, 22,* 59–73.

Montagu, M. F. A. (1971). *Touching: The human significance of the skin.* New York: Columbia University Press.

Morris, D. (1971). *Intimate behaviour.* New York: Random House.

Morris, D. (1977). *Manwatching.* New York: Abrams.

Morry, M. M., & Enzle, M. E. (1994). Effect of gender dominance expectancies for knowledge on self-touching during conversations. *Social Behavior and Personality, 22,* 123–129.

Moyer, C. A., Rounds, J., & Hannum, J. W. (2004). A meta-analysis of massage therapy research. *Psychological Bulletin, 130,* 3–18.

Murphy, A. J. (1972). Effect of body contact on performance of a simple cognitive task. *British Journal of Social and Clinical Psychology, 11,* 402–408.

Nannberg, J. C., & Hansen, C. H. (1994). Post-compliance touch: An incentive for task performance. *Journal of Social Psychology, 134,* 301–307.

Nguyen, M. L., Heslin, R., & Nguyen, T. (1976). The meaning of touch: Sex and marital status differences. *Representative Research in Social Psychology, 7,* 13–18.

Nguyen, T., Heslin, R., & Nguyen, M. L. (1975). The meanings of touch: Sex differences. *Journal of Communication, 25,* 92–103.

Nilsen, W. J., & Vrana, S. R. (1998). Some touching situations: The relationship between gender and contextual variables in cardiovascular responses to human touch. *Annals of Behavioral Medicine, 20,* 270–276.

Older, J. (1982). *Touching is healing: A revolutionary breakthrough in medicine.* New York: Stein and Day.

Patterson, M. L., Powell, J. L, & Lenihan, M. G. (1986). Touch, compliance, and interpersonal affect. *Journal of Nonverbal Behavior, 10,* 41–50.

Pattison, J. E. (1973). Effects of touch on self-exploration and the therapeutic relationship. *Journal of Consulting and Clinical Psychology, 40,* 170–175.

Perdue, V. P., & Connor, J. M. (1978). Patterns of touching between preschool children and male and female teachers. *Child Development, 49,* 1258–1262.

Perper, T. (1989). Theories and observations on sexual selection and female choice in human beings. *Medical Anthropology, 11,* 409–454.

Pisano, M. D., Wall, S. M., & Foster, A. (1986). Perceptions of nonreciprocal touch in romantic relationships. *Journal of Nonverbal Behavior, 10,* 29–40.

Regan, P. C., Jerry, D., Narvaez, M., & Johnson, D. (1999). Public displays of affection among Asian and Latino heterosexual couples. *Psychological Reports, 84,* 1201–1202.

Remland, M. S., Jones, T. S., & Brinkman, H. (1991). Proxemic and haptic behavior in three European countries. *Journal of Nonverbal Behavior, 15,* 215–232.

Rinck, C. M., Willis, F. N., & Dean, L. M. (1980). Interpersonal touch among residents of homes for the elderly. *Journal of Communication, 30,* 44–47.

Roese, N. J., Olson, J. M., Borenstein, M. N., Martin, A., & Shores, A. L. (1992). Same-sex touching behavior: The moderating role of homophobic attitudes. *Journal of Nonverbal Behavior, 16,* 249–259.

Rosenfeld, L. B., Kartus, S., & Ray, C. (1976). Body accessibility revisited. *Journal of Communication, 26,* 27–30.

Shreve, E. G., Harrigan, J. A., Kues, J. R., & Kagas, D. K. (1988). Nonverbal expressions of anxiety in physician-patient interactions. *Psychiatry, 51,* 378–384.

Shuter, R. (1976). Proxemics and tactility in Latin America. *Journal of Communication, 26,* 46–52.

Sigelman, C. K., & Adams, R. M. (1990). Family interactions in public: Parent–child distance and touch. *Journal of Nonverbal Behavior, 14,* 63–75.

Silverman, A. F., Pressman, M. E., & Bartel, H. W. (1973). Self-esteem and tactile communication. *Journal of Humanistic Psychology, 13*, 73–77.

Silverthorne, C., Micklewright, J., O'Donnell, M., & Gibson, R. (1976). Attribution of personal characteristics as a function of the degree of touch on initial contact and sex. *Sex Roles, 2*, 185–193.

Smith, D. E., Willis, F. N., & Gier, J. A. (1980). Success and interpersonal touch in a competitive setting. *Journal of Nonverbal Behavior, 5*, 26–34.

Smith, E. W. L., Clance, P. R., & Imes, S. (1998). *Touch in psychotherapy: Theory, research, and practice.* New York: Guilford.

Spitz, H. H. (1997). *Nonconscious movements: From mystical messages to facilitated communication.* Mahwah, NJ: Erlbaum.

Spitz, R. (1945). Hospitalism: Genesis of psychiatric conditions in early childhood. *Psychoanalytic Study of the Child, 1*, 53–74.

Stier, D. S., & Hall, J. A. (1984). Gender differences in touch: An empirical and theoretical review. *Journal of Personality and Social Psychology, 47*, 440–459.

Summerhayes, D., & Suchner, R. (1978). Power implications of touch in male–female relationships. *Sex Roles, 4*, 103–110.

Sussman, N. M., & Rosenfeld, H. M. (1978). Touch, justification, and sex: Influences on the aversiveness of spatial violations. *Journal of Social Psychology, 106*, 215–222.

Thayer, S. (1982). Social touching. In W. Schiff & E. Foulke (Eds.), *Tactual perception: A sourcebook.* New York: Cambridge University Press.

Thayer, S. (1986). History and strategies of research on social touch. *Journal of Nonverbal Behavior, 10*, 12–28.

Touchy topic: What to do when a handshake isn't enough? (2000, February 16). *Boston Globe*, pp. A1, A20.

Watson, W. H. (1975). The meanings of touch: Geriatric nursing. *Journal of Communication, 25*, 104–112.

Waxer, P. H. (1977). Nonverbal cues for anxiety: An examination of emotional leakage. *Journal of Abnormal Psychology, 86*, 306–314.

Wegner, D. M., Fuller, V. A., & Sparrow, B. (2003). Clever hands: Uncontrolled intelligence in facilitated communication. *Journal of Personality and Social Psychology, 85*, 5–19.

Whitcher, S. J., & Fisher, J. D. (1979). Multidimensional reaction to therapeutic touch in a hospital setting. *Journal of Personality and Social Psychology, 37*, 87–96.

Williams, S. J., & Willis, F. N. (1978). Interpersonal touch among preschool children at play. *Psychological Record, 28*, 501–508.

Williams, T. (1966). Cultural structuring of tactile experience in a Borneo society. *The American Anthropologist, 68*, 27–39.

Willis, F. N., Jr., & Briggs, L. F. (1992). Relationship and touch in public settings. *Journal of Nonverbal Behavior, 16*, 55–63.

Willis, F. N., & Hamm, H. K. (1980). The use of interpersonal touch in securing compliance. *Journal of Nonverbal Behavior, 5*, 49–55.

Willis, F. N., & Hoffman, G. E. (1975). Development of tactile patterns in relation to age, sex, and race. *Developmental Psychology, 11*, 866.

Willis, F. N., & Rawdon, V. A. (1994). Gender and national differences in attitudes toward same-gender touch. *Perceptual and Motor Skills, 78*, 1027–1034.

Willis, F. N., & Reeves, D. L. (1976). Touch interactions in junior high students in relation to sex and race. *Developmental Psychology, 12*, 91–92.

Willis, F. N., Reeves, D. L., & Buchanan, D. R. (1976). Interpersonal touch in high school relative to sex and race. *Perceptual and Motor Skills, 43*, 843–847.

With a handshake, Rabin's fate was sealed. (1995, November 19). *New York Times*.

Chapter 9

THE EFFECTS OF THE FACE
ON HUMAN COMMUNICATION

Your face, my thane, is a book where men
May read strange matters.

—SHAKESPEARE, *MACBETH*, ACT I

The face is rich in communicative potential. It is a primary site for communication of emotional states; it reflects interpersonal attitudes; it provides nonverbal feedback on the comments of others; and some scholars say it is the primary source of information next to human speech. For these reasons, and because of the face's visibility, we pay a great deal of attention to the messages we receive from the faces of others. Frequently, we rely heavily on facial cues when making important interpersonal judgments. This begins when, as infants, we take special interest in the huge face peering over our crib and tending to our needs. Most of the research on facial expressions (and various components of the face) has focused on the display and interpretation of emotional signals. Although this is the major focus of this chapter, we also emphasize that the face may be the basis for judging another person's personality and it can (and does) provide information other than our emotional state.

THE FACE AND PERSONALITY JUDGMENTS

The human face comes in many sizes and shapes. Faces may be triangular, square, or round; foreheads may be high and wide, high and narrow, low and wide, or protruding; complexions may be light, dark, smooth, wrinkled, or blemished; eyes may be close or far apart, or bulging; noses may be short, long, flat, crooked, "humpbacked," or a "ski slope"; mouths may be large or small with thin or thick lips; and cheeks can bulge or appear sunken. Besides the many facial features we can respond to, the face in general receives much attention. *Facial primacy*, or the tendency to give more weight to the face than to other communication channels, is well documented. Facial primacy may result from our belief that the face reveals a great deal about a person's personality or character. This belief goes back hundreds (perhaps thousands) of years. Facial stereotypes have been the topic of some scientific scrutiny. Secord and his colleagues (1959) explored the relationship of facial features and personality judgments and found some consistent stereotypic associations: for example, high foreheads and intelligence, thin lips and conscientiousness, thick lips on females and sexiness, and so on. Undesirable persons were portrayed by Secord's subjects as having more extreme features, that is, features which extended beyond the perceived normative boundaries. More recent research reveals many stereotypes associated with having a youthful-looking face (see chapter 6).

This chapter focuses on the *dynamic* nature of the face—its ability to make practically an infinite number of expressions. Many different muscles are used routinely in making facial expressions (Rinn, 1984). The look of a person's face is due in part to the genetic blueprint that endows it with certain physical features, in part to transient moods that stimulate the muscles to move in distinctive ways, and in part to the lingering imprint of chronically held expressions that seem to set in and become virtually permanent over the years.

People make personality attributions based on facial expressions (Knutson, 1996). For example, the person who smiles at us warmly upon introduction is immediately perceived to be nice (a personality attribution); likewise, we think the sour-faced old man next door is mean and selfish. Little research exists on the validity of such stereotypes; certainly the person with the warm smile might be a cutthroat manipulator, and the mean-looking neighbor may be a tenderhearted soul. One study supporting the validity of facial stereotypes found that college students believe facially expressive individuals are more confident and likable, and, indeed, in a sample of college women, those with more expressive faces were more extraverted according to several different self-report scales (Riggio & Friedman, 1986).

Another study lending support to the validity of facial expression stereotypes was done by Harker and Keltner (2001). The more women's faces showed positive emotional expression (i.e., smiling) in their college yearbook pictures, the more observers of the pictures thought the women would be rewarding to interact with. And, indeed, the women who had more positive expressions had more affiliative personalities and reported experiencing more positive affect not only at age 21 but also decades later, and they were more likely to be married by age 27 than women who had less positive yearbook photos.

Research does not always support the validity of facial expression stereotypes, however. Gifford (1994) studied self-reported personality, others' impressions of personality, and various nonverbal cues emitted during interaction. Although smiling was positively related to observers' impressions of extraversion, agreeableness, and ingenuousness, smiling was not related to targets' own personality ratings of any of these traits.

THE FACE AND INTERACTION MANAGEMENT

Our faces also are used to facilitate and inhibit responses in daily interaction. Parts of the face are used to:

1. Open and close channels of communication
2. Complement or qualify verbal and/or nonverbal responses
3. Replace speech

Behaviors can, of course, serve several functions simultaneously. For example, a yawn may replace the spoken message "I'm bored" and serve to shut down the channels of communication at the same time.

CHANNEL CONTROL

When we want a speaking turn, we sometimes open our mouths in readiness to talk—often accompanied by an inspiration of breath. As noted in chapter 2, the eyebrow flash (frequently accompanied by a smile) is found in greeting rituals and signals a desire to interact. Interestingly, smiles also are found in situations in which there is a desire to close the channels of communication, for example, a smile of appeasement as a person backs away from someone threatening physical harm. Smiling and winking also are used to flirt with others—an invitation that not only opens the channels of communication but also suggests the type of interaction desired. Facial behaviors associated with flirtation seem to have very similar form across different cultures (Eibl-Eibesfeldt, 1974).

Although we usually think of smiles as showing emotion or attitudes, they actually have many complex functions. Brunner (1979) showed that smiles serve as "listener responses" or "back channels" in conversation, in that they signal attentiveness and involvement just as head nods, "uh-huh," and "yeah" do. These smiles do not indicate joy or happiness in the sender but are meant to facilitate and encourage the other's speech.

COMPLEMENTING OR QUALIFYING OTHER BEHAVIOR

In normal conversational give-and-take, there are instances when we wish to underline, magnify, minimize, or contradict messages. The speaker or listener may give these signals. A sad verbal message may acquire added emphasis with the eyebrows' movements that normally accompany the expression of sadness. A smile may temper a message otherwise interpreted as negative. The hand emblem for "A-OK" may be accompanied by a wink, leaving little doubt that approval is being communicated. Thus, facial cues can combine with other cues to avoid confusion and magnify or qualify our messages.

REPLACING SPOKEN MESSAGES

Ekman and Friesen (1975) identified what they call *facial emblems*. Like hand emblems, these displays have a fairly consistent verbal translation. Facial emblems are different from the actual emotional expressions in that the sender is trying to talk *about* an emotion while indicating he or she is not actually feeling it. These facial emblems usually occur in contexts not likely to trigger the actual emotion; they are usually held for a longer or shorter time than the actual expression; and they are usually performed by using only a part of the face. When you drop your jaw and hold your mouth open without displaying other features of the surprise expression, you may be saying the other person's comment is surprising or you were dumbfounded by what was said. Widened eyes (without other features of the surprise and fear expressions) may serve the same purpose as a verbal "Wow!" If you want to comment nonverbally on your disgust for a situation, a nose wrinkle or raising one side of your upper lip should get your message across. Sometimes one or both eyebrows communicate "I'm puzzled" or "I doubt that." Other facial messages with common verbal translations that are not associated with expressions of emotion include the "You know what I mean" wink and sticking your tongue out to convey insult or disapproval (Smith, Chase, & Lieblich, 1974).

Facial movements play an important role in managing conversation (Bavelas & Chovil, 1997; Chovil, 1991/1992). According to Chovil, the most frequent function is *syntactic display*. Syntactic facial displays act as markers for words and clauses; they are directed toward the organizational structure of the conversation, marking beginnings, endings, restarts, continuations, and emphasis. Raising and lowering the eyebrows is a central activity in syntactic displays. Facial actions made by the speaker directly connected with the content of what is being said are called *semantic displays*. These may be redundant with the verbal behavior, or they may involve additional commentary (e.g., personal reactions) on the spoken words. The face also provides *listener responses,* as mentioned earlier. These are primarily facial displays that facilitate the flow of interaction but also include those that give personal reactions and seemingly empathic displays in the form of mimicry. Chovil also noticed facial *adaptors,* that is, biting one's lip or a twitch resulting from physiological activity.

Although the preceding discussion provides an overview of how the face is used in managing the interaction, it does not sufficiently reflect the complexity a thorough analysis requires. For instance, we did not deal with concomitant gaze behavior and other subtle movements such as head tilts. We talked about smiles as if there were only one variety. Brannigan and Humphries (1972) have identified nine smiles (representing various types and degrees of intensity), many of which seem to occur in distinctly separate situations. Ekman and Friesen, using an anatomically based coding system we will describe shortly, have found over 100 distinctly different human smiles!

THE FACE AND EXPRESSIONS OF EMOTION

The intellectual roots of our modern interest in facial expression stem from the mid-19th century. Charles Darwin's *Expression of the Emotions in Man and Animals* (1872), although not as famous as his other writings on natural selection, was a major work of theory and empirical observation that largely focused on the face (Ekman & Oster, 1982). To Darwin, the study of emotional expression was closely tied to his case for evolution, for he held that the capacity to communicate through nonverbal signals had evolved just as the brain and skeleton had. The face becomes increasingly mobile as one moves up the phylogenetic ladder. In many animals, the face is a fixed mask with little to no capacity for mobility, but in primates we see a great variety of expressions (Redican, 1982). Because it would support his theory of evolution, Darwin considered it extremely important to document similarities in the nature of emotional expression across species and across human cultures.

Several strands of contemporary facial research can be traced to Darwin's insights, including conducting judgment studies to find out what meanings observers ascribe to different expressions, undertaking cross-cultural studies, studying the movements of particular facial muscles, and testing the hypothesis that making facial expressions can intensify the expressor's experience of emotion. We review each of these topics.

THE FACE—A COMPLEX STIMULUS

Consider the following situations:

1. A student who feels sure he is doing "C" work is told by his instructor that he is doing "A" work. His immediate reaction is total surprise (probably followed by glee), but how does he react? His face shows mild surprise, and he comments that he thought he was doing pretty good work in the course.
2. A poker player draws his fourth ace in a game with no wild cards. His face would lead the other players to believe he was unmoved.
3. A woman receives a holiday present that she is pleasantly surprised about and happy to receive, but it is nothing spectacular. Her facial expression and comments, however, lead the giver (sitting nearby) to believe it was the only thing she ever wanted in her entire life.
4. The wife of a fledgling executive is forced to attend the boss's party and is told explicitly her behavior will have a profound impact on the promotion of her husband. She is nervous and upset. According to those who describe the party later, however, Mrs. Fledgling was the life of the party, happy, carefree, and content.

These four examples illustrate certain *display rules* we tend to follow (Ekman & Friesen, 1969). The student illustrated a *deintensified affect*—strong surprise was made to look like mild surprise. The poker player was trying to *neutralize an affect*—to make it appear there was no affect at all. The person reacting to the holiday present tried to make mild happiness appear to be strong happiness—an *overintensification of the affect*. Mrs. Fledgling was trying to *mask feelings* of tension or despondency with happiness and confidence. These display rules are learned, but we do not always use them at a conscious level of awareness. We learn there are culturally prescribed norms for when and how much emotion to display; we also develop personal display rules based on our needs or perhaps the demands of our occupation, for example, politicians or salespersons. We learn that some affect displays are appropriate in some places and not others, for some status and role positions and not others, for one sex and not the other; and we may use different expressions responding to the same event at a different time and with different people.

The attempt to use display rules can lead to communication mishaps. After seeing first President Bush smiling while telling about the number of babies born with drug addiction and about other sad statistics on his first television address from the Oval Office, one of his advisers asked in amazement, "What's with the grin?" The answer: Bush is emotional, hates to show it, and overcompensates by lightening up his expression too much ("Why Is This Man Smiling?" 1989).

The existence of display rules helps explain why some anthropologists have believed that emotions are expressed in sharply different ways from culture to culture. In one society, people may weep and moan at a funeral; in another they may celebrate with feast and dance. However, the underlying emotion, grief, is experienced and likely expressed similarly in private. The difference is that in public, cultural norms (display rules) regulate behavior. In one society, the rule says "Show how sad you are," but in another the rule says "Show hope for the future."

Ekman and Friesen (1975) developed a classification system for various styles of facial expressions. The styles are heavily based on personal display rules and represent extremes. A style may be displayed in a less extreme fashion in some situations or at a certain time in the person's life, but some people manifest a given style with consistency. These styles include the following:

1. **The Withholder.** The face inhibits expressions of actual feeling states. There is little facial movement.
2. **The Revealer.** This style is the opposite of the Withholder. The face leaves little doubt how the person feels—continually.
3. **The Unwitting Expressor.** This pattern usually pertains to a limited number of expressions that a person may feel have been masked: for example, "How did you know I was angry?"
4. **The Blanked Expressor.** In this style, the person is convinced an emotion is being portrayed, but others see only a blank face!
5. **The Substitute Expressor.** Here the facial expression shows an emotion other than the one the person thinks is being displayed.
6. **The Frozen-Affect Expressor.** This style manifests at least a part of an emotional display at all times. Some people are born with a facial configuration that, in a relaxed, neutral state, shows the downturned mouth of sadness; others habitually experience an emotion (like sadness) enough so traces of the emotional display are permanently etched into the face. (This is an idea that Darwin proposed.)

Self-presentational desires can also produce distinctive styles of facial expression. Former President Clinton often used a smile we call his "brave smile" (Figure 9-1). It is not a pure expression of happiness, as our discussion of blends and "felt" smiles later in this chapter makes clear. Rather, we think Clinton was trying to convey a complex mixture of pride, determination, concern, and modesty with the combination of the paradoxically down-turned mouth, the set chin, and the "smile wrinkles" around the eyes.

The preceding discussion of display rules and styles of emotional facial expression demonstrates that we have considerable control over our facial expressions, and this control is manifested in a variety of ways. Although we can present facial messages that we do not feel, sometimes we lie imperfectly by enacting an expression at the wrong time, enacting it too often or for too long (as when we insincerely display a smile too long), or using various facial muscles inappropriately. These factors may help us separate genuine from pseudoexpressions of emotion on the face. We undeniably are aware of the communicative potential of our face, and we tend to monitor it carefully by inhibiting or exhibiting when desired. With the constant feedback we receive about our facial expressions, we become rather proficient at controlling them. As Ekman and Friesen (1969) put it,

> Although we usually are aware of our facial affect displays, they may occur with or without a deliberate intention to communicate. Similarly, inhibition of facial display, control of facial display, or dissimulation of an affect (looking cool even when tense), may or may not be intentional. Because we have such good feedback about our facial behavior, we usually are aware of what happens the moment we change facial movements. (p. 76)

FIGURE 9-1

Former President Clinton's brave smile.

As these comments imply, the distinction between spontaneous (i.e., unintentional) facial displays of emotion and deliberate (posed) displays may be quite difficult to make in practice, in part because the concept of intentionality is an extremely slippery one. Often our behavior, our awareness of our behavior, and our conscious intentions occur in complex temporal orderings that preclude a simple understanding of the role of intentionality.

The way we experience emotions can be quite complex. Sometimes we move rapidly from one emotion to another. For example, people reporting the feeling of jealousy indicate that the "jealous flash may move from shock and numbness to desolate pain to rage and anger to moral outrage in a very brief time" (Ellis & Weinstein, 1986). Sometimes we are not sure what emotion we are feeling, and at other times we seem to feel many emotions at once. Simultaneously felt emotions may even be contradictory, as in the case of a woman who described her experience with sadomasochism: "I felt repulsed and attracted at the same time. Indeed, that is what made S & M so attractive." When we experience more than one emotion, we sometimes try to control one while we deal with the other. These are only some of the many ways we experience emotions (Ellis, 1991). Because emotional experience is complex, understanding emotion through facial expression is correspondingly difficult. We do not always portray pure or single emotional states in which all the parts of the face show a single emotion. Instead, the face conveys multiple emotions. These are called *affect blends* and may appear on the face in numerous ways:

1. One emotion is shown in one facial area and another is shown in another area; for example, brows are raised as in surprise and lips are pressed as in anger.
2. Two different emotions are shown in one part of the face; for example, one brow is raised as in surprise and the other is lowered as in anger.
3. A facial display is produced by muscle action associated with two emotions but containing specific elements of neither.

Figure 9-2 shows two examples of facial blends. One photograph shows a blend of happiness (mouth area) and surprise (eyebrows/forehead, eyes/lids, and a slight dropping of the jaw). Such an expression could occur if you thought you were going to get an F on an exam, but you received an A instead. In the other photograph, the brows/forehead area and the eye/lids area show anger while the mouth shows sadness. This combination might occur if your instructor told you that your grade on an exam you considered unfair was an F. You feel sad about the low grade and angry at the instructor.

A final note about the complexity of faces concerns what Haggard and Isaacs (1966) called "micromomentary facial expressions." While searching for indications of nonverbal communication between therapist and patient, they ran films at slow motion and noticed that the expression on the patient's face would sometimes change dramatically—from a smile to a grimace to a smile, for example—within a few frames of the film. Further analysis revealed that when they ran their films at 4 frames per second instead of the normal 24 frames, there were 2.5 times as many changes of expression. At normal speed, expressions lasting about one-fifth second escaped notice; expressions that took about two-fifths second were seen as changes, but the kind of change could not be identified; expressions lasting longer than two-fifths second were usually identified, but not always the same way. It is thought these micromomentary expressions reveal actual emotional states but are condensed in time because of repressive processes. They are often incompatible with both

FIGURE 9-2

Facial blends.

the apparent expression and the patient's words. One patient, saying nice things about a friend, had a seemingly pleasant facial expression; however, slow-motion film revealed a wave of anger across her face. Ekman, Friesen, and Ellsworth (1982b), although agreeing that micromomentary expressions may show conflict, repression, or efforts to conceal an emotion, actually find them to be "very rare events" based on extensive analysis of facial movements. However, this does not mean they do not have an impact (possibly a subliminal one) when they occur.

THE FACIAL EMOTION CONTROVERSY

One tradition, originating with Darwin and associated today with the work of Paul Ekman and Carroll Izard, emphasizes the close connection between facial displays of emotion and concurrently felt emotions, with a corresponding emphasis on emotion-expressive display linkages as biologically grounded (Cornelius, 1996). This approach has fueled ambitious programs of cross-cultural research on the recognition of facial expression, as discussed in chapter 2 and also later in this chapter. A simplistic version of such a theoretical position would hold that a given emotion always produces a certain expression (which could be a single muscle movement or a complex pattern of movements), and conversely that this expression always signifies the occurrence of its associated emotion. According to such a view, facial expressions are always a readout of internal states.

A bit of reflection on everyday experience should make us skeptical of such a simple view, however, and indeed it is unlikely that any theorist holds such a simple position. As we discussed in the previous section, people can feign emotions by willfully putting on different expressions. They also are sensitive to situations in which it would be inappropriate to show certain expressions (for example, a winner who shows too much happiness could be seen as gloating). A rising tide of research now shows that a purely spontaneous nonverbal readout of emotional states may be a rarer event than previously thought (Bonanno & Keltner, 2004; Russell, Bachorowski, & Fernández-Dols, 2003). The term "loosely coupled" is used to describe emotion and expression systems that coincide only occasionally or under certain circumstances.

Many studies support the argument that expressions are not a perfect window into emotional experience. Researchers have sought situations for study in which the experience of an emotion can be confirmed and then see what expressions are produced. People bowling with friends have been observed in the U.S. and Spain. After a good roll and at other moments when they reported feeling happy, bowlers smiled much more when facing their friends than while facing the pins. Similarly, soccer fans watching a match on television smiled much more during happy moments when relating directly to their friends than during happy moments when they were not interacting with them directly; during their noninteractive happy moments, they showed expressions indicative of several different emotions not shown in the interactive happy moments (Fernández-Dols & Ruiz-Belda, 1997; Kraut & Johnston, 1979; Ruiz-Belda et al., 2003).

Further evidence that facial expression and experienced emotion are only loosely coupled, and that the nature of the social situation is a strong determinant of what is displayed on the face, includes the following. Facial "motor mimicry"—displaying what another person is feeling, as when one person winces after a friend stubs his toe or when one grimaces upon hearing a friend tell about a "close call" she has had—decreases when no one is there to see the facial display (Bavelas et al., 1986; Chovil, 1991). Infants' smiles appear to be stimulated by expectations of eye contact with the mother and are greatly suppressed when the infants do not expect their mother to be watching (Jones, Collins, & Hong, 1991). College students watching emotionally provoking slides are more facially expressive when they watch with a friend as opposed to a stranger (Wagner & Smith, 1991), and college students recounting positive and negative experiences showed facial expressions that inconsistently matched their reported affect (Lee & Wagner, 2002). Finally, at the Olympic Games, gold medal winners were filmed at three moments: while standing behind the podium away from public view, while standing on the podium interacting with authorities and the public, and while standing on the podium facing the flagpoles and listening to their national anthem (Fernández-Dols & Ruiz-Belda, 1995). Although their feelings of happiness probably did not vary across these three closely spaced periods, the winners smiled the most during the middle, interactive-public period, suggesting again that facial expression is not due solely to the emotion currently being experienced.

"Audience effects" such as these, studies suggest, may even occur when we are ostensibly alone and behaving "spontaneously," for even then we may respond to fantasies of social interaction. In support of this notion, Fridlund (1991) found that college students watching pleasant films smiled more when watching with a friend than when watching alone, but students watching the same pleasant films in a different room from their friend (but aware the friend was watching) also smiled more than students in the simple alone condition. Thus, the imagined presence or experience of others may serve to stimulate or facilitate facial displays.

Fridlund's "behavioral ecology" theory of facial expression asserts that facial expressions are virtually never simply emotional and are, instead, always enacted for social purposes (Fridlund, 1994, 1997). In Fridlund's view, spontaneous expression of emotion would not have been a selected trait during evolution because it would too often serve others' (possibly rivals') interests rather than the expressor's by depriving the expressor of the ability to deceive. Fridlund's argument that facial expressions are meant to *communicate* rather than simply *reveal* is consistent with many examples of functional expressive behavior in the animal kingdom as well as with everyday observation of human interaction. However, most authors appear not to accept the extreme position that expressions are hardly ever purely emotional. The fact that audience presence effects can sometimes work in reverse, with people showing *less* facial expression with others present rather than more, suggests that people do indeed make spontaneous emotional expressions (Buck, 1984, 1991; Wagner & Lee, 1999). Facial expressions are thus not always put on only for social consumption.

Thus far, the approach described for testing whether expressions match inner feelings involves comparing expressions in different social circumstances. Another way of asking this question is to compare the expressions to some indicator of the feelings themselves. When this was done in a study in which viewers were asked about their emotions during neutral or scary film excerpts, almost no matching occurred (Fernández-Dols et al., 1997); only 2 of 35 viewers who reported a basic emotion showed the expression that theoretically should be produced by that emotion, while 3 showed expressions that suggested entirely different emotions from those reported.

Similarly, a study of actors' expressions in Hollywood movies first obtained good agreement from viewers on which emotions were being expressed in over 100 scenes and then conducted a detailed analysis of the actors' faces (Carroll & Russell, 1997). Only for happy episodes did the expected "happy" pattern of facial movements occur. For other emotions, although particular expected movements occurred more often than chance (e.g., lowered brows in angry episodes), there was little evidence for the expected whole patterns of expression. Considering that actors are likely to make *more* stereotyped expressions than people in real life, these results give a strong indication that emotion is conveyed in many ways other than through prototypical patterns of facial movements.

MEASURING THE FACE

For many years, descriptions of facial movements tended to be impressionistic or idiosyncratic (Ekman, 1982; Rinn, 1984). This changed dramatically with the work of Paul Ekman and Wallace Friesen (1978) and Carroll Izard (1979), teams that independently developed precise systems for describing facial action based on muscle movements. Izard's work has focused on infant expressions; the Ekman-Friesen system has been applied more generally and appears to be the most widely adopted. In this context, the term *widely* is relative, because learning a system comprehensive enough to describe nearly any combination of muscle movements requires many hours of training and practice and is extremely time consuming to apply. Consequently, use of the method is limited to dedicated facial researchers.

Ekman and Friesen developed their Facial Action Coding System, or FACS, by painstakingly (and sometimes painfully) learning how to move all their facial muscles and by studying anatomy texts. They studied the faces of other people who had learned how to control specific muscles and considered what movements an observer could reliably distinguish—important because observers would be the data gatherers. As a consequence, a trained observer can identify which muscles are moving (called "action units"). Sometimes an action unit involves more than one muscle, if those muscles always work in tandem or if an observer cannot see the difference. Altogether, the FACS can identify over 40 distinct action units in the face. Figure 9-3 presents the action units identified by Ekman (1979) for the brow/forehead. Altogether, seven different muscles can influence this region of the face.

The FACS allows emotion researchers to describe objectively what movements have occurred on the face and to categorize a face as showing a given emotion based on extensive data relating those movements to other criteria, mainly observers' judgments of facial

FIGURE 9-3

Action units for the brow/forehead.

SOURCE: From P. Ekman, "About Brows: Emotional and Conversational Signals" in von Cranach, et al., eds. _Human Ethology_, p. 174. Reprinted by permission of Cambridge University Press.

expressions. Through years of collecting such judgments, Ekman and his colleagues have developed a catalogue of movements associated with seven different judged emotions. For example, Ekman and Friesen (1978) determined that in the brow/forehead region (shown in Figure 9-3), action units 1 or 1 + 4 occur in sadness, along with associated movements across the rest of the face. In surprise, we see 1 + 2; in fear, 1 + 2 + 4; in anger, 4; and so forth.

Recall that we discussed the role of the face in interaction management. Ekman tells us how the brow/forehead area contributes to these conversational signals as well:

- Accent a word, 1 + 2 (Woody Allen uses 1 + 4 for this, according to Ekman)
- Underline a phrase, 1 + 2 or 4
- Punctuate (like a visual comma), 1 + 2 or 4
- Question mark, 1 + 2 or 4
- Word search, 4
- Listener response (back channel), 1 + 2
- Indicate lack of understanding, 4

We have gone into detail on the brow/forehead to give you a feel for how the system is applied. Although the method is tedious, the results can be very interesting indeed and possibly quite useful in daily life. For example, facial muscle movements can reveal the occurrence of pain and even distinguish among different pain sources, such as pain from immersion of the hand in cold water, from electric shock, and from surgery or other physical trauma (LeResche, 1982; Patrick, Craig, & Prkachin, 1986). The facial signs of pain, measured in both infants and adults, include a tightening of the muscles surrounding the eye, which narrows the eyes and raises the cheeks; the corrugator and other forehead muscles lower the eyebrows and wrinkle the bridge of the nose; and the levator muscles raise the upper lip and may produce wrinkles at the side of the nose (Prkachin & Craig, 1995). The faces of terminal cancer patients differ according to the stage of disease progression. In the early stages, signs of fear are more prominent ("whole eye tension combined with tension . . . in the lower eyelid") but give way to signs of sadness (in the brow/forehead region) in the late stage (Antonoff & Spilka, 1984–1985).

Some of the most subtle and fascinating work in facial muscle movements concerns different kinds of smiles. The muscle called the zygomatic major, which stretches out the lips when we smile, is the common denominator. Ekman has shown that the frequency, duration, and intensity of action by the zygomatic major differentiated among facial displays made by people watching different kinds of films and also correlated with how much happiness people said they felt while viewing them (Ekman, Friesen, & Ancoli, 1980). However, other muscles besides the zygomatic major are crucial to understanding what the smile really means. Darwin proposed that in a "felt" or genuinely happy smile, the orbicularis oculi muscle (which gives you crow's feet at the corner of your eye) is involved but not in a phony or mechanical smile. Figure 9-4 shows the difference between "felt" and "unfelt" versions of the smile.

In another study, student nurses were shown either a pleasant or a stressful film and asked to act as though the film was pleasant. Thus, those who were watching the stressful film had to lie about their experience. The smiles of those who saw the pleasant film were found to be felt happy smiles (as defined earlier) with no muscular activity associated with any of the negative emotions. Those trying to look pleasant while watching the stressful

FIGURE 9-4

Neutral face, "unfelt" smile, and "felt" smile.

FIGURE 9-4   (Continued)

FIGURE 9-5

Which is the "felt" happy smile?

a   b

c   d

film showed more "masking" smiles involving the zygomatic major but also more movements of the 10 or so muscles associated with fear, disgust, contempt, sadness, or anger (Ekman, Friesen, & O'Sullivan, 1988). Can you tell which of the faces in Figure 9-5 is the felt smile? (See the end of the chapter for the answer.)

The distinction between felt and unfelt smiles (also called Duchenne and non-Duchenne smiles, after the 19th century neurologist who first described them) has been supported in numerous studies, even among infants as young as 10 months of age (Ekman,

Davidson, & Friesen, 1990; Ekman & Friesen, 1982; Fox & Davidson, 1988). Aside from the involvement of the eye muscle, felt smiles are of less variable duration and have a smoother quality than unfelt smiles. Moreover, the two kinds of smiles can be distinguished from one another by naive viewers, even children as young as 9 years old (Frank, Ekman, & Friesen, 1993; Gosselin et al., 2002; Scherer & Ceschi, 2000), although not always with high levels of accuracy (Hess & Kleck, 1990). The distinction between felt and unfelt smiles, although very important, is still a probabilistic one. This means that in any particular instance, there may be uncertainty about the smile's true meaning. Although it is unlikely that a smile involving only the mouth is a true expression of pleasure or happiness, it is possible for a smile involving the eye muscles (a so-called "felt" smile) to be feigned by someone who is aware that such a smile is more convincing than the mouth-only kind. The fact that a felt smile display can be posed (as in Figure 9-4) underscores this point.

Because anatomical description of the face (such as that used in the FACS) is so time consuming to learn and employ, there is strong interest in developing computer programs that can recognize emotions as well as describe facial movement. This is a major challenge because of the many possible muscle movements and the existence of great differences between individual faces in shape and musculature. Some such systems are not very practical in many settings because they require attaching small dots to the face to serve as landmarks for the computerized analysis (Kaiser & Wehrle, 1992). A computerized system that can analyze movement under more natural circumstances has been reported by Bartlett et al. (1999); in a preliminary study, it identified action units correctly over 90% of the time. Eventually such automated systems will contribute greatly to research on facial expression.

Another approach that eliminates human judgment is based on the fact that different emotions produce distinctive facial movements even when the movements are too slight to be seen with the naked eye and are probably not apparent even to the expressors themselves. Electrodes attached to the face measure electromyographic (EMG) responses. Most consistent are results showing that the zygomatic muscle (which expands the mouth) responds under happy conditions and the corrugator muscle (between the brows) responds under sad, angry, and fearful conditions (Cacioppo et al., 1993; Camras, Holland, & Patterson, 1993). Studies that use EMG recording have shown that facial muscles respond in predictable ways simply to seeing others' emotional expressions (Blairy, Herrera, & Hess, 1999; Dimberg, 1982; Lundqvist, 1995). Thus, the face responds with corrugator activity to seeing angry expressions and with zygomaticus activity to seeing happy expressions. The face also responds in mimicking fashion to facial expressions of sadness and disgust. This process of unconscious mimicry may in turn contribute to one's own emotions through facial feedback, as we explain later.

Although much is to be gained from the FACS's fine-grained anatomical analysis and EMG technology, most often researchers employ less highly trained human observers for their facial measurement and judgment tasks. Observers are frequently asked to count the frequency of facial expressions, rate their intensity, or time their duration. For the measurement of a person's total amount of smiling, for example, these methods are the rule rather than the exception (Briton & Hall, 1995). As long as adequate interobserver agreement is obtained, these simpler approaches can have high validity.

JUDGING FACIAL EXPRESSIONS OF EMOTION

An in-depth analysis of all the important studies of facial expression prompted Ekman, Friesen, and Ellsworth (1982a) to draw the following conclusion:

> Contrary to the impression conveyed by previous reviews of the literature that the evidence in the field is contradictory and confusing, our reanalysis showed consistent evidence of accurate judgment of emotion from facial behavior. (p. 86)

Ekman and his colleagues rightly acknowledge that this conclusion pertains primarily to posed expressions, but an increasing number of studies of spontaneous expressions also show accurate perceptions. Because of the difficulty involved in measuring responses to facial expressions, and because so much of the literature concerns these measurement problems, we discuss measurement more than we have previously. How we measure responses to facial expressions is central to any statement about accuracy in judging these expressions. (The methodological issues discussed here are also relevant to measuring judgments in other cue channels, such as voice and body.)

The Response Format

Examine the three faces shown in Figure 9-6, then consider the following methods of responding. Would your responses differ depending on the method used? Is one method easier or harder to use than another? Is one likely to elicit greater accuracy?

1. In the space provided, write in the emotion being expressed in each of the faces you observed.

   A. _____   B. _____   C. _____

2. From the choices given, select the one emotion that best describes Face A, Face B, and Face C.

Face A	Face B	Face C
Rage	Happiness	Sadness
Anger	Joy	Despair
Wrath	Delight	Solemnity
Indignation	Amusement	Despondency
Resentment	Pleasure	Melancholy

3. From this list of emotions, select the one that best describes Face A, Face B, and Face C: Happiness, Sadness, Surprise, Fear, Anger.

This example illustrates one of the many problems involved in testing the accuracy of judgments about facial expressions: the type of response required from the judge. In this case, judgment accuracy would depend a great deal on which set of instructions the judge received. In the first testing condition, we have a totally open or free response from the judge. This will provide a wide range of responses, and researchers will be faced with the problem of deciding whether the judge's label corresponds with their label for the emotion. Sometimes the words used by judges suggest a blend of emotions; for example, "smugness" may contain facial features found in both happiness and anger expressions.

FIGURE 9-6

How should these facial expressions be read?

The labels used by the experimenters or expressors and the judges may be different, but both may respond the same way to the actual emotion in real life or may be thinking of the same emotion. This also raises the problem of the gap between perceiving and naming emotional responses so that others understand.

In the second testing condition, the discrimination task is too difficult—the emotions listed in each category are too much alike. We can predict low accuracy for judges given these instructions. In some cases, the labels all may focus on variants of the same emotion, and the perceiver sees something completely different but is prohibited from adding new categories. For example, photograph "C" seems to be perceived by the researcher as a form of sadness, but a judge might see it as neutral.

The last set of instructions is the opposite of the second set—the discrimination task may be too easy. Because the emotion categories are discrete, we can predict high accuracy for the third condition.

Accuracy is also influenced by biases in judgment patterns. Consider a facial judgment task with equal numbers of sad, happy, and angry faces. If a judge guesses "happy" all the time (to state the extreme case), he or she would score as very accurate on happy faces and we might conclude that such a judge is an excellent judge of happiness. But obviously the judge has no differential accuracy because she or he gave only one answer to all the items. For the same reason, the low accuracy obtained by such a judge on the other emotions is less an index of actual accuracy than of rating bias. Researchers who employ multiple-choice tests have fortunately developed ways of scoring that take rating bias into account (Wagner, 1993). And of course we must keep in mind what level of accuracy would be expected on the basis of guessing alone; with four choices, this level would be 25%, with three, 33%, and so on. Therefore any given level of accuracy cannot be evaluated in absolute terms but rather must be appraised in terms of how much higher or lower it is than the guessing level.

Aside from these methodological factors, others also influence the levels of accuracy that will be obtained by a researcher. As an example, the duration of exposure to the facial expressions will likely have an impact (though accuracy can be obtained with surprisingly short exposures; see Ambady, Bernieri, & Richeson, 2000; Matsumoto et al., 2000).

Creating the Facial Stimulus

Researchers have used varied ways to elicit the emotional expressions that observers are asked to identify. Some simply describe a situation and tell the actor to react as if he or she were in that situation; others give a list of emotions and tell the actor to portray them; and some use candid photos of people in real situations. One early study (Dunlap, 1927) reached an almost comic extreme. A camera was set up in a laboratory, ready to catch the subject's expressions at the proper moment. To elicit an expression of pain, the experimenter bent the subject's finger backward forcibly; to produce a startled look, the experimenter fired a pistol behind the subject at an unexpected moment; apprehension was elicited by telling the subject the pistol would be fired again close to his ear on the count of three (at the count of two the photo was taken); amusement was captured when the experimenter told the subject some jokes; disgust resulted from the subject's smelling a test tube containing tissues of a dead rat; and finally—unbelievably—to elicit an expression of grief, a subject was hypnotized and was told several members of his family had been killed in a car wreck! "Unfortunately," says the experimenter, "the camera could not catch intense grief because the subject bowed his head and cried," so he had to settle for an expression of mild grief to be used in the study!

The idea of presenting subjects with a controlled stimulus and then observing their reactions, although carried to an extreme in Dunlap's study, still underlies much research on spontaneous expressions. Subjects are shown slides or films that differ in their content (funny, disgusting, sexy, heartwarming, and so forth) while a videotape camera unobtrusively records their facial reactions. Judges later observe the subjects' faces and try to guess which slide or film each subject had been viewing (Buck, 1979; Zuckerman et al., 1976). This method can capture completely unpremeditated expressions. However, because expressors are not in a truly communicative situation, their behavior may be no more real or authentic than are expressors' attempts to pose various emotions on the command of the experimenter. Another method, asking subjects to reexperience an emotional event and then talk about it, has been used sometimes as a more natural alternative that blends some elements of deliberate and spontaneous communication (Halberstadt, 1986).

Context or Not?

Though researchers might present faces of strangers out of context, contextual factors obviously influence accuracy. Prior exposure to a face is one such factor. If you are familiar with the face and have seen it express other emotions, you are more likely to correctly identify another emotion you have not seen before. If you are familiar with the person, you have a better reference point for making judgments. For instance, a person who smiles frequently and who you then see not smiling may seem very sad. With another person, absence of a smile may simply be part of a normal, neutral expression.

Several studies make it clear that additional knowledge concerning the context in which a particular facial expression occurs will affect how people judge the emotion expressed. (Context can be visual, as when observers are shown the situation including people who may be in it, or narrative, as when observers are told a background story and then shown a facial expression of a person supposedly in the story.) Observers can label facial expressions of emotion without any knowledge of the context in which they occur, but co-occurring perceptions of the social context, the environment, and other people will surely affect judgments.

Although a number of investigators have pursued the question of whether context or expression dominates perceptions, the issue is far from resolved (Fernández-Dols & Carroll, 1997). Perhaps the most often cited study regarding the influence of context in face judging is the classic one by Munn (1940). Facial expressions taken from popular magazines were shown with and without background context. The background information was very helpful in accurately identifying these facial expressions, as were verbal cues describing the situation.

Another classic demonstration of context effects is Cline's (1956) study of line drawings to test the effect of having another face as part of the total context. He found that the expression on one face influenced interpretation of the other face. When the smiling face was paired with a glum face, the smiling face was seen as that of a vicious, gloating, taunting bully. When paired with a frowning face, the smiling face seemed peaceful, friendly, and happy.

Obviously, the context in which a facial expression is embedded can influence our interpretation of the expression. Sometimes the question is posed in terms of which matters more, expression or context (see the review by Fernández-Dols & Carroll, 1997), but this is too simplistic an approach. Often a judgment depends not on which source of information wins out in observers' judgments, but rather on whether the two sources of information can be meaningfully integrated. Sometimes this is done by reinterpreting the information from one source, for example by deciding that a "sad" story context might actually produce angry feelings, too; other times, a true integration is made, as when a facial expression of "fear" plus a context of "anger" produces the overall interpretation of "pain" (Carroll & Russell, 1996). By manipulating the clarity and potency of either the situation or the expression, it is possible to show that either situational or facial cues exert more influence on people's conclusions about emotional experience (Ekman, Friesen, & Ellsworth, 1982c).

EMOTIONS INFERRED FROM THE FACE

Many factors influence how emotions are inferred from the face, but the compelling fact remains that they can be inferred, and often with extremely high levels of accuracy. Some emotions are more likely to be confused, but six "basic" emotions—happiness, anger, disgust, sadness, surprise, and fear—are judged with very high agreement among observers

Figure 9-7

Surprise: *The brows are raised so they are curved and high. The skin below the brow is stretched. Horizontal wrinkles go across the forehead. The eyelids are opened; the upper lid is raised and the lower lid drawn down; the white of the eye—the sclera—shows above the iris and often below as well. The jaw drops open so the lips and teeth are parted, but there is no tension or stretching of the mouth.*

in many studies. Figures 9-7 to 9-12 show these six basic emotions, with a description of their characteristic facial actions (each of which can also be described in terms of which action units are involved). These expressions are recognized at high levels not only in the United States but also around the globe (see chapters 2 and 3; Ekman, Sorenson, & Friesen, 1969; Izard, 1971). More recently, Biehl and colleagues (1997) demonstrated that seven emotions shown on the faces of both Japanese and Caucasian individuals were judged with high levels of agreement by viewers in Hungary, Japan, Poland, and Sumatra, and by Caucasians and recently immigrated Vietnamese in the United States.

We can argue that in today's world of global media exposure, such a result is not at all surprising. Ekman and his colleagues set about to find out how remote tribal people in New Guinea, who had not been exposed to Western facial expression norms, would respond. Even in New Guinea, photos of U.S. citizens' faces showing six basic emotions (fear, surprise, anger, happiness, sadness, and disgust) were judged correctly for the most part. Moreover, some New Guineans were photographed while showing how they would react in different situations (such as "you feel sad because your child died"), and U.S. respondents later guessed with great accuracy which scenario was being communicated (Ekman & Friesen, 1971).

FIGURE 9-8

Fear: The brows are raised and drawn together. The wrinkles in the forehead are in the center, not across the entire forehead. The upper eyelid is raised, exposing the sclera, and the lower eyelid is tensed and drawn up. The mouth is open and the lips are either tensed slightly and drawn back or stretched and drawn back.

Most cross-cultural research has dealt with depictions of the face showing very pure configurations for the major emotions. However, as noted earlier, facial expressions can be complex blends, with different muscles simultaneously showing elements of different emotions. The question of whether cross-cultural universality also applies to secondary, more subtle, expressions led Ekman and a team of colleagues to introduce a new methodology into the cross-cultural research. These researchers obtained ratings of faces on a variety of emotions from subjects in 10 places around the world, including Estonia, Sumatra, Scotland, Japan, Italy, and Hong Kong. There was dramatic agreement across cultures not only on the primary emotion being shown by the faces but also on the secondary emotion (Ekman et al., 1987).

Although universality of judgment is widely accepted, there has been criticism of the methods employed (Russell, 1994). The most potent of these criticisms is that the forced-choice method that has been used (like example "3" in the methodological exercise earlier) is too easy and also produces artificially high levels of agreement among judges. Frank and Stennett (2001), however, showed that even with a "none of the above" response option included, the great majority of judges agreed on the correct emotion and only a few picked the "none of the above" option. Furthermore, they found that when the correct answer was omitted from the response options and a "none of the above" option was

FIGURE 9-9

Disgust: *The upper lip is raised. The lower lip is also raised and pushed up to the upper lip or is lowered and slightly protruding. The nose is wrinkled. The cheeks are raised. Lines show below the lower lid, and the lid is pushed up but not tense. The brow is lowered, lowering the upper lid.*

included, judges tended to pick "none of the above," suggesting that they knew that the correct emotion had been omitted from the list. This research provides support for the forced-choice method as a valid way to test for accuracy of judgment. However, it remains a fact that accuracy levels could be brought down if the list of options was more like the second example in the exercise, that is, if the choices were made to be much more similar to each other. This discussion should highlight for the reader the fact that accuracy is a relative concept, and that the design of measuring instruments can have very strong effects on accuracy levels.

Although accurate recognition of certain emotions is generally well above chance everywhere it has been tested, variability still exists between individuals and from place to place. We discussed research on differences between individuals in chapter 3. Variation from place to place is still being investigated. Russell (1994) found that facial expressions (which were mainly of Westerners' faces) were more accurately recognized by other Western than by non-Western groups. An *in-group advantage* has been documented showing that people have an advantage when judging cues expressed by members of their own cultural, national, or ethnic group (Elfenbein & Ambady, 2002, 2003). These authors suggested that one reason for such an advantage is the existence of

FIGURE 9-10

Anger: The brows are lowered and drawn together. Vertical lines appear between the brows. The lower lids are tensed and may or may not be raised. The upper lids are tensed and may or may not be lowered by the action of the brow. The eyes have a hard stare and may have a bulging appearance. The lips are in either of two basic positions: pressed firmly together, with the corners straight or down; or open, tensed in a squarish shape as if shouting. The nostrils may be dilated, but this is not essential to the anger facial expression and may also occur in sadness. There is ambiguity unless anger is registered in all three facial areas.

"emotion dialects"—culturally learned ways of expressing different emotional messages through nonverbal cues. Such dialects, when shared between senders and receivers, are hypothesized to promote accurate judgments. Elfenbein and Ambady (2003) measured accuracy in judging photographs of mainland Chinese people (in China) and Caucasian Americans expressing different emotions through the face. The groups whose accuracy was tested were mainland Chinese people in China, mainland Chinese people in the U.S., Chinese Americans (U.S. citizens of Chinese extraction), and non-Asian U.S. citizens. These four groups' accuracy conformed exactly to the authors' "dialect" predictions—the more the group was familiar with mainland Chinese expressions, the better they were on Chinese compared to Caucasian expressions, and the more the group was familiar with American expressions, the better they were on Caucasian compared to Chinese expressions. In addition, an analysis of how long the Chinese Americans' families had been in the U.S. showed that the longer the families had been in the U.S., the better they were at

FIGURE 9-11

Happiness: The corners of lips are drawn back and up. The mouth may or may not be parted, with teeth exposed or not. A wrinkle (the nasolabial fold) runs down from the nose to the outer edge beyond the lip corners. The cheeks are raised. The lower eyelids show wrinkles below them and may be raised but not tense. Crow's-feet wrinkles go outward from the outer corners of the eyes (covered by hair in these photographs).

judging Caucasian compared to Chinese faces. These data lend strong support to the emotion dialects concept.

Although researchers do not agree on how many "basic" emotions there are (Cornelius, 1996), most research describing facial movements associated with emotion has concentrated on the six shown in Figures 9-7 to 9-12. Recently, attention has turned to other expressions. *Contempt* has been found to have a universally recognizable expression—a slight tightening and raising of the corner of the lip on one side (Ekman et al., 1987). Facial signs of *anxiety* have been shown to include increased blinking, more facial movements associated with fear (such as a horizontal mouth stretch), and more facial movements overall (Harrigan & O'Connell, 1996). Increases in smiling and laughing have also been noted in socially anxious situations. *Pride* has been shown to have a recognizable nonverbal expression, though one that may rely on posture and arm position as well as facial expression (Tracy & Robins, 2004). *Embarrassment* has been shown to be signaled by looking down, shifting the eyes, turning the head away, touching the face, and engaging in "controlled smiles" (smiles that one tries to counter with other facial movements)

FIGURE 9-12

Sadness: The inner corners of the eyebrows are drawn up. The skin below the eyebrows is triangulated, with the inner corner up. The upper eyelid inner corners are raised. The corners of the lips are down or the lips are trembling.

(Keltner, 1995). Keltner has also studied the temporal ordering and relative duration of the components of facial embarrassment (Figure 9-13).

PHYSIOLOGY AND THE FACE

We all have at least one friend with a face that remains as still as a rock, no matter how much excitement swirls around him or her. We also have friends with faces that seem as sensitive as a butterfly's wings to every shift of the emotional winds. What we may not know is that these differences, aside from being quite real and enduring, also are associated with differences in physiological functioning. The "internalizers" have little overt expression (that is, on the face) but experience high physiological reactivity (on measures such as heart rate and electrodermal responding); the "externalizers" (the expressive ones) show the opposite pattern (Buck et al., 1972; Lanzetta & Kleck, 1970; Notarius & Levenson, 1979). Most theorizing about this relationship has pointed to learned factors, for example, the notion that society encourages people to suppress their overt emotional reactions, and that individuals who do so must experience their emotions or arousal in some other way, perhaps through internal activation of the nervous system. The metaphor of

Figure 9-13

Prototypical embarrassment response. The mean duration of each action is equal to the interval beginning with the leftmost edge of the photograph and ending with the end of the arrow.

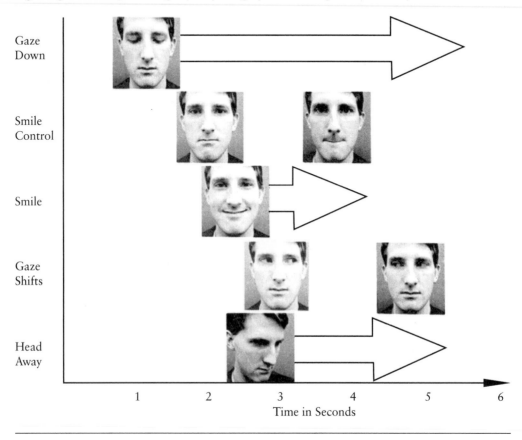

discharge can be applied: The emotion is released *either* externally *or* internally (Notarius & Levenson, 1979). However, research on newborns finds a similar negative relationship between expressiveness and physiological responding (heart rate), suggesting that temperamental factors may also be at work (Field, 1982).

Given these differences, it is intriguing to consider a possible connection between expressiveness and physical health. Could restraining the outward expression of emotion be damaging to health? Friedman and his colleagues (Friedman & Booth-Kewley, 1987; Friedman, Hall, & Harris, 1985) pursued this idea and found that, as predicted, a "repressed" style of expression was related to indications of coronary artery disease and even to the actual occurrence of a heart attack. King and Emmons (1990) found some support for the hypothesis that *ambivalence* over emotional expression would be associated with poorer health. Malatesta, Jonas, and Izard (1987) found that women who showed less expression on their face when talking about an angry experience had more arthritis symptoms, and women who showed less facial expression during a sad account had more skin problems. Promising evidence for a relation of emotional expression/suppression to health comes from research on *alexithymia,* a term used to describe patients who have a pronounced inability to describe their own emotions. These patients are deficient in facial expressiveness and also seem to suffer from a disproportionate number of psychosomatic ailments (Buck, 1993).

Adding to the complexity and fascination of the relation between the face and physiology is the *facial feedback hypothesis* put forth by Darwin. Darwin believed that an emotion freely expressed will be intensified. The facial feedback hypothesis states that expressions on the face can actually *create* emotional experience via direct connections between facial muscles and emotion centers in the brain.

Is the facial feedback hypothesis valid? The idea that emotions can be regulated via facial behavior—that we can create authentic emotional experience from inauthentic outward expressions—has important ramifications for child rearing, psychotherapy, and many other domains (Izard, 1990). The facial feedback hypothesis has been debated at length, for although a majority of studies support it, many are potentially flawed (Matsumoto, 1987). A typical experiment asks subjects to pose their faces in various ways and then measures their emotional state through self-report (Laird, 1974; Tourangeau & Ellsworth, 1979). The flaw in such a study is that expressors may realize their posed expression is meant to look like fear or happiness. If this happens, it is no surprise that they obediently report feeling those emotions.

Fortunately, studies exist that do not share this problem. Some studies measure reactions objectively and not in terms of expressors' self-reports. For example, posing strong reaction (vs. no reaction) to electric shocks produced relative increases in physiological reaction (via electrodermal measures), suggesting that more pain was experienced; posing a strong reaction also led to subjective reports of more pain (Lanzetta, Cartwright-Smith, & Kleck, 1976).

In a shrewd study, a group of investigators disguised the purpose of the facial posing by telling participants they were helping develop ways for persons with disabilities to hold a writing implement; it could be held between the teeth, which naturally expands the lips, or it could be held by the lips, which of course contracts them. Figure 9-14 illustrates these mouth positions. Unknown to the participants, these two manipulations differ in whether the "smiling" muscles around the mouth are activated. Those holding the pen between their teeth (which activates the "smiling" muscles) rated cartoons as funnier than the other participants did (Strack, Martin, & Stepper, 1988). Thus the position of the facial muscles can indeed "feed back" to influence the expressor's emotional state. Subsequent research using this same pencil-in-the-teeth paradigm showed, furthermore, that inducing expressors to activate their eye-corner muscles as well as their mouth-widening muscles (to produce Duchenne smiles) produced higher levels of enjoyment when viewing positive videoclips than occurred when expressors made non-Duchenne smiles (Soussignan, 2002). This makes sense when you consider that the Duchenne smile is said to reflect more genuine positive emotion than the non-Duchenne smile.

Ekman and his colleagues, in a facial feedback experiment, also demonstrated that moving particular facial muscles on command, as well as "reliving" past emotional

FIGURE 9-14

Illustration of the technique used to contract the different facial muscles: LEFT, lips condition; RIGHT, teeth condition.

experiences, produces specific patterns of reaction in the autonomic nervous system (Ekman, Levenson, & Friesen, 1983). Heart rate and finger temperature increased more in anger than in happiness; anger and fear were similar in terms of heart rate increases but differed in finger temperature. Perhaps these results translate into the familiar feelings of being flushed or hot when angry and of having cold hands when afraid.

Strack and Neumann (2000) extended the facial feedback phenomenon beyond emotional responses to the kinds of judgments we make about others. Under the guise of studying how working on a computer produces tension, participants were asked to furrow their brows (or not) while doing a computer judgment task. On the task, participants made ratings of how famous various celebrities and noncelebrities were. Those who maintained the furrowed brow rated the individuals as less famous than those in the control group, perhaps because the furrowed brow unconsciously put them in a skeptical frame of mind.

Though most feedback studies have involved the face, other body parts can also produce feedback effects. In one study, the researchers manipulated posture (upright vs. slumped) by the use of different seating arrangements and showed that if participants were upright rather than slumped when hearing that they had performed well on an earlier task, they experienced more pride in their performance (Stepper & Strack, 1993).

Not much is known about the exact mechanisms that produce psychological changes (e.g., emotions) following face and body movement. Although well-designed studies can rule out a cognitive explanation (that is, people simply report the feelings they know their movements suggest), the nature of the physiological mechanism is still an open question. Although most investigators assume the feedback occurs through the nervous system, a novel theory called the *vascular theory of emotional efference* holds that certain facial movements (and breathing patterns) change the temperature of the blood flowing into the brain, which then influences affective state (cooler blood produces more positive affect) (McIntosh et al., 1997; Zajonc, 1985).

Thus it appears that our own expressions, whether deliberately put on or spontaneously mimicked in response to others' expressions, can produce corresponding emotions or can intensify or deintensify experiences already in progress. The process of "emotional contagion" (Hatfield, Cacioppo, & Rapson, 1994) may contribute to our ability to experience empathy and understand others' emotional states. Indeed, when Surakka and Hietanen (1998) showed the "felt" and "unfelt" smiles shown in Figure 9-4 to viewers, they found that EMG recordings of both eye and cheek muscles were stronger for those who saw the felt smiles. Furthermore, results suggested that more pleasure was subsequently experienced by those who saw those smiles.

Researchers studying the face and physiology also have discovered that posed and spontaneous facial expressions are controlled by different pathways within the brain. This has been demonstrated by certain forms of brain injury that result in a person's losing the ability to produce facial expressions deliberately but not losing the capacity to laugh, cry, frown, and so on when genuinely experiencing an emotion; the reverse form of disability also exists (Rinn, 1984). When brain damage occurs, facial expressiveness is especially impaired when the damage is to the right hemisphere of the brain, which is considered the more nonverbal hemisphere (Buck & Duffy, 1980). Researchers have found that the left side of a person's face tends to be more expressive (Borod et al., 1998; Nicholls el al., 2002; Skinner & Mullen, 1991), because the left half of the face is controlled by the right hemisphere. However, consistent with the notion of separate neural pathways, this asymmetry is present only for posed expressions; spontaneous (more genuine) ones tend to be symmetrical (Ekman, Hager, & Friesen, 1981; Skinner & Mullen, 1991). Perhaps now you will think differently about your friend with the crooked smile!

Thus far we have examined the sending and receiving of messages relevant to emotional state. But researchers also have asked questions that go beyond the momentary expression and judgment of emotion: Does the facial expression of emotion tell us anything about the social consequences that might follow from its occurrence?

THE SOCIAL IMPACT OF FACIAL EXPRESSIONS

Our facial expressions, both intended and spontaneous, exert many influences on those around us. In this section we can present only a sampling of this research. The strong impact of facial expressions takes on special significance because people have a great deal of control over their faces. Most discussions of the face center on emotions—how the face reveals what emotions are being felt. But several times we have mentioned posed versus spontaneous expressions. By its very nature, a posed expression means that we need not actually feel what we are showing. The face becomes a tool of self-presentation (creating a desirable image of ourself in the eyes of others) and of social influence (producing desirable behaviors in someone else). Ironically, we may be particularly vulnerable to manipulation by others' faces because we are likely to assume the face is an honest window into another's true feelings when this might not be the case. Consistent with this, Zuckerman, DePaulo, and Rosenthal (1981) found in a review of deception studies that people are least successful in detecting deception when they are able to see the face of the person they are judging.

An important application of knowledge of facial expressions occurs in the helping professions. One such application is ascertaining the existence and severity of mental disorders. Ekman, Matsumoto, and Friesen (1997) showed that more contempt and more "unfelt" happy expressions at the time of hospital admission were related to less improvement at discharge and that different diagnostic groups showed different facial emotion patterns: People with major depression showed more sadness and disgust; people in a manic condition showed more "felt" and "unfelt" happiness and less anger, disgust, and sadness; and people with schizophrenia showed fear and low levels of all the other coded emotions. Fridlund, Ekman, and Oster (1987) similarly showed that depressed individuals had sadder and less expressive faces than others.

The patient's face may not be the only face that is important in a clinical situation, however. There is reason to believe that physicians' and therapists' facial expressions have an impact on patients. Ambady et al. (2002) found that the facial expressions of physical therapists predicted changes in elderly patients' physical and psychological functioning over the course of treatment. Facial "distancing" (not smiling and not looking at the patient) was associated with decreases in functioning, while facial expressiveness (smiling, nodding, and frowning) was associated with increases in functioning.

The faces of depressed mothers may similarly be an influential stimulus. Extensive work has been conducted on interaction between mothers who have depression and their infants (Field, 2002; Lundy, Field, & Pickens, 1996). These infants have less expressive faces than other infants, do not orient visually as well to adults, and show more facial negativity. Research shows that adults' smiles (and other expressions) influence babies' moods and responses to the environment (Cappella, 1981). In Field's (2002) study, the depressed mothers displayed the same kinds of behaviors that were then seen in their infants (such as more negative facial expressions and less looking), as well as less vocalization and less tactile stimulation.

Savitsky and colleagues (Savitsky et al., 1974) were interested in whether facial expressions of emotion by a "victim" would have any effect on the aggressor's behavior. When individuals thought they were controlling the amount of electric shock that another person (victim) would get, they gave more shocks to victims who responded with expressions of happiness and smiles and fewer to victims who displayed expressions of anger. Expressions of fear and neutrality did not differ from each other in the number of shocks administered, which for both expressions was very low.

Although defendants' faces are scrutinized closely in the courtroom, their faces are not the only influential ones. In a cleverly designed experiment, Hart (1995) obtained videotapes of judges reading standard instructions to juries in real trials, and he also found out how those judges felt about each case—whether they personally leaned toward a guilt or an innocence verdict. These videotapes were then spliced onto a *different* trial and the whole sequence was shown to groups of role-playing jurors. Thus these jurors were being "instructed" by judges who were known to be biased (although about a different case). Jurors' verdicts of guilt and innocence were significantly influenced by the judges' facial expressions (and voice tone), thus demonstrating that judges' expressions can unconsciously influence jurors even though the judges are supposed to remain impartial in their behavior.

Other public settings have produced facial effects, too. One line of research considers the mass media and finds that different television newscasters seem to prefer different political candidates, as revealed by the pleasantness of their faces when mentioning the candidates' names. Viewers' political preferences could be unconsciously altered in this way (Friedman, DiMatteo, & Mertz, 1980; Mullen, 1986).

The possibility that facial expressions are related to discrimination against women was the topic of Butler and Geis's (1990) study of male and female leaders in groups. Male and female (confederate) leaders in their experimentally composed groups offered the same suggestions and arguments, but the group members, who were the subjects of study, displayed more pleased responses (smiling, nodding) and fewer displeased responses (furrowed brow, mouth tightening, head shaking) when they were listening to a male leader than when listening to a female leader. Group members were apparently unaware of their gender-biased behavior, or denied it, for they later revealed no gender bias in written evaluations of the different leaders. Butler and Geis argue that nonverbal signals of devaluation of the female leader could convince others, as well as the female leader herself, that her contributions are weak or wrong.

Another connection between the face and sex discrimination was made by Archer's discovery of the "face-ism" or facial prominence phenomenon: In magazine and newspaper pictures, proportionately more of the picture is devoted to men's faces; pictures of women show more of the body. Archer and his colleagues (Archer et al., 1983) found this pattern in publications from 11 different cultures and in artwork over 6 centuries, as well as in people's amateur drawings. Both Archer and later researchers (Zuckerman, 1986) have made the case that face-ism is a form of devaluing women. Consistent with the view that depicting less of the face devalues the person in the picture, Zuckerman and Kieffer (1994) demonstrated that face-ism favoring whites over blacks also exists in magazines and art (when the artists are white), and the higher the status of the person shown in magazine photos, the larger the proportional depiction of the subject's face.

Not only the relative size of the face, but also which side is shown, makes an impression. As noted earlier, the left side of the face is rated as more expressive. Furthermore, when asked to show emotions people are more likely to show the left side. Portraits of women (who are stereotypically associated with emotion) are especially likely to show the left side of the face (ten Cate, 2002). Portraits of men are inconsistent. Interestingly, the right side is rated as more "scientific" when people judge portraits of professors (ten Cate, 2002). Thus, the depiction of men in portraits may convey more rationality through the choice of head angle. It remains to be seen whether portrait painters, or people posing for portraits, are consciously aware of the different impressions given by each side of the face.

The smile is a profoundly influential social cue that has been studied in many contexts. People reciprocate smiles quite predictably (Cherulnik et al., 2001; Hinsz & Tomhave, 1991; Jorgenson, 1978). You can imagine how, after returning someone's smile, facial feedback or attributional processes ("I just smiled at Jim. I must really like him!") could produce real changes in your emotional state or your attitude toward the smiler. Smiles are positive reinforcers that can change behavior just as other, more traditional, reinforcers can. Receiving a smile from one stranger can make you more helpful toward a different stranger (Guéguen & de Gail, 2003; Solomon et al., 1981), and receiving a smile from your waitperson can lead you to leave a larger tip (Tidd & Lockard, 1978).

Angry faces are a potent stimulus, too. In a series of experiments, Hansen and Hansen (1988) compared people's ability to pick out an angry face in a crowd of happy faces to their ability to pick out a happy face in a crowd of angry faces. As they predicted, picking out the angry face was faster and more error free than picking out the happy face. Perhaps our survival as a species has some relation to our sensitivity to threats.

The influence exerted on us by others' facial expressions is not limited to those faces that we consciously see and take note of. Unconscious (subliminal) perception effects have been uncovered. Murphy and Zajonc (1993) showed people a happy or an angry face for only 4 milliseconds, an interval much too short to allow for conscious perception of the faces, followed by unfamiliar stimuli (written Chinese characters). When the experimenters asked the participants how much they liked each Chinese character, they found that characters preceded by a happy face were liked more than those preceded by an angry face. More recently, Dimberg, Thunberg, and Elmehed (2000) found that subliminally exposing people to happy or angry facial expressions produced corresponding facial movements according to EMG measurements. In this case, both the stimulus (the faces seen) and the response (the small facial movements picked up by EMG recording) occurred unconsciously. The almost uncanny sensitivity of human beings to facial expressions undoubtedly plays an important role in our adaptation to social life.

❖

SUMMARY

The face is a multimessage system. It can communicate information regarding personality, interest and responsiveness during interaction, emotional states, and how people want to present themselves to others. Although we know that people associate certain personality characteristics with certain expressions and facial features, we do not yet know how accurate these impressions are. We know the face is used as a conversational regulator that opens and closes communication channels, complements and qualifies other behaviors, and replaces spoken messages.

Facial expressions are very complex entities to deal with. Of all the areas of the body, the face seems to elicit the best external and internal feedback, which makes it easy for us to follow a variety of facial display rules. Not all facial displays represent single emotions; some are blends of several emotions. Sometimes we show aspects of an emotional display when we are not actually feeling emotional, as with facial emblems that represent commentary on emotions. Other times the emotion we are feeling is not very predictably shown on the face. The question of how often the face spontaneously reveals emotional experiences in daily life is hotly contested.

We noted some measurement issues involved in the study of facial expressions: the complexity of the decisions observers are asked to make, simulated as opposed to real expressions, the method of presenting the face to the observer (films, photos, and the like), knowledge of the context, and others. Naturally, all these factors may impinge on our accuracy in identifying facial expressions of emotion.

Accuracy in judging the face tends to be high, at least when prototypical expressions are presented. Furthermore, certain basic emotions have been found to be accurately judged in cultures around the world: anger, fear, disgust, sadness, happiness, surprise, and contempt. In order to understand what the face actually does during the expression of emotion, anatomically based coding systems, such as the Facial Action Coding System (FACS), have been developed; these systems can identify which muscles are involved in different kinds of expressions.

A psychophysiological approach has added much to our understanding of facial behavior. People with more expressive faces have less activity in their autonomic nervous systems than less expressive people; this is interesting partly because of its health implications. Under certain circumstances, facial movements can influence the emotions being felt by the expressor; thus the face may not only read out emotions but also may actually produce them. Studies of minute facial movements show that people unconsciously mimic the facial expressions of others, even those too quick to be consciously perceived. Finally, researchers are finding out more about which activities of the brain and nervous system are associated with different emotions.

We concluded with a sampling of studies suggesting that facial expressions can have a strong impact on the people in our social environment.

(Answer to Figure 9-5: b. All the others have traces of disgust or sadness.)

QUESTIONS FOR DISCUSSION

1. Facial expressions can show emotions, but they also are used for conversation management. Give examples of each and state which function you consider the most important.

2. Consider men's and women's nonverbal behavior. Does the concept of display rules help you explain any differences between the sexes?

3. As noted in the chapter, the distinction between a feigned or posed facial display and an authentic or spontaneous one may be hard to make. Discuss the issue of intentionality in facial expressions. Is it important to be able to make such a distinction?

4. The chapter gives examples of how the face is a potent influence on others. Think of some other examples of this, and discuss whether the face is more or less influential than other nonverbal channels in terms of its social impact.

BIBLIOGRAPHY

Abelson, R. P., & Sermat, V. (1962). Multidimensional scaling of facial expressions. *Journal of Experimental Psychology, 63,* 546–551.

Ambady, N., Bernieri, F. J., & Richeson, J. (2000). Toward a histology of social behavior: Judgmental accuracy from thin slices of the behavioral stream. In M. P. Zanna (Ed.), *Advances in experimental social psychology,* Vol. 32 (pp. 201–271). San Diego: Academic Press.

Ambady, N., Koo, J., Rosenthal, R., & Winograd, C. H. (2002). Physical therapists' nonverbal communication predicts geriatric patients' health outcomes. *Psychology and Aging, 17,* 443–452.

Andrew, R. J. (1965). The origins of facial expression. *Scientific American, 213,* 88–94.

Antonoff, S. R., & Spilka, B. (1984–1985). Patterning of facial expressions among terminal cancer patients. *Omega, 15,* 101–108.

Archer, D., Iritani, B., Kimes, D. D., & Barrios, M. (1983). Face-ism: Five studies of sex differences in facial prominence. *Journal of Personality and Social Psychology, 45,* 725–735.

Bartlett, M. S., Hager, J. C., Ekman, P., & Sejnowski, T. J. (1999). Measuring facial expressions by computer image analysis. *Psychophysiology, 36,* 253–263.

Bavelas, J. B., Black, A., Lemery, C. R., & Mullett, J. (1986). "I show how you feel": Motor mimicry as a communicative act. *Journal of Personality and Social Psychology, 50,* 322–329.

Bavelas, J. B., & Chovil, N. (1997). Faces in dialogue. In J. A. Russell & J. M. Fernández-Dols (Eds.), *The psychology of facial expression.* Paris: Cambridge University Press.

Biehl, M., Matsumoto, D., Ekman, P., Hearn, V., Heider, K., Kudoh, T., & Ton, V. (1997). Matsumoto and Ekman's Japanese and Caucasian Facial Expressions of Emotion (JACFEE): Reliability data and cross-national differences. *Journal of Nonverbal Behavior, 21,* 3–21.

Blairy, S., Herrera, P., & Hess, U. (1999). Mimicry and the judgment of emotional facial expressions. *Journal of Nonverbal Behavior, 23,* 5–41.

Bonanno, G. A., & Keltner, D. (2004). The coherence of emotion systems: Comparing "on-line" measures of appraisal and facial expressions, and self-report. *Cognition and Emotion, 18,* 431–444.

Borod, J. C., Koff, E., Yecker, S., Santschi, C., & Schmidt, J. M. (1998). Facial asymmetry during emotional expression: Gender, valence, and measurement technique. *Neuropsychologia, 36,* 1209–1215.

Brannigan, C. R., & Humphries, D. A. (1972). Human non-verbal behavior, a means of communication. In N. Blurton Jones (Ed.), *Ethological studies of child behavior.* New York: Cambridge University Press.

Briton, N. J., & Hall, J. A. (1995). Gender-based expectancies and observer judgments of smiling. *Journal of Nonverbal Behavior, 19,* 49–65.

Brunner, L. J. (1979). Smiles can be back channels. *Journal of Personality and Social Psychology, 37,* 728–734.

Buck, R. (1979). Measuring individual differences in the nonverbal communication of affect: The slide-viewing paradigm. *Human Communication Research, 6,* 47–57.

Buck, R. (1984). *The communication of emotion.* New York: Guilford.

Buck, R. (1988). Nonverbal communication: Spontaneous and symbolic aspects. *American Behavioral Scientist, 31,* 341–354.

Buck, R. (1991). Social factors in facial display and communication: A reply to Chovil and others. *Journal of Nonverbal Behavior, 15,* 155–161.

Buck, R. (1993). Emotional communication, emotional competence, and physical illness: A developmental–interactionist view. In H. C. Traue & J. W. Pennebaker (Eds.), *Emotion, inhibition, and health.* Seattle: Hogrefe & Hubner.

Buck, R. (1994). Social and emotional functions in facial expression and communication: The read-out hypothesis. *Biological Psychology, 38,* 95–115.

Buck, R., & Duffy, R. (1980). Nonverbal communication of affect in brain-damaged patients. *Cortex, 16,* 351–362.

Buck, R., Savin, V., Miller, R. E., & Caul, W. F. (1972). Nonverbal communication of affect in humans. *Journal of Personality and Social Psychology, 23,* 362–371.

Bugental, D. E., Love, L. R., & Gianetto, R. M. (1971). Perfidious feminine faces. *Journal of Personality and Social Psychology, 17,* 314–318.

Butler, D., & Geis, F. L. (1990). Nonverbal affect responses to male and female leaders: Implications for leadership evaluations. *Journal of Personality and Social Psychology, 58,* 48–59.

Cacioppo, J. T., Klein, D. J., Berntson, G. G., & Hatfield, E. (1993). The psychophysiology of emotion. In M. Lewis & J. M. Haviland (Eds.), *Handbook of emotions.* New York: Guilford.

Camras, L. A., Holland, E. A., & Patterson, M. J. (1993). Facial expression. In M. Lewis & J. M. Haviland (Eds.), *Handbook of emotions.* New York: Guilford.

Cappella, J. N. (1981). Mutual influence in expressive behavior: Adult–adult and infant–adult dyadic interaction. *Psychological Bulletin, 89,* 101–132.

Carroll, J. M., & Russell, J. A. (1996). Do facial expressions signal specific emotions? Judging emotion from the face in context. *Journal of Personality and Social Psychology, 70,* 205–218.

Carroll, J. M., & Russell, J. A. (1997). Facial expressions in Hollywood's portrayal of emotion. *Journal of Personality and Social Psychology, 72,* 164–176.

Cherulnik, P., D., Donley, K. A., Wiewel, T. S. R., & Miller, S. R. (2001). Charisma is contagious: The effect of leaders' charisma on observers' affect. *Journal of Applied Social Psychology, 31,* 2149–2159.

Chovil, N. (1991). Social determinants of facial displays. *Journal of Nonverbal Behavior, 15,* 141–154.

Chovil, N. (1991/1992). Discourse-oriented facial displays in conversation. *Research on Language and Social Interaction, 25,* 163–194.

Cline, M. (1956). The influence of social context on the perception of faces. *Journal of Personality, 25,* 142–158.

Coats, E. J., Feldman, R. S., & Philippot, P. (1999). The influence of television on children's nonverbal behavior. In P. Philippot, R. S. Feldman, & E. J. Coats (Eds.), *The social context of nonverbal behavior.* Cambridge, UK: Cambridge University Press.

Coleman, J. D. (1949). Facial expressions of emotions. *Psychological Monographs, 63* (1, Whole No. 296).

Cornelius, R. R. (1996). *The science of emotion: Research and tradition in the psychology of emotion.* Upper Saddle River, NJ: Prentice-Hall.

Darwin, C. R. (1872). *The expression of the emotions in man and animals.* London: John Murray.

Dimberg, U. (1982). Facial reaction to facial expressions. *Psychophysiology, 19,* 643–647.

Dimberg, U., Thunberg, M., & Elmehed, K. (2000). Unconscious facial reactions to emotional facial expressions. *Psychological Science, 11,* 86–89.

Duclos, S. E., Laird, J. D., Schneider, E., Sexter, M., Stern, L., & Van Lighten, O. (1989). Emotion-specific effects of facial expressions and postures on emotional experience. *Journal of Personality and Social Psychology, 57,* 100–108.

Dunlap, K. (1927). The role of eye-muscles and mouth-muscles in the expression of the emotions. *Genetic Psychology Monographs, 2,* 199–233.

Eibl-Eibesfeldt, I. (1974). *Love and hate: The natural history of behavior patterns.* New York: Schocken.

Ekman, P. (Ed.). (1973). *Darwin and facial expression.* New York: Academic Press.

Ekman, P. (1979). About brows: Emotional and conversational signals. In V. von Cranach, K. Foppa, W. Lepenies, & D. Ploog (Eds.), *Human ethology.* Cambridge: Cambridge University Press.

Ekman, P. (1982). Methods for measuring facial action. In K. R. Scherer & P. Ekman (Eds.), *Handbook of methods in nonverbal behavior research.* Cambridge: Cambridge University Press.

Ekman, P., Davidson, R. J., & Friesen, W. V. (1990). The Duchenne smile: Emotional expression and brain physiology: II. *Journal of Personality and Social Psychology, 58,* 342–353.

Ekman, P., & Friesen, W. V. (1969). The repertoire of nonverbal behavior: Categories, origins, usage, and coding. *Semiotica, 1,* 49–98.

Ekman, P., & Friesen, W. V. (1971). Constants across cultures in the face and emotion. *Journal of Personality and Social Psychology, 17,* 124–129.

Ekman, P., & Friesen, W. V. (1975). *Unmasking the face.* Englewood Cliffs, NJ: Prentice-Hall.

Ekman, P., & Friesen, W. V. (1978). *The Facial Action Coding System: A technique for the measurement of facial movement.* Palo Alto: Consulting Psychologists Press.

Ekman, P., & Friesen, W. V. (1982). Felt, false, and miserable smiles. *Journal of Nonverbal Behavior, 6,* 238–252.

Ekman, P., & Friesen, W. V. (1986). A new pan-cultural facial expression of emotion. *Motivation and Emotion, 10,* 159–168.

Ekman, P., Friesen, W. V., & Ancoli, S. (1980). Facial signs of emotional experience. *Journal of Personality and Social Psychology, 39,* 1125–1134.

Ekman, P., Friesen, W. V., & Ellsworth, P. (1982a). Does the face provide accurate information? In P. Ekman (Ed.), *Emotion in the human face* (2nd ed.). Cambridge: Cambridge University Press.

Ekman, P., Friesen, W. V., & Ellsworth, P. (1982b). Methodological decisions. In P. Ekman (Ed.), *Emotion in the human face* (2nd ed.). Cambridge: Cambridge University Press.

Ekman, P., Friesen, W. V., & Ellsworth, P. (1982c). What are the relative contributions of facial behavior and contextual information to the judgment of emotion? In P. Ekman (Ed.), *Emotion in the human face* (2nd ed.). Cambridge: Cambridge University Press.

Ekman, P., Friesen, W. V., & O'Sullivan, M. (1988). Smiles when lying. *Journal of Personality and Social Psychology, 54,* 414–420.

Ekman, P., Friesen, W. V., O'Sullivan, M., Chan, A., Diacoyanni-Tarlatzis, I., Heider, K., Krause, R., LeCompte, W. A., Pitcairn, T., Ricci-Bitti, P. E., Scherer, K., Tomita, M., & Tzavaras, A. (1987). Universals and cultural differences in the judgments of facial expressions of emotion. *Journal of Personality and Social Psychology, 53,* 712–717.

Ekman, P., Hager, J. C., & Friesen, W. V. (1981). The symmetry of emotional and deliberate facial actions. *Psychophysiology, 18,* 101–106.

Ekman, P., Levenson, R. W., & Friesen, W. V. (1983). Autonomic nervous system activity distinguishes among emotions. *Science, 221,* 1208–1210.

Ekman, P., Matsumoto, D., & Friesen, W. V. (1997). Facial expression in affective disorders. In P. Ekman & E. Rosenberg (Eds.), *What the face reveals: Basic and applied studies of spontaneous expression using the Facial Action Coding System (FACS).* New York: Oxford University Press.

Ekman, P., & Oster, H. (1982). Review on research, 1970–1980. In P. Ekman (Ed.), *Emotion in the human face* (2nd ed.). Cambridge: Cambridge University Press.

Ekman, P., & Rosenberg, E. (Eds.). (1997). *What the face reveals: Basic and applied studies of spontaneous expression using the Facial Action Coding System (FACS).* New York: Oxford University Press.

Ekman, P., Sorenson, E. R., & Friesen, W. V. (1969). Pan-cultural elements in facial displays of emotions. *Science, 164,* 86–88.

Elfenbein, H. A., & Ambady, N. (2002). On the universality and cultural specificity of emotion recognition: A meta-analysis. *Psychological Bulletin, 128,* 203–235.

Elfenbein, H. A., & Ambady, N. (2003). When familiarity breeds accuracy: Cultural exposure and facial emotion recognition. *Journal of Personality and Social Psychology, 85,* 276–290.

Ellis, C. (1991). Sociological introspection and emotional experience. *Symbolic Interaction, 14,* 23–50.

Ellis, C., & Weinstein, E. (1986). Jealousy and the social psychology of emotional experience. *Journal of Social and Personal Relationships, 3,* 337–357.

Feleky, A. M. (1914). The expression of emotions. *Psychological Review, 21,* 33–41.

Fernández-Dols, J. M., & Carroll, J. M. (1997). Is the meaning perceived in facial expression independent of its context? In J. A. Russell & J. M. Fernández-Dols (Eds.), *The psychology of facial expression*. Paris: Cambridge University Press.

Fernández-Dols, J. M., & Ruiz-Belda, M. A. (1995). Are smiles a sign of happiness? Gold medal winners at the Olympic Games. *Journal of Personality and Social Psychology, 69,* 1113–1119.

Fernández-Dols, J. M., Sanchez, F., Carrera, P., & Ruiz-Belda, M A. (1997). Are spontaneous expressions and emotions linked? An experimental test of coherence. *Journal of Nonverbal Behavior, 21,* 163–177.

Field, T. (1982). Individual differences in the expressivity of neonates and young infants. In R. S. Feldman (Ed.), *Development of nonverbal behavior in children.* New York: Springer-Verlag.

Field, T. (2002). Early interactions between infants and their postpartum depressed mothers. *Infant Behavior & Development, 25,* 25–29.

Fox, N. A., & Davidson, R. J. (1988). Patterns of brain electrical activity during facial signs of emotion in ten-month-old infants. *Developmental Psychology, 14,* 230–236.

Frank, M. G., Ekman, P., & Friesen, W. V. (1993). Behavioral markers and recognizability of the smile of enjoyment. *Journal of Personality and Social Psychology, 64,* 83–93.

Frank, M. G., & Stennett, J. (2001). The forced-choice paradigm and the perception of facial expressions of emotion. *Journal of Personality and Social Psychology, 80,* 75–85.

Fridlund, A. J. (1991). Sociality of solitary smiling: Potentiation by an implicit audience. *Journal of Personality and Social Psychology, 60,* 229–240.

Fridlund, A. J. (1994). *Human facial expression: An evolutionary view.* San Diego: Academic Press.
Fridlund, A. J. (1997). The new ethology of human facial expressions. In J. A. Russell & J. M. Fernández-Dols (Eds.), *The psychology of facial expression.* Paris: Cambridge University Press.

Fridlund, A. J., Ekman, P., & Oster, H. (1987). Facial expressions of emotion: Review of literature, 1970–1983. In A. W. Siegman & S. Feldstein (Eds.), *Nonverbal behavior and communication* (2nd ed.). Hillsdale, NJ: Erlbaum.

Friedman, H. S., & Booth-Kewley, S. (1987). Personality, Type A behavior, and coronary heart disease: The role of emotional expression. *Journal of Personality and Social Psychology, 53,* 783–792.

Friedman, H. S., DiMatteo, M. R., & Mertz, T. I. (1980). Nonverbal communication on television news: The facial expressions of broadcasters during coverage of a presidential election campaign. *Personality and Social Psychology Bulletin, 6,* 427–435.

Friedman, H. S., Hall, J. A., & Harris, M. J. (1985). Type A behavior, nonverbal expressive style, and health. *Journal of Personality and Social Psychology, 48,* 1299–1315.

Gifford, R. (1994). A lens-mapping framework for understanding the encoding and decoding of interpersonal dispositions in nonverbal behavior. *Journal of Personality and Social Psychology, 66,* 398–412.

Gosselin, P., Perron, M., Legault, M., & Campanella, P. (2002). Children's and adults' knowledge of the distinction between enjoyment and nonenjoyment smiles. *Journal of Nonverbal Behavior, 26,* 83–108.

Guégen, N., & deGail, M. (2003). The effect of smiling on helping behavior: Smiling and good samaritan behavior. *Communication Reports, 16,* 133–140.

Hager, J. C., & Ekman, P. (1985). The asymmetry of facial actions is inconsistent with models of hemispheric specialization. *Psychophysiology, 22,* 307–318.

Haggard, E. A., & Isaacs, F. S. (1966). Micromomentary facial expressions as indicators of ego mechanisms in psychotherapy. In L. A. Gottschalk & A. H. Auerback (Eds.), *Methods of research in psychotherapy.* New York: Appleton-Century-Crofts.

Halberstadt, A. G. (1986). Family socialization of emotional expression and nonverbal communication styles and skills. *Journal of Personality and Social Psychology, 51,* 827–836.

Halberstadt, A. G., Hayes, C. W., & Pike, K. M. (1988). Gender and gender role differences in smiling and communication consistency. *Sex Roles, 19,* 589–604.

Hall, J. A. (1984). *Nonverbal sex differences: Communication accuracy and expressive style*. Baltimore: Johns Hopkins University Press.

Hansen, C. H., & Hansen, R. D. (1988). Finding the face in the crowd: An anger superiority effect. *Journal of Personality and Social Psychology, 54*, 917–924.

Harker, L., & Keltner, D. (2001). Expressions of positive emotion in women's college yearbook pictures and their relationship to personality and life outcomes across adulthood. *Journal of Personality and Social Psychology, 80*, 112–124.

Harrigan, J. A., & O'Connell, D. M. (1996). How do you look when feeling anxious? Facial displays of anxiety. *Personality & Individual Differences, 21*, 205–212.

Hart, A. J. (1995). Naturally occurring expectation effects. *Journal of Personality and Social Psychology, 68*, 109–115.

Hatfield, E., Cacioppo, J. T., & Rapson, R. (1994). *Emotional contagion*. Cambridge, UK: Cambridge University Press.

Hess, U., & Kleck, R. E. (1990). Differentiating emotion elicited and deliberate emotional facial expressions. *European Journal of Social Psychology, 20*, 369–385.

Hinsz, V. B., & Tomhave, J. A. (1991). Smile and (half) the world smiles with you, frown and you frown alone. *Personality and Social Psychology Bulletin, 17*, 586–592.

Izard, C. E. (1971). *The face of emotion*. New York: Appleton-Century-Crofts.

Izard, C. E. (1979). *The maximally discriminative facial movement coding system*. Unpublished manuscript, University of Delaware.

Izard, C. E. (1990). Facial expressions and the regulation of emotions. *Journal of Personality and Social Psychology, 58*, 487–498.

Jones, S. S., Collins, K., & Hong, H. (1991). An audience effect on smile production in 10-month-old infants. *Psychological Science, 2*, 45–49.

Jorgenson, D. O. (1978). Nonverbal assessment of attitudinal affect with the smile-return technique. *Journal of Social Psychology, 106*, 173–179.

Kaiser, S., & Wehrle, T. (1992). Automated coding of facial behavior in human–computer interactions with FACS. *Journal of Nonverbal Behavior, 16*, 65–140.

Katsikitis, M. (Ed.). (2002). *The human face: Measurement and meaning*. City: Kluwer.

Keltner, D. (1995). Signs of appeasement: Evidence for the distinct displays of embarrassment, amusement, and shame. *Journal of Personality and Social Psychology, 68*, 441–454.

King, L. A., & Emmons, R. A. (1990). Conflict over emotional expression: Psychological and physical correlates. *Journal of Personality and Social Psychology, 58*, 864–877.

Knutson, B. (1996). Facial expressions of emotion influence interpersonal trait inferences. *Journal of Nonverbal Behavior, 20*, 165–182.

Kraut, R. E., & Johnston, R. E. (1979). Social and emotional messages of smiling: An ethological approach. *Journal of Personality and Social Psychology, 37*, 1539–1553.

Laird, J. D. (1974). Self-attribution of emotion: The effects of expressive behavior on the quality of emotional experience. *Journal of Personality and Social Psychology, 24*, 475–486.

Lanzetta, J. T., Cartwright-Smith, J., & Kleck, R. E. (1976). Effects of nonverbal dissimulation of emotional experience and autonomic arousal. *Journal of Personality and Social Psychology, 33*, 354–370.

Lanzetta, J. T., & Kleck, R. E. (1970). Encoding and decoding of nonverbal affect in humans. *Journal of Personality and Social Psychology, 16*, 12–19.

Lee, V., & Wagner, H. (2002). The effect of social presence on the facial and verbal expression of emotion and the interrelations among emotion components. *Journal of Nonverbal Behavior, 26*, 3–25.

LeResche, L. (1982). Facial expression in pain: A study of candid photographs. *Journal of Nonverbal Behavior, 7*, 46–56.

Lundqvist, D., Esteves, F., & Ohman, A. (1999). The face of wrath: Critical features for conveying facial threat. *Cognition and Emotion, 13,* 691–711.

Lundqvist, L. O. (1995). Facial EMG reactions to facial expressions: A case of facial emotional contagion? *Scandinavian Journal of Psychology, 36,* 130–141.

Lundy, B., Field, T., & Pickens, J. (1996). Newborns of mothers with depressive symptoms are less expressive. *Infant Behavior and Development, 19,* 419–424.

Malatesta, C. Z., Jonas, R., & Izard, C. E. (1987). The relation between low facial expressibility during emotional arousal and somatic symptoms. *British Journal of Medical Psychology, 60,* 169–180.

Matsumoto, D. (1987). The role of facial response in the experience of emotion: More methodological problems and a meta-analysis. *Journal of Personality and Social Psychology, 52,* 769–774.

Matsumoto, D. (1989). Face, culture, and judgments of anger and fear: Do the eyes have it? *Journal of Nonverbal Behavior, 13,* 171–188.

Matsumoto, D. (1992). American-Japanese cultural differences in the recognition of universal facial expressions. *Journal of Cross-Cultural Psychology, 23,* 72–84.

Matsumoto, D., & Ekman, P. (1989). American-Japanese cultural differences in intensity ratings of facial expressions of emotion. *Motivation and Emotion, 13,* 143–157.

Matsumoto, D., LeRoux, J., Wilson-Cohn, C., Raroque, J., Kooken, K., Ekman, P., Yrizarry, N., Loewinger, S., Uchida, H., Yee, A., Amo, L., & Goh, A. (2000). A new test to measure emotion recognition ability: Matsumoto and Ekman's Japanese and Caucasian Brief Affect Recognition Test (JACBART). *Journal of Nonverbal Behavior, 24,* 179–209.

McIntosh, D. N., Zajonc, R. B., Vig, P. S., & Emerick, S. W. (1997). Facial movement, breathing, temperature, and affect: Implications of the Vascular Theory of Emotional Efference. *Cognition and Emotion, 11,* 171–195.

Mullen, B. (1986). Newscasters' facial expressions and voting behavior of viewers: Can a smile elect a president? *Journal of Personality and Social Psychology, 51,* 291–295.

Munn, N. L. (1940). The effect of knowledge of the situation upon the judgment of emotion from facial expression. *Journal of Abnormal and Social Psychology, 35,* 324–338.

Murphy, S. T., & Zajonc, R. B. (1993). Affect, cognition, and awareness: Affective priming with optimal and suboptimal stimulus exposures. *Journal of Personality and Social Psychology, 64,* 723–739.

Nicholls, M. E. R., Wolfgang, B. J., Clode, D., & Lindell, A. K. (2002). The effect of left and right poses on the expression of facial emotion. *Neuropsychologia, 40,* 1662–1665.

Notarius, C. I., & Levenson, R. W. (1979). Expressive tendencies and physiological response to stress. *Journal of Personality and Social Psychology, 37,* 1204–1210.

Osgood, C. E. (1966). Dimensionality of the semantic space for communication via facial expressions. *Scandinavian Journal of Psychology, 7,* 1–30.

Patrick, C. J., Craig, K. D., & Prkachin, K. M. (1986). Observer judgments of acute pain: Facial action determinants. *Journal of Personality and Social Psychology, 50,* 1291–1298.

Prkachin, K. M., & Craig, K. D. (1995). Expressing pain: The communication and interpretation of facial pain signals. *Journal of Nonverbal Behavior, 19,* 191–205.

Redican, W. K. (1982). An evolutionary perspective on human facial displays. In P. Ekman (Ed.), *Emotion in the human face* (2nd ed.). Cambridge: Cambridge University Press.

Riggio, R. E., & Friedman, H. S. (1986). Impression formation: The role of expressive behavior. *Journal of Personality and Social Psychology, 50,* 421–427.

Rinn, W. E. (1984). The neuropsychology of facial expression: A review of the neurological and psychological mechanisms for producing facial expressions. *Psychological Bulletin, 95,* 52–77.

Rozin, P., Lowery, U., & Ebert, R. (1994). Varieties of disgust faces and the structure of disgust. *Journal of Personality and Social Psychology, 66,* 870–881.

Ruiz-Belda, M., Fernández-Dols, J., Carrera, P., & Barchard, K. (2003). Spontaneous facial expressions of happy bowlers and soccer fans. *Cognition and Emotion, 17,* 315–326.

Russell, J. A. (1994). Is there universal recognition of emotion from facial expression? *Psychological Bulletin, 115,* 102–141.

Russell, J. A., Bachorowski, J., & Fernández-Dols, J. (2003). Facial and vocal expressions of emotion. *Annual Review of Psychology, 54,* 329–349.

Russell, J. A., & Fernández-Dols, J. M. (1997). *The psychology of facial expression.* Paris: Cambridge University Press.

Savitsky, J. C., Izard, C. E., Kotsch, W. E., & Christy, L. (1974). Aggressor's response to the victim's facial expression of emotion. *Journal of Research on Personality, 7,* 346–357.

Savitsky, J. C., & Sim, M. E. (1974). Trading emotions: Equity theory of reward and punishment. *Journal of Communication, 24,* 140–146.

Scherer, K. R., & Ceschi, G. (2000). Criteria for emotion recognition from verbal and nonverbal expression: Studying baggage loss in the airport. *Personality and Social Psychology Bulletin, 26,* 327–339.

Schlosberg, H. (1954). Three dimensions of emotion. *Psychological Review, 61,* 81–88.

Secord, P. F., Dukes, W. F., & Bevan, W. (1959). Personalities in faces: I. An experiment in social perceiving. *Genetic Psychology Monographs, 49,* 231–279.

Skinner, M., & Mullen, B. (1991). Facial asymmery in emotional expression: A meta-analysis of research. *British Journal of Social Psychology, 30,* 113–124.

Smith, W. J., Chase, J., & Lieblich, A. K. (1974). Tongue showing: A facial display of humans and other primate species. *Semiotica, 11,* 201–246.

Solomon, H., Solomon, L. Z., Arnone, M. M., Maur, B. J., Reda, R. M., & Roth, E. O. (1981). Anonymity and helping. *Journal of Social Psychology, 113,* 37–43.

Soussignan, R. (2002). Duchenne smile, emotional experience, and autonomic reactivity: A test of the facial feedback hypothesis. *Emotion, 2,* 52–74.

Spitz, R. A., & Wolf, K. M. (1946). The smiling response: A contribution to the ontogenesis of social relations. *Genetic Psychology Monographs, 34,* 57–125.

Stepper, S., & Strack, F. (1993). Proprioceptive determinants of emotional and nonemotional feelings. *Journal of Personality and Social Psychology, 64,* 211–220.

Strack, F., Martin, L. L., & Stepper, S. (1988). Inhibiting and facilitating conditions of the human smile: A nonobtrusive test of the facial feedback hypothesis. *Journal of Personality and Social Psychology, 54,* 768–777.

Strack, F., & Neumann, R. (2000). Furrowing the brow may undermine perceived fame: The role of facial feedback in judgments of celebrity. *Personality and Social Psychology Bulletin, 26,* 762–768.

Surakka, V., & Hietanen, J. K. (1998). Facial and emotional reactions to Duchenne and non-Duchenne smiles. *International Journal of Psychophysiology, 29,* 23–33.

ten Cate, C. (2002). Posing as professor: Laterality in posing orientation for portraits of scientists. *Journal of Nonverbal Behavior, 26,* 175–192.

Thompson, D. F., & Meltzer, L. (1964). Communication of emotional intent by facial expression. *Journal of Abnormal and Social Psychology, 68,* 129–135.

Tidd, K., & Lockard, J. (1978). Monetary significance of the affiliative smile: A case of reciprocal altruism. *Bulletin of the Psychonomic Society, 11,* 344–346.

Tomkins, S. S. (1962–1963). *Affect, imagery, consciousness* (Vols. 1 and 2). New York: Springer.

Tourangeau, R., & Ellsworth, P. C. (1979). The role of facial response in the experience of emotion. *Journal of Personality and Social Psychology, 37,* 1519–1531.

Tracy, J. L., & Robins, R. W. (2004). Show your pride: Evidence for a discrete emotion expression. *Psychological Science, 15*, 194–197.

Wagner, H. L. (1993). On measuring performance in category judgment studies of nonverbal behavior. *Journal of Nonverbal Behavior, 17*, 3–28.

Wagner, H., & Lee, V. (1999). Facial behavior alone and in the presence of others. In P. Philoppot, R. S. Feldman, & E. J. Coats (Eds.), *The social context of nonverbal behavior.* Cambridge, UK: Cambridge University Press.

Wagner, H. L., & Smith, J. (1991). Facial expressions in the presence of friends and strangers. *Journal of Nonverbal Behavior, 15*, 201–214.

Why is this man smiling? (1989, September 18). *Time*, p. 34.

Zajonc, R. B. (1985). Emotion and facial efference: A theory reclaimed. *Science, 228*, 15–21.

Zuckerman, M. (1986). On the meaning and implications of facial prominence. *Journal of Nonverbal Behavior, 10*, 215–229.

Zuckerman, M., DePaulo, B. M., & Rosenthal, R. (1981). Verbal and nonverbal communication of deception. In L. Berkowitz (Ed.), *Advances in experimental social psychology.* (Vol. 14). New York: Academic Press.

Zuckerman, M., Hall, J. A., DeFrank, R. S., & Rosenthal, R. (1976). Encoding and decoding of spontaneous and posed facial expressions. *Journal of Personality and Social Psychology, 34*, 966–977.

Zuckerman, M., & Kieffer, S. C. (1994). Race differences in face-ism: Does facial prominence imply dominance? *Journal of Personality and Social Psychology, 66*, 86–92.

Chapter 10

THE EFFECTS OF EYE BEHAVIOR ON HUMAN COMMUNICATION

He speaketh not; and yet there lies
A conversation in his eyes.

—HENRY WADSWORTH LONGFELLOW

Throughout history, we have been preoccupied with the eye and its effects on human behavior. Do you recall the last time you heard or read one of these phrases?

"She could look right through you."

"It was an icy stare."

"He's got shifty eyes."

"Did you see the gleam in his eye?"

"We're seeing eye to eye now."

"He looked like the original Evil Eye."

"His eyes shot daggers across the room."

"She could kill with a glance."

It is common to associate various eye movements with a wide range of human expressions: Downward glances are associated with modesty; wide eyes with frankness, wonder, naivete, or terror; generally immobile facial muscles and a rather constant stare with coldness; and eyes rolled upward with fatigue or a suggestion that another's behavior is a bit weird. What attribution would you make about the eye shown in Figure 10-1?

Our society has established a number of eye-related norms. For example, we do not look too long at strangers in public places; we are not supposed to look at various body parts except under certain conditions, and so on.

Our fascination with eyes has led to the exploration of almost every conceivable feature of the eyes (size, color, position) and surrounding parts (eyebrows, rings, wrinkles). Eye rings are found mainly in other animals, but some speculate that our eyebrows are residual rings raised during surprise or fear and lowered for focus during threat and anger.

FIGURE 10-1

The human eye.

Eye patches are the colored eyelids sometimes seen in primates. These patches are not a part of the natural human communicative repertoire, although women often use eyeliner and eyeshadow to achieve a similar effect. Another nonhuman feature that has received scholarly attention is eyespots, eye-shaped images located on other body parts. These can be seen on peacock feathers, butterflies, and fish.

Researchers have examined the degree to which eyes open as a reflection of various emotional states. Some feel that excessive blinking may be associated with various stages of anxiety—as if attempting to cut off reality. Psychiatrists report that some patients blink up to 100 times per minute; normal blinking, needed to lubricate and protect the eyeball, occurs about 6 to 10 times per minute in adults. Some evidence shows that when a person is attentive to objects in the environment or deep in concentrated thought, the blinking rate decreases.

Further diversity in the significance of the eyes comes from research on eye color. Blue eyes are a genetically based marker for inhibition and shyness (Rosenberg & Kagan, 1987). Some eye-related behaviors occur without much conscious awareness, such as the crinkles around the eyes when a person is feeling genuine enjoyment, but others are used very deliberately. An example of the latter is the "eye flash" that is used to emphasize particular words, usually adjectives (the eyelids are briefly opened without the accompanying involvement of the eyebrows, for less than a second (Walker & Trimboli, 1983). (The "eyebrow flash" is a different gesture; see chapter 2.)

Of the many eye-related topics of inquiry, this chapter focuses on two: The first is known by such terms as *eye contact, mutual glances, visual interaction, gazing,* or *line of regard;* the other concerns *pupil dilation and constriction* under various social conditions.

GAZE AND MUTUAL GAZE

We begin by looking at the terminology we have chosen: *gaze* and *mutual gaze* (Argyle & Cook, 1976; Kleinke, 1986; Rutter, 1984). *Gaze* refers to an individual's looking behavior, which may or may not be at the other person; *mutual gaze* refers to a situation in which the two interactants are looking at each other, usually in the region of the face (see Figure 10-2). Eye contact (looking specifically in each other's eyes) does not seem to be reliably distinguished by receivers or observers from gazing at the area surrounding the eyes (von Cranach & Ellgring, 1973). In fact, much of what is considered "looking someone in the eye" is a series of rapid, repeated scans of several parts of the face. In one case, an eyemark camera recorded 18 different fixation points for a listener who was apparently maintaining a steady gaze. Indeed, if someone did look fixedly, without moving the eyes, the impression would be one of vacant staring. Gaze and mutual gazing, however, can be reliably assessed. At a distance of 3 meters, face-directed gazing can be distinguished;

FIGURE 10-2

Mutual gaze.

TABLE 10-1   **Amount of Gazing in Two-Person Conversations**

	(%)	(%)	(%)	(%)	(%) MUTUAL	AVERAGE LENGTH OF GAZE	AVERAGE LENGTH OF MUTUAL GAZE
Nielsen	50*	8–73	38	62	—	—	—
Argyle & Ingham	61	—	41	75	31	2.95 sec.	1.18 sec.

* Percentages reflect the amount of time gazing relative to the total interaction time.

shifting the direction of one's gaze by 1 centimeter can reliably be detected from a distance of 1 meter.

We know we do not look at the other person during the entire time we are talking to him or her, nor do we avert our gaze 100% of the time. What are considered normal gazing patterns? Obviously, the answer varies according to the background and personalities of the participants, the topic, the other person's gazing patterns, objects of mutual interest in the environment, and so on. The speaker's fluency also affects gazing patterns. During fluent speech, speakers tend to look at listeners much more than during hesitant speech. We will discuss some of these factors in more detail later in this chapter. Keeping such qualifications in mind, we can get a general idea of normal gazing patterns from two studies of focused interaction between two people, shown in Table 10-1. The table shows that, on average, people gaze about half the time, that there is a huge range (indicating notable individual differences) in the amount of other-directed gaze, and that people gaze more while listening than while talking.

FUNCTIONS OF GAZING

Kendon (1967) has identified four functions of gazing: (1) *regulatory*—responses may be demanded or suppressed by looking; (2) *monitoring*—people may look at their partner to indicate the conclusions of thought units and to check their partner's attentiveness and reactions; (3) *cognitive*—people tend to look away when having difficulty processing information or deciding what to say; and (4) *expressive*—the degree and nature of involvement or arousal may be revealed through looking.

Our discussion follows a similar pattern:

1. Regulating the flow of communication
2. Monitoring feedback
3. Reflecting cognitive activity
4. Expressing emotions
5. Communicating the nature of the interpersonal relationship

These functions do not operate independently; that is, visual behavior not only sends information but it is also one of the primary methods for collecting it. Looking at the other person as you finish an utterance may not only tell the other it is his or her turn to speak but it is also an occasion to monitor feedback regarding the utterance.

REGULATING THE FLOW OF COMMUNICATION

Visual contact occurs when we want to signal that the communication channel is open. In some instances, eye gaze establishes a virtual *obligation* to interact. When you seek visual contact with your server at a restaurant, you are essentially indicating the communication channel is open and that you want to say something to him or her. You may recall instances when an instructor asked the class a question, and you were sure you did not know the answer. Establishing eye contact with the instructor was the last thing you wanted to do. You did not wish to signal the channel was open. We behave the same way when we see someone coming toward us whom we do not wish to talk to. As long as we can avoid eye gaze (in a seemingly natural way), it is much easier to avoid interaction. When confronting unknown others, we typically recognize them with a brief glance, but this initial glance is followed by the avoidance of gaze unless further contact is desired. A length of gaze that exceeds this glance of recognition is likely to signal desire to initiate a conversation (Cary, 1978a), and violation of this "civil inattention" norm (a term coined by Goffman, 1963) can produce negative feelings in the recipients (Zuckerman, Miserandino, & Bernieri, 1983). When you want to disavow social contact, your eye gaze will likely diminish. Thus we see mutual gazing in greeting sequences and greatly diminished gazing when we wish to bring an encounter to a halt.

Within a conversation, gazing at the other can command a nonverbal as well as verbal response. Because speakers gaze less than listeners, it is the speaker's gazing that determines moments of mutual looking. During these moments, there is a heightened likelihood that the listener will respond with a "listener response" (also called a "back-channel response") signifying attention (Bavelas, Coates, & Johnson, 2002). These responses can include smiles and other facial expressions, nods, and sounds such as "mm-hmm." Thus, the speaker's behavior is an important determinant of the timing of these responses. However, gazing is not the only determinant because listener responses also occur when people do not see each other, as on the telephone.

In addition to opening and closing the channel of communication and commanding responses from the other, eye behavior also regulates the flow of communication by providing turn-taking signals. Speakers generally look less often than listeners. But speakers do seem to glance during grammatical breaks, at the end of a thought unit or idea, and at the end of the utterance. Although glances at these junctures can signal the other person to assume the speaking role, we also use these glances to obtain feedback, to see how we are being received, and to see if the other will let us continue. This feedback function is addressed in the next section. The speaker/listener pattern is often choreographed as follows: As the speaker comes to the end of an utterance or thought unit, eye gaze toward the listener will continue as the listener assumes the speaking role; the listener will maintain gaze until the speaking role is assumed, when he or she will look away. Research on naturally emerging and appointed leaders in three-person (male) groups has found that the leader controls the flow of conversation using this cue pattern: The leader shows an increased tendency to engage in prolonged gaze at someone at the end of his or her utterances, as if inviting (possibly instructing) that person to take the floor. Thus, leaders do not only keep the floor for themselves more than others (Schmid Mast, 2002) but, in addition, they orchestrate who gets the floor and when (Kalma, 1992).

Gazing by the speaker at the completion of an utterance may help signal the yielding of a speaking turn, but listener-directed gazes do not always accompany the smooth exchange of speaking turns (Beattie, 1978a; Rutter, Stephenson, & White, 1978). On the other hand, sometimes the speaker glances at the listener when yielding a speaking turn, and the listener delays a response or fails to respond. Further, when a speaker begins an anticipated lengthy response, he or she is likely to delay gazing at the other beyond what would normally be expected. This pattern of adult gazing and looking away during speech seems to have its roots in early childhood development. Observations of the gazing patterns of 3- to 4-month-old infants and their parents revealed temporal similarities between their looking at and looking away sequence and the vocalizing and pausing sequences in adult conversations (Jaffe, Stern, & Peery, 1973).

Monitoring Feedback

When people seek feedback concerning the reactions of others, they gaze at the other person. If the other person is looking at you, it is usually interpreted as a sign of attention to what you are saying. Listener facial expressions and gazing suggest not only attention but also whether or not the listener is interested in what is being said. ("Good. Continue.") Being seen is a profound form of social acknowledgment that may be of crucial importance. A good example is the child on a playground who demands to be watched by his or her parent while doing feats on the monkey bars or slide. Being watched adds safety or security but, much more important, it infuses *meaning* into the child's actions. Without a witness, the actions feel pointless to the child—even unreal. The lack, or even incapacity, for feeling visually acknowledged may be associated with mental illness. People with borderline personality disorder sometimes report feeling invisible. On the other hand, under some circumstances being seen—especially in the sense of being *watched*—can feel like a violation of one's privacy and can be very uncomfortable, especially when one cannot look back at the other person.

People's need to watch and be watched is undoubtedly central to the phenomenon known as *emotional contagion,* whereby one person's mood or emotion is influenced by another's mood or emotion via subtle and mostly unconscious processes (Hatfield, Cacioppo, & Rapson, 1994). When people must communicate without seeing one another, a number of adaptations take place to compensate for this loss of information. For example, they engage in more verbal back-channel responses (responses such as "uh-huh" that are inserted while another is speaking) (Boyle, Anderson, & Newlands, 1994).

Effective monitoring via gaze may have dramatic consequences. In studies of physician–patient interaction, those physicians who engaged in more patient-directed gaze were more accurate at recognizing the patients' degree of psychosocial distress (Bensing, Kerssens, & van der Pasch, 1995), and there was a relation between engaging in more patient-directed gaze and obtaining more psychosocial information from the patient (van Dulmen, Verhaak, & Bilo, 1997).

Reflecting Cognitive Activity

Both listeners and speakers have a tendency to avoid gazing at others when they are trying to process difficult or complex ideas. This averted gaze (which may include closing the eyes) reflects a shift in attention from external to internal matters, as well as an effort to exclude external stimulation. People avoid gaze more on reflective questions than factual ones and on more difficult questions (more difficult in factual content, or more difficult in terms of the length of the temporal search required—as in "Name a professor you have currently" vs. "Name a professor you had two semesters ago") (Glenberg, Schroeder, & Robertson, 1998). Furthermore, when participants were required to answer factual questions either with their eyes closed or while looking directly at the experimenter, performance was better in the eyes-closed condition (Glenberg et al., 1998), thus demonstrating the functional utility of excluding external stimulation while engaging in difficult cognitive activity.

Bakan (Bakan, 1971; Bakan & Strayer, 1973) reported studies in which research participants were asked thought-provoking questions while eye movement was measured. It was found that people tended to look preferentially to the left or right while thinking. Typical questions were as follows:

- "How many letters are there in the word *Washington*?"
- "Multiply twelve by thirteen."
- "What is meant by the proverb 'It is better to have a bad peace than a good war'?"

Then, after classifying "right movers" and "left movers," they collected other data to further characterize the two groups. When a person moves his or her eyes in a particular direction, it is thought to reflect activity in the *opposite* hemisphere of the brain: Left hemisphere activity, often involving intellectual and linguistic tasks, is associated with rightward glances, whereas right hemisphere activity, often involving spatial or emotional processing, is associated with leftward glances (de Gennaro & Violani, 1988; Ehrlichman & Weinberger, 1978; Weisz & Adam, 1993; Wilbur & Roberts-Wilbur, 1985). Studies show that electroencephalic activity (EEG) increases in the hemisphere opposite to the direction of the eye movement, and such activity can actually be stimulated by the movements. Individuals vary in their leftward or rightward eye movement tendencies, with left movers being more susceptible to hypnosis, less scientifically oriented, more involved with feelings and inner experience, more creative, and more prone to psychosomatic symptoms and the psychological defenses of repression and denial.

Expressing Emotions

Sometimes a glance at the eye area provides us with a good deal of information about the emotion being expressed. For example, if we see tears we certainly would conclude the person is emotionally aroused, although without other cues we may not know whether the tears reflect grief, physical pain, joy, anger, or some complex blend of emotions. And as we indicate later, downcast or averted eyes are often associated with feelings of sadness, shame, or embarrassment. The extensive studies of Paul Ekman and Wallace Friesen have given us valuable insights into facial configurations for six common ("basic") emotions. The descriptions here pertain to the brow and eye area, and the photographs are from Ekman and Friesen's collection. As the photographs suggest, it may be difficult to judge what emotion is being expressed without being able to see the brows. Similarly, some expressions may be ambiguous unless the entire face can be seen. Also, in everyday interaction we are likely to see facial blends where the eyes tell one story and other parts of the face another. Recently, it has been shown that the direction in which the eyes are gazing has an influence on judgments of emotion in the face (Adams & Kleck, 2003).

Surprise

Brows are raised so they are curved and high. Skin below the brow is stretched. Eyelids are opened; the upper lid is raised, and the lower lid drawn down; and the white of the eye shows above the iris and often below as well.

Fear

Brows are raised and drawn together. The upper eyelid is raised, exposing the white of the eye, and the lower eyelid is tensed and drawn up.

Disgust

Disgust is shown primarily in the lower face and in the lower eyelids. Lines show below the lower lid, and the lid is pushed up but not tense. The brow is lowered, lowering the upper lid.

Anger

The brows are lowered and drawn together. Vertical lines appear between the brows. The lower lid is tensed and may or may not be raised. The upper lid is tense and may or may not be lowered by the action of the brow. The eyes have a hard stare and may have a bulging appearance.

Happiness

Happiness is shown primarily in the lower face and lower eyelids. The lower eyelid shows wrinkles below it and may be raised but is not tense. Crow's-feet wrinkles go outward from the outer corners of the eyes.

Sadness

The inner corners of the eyebrows are drawn up. The skin below the eyebrow is triangulated, with the inner corner up. The upper-eyelid inner corner is raised.

Only rarely have investigators tested accuracy in judging emotions from the eye area in isolation from the rest of the face. In the earliest study, 51 faces were used as stimuli for judges (Ekman, Friesen, & Tomkins, 1971). The eyes were better than the brows/forehead or lower face for the accurate perception of fear but less accurate for anger and disgust. More recently, Baron-Cohen, Wheelwright, and Jolliffe (1997) tested university students' accuracy at identifying 16 emotions and states, posed by an actress, separately for the eye area (including brows), mouth area, and whole face. The authors included "basic" emotions (such as angry, afraid, and happy) as well as "nonbasic" states (such as admiring, flirtatious, arrogant, and thoughtful). The eye region was not quite as accurately judged as the whole face for the basic emotions, but was indistinguishable for the nonbasic states (see Figure 10-3; answers to this judgment task are at the end of the chapter). Both of these regions were judged much more accurately than the mouth. Consistent with the Ekman et al. (1971) study, accuracy for the mouth region, although not superior to the eye region, was similar to that of the eye region for disgust and anger, and much lower than the eye region for fear.

FIGURE 10-3

Can you judge the emotions in these eyes? (a) happy or surprised, (b) angry or afraid, (c) sad or disgusted, (d) distressed or sad, (e) arrogant or guilty, (f) thoughtful or arrogant, (g) flirting or happy, (h) guilty or arrogant. (See answers at end of chapter.)

a

b

c

d

(Continued)

Figure 10-3   (Continued)

e

f

g

h

COMMUNICATING THE NATURE
OF THE INTERPERSONAL RELATIONSHIP

Gazing and mutual gazing are often indicative of the nature of the relationship between two interactants. Relationships characterized by different status levels may be reflected in the eye patterns; one example was given earlier—the way the leader in a group seems to pick the next speaker by gazing at him or her. Another indicator of status or dominance is the *visual dominance ratio*—the ratio of one's percentage of speaking time spent looking at the other to one's percentage of listening time spent looking at the other. Research on overall gazing levels as a function of status or dominance is not at all clear, however, despite the general belief that people high in "verticality" (status, dominance, or power) claim the lion's share of gazing (Hall, Coats, & Smith LeBeau, 2004). These findings are discussed further in chapter 12.

Several studies testify that we gaze more at people and things perceived as rewarding. Efran and Broughton (1966) found that males gazed more at other males with whom they had participated in a friendly conversation preceding an experiment and who nodded and smiled during the person's presentation. Exline and Eldridge (1967) found that the same verbal communication was decoded as being more favorable when it was associated with more eye gaze than when it was presented with less gaze. Exline and Winters (1965) report that people avoided the eyes of an interviewer and disliked him after he had commented unfavorably on their performance. And mothers of children who have difficult temperaments are reported to look at them less. It makes sense to predict that we will look more at those who like us, if for no other reason than to observe signs of approval and friendliness.

Mehrabian (1972) asked a group of people to imagine they liked another and to engage this person in conversation. Even in this role-playing situation, increased gazing was associated with increased liking. Mutual liking in the form of participants' rating of rapport was similarly related to gazing when interactants debated a controversial topic (Bernieri et al., 1996). Interestingly, when engaging in a more cooperative discussion, eye contact was not related to their rapport judgments.

Increased gazing is often considered in the context of a courtship relationship. The maintenance of mutual gaze longer than otherwise expected is a primary way of signaling desire for heightened intimacy. In movies, we can almost always predict when a first kiss is coming because the characters share a longer than expected mutual gaze. An increased amount of gaze can both signal a wish for more involvement and be an indication that heightened involvement has occurred. Indeed, several sources confirm an increase in gazing between two people who are seeking to develop a more intimate relationship. Rubin's (1970) analysis of engaged couples indicated more mutual gaze, and Kleinke and colleagues (1973) found that longer glances or reciprocated glances were perceived as an indicator of a longer relationship. It may be that the amount of gazing increases as relationships become more intimate, but it may also be true that after maintaining an intimate relationship for years, gazing may return to levels below those used during more intense stages of development.

Argyle and Dean (1965) proposed an intimacy equilibrium model to help explain why and how much people will gaze in an interpersonal interaction. This model suggests that intimacy is a function of the amount of eye gazing, physical proximity, intimacy of topic, and amount of smiling. Thus, gaze is part of a network of other behaviors that have important relations to each other in a total system reflective of the overall psychological intimacy in a given interaction. This model is most applicable to relationships still in the process of establishing themselves. Clearly, other variables might be inserted into the equation, for example, body orientation, the form of address used, tone of voice, facial expression, forward lean, and the like. The central idea behind this proposal is that as one component of the model is changed, one or more of the other components also will change—in the opposite direction as a form of compensation—in order to keep the overall intimacy at a constant, desired level. For example, if one person looks too much, the other may look less, move farther away, smile less, talk less about intimate matters, and so on, to reestablish the initial desired level of intimacy. Also, when one is forced to increase the implied intimacy of a behavior (for example, by standing close to others in a crowded elevator), one will compensate by gazing less, talking less or about personal topics, and so forth.

Although this compensatory model has received support, there are many occasions when, rather than compensate for the other's behavior, people will *reciprocate* it—for example, gazing will elicit gazing and smiling will elicit smiling. Again, context is important, as gazing (in public at any rate) is much more likely to be reciprocated when the gazer is also smiling (Patterson, Webb, & Schwartz, 2002). Several scholars have proposed alternatives to the intimacy equilibrium model (Cappella & Greene, 1982; Patterson, 1976). These theories argue that our tendency to exchange the same behavior (reciprocate) or to offset the other's behavior (compensate) is a result of the type and amount of arousal we feel. A general rule suggests that we tend to reciprocate or match the other's nonverbal behavior when the other's behavior is perceived by us as congruent with our expectations and preferences or when we want to initiate an upward (or downward) spiral in intimacy. When our partner's behavior is not congruent with our expectations and preferences, we are more likely to enact compensatory or offsetting behavior. (See also chapter 12.)

In cities, where it is necessary to interact closely with many strangers, people may stimulate conflicting tendencies with regard to the regulation of interpersonal cues. Tension produced by such contact (for example, standing in a packed subway) may promote compensatory behaviors including less gazing, less conversation, and so forth. However, urban life is sometimes also considered to be too impersonal, despite the large number of people present. Figure 10-4 shows a humorous solution to this problem.

When the relationship between the two communicators is characterized by negative attitudes, we might see a decrease in gazing and mutual gazing, but not always. This is because gaze, like touch, can sometimes serve more to intensify or highlight whatever feeling or intention is present at the moment than to communicate a specific message. Also, gaze does not occur in isolation from other cues—a threatening stare and a long, loving look may both be long, but the rest of the face is likely to be doing quite different things!

To illustrate one of the preceding points, in one study satisfied married couples tended to look at each other *less* than couples who were dissatisfied with their relationship, with this being particularly true when negative messages were exchanged (Noller, 1980). Increased gazing serves to emphasize the confrontational nature of the relationship while simultaneously providing a way to monitor each other's reactions during critical moments. This is a good example of how the immediate context can never be ignored when interpreting the meaning of nonverbal behavior.

FIGURE 10-4

Sometimes people need gaze reciprocation.

A hostile or aggressive orientation may also trigger the use of staring to produce anxiety in others. A gaze of longer than 10 seconds is likely to induce irritation (if not outright discomfort) in many situations; in one study drivers sped more quickly away from an intersection when stared at by a pedestrian (Ellsworth, Carlsmith, & Henson, 1972). Several studies confirm that mutual gaze is physiologically arousing. We can express our hostility toward another by visually and verbally ignoring him or her, especially when the other person knows we are deliberately doing so. But we can insult another person by looking at that person too much, that is, by not according him or her the public anonymity that each of us requires at times. Sometimes you can elicit aggressive behavior from others just because you happen to look too long at a stranger's behavior. Sometimes threats and aggressive motions can be elicited in zoo monkeys by human beings who stare at them too long.

Thus, if we are looking for a unifying thread to link gazing patterns motivated by positive and negative feelings toward the other, it would seem to be this: *People tend to look at those with whom they are interpersonally involved.* Gazing motivated by hostility or affection *both* suggest an interest and involvement in the interpersonal relationship. We must rely on contextual information and other verbal and nonverbal cues to decide whether to interpret extended gazing positively or negatively.

CONDITIONS INFLUENCING GAZING PATTERNS

DISTANCE

As suggested by intimacy equilibrium theory, gazing and mutual gazing often increase as the people interacting increase the physical distance between themselves. In this case, gazing psychologically reduces the distance between the communicators and also allows for better monitoring. Similarly, there may be less visual contact when the two parties feel too close in terms of physical distance, especially if they are not well acquainted. Reducing one's gaze in this situation, then, increases the psychological distance. Several studies by Aiello and colleagues found that extending the conversational distances to as much as 10 feet produced a steady increase in gazing for men, but for women, being beyond 6 feet from their interactant brought a sharp decline in their gazing (Aiello, 1972, 1977a). It is probable that because women prefer closer interaction distances (see chapter 5), they may find it difficult to define interactions at relatively great distances as normal and friendly and may react by ceasing their attempts to maintain involvement.

PHYSICAL CHARACTERISTICS

We would think that when interacting with a person who was perceived as disabled or stigmatized in some way (e.g., identified as an epileptic or made to look like an amputee), gaze would be less frequent. However, Kleck (1968) found the amount of gazing between normal and disabled interactants did not differ significantly from normal/normal interactions. Possible explanations are that in such situations, the normal person is seeking information that might suggest the proper mode of behavior, or the disabled person is a novel stimulus that arouses curiosity. These factors would counteract any tendency to avoid eye gaze. A subsequent study, however, found that when there was a strong possibility the nondisabled person would have to engage the disabled person in conversation, gaze avoidance increased. When conversation was not expected, people without disabilities tended to stare more at disabled persons than nondisabled (Thompson, 1982).

PERSONAL AND PERSONALITY CHARACTERISTICS

Some patterns have emerged in the relations between gazing patterns and personality traits. In actual interaction, of course, gaze patterns reflect the message sender's mood, intent, and situational factors as well as stable dispositions. There are definitely stereotypes about gaze and personality. Kleck and Nuessle (1968) showed a film of people looking at their partners either 15% or 80% of the time to observers, who were asked to select characteristics that typified the interactants. The 15% lookers were labeled as cold, pessimistic, cautious, defensive, immature, evasive, submissive, indifferent, and sensitive; the 80% lookers were seen as friendly, self-confident, natural, mature, and sincere.

Dominance as a personality trait does not appear to have a relation to overall gazing (Hall et al., 2004), but individual studies do produce interesting results. Dependent individuals seem to use eye behavior not only to communicate more positive attitudes but also to elicit such attitudes when they are not forthcoming (Exline & Messick, 1967). Dependent males made more eye gaze with a listener who provided them with few, as opposed to many, social reinforcers, whereas dominant males decreased their eye gaze with less reinforcing listeners. Kalma (1993) distinguished between two personality styles relating to dominance—sociable dominance and aggressive dominance. The sociably dominant person agrees strongly with statements such as "I have no problems talking in front of a group" and "No doubt I'll make a good leader"; the aggressively dominant person agrees strongly with statements such as "I quickly feel aggressive with people" and "I find it important to get my way." In an experimental setting, Kalma observed people who varied on these dominance styles and found that the socially dominant person engaged in more mutual gaze, whereas the aggressively dominant person engaged in more "looking around"—that is, showing disinterest in others.

Self-esteem and self-confidence are associated with gazing patterns. A study of attributions found that interviewees were rated by observers as having increasingly lower self-esteem as their gazing decreased (Droney & Brooks, 1993). Variations in gazing at another person during positive and negative feedback may indeed be related to self-esteem. When receiving favorable feedback on their performance, people with high self-esteem tended to gaze more, while negative feedback reduced their gazing behavior. But the pattern was reversed for those with low self-esteem. These people gazed more during feedback that criticized their performance than during feedback that complimented it (Greene & Frandsen, 1979).

Intelligence is also a trait people display in social interaction. Evidence shows that people who score higher on standard tests of cognitive ability (such as an IQ test) engage in more interpersonal gaze and responsiveness, and that perceivers who watch the people on videotape can use these cues to accurately judge intelligence levels (Murphy, Hall, & Colvin, 2003).

Other personality traits (as measured by self-report of the gazers, not as attributed by observers) have been associated with more gazing—for example extraversion, agreeableness, and openness (Berry & Hansen, 2000; Mobbs, 1968), although some studies do not find relations between gaze and personality. Gifford (1994), for example, failed to find associations between interpersonal gazing and trait measures of ambitiousness, gregariousness, warmth, unassumingness, laziness, aloofness, coldness, and arrogance.

Shyness is related to gazing behavior, but the relation can depend on whether the shy person is of a sociable or unsociable type. In a laboratory experiment, Cheek and Buss (1981) classified college students on both a shyness scale and a sociability scale and observed them in a getting-acquainted session. Although shy individuals engaged in less gaze overall (and also more self-touching and less talking), this effect was mainly present if the person was both shy (e.g., "I am socially somewhat awkward"; "I feel inhibited in social situations") *and* sociable (e.g., "I like to be with people"; "I prefer working with others rather than alone"). Thus the behavioral deficits associated with shyness appear mainly in shy people who crave social interaction; shy people who would just as soon be left alone behaved much like people who were not shy.

Social anxiety, another related concept, is also associated with less gaze; in one study in which socially anxious people were asked to present a viewpoint to two confederates, the socially anxious were especially likely to reduce gaze toward a confederate with opposing views compared to one with agreeing views (Farabee et al., 1993). In an experiment in which participants had choices of which face to look at on a computer screen, Mansell et al. (1999) found that socially anxious persons whose anxiety was heightened by being told they would be giving a public talk avoided faces that showed emotional expressions, preferring to give their visual attention to neutral-expression faces. Under such circumstances the socially anxious person may have an especially strong need to avoid the arousal engendered by emotional faces, which in turn may be related to a history of finding emotionally charged social interactions to be aversive. Highly anxious individuals also avert their eyes sooner from an extended facial display of anger compared to less anxious individuals (Rohner, 2002). Highly anxious individuals are especially quick to use gaze direction as a cue when the gazer has a fearful facial expression, suggesting that these individuals are especially visually attuned to evidence of threat in their environment (Mathews et al., 2003).

A number of research studies suggest special gazing patterns (usually less gaze) in some psychopathological conditions. For example, depressed patients are characterized by nonspecific gaze patterns and looking-down behaviors that revert to more normal patterns with clinical improvement (Schelde & Hertz, 1994). Mothers with depressive symptoms spend less time gazing at their infants, and their infants respond by averting gaze more than control infants (Field, 1995).

Clinicians and researchers on autism cite gaze aversion (among other social interaction deficits) as a characteristic of these patients (Adrien et al., 1993; Hutt & Ounsted, 1966; Walters, Barrett, & Feinstein, 1990), in addition to lack of ability to detect the direction of another's gaze (Senju et al., 2003) and failure to monitor a speaker's gaze direction and direct someone else's gaze via the pointing gesture (Baron-Cohen, Wheelwright, & Jolliffe, 1997). Baron-Cohen et al. (2001) reported that individuals with autism or Asperger's syndrome (related to autism) were less accurate overall than normally functioning participants in judging emotions from the eye region of the face, and Baron-Cohen, Wheelwright, and Jolliffe (1997) also found that the patients were especially impaired for nonbasic (i.e., more complex) expressions and when the eye region alone was being judged as opposed to the full face (see Figure 10-3 for the eye expressions used in this study). Because both groups had normal IQ levels, the result strongly suggests a specific impairment in the autism–Asperger's group with regard to processing information relating to the eyes.

Paranoid schizophrenic patients show a deficit in judging another's gaze direction that is consistent with everyday conceptions of paranoia: They are more likely than comparison subjects to perceive another as looking at them when the person is actually looking away (Rosse et al., 1994).

Finally, males and females differ in the use of gaze. As shown in many studies, females look at others during interaction more than males on almost all measures of gaze frequency, duration, and reciprocity—and such differences have been observed in infancy and early childhood as well as in adulthood (Hall, 1984; Leeb & Rejskind, 2004). (Sex differences are discussed further in chapter 12.)

Most of the results of these efforts to link gazing patterns to personality and/or personal characteristics may be accounted for by the following:

1. *The existing need for affiliation, involvement, or inclusion:* Those with high affiliative needs tend to glance and return glances more often or for longer durations.
2. *Other looking motivations:* Persons who are highly manipulative and/or need much information to control their environment (high Machiavellian types) predictably look more.
3. *The need to avoid unduly high levels of arousal caused by gazing (especially mutual gazing):* Autistic children, for instance, are thought to have a high level of arousal and avoid gaze in order to keep arousal down. The reduced gazing of shy/sociable people may also be related to the control of arousal.
4. *A feeling of shame or low self-esteem:* The lower level of gaze sometimes seen in adolescents may reflect the well-known uncertainties about ourselves that most experience during this period.

TOPICS AND TASKS

Common sense suggests that the topic being discussed and/or the task at hand affect the amount of gazing. We would expect, for instance, more gazing when the topic is happy rather than sad. And we would expect interactants who have not developed an intimate relationship to gaze less when discussing intimate topics, assuming other factors like the need for affiliation or inclusion are controlled. People also may gaze differently during competitive tasks and cooperative tasks. In one study, cooperators used longer gazes and mutual gazes to signal trust, liking, and honesty. Gazes also were used to aid coordination. Competitors, however, seemed to use frequent, short gazes to assess their partner's intentions while not giving away their own (Foddy, 1978).

Discussing topics that cause embarrassment, humiliation, shame, or guilt might be expected to engender less gazing at the other person. Looking away during such situations may be an effort to insulate oneself against threats, arguments, information, or even affection from the other party. When subjects were caused to fail at an anagram task and were publicly criticized for their work, they not only reported feeling embarrassed, but also the amount of gaze slipped from 30% to 18% (Modigliani, 1971). When people want to hide some aspect of their inner feelings, they may try to avoid visual contact—for example, in situations where they are trying to deceive a partner. Exline and his colleagues (1970) designed a fascinating (although possibly ethically suspect) experiment. A paid confederate induced research participants to cheat on an experimental task. Later the experimenter interviewed the participants with the supposed purpose of understanding and evaluating their problem-solving methods. With some participants, the experimenter grew increasingly suspicious during the interview and finally accused him or her of cheating and demanded an explanation. Participants included both those who scored high and low on tests of Machiavellianism. (A Machiavellian person uses cunning and shrewdness to

FIGURE 10-5

Gazing, Machiavellianism, and deception.

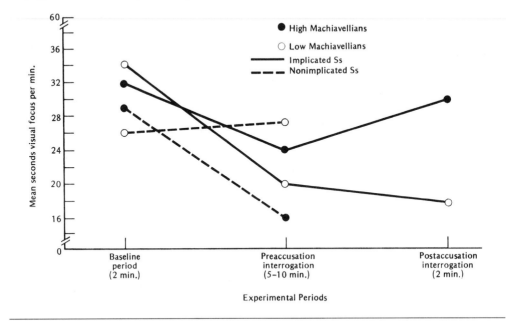

achieve a goal without much regard for how unscrupulous the means might be.) Figure 10-5 shows that the high Machiavellian participants used gazing to present the appearance of innocence after being accused of cheating; low Machiavellian participants, in contrast, continued to look away.

In the Bensing, Kerssens, and van der Pasch study mentioned earlier, physicians' average levels of gaze at patients were much greater when the patients were talking about social and emotional material than when talking about more physiological problems, and when the physicians were verbally conveying empathy or psychosocial interest. Patients were also more satisfied with their visits when the physicians gazed more.

Persuasion is another communicative task we often undertake. We know that gazing can add emphasis to a particular point, but Mehrabian and Williams (1969) found that a person trying to be persuasive gazes more overall. We do not know the actual relationship between attitude change in a listener and speaker gazing, but research shows that listeners do seem to judge speakers who gaze more as more persuasive, informed, truthful, sincere, and credible. Also, compliance with a request can be enhanced if the requester engages in more gaze within an appropriate range (Guéguen & Jacob, 2002).

The application of such findings in a simulated courtroom situation found that witnesses who testified by looking slightly downward rather than directly at their questioner were judged less credible—and the defendant for whom they were testifying was more likely to be judged guilty (Hemsley & Doob, 1978). In another important study, actors reenacted the actual verbal performances of surgery students during medical school oral examinations, using a nonverbal style marked either by direct gaze and a moderate speech rate or by indirect gaze and a slower speech rate. Surgery faculty from 46 medical institutions who judged the competency of these reenacted oral examinations gave significantly higher scores to the actor who used direct gaze and a moderate rate of speech, even though the answers were the same as in the other condition (Rowland-Morin et al., 1991). It is clear from these studies that in real-life situations the presence or absence of gaze can have a profound impact, yet the impact can be highly unfair or damaging: We would not want to be the honest witness, the sincere speaker, or the competent medical student who had the misfortune to gaze less than expected.

CULTURAL BACKGROUND AND RACIAL ATTITUDES

Eye behavior also varies according to the environment in which we learn social norms. Sometimes gazing patterns show differences between "contact" (e.g., Arab) and "non-contact" (e.g., northern European) cultures (see chapters 5, 8, and 13). Sometimes the differences may be in duration of gaze rather than frequency (e.g., it has been said that Swedes looks less frequently, but for longer periods, than the English). Sometimes *where* we observe gaze behavior reveals differences among cultures (e.g., looking more in public places). Sometimes there are cultural rules regarding whom you should or should not look at. One report says that in Kenya conversations between some men and their mothers-in-law are conducted by each party turning his or her back to the other. We may find different patterns within our own culture. Whites are found to gaze significantly more at their partners than African Americans do, and this difference may be especially pronounced with authority figures—a tendency that could create cross-racial misunderstanding. Some research shows African Americans and whites changing gazing patterns in cross-racial encounters, but the research is not consistent (Fehr & Exline, 1987; Halberstadt, 1985). Such findings underscore the variety of factors that may influence gaze in each encounter, and our cultural inclinations may be suppressed, neutralized, or emphasized by other forces attendant to the situation. Although cultural experiences may alter gazing patterns and the total amount of gaze, we may also find that perceived extremes in gaze elicit similar meanings in different cultures. For instance, too much gazing may signal anger, threat, or disrespect; too little may signal dishonesty, inattention, or shyness.

Because people often emit nonverbal behavior without conscious awareness, psychologists have suggested that nonverbal cues may sometimes be subtle indicators of social attitudes, especially those that may be denied or not consciously acknowledged, such as negative feelings toward minority groups (Crosby, Bromley, & Saxe, 1980; Word, Zanna, & Cooper, 1974). Dovidio and colleagues (1997) predicted that the amount of gaze directed by interviewees toward African American versus white interviewers would be related to the interviewees' racial prejudice as measured by an implicit attitudes task (based on reaction time when associating negative words to different racial groups). As predicted, interviewees who had displayed more racial bias on the implicit task gazed less at the African American than the white interviewer (and also blinked more, as predicted—blinking being associated with negative arousal and tension). The nonverbal cues were not related to explicit (and more reactive) paper-and-pencil reports of prejudice.

PUPIL DILATION AND CONSTRICTION

Most of us are aware that the pupils of the eyes constrict in the presence of bright light and dilate in the absence of light. In the early 1960s, however, Eckhard Hess and his colleagues at the University of Chicago renewed the interest of the scientific community in pupil dilation and constriction as a possible indicator of mental and emotional states. At one point, dozens of universities were conducting pupil dilation research, and advertising agencies were testing magazine ads, package designs, television pilot films, and television commercials using the results of Hess's pupil dilation measures.

In an early experiment, Hess and Polt (1960) presented five pictures to male and female subjects. Males' pupils dilated more than females' pupils in response to pictures of female nudes; females' pupils dilated more than males' to pictures of a partially clothed "muscle man," a woman with a baby, and a baby alone. Thus it seemed pupil dilation and interest value of the stimulus were related. Hess, Seltzer, and Shlien (1965) found that pupils of male homosexuals dilated more when viewing pictures of males than the pupils of heterosexual males, whose pupils dilated in response to female pictures. Studies since then have had similar results. Barlow (1969) preselected subjects who actively supported either liberal or conservative candidates. He photographed the pupil of the right eye while they watched slides of political figures. There seemed to be a perfect correlation between pupillary response and political attitudes, with dilation occurring for photographs of liked candidates and constriction occurring for disliked candidates.

Several of Hess's studies suggested that pupil response might be an index of attitudes; pupils dilate for positive attitudes and constrict for negative ones. His oft-cited finding supporting this theory was the constriction of the pupils of subjects who viewed pictures of concentration camp victims, dead soldiers, and a murdered gangster. In Hess's (1975a) words, "The changes in emotions and mental activity revealed by changes in pupil size are clearly associated with changes in attitude." Hess (1975b; Hess & Petrovich, 1987) continued to advocate this position, although he acknowledged the need for more research on the pupil's reaction to negative stimuli. He cited a study that showed photographs like those in Figure 10-6, where the woman's pupils were retouched to appear large in one photo and smaller in the other. Although male subjects did not tend to pick either picture as consistently more friendly or attractive, they tended to associate positive attributes with the woman who had larger pupils and negative attributes with the one with smaller pupils.

Hensley (1990) attempted to replicate Hess's work and obtained the responses of over 500 students to photographs of models with constricted and dilated pupils used by Hess. The students evaluated the photos on 22 characteristics, including attractiveness, social skills, persuasiveness, friendliness, and outgoingness. There were no statistically significant differences between photos of constricted and those of dilated pupils on any of the 22 characteristics—raising doubts about the strength of Hess's claim.

Woodmansee (1970) tried to improve on Hess's methodology and measuring instruments and found no support for pupil dilation and constriction as an index of attitudes toward African Americans. Hays and Plax (1971) found that their subjects' pupils dilated when they received supportive statements ("I am very much interested in your speech"), but constriction did not follow from nonsupportive statements ("I disagree completely

FIGURE 10-6

Some of Hess's stimulus photos with pupil dilation varied.

with the development of your speech"). Some research has found dilation in response to both positive *and* negative feedback (Janisse & Peavler, 1974; Partala & Surakka, 2003). Other research has found the reflex dilation reaction of the pupil to be associated with arousal, attentiveness, interest, and perceptual orientation, but not to be an attitudinal index. Thus the intriguing hypothesis that pupils can be used as a bidirectional indicator of attitudes appears not to be viable.

Even advertising agencies seem to have lost interest in pupils as an involuntary measure of viewer attitudes. Some of the potential problems facing ad testing include the following:

1. The viewer's pupil response may be affected by light and dark colors in the ad itself.
2. It is difficult to know what the viewer is focusing on. In one ad for French fries, viewers' pupils dilated, but subsequent analysis suggested dilation may have been due to a steak that was also pictured in the ad!
3. One advertising executive, commenting on the viability of a theory of attitudes and pupil dilation for his products, asked, "How excited can a person get about a laundry detergent?"
4. In some experiments it was noted that the pupils did not immediately return to their predilated state after seeing an arousing picture. Hence the next stimuli were viewed with still partially dilated eyes.
5. Many stimuli can cause variations in pupil dilation. Tightening muscles anywhere on the body, anticipation of a loud noise, drugs, eyelid closure, and mental effort will alter pupil size.

People also have varying absolute pupil sizes. Children, for instance, have larger absolute pupil sizes than adults. With so many sources of variation, it is difficult to state positively that the dilation is exclusively due to an attitudinal orientation. Another factor contributing to a decline in this kind of research is the expensive nature of the equipment that can measure small changes in pupil size with accuracy and reliability.

Although pupil dilation as measured by a machine can reveal emotional arousal, it is still important to find out how much people notice it or how close they have to be to see it in actual interpersonal interaction. One study suggests that pupil dilation may be influential in selecting interaction partners or even dates. Stass and Willis (1967) dealt with live subjects rather than pictures. Subjects were told they would be in an experiment and they had to choose a partner who was trustworthy, pleasant, and easy to talk to on an intimate basis. They were taken to a room where two other persons waited. These two persons had previously been independently rated as about the same in general attractiveness. Eye gazing and pupil dilation (through use of a drug) were varied. Once the naive subject left the waiting room, the experimenter asked him or her to choose one of the persons and give reasons for the choice. Gazing was an overwhelming factor in choice making, but pupil dilation also was a factor. A few people mentioned visual contact as a reason for their choice, but none mentioned pupil dilation. Thus, for both women and men, pupil dilation seemed to be an influential attraction device for interaction. Perhaps this is not a revelation to those women who, in the Middle Ages, put drops of belladonna into their eyes to enlarge their pupils and thus to increase attractiveness—or to those expert romancers who suggest a dimly lighted meeting place.

❖

Summary

Although researchers have examined the size, color, and position of the eyes, eye rings, eyebrows, and eyespots, our major concern was with gaze and mutual gaze. We said that gazing serves many interpersonal functions:

1. Regulating the flow of communication—opening the channels of communication and assisting in the turn-taking process
2. Monitoring feedback
3. Expressing emotions
4. Communicating the nature of the interpersonal relationship, for example, variations due to status, liking, and disliking

We also outlined a number of factors that influence the amount and duration of gaze in human relationships, for example, distance, physical characteristics, personal and personality characteristics, topics and tasks, and cultural background. From this review, we would predict *more* gazing in the following situations:

- You are male and physically distant from your partner.
- You are discussing easy, impersonal topics.
- You are interested in your partner's reactions—interpersonally involved.
- You like or love your partner.
- You are from a culture that emphasizes visual contact in interaction.
- You are an extravert and not shy.
- You have high affiliative or inclusion needs.
- You are dependent on your partner (and the partner has been unresponsive).
- You are listening rather than talking.
- You are female.
- You do not have a mental disorder like depression, autism, or schizophrenia.
- You are not embarrassed, ashamed, sorrowful, sad, or trying to hide something.

The preceding list is not exhaustive. Indeed, some of the findings depend on certain important qualifications. For example, you may have less gaze and mutual gaze when you are physically close—unless you happen to love your partner and want to get as close, physically and psychologically, as you can! The list is not intended to replace the qualified principles that appear in the chapter.

The last part of this chapter dealt with pupil dilation and constriction. We reviewed the findings of Eckhard Hess and others who have pursued his ideas. At this time, pupil dilation has been associated with arousal, attentiveness, mental effort, interest, and perceptual orientation. Aside from Hess's own work, however, little support has been found for the idea that pupils reflect attitudinal states. Dilation occurs under conditions that seem to represent positive attitudes, but there is less or no support for the belief that constriction of pupils is associated with negative attitudes toward objects and people. Finally, we examined one study that suggests that pupil dilation may be a factor in our desire to interact with another person.

Answers to Figure 10-3: (a) Happy, (b) Afraid, (c) Disgusted, (d) Distressed, (e) Guilty, (f) Thoughtful, (g) Flirting, (h) Arrogant.

QUESTIONS FOR DISCUSSION

1. How do you use gaze in your everyday life? When are you more likely to gaze at someone for a long period of time? For a very short period of time?

2. Watch yourself in a mirror, and try to convey these emotions using only your eyes and eyebrows: fear, anger, disgust, surprise, happiness, sadness. How do your eye positions and movements change? How similar are your expressions to those you see on other people's faces daily?

3. Try to recall a time when you had a conversation with someone with a physical disability—someone on crutches or in a wheelchair, for example. Did your gazing patterns change when interacting with this person, as opposed to an able-bodied person? How?

4. People of higher status are sometimes said to gaze more and for longer periods than people of lower status. What do you think of this? Think of examples that would and would not be supportive.

BIBLIOGRAPHY

Adams, R. B., Jr., Gordon, H. L., Baird, A. A., Ambady, N., & Kleck, R. E. (2003). Effects of gaze on amygdala sensitivity to anger and fear faces. *Science, 300,* 1536.

Adams, R. B., Jr., & Kleck, R. E. (2003). Perceived gaze direction and the processing of facial displays of emotion. *Psychological Science, 14,* 644–647.

Adrien, J. L., Lenoir, P., Martineau, J., Perrot, A., Hameury, L., Larmande, C., & Sauvage, D. (1993). Blind ratings of early symptoms of autism based upon family home movies. *Journal of the American Academy of Child and Adolescent Psychiatry, 32,* 617–626.

Aiello, J. R. (1972). A test of equilibrium theory: Visual interaction in relation to orientation, distance and sex of interaction. *Psychonomic Science, 27,* 335–336.

Aiello, J. R. (1977a). Visual interaction at extended distances. *Personality and Social Psychology Bulletin, 3,* 83–86.

Aiello, J. R. (1977b). A further look at equilibrium theory: Visual interaction as a function of interpersonal distance. *Environmental Psychology and Nonverbal Behavior, 1,* 122–140.

Argyle, M., & Cook, M. (1976). *Gaze and mutual gaze.* Cambridge: Cambridge University Press.

Argyle, M., & Dean, J. (1965). Eye contact, distance and affiliation. *Sociometry, 28,* 289–304.

Argyle, M., & Ingham, R. (1972). Gaze, mutual gaze and proximity. *Semiotica, 6,* 32–49.

Argyle, M., Ingham, R., Alkema, F., & McCallin, M. (1973). The different functions of gaze. *Semiotica, 7,* 19–32.

Argyle, M., Lalljee, M., & Cook, M. (1968). The effects of visibility on interaction in a dyad. *Human Relations, 21*, 3–17.

Argyle, M., Lefebvre, L., & Cook, M. (1974). The meaning of five patterns of gaze. *European Journal of Social Psychology, 4*, 125–136.

Ashear, V., & Snortum, J. R. (1971). Eye contact in children as a function of age, sex, social and intellective variables. *Developmental Psychology, 4*, 479.

Bakan, P. (1971). The eyes have it. *Psychology Today, 4*, 64–67, 96.

Bakan, P., & Strayer, F. F. (1973). On reliability of conjugate lateral eye movements. *Perceptual and Motor Skills, 36*, 429–430.

Barlow, J. D. (1969). Pupillary size as an index of preference in political candidates. *Perceptual and Motor Skills, 28*, 587–590.

Baron-Cohen, S., Wheelwright, S., & Jolliffe, T. (1997). Is there a "language of the eyes"? Evidence from normal adults, and adults with autism or Asperger syndrome. *Visual Cognition, 4*, 311–331.

Baron-Cohen, S., Wheelwright, S., Hill, J., Raste, Y., & Plumb, I. (2001). The "Reading the Mind in the Eyes" test revised version: A study with normal adults, and adults with Asperger syndrome or high-functioning autism. *Journal of Child Psychology & Psychiatry & Allied Disciplines, 42*, 241–251.

Bavelas, J. B., Coates, L., & Johnson, T. (2002). Listener responses as a collaborative process: The role of gaze. *Journal of Communication, 52*, 566–580.

Beattie, G. W. (1978a). Sequential temporal patterns of speech and gaze in dialogue. *Semiotica, 23*, 27–52.

Beattie, G. W. (1978b). Floor apportionment and gaze in conversational dyads. *British Journal of Social and Clinical Psychology, 17*, 7–15.

Bensing, J. M., Kerssens, J. J., & van der Pasch, M. (1995). Patient-directed gaze as a tool for discovering and handling psychosocial problems in general practice. *Journal of Nonverbal Behavior, 19*, 223–242.

Bernieri, F. J., Gillis, J. S., Davis, J. M., & Grahe, J. E. (1996). Dyad rapport and the accuracy of its judgment across situations: A lens model analysis. *Journal of Personality and Social Psychology, 71*, 110–129.

Berry, D. S., & Hansen, J. S. (2000). Personality, nonverbal behavior, and interaction quality in female dyads. *Personality and Social Psychology Bulletin, 26*, 278–292.

Boyle, E. A., Anderson, A. H., & Newlands, A. (1994). The effects of visibility on dialogue and performance in a cooperative problem solving task. *Language and Speech, 37*, 1–20.

Burgoon, J. K., Coker, D. A., & Coker, R. A. (1986). Communicative effects of gaze behavior: A test of two contrasting explanations. *Human Communication Research, 12*, 495–524.

Burgoon, J. K., Manusov, V., Mineo, P., & Hale, J. L. (1985). Effects of gaze on hiring, credibility, attraction and relational message interpretation. *Journal of Nonverbal Behavior, 9*, 133–146.

Burkhardt, J. C., Weider-Hatfield, D., & Hocking, J. E. (1985). Eye contact contrast effects in the employment interview. *Communication Research Reports, 2*, 5–10.

Cappella, J. N., & Greene, J. O. (1982). A discrepancy-arousal explanation of mutual influence in expressive behavior of adult–adult and infant–adult interaction. *Communication Monographs, 49*, 89–114.

Cary, M. S. (1978a). The role of gaze in the initiation of conversation. *Social Psychology, 41*, 269–271.

Cary, M. S. (1978b). Does civil inattention exist in pedestrian passing? *Journal of Personality and Social Psychology, 36*, 1185–1193.

Cheek, J. M., & Buss, A. H. (1981). Shyness and sociability. *Journal of Personality and Social Psychology, 41*, 330–339.

Cook, M., & Lalljee, M. G. (1973). Verbal substitutes for visual signals in interaction. *Semiotica, 6,* 212–221.

Cook, M., & Smith, J. M. C. (1975). The role of gaze in impression formation. *British Journal of Social and Clinical Psychology, 14,* 19–25.

Coss, R. G. (1974). Reflections on the evil eye. *Human Behavior, 3,* 16–22.

Crosby, F., Bromley, S., & Saxe, L. (1980). Recent unobtrusive studies of black and white discrimination and prejudice: A literature review. *Psychological Bulletin, 87,* 546–563.

de Gennaro, L., & Violani, C. (1988). Reflective lateral eye movements: Individual styles, cognitive and lateralization effects. *Neuropsychologia, 26,* 727–736.

Dovidio, J. F., Ellyson, S. L., Keating, C. F., Heitman, K., & Brown, C. E. (1988). The relationship of social power to visual displays of dominance between men and women. *Journal of Personality and Social Psychology, 54,* 233–242.

Dovidio, J. F., Kawakami, K., Johnson, C., Johnson, B., & Howard, A. (1997). On the nature of prejudice: Automatic and controlled processes. *Journal of Experimental Social Psychology, 33,* 510–540.

Droney, J. M., & Brooks, C. I. (1993). Attributions of self-esteem as a function of duration of eye contact. *Journal of Social Psychology, 133,* 715–722.

Efran, J. S. (1968). Looking for approval: Effects on visual behavior of approbation from persons differing in importance. *Journal of Personality and Social Psychology, 10,* 21–25.

Efran, J. S., & Broughton, A. (1966). Effect of expectancies for social approval on visual behavior. *Journal of Personality and Social Psychology, 4,* 103–107.

Ehrlichman, H., & Weinberger, A. (1978). Lateral eye movements and hemispheric asymmetry: A critical review. *Psychological Bulletin, 85,* 1080–1101.

Ekman, P., & Friesen, W. V. (1975). *Unmasking the face.* Eaglewood Cliffs, NJ: Prentice-Hall.

Ekman, P., Friesen, W. V., & Tomkins, S. S. (1971). Facial Affect Scoring Technique: A first validity study. *Semiotica, 3,* 37–58.

Ellsworth, P. C., & Carlsmith, J. M. (1968). Effects of eye contact and verbal content on affective response to a dyadic interaction. *Journal of Personality and Social Psychology, 10,* 15–20.

Ellsworth, P. C., & Carlsmith, J. M. (1973). Eye contact and gaze aversion in an aggressive encounter. *Journal of Personality and Social Psychology, 28,* 280–292.

Ellsworth, P. C., Carlsmith, J. M., & Henson, A. (1972). The stare as a stimulus to flight in human subjects: A series of field experiments. *Journal of Personality and Social Psychology, 21,* 302–311.

Ellsworth, P. C., & Langer, E. J. (1976). Staring and approach: An interpretation of the stare as a nonspecific activator. *Journal of Personality and Social Psychology, 33,* 117–122.

Ellsworth, P. C., & Ludwig, L. M. (1972). Visual behavior in social interaction. *Journal of Communication, 22,* 375–403.

Ellyson, S. L., Dovidio, J. F., & Fehr, B. J. (1981). Visual behavior and dominance in women and men. In C. Mayo & N. M. Henley (Eds.), *Gender and nonverbal behavior.* New York: Springer-Verlag.

Exline, R. V. (1963). Explorations in the process of person perception: Visual interaction in relation to competition, sex and need for affiliation. *Journal of Personality, 31,* 1–20.

Exline, R. V., & Eldridge, C. (1967). Effects of two patterns of a speaker's visual behavior upon the perception of the authencity of his verbal message. Paper presented at a meeting of the Eastern Psychological Association, Boston.

Exline, R. V., Ellyson, S. L., & Long, B. (1975). Visual behavior as an aspect of power role relationships. In P. Pliner, L. Krames, & T. Alloway (Eds.), *Advances in the study of communication and affect* (Vol. 2.) New York: Plenum.

Exline, R. V., & Fehr, B. J. (1978). Applications of semiosis to the study of visual interaction. In A. W. Siegman & S. Feldstein (Eds.), *Nonverbal behavior and communication*. Hillsdale, NJ: Erlbaum.

Exline, R. V., & Fehr, B. J. (1982). The assessment of gaze and mutual gaze. In K. R. Scherer & P. Ekman (Eds.), *Handbook of methods in nonverbal behavior research*. New York: Cambridge University Press.

Exline, R. V., Gray, D., & Schuette, D. (1965). Visual behavior in a dyad as affected by interview content and sex of respondent. *Journal of Personality and Social Psychology, 1*, 201–209.

Exline, R. V., & Messick, D. (1967). The effects of dependency and social reinforcement upon visual behavior during an interview. *British Journal of Social and Clinical Psychology, 6*, 256–266.

Exline, R. V., Thibaut, J., Hickey, C. B., & Gumpert, P. (1970). Visual interaction in relation to Machiavellianism and an unethical act. In P. Christie & F. Geis (Eds.), *Studies in Machiavellianism*. New York: Academic Press.

Exline, R. V., & Winters, L. (1965). Affective relations and mutual glances in dyads. In S. Tomkins & C. Izard (Eds.), *Affect, cognition and personality*. New York: Springer.

Farabee, D. J., Holcom, M. L, Ramsey, S. L., & Cole, S. G. (1993). Social anxiety and speaker gaze in a persuasive atmosphere. *Journal of Research in Personality, 27*, 365–376.

Fehr, B. J., & Exline, R. V. (1987). Social visual interaction: A conceptual and literature review. In A. W. Siegman & S. Feldstein (Eds.), *Nonverbal behavior and communication* (2nd ed.). Hills-dale, NJ: Erlbaum.

Field, T. (1995). Infants of depressed mothers. *Infant Behavior and Development, 18*, 1–13.

Foddy, M. (1978). Patterns of gaze in cooperative and competitive negotiation. *Human Relations, 31*, 925–938.

Fugita, S. S. (1974). Effects of anxiety and approval on visual interaction. *Journal of Personality and Social Psychology, 29*, 586–592.

Galin, D., & Ornstein, R. (1974). Individual differences in cognitive style: I. Reflective eye movements. *Neuropsychologia, 12*, 367–376.

Gibson, J. J., & Pick, A. D. (1963). Perception of another person's looking behavior. *American Journal of Psychology, 76*, 386–394.

Gifford, R. (1994). A lens-mapping framework for understanding the encoding and decoding of interpersonal dispositions in nonverbal behavior. *Journal of Personality and Social Psychology, 66*, 398–412.

Glenberg, A. M., Schroeder, J. L., & Robertson, D. A. (1998). Averting the gaze disengages the environment and facilitates remembering. *Memory & Cognition, 26*, 651–658.

Goffman, E. (1963). *Behavior in public places*. New York: Free Press.

Goldberg, G. N., Kiesler, C. A., & Collins, B. E. (1969). Visual behavior and face-to-face distance during interaction. *Sociometry, 32*, 43–53.

Goldwater, B. C. (1972). Psychological significance of pupillary movements. *Psychological Bulletin, 77*, 340–355.

Greene, J. O., & Frandsen, K. D. (1979). Need-fulfillment and consistency theory: Relationships between self-esteem and eye contact. *Western Journal of Speech Communication, 43*, 123–133.

Guéguen, N., & Jacob, C. (2002). Direct look versus evasive glance and compliance with a request. *Journal of Social Psychology, 142*, 393–396.

Halberstadt, A. G. (1985). Race, socioeconomic status, and nonverbal behavior. In A. W. Siegman & S. Feldstein (Eds.), *Multichannel integrations of nonverbal behavior*. Hillsdale, NJ: Erlbaum.

Hall, J. A. (1984). *Nonverbal sex differences: Communication accuracy and expressive style*. Baltimore: Johns Hopkins University Press.

Hall, J. A., Coats, E. J., & Smith LeBeau, L. Nonverbal behavior and the vertical dimension of social relations: A meta-analysis. Manuscript submitted for publication.

Harper, R. G., Wiens, A. N., & Matarazzo, J. D. (1978). The eye and visual behavior. In R. G. Harper, A. N. Wiens, & J. N. Matarazzo (Eds.), *Nonverbal communication: The state of the art*. New York: Wiley.

Hart, H. H. (1949). The eye in symbol and symptom. *Psychoanalytic Review, 36,* 1–21.

Hatfield, E., Cacioppo, J. T., & Rapson, R. L. (1994). *Emotional contagion.* New York: Cambridge University Press.

Hays, E. R., & Plax, T. G. (1971). Pupillary response to supportive and aversive verbal messages. *Speech Monographs, 38,* 316–320.

Hearn, G. (1957). Leadership and the spatial factor in small groups. *Journal of Abnormal and Social Psychology, 54,* 269–272.

Hemsley, G. D., & Doob, A. N. (1978). The effect of looking behavior on perceptions of a communicator's credibility. *Journal of Applied Psychology, 8,* 136–144.

Henley, N. M. (1977). *Body politics: Power, sex, and nonverbal communication.* Englewood Cliffs, NJ: Prentice-Hall.

Hensley, W. E. (1990). Pupillary dilation revisited: The constriction of a nonverbal cue. *Journal of Social Behavior and Personality, 5,* 97–104.

Hess, E. H. (1965). Attitudes and pupil size. *Scientific American, 212,* 46–54.

Hess, E. H. (1968). Pupillometric assessment. In J. M. Shlien (Ed.), *Research in psychotherapy.* Washington, DC: American Psychological Association.

Hess, E. H. (1975a). The role of pupil size in communication. *Scientific American, 233,* 110–112, 116–119.

Hess, E. H. (1975b). *The tell-tale eye.* New York: Van Nostrand Reinhold.

Hess, E. H., & Petrovich, S. B. (1987). Pupillary behavior in communication. In A. W. Siegman & S. Feldstein (Eds.), *Nonverbal behavior and communication* (2nd ed.). Hillsdale, NJ: Erlbaum.

Hess, E. H., & Polt, J. M. (1960). Pupil size as related to interest value of visual stimuli. *Science, 132,* 349–350.

Hess, E. H., & Polt, J. M. (1964). Pupil size in relation to mental activity during simple problem solving. *Science, 143,* 1190–1192.

Hess, E. H., Seltzer, A. L., & Shlien, J. M. (1965). Pupil response of hetero- and homosexual males to pictures of men and women: A pilot study. *Journal of Abnormal Psychology, 70,* 165–168.

Hindmarch, I. (1973). Eye-spots and pupil dilation in non-verbal communication. In M. von Cranach & I. Vine (Eds.), *Social communication and movement.* New York: Academic Press.

Hobson, G. N., Strongman, K. T., Bull, D., & Craig, G. (1973). Anxiety and gaze aversion in dyadic encounters. *British Journal of Social and Clinical Psychology, 12,* 122–129.

Hutt, C., & Ounsted, C. (1966). The biological significance of gaze aversion with particular reference to the syndrome of infantile autism. *Behavioral Science, 11,* 346–356.

Jaffe, J., Stern, D. N., & Peery, C. (1973). "Conversational" coupling of gaze behavior in prelinguistic human development. *Journal of Psycholinguistic Research, 2,* 321–329.

Janisse, M. P. (1973). Pupil size and affect: A critical review of the literature since 1960. *Canadian Psychologist, 14,* 311–329.

Janisse, M. P., & Peavler, W. S. (1974). Pupillary research today: Emotion in the eye. *Psychology Today, 7,* 60–63.

Jellison, J. M., & Ickes, W. J. (1974). The power of the glance: Desire to see and be seen in cooperative and competitive situations. *Journal of Experimental Social Psychology, 10,* 444–450.

Kalma, A. (1992). Gazing in triads: A powerful signal in floor apportionment. *British Journal of Social Psychology, 31,* 21–39.

Kalma, A. (1993). Sociable and aggressive dominance: Personality differences in leadership style? *Leadership Quarterly, 4,* 45–64.

Kanfer, F. H. (1960). Verbal rate, eyeblink, and content in structured psychiatric interviews. *Journal of Abnormal and Social Psychology, 61,* 341–347.

Kendon, A. (1967). Some functions of gaze-direction in social interaction. *Acta Psychologica, 26,* 22–63.

Kendon, A. (1990). *Conducting interaction: Patterns of behavior in focused encounters.* Cambridge: Cambridge University Press.

Kendon, A., & Cook, M. (1969). The consistency of gaze patterns in social interaction. *British Journal of Psychology, 60,* 481–494.

Kleck, R. (1968). Physical stigma and nonverbal cues emitted in face-to-face interaction. *Human Relations, 21,* 19–28.

Kleck, R. E., & Nuessle, W. (1968). Congruence between the indicative and communicative functions of eye-contact in interpersonal relations. *British Journal of Social and Clinical Psychology, 7,* 241–246.

Kleinke, C. L. (1986). Gaze and eye contact: A research review. *Psychological Bulletin, 100,* 78–100.

Kleinke, C. L., Bustos, A. A., Meeker, F. B., & Staneski, R. A. (1973). Effects of self-attributed and other-attributed gaze in interpersonal evaluations between males and females. *Journal of Experimental Social Psychology, 9,* 154–163.

LaFrance, M., & Mayo, C. (1976). Racial differences in gaze behavior during conversations: Two systematic observational studies. *Journal of Personality and Social Psychology, 33,* 547–552.

Leeb, R. T., & Rejskind, F. G. (2004). Here's looking at you, kid! A longitudinal study of perceived gender differences in mutual gaze behavior in young infants. *Sex Roles, 50,* 1–5.

Lefebvre, L. (1975). Encoding and decoding of ingratiation in modes of smiling and gaze. *British Journal of Social and Clinical Psychology, 14,* 33–42.

Levine, M. H., & Sutton-Smith, B. (1973). Effects of age, sex, and task on visual behavior during dyadic interaction. *Developmental Psychology, 9,* 400–405.

Libby, W. L. (1970). Eye contact and direction of looking as stable individual differences. *Journal of Experimental Research in Personality, 4,* 303–312.

Libby, W. L., & Yaklevich, D. (1973). Personality determinants of eye contact and direction of gaze aversion. *Journal of Personality and Social Psychology, 27,* 197–206.

Macrae, C. N., Hood, B. M., Milne, A. B., Rowe, A. C., & Mason, M. F. (2002). Are you looking at me? Eye gaze and person perception. *Psychological Science, 13,* 460–464.

Mansell, W., Clark, D. M., Ehlers, A., & Chen, Y. (1999). Social anxiety and attention away from emotional faces. *Cognition and Emotion, 13,* 673–690.

Mathews, A., Fox, E., Yield, J., & Calder, A. (2003). The face of fear: Effects of eye gaze and emotion on visual attention. *Visual Cognition, 10,* 823–835.

McAndrew, F. T., & Warner, J. E. (1986). Arousal seeking and the maintenance of mutual gaze in same and mixed sex dyads. *Journal of Nonverbal Behavior, 10,* 168–172.

McCauley, C., Coleman, G., & DeFusco, P. (1978). Commuters' eye contact with strangers in city and suburban train stations: Evidence of short-term adaptation to interpersonal overload in the city. *Environmental Psychology and Nonverbal Behavior, 2,* 215–225.

Mehrabian, A. (1972). *Nonverbal communication.* Chicago: Aldine/Atherton.

Mehrabian, A., & Williams, M. (1969). Nonverbal concomitants of perceived and intended persuasiveness. *Journal of Personality and Social Psychology, 13,* 37–58.

Mobbs, N. (1968). Eye contact in relation to social introversion/extroversion. *British Journal of Social and Clinical Psychology, 7,* 305–306.

Modigliani, A. (1971). Embarrassment, facework and eye-contact: Testing a theory of embarrassment. *Journal of Personality and Social Psychology, 17,* 15–24.

Morris, D. (1967). *The naked ape.* London: Cape.

Mulac, A., Studley, L. B., Wiemann, J. M., & Bradac, J. J. (1987). Male/female gaze in same-sex and mixed-sex dyads: Gender-linked differences and mutual influence. *Human Communication Research, 13,* 323–343.

Murphy, N. A., Hall, J. A., & Colvin, C. R. (2003). Accurate intelligence assessments in social interaction: Mediators and gender effects. *Journal of Personality, 71,* 465–493.

Nevill, D. (1974). Experimental manipulation of dependency motivation and its effects on eye contact and measures of field dependency. *Journal of Personality and Social Psychology, 29,* 72–79.

Nichols, K. A., & Champness, B. G. (1969). Eye gaze and GSR. *Journal of Experimental Social Psychology, 60,* 481–494.

Nielson, G. (1962). *Studies in self confrontation.* Copenhagen: Monksgaard.

Noller, P. (1980). Gaze in married couples. *Journal of Nonverbal Behavior, 5,* 115–129.

Partala, T., & Surakka, V. (2003). Pupil size variation as an indication of affective processing. *International Journal of Human–Computer Studies, 59,* 185–198.

Patterson, M. L. (1976). An arousal model of interpersonal intimacy. *Psychological Review, 83,* 235–245.

Patterson, M. L., Webb, A., & Schwartz, W. (2002). Passing encounters: Patterns of recognition and avoidance in pedestrians. *Basic and Applied Social Psychology, 24,* 57–66.

Pellegrini, R. J., Hicks, R. A., & Gordon, L. (1970). The effects of an approval-seeking induction on eye-contact in dyads. *British Journal of Social and Clinical Psychology, 9,* 373–374.

Pennington, D. C., & Rutter, D. R. (1981). Information or affiliation? Effects on intimacy on visual interaction. *Semiotica, 35,* 29–39.

Rohner, J. (2002). The time-course of visual threat processing: High trait anxious individuals eventually avert their gaze from angry faces. *Cognition & Emotion, 16,* 837–844.

Rosenberg, A., & Kagan, J. (1987). Iris pigmentation and behavioral inhibition. *Developmental Psychobiology, 20,* 377–392.

Rosse, R. B., Kendrick, K., Wyatt, R. J., Isaac, A., & Deutsch, S. I. (1994). Gaze discrimination in patients with schizophrenia: Preliminary report. *American Journal of Psychiatry, 151,* 919–921.

Rowland-Morin, P. A., Burchard, K. W., Garb, J. L., & Coe, N. P. (1991). Influence of effective communication by surgery students on their oral examination scores. *Academic Medicine, 66,* 169–171.

Rubin, Z. (1970). The measurement of romantic love. *Journal of Personality and Social Psychology, 16,* 265–273.

Rutter, D. R. (1973). Visual interaction in psychiatric patients: A review. *British Journal of Psychiatry, 123,* 193–202.

Rutter, D. R. (1984). *Looking and seeing: The role of visual communication in social interaction.* New York: Wiley.

Rutter, D. R., Morley, I. E., & Graham, J. C. (1972). Visual interaction in a group of introverts and extroverts. *European Journal of Social Psychology, 2,* 371–384.

Rutter, D. R., Stephenson, G. M., & White, P. A. (1978). The timing of looks in dyadic conversation. *British Journal of Social and Clinical Psychology, 17,* 17–21.

Schelde, T., & Hertz, M. (1994). Ethology and psychotherapy. *Ethology and Sociobiology, 15,* 383–392.

Scherwitz, L., & Helmreich, R. (1973). Interactive effects of eye contact and verbal content on interpersonal attraction in dyads. *Journal of Personality and Social Psychology, 25,* 6–14.

Schmid Mast, M. (2002). Dominance as expressed and inferred through speaking time: A meta-analysis. *Human Communication Research, 28,* 420–450.

Senju, A., Yaguchi, K., Tojo, Y., & Hasegawa, T. (2003). Eye contact does not facilitate detection in children with autism. *Cognition, 89,* B43–B51.

Shuter, R. (1979). Gaze behavior in interracial and intraracial interaction. In N. Jain (Ed.), *International and intercultural communication annual* (Vol. 5). Falls Church, VA: Speech Communication Association.

Simmel, G. (1921). Sociology of the senses: Visual interaction. In R. E. Park & E. W. Burgess (Eds.), *Introduction to the science of sociology.* Chicago: University of Chicago Press.

Spence, D. P., & Feinberg, C. (1967). Forms of defensive looking: A naturalistic experiment. *Journal of Nervous and Mental Disorders, 145,* 261–271.

Stass, J. W., & Willis, F. N., Jr. (1967). Eye contact, pupil dilation, and personal preference. *Psychonomic Science, 7,* 375–376.

Stephenson, G. M., & Rutter, D. R. (1970). Eye contact, distance and affiliation: A re-evaluation. *British Journal of Psychology, 61,* 385–393.

Stephenson, G. M., Rutter, D. R., & Dore, S. R. (1973). Visual interaction and distance. *British Journal of Psychology, 64,* 251–257.

Strongman, K. T., & Champness, B. G. (1968). Dominance hierarchies and conflict in eye contact. *Acta Psychologica, 28,* 376–386.

Thayer, S. (1969). The effect of interpersonal looking duration on dominance judgments. *Journal of Social Psychology, 79,* 285–286.

Thompson, T. L. (1982). Gaze toward and avoidance of the handicapped: A field experiment. *Journal of Nonverbal Behavior, 6,* 188–196.

van Dulmen, A. M., Verhaak, P. F. M., & Bilo, H. J. G. (1997). Shifts in doctor–patient communication during a series of outpatient consultations in non-insulin–dependent diabetes mellitus. *Patient Education and Counseling, 30,* 227–237.

Vine, I. (1971). Judgment of direction of gaze: An interpretation of discrepant results. *British Journal of Social and Clinical Psychology, 10,* 320–331.

von Cranach, M., & Ellgring, J. H. (1973). Problems in the recognition of gaze direction. In M. von Cranach & I. Vine (Eds.), *Social communication and movement.* New York: Academic Press.

Walker, M. B., & Trimboli, C. (1983). The expressive function of the eye flash. *Journal of Nonverbal Behavior, 8,* 3–13.

Walters, A. S., Barrett, R. P., & Feinstein, C. (1990). Social relatedness and autism: Current research, issues, directions. *Research in Developmental Disabilities, 11,* 303–326.

Webbink, P. (1986). *The power of the eyes.* New York: Springer.

Weisz, J., & Adam, G. (1993). Hemispheric preference and lateral eye movements evoked by bilateral visual stimuli. *Neuropsychologia, 31,* 1299–1306.

Wilbur, M. P., & Roberts-Wilbur, J. (1985). Lateral eye-movement responses to visual stimuli. *Perceptual and Motor Skills, 61,* 167–177.

Williams, E. (1978). Visual interaction and speech patterns: An extension of previous results. *British Journal of Social and Clinical Psychology, 17,* 101–102.

Woodmansee, J. J. (1970). The pupil response as a measure of social attitudes. In G. F. Summers (Ed.), *Attitude measurement.* Chicago: Rand McNally.

Word, C. O., Zanna, M. P., & Cooper, J. (1974). The nonverbal mediation of self-fulfilling prophecies in interracial interaction. *Journal of Experimental Social Psychology, 10,* 109–120.

Zuckerman, M., Miserandino, M., & Bernieri, F. J. (1983). Civil inattention exists—in elevators. *Personality and Social Psychology Bulletin, 9,* 578–586.

Chapter 11

THE EFFECTS OF VOCAL CUES
THAT ACCOMPANY SPOKEN WORDS

I understand a fury in your words
But not the words.

—SHAKESPEARE, *OTHELLO*, ACT IV

I deally, this chapter would not be in written form. Instead, it should be a recording you can listen to. A recording would give you a greater appreciation for the vocal nuances that are the subject of this chapter—or, as the cliché goes, "*how* something is said rather than *what* is said." But the dichotomy set up by this cliché is misleading, because *how* something is said is frequently *what* is said.

Some responses to vocal cues are elicited because we deliberately try to manipulate our voice in order to communicate various meanings. Robert J. McCloskey, spokesperson for the State Department during the Nixon administration, reportedly exemplified such behavior:

> McCloskey has three distinct ways of saying, "I would not speculate": spoken without accent, it means the department doesn't know for sure; emphasis on the "I" means "I wouldn't, but you may—and with some assurance"; accent on "speculate" indicates that the questioner's premise is probably wrong. (*Newsweek*, 1970, p. 106)

Most of us do the same kind of thing when we emphasize a particular part of a message. *Prosody* is the word used to describe all the variations in the voice that accompany speech and help to convey its meaning. Notice how different vocal emphases influence the interpretation of the following message:

1. *He's* giving this money to Herbie. (*He* is the one giving the money, nobody else.)
2. He's *giving* this money to Herbie. (He is *giving*, not lending, the money.)
3. He's giving *this* money to Herbie. (The money being exchanged is not from another fund or source; it is *this* money.)
4. He's giving this *money* to Herbie. (*Money* is the unit of exchange, not flowers or beads.)
5. He's giving this money to *Herbie*. (The recipient is *Herbie*, not Eric or Bill or Rod.)

We manipulate our pitch to indicate the end of a declarative sentence (by lowering it) or a question (by raising it). Sometimes we consciously manipulate our tone to contradict the verbal message, as in sarcasm. For instance, you can say the words "I'm having a wonderful time" so they mean "I'm having a terrible time." If you are perceived as being sarcastic, the vocal cues you have given probably superseded the verbal.

Such an assumption (the predominance of vocal cues in forming attitudes based on contradictory vocal and verbal content) initiated some work of Mehrabian and his colleagues. In one study, he presented single words, previously rated as positive, neutral, or negative, to listeners in positive or negative vocal tones (Mehrabian & Wiener, 1967). From this experiment, he concluded the following:

> The variability of inferences about communicator attitude on the basis of information available in content and tone combined is mainly contributed by variations in tone alone. For example, when the attitude communicated in content contradicted the attitude communicated by negative tone, the total message was judged as communicating negative attitude. (p. 109)

A similar study, pitting vocal cues against facial and verbal cues, found the facial more influential (Mehrabian & Ferris, 1967). From these studies, Mehrabian devised a formula that illustrates the differential impact of verbal, vocal, and facial cues:

Perceived attitude = .07 (verbal) + .38 (vocal) + .55 (facial)

Obviously the formula is limited by the design of Mehrabian's experiments. For instance, we do not know how the formula might change if some of the variables were manipulated more vigorously, or if more or different people did the judging; we do not know whether the formula would apply to verbal materials longer than one word; and we do not know whether these respondents were reacting to the inconsistency itself as a source of attitudinal information (see Lapakko, 1997, for a critique). Just the fact that subjects resolved their inconsistency by relying on nonverbal cues does not mean evaluative information is conveyed by nonverbal cues alone. Indeed, Friedman (1979) found that for some kinds of messages, the words mattered more than the facial expressions. Moreover, the preference to base interpretations on words versus vocal cues changes with age: young children rely much more on verbal content, older children show a mixed pattern, and adults rely much more on nonverbal tonal qualities (Bugental, Kaswan, & Love, 1970; Morton & Trehub, 2001).

Studies comparing impressions made by the voice to those made by the face have found the voice especially suited to convey degrees of dominance or potency. The face has a greater impact on judgments of pleasantness or positivity (Zuckerman & Driver, 1989; Zuckerman et al., 1982), and the face is a more effective channel than the voice by which to judge people's rapport (Grahe & Bernieri, 1999). Clues to dominance in the voice include speed and loudness; the most obvious clue to pleasantness in the face is the smile. However, each modality can convey through more subtle variations a wealth of other messages. For example, the presence of a smile can be evident in the voice alone; in smiling, the vocal tract is shortened with the effect of raising the resonances (Scherer, 1986). Some actors who do voice-overs on television advertisements are skilled in conveying a cheerful attitude through their voice quality alone.

Thus, even though the impact of the voice relative to other channels of communication may vary according to many factors, there is no doubt that vocal cues exert a great deal of influence on listener perceptions. Often, these responses are based on stereotypes associated with various vocal qualities. Not surprisingly, the existence of such stereotypes means that some vocal qualities are preferred over others. Zuckerman and Driver (1989) have documented that listeners generally agree on whether a voice is attractive or not, and that people whose voices are considered more attractive are believed to have personality traits such as dominance, competence, industriousness, sensitivity, and warmth. Other stereotypes relating to the voice will be described later in this chapter.

THE INGREDIENTS AND METHODS OF STUDYING PARALANGUAGE

The physical mechanisms for producing nonverbal vocal qualities and sounds (also called *paralanguage*) are extremely complex. Figure 11-1 illustrates the many muscles and other structures involved, which include the throat, nasal cavities, tongue, lips, mouth, and jaw. In this chapter, however, we focus on the impact of paralanguage rather than the mechanisms by which it is produced. Many techniques and methods have been developed for studying the role of vocal nonverbal cues in the communication process (Scherer, 2003). We provide just a short introduction here.

In one approach to studying the nonverbal vocal communication, listeners are asked for their impressions or inferences about a voice sample, for example, how anxious or competent the voice sounds. Using this method, a researcher may gain insight into the social meanings of vocal cues because listeners' impressions are based on their store of experience, knowledge, and beliefs; however, a researcher learns little about specific vocal cues that created a given impression because the listeners are interpreting the vocal cues in an implicit way to reach a final impression. Thus a listener may know an angry voice when she hears one, but may not be able to pinpoint the acoustic properties that made it sound angry.

In contrast, sometimes researchers want and need to measure specific vocal characteristics (also called *acoustic properties*), and for this they use automated devices or trained coders. Voice researchers use automated measurement (done by computers, for example) much more than do researchers who study nonvocal modalities of communication, in part because the technology exists for doing so. Some commonly measured acoustic properties are *speech rate* (words per unit of time); *fundamental frequency* (F_0), which is the vibration rate of the vocal folds in the throat and the main contributor, along with the harmonics and resonances it produces, to our perception of pitch; and *intensity,* which is the energy value for a speech sound, perceived as loudness. Each of these can be measured as an average value over an utterance or other unit of time or can be described more dynamically in terms of range, variation, and contour (Scherer, 1986).

It is also possible to assess vocal nonverbal behavior at a level *between* these impressionistic and purely descriptive extremes. A listener might be asked to characterize a voice as whiny, breathy, or abrupt but not to go to the next level of subjectivity by inferring a trait or mood; for example, from the three adjectives just named a listener might infer that

FIGURE 11-1

Muscles and structures involved in speech and paralanguage.

SOURCE: From Fernando Poyatos, *Paralanguage: A Linguistic Approach to Interactive Speech and Sound*, 1993, p. 49.
Reprinted by permission of John Benjamins Publishing Company, Amsterdam/Philadelphia.www.benjamins.com

the speaker is weak, sexy, or rude, respectively. You can see that the last three descriptions are further removed from the actual vocal cues and more inferential than the first three. Studying perceptions at this midway point is a crucial link in understanding the relationship between acoustic features of voices and their social impact (Scherer, 1982).

The fact that the voice has acoustic features perceived and interpreted by a listener according to his or her knowledge, stereotypes, and other cognitions is part of what is called the "lens" model of nonverbal judgment (Scherer, 2003). According to this model, a full understanding of vocal (and other nonverbal) phenomena must acknowledge a series of interlocking steps: A person's state or trait (A) is reflected in acoustic behavior (B), which is perceived by a listener (C), who forms an impression or attribution (D), which may then be the basis for behavioral reaction or change in the listener (E). Studies hardly ever include all of these elements. One study might document how a speaker's emotional state is reflected in acoustic changes (A–B), while another might relate acoustic properties of the voice to listeners' impressions of personality (B–D), and so forth.

All approaches for measuring vocal behavior have strengths and weaknesses. The choice depends on the questions being asked in a particular study. Hall, Roter, and Rand (1981), for example, were interested in the impact of physicians' and patients' communication of emotion during the medical visit. Accordingly, they asked listeners to rate the emotions conveyed in content-masked audiotapes of doctors and patients talking during medical office visits. (Content masking obscures the verbal information while retaining nonverbal vocal properties, as explained in chapter 3 and later in this chapter.) They found that if the physician sounded angry (or anxious or contented), so did the patient and vice versa—in other words, there was a reciprocation of expressed feelings. In that study, gathering only judges' impressions made more sense than measuring acoustic properties such as fundamental frequency or loudness because the interest was in social impact, not on the specific cues. But another researcher might focus on uncovering the relationship *between* the descriptive and impressionistic levels, that is, finding out what increased fundamental frequency, intensity, and so forth mean in terms of listeners' perceptions. For example, a voice tone we would label as "breathy" is produced by narrowing the glottis a little while letting through more air than for a normal voice and making the vocal folds vibrate without fully closing (Poyatos, 1993). Researchers of the vocal communication of emotion have been particularly active in trying to uncover what cues are used to convey different emotions.

The voice is capable of a great variety of sounds (Poyatos, 1993; Trager, 1958). The components most closely tied to speech include three already mentioned (frequency, intensity, and speed) as well as vocal lip control (sharp or smooth transition), articulation control (forceful, relaxed), rhythm control (smooth, jerky), and resonance (resonant, thin). Other nonverbal vocal behaviors are less tied to speech and may even substitute for speech. These include laughing, crying, whispering, snoring, yelling, moaning, yawning, whining, sighing, and belching, along with the common "uh," "um," "mmm," "uh-huh," and other such sounds, some of which merge with our definitions of linguistic behavior. Also included as paralanguage are *nonsounds:* pauses between words or phrases in someone's speech and pauses when a new speaker begins (also called a *switching pause* or *speech latency*). Some related phenomena, which Mahl and Schulze (1964) placed under the broad heading of *extralinguistic* phenomena, are also relevant to any discussion of communication and vocal behavior. These include dialect or accent, nonfluencies, duration of utterance, and interaction rates.

Now that we have a sense of the ingredients of paralanguage, we can ask the next logical question: What reactions do vocal cues elicit, and how are they important in communicating?

VOCAL CUES AND SPEAKER RECOGNITION

You may have had this experience: You pick up the phone and say, "Hello." The voice on the other end says, "Hi, how ya doin'?" At this point you realize two things: (1) The greeting suggests an informality found among people who are supposed to know each other, and (2) you don't know who it is! So you try to extend the conversation without admitting your ignorance, hoping some verbal cue will be given or that you eventually will recognize the caller's voice. As a result, you say something like, "Fine. What have you been up to?" Speaker recognition is important not only to all of us in everyday life but also to law enforcement officials and governments. Joseph Stalin assigned teams of imprisoned scientists and engineers to develop speaker recognition technology so Stalin's police could easily identify "enemies of the state" (Hollien, 1990).

Each time you speak, you produce a complex acoustic signal. It is not exactly the same each time you speak (even if it is the same word), nor is the acoustic signal you produce exactly the same as the one produced by other speakers. The probability that there are greater differences between the voices of two different speakers than the voice of a single speaker at two different times has led to considerable interest in the process of identifying speakers by their voices alone.

There are three primary methods for identifying speakers:

1. Listening
2. Visual comparison of spectrograms (voiceprints)
3. Recognition by computers, which compare the acoustic patterns of a standard spoken message to stored versions of the same message previously spoken by the same speaker

Although machines are credited with many accomplishments in today's society, ordinary human listening compares favorably with the other two techniques for accuracy in most speaker recognition tasks. Under certain circumstances, human beings can recognize speakers with a high degree of accuracy. In one study, a single sentence was enough to identify 8 to 10 work colleagues at more than 97% accuracy (van Lancker, Kreiman, & Emmorey, 1985). In another study, 83% accuracy for 29 familiar speakers was achieved (Ladefoged & Ladefoged, 1980).

Even when listeners accurately identify a speaker from his or her voice, they are probably not able to explain the perceptual bases for their decision. Of the many characteristics of the voice, listeners probably utilize very few in speaker recognition.

Law enforcement and judicial agencies have had a special concern for identifying speakers objectively from their vocal characteristics. At the famous trial of Bruno Hauptman, the kidnapper of Charles and Anne Morrow Lindbergh's baby, Charles Lindbergh claimed he recognized Hauptman's voice as the voice of the kidnapper even though it had been about 3 years since he had heard it. Skeptical about the accuracy of this identification, McGehee (1937) conducted research that found accuracy tends to drop off sharply after 3 weeks, and after 5 months it dips to about 13%. Other research finds that accuracy of identification by listeners falls dramatically as the speech samples are made shorter, when various distortions occur (e.g., more speakers, disguised voices, whispering, and dialects), and when the target voice is paired with another that sounds similar to it (Hollien, 1990). And, of course, accuracy varies with how many times one has heard the voice in question.

Many factors affect listening accuracy, but similar problems plague efforts to devise more "objective" methods of speaker recognition—not the least of which is the knowledge that no single set of acoustic cues reliably distinguishes speakers.

One effort to find a more objective method of speaker identification involves the *spectrogram*, also called a *voiceprint*, which is a visual picture of a person's speech. A spectrogram is a plot of vocal energy in different frequency bands as a function of time. Although some have made strong claims for the accuracy and reliability of spectrographic analysis, it seems to be very fallible (Bolt et al., 1973). Errors in human judgment occur as interpretations of the visual data are made. The interpreter's skill becomes particularly relevant when we look at Figure 11-2. These two similar spectrograms of two different people uttering a

FIGURE 11-2

Similar spectrograms of the word "you" uttered by two arbitrarily selected speakers.

single word make it sufficiently clear that we must weigh our reliance on spectrograms as evidence at trials very carefully (Hollien, 1990). Spectrograms are not like fingerprints. True, no two voices are exactly alike, but depending on the voice sample obtained and the equipment used, two different voices may appear very similar. In contrast, fingerprints, unlike voices, show little variability from one time to the next, unless, of course, smudges or smears have occurred. One study asked speakers to produce the same sentence using their normal voice and a number of "disguises"—speaking like an old person, using a hypernasal voice, a hoarse voice, a slow rate of speech, and a disguise of one's own choosing. These voice samples were then submitted to spectrographic analysis by experts who were paid $50 if they achieved the highest accuracy of identification. Normal voices were matched with about 57% accuracy, but all the disguises significantly interfered with identification. The least accuracy was achieved when speakers chose their own type of disguise (Reich, Moll, & Curtis, 1976). Hollien (1990) concluded that spectrographic speaker recognition is a still unvalidated methodology.

VOCAL CUES AND PERSONALITY

One cultural syndrome that aptly illustrates our association of vocal cues with certain personality characteristics concerns the low, deep voice associated with men and masculinity. Salespeople, radio and television announcers, lawyers, and many others try to emulate low vocal tones, which they perceive as being more sophisticated, appealing, sexy, or masculine than higher pitched voices.

Numerous research efforts have tried to determine whether certain personality traits are actually expressed in the voice and whether listeners are sensitive to these cues. It is common to find the following:

1. High agreement among judges of the voices regarding the presence of certain personality characteristics
2. Inconsistent agreement between the judges' personality perceptions and the speaker's actual score on personality tests
3. For some voices and some personality traits, a very high correspondence between the judges' perceptions and actual criterion measures

We can make several points about these findings. First, the criterion measures (personality tests) are also frequently imperfect measures, meaning there might be a higher correspondence than the data seem to indicate. Furthermore, research has often ignored differences among listeners with respect to personality, culture, and developmental traits, which may profoundly impact the listener's accuracy in perceiving personality traits based on vocal cues. Research also suggests that a given personality trait may not be expressed similarly in the voices of people from different cultures.

The finding that listeners cannot always detect personality from vocal cues does not mean the voice does not contain any cues to personality. There are several lines of positive evidence on this issue. Extraversion/introversion is the trait dimension best documented in vocal cues of American speakers. Cues associated with a speaker's actual (not just perceived) extraversion, when compared to introversion, are more fluency (shorter pauses when the speaking turn switches from one speaker to another, shorter silent pauses within a person's speech, fewer hesitations); faster rate; louder speech; more dynamic contrast; higher pitch (up to a point); and more variable pitch. In addition, extraverted people have been shown to talk more, in both number of words and total speaking time (Lippa, 1998; Siegman, 1987). In light of these robust vocal manifestations of extraversion, it is not surprising that people use vocal cues (such as loudness, fullness, and enunciation) as a basis for judging extraversion (Lippa, 1998).

Lippa (1998) also inquired about several dimensions of "masculinity–femininity" in college students in relation to vocal qualities, defining the masculinity–femininity dimensions in terms of gender-typical preferences for occupations, hobbies, and other activities. Among men, those who were more "masculine" by this definition had less expressive, lower pitched, slower, and louder voices, and had poorer enunciation; among women, there was a correlation only for voice pitch (more "masculine" women had lower pitched voices). Viewers' perceptions partially matched these associations; higher ratings of masculinity were given to targets whose voices were less expressive and lower pitched.

Another intriguing set of results has emerged regarding the "Type A" personality, a syndrome of attitudes and behaviors linked to the development of coronary heart disease. Current theory points to hostility or anger as an important feature of this syndrome. Early in the research on these hard-driving, aggressive Type A's, it was found that speech style was very distinctive. In particular, fast or accelerating speech, uneven speech rate, short latencies, interruptions, a loud or explosive voice, and a hard or staccato voice are more pronounced in Type A individuals. Many of these qualities also have been shown independently to be associated with heart disease, for example, loud, vigorous, and explosive speech (Hall, Friedman, & Harris, 1984).

The trait of dominance also has been documented to have an associated speech style; some of its elements overlap with those found for extraversion and Type A personality. Individuals who speak louder are perceived as more dominant (Harrigan et al., 1989; Tusing & Dillard, 2000), and indeed more dominant individuals do tend to have voices that are louder than less dominant individuals (Siegman, 1987; Weaver & Anderson, 1973). Because the stereotype and the actual behavior associated with dominance coincide, it is not surprising that Berry (1991) found that judges' ratings of assertiveness in voices recorded while expressors recited the alphabet were accurate.

How personality is actually expressed in speech may be complex, but there is no dearth of evidence that people *believe* speech contains clues to personality. Addington (1968) conducted one of the most complete studies in this area. Male and female speakers simulated 9 vocal characteristics, and judges responded to the voices by rating them on 40 personality characteristics. Judges were most reliable (i.e., they agreed most with each other) in ratings of masculine/feminine, young/old, enthusiastic/apathetic, energetic/lazy, and attractive/ugly. Addington concluded that the male personality generally was perceived in terms of physical and emotional power, whereas the female personality was apparently perceived in terms of social faculties. Table 11-1 summarizes his results.

Addington posed some interesting questions for researchers studying vocal cues and personality. To what extent are these stereotyped impressions of personality maintained in the face of conflicting personality information? And what is the relationship between a given personality impression and vocal cue? For example, Addington's research indicated

TABLE 11-1   **Simulated Vocal Cues and Personality Stereotypes**

SIMULATED VOCAL CUE	SPEAKERS	STEREOTYPED PERCEPTIONS
Breathiness	Males	Younger, more artistic
	Females	More feminine; prettier, more petite, effervescent, high-strung; shallower
Thinness	Males	Did not alter listener's image of the speaker; no significant correlations
	Females	Increased social, physical, emotional, and mental immaturity; increased sense of humor and sensitivity
Flatness	Males	More masculine, more sluggish, colder, more, withdrawn
	Females	More masculine, more sluggish, colder, more withdrawn
Nasality	Males	A wide array of socially undesirable characteristics
	Females	A wide array of socially undesirable characteristics
Tenseness	Males	Older, more unyielding, cantankerous
	Females	Younger; more emotional, feminine, high-strung; less intelligent
Throatiness	Males	Older; more realistic; mature; sophisticated; well adjusted
	Females	Less intelligent; more masculine; lazier; more boorish, unemotional, ugly, sickly, careless, inartistic, naive, humble, neurotic, quiet, uninteresting, apathetic
Increased Rate	Males	More animated and extraverted
	Females	More animated and extraverted
Increased Pitch Variety	Males	More dynamic, feminine, esthetically inclined
	Females	More dynamic and extraverted

that increased pitch variety led to more positive personality impressions, but is it not possible that at some point, increasing pitch variety could become so exaggerated as to evoke negative perceptions? Zuckerman's research on vocal attractiveness suggests this may be so, because extremes of pitch, pitch range, shrillness, and squeakiness produce more negative impressions.

People with more attractive sounding voices are, in general, rated as having better personalities (less neurotic and more extraverted, open, warm, agreeable, powerful, honest, and conscientious) than people with less attractive sounding voices (Berry, 1992; Zuckerman, Hodgins, & Miyake, 1990; Zuckerman & Miyake, 1993). Zuckerman's research also uncovered the particular speech qualities that produced higher ratings on vocal attractiveness. More attractive-rated voices were more resonant, less monotonous, less nasal, and lower in pitch (the latter for male voices only); more nasality was also judged negatively in the voices of adults (Bloom, Zajac, & Titus, 1999) and even in the voices of infants only 3 months old (Bloom, Moore-Schoenmakers, & Masataka, 1999).

Personality stereotypes also exist about people with babyish voices. Both adults and young children with more babyish voices are perceived as more warm and honest, but less powerful and competent, than people with more mature-sounding voices. It seems the general qualities attributed to children are attributed to people with younger sounding voices no matter what their actual age (Berry, 1992; Berry et al., 1994).

VOCAL CUES AND GROUP PERCEPTIONS

A related line of study involves associating various characteristics with voices representative of groups of people. These studies deal with judgments of group personality rather than individual personality. The study of dialects and accents is illustrative. In George Bernard Shaw's play *Pygmalion* and its musical adaptation, *My Fair Lady,* Eliza Doolittle spent considerable time and effort trying to correct her dialect so she could rise in social standing. (Professor Higgins says, "Look at her—a pris'ner of the gutters; Condemned by ev'ry syllable she utters." *My Fair Lady,* Act I, Scene 1.) Eliza's training, according to one study, was most appropriate. It suggests that if we expect a speaker to reflect a nonstandard and/or "lower-class" dialect and the speaker actually presents himself or herself in accord with standard or "upper-class" models, the evaluation will be very positive. The reverse also was true; speakers expected to speak "up" but who spoke "down" were evaluated negatively (Aboud, Clement, & Taylor, 1974). Sometimes, though, there may be a fine line between adapting to our audience and violating expectations based on our own background. If an audience thinks we are faking something or concealing who we "really are," they might judge us harshly.

Although there are some exceptions, ordinarily dialects other than the one spoken by the listener/evaluator receive less favorable evaluations than those considered standard. Generally, these negative responses occur because the listener associates the speaker's dialect with an ethnic or regional stereotype and then evaluates the voice in accord with the stereotype.

Do regional varieties of speech in the United States differ in prestige value? Listeners in Maine, Louisiana, New York City, Arkansas, and Michigan rated 12 voice samples of American dialects and one foreign accent (Wilke & Snyder, 1941). The most unfavorably regarded were the foreign accent and so-called New Yorkese. Although this study is more than 60 years old, dialects and accent stereotypes continue to influence our judgments of speakers. Many people tested their accent stereotypes in the political realm as they evaluated the Boston Brahmin accent of John F. Kennedy, the Southern accent of Jimmy Carter, and the European accent of Teresa Heinz Kerry.

Several investigators have pursued the question of exactly how we judge the speech and dialects of others. By far the most extensive work in this direction was done by Mulac (1976). Mulac's experiments have used regional and foreign dialects, broadcasters, various speech pathologies, prose and spontaneous speech, and different modes of presentation, such as written, audiotape, videotape, and sound film. This work shows we tend to respond to samples of speech along three primary dimensions:

1. *Sociointellectual status,* that is, high or low social status, blue or white collar, rich or poor, and literate or illiterate
2. *Aesthetic quality,* that is, pleasing or displeasing, nice or awful, sweet or sour, beautiful or ugly
3. *Dynamism,* that is, aggressive or unaggressive, active or passive, strong or weak, loud or soft

These results confirm studies in many other areas of perception that show we tend to see our world and the things in it according to power, evaluation, and activity dimensions.

Over 70 years ago, Pear (1931) did pioneering work on vocal cues and judgments of personal characteristics. Using 9 speakers and over 4,000 radio listeners, he found a speaker's age could be estimated fairly accurately, the speaker's sex with remarkable accuracy, birthplace with little accuracy, and occasionally vocation with surprising accuracy. The actor and clergy were consistently identified from among the nine professionals represented. Since that time, others have been interested in judgments of such characteristics as body type, height, weight, age, occupation, status or social class, race, sex, education, and dialect region. Three characteristics judged accurately with some consistency are sex, age, and social class/status.

SEX

Listeners who heard 6 recorded vowels of 20 speakers were able to identify the sex of the speaker 96% of the time when the tape was not altered in any way. Accuracy decreased to 91% for a filtered tape and to 75% for a whispered voice sample (Lass et al., 1976). These authors argue that the fundamental frequency is a more important acoustic cue in speaker sex identification than the resonance characteristics of the voices. It is certainly the case that women typically speak with a higher fundamental frequency (perceived as higher pitch) than men (Viscovich et al., 2003). Sometimes women and men may be identified by their intonation patterns. Women's voices are more variable (i.e., expressive) than men's, and women sometimes end a sentence on a higher pitch, relative to where they started the sentence, than men (in some age groups, at any rate).

It has been said that women speak in an even higher pitch than their anatomy requires. This is notably true in Japan, where women have traditionally spoken with extremely high voices and have been censured for not doing so. Because a high voice is seen as conveying politeness, its extreme is most often heard in women in service occupations, such as elevator operators. Bilinguals of both sexes seem to speak in a higher pitch when speaking Japanese than when speaking English. Recent trends suggest, however, that the voices of Japanese women are steadily deepening as their status becomes more equal to that of men ("Japan's Feminine Falsetto," 1995).

Thus pitch is a likely basis for differentiating male and female voices. Again, the nature of the vocal stimuli is most influential in determining exactly how well we can discriminate between male and female voices. For instance, males and females *interacting* with each other may manifest different vocal cues than when they present monologues or interact with a member of the same sex (Markel, Prebor, & Brandt, 1972). The topic of discussion also may affect voice production and perceptions. And if there is a gradual narrowing of differences as adaptations to the social community are made, we might speculate that the vocal tones of working women in predominantly male organizations may be harder to distinguish—particularly if the sample is taken in the work milieu.

At the borderline between verbal and nonverbal behavior falls an area of study concerned with speech styles, or *speech registers*. A speech register is a total way of communicating through speech, which can include verbal forms, and it is believed to vary systematically with social characteristics of the speakers—for example, how socially powerful a person is (Erickson et al., 1978). This research is pertinent to our discussion of speaker sex because it has been suggested that certain verbal forms associated with power differentiate the sexes (Lakoff, 1975). Examples of less powerful speech sometimes associated with females include tag questions ("It's a nice day, *isn't it?*"), hedges and qualifiers ("sort of," "maybe"), disclaimers ("I don't know, but"), and intensifiers ("The puppy was *so* cute").

Interruptions, another interactional strategy that can reflect dominance, also have been hypothesized to differentiate between men and women in the direction we might expect based on stereotype. People certainly do have well-developed stereotypes about how the sexes speak, but the evidence supporting the hypothesis of sex differences in language use and interruptions is extremely mixed (Aries, 1987; Dindia, 1987; Hirschman, 1994; Irish & Hall, 1995; Kramer, 1978; Marche & Peterson, 1993; Mulac, Lundell, & Bradac, 1986; Nohara, 1992; Turner, Dindia, & Pearson, 1995). The fact that interruptions can signify enthusiastic, active participation in the conversation rather than efforts to attain or express dominance is probably one reason why studies are mixed as to which sex interrupts more; whereas early studies tended to find that men interrupted more, more recent studies often find no difference, and some find that females interrupt more than males.

People's expectations or beliefs about how each sex speaks may shape not only their perceptions and interpretations of speech but also their own behavior in such a way that it actually elicits the expected behavior. For example, if a man expects a woman to speak in a weak or indecisive way, he might treat her in a strong or protective manner that elicits a complementary weak and dependent response. Though stereotypes can change over time, they will likely always exist not only for sex but for other social categories. Perhaps the best a person can do is to maintain an awareness of stereotypes and the many subtle ways in which they may influence our attitudes and behavior.

AGE

As we mentioned, studies show age to be fairly accurately assessed from vocal cues, and something is known about how these judgments are made. With advancing age, speech slows down and there are more dysfluencies and perturbations in fundamental frequency (Hummert, Mazloff, & Henry, 1999). Several studies have investigated pitch of males during infancy, childhood, adolescence, early adulthood, and middle and advanced age. There is a general lowering of pitch level from infancy through middle age, with some studies finding a reversal such that pitch level rises slightly with advancing age. If, as some studies suggest, our voices change in pitch flexibility, rate, loudness, vocal quality, articulatory control, and the like, the voice may give clues to age we are largely unaware of.

SOCIAL CLASS/STATUS

Several studies show listeners to be amazingly accurate in judging social class or status on the basis of voice alone. Harms (1961) used a standard system to determine social class for nine speakers. Each speaker recorded a 40- to 60-second conversation in which he responded to questions and statements such as "How are you?" and "Ask for the time."

many of them said they made their decision after only 10 to 15 seconds of listening to the recording.

TARGET EFFECTS

So far we have been discussing ways in which a speaker's personal characteristics are reflected in his or her nonverbal speech style. But it would be very surprising if a person's speech style did not also reflect characteristics of the *other* person in an interaction. After all, we react to different kinds of people with many emotions and thoughts that may be reflected in our vocal expression, and we also have notions about how we *ought* to talk to different kinds of people.

A well-studied example of such a "target effect" is baby talk (also called *motherese*), which is the high-pitched, singsong, slow, rhythmic, repetitive, simplified way that parents (fathers as well as mothers) around the world talk to young children (Grieser & Kuhl, 1988; Snow & Ferguson, 1977; Trainor, Austin, & Desjardins, 2000). Even young children know how to talk this way to babies or pets. Furthermore, infants prefer baby talk to normal adult speech style. Various purposes have been proposed for baby talk, including getting the infant's attention, promoting language development, clarifying the speaker's message, and creating an emotional bond. The last of these propositions was supported by Trainor, Austin, and Desjardins's (2000) research, which showed that baby talk contained more free emotional expression than typical adult-directed talk did, but was very similar in terms of acoustic characteristics to adult-directed speech that emphasized the communication of emotion. What makes baby talk distinctive, the authors argued, is that it contains more freely expressed emotion than typical adult-directed talk does.

Certain groups of adults who are attributed childlike qualities or who are perceived (often erroneously) as cognitively impaired, such as the institutionalized elderly or the deaf, are also spoken to in a way that resembles baby talk. Psychologists are especially interested in this kind of "secondary" baby talk because of the possibility that it contributes to the stigmatizing of groups perceived as dependent or incompetent (Caporael, 1981).

With this in mind, DePaulo and Coleman (1986, 1987) compared the warmth of speech to children, adults with mental retardation, non-native adult speakers of English, and native adult English speakers, hypothesizing that warmth (one component of baby talk) would decrease across these four groups. The prediction was supported. In addition, when considering those with mental retardation alone, speakers displayed more vocal warmth when speaking to the more retarded than to the less retarded individuals. Particular ways of using the language also differed among the groups: Speech to children was clearer, simpler, and more attention maintaining and had longer pauses; speech to those with retardation was very similar to this; speech to foreigners, however, was more similar to that addressed to "normal people" except for being more repetitive. Zebrowitz, Brownlow, and Olson (1992) found that adults used baby talk more to children with babyish faces than to same-age children who had more mature-looking faces.

The sex of the person being spoken to also influences how we speak. Men are spoken to more loudly than women are by both men and women (Markel, Prebor, & Brandt, 1972). Similarly, in a study of people's voices on television dramas and talk shows, men were spoken to more dominantly, condescendingly, and unpleasantly than women were by both men and women (Hall & Braunwald, 1981). However, listeners who heard the speaker without knowing the sex of the recipient erroneously thought that women spoke meekly to men when in fact women and men both spoke more powerfully to men.

VOCAL CUES AND EMOTION

Vocal cues are widespread among many animal species for communication about territory, relationship, identity, alarm, physical states, and emotion (Marler, Evans, & Hauser, 1992; Kitchen, Cheney, & Seyfarth, 2003). Darwin viewed the voice as a primary channel for emotional signals in both humans and animals. In this section we examine what is known about emotional expression in the human voice.

One persistent question is whether people can identify emotions in the voice. Davitz's (1964) early conclusion was positive: "Regardless of the technique used, all studies of adults thus far reported in the literature agree that emotional meanings can be communicated accurately by vocal expression" (p. 23). More recent reviews strongly concur and also demonstrate that there is substantial accuracy even when speakers and listeners are not from the same culture, and that listeners in different cultures tend to make the same errors and confusions when judging emotions in the voice, though there appears also to be an advantage in judging voices from one's own culture (Juslin & Laukka, 2003; Scherer, 2003; Scherer, Banse, & Wallbott, 2001). Pittam and Scherer (1993) concluded that the recognition of emotion from the voice is four to five times what would be expected if listeners were simply guessing. Neumann and Strack (2000) have further demonstrated that hearing voices expressing different emotions also elicits the corresponding emotional feelings, as reflected both in the listener's own voice tone and in self-ratings of mood. These, like other findings on "emotional contagion" (see chapter 9), show that emotions can be conveyed and shared as a largely unconscious process (Chartrand & Bargh, 1999).

The notion that a listener might respond with the same kind of emotion as expressed in the speaker's voice suggests a parallel situation that we experience very often when we listen to music. Music can create potent emotional effects, and indeed experimenters sometimes use music to induce emotions in laboratory studies. Some researchers have studied accuracy of identifying emotions in music using methods very similar to those used to study the communication of emotion in the voice. For example, a performer might be asked to play a passage on the piano so as to convey anger or happiness. Accuracy on the part of listeners can then be measured. Juslin and Laukka (2003) found, in reviewing these studies, that accuracy for judging emotions in music is very similar to accuracy in judging emotions in the voice, and furthermore that many of the same acoustic qualities account for the effects. As illustration, tempo and intensity increase in anger and happiness in both modalities, and variability in intensity is increased for anger and fear but is decreased for sadness and tenderness in both modalities.

Several methods have been used to eliminate or control the verbal information usually accompanying vocal cues. Accuracy may vary depending on the method used. Some studies use "meaningless content," usually having the speaker say numbers or letters while trying to convey various emotional states. As early as 1959, Davitz and Davitz conducted a study of this type. Speakers were instructed to express 10 different feelings while reciting parts of the alphabet. These expressions were recorded and played to judges who were asked to identify the emotion being expressed from the list of 10 emotions. Generally, emotions or feelings were communicated far beyond chance expectation. It is difficult to tell, of course, whether the communicators were using the same tonal or vocal cues they would use in real-life emotional reactions.

Other studies have attempted to control verbal cues by using "constant content." A speaker reads a standard passage while attempting to simulate different emotional states. The underlying assumption is that the passage selected is neutral in emotional tone. Another approach is to try to ignore content and focus attention on the pauses, breathing rate, and other characteristics that suggest the person's emotional state. This method is frequently used in psychotherapy to identify signs of anxiety.

Some studies have used electronic filtering to eliminate verbal content (Rogers, Scherer, & Rosenthal, 1971). A low-pass filter will hold back the higher frequencies of speech on which word recognition depends. The finished product sounds much like a mumble heard through a wall. One common problem with the electronically filtered technique is that some of the nonverbal vocal cues may be eliminated in the filtering process, creating an artificial stimulus. Although some aspects of vocal quality may be lost in the filtering process, a listener can still adequately perceive pitch, rate, and loudness in order to judge emotional content. An advantage of the filtering method is that naturally occurring speech can be used, in contrast to the previous methods which require the speaker to recite a standard text.

Filtered speech is the most popular method of making words unintelligible and has produced some very intriguing results, some of which we summarize here. In a study of doctors, Milmoe and her colleagues (1967) found that the more anger was perceived in the filtered voices of doctors talking about their alcoholic patients, the less successful they were in getting those patients into therapy. Later research verified that the tone of voice used when talking *about* patients carries over into the way doctors talk *to* patients (Rosenthal, Vanicelli, & Blanck, 1984). Another study of physicians found that those who provided more medical information to their patients and were more competent according to technical standards (conducting a proper interview, diagnosing correctly, and so forth) were those with the lowest ratings of boredom in short filtered clips of their voices (Hall, Roter, & Katz, 1987). It has also been found that a patient's satisfaction with a medical visit is greatest when the physician's words are rated as more pleasant and when the physician's filtered voice tone is rated as more angry and anxious. The combination of pleasant words and not-so-pleasant voice may convey a desirable message of concern and involvement in the patient's problems (Hall, Roter, & Rand, 1981). Consistent with this finding is a study of surgeons talking to their patients (Ambady et al., 2002) that did not use filtered speech but rather ratings of the surgeons' unfiltered voices plus statistical controls for the verbal content. That study found that surgeons whose voices were less dominant and more anxious were less likely to have been sued by patients.

Another study analyzed the filtered speech of airline passengers talking to airport agents about their lost baggage (Scherer & Ceschi, 2000). In that study, the number of "felt" and "unfelt" smiles (see chapter 9) was counted, and judges made ratings of the passengers' filtered speech. A higher frequency of felt (enjoyment) smiles was related to less vocal anger, worry, and resignation and to more rated good humor; inauthentic or "un-felt" smiles were unrelated to the voice ratings. This study supports the validity of filtered speech ratings as an indicator of authentic feelings.

Studies vary in how accurately emotions are judged from voice cues. One reason for this involves the differing methods by which such observations may be made—for example, how long the voice samples are, which content-masking technique is used, or how dissimilar the response alternatives are. Another reason is that speakers (and listeners) vary widely in how accurately they can express (and recognize) different emotions (see chapter 3). For example, in the Davitz and Davitz (1959) study, one speaker's expressions were identified correctly only 23% of the time, whereas another speaker communicated accurately over 50% of the time. In that study, like many others, accuracy was defined in terms of how well listeners could identify the emotion the speaker was asked to express. Listeners' accuracy in recognizing the intended emotion varied widely, just as the speakers' sending accuracy did.

Thus, depending on the skills that individuals bring to a communication situation, they may or may not succeed in sending and receiving vocal emotion cues well. Accuracy in judging emotions from the voice develops with age and appears to be correlated with similar psychological characteristics as is skill in judging other nonverbal cues (Baum & Nowicki, 1998) (see chapter 3). As one example, persons with autism and Asperger syndrome score lower than comparison groups on judging both vocal and facial emotion cues (Rutherford, Baron-Cohen, & Wheelwright, 2002), and the same is true for persons with anorexoria nervosa (Kucharska-Pietura et al., 2004). Some research questions are intrinsically more relevant to the voice than to other cue channels. For example, Thompson, Schellenberg, and Husain (2004) demonstrated that studying music helps a person's accuracy in decoding emotions conveyed in the voice. (By the same token, one might predict that studying painting or sculpture might improve a person's accuracy in judging emotions through the face or body. To our knowledge, this research has not been done.)

Another qualification to any statement about the voice's overall ability to communicate emotions is that some emotions are easier to communicate than others. For example, one study found anger identified 63% of the time, whereas pride was identified correctly only 20% of the time. Another study found that joy and hate were easily recognized, but shame and love were the most difficult to recognize. In general, anger, joy, and sadness are easier to recognize than fear and disgust in the voice (Banse & Scherer, 1996; Pittam & Scherer, 1993). The similarity of some feelings may account for some of the difference. For instance, certain errors are consistent in some studies: Fear is mistaken for nervousness, love is mistaken for sadness, and pride is mistaken for satisfaction. It is also possible that in more real-life situations, we can use context to discriminate emotions with similar characteristics. But when confronted with such cues and no context, we find discriminations difficult.

The most significant work on how emotion is revealed in the voice is by Klaus Scherer, who brings together knowledge of acoustical features of the voice, theory on how different emotions affect the voice, and results of actual research. One thing is clear: There is no "dictionary" of emotion cues for the voice, any more than there is for any nonverbal channel. You cannot identify key acoustic features and then look them up in a book somewhere to see which emotion is being expressed. Many factors enter into the total picture of

TABLE 11-2   Speech Disturbance Categories, Frequency of Occurrence, and Examples

CATEGORY	% OF TOTAL	EXAMPLE
1. "Er," "Ah," or "Um"	40.5	Well . . . er . . . when I go home
2. Sentence change	25.3	I have a book which . . . the book I
3. Repetition	19.2	I often . . . often work at night.
4. Stutter	7.8	It sort of l . . . l . . . leaves me.
5. Omission (leaving out a word or leaving it unfinished)	4.5	I went to the lib . . . the Bod.
6. Sentence incompletion	1.2	He said the reason was . . . anyway I
7. Tongue slip	0.7	I haven't much term (that is, time)
8. Intruding incoherent sound	1.2	I don't really know why . . . dh . . .

SOURCE: From M. Cook, "Anxiety, speech disturbances and speech," *Journal of Clinical Psychology*, Vol. 4, 1969, 107. Reprinted by permission of John Wiley and Sons.

emotional expression: contextual cues, the words being spoken, other nonverbal behaviors, individual differences in the people, and the fact that there is undoubtedly more than one way to express a given emotion.

The emotion of anxiety well illustrates this complexity. There are wide individual differences in vocal expression by anxious people. Some say anxious people talk slower under experimentally induced anxiety, but those not normally anxious speak faster under such conditions. Anxiety induced in a particular circumstance often is associated with more nonfluencies or speech disruptions (Mahl, 1956; Siegman, 1987). Table 11-2 presents the categories of speech disturbance investigated by Cook (1965). "Non-Ah" speech errors (categories 2 through 8) seem to increase with induced anxiety or discomfort; "Ah" errors (category 1) do not (see the section Hesitations, Pauses, Silence, and Speech later in this chapter). Personality dimensions related to anxiety have also been studied in relation to the production of speech disturbances. Harrigan, Suarez, and Hartman (1994) obtained anxiety ratings of verbatim transcripts of the speech of individuals who varied in state and trait anxiety as well as in repression (the need to deny negative thoughts, impulses, or behaviors). Repressors' speech was judged to be the most anxious, more so even than the speech of people who were high trait-anxious but not repressive. The authors attributed these effects to differences in the frequency of speech disturbances among groups. Although repressors do not view themselves as high on trait anxiety, their vocal behavior says otherwise. Perhaps anxious people are more aware of their anxiety and can take steps to conceal or control it, whereas repressive people are not aware of it, increasing the chances that anxiety cues will "leak" out through the voice.

Acoustic analyses of actors' voices portraying anger, fear, sorrow, and neutral mood were found by Williams and Stevens (1972) to vary in their frequency contours; for example, for sadness the contours were relatively flat. The average frequencies were lowest for sorrow and highest for anger, with neutral and fear in between. These researchers went outside the laboratory also for more evidence; they analyzed recordings of the radio announcer who described, live, the explosion and burning of the hydrogen-filled zeppelin

TABLE 11-3   **Acoustic Concomitants of Emotional Dimensions**

Amplitude variation	Moderate	Pleasantness, activity, happiness
Pitch variation	Moderate	Anger, boredom, disgust, fear
Pitch contour	Down	Pleasantness, boredom, sadness
	Up	Potency, anger, fear, surprise
Pitch level	Low	Pleasantness, boredom, sadness
Tempo	Slow	Boredom, disgust, sadness
	Fast	Pleasantness, activity, potency, anger, fear
Duration (shape)	Round	Potency, boredom, disgust, fear, sadness
Filtration (lack of overtones)	Low	Sadness, pleasantness, boredom, happiness
	Moderate	Potency, activity
Tonality	Atonal	Disgust
	Tonal—minor	Anger
Rhythm	Not rhythmic	Boredom
	Rhythmic	Activity, fear, surprise

Hindenburg at Lakehurst, New Jersey, in 1937. Comparison of his voice before and immediately after the disaster showed the fundamental frequency rose afterwards, with much less fluctuation in frequency. Later investigations have confirmed that the voice rises in pitch when the speaker is in a state of stress.

Scherer's work has encompassed a broad range of emotions. In a 1974 study, he used artificial sounds rather than spontaneous speech to approach the question of which vocal features are associated with which emotions. Subjects rated synthesized tones on 10-point scales of pleasantness, potency, activity, and evaluation and indicated whether the stimuli could or could not be an expression of interest, sadness, fear, happiness, disgust, anger, surprise, elation, or boredom. Generally speaking, tempo and pitch variation seem to be very influential factors for a wide range of judgments about emotional expressions. Table 11-3 summarizes the results of several of Scherer's studies.

Scherer (1986) expanded his predictions to include 12 different emotions (such as irritation/cold anger, grief/desperation, elation/joy) and 18 different acoustic variables (such as average fundamental frequency, variability in loudness, and speech rate). In comparing these theoretical predictions to actual research, Scherer found some impressive consistencies but also considerable variation, partly due to great differences in how the studies were conducted and the number of studies conducted. Joy/elation is well studied and associated with higher average frequency (pitch), greater frequency range, greater frequency variability, higher average intensity (loudness), and faster rate. Anger is conveyed by higher frequency and intensity, and greater frequency range and faster speech rate for "hot" anger. Fear is shown by higher frequency, especially high-frequency energy, and faster speech rate. Sadness (at least the quiet, resigned sort) involves lower average frequency and intensity, has downward-directed contours, and is slower (Pittam & Scherer, 1993; Scherer et al., 1991). Research is progressing on identifying emotions from acoustic variables, so that someday computers may be able to "recognize" vocal emotions almost as well as human listeners do (Banse & Scherer, 1996).

VOCAL CUES, COMPREHENSION, AND PERSUASION

In addition to its role in personality and emotional judgments, the voice also plays a part in retention and attitude change, which has been primarily studied in public speaking. For many years introductory public speaking textbooks have stressed the importance of the ancient canon of delivery to the rhetorical situation. Delivery of the speech (rather than content) was perhaps the first area of rhetoric to receive quantitative examination by speech researchers. Almost every study that isolated delivery as a variable showed that delivery did matter. It had positive effects on the amount of information remembered, the amount of attitude change elicited from the audience, and the amount of credibility audience members attributed to the speaker. Some authors maintain that poor delivery decreases our chances for accomplishing intended goals, but that good delivery, in itself, does not produce desirable changes—it only allows such effects to take place.

Rather than arguing the merits of good delivery, we are only concerned with one aspect of this larger concept. We want to know whether vocal cues alone (excluding gestures, facial expressions, movements, and other elements of delivery) significantly affect comprehension, attitude change, and speaker credibility.

Typical prescriptions for use of the voice in delivering a public speech include the following:

1. Use variety in volume, rate, pitch, and articulation. The probability of desirable outcomes is less when we use a constant rate, volume, pitch, and articulation. Being consistently overprecise may be as ineffective as being overly sloppy in articulation. Although it has not been formally studied, it is quite possible that when vocal variety is perceived as rhythmic or patterned, it is no longer variety, and this decreases the probability of desirable outcomes.
2. Base decisions concerning loud/soft, fast/slow, precise/sloppy, or high/low on what is appropriate for a given audience in a given situation.
3. Avoid excessive nonfluencies.

Vocal Cues, Comprehension, and Retention

Several studies tend to support the prescriptions for vocal variety in increasing audience comprehension or retention. Woolbert (1920), in perhaps the earliest study of this type, found that large variations of rate, force, pitch, and quality produced high audience retention when compared with a no-variation condition. Glasgow (1952), using prose and poetry, established two conditions for study: "good intonation" and "mono-pitch." Multiple-choice tests, following exposure to these differing vocal samples, showed that mono-pitch decreased comprehension by more than 10% for both prose and poetry. Other research suggests that moderately poor vocal quality, pitch patterns, nonfluencies, mispronunciation, and even stuttering do not interfere significantly with comprehension, although listeners generally find these conditions unpleasant (Kibler & Barker, 1972; Klinger, 1959; Utzinger, 1952). All of these studies indicate that listeners are rather adaptable. It probably takes constant and extreme vocal unpleasantries to affect comprehension, and even then the listener may adapt. Poor vocal qualities probably contribute more to a listener's perception of the speaker's personality or mood than to a decrease in comprehension.

The study of speaking rate by itself yields additional evidence of listener flexibility and the lack of impact on comprehension of seemingly poor voice-related phenomena. The normal speaking rate is between 125 and 190 words per minute. Some researchers believe comprehension begins to decrease once the rate exceeds 200 words per minute, but other experts in speeded speech place the level of significant decline in comprehension at between 250 and 275 words per minute. King and Behnke (1989) point out that time-compressed speech adversely affects comprehensive listening (understanding a message and remembering it for the future) but does not adversely affect short-term listening (40 seconds or less) or interpretive listening (reading between the lines) until very high levels of compression are reached, that is, 60%. Obviously, individual ability to process information at rapid rates differs widely. The inescapable conclusion from studies of speech rate, however, is that we can comprehend information at much more rapid rates than we ordinarily are exposed to. In an experiment in which individual listeners were allowed to vary the rates of presentation at will, the average choice was 1.5 times normal speed (Orr, 1968).

VOCAL CUES AND PERSUASION

What is the role of the voice in persuasive situations? It is clear we can communicate various attitudes with our voice alone, for example, friendliness, hostility, superiority, and submissiveness. Then what contribution, if any, do vocal cues make toward changing people's attitudes?

Mehrabian and Williams (1969) conducted a series of studies on the nonverbal correlates of intended and perceived persuasiveness. The following vocal cues were associated with both "increasing intent to persuade and decoded as enhancing the persuasiveness of a communication": more speech volume, higher speech rate, and less halting speech. This early study has been followed by many studies on the relation of vocal cues to attitude change. Burgoon and her colleagues (1990) concluded, after reviewing this research, that the following vocal cues are associated with greater perceived persuasiveness, credibility, competence, or actual attitude change. (There are probably upper limits to the effective range on each of these variables, so that extremes would produce less, not more, credibility or persuasion.)

- ◆ Fluent, nonhesitant speech
- ◆ Shorter response latencies (length of pause when speakers switch turns)
- ◆ More pitch variation
- ◆ Louder voice
- ◆ Faster speech (as measured by words per minute or length of pauses)

Of all these cues, faster speech has received the most attention in its relation to the persuasion process (Miller et al., 1976; Street, Brady, & Lee, 1984). Why is fast speech persuasive? Is it because faster speech seems more credible? Considerable evidence indicates that a speaker's perceived credibility is a potent factor in persuasion (Hass, 1981). Although this position is the most widely accepted, other explanations have been offered. When listening to a faster-speaking persuader, we may be kept so busy processing the message that we have little chance to develop counterarguments in our heads. Or we may be simply distracted by noticing the faster speech, and this interferes with our ability to focus on the message and develop counterarguments (Woodall & Burgoon, 1983). It is also important to note that faster speech does not *always* produce more persuasion. Smith and Shaffer (1991) found that faster speech increased persuasion when the message was counterattitudinal (i.e., favored a position that opposed the listener's pre-existing attitude), but decreased persuasion when the message was consistent with the listener's pre-existing attitude.

At this point you may legitimately ask, "So what?" What if we know the voice's potential for eliciting various responses related to comprehension, attitude change, and speaker credibility? Obviously in real-life situations there are visual and verbal cues, prior publicity and experiences with the speaker, and a multitude of other interacting factors that greatly reduce the importance of vocal cues. In short, specific nonverbal cues do not operate in isolation in human interaction as they do in the experiments reported here. For the most part, we do not know what their role is in context—that is, in combination with other cues and in settings outside the laboratory. DeGroot and Motowidlo's (1999) study takes us a step in that direction. These investigators asked managers in companies to let themselves be interviewed as though they were applying for their job; the managers' vocal cues were then related to their actual supervisors' performance ratings of them and also to naive observers' impressions of the taped interviews. A vocal composite that consisted of faster speech rate, more pitch variability, fewer pauses, lower pitch, and less amplitude variability was a significant predictor of both the performance ratings and the favorability of listeners' reactions. The authors believe that people who speak with this desirable set of vocal characteristics will be better able to perform well on a job owing to the favorability of people's responses to them. Burgoon, Birk, and Pfau (1990) also examined a wide range of different cues, vocal as well as those relating to face and body, in a study of credibility and persuasiveness. Controlling for other nonverbal behaviors, vocal fluency remained the strongest predictor of judged competence (a dimension of credibility), and it was one of the two strongest predictors of judged persuasiveness.

VOCAL CUES AND TURN TAKING IN CONVERSATIONS

Thus far we have discussed the role of vocal cues in communicating interpersonal attitudes, emotions, and information about oneself. Vocal cues also play an important role in managing the interaction. Vocal cues are part of a system of cues that helps us structure our interactions—that is, who speaks, when, to whom, and for how long. Rules for turn taking, or floor apportionment, may have as much to do with how a conversation is perceived as does the actual verbal content of the interaction (Duncan, 1973; Wiemann & Knapp, 1975). You can probably recall instances where turn-taking rules played a significant role in your responses: for example, when a long-winded speaker would not let you get a word in edgewise; when a passive interactant refused to "take the conversational ball" that you offered; when you were confronted with an "interrupter"; or those awkward moments when two people started talking simultaneously. Obviously, vocal cues are only some of the signals we use to manage our turn taking (see chapter 12). Only rarely do we explicitly verbalize this information—for example, "OK, Lillian, I'm finished talking. Now it's your turn to talk."

Our use of these signals is mostly unconscious but conforms to definite rules of usage nonetheless. These have been described extensively by Duncan and Fiske (1977) in their analyses of two-person conversations held in a laboratory setting. They found that certain cues were almost invariably present when smooth turn taking took place, five of which were vocal (verbal or nonverbal). None of these cues seems to be more important than the others; rather it seems that a smooth switch is best predicted by the sheer number of these cues. In other words, redundancy—sending several equivalent-meaning cues simultaneously—promotes smooth regulation of conversation. These cues included the speaker's pitch or a drawl at the end of a unit of speech, the grammatical completion of a unit of speech, and the use of certain routine verbal phrases. The next sections elaborate on these and other turn-regulating behaviors identified in research (Cappella, 1985; Rosenfeld, 1987).

TURN YIELDING

To yield a turn means to signal you are finished and the other person can start talking. Sometimes we do this by asking a question—causing the pitch to rise at the end of our comment. Another unwritten rule most of us follow is that questions require (or demand) answers. We also can drop our pitch (sometimes with a drawl on the last syllable) when finishing a declarative statement that concludes our intended turn. If the cues are not sufficient for the other person to start talking, we may have to add a trailer on the end. The trailer may be silence or a form of a filled pause, for example, "ya know," "so, ah," or "or something." The filled pauses reiterate the fact that you are yielding and fill a silence that might otherwise indicate the other's insensitivity to your signals (or your own inability to make them clear!).

TURN REQUESTING

We can also use vocal cues to show others that we want to say something. Although an audible inspiration of breath alone may not be a sufficient cue, it does help signal turn requesting. The mere act of interrupting or simultaneous talking may signal an impatience to get the speaking turn. Sometimes you can inject vocalizations during normal pausing of the other speaker. These "stutter starts" may be the beginning of a sentence ("I . . . I . . . I . . .") or just vocal buffers ("Ah . . . Er . . . Ah . . ."). Another method for requesting a turn is to assist the other person in finishing quickly. This can be done by increasing the rapidity of our responses, much like the increased rapidity of the head nods when we are anxious to leave a situation in which another person has the floor. Normally, back-channel cues, such as "Uh-huh," "Yeah," and "Mmm-hmm," are used to encourage the other to continue speaking and to signal attentiveness. However, when these are used rapidly, the message can be "Get finished so I can talk."

TURN MAINTAINING

Sometimes we want to keep the floor. It may be to show our status or to avoid unpleasant feedback, or perhaps it reflects some exaggerated sense of the importance of our own words and ideas. Common vocal cues in these instances may include the following:

1. Increasing volume and rate when turn-requesting cues are sensed
2. Increasing the frequency of filled pauses
3. Decreasing the frequency and duration of silent pauses (Maclay & Osgood, 1959)

Although Lalljee and Cook's (1969) research does not support the use of pauses for control, Rochester (1973) cites several studies that support the following conclusions:

1. More filled pauses and fewer silent pauses are found in dialogue than monologue.
2. More filled pauses and fewer silent pauses are not found when people want to break off speaking.
3. More filled pauses and fewer silent pauses are more likely when the speaker lacks visual means of controlling the conversation (as on the telephone).

Turn Denying

In some instances, we may want the other person to keep talking—to deny the turn when offered. The back-channel cues we noted earlier may keep the other person talking by giving reinforcement for what is being said. The rate with which these are delivered, however, is probably slower than when we are requesting a turn. And, of course, just remaining silent may dramatically communicate a turn denial. Silence and pauses are the subjects of our next section.

We wish to reiterate that conversational regulation is a delicate matter involving a complex coordination of verbal behavior, vocal behavior, gaze, and body movement. As examples, research finds that even if we would predict a turn switch based on words and voice, a switch is very unlikely if the speaker looks away from the listener during the likely switching point or engages in a hand gesture that is maintained or not returned to a resting state.

HESITATIONS, PAUSES, SILENCE, AND SPEECH

Spontaneous speech is actually highly fragmented and discontinuous. Goldman-Eisler (1968) said that even when speech is at its most fluent, two-thirds of spoken language comes in chunks of less than six words—strongly suggesting that the concept of fluency in spontaneous speech is an illusion. Pauses range in length from milliseconds to minutes. Pauses are subject to considerable variation based on individual differences, the kind of verbal task, the amount of spontaneity, and the pressures of the particular social situation.

Location or Placement of Pauses

Pauses are not evenly distributed throughout the speech stream. Goldman-Eisler (1968, p. 13) outlined places where pauses do occur—at both grammatical and nongrammatical junctures.

Grammatical

1. "Natural" punctuation points, for example, the end of a sentence.
2. Immediately preceding a conjunction whether (a) coordinating, such as *and, but, neither, therefore*, or (b) subordinating, such as *if, when, while, as, because.*
3. Before relative and interrogative pronouns, for example, *who, which, what, why, whose.*
4. When a question is direct or implied: "I don't know whether I will."
5. Before all adverbial clauses of time (when), manner (how), and place (where).
6. When complete parenthetical references are made: "You can tell that the house— the one on the corner—is falling into disrepair."

Nongrammatical

1. Where a gap occurs in the middle or at the end of a phrase: "In each of//the cells of the body// . . ."
2. Where a gap occurs between words and phrases repeated: (a) "The question of the//of the economy" and (b) "This attitude is narrower than that//that of many South Africans."
3. Where a gap occurs in the middle of a verbal compound: "We have//taken issue with them and they are//resolved to oppose us."
4. Where the structure of a sentence is disrupted by a reconsideration or a false start: "I think the problem of France is the//what we have to remember about France is . . ."

Analysis of spontaneous speech shows that only 55% of the pauses fall into the grammatical category, whereas oral readers of prepared texts are extremely consistent in pausing at clause and sentence junctures.

Types of Pauses

The two major types of pauses are the unfilled pause (silent) and the filled pause. *A filled pause* is filled with some type of phonation such as "um" or "uh." A variety of sources associate filled pauses with a range of generally undesirable characteristics. Some people associate filled pauses and repetitions with emotional arousal; some feel filled pauses may reduce anxiety but jam cognitive processes. Goldman-Eisler (1961) found, in four studies, that unfilled pausing time was associated with "superior (more concise) stylistic and less probable linguistic formulations," whereas higher rates of filled pauses were linked to "inferior stylistic achievement (long-winded statement) of greater predictability." Livant (1963) found the time required to solve addition problems was significantly greater when the subject filled his pauses than when he was silent. Several experimenters reached similar conclusions: When speakers fill pauses, they also impair their performance. Thus in a heated discussion you may maintain control of the conversation by filling the pauses, but you may also decrease the quality of your contribution. Too many filled or unfilled pauses may receive negative evaluations from listeners (Christenfeld, 1995). Lalljee (1971) found that too many unfilled pauses by the speaker caused listeners to perceive the speaker as anxious, angry, or contemptuous; too many filled pauses evoked perceptions of the speaker as anxious or bored. Although these studies suggest that filled pauses are generally to be avoided, research also finds that in university lecturers their use is correlated with more complex thought processes and use of a larger vocabulary (Schachter et al., 1991; Schachter et al., 1994).

Filled pauses show up, interestingly, much more in the speech of men than of women (Hall, 1984). We might think of men as more assertive in general, but Siegman (1987) observed that more filled pauses are usually associated with "cautious and hesitant speech" (p. 398). Perhaps men are more socially uncomfortable than women are. It may be, however, that filled pauses are serving another function altogether—keeping the speaker's turn from being taken over by the other person, which may be of more concern for men.

Reasons Why Pauses Occur

During the course of spontaneous speech, we are confronted with situations that require decisions as to what to say and what lexical or structural form to put it in. One school of thought relates hesitancy in speech to the uncertainty of predicting the cognitive and lexical activity while speaking. The speaker may be reflecting on decisions about the immediate message or may even be projecting into the past or future—that is, "I don't think she understood what I said earlier" or "If she says no, what do I say then?" Thus the assumption is that these hesitation pauses are actually delays due to competing processes taking place in the brain. Goldman-Eisler indeed found that pause time while "interpreting" cartoons was twice as long as while "describing" them. It also was observed that with each succeeding trial (a reduction in spontaneity), there was a decline in pausing. Recent research continues to support the theory that longer speech latencies and a relatively large number of pauses are sometimes due to the complexity of the message being formulated (Greene & Ravizza, 1995).

Another possible explanation for some pausing behavior involves what is described as disruption behavior. Instead of representing time for planning, the pause may indicate a disruption due to an emotional state that may have developed from negative feedback or time pressures. These disruptions may take many forms: fears about the subject matter under discussion, desire to impress the listener with verbal and/or intellectual skills, pressure to perform other tasks simultaneously, or pressure to produce verbal output immediately.

Influence and Coordination within the Dyad

Thus far we have considered hesitations and pauses primarily from the speaker's standpoint. Now we consider the interaction process and the effect of one person's interpersonal timing on another. For many years, Chapple (1949, 1953; Chapple & Sayles, 1961) explored the rhythms of dialogue, that is, the degree of synchrony found in the give-and-take of conversations. This involved noting who talks, when, and for how long. He developed a standardized interview in which the interviewer alternates "normal" attentive responding with silences and, later, interruptions. As you might suspect, there are many reactions. Some people respond to a nonresponse, or silence, by speeding up; others match the nonresponse; and most try some combination of the two.

Matarazzo's studies of interviewing behavior found most latencies of response were between 1 and 2 seconds, with the mean about 1.7 seconds (Matarazzo, Wiens, & Saslow, 1965). The interviewer, however, can have considerable influence on the length of pauses. For example, when the interviewer did not respond to a statement by the interviewee, almost 65% of the interviewees began to talk again, but the pause was now closer to 4.5 seconds. In the same manner, Matarazzo demonstrated response matching, showing how the interviewer can also control the length of utterance by increasing the length of his own utterances. Figures 11-3 and 11-4 show the results of several experiments involving three 15-minute segments of a 45-minute interview with the interviewer varying his responses during different periods. As the interviewer extended the length of his responses, there was a corresponding increase in the length of responses from the interviewee. In the same manner, there must be times when pauses beget pauses. The interviewer also can control response duration by head nodding or saying "Mmm-hmm" during the interviewee's response, as shown in Figure 11-4. This demonstrates that these back-channel responses do indeed encourage a speaker to continue speaking.

FIGURE 11-3

The influence of interviewer response duration on interviewee response duration.

SOURCE: Courtesy of D. W. Addington

FIGURE 11-4

The influence of interviewer head nods and "Mm-hmm" on interviewee response duration.

SOURCE: Courtesy of D. W. Addington

SILENCE

Most of the hesitations and pauses we have discussed are relatively short. Sometimes silences may be extended. They may be imposed by the nature of the environment, for example, in churches, libraries, courtrooms, or hospitals; they may be imposed for the duration of a given event, for example, at a funeral, during the playing of taps, when praying, or when singing the national anthem; or they may be self-imposed, for example, remaining quiet in the woods to hear other sounds or enjoying with a lover the mutual closeness that silence may bring. Silence can mean virtually anything. Silence is charged with those words that have just been exchanged; words that have been exchanged in the past; words that have not or will not be said but are fantasized; and words that may actually be said in the future. For these reasons, it would be absurd to provide a list of meanings for silence. The meaning of silence, like the meaning of words, can only be deduced after careful analysis of the communicators, subject matter, time, place, culture, and so forth.

Some of the many interpersonal functions served by silence include the following:

- Punctuation or accenting, drawing attention to certain words or ideas
- Evaluating, providing judgments of another's behavior, showing favor or disfavor, agreement or disagreement, attacking (e.g., not responding to a comment, greeting, or letter)
- Revelation, making something known or hiding something by being silent
- Expression of emotions, the silence of disgust, sadness, fear, anger, or love
- Mental activity, showing thoughtfulness and reflection or ignorance through silence (preceding list from Bruneau, 1973; Jaworski, 1993; Jensen, 1973)

❖

Summary

In the course of reading this chapter, you have been exposed to a considerable number of research studies and amount of descriptive material. What do they mean for you as a communicator and as an observer of nonverbal behavior in human interaction?

Generally, this chapter should leave you with the overall impression that vocal cues frequently play a major role in determining responses in human communication situations. You should be quick to challenge the cliché that vocal cues only concern how something is said; frequently they are what is said. What is said might be an attitude ("I like you" or "I'm superior to you"); it might be an emotion; it might be the coordination and management of the conversation; or it might be the presentation of some aspect of your personality, background, or physical features.

As a communicator and observer of the human species, also recognize the important role vocal stereotypes play in determining responses. Whether judges are trying to estimate your occupation, sociability, race, degree of introversion, body type, or any of various other qualities about you, they will be very apt to respond to well-learned stereotypes. These stereotypes may not accurately describe you, but they will be influential in the interaction between you and the judge. Almost all the research reviewed in this chapter demonstrated considerable interjudge agreement. So far it is difficult to identify many personality traits that seem to be judged with consistent accuracy. This is partly due, of course, to the imperfect nature of the personality measures. Moreover, a particular person, judging a particular voice, may be very accurate in judging the personality behind that voice. Our judgments of large groups of people are also influential in our judgments of a single person's vocal personality. Although it is not uncommon for a person speaking a dialect other than one's own to be perceived negatively, speakers who try to correct for speech differences and severely violate expectations for their speech may also be perceived negatively.

Accurate judgments (beyond chance) of age, sex, and status from vocal cues alone tend to be fairly consistently reported in the literature. Furthermore, under certain circumstances we are able to identify specific speakers from their voice alone.

Although studies of judgments of emotions from vocal cues have used different methods, different emotions, listeners with differing sensitivity, and speakers with differing abilities for portraying emotions, the results reveal that we can make quite accurate judgments of emotions and feelings from wordless vocal messages. Obviously, we must consistently remind ourselves that any given individual may vocally express the same emotion differently on different days, in different situations, and with different provoking stimuli.

Some indications are that moderately poor vocal behaviors do not interfere with a listener's comprehension of a message, and that if we use variety in our volume, pitch, and rate, we may increase our chances of achieving audience comprehension in public speeches. Unchanging, constant vocal behavior (particularly at the extremes) may be less advantageous in achieving audience comprehension.

Preliminary findings also suggest that the voice may be important in some aspects of persuasion. More fluency, higher rate, more volume, and less halting speech seem related to intent to persuade and perceived persuasiveness. We know the credibility of the speaker plays an important role in persuasion in some situations. We now know that some decisions concerning credibility (trustworthiness, dynamism, likableness, competency) are made from word-free samples of the voice alone.

Vocal cues also help us manage the give-and-take of speaking turns. In turn yielding, turn requesting, turn maintaining, and turn denying, we use vocal cues to make our intentions clear.

We also discussed the important role of hesitations or pauses in spontaneous speech. Such pauses, ordinarily between 1 and 2 seconds long, may be greatly influenced by the other interactant, the topic being discussed, and the nature of the social situation. Pauses may be the overt manifestation of time used to make decisions about what to say and how to say it, or they may represent disruptions in the speech process.

Taken together, these findings show that vocal cues alone can give much information about a speaker, and our total reaction to another individual is at least somewhat colored by our reactions to these vocal cues. Our perceptions of verbal cues combine with other verbal and nonverbal stimuli to mold conceptions used as a basis for communicating. Perhaps future study will provide some information on how our responses to our own voices affect self-images and, hence, our communication behavior. First, however, we need to give more attention to voices manifested in naturalistic interaction, particularly with partners other than strangers. Some of the preceding results may need modifying as we look at spontaneous speech at different stages in relationships.

Questions for Discussion

1. Consider stereotypes you have about the voice—for example, about high or low voices, fast or slow voices, voices with different accents, and so forth. Discuss what truth you think there is to them, based on as many real examples as you can think of.

2. Analyze the phenomenon of sarcasm in terms of the voice as well as the other cues that might be associated with it. Act out a variety of different comments in a sarcastic manner, and specify the cues you use.

3. Review the different methods for making voices "content free." Why does the chapter argue that the term *content free* is a misnomer?

4. Theorists argue that some nonverbal channels are easier than others to self-monitor and control. Compare the vocal channel to the face and body channels. How would you rank these three channels in terms of how easy they are to monitor and control? Why?

BIBLIOGRAPHY

Aboud, F. E., Clement, R., & Taylor, D. M. (1974). Evaluational reactions to discrepancies between social class and language. *Sociometry, 37,* 239–250.

Addington, D. W. (1968). The relationship of selected vocal characteristics to personality perception. *Speech Monographs, 35,* 492–503.

Allport, G., & Cantril, H. (1934). Judging personality from voice. *Journal of Social Psychology, 5,* 37–54.

Ambady, N., LaPlante, D., Nguyen, T., Rosenthal, R., Chaumeton, N., & Levinson, W. (2002). Surgeons' tone of voice: A clue to malpractice history. *Surgery, 132,* 5–9.

Anisfeld, M., Bogo, N., & Lambert, W. (1962). Evaluation reactions to accented English speech. *Journal of Abnormal and Social Psychology, 65,* 223–231.

Aries, E. (1987). Gender and communication. In P. Shaver & C. Hendrick (Eds.), *Review of personality and social psychology* (Vol. 7). Newbury Park, CA: Sage.

Banse, R., & Scherer, K. R. (1996). Acoustic profiles in vocal emotion expression. *Journal of Personality and Social Psychology, 70,* 614–636.

Baum, K. M., & Nowicki, S., Jr. (1998). Perception of emotion: Measuring decoding accuracy of adult prosodic cues varying in intensity. *Journal of Nonverbal Behavior, 22,* 89–107.

Beier, E. G., & Zautra, A. (1972). Identification of vocal communication of emotions across culture. (ERIC Document Reproduction Service No. ED 056504).

Berry, D. S. (1991). Accuracy in social perception: Contributions of facial and vocal information. *Journal of Personality and Social Psychology, 61,* 298–307.

Berry, D. S. (1992). Vocal types and stereotypes: Joint effects of vocal attractiveness and vocal maturity on person perception. *Journal of Nonverbal Behavior, 16,* 41–54.

Berry, D. S., Hansen, J. S., Landry-Pester, J. C., & Meier, J. A. (1994). Vocal determinants of first impressions of young children. *Journal of Nonverbal Behavior, 18,* 187–197.

Bloom, K., Moore-Schoenmakers, K., & Masataka, N. (1999). Nasality of infant vocalizations determines gender bias in adult favorability ratings. *Journal of Nonverbal Behavior, 23,* 219–236.

Bloom, K., Zajac, D. J., & Titus, J. (1999). The influence of nasality of voice on sex-stereotyped perceptions. *Journal of Nonverbal Behavior, 23,* 271–281.

Bolt, R., Cooper, F., Davis, E., Jr., Denes, P., Pickett, J., & Stevens, K. (1973). Speaker identification by speech spectrograms. *Journal of the Acoustical Society of America, 54,* 531–537.

Boomer, D. S. (1965). Hesitation and grammatical encoding. *Language and Speech, 8,* 148–158.

Boomer, D. S., & Dittmann, A. T. (1962). Hesitation pauses and juncture pauses in speech. *Language and Speech, 5,* 215–220.

Boomer, D. S., & Dittmann, A. T. (1964). Speech rate, filled pause, and body movements in interviews. *Journal of Nervous and Mental Disease, 139,* 324–327.

Bruneau, T. J. (1973). Communicative silences: Forms and functions. *Journal of Communication, 23,* 17–46.

Buck, J. (1968). The effects of Negro and white dialectical variations upon attitudes of college students. *Speech Monographs, 35,* 181–186.

Bugental, D. E., Kaswan, J. W., & Love, L. R. (1970). Perception of contradictory meanings conveyed by verbal and nonverbal channels. *Journal of Personality and Social Psychology, 16,* 647–655.

Buller, D. B., & Aune, R. K. (1988). The effects of vocalics and nonverbal sensitivity on compliance: A speech accommodation theory explanation. *Human Communication Research, 14,* 301–332.

Buller, D. B., & Burgoon, J. K. (1986). The effects of vocalics and nonverbal sensitivity on compliance: A replication and extension. *Human Communication Research, 13,* 126–144.

Burgoon, J. K., Birk, T., & Pfau, M. (1990). Nonverbal behaviors, persuasion, and credibility. *Human Communication Research, 17,* 140–169.

Caporael, L. R. (1981). The paralanguage of caregiving: Baby talk to the institutionalized aged. *Journal of Personality and Social Psychology, 40,* 876–884.

Cappella, J. N. (1985). Controlling the floor in conversation. In A. W. Siegman & S. Feldstein (Eds.), *Multichannel integrations of nonverbal behavior.* Hillsdale, NJ: Erlbaum.

Chapple, E. D. (1949). The interaction chronograph: Its evolution and present application. *Personnel, 25,* 295–307.

Chapple, E. D. (1953). The standard experimental (stress) interview as used in interaction chronograph investigations. *Human Organizations, 12,* 23–32.

Chapple, E. D., & Sayles, L. R. (1961). *The measure of management.* New York: Macmillan.

Chartrand, T. L., & Bargh, J. A. (1999). The chameleon effect: The perception–behavior link and social interaction. *Journal of Personality and Social Psychology, 76,* 893–910.

Christenfeld, N. (1995). Does it hurt to say um? *Journal of Nonverbal Behavior, 19,* 171–186.

Cook, M. (1965). Anxiety, speech disturbances, and speech rate. *British Journal of Social and Clinical Psychology, 4,* 1–7.

Corsi, P. (1982). Speaker recognition: A survey. In J. P. Haton (Ed.), *Automatic speech analysis and recognition.* Dordrecht, Holland: Reidel.

Crosby, F., & Nyquist, L. (1977). The female register: An empirical study of Lakoff's hypothesis. *Language in Society, 6,* 313–322.

Davitz, J. R. (1964). *The communication of emotional meaning.* New York: McGraw-Hill.

Davitz, J. R., & Davitz, L. (1959). The communication of feelings by content-free speech. *Journal of Communication, 9,* 6–13.

DeGroot, T., & Motowidlo, S. J. (1999). Why visual and vocal interview cues can affect interviewers' judgments and predict job performance. *Journal of Applied Psychology, 84,* 986–993.

DePaulo, B. M., & Coleman, L. M. (1986). Talking to children, foreigners, and retarded adults. *Journal of Personality and Social Psychology, 51,* 945–959.

DePaulo, B. M., & Coleman, L. M. (1987). Verbal and nonverbal communication of warmth to children, foreigners, and retarded adults. *Journal of Nonverbal Behavior, 11,* 75–88.

Dindia, K. (1987). The effects of sex of subject and sex of partner on interruptions. *Human Communication Research, 13,* 345–371.

Dittmann, A. T, & Llewellyn, L. G. (1967). The phonemic clause as a unit of speech decoding. *Journal of Personality and Social Psychology, 6,* 341–349.

Dittmann, A. T., & Llewellyn, L. G. (1969). Body movement and speech rhythm in social conversation. *Journal of Personality and Social Psychology, 11,* 98–106.

Doddington, G. (1985). Speaker recognition: Identifying people by their voices. *Proceedings of the IEEE, 73,* 1651–1664.

Duncan, S. (1972). Some signals and rules for taking speaking turns in conversations. *Journal of Personality and Social Psychology, 23,* 283–292.

Duncan, S. (1973). Toward a grammar for dyadic conversation. *Semiotica, 9,* 24–46.

Duncan, S., & Fiske, D. W. (1977). *Face-to-face interaction.* Hillsdale, NJ: Erlbaum.

Ellgring, H., & Scherer, K. R. (1996). Vocal indicators of mood change in depression. *Journal of Nonverbal Behavior, 20,* 83–110.

Ellis, D. S. (1967). Speech and social status in America. *Social Forces, 45,* 431–451.

Erickson, B., Lind, E. A., Johnson, B. C., & O'Barr, W. M. (1978). Speech style and impression-formation in a court setting: The effects of "powerful" and "powerless" speech. *Journal of Experimental Social Psychology, 14,* 266–279.

Fay, P., & Middleton, W. (1940). Judgment of occupation from the voice as transmitted over a public address system. *Sociometry, 3,* 186–191.

Frick, R. W. (1985). Communicating emotion: The role of prosodic features. *Psychological Bulletin, 97,* 412–429.

Friedman, H. S. (1979). The interactive effects of facial expressions of emotion and verbal messsage on perceptions of affective meaning. *Journal of Experimental Social Psychology, 15,* 453–469.

Gates, G. S. (1927). The role of the auditory element in the interpretation of emotions. *Psychological Bulletin, 24,* 175.

Giles, H. (1971). Ethnocentrism and the evaluation of accented speech. *British Journal of Social and Clinical Psychology, 10,* 187–188.

Giles, H., & Bourhis, R. Y. (1976). Voice and racial categorization in Britain. *Communication Monographs, 43,* 108–114.

Giles, H., Henwood, K., Coupland, N., Harriman, J., & Coupland, J. (1992). Language attitudes and cognitive mediation. *Human Communication Research, 18,* 500–527.

Giles, H., & Powesland, P. F. (1975). *Speech style and social evaluation.* New York: Academic Press.

Gill, M. M. (1994). Accent and stereotypes: Their effect on perceptions of teachers and lecture comprehension. *Journal of Applied Communication Research, 22,* 348–361.

Glasgow, G. M. (1952). A semantic index of vocal pitch. *Speech Monographs, 19,* 64–68.

Goldman-Eisler, F. (1961). A comparative study of two hesitation phenomena. *Language and Speech, 4,* 18–26.

Goldman-Eisler, F. (1968). *Psycholinguistics: Experiments in spontaneous speech.* London & New York: Academic Press.

Grahe, J. E., & Bernieri, F. J. (1999). The importance of nonverbal cues in judging rapport. *Journal of Nonverbal Behavior, 23,* 253–269.

Greene, J. O., & Ravizza, S. M. (1995). Complexity effects on temporal characteristics of speech. *Human Communication Research, 21,* 390–421.

Grieser, D. L., & Kuhl, P. K. (1988). Maternal speech to infants in a tonal language: Support for universal prosodic features in motherese. *Developmental Psychology, 24,* 14–20.

Hall, J. A. (1980). Voice tone and persuasion. *Journal of Personality and Social Psychology, 38,* 924–934.

Hall, J. A. (1984). *Nonverbal sex differences: Communication accuracy and expressive style.* Baltimore: Johns Hopkins University Press.

Hall, J. A., & Braunwald, K. G. (1981). Gender cues in conversations. *Journal of Personality and Social Psychology, 40,* 99–110.

Hall, J. A., Friedman, H. S., & Harris, M. J. (1984). Nonverbal cues, the Type A behavior pattern, and coronary heart disease. In P. D. Blanck, R. Buck, & R. Rosenthal (Eds.), *Nonverbal communication in the clinical context.* University Park: Pennsylvania State University Press.

Hall, J. A., Roter, D. L., & Katz, N. R. (1987). Task versus socioemotional behaviors in physicians. *Medical Care, 25,* 399–412.

Hall, J. A., Roter, D. L., & Rand, C. S. (1981). Communication of affect between patient and physician. *Journal of Health and Social Behavior, 22,* 18–30.

Harms, L. S. (1961). Listener judgments of status cues in speech. *Quarterly Journal of Speech, 47,* 164–168.

Harrigan, J. A., Gramata, J. F., Luck, K. S., & Margolis, C. (1989). It's how you say it: Physicians' vocal behavior. *Social Science & Medicine, 28,* 87–92.

Harrigan, J. A., Suarez, I., & Hartman, J. S. (1994). Effect of speech errors on observers' judgments of anxious and defensive individuals. *Journal of Research in Personality, 28,* 505–529.

Hass, R. G. (1981). Effects of source characteristics on cognitive responses and persuasion. In R. E. Petty, T. M. Ostrom, & T. C. Brock (Eds.), *Cognitive responses in persuasion.* Hillsdale, NJ: Erlbaum.

Hecker, M. H. L. (1971). Speaker recognition: An interpretive survey of the literature. *ASHA Monographs, 16.* Washington, DC: American Speech and Hearing Association.

Hirschman, L. (1994). Female–male differences in conversational interaction. *Language in Society, 23,* 427–442.

Hollien, H. (1990). *The acoustics of crime: The new science of forensic phonetics.* New York: Plenum.

Hummert, M. L., Mazloff, D., & Henry, C. (1999). Vocal characteristics of older adults and stereotyping. *Journal of Nonverbal Behavior, 23,* 111–132.

Irish, J. T., & Hall, J. A. (1995). Interruptive patterns in medical visits: The effects of role, status, and gender. *Social Science & Medicine, 41,* 873–881.

Japan's feminine falsetto falls right out of favor. (1995, December 13). *New York Times,* pp. A-1, A-4.

Jaworski, A. (1993). *The power of silence: Social and pragmatic perspectives.* Newbury Park, CA: Sage.

Jensen, J. V. (1973). Communicative functions of silence. *ETC, 30,* 249–257.

Juslin, P. N., & Laukka, P. (2003). Communication of emotions in vocal expression and music performance: Different channels, same code? *Psychological Bulletin, 129,* 770–814.

Kappas, A., Hess, U., & Scherer, K. R. (1991). Voice and emotion. In R. S. Feldman & B. Rime (Eds.), *Fundamentals of nonverbal behavior.* New York: Cambridge University Press.

Kasl, S. V., & Mahl, G. F. (1965). The relationship of disturbances and hesitations in spontaneous speech to anxiety. *Journal of Personality and Social Psychology, 1,* 425–433.

Kibler, R. J., & Barker, L. L. (1972). Effects of selected levels of misspelling and mispronunciation on comprehension and retention. *Southern Speech Communication Journal, 37,* 361–374.

King, P. E., & Behnke, R. R. (1989). The effect of time-compressed speech on comprehensive, interpretive, and short-term listening. *Human Communication Research, 15,* 428–443.

Kitchen, D. M., Cheney, D. L., & Seyfarth, R. M. (2003). Female baboons' responses to male loud calls. *Ethology, 109,* 401–412.

Klinger, H. N. (1959). *The effects of stuttering on audience listening comprehension.* Unpublished doctoral dissertation, New York University.

Kramer, C. (1978). Female and male perceptions of female and male speech. *Language and Speech, 20,* 151–161.

Kramer, E. (1963). Judgment of personal characteristics and emotions from non-verbal properties. *Psychological Bulletin, 60,* 408–420.

Kramer, E. (1964). Personality stereotypes in voice: A reconsideration of the data. *Journal of Social Psychology, 62,* 247–251.

Kucharska-Pietura, K., Nilolaou, V., Masiak, M., & Treasure, J. (2004). The recognition of emotion in the faces and voice of anorexia nervosa. *International Journal of Eating Disorders, 35,* 42–47.

Ladefoged, P., & Ladefoged, J. (1980). The ability of listeners to identify voices. *UCLA Working Papers in Phonetics, 49,* 43–51.

Ladefoged, P., & Vanderslice, R. (1967). The voiceprint mystique. *UCLA Working Papers in Phonetics, 7.*

Lakoff, R. (1975). *Language and women's place*. New York: Harper & Row.

Lalljee, M. G. (1971). *Disfluencies in normal English speech*. Unpublished doctoral dissertation, Oxford University, Oxford.

Lalljee, M. G., & Cook, M. (1969). An experimental investigation of the filled pauses in speech. *Language and Speech, 12*, 24–28.

Lapakko, D. (1997). Three cheers for language: A closer examination of a widely cited study of non-verbal communication. *Communication Education, 46*, 63–67.

Lass, N. J., & Davis, M. (1976). An investigation of speaker height and weight identification. *Journal of the Acoustical Society of America, 60*, 700–703.

Lass, N. J., & Harvey, L. A. (1976). An investigation of speaker photograph identification. *Journal of the Acoustical Society of America, 59*, 1232–1236.

Lass, N. J., Hughes, K. R., Bowyer, M. D., Waters, L. T., & Broune, V. T. (1976). Speaker sex identification from voiced, whispered and filtered isolated vowels. *Journal of the Acoustical Society of America, 59*, 675–678.

Levin, S., Hall, J. A., Knight, R. A., & Alpert, M. (1985). Verbal and nonverbal expression of affect in speech of schizophrenic and depressed patients. *Journal of Abnormal Psychology, 94*, 487–497.

Lippa, R. (1998). The nonverbal display and judgment of extraversion, masculinity, femininity, and gender diagnosticity: A lens model analysis. *Journal of Research in Personality, 32*, 80–107.

Livant, W. P. (1963). Antagonistic functions of verbal pauses: Filled and unfilled pauses in the solution of additions. *Language and Speech, 6*, 1–4.

Mahl, G. F. (1956). Disturbances and silences in the patient's speech in psychotherapy. *Journal of Abnormal and Social Psychology, 53*, 1–15.

Mahl, G. E, & Schulze, G. (1964). Psychological research in the extralinguistic area. In T. Sebeok, A. S. Hayes, & M. C. Bateson (Eds.), *Approaches to semiotics*. The Hague: Mouton.

Marche, T. A., & Peterson, C. (1993). The development and sex-related use of interruption behavior. *Human Communication Research, 19*, 388–408.

Markel, N. N., Meisels, M., & Houck, J. E. (1964). Judging personality from voice quality. *Journal of Abnormal and Social Psychology, 69*, 458–463.

Markel, N. N., Prebor, L. D., & Brandt, J. F. (1972). Biosocial factors in dyadic communication: Sex and speaking intensity. *Journal of Personality and Social Psychology, 23*, 11–13.

Markel, N. N., & Robin, G. L. (1965). The effect of content and sex-of-judge on judgments of personality from voice. *International Journal of Social Psychiatry, 11*, 295–300.

Marler, P., Evans, C. S., & Hauser, M. D. (1992). Animal signals: Motivational, referential, or both? In H. Papousek, U. Jurgens, & M. Papousek (Eds.), *Nonverbal vocal communication: Comparative and developmental approaches* (pp. 66–86). Paris: Cambridge University Press.

Matarazzo, J. D., Wiens, A. N., & Saslow, G. (1965). Studies in interview speech behavior. In L. Krasner & U. P. Ullman (Eds.), *Research in behavior modification*. New York: Holt, Rinehart & Winston.

McClone, R. E., & Hollien, H. (1963). Vocal pitch characteristics of aged women. *Journal of Speech and Hearing Research, 6*, 164–170.

McGehee, F. (1937). The reliability of the identification of the human voice. *Journal of General Psychology, 17*, 249–271.

Mehrabian, A. (1972a). Nonverbal communication. In J. Cole (Ed.), *Nebraska symposium on motivation 1971*. Lincoln: University of Nebraska Press.

Mehrabian, A. (1972b). *Silent messages*. Belmont, CA: Wadsworth.

Mehrabian, A., & Ferris, S. R. (1967). Inference of attitudes from nonverbal communication in two channels. *Journal of Counseling Psychology, 31*, 248–252.

Mehrabian, A., & Wiener, M. (1967). Decoding of inconsistent communication. *Journal of Personality and Social Psychology, 6,* 109–114.

Mehrabian, A., & Williams, M. (1969). Nonverbal concomitants of perceived and intended persuasiveness. *Journal of Personality and Social Psychology, 13,* 37–58.

Miller, D. T. (1975). The effect of dialect and ethnicity on communicator effectiveness. *Speech Monographs, 42,* 69–74.

Miller, N., Maruyama, G., Beaber, R. J., & Valone, K. (1976). Speed of speech and persuasion. *Journal of Personality and Social Psychology, 34,* 615–624.

Milmoe, S., Rosenthal, R., Blane, H. T., Chafetz, M. E., & Wolf, I. (1967). The doctor's voice: Postdictor of successful referral of alcoholic patients. *Journal of Abnormal Psychology, 72,* 78–84.

Morton, J. B., & Trehub, S. E. (2001). Children's understanding of emotions in speech. *Child Development, 72,* 834–843.

Mulac, A. (1976). Assessment and application of the revised speech dialect attitudinal scale. *Communication Monographs, 43,* 238–245.

Mulac, A., Hanley, T. D., & Prigge, D. Y. (1974). Effects of phonological speech foreignness upon three dimensions of attitude of selected American listeners. *Quarterly Journal of Speech, 60,* 411–420.

Mulac, A., Lundell, T. L., & Bradac, J. J. (1986). Male/female language differences and attributional consequences in a public speaking situation: Toward an explanation of the gender-linked language effect. *Communication Monographs, 53,* 115–129.

Neumann, R., & Strack, F. (2000). "Mood contagion": The automatic transfer of mood between persons. *Journal of Personality and Social Psychology, 79,* 211–223.

Newsweek. (1970, October 5). p. 106.

Nohara, M. (1992). Sex differences in interruption: An experimental reevaluation. *Journal of Psycholinguistic Research, 21,* 127–146.

Orr, D. B. (1968). Time compressed speech—A perspective. *Journal of Communication, 18,* 288–292.

Ostwald, P. F. (1961). The sounds of emotional disturbance. *Archives of General Psychiatry, 5,* 587–592.

O'Sullivan, M., Ekman, P., Friesen, W., & Scherer, K. (1985). What you say and how you say it: The contribution of speech content and voice quality to judgments of others. *Journal of Personality and Social Psychology, 48,* 54–62.

Pear, T. H. (1931). *Voice and personality.* London: Chapman & Hall.

Pittam, J. (1994). *Voice in social interaction: An interdisciplinary approach.* Thousand Oaks, CA: Sage.

Pittam, J., & Scherer, K. S. (1993). Vocal expression and communication of emotion. In M. Lewis & J. M. Haviland (Eds.), *Handbook of emotions.* New York: Guilford.

Poyatos, F. (1993). *Paralanguage: A linguistic and interdisciplinary approach to interactive speech and sound.* Amsterdam: John Benjamins.

Reich, A., & Duke, J. (1979). Effects of selected vocal disguises upon speaker identification by listening. *Journal of the Acoustical Society of America, 66,* 1023–1028.

Reich, A. R., Moll, K. L., & Curtis, J. F. (1976). Effects of selected vocal disguises upon spectrographic speaker identification. *Journal of the Acoustical Society of America, 60,* 919–925.

Rochester, S. R. (1973). The significance of pauses in spontaneous speech. *Journal of Psycholinguistic Research, 2,* 51–81.

Rogers, P. L., Scherer, K. R., & Rosenthal, R. (1971). Content filtering human speech: A simple electronic system. *Behavior Research Methods and Instrumentation, 3,* 16–18.

Rosenfeld, H. M. (1987). Conversational control functions of nonverbal behavior. In A. W. Siegman & S. Feldstein (Eds.), *Nonverbal behavior and communication* (2nd ed.). Hillsdale, NJ: Erlbaum.

Rosenthal, R., Hall, J. A., DiMatteo, M. R., Rogers, P. L., & Archer, D. (1979). *Sensitivity to non-verbal communication: The PONS test*. Baltimore: Johns Hopkins University Press.

Rosenthal, R., Vanicelli, M., & Blanck, P. (1984). Speaking to and about patients: Predicting therapists' tone of voice. *Journal of Consulting and Clinical Psychology, 52*, 679–686.

Rutherford, M. D., Baron-Cohen, S., & Wheelwright, S. (2002). Reading the mind in the voice: A study with normal adults and adults with Asperger syndrome and high functioning autism. *Journal of Autism and Developmental Disorders, 32*, 189–194.

Sachs, J., Lieberman, P., & Erickson, D. (1973). Anatomic and cultural determinants of male and female speech. In R. W. Shuy & R. W. Fasold (Eds.), *Language attitudes: Current trends and prospects*. Washington, DC: Georgetown University Press.

Schachter, S., Christenfeld, N., Ravina, B., & Bilous, F. (1991). Speech disfluency and the structure of knowledge. *Journal of Personality and Social Psychology, 60*, 362–367.

Schachter, S., Rauscher, F., Christenfeld, N., & Crone, K. T. (1994). The vocabularies of academia. *Psychological Science, 5*, 37–41.

Scherer, K. R. (1971). Randomized splicing: A note on a simple technique for masking speech content. *Journal of Experimental Research in Personality, 5*, 155–159.

Scherer, K. R. (1974). Acoustic concomitants of emotional dimensions: Judging affect from synthesized tone sequences. In S. Weitz (Ed.), *Nonverbal communication: Readings with commentary*. New York: Oxford University Press.

Scherer, K. R. (1979). Personality markers in speech. In K. R. Scherer & H. Giles (Eds.), *Social markers in speech*. London: Cambridge University Press.

Scherer, K. R. (1982). Methods of research on vocal communication: Paradigms and parameters. In K. R. Scherer & P. Ekman (Eds.), *Handbook of methods in nonverbal behavior research*. Cambridge, UK: Cambridge University Press.

Scherer, K. R. (1986). Vocal affect expression: A review and a model for future research. *Psychological Bulletin, 99*, 143–165.

Scherer, K. R. (2003). Vocal communication of emotion: A review of research paradigms. *Speech Communication, 40*, 227–256.

Scherer, K. R., Banse, R., & Wallbott, H. G. (2001). Emotion inferences from vocal expression correlate across languages and cultures. *Journal of Cross-Cultural Psychology, 32*, 76–92.

Scherer, K. R., Banse, R., Wallbott, H. G., & Goldbeck, T. (1991). Vocal cues in emotion encoding and decoding. *Motivation and Emotion, 15*, 123–148.

Scherer, K. R., & Ceschi, G. (2000). Criteria for emotion recognition from verbal and nonverbal expression: Studying baggage loss in the airport. *Personality and Social Psychology Bulletin, 26*, 327–339.

Scherer, K. R., Koivumaki, J., & Rosenthal, R. (1972). Minimal cues in the vocal communication of affect: Judging emotions from content-masked speech. *Journal of Psycholinguistic Research, 1*, 269–285.

Siegman, A. W. (1987). The telltale voice: Nonverbal messages of verbal communication. In A. W. Siegman & S. Feldstein (Eds.), *Nonverbal behavior and communication* (2nd ed.). Hillsdale, NJ: Erlbaum.

Smith, S. M., & Shaffer, D. R. (1991). Celerity and cajolery: Rapid speech may promote or inhibit persuasion through its impact on message elaboration. *Personality and Social Psychology Bulletin, 17*, 663–669.

Snow, C. E., & Ferguson, C. A. (Eds.). (1977). *Talking to children*. Cambridge, UK: Cambridge University Press.

Starkweather, J. A. (1961). Vocal communication of personality and human feelings. *Journal of Communication, 11*, 69.

Street, R. L., Jr. (1990). The communicative functions of paralanguage and prosody. In H. Giles & W. P. Robinson (Eds.), *Handbook of language and social psychology.* Chichester, UK: Wiley.

Street, R. L., Jr., Brady, R. M., & Lee, R. (1984). Evaluative responses to communicators: The effects of speech rate, sex, and interaction context. *Western Journal of Speech Communication, 48,* 14–27.

Thompson, W. F., Schellenberg, E. G., & Husain, G. Decoding speech prosody: Do music lessons help? *Emotion, 4,* 46–64.

Trager, G. L. (1958). Paralanguage: A first approximation. *Studies in Linguistics, 13,* 1–12.

Trainor, L. J., Austin, C. M., & Desjardins, R. N. (2000). Is infant-directed speech prosody a result of the vocal expression of emotion? *Psychological Science, 11,* 188–195.

Turner, L. H., Dindia, K., & Pearson, J. C. (1995). An investigation of female/male verbal behaviors in same-sex and mixed-sex conversations. *Communication Reports, 8,* 86–96.

Tusing, K. J., & Dillard, J. P. (2000). The sounds of dominance: Vocal precursors of perceived dominance during interpersonal influence. *Human Communication Research, 26,* 148–171.

Utzinger, V. A. (1952). *An experimental study of the effects of verbal fluency upon the listener.* Unpublished doctoral dissertation, University of Southern California, San Diego.

van Lancker, D., Kreiman, J., & Emmorey, K. (1985). Familiar voice recognition: Patterns and parameters—Recognition of backward voices. *Journal of Phonetics, 13,* 19–38.

Viscovich, N., Borod, J., Pihan, H., Peery, S., Brickman, A. M., Tabert, M., Schmidt, M., & Spielman, J. (2003). Acoustical analysis of posed prosodic expressions: Effects of emotion and sex. *Perceptual and Motor Skills, 96,* 759–771.

Weaver, J. C., & Anderson, R. J. (1973). Voice and personality interrelationships. *Southern Speech Communication Journal, 38,* 262–278.

Weitz, S. (1972). Attitude, voice, and behavior: A repressed affect model of interracial interaction. *Journal of Personality and Social Psychology, 24,* 14–21.

Wiemann, J. M., & Knapp, M. L. (1975). Turn-taking in conversations. *Journal of Communication, 25,* 75–92.

Wilke, W., & Snyder, J. (1941). Attitudes toward American dialects. *Journal of Social Psychology, 14,* 349–362.

Williams, C. E., & Stevens, K. N. (1972). Emotions and speech: Some acoustical correlates. *Journal of the Acoustical Society of America, 52,* 1238–1250.

Williams, F. (1970). The psychological correlates of speech characteristics: On sounding "disadvantaged." *Journal of Speech and Hearing Research, 13,* 472–488.

Woodall, W. G., & Burgoon, J. K. (1983). Talking fast and changing attitudes: A critique and clarification. *Journal of Nonverbal Behavior, 8,* 126–142.

Woolbert, C. (1920). The effects of various modes of public reading. *Journal of Applied Psychology, 4,* 162–185.

Zebrowitz, L. A., Brownlow, S., & Olson, K. (1992). Baby talk to the babyfaced. *Journal of Nonverbal Behavior, 16,* 143–158.

Zuckerman, M., Amidon, M. D., Biship, S. E., & Pomerantz, S. D. (1982). Face and tone of voice in the communication of deception. *Journal of Personality and Social Psychology, 43,* 347–357.

Zuckerman, M., & Driver, R. E. (1989). What sounds beautiful is good: The vocal attractiveness stereotype. *Journal of Nonverbal Behavior, 13,* 67–82.

Zuckerman, M., Hodgins, H., & Miyake, K. (1990). The vocal attractiveness stereotype: Replication and elaboration. *Journal of Nonverbal Behavior, 14,* 97–112.

Zuckerman, M., & Miyake, K. (1993). The attractive voice: What makes it so? *Journal of Nonverbal Behavior, 17,* 119–135.

Part Five

Communicating Important Messages

Our book concludes with a discussion of how the variety of nonverbal signals discussed earlier in the book combine as communicators pursue critical and familiar outcomes. Chapter 12 focuses on how nonverbal signals help us effectively communicate such things as intimacy, power, involvement, identity, and deception in daily interaction. Chapter 13 examines nonverbal messages in advertising, politics, education, culture, and health care. Together, these two chapters show how important it is to understand nonverbal behavior in order to effectively manage life's most important tasks.

Chapter 12

USING NONVERBAL BEHAVIOR
IN DAILY INTERACTION

Nothing in nature is isolated; nothing is without connection to the whole.

—GOETHE

Try to imagine yourself telling a high school student how to be a successful college student. Your approach probably would break up the process into its component parts, such as social life (dating, partying); intellectual life (studying, taking notes, relating to teachers); organizational life (what campus and social groups to join); financial life (how to get by with little money); and so on. As informative as your explanations and advice in these separate areas may be, you know it is not enough. You also need to point out how these parts go together to create complex situations; for example, a long-sought date has agreed to go out with you, but it is the night before a big test and it is going to cost a lot of money.

In the same way, this book is designed to make you more knowledgeable about human interaction and about nonverbal behavior in particular. The preceding chapters focused on individual parts of the total system: eyes, face, gestures, physical appearance, voice, and so forth. In this chapter, we show how these component parts combine to achieve the various communicative outcomes we seek daily.

To fully understand any process, we continually must look at the isolated parts that make up the system and at how they combine to achieve the system's purpose. Throughout the book, we have made occasional references to multisignal effects—for example, the role of verbal behavior in judgments of physical attractiveness and the close interrelationship of gestures with verbal behavior. Edward T. Hall, who coined the term *proxemics*, currently used to identify the study of distance and space, believed we have to consider 19 different behavioral signals to fully understand proximity in human transactions. In this chapter, we look at how various nonverbal signals help us accomplish the following goals: communicating intimacy; communicating status and power; managing the interaction; communicating our identity; and deceiving others. These outcomes, along with expressing emotion and achieving understanding, seem to cover adequately the most critical interaction goals.[1]

COMMUNICATING INTIMACY

Scholars have studied nonverbal signals associated with intimacy from four different perspectives, and we will discuss each of them in this chapter: the display behaviors associated with romantic courtship; courtship behaviors displayed in nonromantic situations; nonverbal behaviors that signal closeness with strangers and acquaintances; and nonverbal behaviors that signal closeness in more well-established intimate relationships.

COURTSHIP BEHAVIOR

We know that some men and women can exude such messages as "I'm available," "I'm knowledgeable," or "I want you" without saying a word. These messages can be expressed by the thrust of one's hips, touch gestures, extra-long eye contact, carefully looking at the other's body, showing excitement and desire in fleeting facial expressions, and gaining close proximity. When subtle enough, these moves will allow both parties to deny that either had committed themselves to a courtship ritual.

Studies involving flirtation behavior between men and women in bars (singles bars, hotel cocktail lounges, bars within restaurants, etc.) provide some observational data on the role of nonverbal signals in the courtship process (McCormick & Jones, 1989; Moore, 1985; Perper & Weis, 1987). Most of the early signaling seemed to be performed by women. The most frequently observed behaviors included 3 types of eye gaze (a room-encompassing glance; a short, darting glance at a specific person; and a fixed gaze of at least 3 seconds at a specific other); smiling at a specific other person; laughing and giggling in response to another's comments; tossing one's head, a movement sometimes accompanied by stroking of the hair; grooming, primping, and adjustment of clothes; caressing objects such as keys or a glass; a solitary dance (keeping time to the music with visible movements); and a wide variety of seemingly "accidental" touching of a specific other.

---

[1] These goals have been identified in several sources. See the following: Patterson, M. L. (1983). *Nonverbal behavior: A functional perspective*. New York: Springer-Verlag; Siegman, A. W., & Feldstein, S. (Eds.). (1985). *Multichannel integrations of nonverbal behavior*. Hillsdale, NJ: Erlbaum; Burgoon, J. K. & Hoobler, G. D. (2002) Nonverbal signals. In M. L. Knapp & J. A. Daly (Eds.), *Handbook of interpersonal communication*. Thousand Oaks, CA: Sage. The goals of communicating emotion, understanding, and persuasion are not covered in this chapter because it would duplicate too much material in other chapters. See especially chapters 9 and 11 for the expression of emotion; chapters 3 and 7 for achieving understanding; and chapter 11 for persuasion cues. For multisignal treatments of persuasion, see Burgoon, J. K., Birk, T., & Pfau, M. (1990). Nonverbal behaviors, persuasion, and credibility. *Human Communication Research, 17,* 140–169; and Burgoon, J. K. (2002). Nonverbal influence. In J. P. Dillard & M. Pfau (Eds.), *The persuasion handbook: Developments in theory and practice* (pp. 445–473). Thousands Oaks, CA: Sage. Also see: Brinol, P. & Petty. R. E. (2003). Overt head movements and persuasion: A self-validation analysis. *Journal of Personality and Social Psychology, 84,* 1123–1139.

The researchers did not specifically examine the type of clothing, nor did they examine the tone of voice used—both of which are likely to be influential flirtation behaviors. In an effort to determine whether these behaviors were more likely to occur in a context where signaling interest in and attraction to others was expected, the researchers observed the behavior of women and men in snack bars, meetings, and libraries. None of these contexts revealed anything close to the number of flirting behaviors found in bars.

Does the courtship process proceed according to a sequence of steps? Perper (1985) describes courtship's "core sequence" like this: The *approach* involves getting the two people in the same general proximity; *acknowledging and turning toward the other* is the invitation to begin talking; during *talk*, there will be an increasing amount of fleeting, *non-intimate touching and a gradually increasing intensity in eye gaze;* finally, Perper says the two will exhibit *more and more synchrony in their movements.* Obviously, either person can short-circuit the sequence at any point.

Nielsen (1962), citing Birdwhistell, described the "courtship dance" of the American adolescent. He claimed to have identified 24 steps from the "initial contact between the young male and female and the coitional act." These steps, he maintained, occur in a particular sequence: When a boy begins holding a girl's hand, he must wait until she presses his hand (signaling a go-ahead) before he can take the next step of allowing his fingers to intertwine with hers. Girls and boys are labeled "fast" or "slow" according to whether they follow the order of the steps. If a step is skipped or reversed, the person who does so is labeled "fast." If a person ignores the signal to move on to the next step or takes actions to prevent the next step, he or she is considered "slow."

Morris (1971) also believes that heterosexual couples in Western culture go through a sequence of steps, like courtship patterns of other animals, on the road to sexual intimacy. Notice the predominant nonverbal theme:

1. Eye to body
2. Eye to eye
3. Voice to voice
4. Hand to hand
5. Arm to shoulder
6. Arm to waist
7. Mouth to mouth
8. Hand to head
9. Hand to body
10. Mouth to breast
11. Hand to genitals
12. Genitals to genitals and/or mouth to genitals

Morris, like Nielson, believes these steps generally follow the same order, although he admits there are variations. Skipping steps or moving to a level of intimacy beyond what would be expected is found in socially formalized types of bodily contact, for example, a good-night kiss. It should be noted that any of the behaviors identified by Neilson and Morris can be performed in a more or less intimate way. Mouth-to-mouth kisses, for example, may be performed with little intimacy or with a great deal of it. It should also be noted that gazing, touching, and other nonverbal behavior associated with heterosexual courtship patterns is also an important part of homosexual courtship as well (Delph, 1978).

QUASI-COURTSHIP BEHAVIOR

Scheflen (1965) identified some behaviors he called "quasi-courtship" behavior—meaning they could be used during courtship, but they could also be used to communicate affiliative interest of a nonromantic type. Depending on the context, then, a particular cluster of behavior could be considered friendly, flirting, or seductive. Potential misunderstandings associated with such behavior are at the heart of many cases involving sexual harassment and date rape. It is not uncommon, for example, for men to perceive more sexual intent in the friendly behavior of women than women see in the friendly behavior of men (Abbey & Melby, 1986; Egland, Spitzberg, & Zormeier, 1996; Koeppel et al., 1993; Simpson, Gangestad, & Nations, 1996).

Quasi-courtship behavior has some elements of courting (relating to another for romantic purposes), but these behaviors are qualified by other co-occurring behavior that says, "This is not courtship even though you see some similarities to that behavior." In some cases, quasi-courtship behavior is used to build rapport; in some cases, it is a form of play. The overall message is one of affiliation. Scheflen (1965) made sound films of numerous therapeutic encounters, business meetings, and conferences. His content analysis of these films led him to conclude that consistent and patterned quasi-courtship behaviors were exhibited in these settings. He then developed a set of classifications for such behaviors:

* *Courtship readiness* defines a category of behaviors characterized by constant manifestations of high muscle tone, reduced eye bagginess and jowl sag, lessening of slouch and shoulder hunching, and decreasing belly sag.
* *Preening behavior* is exemplified by such things as stroking of the hair, rearrangement of makeup, glancing in the mirror, rearranging clothes in a sketchy fashion, leaving buttons open, adjusting suit coats, tugging at socks, and readjusting tie knots.
* *Positional cues* were reflected in seating arrangements that suggested, "We're not open to interaction with anyone else." Arms, legs, and torsos were arranged to inhibit others from entering the conversation.
* *Actions of appeal or invitation* included flirtatious glances, gaze holding, rolling of the pelvis, crossing legs to expose a thigh, exhibiting wrist or palm, protruding the breasts, and others.

Others have discussed Scheflen's positional cues in terms of who is excluded and who is included. The positioning of arms and legs in Figure 12-1 clearly suggests, "We're not open to others" in *a* and "I'm with you—not him" in *b*.

LIKING BEHAVIOR (IMMEDIACY)

In the late 1960s and early 1970s, Mehrabian (1972) conducted a number of experimental studies of what he called *immediacy*, that is, behaviors that indicate greater closeness

FIGURE 12-1

Positional cues.

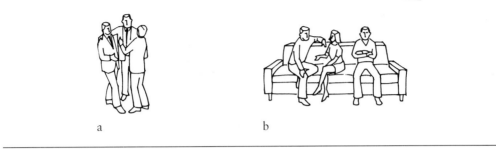

a   b

or liking. His research identified the following cluster of signals that distinguished a positive evaluation of an interaction partner from a negative one.

- More forward lean
- Closer proximity
- More eye gaze
- More openness of arms and body
- More direct body orientation
- More touching
- More postural relaxation
- More positive facial and vocal expressions

Low frequency of these behaviors, particularly when expected, or the manifestation of opposite behaviors tended to be associated with less intimacy or even disliking. Some combinations of these immediacy behaviors also have been found when people are trying to communicate support (Trees, 2000) and politeness (Trees & Manusov, 1998), too. And as we note in chapter 13, a teacher's immediacy behaviors with his or her students have been linked to positive student attitudes (toward the instructor and the course) as well as learning course material (Rodriguez, Plax, & Kearney, 1996).

The work by Mehrabian and others provides a useful perspective for understanding how positive and negative evaluations of interaction partners can be given through clusters of nonverbal signals. In theory, the greater the number of signals activated, the more powerful the message. Immediacy cues can instruct us on what signals to exhibit or look for in our culture during initial interactions with people we do not know very well. They do not tell us much about how people whose relationship has a history (friends, lovers) communicate intimacy. Close relationships to spouses, for example, cannot be accurately judged by the amount of time spent leaning forward with more direct body orientation, in close proximity with more eye gaze, and so on. Because much of this stereotypical immediacy behavior has happened early in the relationship, it needs to be done only on certain occasions once the relationship is mutually agreed to be an intimate one. There are times in established relationships when it is imperative to communicate closeness with utmost clarity, for example, when the relationship has been threatened. At such times, we are likely to see again the cluster of immediacy signals by the partner or partners who wish to offset the threat to the current level of intimacy. Partners in an established close relationship also use these stereotyped signals of intimacy when they want to communicate their closeness to outsiders. Outsiders may not understand the subtle and sometimes idiosyncratic ways intimates come to communicate their intimacy to one another; they will understand close proximity, gazing into one another's eyes, touching, and all the other signals associated with the stereotyped immediacy cluster.

Time is an important limitation of much of the work on nonverbal behavior associated with intimacy, affiliation, or liking. Mehrabian's cluster of immediacy signals is primarily limited to one-time encounters. Ongoing relationships express different levels of intimacy over time, often indicating liking and disliking in quick succession. Clore and his colleagues (1975a, 1975b) realized that the sequencing of immediacy behaviors may have an important influence. They first collected a large number of verbal statements describing nonverbal liking and disliking. These behaviors were limited to a female's actions toward a male. The large number of behavioral descriptions was narrowed by asking people to rate the extent to which the behavior accurately conveyed liking or disliking. Table 12-1 lists (in order) the behaviors rated highest and lowest. An actress then portrayed these behaviors in an interaction with a male, and the interaction was videotaped. To no one's surprise, viewers of the tape felt the warm behaviors would elicit greater liking from the male

TABLE 12-1   **Behaviors Rated as Warm and Cold**

WARM BEHAVIORS	COLD BEHAVIORS
Looks into his eyes	Gives a cold stare
Touches his hand	Sneers
Moves toward him	Gives a fake yawn
Smiles frequently	Frowns
Works her eyes from his head to his toes	Moves away from him
Has a happy face	Looks at the ceiling
Smiles with mouth open	Picks her teeth
Grins	Shakes her head negatively
Sits directly facing him	Cleans her fingernails
Nods head affirmatively	Looks away
Puckers her lips	Pouts
Licks her lips	Chain smokes
Raises her eyebrows	Cracks her fingers
Has eyes wide open	Looks around the room
Uses expressive hand gestures while speaking	Picks her hands
Gives fast glances	Plays with her hair's split ends
Stretches	Smells her hair

SOURCE: Adapted from *Journal of Consulting and Clinical Psychology, 43,* p. 493, 1975. Copyright © 1975 by the American Psychological Association. Adapted with permission.

addressee. The interesting aspect of the studies is what happened when viewers were exposed to a combined tape in which the actress's behavior was initially warm, then turned cold; or when her behavior was initially cold, then turned warm. The reactions to these videotapes were compared with responses to videotapes showing totally warm or totally cold portrayals by the actress. People judged that the man on the videotape would be more attracted to the woman who was cold at first and warm later than he would be to the woman who was warm for the entire interaction. Further, people felt the woman whose behavior turned from warm to cold was less attractive to the man than the woman who was cold during the entire interaction. Why? It probably has to do with the extent to which the judges felt the male had responsibility for the female's change in behavior. If the man had a part in turning a "cold" female "warm," they felt he could take credit for the change and, thereby, feel better about the interaction.

BEING CLOSE IN CLOSE RELATIONSHIPS

Once people have established a close relationship (friends, lovers), we are likely to see some variations in the way nonverbal signals communicate closeness. Ironically, intimates in established romantic relationships may exhibit quantitatively less nonverbal behavior typically associated with affection and intimacy than they did in forming the relationship. To establish these relationships usually means a high frequency of hugs, kisses, hand holding, and so forth; to maintain the relationship, though, it is often the quality of the act, not the frequency, that is important. Perceived sincerity, magnitude of the expression, and perfect timing are examples of qualitative factors. A hand held out to our partner at just the right moment after a fight may be the equivalent of 10 hand holdings at an earlier point in the relationship. The frequency of nonverbal acts of intimacy becomes important in established relationships when it is necessary to offset a threat to the relationship.

As intimate relationships develop, nonverbal behavior is also likely to change. To communicate a wider range of emotional states, more facial and vocal blends may occur. Sharply defined territories become more permeable. Conventionally performed nonverbal acts gradually give way to performances unique to the couple. The increasing familiarity with auditory, visual, and olfactory signals creates a condition for greater accuracy and efficiency in communicating, but it may also engender an overconfidence leading to decoding problems. More than acquaintances, intimates rely on a variety of nonverbal signals to communicate the same message. Long-term intimates also are subject to acquiring one another's facial, postural, and gestural styles, making them look alike. Intimacy brings with it exposure to more personal nonverbal acts and more talk about them. We would also expect more overt evaluations (approval/disapproval) of nonverbal behavior among intimates than among acquaintances (Knapp, 1983).

In the next section we discuss how closeness or intimacy is created by the contributions of both parties. But matching or reciprocity in established close relationships has the potential to differ from reciprocity among strangers or acquaintances. For example, they may not reciprocate the same kind of behavior, only its equivalent. The extent to which the behavior is equivalent to another is negotiated by the relationship partners. Thus almost any behavior can communicate intimacy in established relationships if the partners to the relationship agree that it does. Intimates also may respond (either with compensation or reciprocity), but not in the same immediate time frame.

MUTUAL INFLUENCE

Whatever nonverbal behavior is used to communicate liking or disliking is inevitably the result of what both interactants do. This perspective prompted Argyle and Dean to propose equilibrium theory in 1965. Equilibrium theory maintains that interactants seek an intimacy level comfortable for both of them. Eye gaze, proximity, smiling, and topic intimacy, according to this theory, signal the degree of intimacy. If the nonverbal behavior in one or more of these areas signals an increase or decrease in intimacy, the other interactant compensates by engaging in behaviors necessary to achieve equilibrium. For example, if a mere acquaintance looked at you too much, stood too close, and talked to you about intimate topics, equilibrium theory would predict that you would increase distance, look away, and try to change the topic to something less intimate. Although some attempts to test this theory found support for the predicted compensatory reactions, others found the opposite pattern—reciprocating changes in intimacy rather than offsetting them. This finding led to Patterson's (1976) arousal model of interpersonal intimacy, which maintained that gaze, touch, and proximity with another person creates arousal. This arousal state is then labeled either positive or negative. If it is negative (dislike, embarrassment, anxiety), the reaction will be to compensate or offset the behavior. If the arousal state is considered positive (liking, relief, love), the reaction will be matching or reciprocity of behavior. Although this theory explained why we sometimes compensate for and sometimes reciprocate the behavior of our partner, it required time-consuming cognitive labeling of another's behavior. In many encounters, these changes are too quick to involve this kind of mental processing. This consideration prompted Cappella and Greene (1982) to posit a discrepancy arousal theory. This model suggests we all have expectations about other people's expressive behavior. Increases and decreases in involvement by one person that violate the other person's expectations will lead to arousal or cognitive activation. Moderate arousal results from moderate discrepancies from expectancies; these are pleasurable, and reciprocity ensues. Large discrepancies from what is expected are highly arousing, leading to negative affective response and compensation. Little or no discrepancy from expectations is not arousing, so we would not expect to see any compensatory or reciprocal adjustments made.

Burgoon (1978) and her colleagues proposed and tested a model specifically focused on one element of immediacy—proximity. Since then it has also been used to study and predict involvement in general (Burgoon & Hale, 1988; LePoire & Burgoon, 1994). This model is an important contribution toward our understanding of reciprocal and compensatory reactions, however, because it (1) relies on both arousal and cognitive responses; and (2) explicates the important role of the communicator's perceived rewardingness.

The violations of expectations model posits that we all develop expectations for appropriate proximity in conversations from our culture, from our personal experiences, and from our knowledge of specific interactants. When our expectations for proxemic immediacy are met, arousal is not likely to play an important role. When violations occur (too far or too close), arousal is heightened and directs our attention to the nature of the interpersonal relationship. Interpretations then are made that guide our response. Interpretations vary, according to Burgoon's work, based on the perceptions of the violator's rewardingness. If the person is rewarding (high credibility, high status, positive feedback), the violation of expectations will be perceived more positively than for nonrewarding interactants.

In an elaboration of the violations of expectations model, Burgoon and her colleagues proposed interaction adaptation theory (Burgoon, Stern, & Dillman, 1995). This theory assumes that each interactant enters a conversation with requirements, expectations, and desires. Requirements are what we deem absolutely necessary (like being close enough to hear someone); expectations are what we anticipate happening based on the norms, the people involved, and the situation; and desires are our personal goals and preferences for the interaction. This combination of what is believed to be needed, anticipated, and preferred is called an "interaction position" and is used as the standard against which our interaction partner's behavior is judged. When our interaction partner's behavior is closely aligned with our interaction position, this theory predicts reciprocity of behavior. Reciprocity is also expected when our partner engages in major deviations that are more positive than our interaction position. However, major deviations by our interaction partner that are more negative than our interaction position are likely to make us respond with compensatory behavior. In one study, romantic partners tended to reciprocate both increases and decreases in immediacy behaviors from their partners (Guerrero, Jones, & Burgoon, 2000). Compensating behavior with romantic partners who manifest decreases in immediacy is most likely when there is a strong desire to change or neutralize the partner's decreased intimacy. Otherwise, there seems to be a natural pull to match it. Keep in mind that interaction is an ongoing, sometimes rapidly changing, process. For example, we may be surprised by a close friend who engages in more immediacy behavior than we anticipated (or desired), and we may initially respond with compensatory behavior. But in a split second our friend observes our reaction, and he or she begins acting more in line with our expectations, preferences, and desires. Then our behavior becomes more reciprocal.

What are we to make of these theories that try to predict when we reciprocate our partner's behavior and when we engage in compensatory behavior? Obviously, a simple bottom-line statement cannot take into account the many subtleties and variations associated with every human transaction, but as a general rule of thumb, we would do well to remember the following: *With strangers and acquaintances we tend to reciprocate or match their nonverbal behavior when it is perceived as generally congruent with our expectations and involvement preferences. We tend to compensate or offset another's nonverbal behavior when it is perceived as a major violation of our expectations and preferences.*

COMMUNICATING DOMINANCE/STATUS

Tired of feeling weak and unimportant? Want to unlock the secrets of those who have gained authority and power? Want to know how to dominate friends, enemies, and business associates, just about anyone, with a few simple tips?

Sorry, but we can't tell you. You can find this kind of advice in popular books on nonverbal behavior. Some "tips" from these books include the following: Put the desk between you and the person you wish to dominate. Position yourself physically higher than the other. Sit in a relaxed posture (preferably with hands behind head). Take up as much space as possible. Be sparing with your smiles. Press your palms firmly downwards on the table in front of you. Don't use speedy or jerky gestures. Keep your thumbs sticking out when you put your hands in your jacket pockets. Shake hands so your hand is on top of the other person's hand. The list goes on, but you should be very skeptical of such glib advice. We can summarize the research on dominance and nonverbal behavior for you, but there are no pat answers. The desire for a simple how-to manual is probably greatest in this area, yet the research is much too complex to warrant any such thing.

Even the basic concepts are complicated. The terms *status, dominance,* and *power* are often used interchangeably, but many authors have noted their ambiguities and have offered many (and sometimes contradictory) definitions (Edinger & Patterson, 1983; Ellyson & Dovidio, 1985; Harper, 1985). The concepts are certainly related, but not perfectly: A figurehead leader has status without power, whereas a low-status member of an organization may wield considerable influence by virtue of personal contacts, shrewd insight, and social interaction skill. Status often connotes a socially valued quality that a person carries with her or him into different situations, whereas power and dominance are more likely to be situationally defined. But dominance can also be seen as a personality trait (a "dominant" person) in addition to a situational condition. Some researchers would say that any kind of aggressive act is dominant, but for others a behavior is dominant only if it is followed by clear evidence of submission from another individual. In research, many operational definitions have been used to represent these concepts. The following are some illustrations:

- For status: attire, occupation, education, military rank, socioeconomic status, role (e.g., professor)
- For dominance: initiation of contacts, children's attempts to gain precedence in play, giving orders, boasts, not submitting to others, controlling others' behaviors, attacks
- For power: control of resources, expertise, experience, autonomy

Other issues complicate this discussion, which we must consider before going further. One issue is whether the nonverbal behaviors used to try to attain dominance or status may be different from those used by someone who has already achieved this goal (Argyle, 1988; Heslin & Patterson, 1982). Thus, acquiring and expressing dominance may not involve the same cues. Recognition of this possibility may help us sort out contradictory results. For example, research finds that more gazing is perceived as dominant; that people with more dominant personalities, people who initiate speech more in groups, and people who attain higher status in groups are also less likely to be the first to break a mutual glance in face-to-face interaction; and that high-status people gaze more freely at others (Dovidio & Ellyson, 1985; Kleinke, 1986; Lamb, 1981; Rosa & Mazur, 1979; Snyder & Sutker, 1977; Thayer, 1969). Many authors have noted that gaze can carry connotations of threat and coercion, and it is often assumed that higher levels of gazing are a hallmark of a dominant, powerful, or high-status individual.

We might think everything adds up—higher status people gaze more—until we also read that people with dependent personalities tend to gaze more; that people who are gazed at by a confederate feel less dominant; that people made to feel dependent gaze longer at an experimenter; and that higher status people gaze less at lower status addressees (Kleinke, 1986; Mehrabian, 1972; Nevill, 1974; Thayer, 1969). These apparent contradictions may be reconciled if we consider that a person of high status or dominance may feel either secure or defensive, and a person of lower status or dominance may be struggling to gain status or may be signaling to more powerful others that he or she is no threat. The nonverbal behaviors, gaze or otherwise, that people use in these different states could differ radically. For example, the person who feels out of control but is striving to gain control might engage in high levels of gaze, whereas the person who accepts a low-status role might avert his or her eyes so as not to appear threatening. Gaze, like touch and most other nonverbal behaviors, takes its meanings in a complex way from the situation and other co-occurring nonverbal behaviors.

Fehr and Exline (1987) suggest another intriguing resolution to the contradictory findings on gaze. They suggest that the higher status person is accorded the privilege of violating norms; in public situations, the norm is not to look much at others, whereas in more personal, conversational situations, the norm is to look a fair amount at others. Fehr and Exline suggest that the behavior of the higher status person is to gaze more than the norm in situations involving strangers but to gaze less than the norm in conversations of a more personal nature. This interesting theory has not been fully explored.

Another important issue is the difference between the impression made by a particular nonverbal behavior and the actual behavior of people having different degrees of dominance, power, or status. Here are two examples: A nonsmiling face is sometimes perceived as dominant (Keating, 1985), and seeing someone touch another raises the viewer's perception of the toucher's dominance (Major & Heslin, 1982). But these findings do not necessarily mean that dominant or high-status people smile less and touch more. The evidence is mixed for both, with no overall trends either way (Hall, 1996; Hall & Friedman, 1999; Johnson, 1994; Stier & Hall, 1984).

In general, people have well-developed beliefs about how dominance, status, or power (all of which we will call "dominance") relate to nonverbal behavior. Carney, Hall, and Smith LeBeau (in press) asked college students to imagine interactions among people with differing dominance—more or less dominant personalities or more or less status in the workplace. A large number of beliefs were expressed by the students. The higher dominant person was believed to pay less attention to the other person, engage in more "invasive" behaviors, touch the other more, touch the self less, stand at a close distance, show emotions successfully, glare and gaze more, stand more erect, and interrupt more (among many others). Another way to examine people's beliefs is to show them nonverbal behavior (on videotape, for example) and ask them to rate how dominant the individuals seem. Many studies have done this. In general, the behaviors that are rated as more dominant concur with those expressed more explicitly in Carney and colleagues' study (Hall, Coats, & Smith LeBeau, 2004).

However, when studies were examined that related the expressors' actual degree of dominance to their nonverbal behavior, many fewer relations were found on average (Hall, Coats, & Smith LeBeau, 2004). High actual dominance was associated with more facial expressiveness, more bodily openness, smaller interpersonal distances, better posed expression skill, less vocal variability, louder voices, more interruptions, fewer back-channel responses, fewer filled pauses, and more relaxed-sounding voice. But many other behaviors for which beliefs exist did not show overall effects. However, because high and low dominance can have many different emotions and motives associated with it, we should perhaps not expect strong overall relations. For example, a person low in dominance who is feeling hostile would smile a very different amount from the same person who is feeling the need to please the other person. Also the nonverbal behaviors themselves can have ambiguous meaning such that a clear dominance interpretation is not always clear. For instance, although interrupting others in conversation can be a dominance behavior (Henley, 1977; Kollock, Blumstein, & Schwartz, 1985; Leffler, Gillespie, & Conaty, 1982; Robinson & Reis, 1989), we should not take this interpretation for granted. Interruption is sometimes indicative of a highly involved conversation and not necessarily a sign of a power struggle in progress (Dindia, 1987; Kennedy & Camden, 1983).

One behavior that has consistently been associated with dominance is the visual dominance ratio (Ellyson, Dovidio, & Fehr, 1981; Exline, Ellyson, & Long, 1975). Experiments that defined status, power, and dominance in different ways have found that among white college students, the higher status person gazes roughly the same amount while listening and while speaking, whereas the lower status person gazes relatively more while listening than while speaking. When a male and a female interact and one is made to be the expert or accorded higher status, that individual, regardless of sex, will engage in the visual dominance pattern. Although subtle, the visual dominance ratio does not go unnoticed. When subjects were asked to judge the relative power or potency of individuals engaging in different amounts of eye gaze, they gave higher ratings to individuals engaging in relatively more looking while speaking than to those engaging in relatively more looking while listening.

Though not strictly a nonverbal behavior, how much a person talks in a group is also a very consistent and rather strong indicator of status rank, both in terms of observers' perceptions and in terms of actual rank (Schmid Mast, 2002). However, even here there are exceptions. In an interview situation, the interviewee (lower power) is likely to talk more than the interviewer (higher power). And in extant groups, sometimes a person with well-established status or power can afford to sit back and say very little, knowing that others will attend fully whenever he or she chooses to speak.

Murphy, Driscoll, and Kelly (1999) connected nonverbal dominance to the likelihood that college males would engage in sexual harassment. These authors found that males who scored higher on a scale that had previously been shown to predict sexual harassment engaged in several behaviors that the authors predicted would show dominance (more open body postures, more direct eye contact, and less direct body orientation). Nonverbal behaviors that might be construed as sexual were not predicted by the scale, however (smiling, tilting head, and flirtatious glances), leading the authors to conclude that sexual harassment is more dominance than sexuality related.

In sum, the relation of nonverbal communication to dominance is complex and does not lend itself to simple formulaic approaches. Perhaps this is fortunate, in that it would be troubling if it were truly easy to dominate others through nonverbal behavior.

MANAGING THE INTERACTION

Most of the time, we do not engage in much conscious thinking about how to greet people, request a speaking turn, show our conversational partner we believe what he or she was saying, or say good-bye. We do these things to structure the interaction—to regulate the processes of coming together, the back and forth nature of speaking and listening, and departure. As we note later, however, these acts are also rich in content. When such acts are the subject of conscious reflection, we appreciate the importance of the messages involved.

GREETING BEHAVIOR

Greetings perform a regulatory function by signaling the beginning of interaction. Greetings also convey information about the relationship between the two communicators that helps structure the ensuing dialogue. Verbal and nonverbal behavior during greetings may signal status differences (subordinate/supervisor), degree of intimacy (acquaintance/lover), or a current feeling or attitude (aversiveness/interest). An emotionally charged greeting may reflect our desired involvement with the other person or it may reflect a long absence of contact. Goffman (1971) proposed an attenuation rule, which states that the expansiveness of a greeting with a particular person will gradually subside with continual contact with that person, for example, a co-worker at an office. Kendon and Ferber (1973) found the following six stages characterized greetings initiated from a distance.

1. **Sighting, Orientation, and Initiation of the Approach.** A greeting, like any other transaction, requires participation by both interactants. Sometimes both will agree that "acknowledgment" is enough. After mutual recognition, there is an immediate and sustained withdrawal of attention. Goffman (1963) called this common action "civil inattention." When the greeting continues, we move to stage 2.
2. **The Distant Salutation.** This is the "official ratification" that a greeting sequence has been initiated and who the participants are. A wave, smile, or call may be used for recognition. Two types of head movements were noted at this point. One, the head toss, is a fairly rapid back and forward tilting motion. Some people tended to lower their head, hold it for a while, and then slowly raise it.
3. **The Head Dip.** Researchers have noted this movement in other contexts as a marker for transitions between activities or shifts in psychological orientation. Interestingly, this movement was not observed by Kendon and Ferber if the greeter did not continue to approach his or her partner.
4. **Approach.** As the greeting parties continued to move toward each other, several behaviors were observed. Gazing behavior probably helped signal that the participants were cleared for talking. An aversion of this gaze was seen just prior to the close salutation stage, however. Grooming behavior and one or both arms moved in front of the body were also observed at this point.
5. **Final Approach.** Now the participants are less than 10 feet from each other. Mutual gazing, smiling, and a positioning of the head not seen in the sequence thus far are now seen. The palms of the hands may also be turned toward the other person.

6. **Close Salutation.** As the participants negotiate a standing position, we will hear the more stereotyped, ritualistic verbalizations so characteristic of the greeting ceremony—for example, "Hi, Steve! How ya doin'?" and so on. If the situation calls for body contact (handshakes, embraces, and the like), it will occur at this time. Even though the handshake is very common in the United States, this kind of greeting behavior is not shared in some other cultures.

The specific nature of greetings varies according to the relationship of the communicators, the setting, and the attendant verbal behavior. Our major concern here is with the nonverbal behavior. The greetings observed by Krivonos and Knapp (1975) were frequently initiated by a vertical or sideways motion of the head accompanied by eye gaze. Smiles, regardless of the degree of acquaintanceship, were also common. Perhaps the smile serves the function of setting a positive, friendly initial mood. The eye gaze signals that the communication channels are open and an obligation to communicate exists. Other eye-related greeting behaviors included winks and the eyebrow flash (discussed in chapter 2). The hands are often active in the greeting process with salutes, waves, handshakes (Schiffrin, 1974), hand slaps, and various emblematic gestures such as the peace sign, the raised fist, or the thumbs-up gesture. Hands used in greetings have traditionally been open, but in recent years the "fist bump" has been used by some in the United States. When fists lightly touch each other in greeting, the greeters are signaling friendliness by showing that a potentially threatening gesture is being used in a nonthreatening way. Hands also may be engaged in grooming, that is, running fingers through one's hair. Touching may take the form of embraces, kisses, or hitting on the hands or arm. The mouth may smile or assume an oval shape, suggesting a possible readiness for talk.

TURN-TAKING BEHAVIOR

Conversations begin and they are eventually terminated. Between these two points, however, it is necessary to exchange speaking and listening roles, that is, to take turns. Without much awareness of what we are doing, we use body movements, vocalizations, and some verbal behavior that often seem to accomplish this turn taking with surprising efficiency. The act of smoothly exchanging speaking and listening turns is an extension of our discussion of interaction synchrony in chapter 7. And, because a number of the turn-taking cues are visual, it is understandable that we might have a harder time synchronizing our exchanges during telephone and intercom conversations.

Turn-taking behavior is not just an interesting curiosity of human behavior. We seem to base important judgments about others on how the turns are allocated and how smoothly exchanges are accomplished. Effective turn taking may elicit the perception that you and your partner "really hit it off well" or that your partner is a very competent communicator; ineffective turn taking may prompt evaluations of "rude" (too many interruptions), "dominating" (not enough turn yielding), or "frustrating" (unable to make an important point).

The turn-taking behaviors we are about to outline have generally been derived from analyses of adult, white, and middle- and upper–socioeconomic-class interactants. Some of these behaviors and behavior sequences may not apply to other groups. Blacks, for example, seem to gaze less than whites during interaction (Halberstadt, 1985). Other groups may develop speaking patterns with more unfilled pauses, which may communicate turn yielding to those unfamiliar with the group norm. Children who are learning turn-taking rules engage in behaviors we rarely see in adults, such as tugging at their parent's clothing and hand raising to request a speaking turn.

Speakers engage in two turn-taking behaviors: (1) turn yielding and (2) turn maintaining. Listeners also initiate two types of turn-taking behaviors: (1) turn requesting and (2) turn denying. The behaviors associated with these acts are derived from careful analyses of both audio and visual elements enacted at junctures where interactants exchange or maintain the speaking turn (Duncan, 1975; Duncan & Fiske, 1977; Wiemann & Knapp, 1975; Wilson, Wiemann, & Zimmerman, 1984). Any individual behavior associated with speaker or listener intentions will contribute toward a smooth turn exchange, but the greater the number of signals, the greater the chances for a smooth exchange. Note, however, that a familiarity with the rules of interaction is also an important part of effective turn taking. For example, before any specific turn-taking behaviors are observed, most people enter conversations knowing that speaking roles will generally alternate in an ABABAB sequence and that when one person "finishes" an utterance, the other person is generally obligated to "take the conversational ball." Cultures with different conversational rules and specialized systems of communication like sign language require somewhat different turn-exchange processes.

Turn Yielding

To *yield* literally means you are giving up your turn and you expect the other person to start talking. As noted in Figure 7-14, the termination of one's utterance can be communicated with kinesic markers that rise or fall with the speaker's pitch level. Questions are clearly an indication that a speaker yields his or her turn and expects the partner to respond. If it is a rhetorical question the speaker plans to answer, we probably will see some turn-maintaining cues, but if the listener is eager to get into the conversation, he or she may attempt to answer even the rhetorical question. Vocally, we also can indicate the end of our utterance by a decreased loudness, a slowed tempo, a drawl on the last syllable, or an utterance trailer such as "you know," "or something," or "but, uh." Naturally an extended unfilled pause also is used to signal turn yielding. More often than not, however, the silence becomes awkward, and the speaker adds a trailer onto the utterance. Body movements that have been accompanying the speech may also be terminated; for example, illustrative gestures come to rest, body tenseness becomes relaxed. Gazing at the other person also will help signal the end of an utterance. If the listener does not perceive these yielding cues (and gives no turn-denying cues), the speaker may try to convey more explicit cues, such as touching the other, raising and holding the eyebrows in expectation, or saying something like "Well?"

Turn Maintaining

If, for some reason, the speaker does not want to yield a speaking turn, we are likely to see several behaviors. Voice loudness probably will increase as turn-requesting signals are perceived in the listener. Gestures probably will not come to rest at the end of the verbal utterances, creating a gestural equivalent to the filled pause. Filled pauses probably will increase while the frequency and duration of silent pauses decrease. This minimizes the opportunities for the other person to start speaking without interrupting or speaking simultaneously. Sometimes we see a light touching of the other person by the speaker, which seems to say, "Hold on a little bit longer. I want to make a few more points and then you can talk." This touching is sometimes accompanied by a patting motion as if to soothe the impatient auditor. In some respects, this touch has the effect of the speaker putting his or her hand over the mouth of the auditor—an act not allowed in interpersonal etiquette in our society.

Turn Requesting

When we do not have the floor and we want to talk, we may exhibit one or more of the following behaviors. An upraised index finger seems to symbolize an instrument for creating a conversational hole in the speaker's stream of words, but it also approximates a familiar, formal turn-requesting signal learned in school—a raised hand. Sometimes this upraised index finger is accompanied by an audible inspiration of breath and a straightening and tightening of posture, signaling the imminence of talk. In some cases, certain self-adaptors classified as preening behavior also may signal preparation for a new role. The very act of simultaneous talking (extended interruption) will convey your request for a speaking turn, but to make sure that request is granted, you have to speak louder than your partner, begin gesturing, and look away as if the turn was now yours. When the speaker and listener are well synchronized, the listener will anticipate the speaker's juncture for yielding and will prepare accordingly by getting the rhythm before the other person has stopped talking, much like a musician tapping his or her foot preceding a solo performance. If the requestor's rhythm does not fit the speaker's, we might observe some stutter starts—for example, "I . . . I . . . I wa . . ." Sometimes the turn-requesting mechanism consists of efforts to speed up the speaker, realizing that the sooner one speaker has his or her say, the sooner the requestor will get his or hers. This same behavior was noted when people were anxious to terminate a conversation (Knapp et al., 1973). The most common method for encouraging a speaker to finish quickly is the use of rapid head nods, often accompanied by verbalizations of pseudo agreement such as "yeah," "mmm-hmm," and so forth. The requestor hopes the speaker perceives that these comments are being given much too often and do not logically enough follow ideas expressed to be genuine signs of reinforcement.

Turn Denying

Sometimes we receive turn-yielding cues from the speaker, but we do not want to talk. At such times, we probably maintain a relaxed listening pose, maintain silence, or gaze intently at something in the surrounding environment. More often, we exhibit behavior that shows our continuing involvement in the content of the speaker's words but denies we are seeking a turn. This might take the form of smiling, nodding, or shaking the head; completing a sentence started by the speaker; briefly restating what the speaker just said;

briefly requesting clarification of the speaker's remarks; or showing approval by appropriately placed "mmm-hmm's," "yeah's," or other noises such as the "clicking" sound that suggests "You shouldn't have said that."

The preceding repertoire of turn-taking behaviors, although accurate, may be misleading. The exchange of turns in conversation is a jointly negotiated process and not merely the display of one or more signals associated with yielding, maintaining, requesting, or denying. Sometimes it is hard to tell who is playing the speaker role and who is playing the auditor role. For example, before an auditor does any requesting behavior, a speaker may provide signals that essentially project the completion of his or her turn—thereby acknowledging a request before it has occurred. Sometimes an auditor uses gestures that simultaneously signal the desire for a turn, project the type of talk to ensue, and avoid disrupting the speaker's turn.

Many of the actions auditors perform during a speaker's turn are called back-channel feedback (Duncan, 1974; Rosenfeld, 1987; Rosenfeld & Hancks, 1980). These listener responses help regulate the flow of information and signal the energy expended in the decoding process. Listener responses can affect the type and amount of information given by the speaker, the length of his or her turn, the clarity of the speaker's content, and the extent to which the speaker communicates in a qualified or specific manner. At key points in the telling of a story, a speaker will look into the face of his or her listener—an act that is likely to produce a back-channel response such as a nod, an "mmm-hmm," or the like from the listener (Bavelas, Coates, & Johnson (2002). Back-channel responses by the listener normally occur at the juncture of phonemic clauses by the speaker. The primary nonverbal signals are head nods, but postural changes, smiles, frowns, eyebrow flashes, and laughter (Vettin & Todt, 2004) also occur. Common verbal and vocal back-channel signals include saying "yeah," "mmm-hmm," repeating the speaker's words, asking a clarifying question, or completing a sentence for the speaker. Sometimes the auditor provides these signals prior to the phonemic clause juncture, which may indicate he or she is "ahead" of the speaker. When such signals are "late," it is acknowledgment of what is being said but may also indicate a lack of full understanding. Once again, though, back-channel cues only affect the speaker if he or she is both motivated to attend to them and motivated to act on the feedback given.

LEAVE-TAKING BEHAVIOR

Having managed our way through the conversation thus far, it is now time to terminate it. Leave taking seems to serve three valuable functions in daily interaction (Knapp et al., 1973). The primary regulatory function is signaling the end of the interaction; that is, immediate physical and/or vocal contact soon will be terminated. Again, specific nonverbal manifestations of these functions vary with the relationship between the communicators, the preceding dialogue, body position (standing/sitting), the anticipated time of separation, and other factors. Decreasing eye gaze and positioning one's body toward the nearest exit were the two most frequent nonverbal behaviors observed in this study and seem to adequately signal impending absence. Leave-taking rituals also summarize the substance of the discourse sometimes. This is usually accomplished verbally, but a good-night kiss may sufficiently capture the evening's pleasantries to qualify as a summarizer. Finally, departures tend to signal supportiveness, which can offset any negativity that might arise from encounter-termination signals while simultaneously setting a positive mood for the next encounter—that is, our conversation has terminated, but our relationship has not. Nonverbal supportiveness may be found in a smile, a handshake, a touch, head nodding, and forward body lean. Because signaling supportiveness seems so important, we often use the more direct verbal signals—for example, "Thanks for your time. I'm glad we got a chance to talk."

Head nodding and forward lean, of course, serve several simultaneous functions. Rapid head nodding toward the end of a conversation reinforces what the speaker is saying, but it is a rather empty reinforcement because it also signals a desire to terminate the conversation. After all, if there is no apparent disagreement or lack of understanding, the speaker will feel no need to expand on his or her remarks. And, although it is true that people accompany their feelings of liking by sometimes leaning toward another person, it is also necessary to lean forward in order to stand up prior to exiting. So, like words, movements have multiple meanings and serve several functions.

Other nonverbal leave-taking behaviors included looking at one's watch; placing hands on thighs for leverage in getting up (which also signals the other person that the catapult is imminent); gathering one's possessions together in an orderly fashion; and accenting the departure ritual by nonvocal sounds, such as slapping the thighs when rising, stomping the floor with the feet when rising, or tapping a desk or wall with the knuckles or palm. Finally, researchers noticed that nearly all the nonverbal variables studied tended to increase in frequency during the last minute of interaction, with a peak during the 15 seconds just prior to standing. This increasing activity in at least 10 body areas just prior to termination may suggest why we are so frustrated when our partings "fail," that is, when our partner calls us back with "Oh, just one more thing . . ." It means we have to go through the entire process of leave-taking again!

COMMUNICATING OUR IDENTITY

The evening news shows a group of men entering a building. The narrator tells us that a fugitive sought in several states has been apprehended by the FBI. But did we need to be told? Even without the narrative, we can tell a great deal about the people and what is going on. The bearing and demeanor of some have "federal agent" written all over them. They are likely to be large and burly and to wear their hair conservatively short and keep their faces closely shaved; sunglasses might be worn; and the attire is undistinguished but is likely to be a plain dark business suit. They do not smile—indeed, they look completely humorless, erect, and controlling. And what of the suspected criminal? His posture is likely to be slumped, with his head bowed, face wearing a dismal expression, and eyes averted from the camera.

You can imagine variations on this scene. The agents might be seedily dressed undercover agents or uniformed police officers, the suspect might look angry or defiant, and so forth. But the point is the same: Appearance and behavior reveal significant information about people's identity—who they are or, in many cases, who they would like to be. Identity includes a person's social attributes, personality, and those attitudes and roles he or she regards as self-defining. Thus, being a police officer is a role likely to be deeply connected to one's self-definition and portraying that identity is likely to be very important to the person holding it. Being an arrested suspect is a more fleeting role but could be integral to the self-concept in the case of a career criminal. Sometimes it is hard to tell when behavior reflects transient emotions and roles or is part of a more enduring identity portrayal. A suspect's slumped or defiant posture could be either one.

People have a great need to convey their identity. In previous chapters, we talked about ways in which aspects of identity such as age, occupation, culture, and personality are expressed in dress and in nonverbal behaviors. The communication of identity is, in part, self-validating: We confirm for ourselves our sense of who we are. We also show our identities for the benefit of others—both those in our group (to build solidarity and signal belonging) and those not in our group (to emphasize that they are not one of us and vice versa). Michael Argyle has suggested that people want to know about others' social attributes partly to help maintain the belief that the world is a predictable place. Clues to another's identity also help us decide how to act toward that person. But direct, concrete evidence of others' identities is sometimes hard to come by, so people rely on cues and gestures (Argyle, 1988). In the case of social class, for example, one's way of dressing tells us a great deal, as do other accoutrements, such as pens, briefcases, hairstyles, makeup, and jewelry. Sometimes people orchestrate these aspects of their material selves to present an "improved version of the self," in the hope of winning acceptance or approval.

PERSONAL IDENTITY

The concept of identity can be construed at both the personal and social levels. Personal identity consists of a unique configuration of characteristics—personality, attitudes, tastes, values, and features—that the individual perceives as personally defining. Nonverbal styles of expression can also be so distinctive that they become an aspect of identity. Davis and Dulicai (1992) provide an analysis of Adolf Hitler's movement and gestural mannerisms during public appearances. Some of Hitler's movements include finger wagging (the "scolding Dutch uncle"), forward stabs, pounding, slicing, crushing fists, and snapping-punching, all of which are performed with extreme control and inward stress. Davis and Dulicai summarize the uniqueness of Hitler's movement style as follows:

> Hitler's movement is very difficult to imitate. In seminars with people who are sophisticated about movement analysis and performance such as dancers and dance therapists, most cannot even approximate the ways in which he controls the action . . . and sustains such a violent intensity throughout a series of batons (pointing getures). Those who come close want to stop. It is tortured, painful, relentless, and unyielding motion. To move this way is to be at war with one's body and it is notable that, for all of the aggression that Hitler's oratory displays, it is this war with himself that stands out. (p. 161)

Personality is one of the ways we define personal identity. Personality is consistent across situations and time. In many chapters of this book we have described nonverbal behaviors displayed by people with various personality traits. Extraversion, for example, has a number of nonverbal correlates such as faster and louder speech.

An important question is how beliefs about behavior-trait associations differ from the actual associations. People may have beliefs that are not substantiated when observational

FIGURE 12-2

A diagram of a judgment lens model of social perception.

research is done. A useful way of conceptualizing this question is the "lens model," which we have mentioned in other chapters. As shown in Figure 12-2, the lens model encompasses the relation of both perceived and actual behavior to a criterion (such as a personality trait), as well as the relation between the perceived and actual trait (that is, the degree to which observers can judge which targets have the trait in question).

Table 12-2 summarizes the lens-model results of Gifford's (1994) study of 60 undergraduates videotaped in conversation. Over 20 nonverbal behaviors were coded from these tapes and then related both to the participants' self-descriptions of personality and the impressions of personality made by observers who watched the tapes with the sound turned off. Table 12-2 shows that for the trait "ambitious–dominant" there were associations between nonverbal behaviors and the personality ratings made by observers. However, actual ambition–dominance (i.e., the self-ratings by those in the tape) related to fewer behaviors, only two of which appeared on the list of behaviors correlated with observers' ratings. This suggests that observers (who were other college students) had a correct naive theory as far as these two cues were concerned, but held misconceptions for all the others shown on the left side of the table; in other words, they thought that more ambitious–dominant people would display these cues, but they were wrong (at least for the people they were observing). The observers did, however, extract enough information to form a significantly accurate overall impression of the targets' ambition–dominance; possibly, they based their impression on additional cues that were not measured, as well as the two they used correctly. Other lens-model studies relating a wide array of nonverbal cues to perceived and actual personality traits have been done by Berry and Hansen (2000), Borkenau and Liebler (1995), Lippa (1998), and Murphy, Hall, and Colvin (2003).

Another characteristic that is central to our identity is our sense of how intelligent we are. Despite the debate surrounding the intelligence concept, nevertheless it is a thing of abiding importance to people in modern society. All of us have at some point, and

TABLE 12-2   **Perceived and Actual Correlates of "Ambition–Dominance"**

CORRELATED WITH PERCEIVED TRAIT ONLY	CORRELATED WITH BOTH PERCEIVED TRAIT AND ACTUAL TRAIT	CORRELATED WITH ACTUAL TRAIT ONLY
Head, trunk, and legs more directly facing other	More gestures	More leg lean
Head more tilted back	Legs more extended	Less manipulating objects
Arms less wrapped		
More touching self		
More headshaking		

Adapted from R. Gifford (1994) *Journal of Personality and Social Psychology,* 66, p. 401.

perhaps often, worried about how we compare to others in intelligence (and in other characteristics that are related, or perceived to be related, such as SAT scores, colleges attended, etc.), and whether others will think we are as smart as we would like them to. In daily life we do a great deal of assessing others' intelligence as well as projecting our own as we would like others to see it. Murphy, Hall, and Colvin (2003) asked what cues people look for when judging others' intelligence and whether those cues are correct. When making intelligence ratings based on one-minute clips of conversational behavior, perceivers associated many cues with higher intelligence, including having a pleasant speech style, talking with the hands, sitting up straight, talking fast, looking at the partner while speaking, and behaving in a responsive manner to the partner. However, only a few of these were valid cues to higher intelligence, most notably looking more at the partner while speaking. Whether people higher in intelligence are aware of engaging in such behavior is not known, but certainly it is possible that if such an association is strong and constant enough, the person will incorporate that behavior into their sense of "who they are" and others will do the same.

SOCIAL IDENTITY

Our race and gender are among the most salient aspects of social identity (i.e., identification with social and cultural groups), and it is not surprising that research has turned up nonverbal communication differences associated with these categories. It is, of course, an oversimplification to think of these categories as though everyone in them behaves the same. Stereotypic thinking promotes many judgment errors and undesirable behaviors. Obviously, a woman may express her womanhood differently at home than at the office (let's hope she does!); similarly, a minority student may have a different behavior style when with friends of the same social group than in a predominantly majority classroom. Also remember that distinctions such as male/female and African American/white are often confounded with other distinctions, such as social class and status. It can be unclear what factors explain a given nonverbal behavior.

At various places in this book we have documented differences between the nonverbal behavior of African Americans and whites in the United States. Although African American/

white differences in nonverbal behavior have not been studied extensively, there appear to be differences (at least in the limited populations observed) in style of walking, interpersonal distance, orientation, gaze, and conversational regulators (Burgoon, Buller, & Woodall, 1989; Halberstadt, 1985; Johnson, 1972). It is important to note that some of the findings may pertain only to subgroups and not to the larger group. For example, a distinctive walk that may be evident in urban African-American teenagers is probably not the same walk that would characterize African-American housewives or executives. Keeping this in mind, research suggests that among adults, the distance maintained between interactants is typically greater and the body orientation is less direct among African Americans than among European Americans. As an interesting contradiction to this pattern of reduced sensory involvement, studies have found African Americans to touch more than European Americans do. Perhaps the greater amount of touching reestablishes a sense of involvement.

Some research suggests that African Americans gaze less than European Americans during conversation and gaze especially little with authorities (whereas among European Americans, gaze often increases with authorities). Erickson's (1979) analysis of films of conversations pointed to distinct African-American and European-American norms for conversational turn taking and signaling attention. African-American speakers used less subtle and less frequent cues indicating that a listener should give a "listener response" (a signal that the listener is paying attention). But, as listeners, African Americans employed listener responses that were more subtle and likely to be missed by a speaker from outside that group. Erickson suggested that these differences could lead to a situation in which a European-American speaker concludes an African-American partner is either not listening or not understanding. The European American then repeats himself, which is, in turn, perceived as "talking down" by the African-American. Although Erickson found evidence that African-American subjects displayed bicultural competence (a kind of nonverbal bilingualism), there remained differences in conversational behavior. The potential for serious interracial misunderstanding stemming from cultural differences is obvious and has been noted by educators and others concerned with race relations.

Gender differences in nonverbal behavior also reflect the different identities of males and females. Nonverbal differences appear early in life. *Gender roles* are collections of attitudes, behaviors, and traits deemed desirable for males versus females. In our society, the male gender role includes autonomy, assertiveness, dominance, and task orientation; for women, gentleness, empathy, and interpersonal orientation are stereotypical (Cross & Madson, 1997). To a great extent, nonverbal differences correspond to these role prescriptions. It is as if the social display of sexual identity and gender role has special importance. Thus we may want to show the world not only that we are men (women) but also that we behave as men (women) are expected to behave. We discuss some of the findings from research next (Hall, 1984; Hall, Carter, & Horgan, 2000; LaFrance & Hecht, 2000); other differences have been discussed earlier in the book. Men, compared to women,

- Have less skill in sending and receiving nonverbal, especially emotional, cues
- Are less likely to notice (or to be influenced by) people's appearance and nonverbal behavior

- Have less expressive faces and use fewer expressive gestures
- Smile and laugh less
- Look at others less
- Keep greater distances from others

A difference involving much debate concerns interpersonal touching. When it comes to same-gender touch, the evidence is rather clear that heterosexual men are particularly averse to touching other men, except in certain prescribed settings such as team sports (both as part of the game and as expressions of team spirit). Both self-report and observational data indicate that same-gender touching is avoided by men but is quite welcome by women. One hypothesis for the men's avoidance is homophobic attitudes and the fear that touching will be seen as homosexual. Indeed, research by Roese et al. (1992) found that, among men, those with the least stated liking for same-gender touching had the highest scores on a homophobia scale (with items such as "Homosexuality is a sin and just plain wrong," and "Homosexual behavior disgusts me"). In a second study, college students who were observed to engage in less same-gender touching in a cafeteria had stronger homophobic attitudes when surveyed by the researchers; this was the case for both men and women (Roese et al., 1992).

Studies on opposite-gender touching have been more debated (Henley, 1977; Stier & Hall, 1984), but there is some concurrence that when the individuals are young adults or the touch is with the hand or the arm is put around the other person, males do take the touching initiative. However, the woman is more likely to touch the man than vice versa when the couple is in their 40s or older, when the touch is either brief or involves linking her arm through the man's or initiating hand holding (Hall & Veccia, 1990), and when the couple is married rather than dating (Guerrero & Andersen, 1994; Willis & Briggs, 1992).

Although exhaustive research over the life span has not been conducted, there is reason to believe that nonverbal gender differences are especially pronounced in adolescence and the college years, when gender roles are especially salient. For example, the gender difference in smiling is not evident in young children (Dodd, Russell, & Jenkins, 1999; Hall, 1984); it peaks in adolescence and decreases after that, though never completely (LaFrance, Hecht, & Levy Paluck, 2003). Most nonverbal gender differences have been investigated among college students observed in a laboratory situation, but there is also abundant evidence from more naturalistic settings as well. For example, male physicians when interacting with patients engage in less smiling, nodding, and back-channeling (saying "mmm-hmm") than female physicians do (Hall et al., 1994).

The nonverbal behaviors that women engage in more than men suggest more openness, sensitivity, and involvement. In some circumstances, these traits may work to women's disadvantage (Henley, 1977). Their smiling may make them appear weak, "too nice," or even insincere; their higher levels of gazing may connote dependency; their nonverbal style may not be distant or threatening enough to win automatic respect in the professional world. However, if this is the case we would argue that the problem is with the stereotypic beliefs rather than with the behavior per se. Furthermore, one can also argue that it is only because of cultural blinders that we tend to see men's behavior as "normal" and women's behavior as different or in need of correction. Because most evidence suggests that the kinds of nonverbal skills and behavior shown more by women are an asset in daily life, it may make more sense to focus on men as deficient and handicapped in social relations.

Women's greater emotional expressivity is consistent with the stereotype that women are more emotional than men. However, several studies have found that self-reports of the intensity of emotional experience do not differ when assessed concurrently with the experience (e.g., Kring & Gordon, 1998), but studies that ask about emotional intensity in general or retrospective terms find a consistent gender difference in self-reported emotional intensity (e.g., Diener, Sanvik, & Larsen, 1985). The latter difference may be biased by the influence of gender stereotypes on self-ratings; alternatively, women may do more subsequent thinking and processing of emotional experiences, which amplifies their intensity with the passage of time. At any rate, although it is clear that women are more emotionally expressive than men, it is not clear that they are also more emotional in terms of their inner experience.

Sometimes the claim is made that women are false in their nonverbal expressions—for example, that their smiles are constant and insincere. An early study, cited often, found that women tended to smile even when their words did not contain congruently happy messages, but men's smiles were more in accord with their words (Bugental, Love, & Gianetto, 1971). Bugental called women's behavior "perfidious." Here is a pattern that could certainly have social impact and the label is very derogatory. However, a subsequent study done that tested this same hypothesis found exactly the *opposite* pattern, with women being more consistent across channels than men were (Halberstadt, Hayes, & Pike, 1988). Clearly, it is premature to conclude that inconsistent displays are the province of women.

As with race and other group differences, male/female nonverbal differences are not large in absolute terms, and we should not overestimate the size of these differences. Though some of them are large relative to other psychological differences between the sexes, nevertheless they are still of modest magnitude, and even the largest nonverbal gender difference shows more similarity than difference between males and females. Stated differently, there is a great deal of overlap in the male and female repertoires. Nevertheless, there is a striking correspondence between people's beliefs about these differences and the actual size of the differences (Briton & Hall, 1995; Hall & Carter, 1999), which strongly suggests that people can see these differences in daily life. Of course, societal beliefs can also translate into self-fulfilling prophecies, such that men and women come to have the behaviors that others expect them to have (Zanna & Pack, 1975).

The gender differences are also not invariant. They vary considerably as a function of setting and context, including the nature of the situation, the affective tone of an interaction, other nonverbal behaviors, and the characteristics of the other person involved (Aiello & Aiello, 1977; Hall & Halberstadt, 1986; LaFrance, Hecht, & Levy Paluck, 2003; Putnam & McCallister, 1980). As examples of this variation, the gender difference in gazing is much more evident when people are within conversational distance of one another than when they are standing farther apart. The tendency for women to smile more than men is largest when people know they are being observed, when they are interacting with others, when they are not very familiar with the other people, when the circumstances make them feel more anxious, and when they are Caucasian. Finally, people act in the most sex-stereotypic ways when with others of their own sex; in opposite-sex encounters males and females often accommodate to the other's norms. So, for example, gazing is highest between females, lowest between males, and intermediate in male/female interaction (Hall, 1984; Vrugt & Kerkstra, 1984). The fact that nonverbal gender differences vary with these contextual factors demonstrates that we still have a great deal to learn about the origins of male and female behavior.

Interpretations of sex differences in gaze have concentrated on the competing themes of affiliation–warmth versus dominance–power. Because nonverbal cues do not typically have fixed meanings, this ambiguity is difficult to resolve. Smiling and gazing, for example, can have multiple meanings. However, the visual dominance ratio described earlier is less ambiguous than some other nonverbal behaviors; the visual dominance ratio has been linked to differences in status, power, dominance, or expertise in a variety of studies, but to our knowledge no one has suggested that it varies with the warmth or friendliness of the interaction. Dovidio and his colleagues (1988) performed two experiments involving mixed-gender pairs of interactants in which the relative status of the interactants was experimentally manipulated. When a status difference was created between the interactants, the party having the higher status (whether male or female) had a higher visual dominance ratio, consistent with research already described. However, when status was *not* manipulated, men behaved in the visually dominant way that high-status communicators display, and women showed the less visually dominant behavior typical of people in low-status roles. This finding suggests a connection between dominance and gender differences in gazing patterns.

The well-established finding that women score higher on tests of judging the meanings of nonverbal cues has also been theorized to stem from dominance and status differences (Henley, 1977), but, in fact, little is known about why females are so often better at decoding nonverbal cues despite much debate and discussion (Hall, 1984; Hall & Halberstadt, 1996; Henley, 1977; Noller, 1986). So far, there is little evidence for the dominance/status interpretation (Hall, Halberstadt, & O'Brien, 1997). Noller (1986), like most other social psychologists, believes that females are socialized to be expert in various aspects of social interaction, including knowing the general social rules governing interpersonal relations, knowing the general display and decoding rules appropriate to various situations, and knowing the more specific rules governing the use of nonverbal cues in particular. It is society's expectation not only that females will be attuned to social interactions, but also that they will be responsible for how social interactions proceed. These pressures and expectations could easily produce the skill differences that are documented in research.

Similarly, there is only very limited support for dominance/status interpretations for gender differences in other nonverbal behaviors. Smiling, in particular, has been hypothesized to vary with dominance/status (such that the lower-power person smiles more), and it has been suggested that differences in dominance/status can explain why women smile more than men. However, research on smiling and dominance/status finds no overall connection between the two (Hall, Coats, & Smith LeBeau, 2004). It is likely that how much smiling is shown by people with different degrees of dominance or status depends on factors such as how pleasant, ingratiating, hostile, nervous, or preoccupied they are rather than dominance or status per se.

DECEIVING OTHERS

One of the most common communicative outcomes we seek is to persuade or influence others. In previous chapters, we cited research aimed at identifying the contribution of physical attraction, distance, eye gaze, touch, and vocal cues to perceptions of authoritativeness (expertise) and character (trustworthiness)—the two central factors in the persuasive process. But the area of influence that has captured the attention of the American public and university researchers the most in recent years is the act of lying.

These are the three major questions driving the research in this area:

1. What behaviors distinguish liars from truth tellers?
2. What cognitive/emotional processes are at work during acts of lying?
3. How accurate are we at detecting lies?

Identifying behaviors exhibited by liars has, until recently, focused predominantly on nonverbal signals. It was incorrectly assumed that liars could manipulate their verbal behavior easily but could not or would not control their nonverbal behavior to the same extent, thereby revealing they were lying. Ekman and Friesen (1969) believed it was more likely that clues to deception would be found in the feet/legs area first, the hands next, and the face last. Because the face is more likely to be controlled by the liar, Ekman and Friesen argued that facial clues would be more difficult to detect. Later work by these researchers (1975), however, indicated several ways the face reveals deception, such as micromomentary expressions and the timing and location of the expression. For example, smiles made when people were trying to cover up negative feelings included traces of muscular actions associated with disgust, fear, contempt, or sadness (Ekman, Friesen, & O'Sullivan, 1988).

Attempts to develop a list of behaviors that distinguish liars from truth tellers always have faced the problem that there are many types of lies (prepared or not, short answer or extended narrative, interrogated or not) and many motivations for lying (protecting oneself or someone else, getting out of an obligation or promise, avoiding conflict). For the lies that comprise most of our daily interaction, people report they are not serious, largely unplanned, and do not make them fearful of being caught (DePaulo et al., 1996). In addition, no behavior occurring during a lie is completely unique to lying (Buck, 1984; Zuckerman, DePaulo, & Rosenthal, 1981). Ekman (1992, p. 80) put it this way: "There is no sign of deceit itself—no gesture, facial expression, or muscle twitch that in and of itself means that a person is lying." Still, attempts have been made to examine the behavioral indicators of lying regardless of how lying was operationalized. DePaulo et al. (2003) conducted the most recent meta-analysis. When compared with truth tellers, they concluded the following about liar behavior:

- *Liars are less forthcoming.* As a result, they are likely to manifest shorter responses, less elaboration, appear to be holding back, speak at a slower rate, and have longer response latencies.
- *Liars tell stories that seem less plausible and with fewer details.* Thus, stories by liars are likely to have more discrepancies, be less engaging (e.g., more word/phrase

repetitions), be less direct, use fewer self-references, be more uncertain, less fluent (more hesitations, errors, pauses), and be presented in a less active manner (fewer gestures).

- *Liars make fewer spontaneous corrections while telling their story and are less likely to admit they can't remember something.*
- *Liars make a more negative impression.* Overall, they seem less cooperative, make more negative statements, use more words denoting anger and fear, more likely to use offensive language, complain, smile less, and seem more defensive.
- *Liars are more tense.* Their voices are likely to have a higher pitch; their pupils are more likely to be dilated for a longer period of time; and they are more likely to exhibit fidgeting.

One behavior many people expect of liars is a sharp decrease in eye gaze. Although this behavior may occur with some liars in some situations, it has become so stereotypically associated with lying in this culture that liars often consciously seek to control it. Sometimes, of course, the ability to display a normal pattern of gaze is deficient, and the liar ends up staring. And too much gazing signals that something is wrong just as too little gazing does.

If it is difficult to find behaviors that always characterize liars, it is easier to identify behaviors associated with key underlying cognitive and emotional processes that occur during lies (Knapp, Cody, & Reardon, 1987). The two most commonly studied processes are *arousal* and *cognitive difficulty*. Nonpathological liars who know they are lying and who know there will be important consequences if they are caught are likely to experience one or both of these states. Nonverbally, arousal is indicated by pupil dilation, blinking, speech errors, and higher pitch. Verbally, we might see excessive responses (e.g., "WHY DO YOU ALWAYS HAVE TO QUESTION ME?!" in response to a seemingly natural, nonthreatening question), curt replies, or extremes in language usage. Obviously, people experience arousal for reasons other than lying, but aroused truth tellers and aroused liars do not seem to behave the same. Liars commonly experience cognitive difficulty as well. This may be manifested in speech hesitations, shorter responses, pupil dilation, speech errors, incongruous verbal and nonverbal behavior, and lack of specific references.

Two other processes typical of the lie experience involve *attempted control* and the *display of an affective state.* Less spontaneous or what seems to be rehearsed behavior would indicate attempted control. In 1991 military prisoners of war who were forced to make anti-U.S. statements on Iraqi television were reportedly trained prior to their capture to speak and behave in a wooden and mechanical manner to indicate they were lying. Indirect responses to direct questions also may signal an attempt to control one's behavior. The expected affective state is one of anxiety commonly reflected in fidgeting, stammering, and the like. But other emotional states are also relevant to deception. Anger is very common and reflected in liars' tendencies to be negative and disaffiliative in their responses. Some liars feel enough guilt so that looking away for long periods or covering their eyes with their hands is not uncommon. Duping delight, the pleasure one may experience in deceiving another, occurs sometimes as well and may be reflected in a smile at the wrong time or a sneer of contempt.

Given what we have said about the nature of liar behavior, it should be no surprise that strangers, without the aid of any mechanical equipment such as a polygraph, are only about 50% to 60% accurate in identifying liars. Since accuracy judgments usually combine the accuracy of people judging truthful and deceptive speakers and since truthful speakers are usually judged with a much higher degree of accuracy, our ability to detect liars may be well below 50% (Levine, Park, & McCornack, 1999). Most studies assessing accuracy are based on observer judgments, not those who are actually participating in the conversation. Some evidence suggests participants are less accurate than observers. Higher detection rates have been obtained from professionals who are highly motivated to detect deception and reputed to be good detectors (Ekman, O'Sullivan, & Frank, 1999); people who focus on vocal cues as a good source of information about deception (Anderson et al., 1999; Zuckerman et al., 1982); and aphasics who have poor language skills when the detection process involves judging emotion (Etcoff et al., 2000). Analyzing both verbal and nonverbal signals is also more likely to reveal a liar than observing either one alone (Vrij et al., 2000). Getting feedback during training and practice in deception detection also seems to improve accuracy somewhat (deTurck, 1991; deTurck, Feeley, & Roman, 1997). DePaulo and her colleagues (1988) believe liars are more likely to reveal themselves nonverbally when the lie is very important to them. They called this the motivational impairment hypothesis. Burgoon and Floyd (2000), however, found that liars who were highly motivated to lie often performed it more skillfully and were less apt to be uncovered through their nonverbal behavior.

Although some may bemoan the fact that our detection rate is not higher, others believe it would be undesirable to get too accurate at detecting lies. The ability to withhold information and mislead, it is argued, is just as crucial to the well-being of our society as disclosure, openness, and honesty. Overzealous lie detectors may find lies that are not there and sometimes even elicit lies from people who might not have otherwise intended to lie. We hope these and other issues related to truth and deception will continue to be hotly debated. Only when we stop searching for answers to questions of truth and deception will we be morally bankrupt.

Are machines any better than human beings at detecting lies? Polygraphs, which measure various physiological indicators like heart rate and blood pressure, are sometimes reported to detect liars with more accuracy than most human observers. But because they too often identify truth tellers and liars incorrectly, they are barred as courtroom evidence in most states (Robinson, 1996; Vrij, 2000). Furthermore, polygraphs can be beaten. People whose lies were detected at about 80% then received either biofeedback or relaxation training. After they were better able to control their bodily responses, the accuracy of the polygraphs was reduced to about 20% (Corcoran, Lewis, & Garver, 1978). In addition to polygraphs, many products on the market claim to measure vocal microtremors. Like the polygraph, these devices are based on the assumption that liars experience anxiety, and behaviors associated with anxiety will identify them. According to Hollien (1990), these voice stress analyzers accurately identify liars at slightly above chance—that is, not any better than most human beings could do on their own. A device that measures brain wave responses to crime-relevant words or pictures presented on a computer screen, called "brain fingerprinting," claims to have been 100% accurate in identifying liars in 120 tests (Farwell & Smith, 2001).

What about people in close relationships? Shouldn't they be more accurate at detecting lies? Because trust is the fundamental reason couples have close relationships, either party is likely to get away with lying quite easily at first. But once suspicion is aroused, those who know a person's behavior well are likely to be the best detectors (Comadena, 1982; McCornack & Parks, 1986). However, it is not uncommon for people in close relationships not to engage in the close monitoring necessary to detect deception. They may not want to confront the lie, or they may be afraid of destroying intimacy if they show distrust by their close monitoring (Knapp, in press).

A PERSPECTIVE FOR COMMUNICATORS

Throughout this chapter, we have emphasized the idea that communicators mutually construct their reality. One person's behavior can only be understood as we see how it interacts with the behavior of another interactant. In the abstract, this proposition seems reasonable—one that would not be hard to memorize and recall for a test. But what does the concept of mutual influence mean in practical application to our everyday lives? Two things seem to be particularly important: (1) If the outcome of any transaction is the product of behavior by both interactants, it means we must be very careful in judging and ascribing meaning to the nonverbal behavior of a single person or generalizing a person's behavior with one person to all others. This does not suggest that people do not have a style of communicating they may carry from one encounter to another. The parts of that style that are emphasized and deemphasized, however, can change dramatically depending on whom one is interacting with. (2) If the outcome of any transaction is the product of behavior by both interactants, each interactant must share the responsibility for the outcome. This does not mean that in some encounters one person may not take or deserve more of the responsibility than the other. It does mean that we should, perhaps more than we would like to, examine our own verbal and nonverbal behavior to determine how it contributed to the interpersonal outcome. In social life, it is rare indeed for one person to be doing everything "right" and the other to be doing everything "wrong." Unpleasant outcomes are usually constructed mutually.

These notions return us to the self-fulfilling prophecy described in chapter 1. The most important lessons about social life probably are these: We see what we expect to see, and what we expect of others will likely come true. Through our verbal and nonverbal behavior, we unconsciously shape other people into conformance with our expectations, in all areas of life including educational settings (Harris & Rosenthal, 1985), psychological experiments (Rosenthal, 1976), and ordinary interpersonal relationships (Snyder, Tanke, & Berscheid, 1977; Spitz, 1997). Your nonverbal behavior does make a difference.

❖

Summary

Every day we have to accomplish goals that require the effective management and reading of nonverbal signals. This chapter identified what we know about five of those goals.

We began by discussing the various ways we manifest our liking and disliking for others. Even though there are certain nonverbal signals that have been associated with courtship and romantic flirtation, we also know that similar behaviors occur when people are trying to communicate friendliness, interest, and playfulness. These "quasi-courtship" behaviors can lead to misunderstandings and remind us how important context is for interpreting nonverbal signals. The cluster of nonverbal behavior comprising immediacy or liking behavior can be usefully applied to a variety of situations in which we want to signal positive responses to strangers and acquaintances. Immediacy occurs in established close relationships, too, but mainly when it is important to be clear about one's feelings, when the relationship is threatened, or when a couple wants to communicate their closeness to outsiders. Otherwise, people in close relationships employ a more unique and varied nonverbal repertoire. We concluded this section by noting the ways people adjust the intimacy level through reciprocal or compensatory behavior.

Nonverbal behavior is also highlighted in acts of dominance and efforts to show one's status. Like intimacy, sometimes people will manifest different nonverbal behavior when seeking it than after they have achieved it. But, again, context and individual differences are important. An aspiring executive may engage in a lot of eye gaze while seeking the top position in the company, but another executive, equally motivated, may engage in far less eye gaze with his superiors as a sign of respect. There are a number of behaviors that have been associated with dominance and status. Some research indicates that higher status men and women tend to manifest the visual dominance ratio (the tendency to look more while speaking than listening).

Nonverbal signals are also crucial in initiating, managing, and terminating everyday conversations. Smooth turn exchanges are negotiated when speakers signal turn yielding cues and listeners signal turn requesting dues. There are times, however, when listeners do not want to assume the speaking turn and speakers do not want to give it up. These, too, are highly dependent on the manifestation of certain nonverbal signals.

We tell others (and ourselves) who we are when we communicate our identity through nonverbal signals. Identity may be personal (e.g., personality) or social (e.g., our race or gender). Research has found important differences in the nonverbal behavior of men and women, for example, but often these differences are not large.

Even though we would not like to think of ourselves as deceivers, research indicates we often use deception to manage our social worlds. There is no behavior that is always associated with lying, but research shows that liars tend to be less forthcoming, provide fewer details, give off a negative impression, exhibit more tenseness, and make fewer spontaneous corrections in their speech. Arousal and cognitive difficulty often trigger the observed behaviors seen in high stakes lying, but most of us are not very accurate (about 50–60%) in identifying liars whom we do not know.

QUESTIONS FOR DISCUSSION

1. Research tells us men typically smile, laugh, and gaze at their conversational partners far less than women do. Speculate on why and the extent to which it is functional or dysfunctional behavior.

2. What does it mean to collaborate in a lie? Are collaborators and liars subject to similar ethical standards?

3. Identify situations when controlling behavior is likely to be reciprocated and when it is likely to elicit compensatory behavior. Why?

4. Try to imagine a social world in which lies could be detected accurately 99% of the time. Describe it.

5. Write a paragraph describing a situation where you felt your partner's verbal and nonverbal behavior had little to do with your own. Exchange your description with another person who has done the same thing. With additional questioning, each of you should now try to convince the other person that the episode he or she described omitted a lot of the partner's influence.

BIBLIOGRAPHY

INTIMACY

Abbey, A., & Melby, C. (1986). The effect of nonverbal cues on gender differences in perceptions of sexual intent. *Sex Roles, 15,* 283–298.

Afifi, W. A., & Johnson, M. L. (1999). The use and interpretation of tie signs in a public setting: Relationship and sex differences. *Journal of Social and Personal Relationships, 16,* 9–38.

Andersen, P. A. (1985). Nonverbal immediacy in interpersonal communication. In A. W. Siegman & S. Feldstein (Eds.), *Multichannel integrations of nonverbal behavior.* Hillsdale, NJ: Erlbaum.

Andersen, P. A., & Andersen, J. F. (1984). The exchange of nonverbal intimacy: A critical review of dyadic models. *Journal of Nonverbal Behavior, 8,* 327–349.

Andersen, P. A., Guerrero, L. K., Buller, D. B., & Jorgensen, P. F. (1998). An empirical comparison of three theories of nonverbal immediacy exchange. *Human Communication Research, 24,* 501–535.

Argyle, M., & Dean, J. (1965). Eye contact, distance and affiliation. *Sociometry, 28,* 289–304.

Burgoon, J. K. (1978). A communication model of personal space violations: Explication and an initial test. *Human Communication Research, 4,* 129–142.

Burgoon, J. K., & Aho, L. (1982). Three field experiments on the effect of violations of conversation distance. *Communication Monographs, 49,* 71–88.

Burgoon, J. K., & Hale, J. L. (1988). Nonverbal expectancy violations: Model elaboration and application to immediacy behaviors. *Communication Monographs, 55,* 58–79.

Burgoon J. K., & Jones, S. B. (1976). Toward a theory of personal space expectations and their violations. *Human Communication Research, 2,* 131–146.

Burgoon, J. K., Stern, L. A., & Dillman, L. (1995). *Interpersonal adaptation: Dyadic interaction patterns.* New York: Cambridge University Press.

Cappella, J. N. (1981). Mutual influence in expressive behavior: Adult–adult and infant–adult interaction. *Psychological Bulletin, 89,* 101–132.

Cappella, J. N., & Greene, J. O. (1982). A discrepancy-arousal explanation of mutual influence in expressive behavior for adult and infant–adult interaction. *Communication Monographs, 49,* 89–114.

Clore, G. L., Wiggins, N. H., & Itkin, S. (1975a). Gain and loss in attraction: Attributions from nonverbal behavior. *Journal of Personality and Social Psychology, 31,* 706–712.

Clore, G. L., Wiggins, N. H., & Itkin, S. (1975b). Judging attraction from nonverbal behavior: The gain phenomenon. *Journal of Consulting and Clinical Psychology, 43,* 491–497.

Delph, E. W. (1978). *The silent community: Public homosexual encounters.* Beverly Hills, CA: Sage.

DePaulo, B. M., & Coleman, L. M. (1987). Verbal and nonverbal communication of warmth to children, foreigners, and retarded adults. *Journal of Nonverbal Behavior, 11,* 75–88.

Egland, K. L., Spitzberg, B. H. & Zormeier, M. M. (1996). Flirtation and conversational competence in cross-sex platonic and romantic relationships. *Communication Reports, 9,* 105–117.

Floyd, K., & Burgoon, J. K. (1999). Reacting to nonverbal expressions of liking: A test of interaction adaptation theory. *Communication Monographs, 66,* 219–239.

Guerrero, L. K., Jones, S. M., & Burgoon, J. K. (2000). Responses to nonverbal intimacy change in romantic dyads: Effects of behavioral valence and degree of behavioral change on nonverbal and verbal reactions. *Communication Monographs, 67,* 325–346.

Knapp, M. L. (1983). Dyadic relationship development. In J. M. Wiemann & R. P. Harrison (Eds.), *Nonverbal interaction.* Beverly Hills, CA: Sage.

Koeppel, L. B., Montagne-Miller, Y., O'Hair, D., & Cody, M. J. (1993). Friendly? Flirting? Wrong? In P. J. Kalbfleisch (Ed.), *Interpersonal communication: Evolving interpersonal relationships.* Hillsdale, NJ: Erlbaum.

LePoire, B. A. (1991). Orientation and defensive reactions as alternatives to arousal in theories of nonverbal reactions to changes in immediacy. *Southern Communication Journal, 56,* 138–146.

LePoire, B. A., & Burgoon, J. K. (1994). Two contrasting explanations of involvement violations: Expectancy violations theory versus discrepancy arousal theory. *Human Communication Research, 20,* 560–591.

McCormick, N. B., & Jones, A. I. (1989). Gender differences in nonverbal flirtation. *Journal of Sex Education and Therapy, 15,* 271–282.

Mehrabian, A. (1968a). Inference of attitude from the posture, orientation, and distance of a communicator. *Journal of Consulting and Clinical Psychology, 32,* 296–308.

Mehrabian, A. (1968b). Relationship of attitude to seated posture, orientation, and distance. *Journal of Personality and Social Psychology, 10,* 26–30.

Mehrabian, A. (1968c). Significance of posture and position in the communication of attitude and status relationships. *Psychological Bulletin, 71,* 359–372.

Mehrabian, A. (1972). *Nonverbal communication.* Chicago: Aldine.

Moore, M. M. (1985). Nonverbal courtship patterns in women: Content and consequences. *Ethology and Sociobiology, 6,* 237–247.

Morris, D. (1971). *Intimate behavior.* New York: Random House.

Nielsen, G. (1962). *Studies in self-confrontation.* Copenhagen: Munksgaard; Cleveland: Howard Allen.

Noller, P. (1984). *Nonverbal communication and marital interaction.* New York: Pergamon.

Patterson, M. L. (1976). An arousal model of interpersonal intimacy. *Psychological Review, 83,* 235–245.

Patterson, M. L. (1983). *Nonverbal behavior: A functional approach.* New York: Springer-Verlag.

Patterson, M. L. (Ed.). (1985). Nonverbal intimacy and exchange. *Journal of Nonverbal Behavior, 8,* 233–393.

Patterson, M. L., Reidhead, S. M., Gooch, M. V., & Stopka, S. J. (1984). A content-classified bibliography of research on the immediacy behaviors: 1965–82. *Journal of Nonverbal Behavior, 8,* 360–393.

Perper, T. (1985). *Sex signals: The biology of love.* Philadelphia: ISI Press.

Perper, T., & Weis, D. L. (1987). Proceptive and rejective strategies of U.S. and Canadian college women. *Journal of Sex Research, 23,* 455–480.

Reece, M., & Whitman, R. (1962). Expressive movements, warmth, and verbal reinforcement. *Journal of Abnormal and Social Psychology, 64,* 234–236.

Richmond, V. P., McCroskey, J. C., & Johnson, A. D. (2003). Development of the nonverbal immediacy scale (NIS): Measures of self- and other-perceived nonverbal immediacy. *Communication Quarterly, 51,* 504–517.

Rodriguez, J. I., Plax, T. G., & Kearney, P. (1996). Clarifying the relationship between teacher nonverbal immediacy and student cognitive learning: Affective learning as the central causal mediator. *Communication Education, 45,* 293–305.

Rosenfeld, H. M. (1966a). Approval-seeking and approval-inducing functions of verbal and nonverbal responses in the dyad. *Journal of Personality and Social Psychology, 4,* 597–605.

Rosenfeld, H. M. (1966b). Instrumental affiliative functions of facial and gestural expressions. *Journal of Personality and Social Psychology, 4,* 65–72.

Scheflen, A. E. (1965). Quasi-courtship behavior in psychotherapy. *Psychiatry, 28,* 245–257.

Simpson, J. A., Gangestad, S. W., & Nations, C. (1996). Sociosexuality and relationship initiation: An ethological perspective of nonverbal behavior. In G. J. O. Fletcher & J. Fitness (Eds.), *Knowledge structures in close relationships.* Mahwah, NJ: Erlbaum.

Tickle-Degnen, L., & Rosenthal, R. (1990). The nature of rapport and its nonverbal correlates. *Psychological Inquiry, 1,* 285–293.

Trees, A. R. (2000). Nonverbal communication and the support process: Interactional sensitivity in interactions between mothers and young adult children. *Communicaiton Monographs, 67,* 239–261.

Trees, A. R. & Manusov, V. (1998). Managing face concerns in criticism: Integrating nonverbal behaviors as a dimension of politeness in female friendship dyads. *Human Communication Research, 24,* 564–583.

DOMINANCE/STATUS

Argyle, M. (1988). *Bodily communication* (2nd ed.). London: Methuen.

Berger, J., Rosenholtz, S. J., & Zelditch, M., Jr. (1980). Status organizing processes. *Annual Review of Sociology, 6,* 479–508.

Burgoon, J. K., Buller, D. B., & Woodall, W. G. (1989). *Nonverbal communication: The unspoken dialogue.* New York: Harper & Row.

Burroughs, W., Schulz, W., & Aubrey, S. (1973). Quality of argument, leadership roles and eye contact in three-person leaderless groups. *Journal of Social Psychology, 90,* 89–93.

Carney, D. R., Hall, J. A., & Smith LeBeau, L. (in press). Beliefs about the nonverbal expression of social power. *Journal of Nonverbal Behavior.*

Dindia, K. (1987). The effects of sex of subject and sex of partner on interruptions. *Human Communication Research, 13,* 345–371.

Dovidio, J. F., Brown, C. E., Heitman, K., Ellyson, S. L., & Keating, C. F. (1988). Power displays between women and men in discussions of gender-linked tasks: A multichannel study. *Journal of Personality and Social Psychology, 55,* 580–587.

Dovidio, J. F., & Ellyson, S. L. (1985). Patterns of visual dominance behavior in humans. In S. L. Ellyson & J. F. Dovidio (Eds.), *Power, dominance, and nonverbal behavior.* New York: Springer-Verlag.

Dovidio, J. F., Ellyson, S. L., Keating, C. F., Heitman, K., & Brown, C. E. (1988). The relationship of social power to visual displays of dominance between men and women. *Journal of Personality and Social Psychology, 54,* 233–242.

Edinger, J. A., & Patterson, M. L. (1983). Nonverbal involvement and social control. *Psychological Bulletin, 93,* 30–56.

Ellyson, S. L., & Dovidio, J. F. (1985). Power, dominance, and nonverbal behavior: Basic concepts and issues. In S. L. Ellyson & J. F. Dovidio (Eds.), *Power, dominance, and nonverbal behavior.* New York: Springer-Verlag.

Ellyson, S. L., Dovidio, J. F., & Fehr, B. J. (1981). Visual behavior and dominance in women and men. In C. Mayo & N. M. Henley (Eds.), *Gender and nonverbal behavior.* New York: Springer-Verlag.

Exline, R. V. (1971). Visual interaction: The glances of power and preference. *Nebraska Symposium on Motivation, 19,* 163–206.

Exline, R. V., Ellyson, S. L., & Long, B. (1975). Visual behavior as an aspect of power relationships. In P. Pliner, L. Kramer, & T. Alloway (Eds.), *Nonverbal communication of aggression.* New York: Plenum.

Fehr, B. J., & Exline, R. V. (1987). Social visual interaction: A conceptual and literature review. In A. W. Siegman & S. Feldstein (Eds.), *Nonverbal behavior and communication* (2nd ed.). Hillsdale, NJ: Erlbaum.

Goldstein, A. G., & Jeffords, J. (1981). Status and touching behavior. *Bulletin of the Psychonomic Society, 17,* 79–81.

Halberstadt, A. G., Dovidio, J. F., & Davidson, L. A. (1988, October). *Power, gender, and smiling.* Paper presented at the meeting of the Society of Experimental Social Psychology.

Halberstadt, A. G., & Saitta, M. B. (1987). Gender, nonverbal behavior, and perceived dominance: A test of the theory. *Journal of Personality and Social Psychology, 53,* 257–272.

Hall, J. A. (1984). *Nonverbal sex differences: Communication accuracy and expressive style.* Baltimore: Johns Hopkins University Press.

Hall, J. A. (1996). Touch, status, and gender at professional meetings. *Journal of Nonverbal Behavior, 20,* 23–44.

Hall, J. A., Coats, E. J., & Smith LeBeau, L. (2004). Nonverbal behavior and the vertical dimension of social relations: A meta-analysis. Manuscript submitted for publication.

Hall, J. A., & Friedman, G. B. (1999). Status, gender, and nonverbal behavior: A study of structured interactions between employees of a company. *Personality and Social Psychology Bulletin, 25,* 1082–1091.

Harper, R. G. (1985). Power, dominance, and nonverbal behavior: An overview. In S. L. Ellyson & J. F. Dovidio (Eds.), *Power, dominance, and nonverbal behavior.* New York: Springer-Verlag.

Henley, N. M. (1977). *Body poliltics: Power, sex, and nonverbal communication.* Englewood Cliffs, NJ: Prentice-Hall.

Heslin, R., & Patterson, M. L. (1982). *Nonverbal behavior and social psychology.* New York: Plenum.

Johnson, C. (1994). Gender, legitimate authority, and leader–subordinate conversations. *American Sociological Review, 59,* 122–135.

Keating, C. F. (1985). Human dominance signals: The primate in us. In S. L. Ellyson & J. F. Dovidio (Eds.), *Power, dominance, and nonverbal behavior.* New York: Springer-Verlag.

Kennedy, C. W., & Camden, C. T. (1983). A new look at interruptions. *Western Journal of Speech Communication, 47,* 45–58.

Kleinke, C. L. (1986). Gaze and eye contact: A research review. *Psychological Bulletin, 100,* 78–100.

Kollock, P., Blumstein, P., & Schwartz, P. (1985). Sex and power in interaction: Conversational privileges and duties. *American Sociological Review, 50,* 34–46.

Lamb, T. A. (1981). Nonverbal and paraverbal control in dyads and triads: Sex or power differences. *Social Psychology Quarterly, 44,* 49–53.

Latta, R. M. (1978). Relation of status incongruence to personal space. *Personality and Social Psychology Bulletin, 4,* 143–146.

Leffler, A., Gillespie, D. L., & Conaty, J. C. (1982). The effects of status differentiation on nonverbal behavior. *Social Psychology Quarterly, 45,* 153–161.

Lott, D. F., & Sommer, R. (1967). Seating arrangements and status. *Journal of Personality and Social Psychology, 7,* 90–95.

Major, B., & Heslin, R. (1982). Perceptions of cross-sex and same-sex nonreciprocal touch: It is better to give than to receive. *Journal of Nonverbal Behavior, 6,* 148–162.

Mehrabian, A. (1972). *Nonverbal communication.* Chicago: Aldine/Atherton.

Mullen, B., Salas, E., & Driskell, J. E. (1989). Salience, motivation, and artifact as contributions to the relation between participation rate and leadership. *Journal of Experimental Social Psychology, 25,* 545–559.

Murphy, J. D., Driscoll, D. M., & Kelly, J. R. (1999). Differences in nonverbal behavior of men who vary in the likelihood to sexually harass. *Journal of Social Behavior & Personality, 14,* 113–128.

Nevill, D. (1974). Experimental manipulation of dependency motivation and its effects on eye contact and measures of field dependency. *Journal of Personality and Social Psychology, 29,* 72–79.

Ridgeway, C. L. (1987). Nonverbal behavior, dominance, and the basis of status in task groups. *American Sociological Review, 52,* 683–694.

Ridgeway, C. L., Berger, J., & Smith, L. (1985). Nonverbal cues and status: An expectation states approach. *American Journal of Sociology, 90,* 955–978.

Robinson, L. F., & Reis, H. T. (1989). The effects of interruption, gender, and status on interpersonal perceptions. *Journal of Nonverbal Behavior, 13,* 141–153.

Rosa, E., & Mazur, A. (1979). Incipient status in small groups. *Social Forces, 58,* 18–37.

Schwartz, B., Tesser, A., & Powell, E. (1982). Dominance cues in nonverbal behavior. *Social Psychology Quarterly, 45,* 114–120.

Schmid Mast, M. (2002). Dominance as expressed and inferred through speaking time: A meta-analysis. *Human Communication Research, 28,* 420–450.

Siegel, S. M., Friedlander, M. L., & Heatherington, L. (1992). Nonverbal relational control in family communication. *Journal of Nonverbal Behavior, 16,* 117–139.

Snyder, R. A., & Sutker, L. W. (1977). The measurement of the construct of dominance and its relation to nonverbal behavior. *Journal of Psychology, 97,* 227–230.

Stier, D. S., & Hall, J. A. (1984). Gender differences in touch: An empirical and theoretical review. *Journal of Personality and Social Psychology, 47,* 440–459.

Thayer, S. (1969). The effect of interpersonal looking duration on dominance judgments. *Journal of Social Psychology, 79,* 285–286.

Tiedens, L. Z., & Fragale, A. R. (2003). Power moves: Complementarity in dominant and submissive nonverbal behavior. *Journal of Personality and Social Psychology, 84,* 558–568.

INTERACTION MANAGEMENT

Ayres, J. (1975). Observers' judgments of audience members' attitudes. *Western Speech, 39,* 40–50.

Baker, C. (1977). Regulators and turn-taking in American sign language discourse. In L. A. Friedman (Ed.), *On the other hand: New perspectives on American sign language.* New York: Academic Press.

Bavelas, J. B., Coates, L., & Johnson, T. (2002). Listener responses as a collaborative process: The role of gaze, *Journal of Communication, 52,* 566–580.

Beattie, G. W. (1980). The skilled art of conversational interaction: Verbal and nonverbal signals in its regulation and management. In W. T. Singleton, P. Spurgeon, & R. B. Stammers (Eds.), *The analysis of social skill.* New York: Plenum.

Beattie, G. W. (1981). The regulation of speaker turns in face-to-face conversation: Some implications for conversation in sound-only communication channels. *Semiotica, 34,* 55–70.

Brunner, L. J. (1979). Smiles can be back channels. *Journal of Personality and Social Psychology, 37,* 728–734.

Cappella, J. N. (1985). Controlling the floor in conversation. In A. W. Siegman & S. Feldstein (Eds.), *Multichannel integrations of nonverbal behavior* (pp. 69–103). Hillsdale, NJ: Erlbaum.

Cegala, D. J., Savage, G. T., Brunner, C. C., & Conrad, A. B. (1982). An elaboration of the meaning of interaction involvement: Toward the development of a theoretical concept. *Communication Monographs, 49,* 229–248.

Coker, D. A., & Burgoon, J. K. (1987). The nature of conversational involvement and nonverbal encoding patterns. *Human Communication Research, 13,* 463–494.

Dickens, M., & Krueger, D. H. (1969). Speakers' accuracy in identifying immediate audience response during a speech. *Speech Teacher, 18,* 303–307.

Duncan, S. D., Jr. (1972). Some signals and rules for taking speaking turns in conversations. *Journal of Personality and Social Psychology, 23,* 283–292.

Duncan, S. D., Jr. (1973). Toward a grammar for dyadic conversation. *Semiotica, 9,* 29–46.

Duncan, S. D., Jr. (1974). On the structure of speaker-auditor interaction during speaking turns. *Language in Society, 2,* 161–180.

Duncan, S. D., Jr. (1975). Interaction units during speaking turns in dyadic face-to-face conversations. In A. Kendon, R. M. Harris, & M. R. Key (Eds.), *Organization of behavior in face-to-face interaction.* Chicago: Aldine.

Duncan, S. D., Jr., & Fiske, D. W. (1977). *Face-to-face interaction: Research, methods, and theory.* Hillsdale, NJ: Erlbaum.

Duncan, S. D., Jr., & Niedereche, G. (1974). On signaling that it's your turn to speak. *Journal of Experimental Social Psychology, 10,* 234–254.

Edinger, J. A., & Patterson, M. L. (1983). Nonverbal involvement and social control. *Psychological Bulletin, 93,* 30–56.

Feldstein, S., & Welkowitz, J. (1987). A chronography of conversation: In defense of an objective approach. In A. W. Siegman & S. Feldstein (Eds.), *Nonverbal behavior and communication* (2nd ed.). Hillsdale, NJ: Erlbaum.

Firth, R. W. (1972). Verbal and bodily rituals of greeting and parting. In J. S. Fontaine (Ed.), *Interpretation of ritual.* London: Tavistock.

Gardiner, J. C. (1971). A synthesis of experimental studies of speech communication feedback. *Journal of Communication, 21,* 17–35.

Givens, D. (1978). Greeting a stranger: Some commonly used nonverbal signals of aversiveness. *Semiotica, 22,* 351–367.

Goffman, E. (1963). *Behavior in public places.* New York: Free Press.

Goffman, E. (1971). *Relations in public.* New York: Basic.

Greenbaum, P. E., & Rosenfeld, H. M. (1980). Varieties of touching in greetings: Sequential structure and sex-related differences. *Journal of Nonverbal Behavior, 5,* 13–25.

Halberstadt, A. G. (1985). Race, socioeconomic status, and nonverbal behavior. In A. W. Siegman & S. Feldstein (Eds.), *Multi-channel integrations of nonverbal behavior.* Hillsdale, NJ: Erlbaum.

Karns, C. F. (1969). Speaker behavior to nonverbal aversive stimuli from the audience. *Speech Monographs, 36,* 26–30.

Kendon, A., & Ferber, A. (1973). A description of some human greetings. In R. P. Michael & J. H. Crook (Eds.), *Comparative ecology and behavior of primates.* London: Academic Press.

Knapp, M. L., Hart, R. P., Friedrich, G. W., & Shulman, G. M. (1973). The rhetoric of goodbye: Verbal and nonverbal correlates of human leave-taking. *Speech Monographs, 40,* 182–198.

Knuf, J. (1990/1991). Greeting and leave-taking: A bibliography of resources for the study of ritualized communication. *Research on Language and Social Interaction, 24,* 405–448.

Kraut, R., & Lewis, S. H. (1984). Some functions of feedback in conversation. In H. E. Sypher & J. L. Applegate (Eds.), *Communication by children and adults.* Beverly Hills, CA: Sage.

Krivonos, P. D., & Knapp, M. L. (1975). Initiating communication: What do you say when you say hello? *Central States Speech Journal, 26,* 115–125.

LaFrance, M., & Mayo, C. (1976). Racial differences in gaze behavior during conversations: Two systematic observational studies. *Journal of Personality and Social Psychology, 33,* 547–552.

Laver, J. (1975). Communication functions of phatic communion. In A. Kendon, R. M. Harris, & M. R. Key (Eds.), *Organization of behavior in face-to-face interaction.* Chicago: Aldine.

Leathers, D. (1979). The informational potential of the nonverbal and verbal components of feedback responses. *Southern Speech Communication Journal, 44,* 331–354.

Norton, R. W., & Pettegrew, L. S. (1979). Attentiveness as a style of communication: A structural analysis. *Communication Monographs, 46,* 13–36.

O'Leary, M. J., & Gallois, C. (1985). The last ten turns: Behavior and sequencing in friends' and strangers' conversational endings. *Journal of Nonverbal Behavior, 9,* 8–27.

Pike, K. (1975). On kinesic triadic relations in turn-taking. *Semiotica, 13,* 389–394.

Rosenfeld, H. M. (1987). Conversational control functions of nonverbal behavior. In A. W. Siegman & S. Feldstein (Eds.), *Nonverbal behavior and communication* (2nd ed.). Hillsdale, NJ: Erlbaum.

Rosenfeld, H. M., & Hancks, M. (1980). The nonverbal context of verbal listener responses. In M. R. Key (Ed.), *The relationship of verbal and nonverbal communication.* The Hague: Mouton.

Scheflen, A. E. (1964). Communication and regulation in psychotherapy. *Psychiatry, 27,* 126–136.

Schiffrin, D. (1974). Handwork as ceremony: The case of the handshake. *Semiotica, 12,* 189–202.

Vettin, J., & Todt, D. (2004). Laughter in conversation: Features of occurrence and acoustic structure. *Journal of Nonverbal Behavior, 28,* 93–115.

Walker, M. B., & Trimboli, C. (1982). Smooth transitions in conversational interactions. *Journal of Social Psychology, 117,* 305–306.

Walker, M. B., & Trimboli, C. (1984). The role of nonverbal signals in co-ordinating speaking turns. *Journal of Language and Social Psychology, 3,* 257–272.

Wiemann, J. M., & Knapp, M. L. (1975). Turn-taking in conversations. *Journal of Communication, 25,* 75–92.

Wilson, T. P., Wiemann, J. M., & Zimmerman, D. H. (1984). Models of turn-taking in conversational interaction. *Journal of Language and Social Psychology, 3,* 159–184.

Yngve, V. H. (1970). On getting a word in edgewise. In M. A. Campbell et al. (Eds.), *Papers from the sixth regional meeting, Chicago Linguistics Society.* Chicago: Department of Linguistics, University of Chicago.

IDENTITY

Aiello, J. R., & Aiello, T. D. (1977). Visual interaction at extended distances. *Personality and Social Psychology Bulletin, 3,* 83–86.

Argyle, M. (1988). *Bodily communication* (2nd ed.). London: Methuen.

Berry, D. S., & Hansen, J. S. (2000). Personality, nonverbal behavior, and interaction quality in female dyads. *Personality and Social Psychology Bulletin, 26,* 278–292.

Borkenau, P., & Liebler, A. (1995). Observable attributes as manifestations and cues of personality and intelligence. *Journal of Personality, 63,* 1–25.

Briton, N. J., & Hall, J. A. (1995). Beliefs about female and male nonverbal communication. *Sex Roles, 32,* 79–90.

Bugental, D. E., Love, L. R., & Gianetto, R. M. (1971). Perfidious feminine faces. *Journal of Personality and Social Psychology, 17,* 314–318.

Burgoon, J. K., Buller, D. B., & Woodall, W. G. (1989). *Nonverbal communication: The unspoken dialogue.* New York: Harper & Row.

Cross, S. E., & Madson, L. (1997). Models of the self: Self-construals and gender. *Psychological Bulletin, 122,* 5–37.

Davis, M., & Dulicai, D. (1992). Hitler's movement signature. *The Drama Review, 36,* 152–172.

Diener, E., Sandvik, E., & Larsen, R. (1985). Age and sex effects for emotional intensity. *Developmental Psychology, 21,* 542–546.

Dodd, D. K., Russell, B. L., & Jenkins, C. (1999). Smiling in school yearbook photos: Gender differences from kindergarten to adulthood. *Psychological Record, 49,* 543–554.

Dovidio, J. F., Brown, C. E., Heitman, K., Ellyson, S. L., & Keating, C. F. (1988). Power displays between women and men in discussions of gender-linked tasks: A multichannel study. *Journal of Personality and Social Psychology, 55,* 580–587.

Erickson, F. (1979). Talking down: Some cultural sources of miscommunication in interracial interviews. In A. Wolfgang (Ed.), *Nonverbal behavior: Applications and cultural implications.* New York: Academic Press.

Gifford, R. (1994). A lens-mapping framework for understanding the encoding and decoding of interpersonal dispositions in nonverbal behavior. *Journal of Personality and Social Psychology, 66,* 398–412.

Guerrero, L. K., & Andersen, P. A. (1994). Patterns of matching and initiation: Touch behavior and touch avoidance across romantic relationship stages. *Journal of Nonverbal Behavior, 18,* 137–153.

Halberstadt, A. G. (1985). Race, socioeconomic status, and nonverbal behavior. In A. W. Siegman & S. Feldstein (Eds.), *Multichannel integrations of nonverbal behavior.* Hillsdale, NJ: Erlbaum.

Halberstadt, A. G., Hayes, C. W., & Pike, K. M. (1988). Gender and gender role differences in smiling and communication consistency. *Sex Roles, 19,* 589–604.

Hall, J. A. (1984). *Nonverbal sex differences: Communication accuracy and expressive style.* Baltimore: Johns Hopkins University Press.

Hall, J. A. (1987). On explaining gender differences: The case of nonverbal communication. In P. Shaver & C. Hendrick (Eds.), *Review of personality and social psychology* (Vol. 7). Beverly Hills, CA: Sage.

Hall, J. A., & Carter, J. D. (1999). Gender-stereotype accuracy as an individual difference. *Journal of Personality and Social Psychology, 77,* 350–359.

Hall, J. A., Carter, J. D., & Horgan, T. G. (2000). Gender differences in nonverbal communication of emotion. In A. Fischer (Ed.), *Gender and emotion.* Paris: Cambridge University Press.

Hall, J. A., Coats, E. J., & Smith LeBeau, L. (2004). Nonverbal behavior and the vertical dimension of social relations: A meta-analysis. Manuscript submitted for publication.

Hall, J. A., & Halberstadt, A. G. (1986). Smiling and gazing. In J. S. Hyde & M. Linn (Eds.), *The psychology of gender: Advances through meta-analysis.* Baltimore: Johns Hopkins University Press.

Hall, J. A., Halberstadt, A. G., & O'Brien, C. E. (1997). "Subordination" and nonverbal sensitivity: A study and synthesis of findings based on trait measures. *Sex Roles, 37,* 295–317.

Hall, J. A., Irish, J. T., Roter, D. L., Ehrlich, C. M., & Miller, L. H. (1994). Gender in medical encounters: An analysis of physician and patient communication in a primary care setting. *Health Psychology, 13,* 384–392.

Hall, J. A., & Veccia, E. M. (1990). More "touching" observations: New insights on men, women, and interpersonal touch. *Journal of Personality and Social Psychology, 59,* 1155–1162.

Henley, N. M. (1977). *Body politics: Power, sex, and nonverbal communication.* Englewood Cliffs, NJ: Prentice-Hall.

Johnson, K. R. (1972). Black kinesics—some nonverbal communication patterns in the black culture. In L. A. Samovar & R. E. Porter (Eds.), *Intercultural communication: A reader.* Belmont,
CA: Wadsworth.

Kring, A. M. & Gordon, A. H. (1998). Sex differences in emotion: Expression, experience, and
physiology. *Journal of Personality and Social Psychology, 74,* 686–703.

LaFrance, M., & Hect, M. A. (2000). Gender and smiling: A meta-analysis. In A. H. Fischer (Ed.),
Gender and emotion: Social psychological perspectives (pp. 118–142). New York: Cambridge
University Press.

LaFrance, M., Hecht, M. A., & Levy Paluck, E. (2003). The contingent smile: A meta-analysis of sex
differences in smiling. *Psychological Bulletin, 129,* 305–334.

Lippa, R. (1998). The nonverbal display and judgment of extraversion, masculinity, femininity, and
gender diagnosticity: A lens model analysis. *Journal of Research in Personality, 32,* 80–107.

Murphy, J. D., Driscoll, D. M., & Kelly, J. R. (1999). Differences in the nonverbal behavior of men
who vary in the likelihood to sexually harass. *Journal of Social Behavior and Personality, 14,*
113–128.

Murphy, N. A., Hall, J. A., & Colvin, C. R. (2003). Accurate intelligence assessments in social interaction: Mediators and gender effects. *Journal of Personality, 71,* 465–493.

Putnam, L. L., & McCallister, L. (1980). Situational effects of task and gender on nonverbal display.
In D. Nimmo (Ed.), *Communication yearbook 4.* New Brunswick, NJ: Transaction.

Roese, N. J., Olson, J. M., Borenstein, M. N., Martin, A., & Shores, A. L. (1992). Same-sex touching behavior: The moderating role of homophobic attitudes. *Journal of Nonverbal Behavior,
16,* 249–259.

Rosenthal, R., & DePaulo, B. M. (1979). Sex differences in eavesdropping on nonverbal cues. *Journal of Personality and Social Psychology, 37,* 273–285.

Stier, D. S., & Hall, J. A. (1984). Gender differences in touch: An empirical and theoretical review.
Journal of Personality and Social Psychology, 47, 440–459.

Tucker, J. S., & Friedman, H. S. (1993). Sex differences in nonverbal expressiveness: Emotional
expression, personality, and impressions. *Journal of Nonverbal Behavior, 17,* 103–117.

Vrugt, A., & Kerkstra, A. (1984). Sex differences in nonverbal communication. *Semiotica, 50,* 1–41.

Willis, F. N., Jr., & Briggs, L. F. (1992). Relationship and touch in public settings. *Journal of Nonverbal Behavior, 16,* 55–63.

Zanna, M. P., & Pack, S. J. (1975). On the self-fulfilling nature of apparent sex differences in behavior. *Journal of Experimental Social Psychology, 11,* 583–591.

DECEPTION

Anderson, D. E., DePaulo, B. M., Ansfield, M. E., Tickle, J. J., & Green, E. (1999). Beliefs about
cues to deception: Mindless stereotypes or untapped wisdom? *Journal of Nonverbal Behavior,
23,* 67–89.

Buck, R. (1984). *The communication of emotion.* New York: Guilford.

Burgoon, J. K., & Floyd, K. (2000). Testing for the motivational impairment effect during deceptive
and truthful interaction. *Western Journal of Communication, 64,* 243–267.

Comadena, M. E. (1982). Accuracy in detecting deception: Intimate and friendship relationships. In
M. Burgoon (Ed.), *Communication yearbook 6.* Newbury Park, CA: Sage.

Corcoran, J. F. T., Lewis, M. D., & Garver, R. B. (1978). Biofeedback—conditioned galvanic skin
response and hypnotic suppression of arousal: A pilot study of their relation to deception. *Journal of Forensic Sciences, 23,* 155–162.

DePaulo, B. M., Kashy, D. A., Kirkendol, S. E., Wyer, M. M., & Epstein, J. A. (1996). Lying in
everyday life. *Journal of Personality and Social Psychology, 70,* 979–995.

DePaulo, B. M., Kirkendol, S. E., Tang, J., & O'Brien, T. P. (1988). The motivational impairment effect in the communication of deception: Replications and extensions. *Journal of Nonverbal Behavior, 12,* 177–202.

DePaulo, B. M. Lindsay, J. J., Malone, B. E., Muhlenbruck, L., Charlton, K., & Cooper, H. (2003). Cues to deception. *Journal of Personality and Social Psychology, 129,* 74–118.

deTurck, M. A. (1991). Training observers to detect spontaneous deception: Effects of gender. *Communication Reports, 4,* 79–89.

deTurck, M. A., Feeley, T. H., & Roman, L. A. (1997). Vocal and visual cue training in behavioral lie detection. *Communication Research Reports, 14,* 249–259.

Ekman, P. (1992). *Telling lies* (2nd ed). New York: Norton.

Ekman, P., & Friesen, W. V. (1969). Nonverbal leakage and clues to deception. *Psychiatry, 32,* 88–106.

Ekman, P., & Friesen, W. V. (1975). *Unmasking the face.* Englewood Cliffs, NJ: Prentice-Hall.

Ekman, P., Friesen, W. V., & O'Sullivan, M. (1988). Smiles when lying. *Journal of Personality and Social Psychology, 54,* 414–420.

Ekman, P., & O'Sullivan, M. (1991). Who can catch a liar? *American Psychologist, 46,* 913–920.

Ekman, P., O'Sullivan, M., & Frank, M. G. (1999). A few can catch a liar. *Psychological Science, 10,* 263–266.

Etcoff, N. L., Ekman, P., Magee, J. J., & Frank, M. G. (2000). Lie detection and language comprehension. *Nature, 405,* 139.

Farwell, L. A., & Smith, S. S. (2001). Using brain MERMER testing to detect concealed knowledge despite efforts to conceal. *Journal of Forensic Sciences, 46,* 1–9. Also see http://brainwavescience.com

Feeley, T. H., & Young, M. J. (1998). Humans as lie detectors: Some more second thoughts. *Communication Quarterly, 46,* 109–126.

Hollien, H. (1990). *The acoustics of crime: The new science of forensic phonetics.* New York: Plenum.

Knapp, M. L. (In press). Lying and deception in close relationships. In A. L. Vangelisti and D. Perlman (Eds.), *Cambridge handbook of personal relationships.* New York: Cambridge University Press.

Knapp, M. L., Cody, M. J., & Reardon, K. K. (1987). Nonverbal signals. In C. R. Berger & S. H. Chaffee (Eds.), *Handbook of communication science.* Beverly Hills, CA: Sage.

Knapp, M. L., & Comadena, M. F. (1979). Telling it like it isn't: A review of theory and research on deceptive communications. *Human Communication Research, 5,* 270–285.

Knapp, M. L., Hart, R. P., & Dennis, H. S. (1974). An exploration of deception as a communication construct. *Human Communication Research, 1,* 15–29.

Kraut, R. E. (1978). Verbal and nonverbal cues in the perception of lying. *Journal of Personality and Social Psychology, 36,* 380–391.

Kraut, R. E., & Poe, D. (1981). Behavioral roots of person perception: Deception judgments of customs inspectors and laymen. *Journal of Personality and Social Psychology, 39,* 784–798.

Levine, T. R., Park, H. S., & McCornack, S. A. (1999). Accuracy in detecting truths and lies: Documenting the "veracity effect." *Communication Monographs, 66,* 125–144.

Lewis, M., & Saarni, C. (Eds.). (1993). *Lying and deception in everyday life.* New York: Guilford.

McCornack, S. A., & Parks, M. R. (1986). Deception detection and relationship development: The other side of trust. In M. L. McLaughlin (Ed.), *Communication yearbook 9.* Newbury Park, CA: Sage.

Mitchell, R. W., & Thompson, N. S. (Eds.). (1986). *Deception: Perspectives on human and nonhuman deceit.* Albany: SUNY Press.

Nyberg, D. (1993). *The varnished truth: Truth telling and deceiving in ordinary life.* Chicago: University of Chicago Press.

Robinson, W. P. (1996). *Deceit, delusion, and detection.* Thousand Oaks, CA: Sage.

Vrij, A. (2000). *Detecting lies and deceit.* New York: Wiley.

Vrij, A., Edward, K., Roberts, K. P., & Bull, R. (2000). Detecting deceit via analysis of verbal and nonverbal behavior. *Journal of Nonverbal Behavior, 24,* 239–263.

Zebrowitz, L. A., Voinescu, L., & Collins, M. A. (1996). "Wide-eyed" and "crooked-faced": Determinants of perceived and real honesty across the life span. *Personality and Social Psychology Bulletin, 22,* 1258–1269.

Zuckerman, M., DePaulo, B. M., & Rosenthal, R. (1981). Verbal and nonverbal communication of deception. In L. Berkowitz (Ed.), *Advances in experimental social psychology* (Vol. 14). New York: Academic Press.

Zuckerman, M., Spiegel, N. H., DePaulo, B. M., & Rosenthal, R. (1982). Nonverbal strategies for decoding deception. *Journal of Nonverbal Behavior, 6,* 171–187.

SELF-FULFILLING PROPHECY

Blanck, P. D. (Ed.). (1993). *Interpersonal expectations: Theory, research, and applications.* New York: Cambridge University Press.

Harris, M. J., Milich, R., Johnston, E. M., & Hoover, D. W. (1990). Effects of expectancies on children's social interactions. *Journal of Experimental Social Psychology, 26,* 1–12.

Harris, M. J., & Rosenthal, R. (1985). Mediation of interpersonal expectancy effects: 31 meta-analyses. *Psychological Bulletin, 97,* 363–386.

Rosenthal, R. (1976). *Experimenter effects in behavioral research* (enlarged ed.). New York: Irvington.

Snyder, M., Tanke, E. D., & Berscheid, E. (1977). Social perception and interpersonal behavior: On the self-fulfilling nature of social stereotypes. *Journal of Personality and Social Psychology, 35,* 656–666.

Spitz, H. H. (1997). *Nonconscious movements: From mystical messages to facilitated communication.* Mahwah, NJ: Erlbaum.

Sullins, E. S., Friedman, H. S., & Harris, M. J. (1985). Individual differences in expressive style as a mediator of expectancy communication. *Journal of Nonverbal Behavior, 9,* 229–238.

Word, C. O., Zanna, M. P., & Cooper, J. (1974). The nonverbal mediation of self-fulfilling prophecies in interracial interaction. *Journal of Experimental Social Psychology, 10,* 109–120.

Chapter 13

NONVERBAL MESSAGES
IN SPECIAL CONTEXTS

The context is the frame of reference for interpreting an action.
—S. W. LITTLEJOHN

If asked what the word "fast" means, you are likely to pause because you know the word has different meanings in different contexts. If the subject is running, fast is associated with speed; if the subject is food, fast may be associated with not eating or take-out food. Nonverbal behavior has the same multimeaning potential: Nonverbal signals may be interpreted differently in different contexts. People who are sad look down at the floor, but so do people who are submissive or shy. Knowing which meaning to select requires a knowledge of the context. A smile displayed by a powerful and energetic person to a submissive and passive person may be seen as sinister, but the very same smile by the same person with another powerful and energetic person may be viewed as a happy smile. If any given facial expression can be interpreted in multiple ways—as delight, contentment, pleasure, approval, interest, or sexually inviting—then we need a knowledge of various contextual features to help us pinpoint the most likely meaning.

What is context? Those features of a social encounter that provide key markers for the meaning of any given behavior are usually identified as the context. Philippot, Feldman and Coats (1999, p. 13) say that "nonverbal behavior can be fully understood only when considered within its social context."[1] For example, you may feel like you understand the meaning of a particular nonverbal behavior because you are aware of: 1) some personal or background characteristics of the people involved—their relationship, their age, their group membership, their gender; or 2) some environmental features—the number of people involved, the accompanying lighting or noise, the time of day, the furniture configuration; or 3) the expectations and norms for the situation—learning, therapy, fun; or 4) various message features—the topic, the emphasis given the behavior, what other verbal

---

[1] Philippot, P., Feldman, R. S., & Coats, E. J. (1999). Introducing nonverbal behavior within a social context. In P. Philippot, R. S. Feldman, & E. J. Coats (Eds.), *The social context of nonverbal behavior* (3–14). New York: Cambridge University Press.

and nonverbal behavior preceded and followed the behavior in question, and so on. These features of context give meaning to nonverbal messages, but whenever we produce nonverbal messages, they have the potential to change contextual features too.

In this chapter, we discuss nonverbal messages in the context of advertising, politics. education, culture, and therapy.

ADVERTISING MESSAGES

No one in modern society needs to be told that we are surrounded by advertising. Nevertheless, people routinely underestimate the broad scope of its influence. Television, magazines, and other forms of media do far more than bombard us with direct appeals to buy products. To buy a product, you have to lay down your money. But the media exert a powerful influence on us even when nothing is bought. By immersing us in images, concepts, and associations, the media and the advertisers shape the very assumptions and expectations by which we live. What does success mean? How does one measure beauty? How should we behave in order to be socially acceptable? How do people belonging to different groups behave and what do they value? Advertising does far more than just supply answers to these questions. It legitimizes the underlying premises that success, beauty, and social acceptance are the keys to happiness and that stereotypes have validity. And it does so without our putting a penny on the counter; indeed, almost without our noticing.

Many commentators have railed at the subtle influence and the homogenizing power of the concepts and assumptions that are planted in our minds by advertising. But people are likely to deny the influence when it comes to themselves. Partly, it's the "fish don't know they are wet" phenomenon: If all we know is the images, then that is the only reality we know—so how can we imagine an alternative? People also routinely deny social influences on themselves that they can readily see influencing others. This "I'm immune to what influences other people" fallacy is common; we see it when people deny that smoking will harm their health, that they are victims of discrimination, or that they engage in faulty ways of social thinking, while at the same time acknowledging that all of these happen to other people.

Thus, we have a built-in bias against recognizing what influences us. Social psychologists have documented this in countless studies (Nisbett & Wilson, 1977; Wegner, 2002). The sheer fact that one can conduct a social psychological experiment in which situational factors can be manipulated to influence behavior without participants ever being aware of it proves that people's insight into the sources of their behavior is frighteningly weak.

On those occasions when we are on guard for attempted influence, we are most likely to attend to what is being *said*. Is this person telling me the truth? Misrepresenting the product or the issues? Claiming to be better than he or she is? But the kinds of influence that are most likely to be unnoticed and out of awareness are—you guessed it—*nonverbal* in nature. In advertising, nonverbal information accounts for an overwhelming amount of the total message, especially if we include information provided by settings, backgrounds, props, possessions, clothes, hair, make-up, music, and physical and group characteristics of the people shown, in addition to obviously nonverbal variables such as facial expression, tone of voice, and body movements. The unconscious conclusions we draw rest more on the nature and juxtaposition of these images and sounds than on what is actually said. As we all know, the verbal messages contained in advertisements are often silly, irrelevant, meaningless, or not likely to promote distinctive associations to the product. Yet the message can be powerful indeed.

That the influences are mainly nonverbal means that we are less guarded against their influence and less critical of their content. But to make matters worse, we are most vulnerable to such influences when we are distracted or when we are not closely attending to, or resisting, the advertiser's persuasion attempt (Petty, Cacioppo, & Schumann, 1983). Unfortunately, those are precisely the circumstances under which we experience most advertising. Furthermore, laboratory research shows that nonverbal cues that are impossible to notice consciously (i.e., are presented subliminally) can serve as primes that influence subsequent behavior—such as behavior towards racial groups (Chen & Bargh, 1997). The images, associations, and stereotypes represented in advertising penetrate our minds through constant repetition and their seemingly peripheral nature. But peripheral they are not—they *are* the message.

It doesn't require empirical research for you to see the validity of this analysis, yet research does exist. One area of intense study is the representation of gender in advertisements. Goffman (1979) listed several ways in which the nonverbal portrayal of women suggests demeaned status relative to men: the relative size of men versus women, how objects or the self are touched or grasped, which gender appears to be in charge of the activity, the presence of ritualized subordination gestures (such as averting the eyes), "unserious" (clowning or childlike) poses, and the occurrence of "licensed withdrawal" (separating themselves from the activity). Of course, one can add other specific ways in which the genders are shown in stereotypic ways: the specific roles assigned to men and women (e.g., male worker vs. female homemaker, or male narrator vs. female onscreen character); the distribution of products to male and female onscreen characters (e.g., men are shown advertising life insurance, electronic products, and financial services, whereas women are shown advertising health and beauty products and retail stores); and gender disparities in body display and sexualization (Bartsch et al., 2000; Ganahl, Prinsen, & Netzley, 2003; Goffman, 1979; Kang, 1997). Gender stereotypes are easy to detect even in television commercials aimed at children. For example, boys demonstrate or sell products more, even when the product is not gender-typed (Browne, 1998).

Specific nonverbal cues are enacted differently by males and females, too. In advertising aimed at children, boys are dominant, aggressive, effective, victorious, and likely to manipulate objects whereas girls act shy, giggle, cover the face, avert the head or eyes, lower or tilt the head, and touch objects gently (Browne, 1998). In advertising showing adult characters, women smile more and stand in a more canted position (weight unevenly distributed between the legs) (Halberstadt & Saitta, 1987). Because such gender-stereotypical portrayals feel very normal and expected, it is difficult for us to grasp how profound are the assumptions on which they are based. Only if boys acted "like girls" and vice versa would the viewer suddenly see the stereotyping in action. One might counter that the portrayals of men and women are simply reflecting the way men and women behave in real life.

Though to some extent this is true, many of the nonverbal expressions and mannerisms shown in advertising are strong exaggerations of real-life gender differences or show behaviors that ordinary men and women don't actually engage in.

The tendency for magazines and television to show relatively more of men's faces and relatively more of women's bodies is also well documented (Archer et al., 1983; Copeland, 1989; Dodd et al., 1989), and the disturbing—unspoken—message of these depictions is that photos showing more of the face are seen as more intelligent and dominant (Schwarz & Kurz, 1989; Zuckerman, 1986). Again, a nonconscious cue manipulates our impressions of men and women.

Advertising manipulates not only how we think about products but also how we feel emotionally, how we think about social groups, and how we think about ourselves. Images of beautiful people who seem very successful and happy simultaneously invite us to identify with them ("If I drink this beer, I can become just like them") *and* to think we are sadly inadequate by contrast ("My boyfriend isn't that cute, my sex life doesn't seem that good, I don't have such a nice car, and my thighs will never look that good"). The subtle message that the viewer is inadequate is a large part of advertising's lethal power. Even the current fad for television ads to be fast video montages—many images that change so quickly you hardly know what you saw—is more than just a way to get the viewer's attention. It is a way to make viewers feel slow, dull, and excluded from the exciting, fast-paced life of the people on the screen.

Advertisers use both research and common sense in planning their strategies. No doubt a great deal of advertising research is done in-house and is never published in journals. But there is no shortage of published advertising research, some of it very early indeed. An article from 1923 asked the reasonable question, "How much smiling should an actor show for different kinds of products?" (Burtt & Clark, 1923). Research participants were shown faces with different degrees of smiling and were asked to name products that would sell best with each kind of smile. They thought that clothing would be sold best by a relatively unsmiling face, whereas toilet articles, amusements, and food would sell better if the actors smiled more.

Of course, asking people what kind of advertising messages they think would work best is not the only, or the best, way to evaluate effectiveness. An advertiser would want to know about actual consumers' responses and about their purchasing choices. Current advertising researchers are especially interested in indirect methods of understanding viewers' emotional responses by measuring brain activity, by recording tiny electric impulses in the facial muscles that are associated with different emotions, and by cataloguing which facial muscles move visibly (Hazlett & Hazlett, 1999; Raskin, 2003; Young, 2002). For example, such methods may reveal the difference between a viewer's true enjoyment smile and the polite smile of a viewer who is just saying what the researcher wants to hear. In chapter 10 we also described early interest in using changes in pupil size as an indicator of viewers' product preferences.

Should you be worried about advertising's power to exploit and manipulate you with nonverbal cues and images? Yes! But considering that a person can hardly go live on a desert isle (assuming there would be no advertising there), the best you can hope for is that by developing your knowledge of nonverbal communication and the use of psychological tactics (Cialdini, 1993), you can arm yourself against these effects.

POLITICAL MESSAGES

Politicians have long recognized the important role of nonverbal behavior. President Lyndon Johnson is said to have been very sensitive to what nonverbal cues can communicate. He reportedly cautioned his staff not to stand in front of the windows and look across the street at the White House the day after President John F. Kennedy's assassination for fear it would appear they were looking for power. In journalist Bob Woodward's (2004) book about how and why President Bush and his staff initiated a preemptive attack on Iraq, he notes how members of Bush's cabinet paid close attention to his body language. In the following excerpt involving General Tommy Franks, we can see that Bush, too, felt nonverbal signals played a critical role in understanding a person's reaction:

> "I'm trying to figure out what intelligent questions to ask a commander who has just impressed me in Afghanistan. I'm looking for the logic. I'm watching his body language very carefully," Bush recalled. He emphasized the body language, the eyes, the demeanor. It was more important than some of the substance. It was also why he wanted Franks there in Crawford and not as another face on a wall of screens. (p. 66)

Television, and specifically the televised presidential debates, can highlight nonverbal signals. Some argue that the candidates have become so preoccupied with their image that it diminishes their concern for arguments supporting their policies. But physically unappealing candidates and candidates whose behavior does not signal energy and confidence are not likely to play well on television. The average American watches between 30 and 40 hours of television each week. Television has certainly helped to structure some of our nonverbal perceptions, and more and more political candidates recognize the tremendous influence these perceptions may have on the eventual election outcome. Television seems especially well suited to nonverbal signals that express positive relationship messages (e.g., facial expressions that communicate sincerity, body positions that suggest immediacy, or vocal tones that are perceived as caring). Television requires what Jamieson (1988) calls "a new eloquence—a softer, warmer style of communication." This in no way minimizes the necessity of a candidate also displaying nonverbal signals that would help to communicate assertiveness and energy. How have our presidential candidates fared?

During the first of the 1960 television debates between presidential candidates Richard Nixon and John Kennedy, analysts often discussed Nixon's loss in terms of how he presented himself on television, that is, his five o'clock shadow showing through the stage makeup, lighting conditions that accentuated a tired face, a suit that blended into the background, and so forth. Nixon has been quoted as saying he spent too much time studying and not enough time on his physical appearance (Bryski & Frye, 1979–1980; Tiemens, 1978). A movement analysis by Davis (1995, p. 213) indicates Nixon's appearance was only one of his nonverbal drawbacks.

> Nixon sits with a tense, narrow posture, whereas Kennedy sits with legs crossed, hands resting easily, his weight centered. In the medium camera shots, Nixon can be seen gripping the lectern tightly and not gesticulating for long periods of time, although his head movements are clear and emphatic. And Nixon displays a disastrous pattern of hyperblinking— not just abnormally frequent (more than one per second), but at times with such rapid flutters that his eyes momentarily close. By comparison Kennedy clearly wins despite his rather ordinary and constricted showing.

FIGURE 13-1

John Kerry and George Bush debate in the 2003 Presidential election campaign.

It was widely reported and believed that radio listeners judged the debate a draw, whereas television viewers felt Kennedy was the winner. Even though the accuracy of this conclusion has been questioned, the belief that it was true may have been largely responsible for subsequent concern about the influence of nonverbal signals in political campaigns and debates (Kraus, 1996; Vancil & Pendell, 1987). By 1968, though, candidate Nixon felt he knew a great deal more about the role of nonverbal signals and the use of television. Joe McGinniss's book *The Selling of the President 1968* presents a vivid, if not alarming, picture of the role nonverbal signals were expected to play in televised politics:

> Television seems particularly useful to the politician who can be charming but lacks ideas. . . . On television it matters less that he does not have ideas. His personality is what the viewers want to share. He need be neither statesman nor crusader; he must only show up on time. Success and failure are easily measured: how often is he invited back? Often enough and he reaches his goal—to advance from "politician" to "celebrity," a status jump bestowed by grateful viewers who feel that finally they have been given a basis for making a choice.
>
> The TV candidate, then, is measured not against his predecessors—not against a standard of performance established by two centuries of democracy—but against Mike Douglas. How well does he handle himself? Does he mumble, does he twitch, does he make me laugh? Do I feel warm inside? (pp. 29–30)

The words would be the same ones Nixon always used—the words of the acceptance speech. But they would all seem fresh and lively because a series of still pictures would flash on the screen while Nixon spoke. If it were done right, it would permit Treleaven to create a Nixon image that was entirely independent of the words. Nixon would say his same old tiresome things but no one would have to listen. The words would become Muzak. Something pleasant and lulling in the background. The flashing pictures would be carefully selected to create the impression that somehow Nixon represented competence, respect for tradition, serenity, faith that the American people were better people than people anywhere else, and that all these problems others shouted about meant nothing in a land blessed with the tallest building, strongest armies, biggest factories, cutest children, and rosiest sunsets in the world. Even better: through association with these pictures, Richard Nixon could become these very things. (p. 85)

Since 1968, the strategies used to create favorable images of political candidates at speeches and on television have become more widespread and more sophisticated. The environment is carefully constructed. At a 2004 campaign speech in Indianapolis, White House aides asked people in the crowd behind President Bush to take off their ties so they would look more like the people who would benefit from his tax cut. Backdrops with pictures and slogans accompanied most of Bush's speeches and became a part of any photo of Bush, the speaker. For some who saw the photo in the newspaper the next day, the composite message of Bush and the backdrop summed up the speech completely (see Figure 13-2). When President Bush selected a small shipping company to deliver a speech on how his economic plan would favor small business, his aides put up American flags and a backdrop saying "Strengthening the Economy." Boxes near the podium that were stamped "Made in China," however, were covered over and a backdrop of boxes with the label "Made in USA" was added.

Analysts of the 1976 Carter–Ford presidential debates argue that Gerald Ford's loss was attributable to less eye gaze with the camera, grimmer facial expressions, and less favorable camera angles (Tiemens, 1978). Subsequently, Jimmy Carter's loss to Ronald Reagan in the 1980 debate was attributed to Carter's visible tension and his inability to "coordinate his nonverbal behavior with his verbal message" (Ritter & Henry, 1990). Effective leaders are often seen as people who confidently take stock of a situation, perform smoothly, and put those around them at ease. Many saw Reagan's nonverbal behavior this way. In 1984 Reagan's expressiveness and physical attractiveness were evident, whereas his opponent, Walter Mondale, was perceived as low in expressiveness and attractiveness (Patterson et al., 1992). Expressions of fear may be the biggest turnoff for voters. These include looking down; hesitating; making rapid, jerky movements; or seeming to freeze, as Dan Quayle did when Lloyd Bentsen told him in the 1988 vice presidential debate, "You're no Jack Kennedy." Some even associated Walter Mondale's tense smile with a fear grimace (Masters, 1989; Sullivan et al., 1991). The fact that presidential faces are so prominent on television may mean that attention to the candidate's make-up will become more detailed in the future. Keating, Randall, and Kendrick (1999), for example, digitized the faces of Presidents Clinton, Reagan, and Kennedy and made them look more or less mature by altering the size of the eyes and lips. A less mature Clinton (bigger eyes and lips) was perceived as more honest and attractive, even by those who did not support him in the 1996 election. Clinton's power ratings were not affected by his youthful look,

Figure 13-2

Bush using backdrop to create an image.

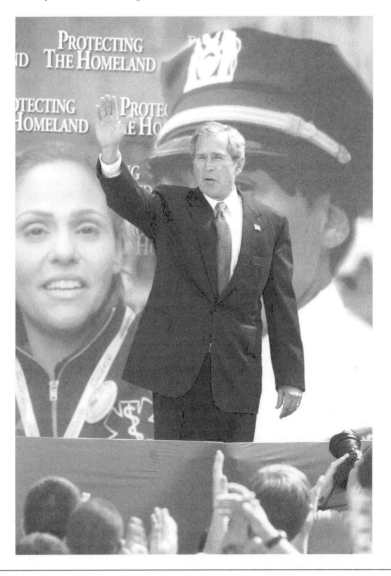

but Reagan and Kennedy were seen as less powerful when their faces were made to look less mature.

Fortunately, the image advisors are not yet in control of all the variables—none the least of which is the public's increasing knowledge of how political images can be molded. Carefully controlled appearance and scripted verbal behavior can readily be offset or put in perspective when the candidates engage in spontaneous talk and interactive dialogue about substantive issues.

TEACHER–STUDENT MESSAGES

Whether it takes place in the classroom itself or not, the teaching/learning process is a gold mine for discovering the richness and importance of nonverbal behavior (Andersen & Andersen, 1982; Babad, 1992; Philippot, Feldman, & McGee, 1992; Woolfolk & Brooks, 1983).

Acceptance and understanding of ideas and feelings by both teacher and student, encouraging and criticizing, silence, and questioning all involve nonverbal elements. Consider the following instances as representative of the variety of classroom nonverbal cues:

1. The frantic hand-waver who is sure he or she has the correct answer
2. The student who is sure she or he does not know the answer and tries to avoid eye contact with the teacher
3. The effects of student dress, hair length, and adornment on teacher–student interaction
4. The glowering facial expressions, threatening gestures, and critical tone of voice frequently used for discipline in elementary schools
5. Teachers who request student questioning and criticism, but whose nonverbal actions make it clear they will not be receptive
6. The way arrangement of seating and monitoring behavior during examinations reveal a teacher's degree of trust in students
7. Professors who announce they have plenty of time for student conferences, but whose fidgeting and glancing at a watch suggest otherwise
8. Teachers who try to assess visual feedback to determine student comprehension
9. The ways different classroom designs (wall colors, space between seats, windows) influence student participation and learning
10. The nonverbal cues that signal student–teacher closeness or distance

Subtle nonverbal influence in the classroom can sometimes have dramatic results, as Rosenthal and Jacobson (1968) found. Intelligence quotient (IQ) tests were given to elementary school pupils prior to their entering for the fall term. Randomly (that is, not according to scores), some students were labeled as high scorers on an "intellectual blooming test" indicating they would show unusual intellectual development in the following year. Teachers were given this information. These students showed a sharp rise on IQ tests given at the end of the year, which experimenters attributed to teacher expectations and to the way these students were treated.

> To summarize our speculations, we may say that by what she said, by how and when she said it, by her facial expressions, postures, and perhaps by her touch, the teacher may have communicated to the children of the experimental group that she expected improved intellectual performance. Such communications together with possible changes in teaching techniques may have helped the child learn by changing his self-concept, his expectations of his own behavior, and his motivation, as well as his cognitive style and skills. (p. 180)

In an effort to identify the cues associated with teacher expectancies, Chaikin, Sigler, and Derlega (1974) asked people to tutor a 12-year-old boy. The boy was described as either bright or dull to some, and a third group was given no information about the boy's intelligence. A 5-minute videotape of the tutoring was analyzed for behaviors indicating liking and approval. Tutors of the so-called bright boy smiled more, had more direct eye contact, leaned forward more, and nodded more than either of the other two groups. In general, then, people who expect others to do well (as compared to those who expect poor performance) seem to:

1. Create a warm socioemotional climate.
2. Provide more differentiated performance feedback.
3. Give more (and more difficult) material.
4. Give more opportunities for the performer to respond (Blanck, 1993; Rosenthal, 1985).

A related line of research has examined teachers who are perceived as more and less "immediate" in their style of teaching (Harris, in press; McCroskey & Richmond, 1992). Immediacy behavior signals liking, warmth, and positive affect (see chapter 12). Sometimes immediacy is shown when teachers move around the classroom and gain proximity to their students. Sometimes it involves more teacher smiling, facial expressions of interest when students are talking, maintaining eye gaze with students, using a friendly vocal tone, or other behaviors that students associate with liking and warmth. Numerous studies show that when college students associate nonverbal immediacy with their teacher, they are more likely to like the teacher and the course. There is more teacher–student interaction in these classes. Students also report that they would like to take another course from that instructor. Students feel like they learn more from teachers who exhibit immediacy behavior, which is an important outcome from a motivational standpoint, but the data available at present does not provide consistent and conclusive evidence that students actually do learn more from teachers who exhibit more immediacy behavior.

Even though there is plenty of evidence to support the conclusion that perceived teacher immediacy behavior has a positive impact on some important student perceptions, the exact nature of that behavior and the way it is displayed throughout the length of the class are not well known. For example, does a teacher have to exhibit immediacy behavior throughout every class period to be perceived as immediate or is the optimum style a mix of immediate and less immediate behavior? When does immediacy behavior signal that the course is "easy" or that the teacher is a "pushover"? Can a teacher be stern, strict, and businesslike and also communicate positive affect to his or her students? Woolfolk (1978) and others have found that even negative nonverbal behavior can elicit quality student performance sometimes—but it is unlikely to be an effective teaching style if used for the duration of the class. And even though we know the types of behavior associated with immediacy, it is still not clear how such behaviors should be enacted in order to be perceived as having an immediate teaching style.

Thus far we've been focusing on teacher behavior, but the classroom is a two-way street in which teachers and students mutually influence one another. As we've observed, teacher immediacy behavior elicits a number of positive outcomes from students. But students who exhibit immediacy can also elicit positive outcomes from the teacher (Baringer

& McCroskey, 2000). We have much to learn about the nonverbal communication of warmth and closeness in learning environments, and this knowledge will be increasingly important as distance education continues to increase (Guerrero & Miller, 1998; Mottet, 2000).

Sometimes teachers treat some students better or worse than others—for example, because of race, gender, unpleasant interactions with them and so on. Do students perceive these teacher biases even when the teachers believe they are controlling them? Not always, but certainly much more than teachers believe. Students are often keenly aware of subtle nonverbal signals that convey messages teachers believe they are effectively masking. Babad (1992) argues that teachers need to admit their biases to themselves and recognize they are likely to be perceived by others. Once that is done, more realistic goals for student–teacher communication can be developed.

CULTURAL MESSAGES

When we learn the rules and/or norms people expect our behavior to match, we are learning about culture. All of us exist within several cultures—our family, our religious group, our social class, our age group, our school, the place we work, our gender, and our society. So some cultural teaching is a part of all our communication behavior. Culture in this section focuses on large groups of people, possibly millions, who vary in age, sex, gender, and social class, but share a set of nonverbal behaviors which help to define them as a culture.

Any behavior identified as characteristic of a large group of people, however, does not mean that every person or every conversation in that culture will always exhibit that behavior. For example, a culture described as one in which people touch each other a lot may also have: 1) some people whose conversations do not involve a lot of touching; and 2) some conversations that are devoid of touching even though the interactants normally do a lot of touching. When touching is identified as a characteristic of a culture, it simply means that this group of people generally tends to touch each other more when compared with other groups of people.

Scholars believe cultures differ on a variety of dimensions (Gudykunst & Ting-Toomey, 1988), but three seem particularly useful for examining variations in nonverbal behavior: 1) high-contact versus low-contact cultures; 2) cultures that value collectivism versus cultures that value individualism; and 3) high-context versus low-context cultures.

HIGH-CONTACT VERSUS LOW-CONTACT CULTURES

People in high-contact cultures establish close interaction distances and touch each other frequently (Hall, 1966). They enjoy the olfactory and tactile stimulation that comes with this kind of interpersonal involvement. Central and South America, southern Europe, and the Mideast are often classified as high-contact regions while Asia and northern Europe are viewed as low contact.

The United States has traditionally been labeled a low-contact culture. Informal observations by Jourard (1966) would seem to support this designation. He counted the frequency of contact between couples in cafés in various cities and reported the following contacts per hour: San Juan, Puerto Rico, 180; Paris, 110; Gainesville, Florida, 2; London, 0. Cultural habits do change and people in the United States may be touching more now than at any time in their history (see "Touchy Topic," 2000; Willis & Rawdon, 1994). In the early 1970s, Barnlund (1975) conducted a comparative study of Japanese and U.S. touching patterns using 120 college students in each culture. In almost every category, the amount of physical contact reported in the United States was twice that reported by the Japanese. A much more recent observational study on a U.S. campus of romantically in-volved cross-sex couples found that Asian couples were far less likely to walk with arms around one another than were Latino couples (Regan et al., 1999). Similarly, McDaniel and Andersen (1998), in a study of cross-sex touch between travelers in a U.S. airport, found that travelers from the United States touched notably more body regions than did northeast Asians, who touched less than any group observed (including southeast Asians, Caribbean/Latin Americans, and northern Europeans). Although this study measures ex-tent of touch, not frequency of touch, it does suggest (like the other studies reviewed here) that whereas Asia, especially northeast Asia, may indeed have low contact as its norm, the United States seems to have norms that are further in the "contact" direction. As the U.S. population grows ever more ethnically diverse, any broad label would probably be an oversimplification.

Field (1999) speculated that patterns of touching in public might be related to cultural tendencies toward aggression. Field chose France and the United States because they dif-fer dramatically in their rates of societal violence. Comparing French and U.S. adolescents interacting with their peers in McDonald's restaurants in Paris and Miami, she found that the U.S. sample engaged in less leaning, stroking, kissing, and hugging of their friends but more self-touching than did the French sample (consistent with France being more of a contact culture).

Classifying cultures as either high or low contact inevitably covers up differences. For example, Central and South America are both classified as "high contact," but Shuter's (1976) systematic observation of people interacting in natural settings suggests that public touching and holding decreases as one moves south from Costa Rica to Panama to Columbia. And as we noted earlier, when we label a culture as high or low contact we should not forget that there are likely to be important variations within a culture. Halberstadt (1985), for example, reviewed race differences and nonverbal behavior and found African Americans tend to establish larger interpersonal distances for conversation than whites do, but they also engage in *more* touch. As we reflect on high- and low-contact cultures, we should also recognize the importance of distinguishing between *frequency* and *meaning*. Two cultures may display different frequencies of touch (especially in public), but it is a sep-arate question as to whether the meanings attached to those touches are different as well. Communicating intimacy through touch, for example, can be accomplished with a lot of contact or a little contact.

INDIVIDUALISM VERSUS COLLECTIVISM

Cultures have also been distinguished from one another by the extent to which they manifest individualism or collectivism (Hofstede, 1980; Triandis, 1994). Individualistic cultures emphasize things like personal rights, responsibilities, achievements, privacy, self-expression, individual initiative, and identity based on personal attributes. Regions said to typically manifest behavior aligned with this orientation include the United States, Australia, Great Britain, Canada, the Netherlands, New Zealand, Germany, Belgium, and Denmark. Nonverbal signals that support individualism may include such things as: 1) environments designed for privacy; 2) eye gaze and vocal signals which exude confidence, strength, and dynamism; and 3) distinctive clothing. Dion (2002) argues that stereotyping based on facial attractiveness will also be more prevalent among members of individualistic cultures because facial attractiveness is another way to highlight one's distinctiveness.

Cultures with a collective orientation tend to emphasize things that show the value they put on their group membership. Of special concern would be things like interests shared with group members, collaborating for the good of the group, maintaining harmony within the group to ensure it functions well, and maintaining traditions which emphasize group values and successes. Global regions typically associated with collectivism include Venezuela, Japan, Pakistan, Peru, Taiwan, Thailand, Brazil, Kenya, and Hong Kong. Among other things, we would expect nonverbal signals in collective cultures to exhibit: 1) familiar routines, rituals, and ways of behaving that are widely known and practiced in the culture; 2) a high frequency of deference behavior (e.g., bowing, gaze avoidance) and politeness routines—including the suppression of emotional displays that might offend the group; and 3) behavior designed to avoid calling attention to the actions of an individual when it could be detrimental to the group.

High-Context versus Low-Context Cultures

According to Hall (1976), low-context cultures tend to rely on verbal messages. Words are valued because they are believed to provide information in a direct, explicit manner. Saying what you want to say as unambiguously as possible is valued. There is not a high tolerance for ambiguity. In contrast, high-context cultures are more likely to rely on implicit and indirect messages. Nonverbal behavior is valued and messages gain their meaning by knowing the context. "What everyone knows" is the key to understanding and there is a higher tolerance for ambiguity.

Effective communication in some cultures may rely more on contextual knowledge than other cultures, but the need to understand context is an issue that permeates any cross-cultural encounter. Ignorance of context leads to misunderstandings. "Outsiders," or people who are less knowledgeable about a culture, are less knowledgeable about contextual cues that give meaning to certain behaviors. On the other hand, the knowledge necessary to properly interpret a message comes much more easily to a cultural "insider."

Similarities Across Cultures

The fact that cultures exhibit different nonverbal behaviors gets a lot of attention. It should. These differences often lead to problematic encounters. But it is also important to understand that there are similarities across cultures as well. Some of these similarities occur because people in one or more cultures adopt a behavior exhibited in another culture. Today information flows freely across cultures, so it is not difficult to imagine how a gesture or style of adorning the body becomes a multicultural phenomenon. Information about behavior in other cultures is regularly exchanged via travelers, magazines, movies, the Internet, and other ways.

Similarities in nonverbal behavior also occur across cultures for another reason as well. They may be part of an inherited neurological program that members of the human species acquire. In chapter 2, we noted that the eyebrow raise or flash has been observed in greeting behavior in cultures around the world. Chapter 2 also reported the work of Ekman and his colleagues (Ekman, 2003; Ekman, Sorenson, & Friesen, 1969) who found people in literate and nonliterate cultures around the world who: 1) could decode six facial expressions of emotion with a high degree of accuracy and 2) could make these same expressions which were, in turn, decoded by people from other cultures with a high degree of accuracy. Researchers have also found considerable cross-cultural agreement on which faces are attractive and unattractive—with some scholars speculating that this agreement occurs because it is linked to the survival of the species (Cunningham, Barbee, & Philhower, 2002; Dion, 2002; Etcoff, 1999; Rhodes et al., 2002). The list of cross-cultural similarities in nonverbal behavior is not a long one at this time, but the following seem to be fruitful areas to explore—meanings associated with extremes of eye gaze, caregiver touching behavior with neonates, and the need for territory. Some research on refusal and greeting sequences, reported in chapters 2 and 12, suggests the species may even have hard-wired *patterns* of behavior. These underlying similarities among us are not always readily visible because cultural teachings may direct members to mask or minimize them.

THERAPEUTIC SETTINGS

Anyone who has ever visited a medical doctor or a psychotherapist knows that the nonverbal cues that are exchanged in such a visit are important to the outcome of the visit. In this section we wish to suggest four ways in which nonverbal communication matters in understanding illness and therapy, whether physical or mental:

1. **Understanding the disorder.** How do we define different conditions, such as depression?
2. **Diagnosis.** Does the clinician reach the correct conclusions about the client's problems, states, and progress?
3. **Therapy.** Is the clinician able to help the client solve his or her problems and maintain good physical and psychological functioning?
4. **Relationship.** Do the clinician and client develop a positive and trusting interpersonal relationship?

For each of these goals, nonverbal cues play an important part (Hall, Harrigan, & Rosenthal, 1995). In terms of understanding the disorder, studying nonverbal behavior and skill can help researchers to develop theories about what the disorder is all about. Nonverbal behavior might be part of the definition. For example, the definition of depression might include the expression of sadness and the definition of schizophrenia might include the display of inappropriate nonverbal behavior. Similarly, autism may be defined in part by the idea that such patients lack the will or the ability to infer what's going on in someone else's head; therefore, a deficit in ability to judge emotional expressions would be a definitional element. As summarized in previous chapters and by Perez and Riggio (2003), many groups with psychological disorders, including depression, schizophrenia, alcoholism (Philippot, Kornreich, & Blairy, 2003), and autism (McGee & Morrier, 2003), score lower on accuracy in judging the meanings of nonverbal cues than do control groups. At present, it is not clear to what extent this deficit is tied uniquely to the nature of the disorders or instead reflects other factors such as a general deficit in cognitive ability, lowered motivation to focus on experimental tasks, or the effect of medications. Studies will need to include appropriate control tests along with nonverbal sensitivity tests in order to resolve this question.

Nonverbal cues are also important in the process of diagnosis by practicing clinicians. Though the process of clinical care (either by medical doctors or psychotherapists) involves expert knowledge and cognitive skills acquired through training, nevertheless most of what clinical care consists of is interpersonal interaction. Basically, clinicians and clients talk to each other and it is through the talking medium that therapeutic action occurs. Naturally, nonverbal behavior is a crucial component of this interaction.

The clinician routinely studies the patient for nonverbal signs that will shed light on problems and progress. In a psychotherapy visit, the therapist's ability to read signs of emotion—especially those that signal issues not brought up verbally or that are especially upsetting to clients—is central. But even in medical visits, the physician is attuned to emotional and psychosocial issues that might be causing, or be caused by, a medical condition. For instance, a patient might start experiencing depression in the aftermath of a heart attack.

Many studies have investigated the display of different nonverbal cues in relation to different psychological disorders. For example, researchers have shown that the stereotype of the depressed person as downcast and slow in response has validity. Evidence of decreased general movement; decreased expressiveness; decreased speech, gestures, eye contact, and smiling; halting speech; and a deficit in ability to express emotions have all been documented in depressed persons (Bouhuys, 2003; Ekman & Friesen, 1974; Ellgring, 1986; Perez & Riggio, 2003; Waxer, 1976).

Some forms of schizophrenia are marked by a voice that is very flat and monotonous in its tone, and there is also an increase in very subtle muscle activation in the corrugator muscle of the face (the muscle associated with distressed-looking eyebrows) compared to control participants, even when viewing positive stimuli (Kring & Earnst, 2003). Other nonverbal characteristics of schizophrenia include lack of facial expression, inappropriate affect displays, increased self-touching, and less interpersonal gazing. As discussed in chapter 10, there are also nonverbal behaviors distinctively associated with autism and related conditions (such as Asperger syndrome), most notably gaze avoidance and also less smiling and gesturing (McGee & Morrier, 2003).

Another illustration of the diagnostic use of nonverbal cues is in the detection of pain. Researchers have documented the configuration of facial cues indicative of different kinds of pain in both infants and adults (Patrick, Craig, & Prkachin, 1986; Prkachin, 1992a). Some common indicators include lowering the brows, narrowing the eye openings, raising the cheeks, raising the upper lip, and wrinkling the nose. Analysis of cues may reveal information not forthcoming from self-reports provided by patients. For example, chronic and acute sufferers of temporomandibular disorder (jaw movement pain) reported the same amounts of pain, but the chronic group showed more facial indications of pain both when alone and when experiencing painful procedures (LeResche et al., 1992). Nonverbal cues can also reveal differences in the behavior of people actually experiencing pain versus pretending (Prkachin, 1992b).

As discussed in chapter 11, there are also nonverbal behaviors associated with the Type A personality syndrome (a risk factor for heart attack). These include loud and explosive speech, suggestive of hostility. Indeed, many studies implicate hostility as a precursor to heart disease. In a recent study, facial expressions coded by the FACS (see chapter 9) were associated with transient occurrences of ischemia, a condition in which there is insuffient blood supply to the muscles of the heart (a predictor of serious and even fatal coronary events). Men with existing heart conditions were interviewed while their faces were videotaped and physiological measurements were made. Those experiencing episodes of ischemia showed more expressions suggestive of anger and more nonenjoyment smiles than those not showing ischemia (Rosenberg et al., 2001). Results such as these could influence physicians' care of these patients.

During medical education, physicians receive only a limited amount of training in communicating with patients, including recognizing patients' states and conditions through monitoring nonverbal cues. Clearly, physicians can use this kind of knowledge. However, it is also important that they make appropriate interpretations of the cues they see. In chapter 10 we reviewed a study in which surgery professors (erroneously) thought medical students knew less if the students used averted gaze during an oral examination. Picking up on nonverbal cues is good, but it is also crucial that the correct inferences are made about them. Nonverbal cues can also be tied to diagnostic judgments by considering them as an unobtrusive source of information on the patient's progress. Ellgring and Scherer (1996), Ostwald (1961), and others have found that vocal qualities, smiling, movement and other nonverbal behaviors can change following psychotherapy.

Thus far, we have discussed ways in which the clinician makes use of the client's cues. The client also studies the clinician's cues for signs of understanding, interest, approval, rejection, and reassurance. The clinician's nonverbal behavior may facilitate a good relationship, a high level of trust, and a good exchange of information—what are together called the "therapeutic alliance"—or it may make the client feel disregarded and misunderstood. Both patients and physicians are able to judge with some (though not great) accuracy how much they are liked by the other, certainly an impression that could have far-reaching consequences (Hall et al., 2002). In that study, patients whose doctors liked them less were less satisfied and more likely to consider changing doctors over the following year. Greater satisfaction and attributions of empathy are associated with doctors who gaze, lean forward, nod, gesture, and establish closer interpersonal distances (summarized in Hall, Harrigan, & Rosenthal, 1995). Sometimes certain combinations of physician cues have the best effect. Hall, Roter, and Rand (1981) found that patients were most satisfied when their physicians' voice tone was negative (e.g., anxious) combined with words that were positive. Sometimes physicians' nonverbal behaviors can signal a troubled history with patients. As noted in chapter 11, surgeons who were sued more had voices that suggested more dominance.

As noted in chapter 3, physicians who are better able to decode the meanings of nonverbal cues have patients who are more satisfied and more likely to keep their appointments (DiMatteo et al., 1980; DiMatteo, Hays, & Prince, 1986). Those researchers also found that physicians who were more accurate at expressing nonverbal emotion cues in a posed task had more satisfied and compliant patients. So far it is not known how these nonverbally skilled physicians put their skills into action in the medical encounter, but we can imagine that they might be good at showing empathy, creating a warm atmosphere, or picking up on the patient's unmentioned issues.

Medical educators now stress the importance of developing a good relationship with patients. It is a fallacy to think that physicians and patients are just enacting well-learned roles, or that physicians are cognitive machines that crank out professional behavior without feeling or showing emotions. Clinicians and clients (of all sorts) develop relationships—relationships of a unique and highly structured kind, but relationships nonetheless. Therefore, all that we know about the role nonverbal behavior in attraction, attitudes, impressions, rapport, emotions, and persuasion are relevant.

❖❖
❖

SUMMARY

Understanding the meaning of nonverbal behavior requires an understanding of context. This chapter examined various forms of nonverbal behavior in several familiar contexts—advertising, politics, education, culture, and therapy.

Nonverbal messages embedded in advertising can be extremely influential. A wide variety of nonverbal signals including music, hairstyle, clothing, possessions, responsiveness, and such are used to influence the viewer and/or hearer. When the target of the ads is distracted during the processing of the ad's information and there are multiple exposures to the ad, the impact can be even more powerful. These nonverbal signals not only help sell products, but they can also influence the viewer and/or hearer's expectations, perceptions, and attitudes related to actual daily social interaction.

Sometimes it seems like political candidates are obsessed with creating the "right" image, and more often than not displaying the "right" nonverbal signals is a compelling part of that image. Images of the candidate can be honed by carefully structuring the environment within which he or she is viewed (music, backdrops, others present) or it may be done through the candidate's looks (makeup, clothes, hairstyle) and behavior ("act more assertive"). On several occasions, the outcome of televised presidential debates have been attributed to nonverbal signals—calm demeanor versus tension, confidence versus uncertainty, warmth versus coldness, short versus tall, listening with interest versus smirking, and so on.

The learning process in elementary, secondary, and college classrooms is also influenced by nonverbal messages. Students whose nonverbal signals communicate liking and warmth get positive outcomes from their teachers, and they also believe they learn more from teachers who exhibit such behaviors. Some research, however, indicates that negative nonverbal behavior by a teacher can have positive outcomes for learning in the short run.

Some nonverbal behavior is common to human beings throughout the planet, but many of the behaviors we exhibit are taught to us by our culture. We explored three dimensions along which cultures vary in order to highlight cultural differences in nonverbal behavior. These dimensions focused on close versus distant behavior; behavior focused on highlighting the individual versus highlighting the group; and behavior which assumes a lot of contextual knowledge for interpretation versus behavior which assumes little contextual knowledge for interpretation. While these broad cultural characterizations are a useful place to start, it is important to remember that there are cultural variations that exist within them.

Therapy is another context in which nonverbal messages are crucial. Therapists rely on nonverbal signals to assist them in understanding and diagnosing depression, schizophrenia, autism, and pain, among others. Equally important are nonverbal signals which occur as part of the communication between therapist and patient during therapy. Both patient and therapist are especially attuned to cues that may signal emotions being felt.

In a similar manner physicians can learn to read nonverbal signals emanating from their patients, which can be valuable signs of an illness, fear, or how the patient feels about his or her physician. In the same way patients can use nonverbal signals to assess how their physician feels about their illness and their relationship.

QUESTIONS FOR DISCUSSION

1. Discuss how the nonverbal behavior of a patient and physician can mutually influence one another.

2. You are a consultant to a vibrant, physically appealing presidential candidate who is not a "deep thinker" and unable to make good arguments for his or her platform. What would you do to get this person elected? Now reverse the situation. You are advising a person who is a "deep thinker" and who is able to make good arguments for his or her platform, but this person is not dynamic and is physically unappealing. What do you do to get this person elected?

3. Suppose you were hired to advise incoming college freshmen on what nonverbal behavior they should enact to impress their teachers. What advice would you give?

4. In what ways do you think advertising influences your nonverbal behavior? Your perceptions of other people's nonverbal behavior?

5. Different cultures exhibit different nonverbal behavior and sometimes it causes communication problems when people from those different cultures interact. But it is also true that sometimes these differences occur and there are no problems. Under what conditions do you think problems would or would not occur?

BIBLIOGRAPHY

ADVERTISING MESSAGES

Archer, D., Iritani, B., Kimes, D. D., & Barrios, M. (1983). Face-ism: Five studies of sex differences in facial prominence. *Journal of Personality and Social Psychology, 45,* 725–735.

Bartsch, R. A., Burnett, T., Diller, T. R., & Rankin-Williams, E. (2000). Gender representation in television commercials: Updating an update. *Sex Roles, 43,* 735–743.

Browne, B. A. (1998). Gender stereotypes in advertising on children's television in the 1990s: A cross-national analysis. *Journal of Advertising, 27(1),* 83–96.

Burtt, H. E., & Clark, J. C. (1923). Facial expression in advertisements. *Journal of Applied Psychology, 7,* 114–125.

Chen, M., & Bargh, J. A. (1997). Nonconscious behavioral confirmation processes: The self-fulfilling consequences of automatic stereotype activation. *Journal of Experimental Social Psychology, 33,* 541–560.

Cialdini, R. B. (1993). *Influence: Science and practice,* 3rd ed. New York: HarperCollins.

Copeland, G. A. (1989). Face-ism and primetime television. *Journal of Broadcasting and Electronic Media, 33,* 209–214.

Cortese, A. J. (1999). *Provocateur: Images of women and minorities in advertising.* New York: Rowman & Littlefield.

Dodd, D. K., Harcar, V, Foerch, B. J., & Anderson, H. T. (1989). Face-ism and facial expressions of women in magazine photos. *Psychological Record, 39,* 325–331.

Ganahl, D. J., Prinsen, T. J., & Netzley, S. B. (2003). A content analysis of prime time commercials: A contextual framework of gender representation. *Sex Roles, 49,* 545–551.

Goffman, E. (1979). *Gender advertisements.* Cambridge, MA: Harvard University Press.

Halberstadt, A. G., & Saitta, M. B. (1987). Gender, nonverbal behavior, and perceived dominance: A test of the theory. *Journal of Personality and Social Psychology, 53,* 257–272.

Hazlett, R. L., & Hazlett, S. Y. (1999). Emotional response to television commercials: Facial EMG vs. self-report. *Journal of Advertising Research, 39,* 7–23.

Kang, M. (1997). The portrayal of women's images in magazine advertisements: Goffman's gender analysis revisited. *Sex Roles, 37,* 979–996.

Nisbett, R. E., & Wilson, T. D. (1977). Telling more than we can know: Verbal reports on mental processes. *Psychological Review, 84,* 231–259.

Petty, R. E., Cacioppo, J. T., & Schumann, D. (1983). Central and peripheral routes to advertising effectiveness: The moderating role of involvement. *Journal of Consumer Research, 10,* 135–146.

Raskin, A. (2003). A face any business can trust. *Business 2.0,* December, 58, 60.

Schwarz, N., & Kurz, E. (1989). What's in a picture? The impact of face-ism on trait attribution. *European Journal of Social Psychology, 19,* 311–316.

Wegner, D. M. (2002). *The illusion of conscious will.* Cambridge, MA: MIT Press.

Young, C. (2002). Brain waves, Picture Sorts, and branding moments. *Journal of Advertising Research, 42,* 42–53.

Zuckerman, M. (1986). On the meaning and implications of facial prominence. *Journal of Nonverbal Behavior, 10,* 215–229.

POLITICAL MESSAGES

Bryski, B. G., & Frye, J. K. (1979–1980). Nonverbal communication in presidential debates. *Australian Scan, 7* and *8,* 25–31.

Davis, M. (1995). Presidential body politics: Movement analysis of debates and press conferences. *Semiotica, 106,* 205–244.

Jamieson, K. H. (1988). *Eloquence in an electronic age.* New York: Oxford University Press.

Keating, C. F., Randall, D., & Kendrick, T. (1999). Presidential physiognomies: Altered images, altered perceptions. *Political Psychology, 20,* 593–610.

Kraus, S. (1996). Winners of the first 1960 televised presidential debate between Kennedy and Nixon. *Journal of Communication, 46,* 78–94.

Masters, R. D. (1989). *The nature of politics.* New Haven, CT: Yale University Press.

McGinnis, J. (1969). *The selling of the president 1968.* New York: Simon & Schuster.

Patterson, M. L., Churchill, M. E., Burger, G. K., & Powell, J. L. (1992). Verbal and nonverbal modality effects on impressions of political candidates: Analysis from the 1984 presidential debates. *Communication Monographs, 59,* 231–242.

Ritter, K., & Henry, D. (1990). The 1980 Reagan–Carter presidential debate. In R. V. Friedenberg (Ed.), *Rhetorical studies of national political debates: 1960–1988.* New York: Praeger.

Sullivan, D. G., Masters, R. D., Lanzetta, J. T., McHugo, G. J., Plate, E., & Englis, B. G. (1991). Facial displays and political leadership. In G. Schubert & R. Masters (Eds.), *Primate politics.* Carbondale: University of Southern Illinois Press.

Tiemens, R. K. (1978). Television's portrayal of the 1976 presidential debates: An analysis of visual content. *Communication Monographs, 45,* 362–370.

Vancil, D. L., & Pendell, S. D. (1987). The myth of viewer–listener disagreement in the first Kennedy–Nixon debate. *Central States Speech Journal, 38,* 16–27.

Woodward, B. (2004). *Plan of attack.* New York: Simon & Schuster.

TEACHER–STUDENT MESSAGES

Andersen, P. A., & Andersen, J. (1982). Nonverbal immediacy in instruction. In L. L. Barker (Ed.), *Communication in the classroom.* Englewood Cliffs, NJ: Prentice-Hall.

Babad, E. (1992). Teacher expectancies and nonverbal behavior. In R. S. Feldman (Ed.), *Applications of nonverbal behavioral theories and research.* Hillsdale, NJ: Erlbaum.

Baringer, D. K., and McCroskey, J. C. (2000). Immediacy in the classroom: Student immediacy. *Communication Education, 49,* 178–186.

Blanck, P. D. (Ed.). (1993). *Interpersonal expectations: Theory, research, and applications.* New York: Cambridge University Press.

Chaikin, A. L., Sigler, E., & Derlega, V. J. (1974). Nonverbal mediators of teacher expectancy effects. *Journal of Personality and Social Psychology, 30,* 144–149.

Feldman, R. S. (1985). Nonverbal behavior, race, and the classroom teacher. *Theory Into Practice, 24,* 45–49.

Freedman, D. P., & Holmes, M. S. (2003). *The teacher's body: Embodiment, authority, and identity in the academy.* Albany, NY: State University of New York Press.

Goldin-Meadow, S., Kim, S., & Singer, M. (1999). What the teacher's hands tell the student's mind about math. *Journal of Educational Psychology, 91,* 720–730.

Guerrero, L. K. & Miller, T. A. (1998). Associations between nonverbal behaviors and initial impressions of instructor competence and course content in videotaped distance education courses. *Communication Education, 47,* 30–42.

Harris, M. J., & Rosenthal, R. (1985). The mediation of interpersonal expectancy effects: 31 meta-analyses. *Psychological Bulletin, 97,* 363–386.

Harris, M. J., & Rosenthal, R. (in press). Nonverbal behavior and education. In R. E. Riggio & R. S. Feldman (Eds.), *Applications of nonverbal communication.* Mahwah, NJ: Erlbaum.

McCroskey, J. C., & Richmond, V. P. (1992). Increasing teacher influence through inmediacy. In V. P. Richmond & J. C. McCroskey (Eds.), *Power in the classroom: Communication, control, and concern* (pp. 101–119). Hillsdale, NJ: Erlbaum.

Mottet, T. P. (2000). Interactive television instructors' perceptions of students' nonverbal responsiveness and their influence on distance teaching. *Communication Education, 49,* 146–164.

Mottet, T. P., Beebe, S. A., Raffeld, P. C., & Paulsel, M. L. (2004). The effects of student verbal and nonverbal responsiveness on teachers' liking of students and willingness to comply with student requests. *Communication Quarterly, 52,* 27–38.

Philippot, P., Feldman, R. S., & McGee, G. (1992). Nonverbal behavioral skills in an educational context: Typical and atypical populations. In R. S. Feldman (Ed.), *Applications of nonverbal behavioral theories and research*. Hillsdale, NJ: Erlbaum.

Rosenthal, R. (1985). Nonverbal cues in the mediation of interpersonal expectancy effects. In A. W. Siegman & S. Feldstein (Eds.), *Multichannel integration of nonverbal behavior* (pp. 105–128). Hillsdale, NJ: Erlbaum.

Rosenthal, R. (2002). Covert communication in classrooms, clinics, courtrooms, and cubicles. *American Psychologist, 57,* 839–849.

Rosenthal, R., & Jacobson, L. (1968). *Pygmalion in the classroom.* New York: Irvington.

Wolfgang, A. (Ed.). (1984). *Nonverbal behavior: Perspectives, applications, intercultural insights.* New York: Hogrefe.

Woolfolk, A. E., & Brooks, D. M. (1983). Nonverbal communication in teaching. In E. Gordon (Ed.), *Review of Research in Education, 10*. Washington, DC: American Educational Research Association.

Woolfolk, R. L. (1978). Student learning and performance under varying conditions of teacher verbal and nonverbal evaluative communication. *Journal of Educational Psychology, 70,* 87–94.

Cultural Messages

Aiello, J. R., & Thompson, D. E. (1980). Personal space, crowding, and spatial behavior in a cultural context. In I. Altman, A. Rapoport, & J. F. Wohlwill (Eds.), *Human behavior and environment* (Vol. 4). New York: Plenum.

Altman, I., & Chemers, M. M. (1988). *Culture and environment.* New York: Cambridge University Press.

Andersen, P. A., Hecht, M. L., Hoobler, G. D., & Smallwood, M. (2002). Nonverbal communication across cultures. In W. B. Gudykunst & B. Moody (Eds.), *Handbook of international and intercultural communication* (pp. 89–106). 2nd ed. Thousand Oaks, CA: Sage.

Armstrong, N., & Wagner, M. (2003). *Field guide to gestures.* Philadelphia: Quirk Books.

Barnlund, D. C. (1975). Communicative styles in two cultures: Japan and the United States. In A. Kendon, R. M. Harris, & M. R. Key (Eds.), *Organization of behavior in face-to-face interaction.* The Hague: Mouton.

Collett, P. (1971). Training Englishmen in the non-verbal behavior of Arabs: An experiment of intercultural communication. *International Journal of Psychology, 6,* 209–215.

Cunningham, M. R., Barbee, A. P., & Philhower, C. L. (2002). Dimensions of facial physical attractiveness: The intersection of biology and culture. In G. Rhodes & L. A. Zebrowitz (Eds.), *Facial attractiveness* (pp. 193–238). Westport, CT: Ablex.

Dion, K. K. (2002). Cultural perspectives on facial attractiveness. In G. Rhodes & L. A. Zebrowitz (Eds.), *Facial attractiveness* (pp. 239–259). Westport, CT: Ablex.

Draper, P. (1973). Crowding among hunter-gatherers: The !Kung bushmen. *Science, 182,* 301–303.

Ectoff, N. (1999). *Survival of the prettiest.* New York: Random House.

Ekman, P. (2003). *Emotions revealed*. New York: Times Books.

Ekman, P., Sorenson, E. R., & Friesen, W. V. (1969). Pan-cultural elements in facial displays of emotions. *Science, 164,* 86–88.

Evans, G. W., Lepore, S. J., & Allen, K. M. (2000). Cross-cultural differences in tolerance for crowding: Fact or fiction? *Journal of Personality and Social Psychology, 79,* 204–210.

Field, T. (1999). American adolescents touch each other less and are more aggressive toward their peers as compared with French adolescents. *Adolescence, 34,* 753–758.

Garber, L. L., Jr. & Hyatt, E. M. (2003). Color as a tool for visual persuasion, in L. M. Scott and R. Batra (Eds.), *Persuasive imagery: A consumer response perspective* (pp. 313–336). Mahwah, NJ: Erlbaum.

Gudykunst, W. B., & Ting-Toomey, S. (1988). *Culture and interpersonal communication.* Newbury Park, CA: Sage.

Halberstadt, A. G. (1985). Race, socioeconomic status, and nonverbal behavior. In A. W. Siegman and S. Feldstein (Eds.), *Multichannel integrations of nonverbal behavior.* Hillsdale, NJ: Erlbaum.

Hall, E. T. (1966). *The hidden dimension.* New York: Doubleday Anchor.

Hall, E. T. (1976). *Beyond culture.* Garden City, NY: Doubleday/Anchor Books.

Hofstede, G. (2001). *Culture's consequences* (2nd Ed.). Thousand Oaks, CA: Sage.

Jourard, S. M. (1966). An exploratory study of body-accessibility. *British Journal of Social and Clinical Psychology, 26,* 235–242.

Langlois, J. H., Roggman, L. A., & Rieser-Danner, L. A. (1990). Infants' differential social responses to attractive and unattractive faces. *Developmental Psychology, 26,* 153–159.

Lee, M. E., Matsumoto, D., Kobayashi, M., Krupp, D., Maniatis, E. F., & Roberts, W. (1992). Cultural influences on nonverbal behavior in applied settings. In R. S. Feldman (Ed.), *Applications of nonverbal behavioral theories and research* (pp. 239–261). Hillsdale, NJ: Erlbaum.

Levine, R. (1997). *A geography of time: The temporal misadventures of a social psychologist or how every culture keeps time just a little bit differently.* New York: Basic.

Matsumoto, D. (2001). Culture and emotion. In D. Matsumoto (Ed.), *The handbook of culture and psychology* (pp. 171–194). New York: Oxford University Press.

Matsumoto, D., & Yoo, S. H. (in press). Culture and applied nonverbal communication. In R. E. Riggio & R. S. Feldman (Eds.), *Applications of nonverbal communication.* Mahwah, NJ: Erlbaum.

McDaniel, E., & Andersen, P. A. (1998). International patterns of interpersonal tactile communication: A field study. *Journal of Nonverbal Behavior, 22,* 59–73.

Morris, D., Collett, P., Marsh, P., & O'Shaughnessy, M. (1980). *Gestures: Their origins and distribution.* New York: Scarborough.

Munroe, R. L., & Munroe, R. H. (1972). Population density and affective relationships in three East African societies. *Journal of Social Psychology, 88,* 15–20.

Poyatos, F. (Ed.) (1988). *Cross-cultural perspectives in nonverbal communication.* Toronto: C.J. Hogrefe.

Regan, P. C., Jerry, D., Narvaez, M., & Johnson, D. (1999). Public displays of affection among Asian and Latino heterosexual couples. *Psychological Reports, 84,* 1201–1202.

Remland, M. S., Jones, T. S., & Brinkman, H. (1991). Proxemic and haptic behavior in three European countries. *Journal of Nonverbal Behavior, 15,* 215–232.

Rhodes, G., Harwood, K., Yoshikawa, S., Nishitani, M., & McLean, I. (2002). The attractiveness of average faces: Cross-cultural evidence and possible biological basis. In G. Rhodes & L. A. Zebrowitz (Eds.), *Facial attractiveness* (pp. 35–58). Westport, CT: Ablex.

Rosenthal, R., Hall, J. A., DiMatteo, M. R., Robers, P. L., & Archer, D. (1979). *Sensitivity to nonverbal communication: The PONS test.* Baltimore: Johns Hopkins University Press.

Shuter, R. (1976). Proxemics and tactility in Latin America. *Journal of Communication, 26,* 46–52.

Shuter, R. (1977). A field study of non-verbal communication in Germany, Italy and the United States. *Communication Monographs, 44,* 298–305.

Touchy topic: What to do when a handshake isn't enough? (2000, February 16). *Boston Globe,* pp. A1, A20.

Triandis, H. C. (1994). Theoretical and methodological approaches to the study of collectivism and individualism. In U. Kim, H. Triandis, C. Kâgitçibasi, S.-C. Choi, & G. Yoon (Eds.), *Individualism and collectivism: Theory, methods, and applications* (pp. 41–51). Thousand Oaks, CA: Sage.

Willis, F. N., & Rawdon, V. A. (1994). Gender and national differences in attitudes toward same-gender touch. *Perceptual and Motor Skills, 78,* 1027–1034.

THERAPEUTIC SETTINGS

Bensing, J. M., Kerssens, J. J., & van der Pasch, M. (1995). Patient-directed gaze as a tool for discovering and handling psychosocial problems in general practice. *Journal of Nonverbal Behavior, 19,* 223–242.

Bouhuys, A. L. (2003). Ethology and depression. In P. Philippot, R. S. Feldman, & E. J. Coats (Eds.), *Nonverbal behavior in clinical settings.* Oxford, UK: Oxford University Press.

DiMatteo, M. R., Hays, R. D., & Prince, L. M. (1986). Relationship of physicians' nonverbal communication skill to patient satisfaction, appointment noncompliance, and physician workload. *Health Psychology, 5,* 581–594.

DiMatteo, M. R., Taranta, A., Friedman, H. A., & Prince, L. M. (1980). Predicting patient satisfaction from physicians' nonverbal communication skills. *Medical Care, 18,* 376–387.

Ekman, P., & Friesen, W. V. (1974). Nonverbal behavior and psychopathology. In R. J. Friedman & M. M. Katz (Eds.), *The psychology of depression: Contemporary theory and research.* Washington, DC: Winston and Sons.

Ellgring, H. (1986). Nonverbal expression of psychological states in psychiatric patients. *European Archives of Psychiatric Neurological Science, 236,* 31–34.

Ellgring, H., & Scherer, K. R. (1996). Vocal indicators of mood change in depression. *Journal of Nonverbal Behavior, 20,* 83–110.

Hall, J. A., Harrigan, J. A., & Rosenthal, R. (1995). Nonverbal behavior in clinician–patient interaction. *Applied and Preventive Psychology, 4,* 21–37.

Hall, J. A., Horgan, T. G., Stein, T. S., & Roter, D. L. (2002). Liking in the physician–patient relationship. *Patient Education and Counseling, 48,* 69–77.

Hall, J. A., Roter, D. L., & Rand, C. S. (1981). Communication of affect between patient and physician. *Journal of Health and Social Behavior, 22,* 18–30.

Irish, J. T., & Hall, J. A. (1995). Interruptive patterns in medical visits: The effects of role, status, and gender. *Social Science & Medicine, 41,* 873–881.

Kring, A. M., & Earnst, K. S. (2003). Nonverbal behavior in schizophrenia. In P. Philippot, R. S. Feldman, & E. J. Coats (Eds.), *Nonverbal behavior in clinical settings.* Oxford, UK: Oxford University Press.

LeResche, L., Dworkin, S. F., Wilson, L., & Ehrlich, K. J. (1992). Effect of temporomandibular disorder pain duration on facial expressions and verbal report of pain. *Pain, 51,* 289–295.

McGee, G., & Morrier, M. (2003). Clinical implications of research in nonverbal behavior of children with autism. In P. Philippot, R. S. Feldman, & E. J. Coats (Eds.), *Nonverbal behavior in clinical settings.* Oxford, UK: Oxford University Press.

Ostwald, P. F. (1961). The sounds of emotional disturbance. *Archives of General Psychiatry, 5,* 587–592.

Patrick, C. J., Craig, K. D., & Prkachin, K. M. (1986). Observer judgments of acute pain: Facial action determinants. *Journal of Personality and Social Psychology, 50,* 1291–1298.

Perez, J. E., & Riggio, R. E. (2003). Nonverbal social skills and psychopathology. In P. Philippot, R. S. Feldman, & E. J. Coats (Eds.), *Nonverbal behavior in clinical settings.* Oxford, UK: Oxford University Press.

Philippot, P., Feldman, R. S., & Coats, E. J. (Eds.). (2003). *Nonverbal behavior in clinical settings.* Oxford, UK: Oxford University Press.

Philippot, P., Kornreich, C., & Blairy, S. (2003). Nonverbal deficits and interpersonal regulation in alcoholics. In P. Philippot, R. S. Feldman, & E. J. Coats (Eds.), *Nonverbal behavior in clinical settings.* Oxford, UK: Oxford University Press.

Prkachin, K. M. (1992a). The consistency of facial expressions of pain: A comparison across modalities. *Pain, 51,* 297–306.

Prkachin, K. M. (1992b). Dissociating spontaneous and deliberate expressions of pain: Signal detection analyses. *Pain, 51,* 57–65.

Rosenberg, E. L., Ekman, P., Jiang, W., Babyak, M., Coleman, R. E., Hanson, M., O'Connor, C., Waugh, R., & Blumenthal, J. A. (2001). Linkages between facial expressions of anger and transient myocardial ischemia in men with coronary artery disease. *Emotion, 1,* 107–115.

Waxer, P. (1976). Nonverbal cues for depth of depression: Set versus no set. *Journal of Consulting and Clinical Psychology, 44,* 493.

PHOTO CREDITS

AUTHOR INDEX

This index refers the reader only to those authors and their works cited in the text itself. Additional references to these authors and others not cited here can be found in the bibliographies at the end of each chapter and in the Photo Credits on page 476.

SUBJECT INDEX

Note: Photographs, illustrations, tables, figures, discussion questions, and bibliography are not indexed.

Discrepancy, 12–15, 371, 436, 458. (*See also* Contradictory cues, Joking, Sarcasm.)
Discrepancy arousal theory, 418
Discrimination, 191, 194, 198–200, 327, 453
Disgust, 10, 34, 39, 54, 56–57, 80, 226, 297, 310–311, 314–316, 326, 329, 345–346, 386, 388, 398, 436
Display rules, 32, 35, 56, 58, 82–84, 299–300, 328
Distance, 22, 52, 89, 101, 104, 106–107, 120, 125–129, 141–142, 147–155, 191, 247, 266, 352, 361, 418, 421, 432–434, 436, 460, 462, 467, 469. (*See also* Personal Space, Proxemics/proximity.)
Distance education, 462
Distress, 38, 45, 286, 343
Doctor/nurse-patient communication, 14, 22
Dominance, 11, 23, 52, 57, 64, 79, 81–84, 107, 129, 138, 143–144, 154–156, 162, 196, 199, 207, 253, 267, 270, 349, 353, 371–372, 378, 382, 384–385, 395, 419–422, 424, 430, 432, 435, 440, 454–456, 468. (*See also* Power, Status, Submissiveness, Subordinates.)
Dormitories, 124–125, 129
Dousing rod, 283
Dress, 18, 21, 141–142, 171, 173, 179, 196, 200, 202–209, 279, 284, 287, 412–414, 420, 425, 428–429, 453, 455–456, 458, 460, 464, 468. (*See also* Artifacts, Jewelry, Uniforms.)
Dress codes, 204
Drivers, 111, 140, 351
Duchenne smiles, 307–311, 323, 325–326, 339, 385–386. (*See also* Enjoyment/nonenjoyment smiles.)
Duping delight, 437

Ears, 186, 198, 204, 284
Ecological validity, 72
Ectomorph, 19, 188–191
Education, 23, 183, 192, 381, 420, 439, 453, 467–468. (*See also* Schools, Social class, Teachers.)
Elderly. (*See* Aging.)
Electric shock, 66, 85, 323, 326
Electromyographic responses (EMG), 311, 325, 328
Electronic filtering, 69
Elevation, 420
Elevators, 107–108, 145
Elocution, 18
Embarrassment, 15, 53, 142, 195, 271, 320–321, 344, 355, 361, 418
Emblems, 20, 226–236, 297, 424. (*See also* Facial emblems.)
Embrace, 45, 48, 268, 271, 281, 417, 424, 463
Emotions, 9–12, 15–16, 19, 32, 35, 38–39, 45, 53–57, 63–65, 68–70, 72, 74, 79, 81–84, 86, 107, 109, 113, 129, 142, 150, 153, 196–197, 250, 253, 265, 266, 268, 271, 273, 275, 277, 281, 286, 288, 295, 297–307, 312–329, 339, 341, 343–345, 354–356, 358, 360–361, 374, 383–389, 391, 394–395, 398, 411, 417,

422–423, 429, 432, 434, 436–438, 455, 464, 466, 468–469. (*See also* specific emotions.)
Emotion blends, 32, 45, 47, 300, 302, 312, 344, 417
Emotion dialects, 319
Emotional contagion, 250, 325, 343, 384. (*See also* Mimicry, Motor mimicry, Reciprocation, Synchrony.)
Emotional disturbance, 78
Emotional intelligence, 63
Emotional intensity, 434
Emotional suppression, 83
Empathic accuracy paradigm, 72, 76
Empathy, 45, 64, 76–77, 154, 250, 325, 356, 432, 467–468
Encoding. (*See* Accuracy of expression.)
Encoding-decoding relation, 85, 90
Endomorph, 19, 154, 188–191
Enjoyment/nonenjoyment smiles, 77, 339, 385–386, 455, 467. (*See also* Duchenne smiles.)
Environment, 7–8, 18–19, 24, 32–33, 41, 52–53, 85, 87, 101–130, 144–145, 198, 275, 281, 283–284, 288, 314, 326, 341, 354–355, 397, 452, 458, 464, 468
Equilibrium theory, 418. (*See also* Intimacy equilibrium model.)
Ethnicity, 33, 78, 105, 127, 140, 147, 149, 151–152, 162, 192, 205, 240, 266, 269, 318, 380, 422, 463. (*See also* African-American, Culture, In-group advantage, Race.)
Evolution, 33–34, 298, 305, 465. (*See also* Phylogeny.)
Expectations, 74, 88, 350, 380, 382, 398, 418–419, 434–435, 439, 452–453, 460–462, 468
Exposure time, 72, 81
Expressiveness, 82–85, 296, 321–323, 325–326, 329, 378, 381, 418, 422, 433–434, 458, 466
Extralinguistic phenomena. (*See* Vocal behavior.)
Extrasensory perception, 76
Extraversion, 44, 74, 77, 83–84, 116, 154–155, 160–161, 207, 296, 353, 358, 361, 377–379, 398, 429. (*See also* Shyness.)
Eye behavior, 10–11, 16–22, 24, 33–34, 39, 45, 52–53, 85, 87, 101–130, 120, 125, 140–142, 149 151, 156, 158–159, 174, 229, 250, 274, 284, 297, 320, 326, 338–362, 412–414, 431, 433, 452, 456, 461, 466; movements to left or right, 344. (*See also* Eye blink, Eye flash, Eyebrow flash, Eyes, Gaze, Gaze aversion/gaze avoidance, Visual dominance ratio.)
Eye blink, 244, 320, 339, 357, 437, 456
Eye color, 338–339
Eye contact. (*See* Eye behavior, Gaze.)
Eye flash, 239, 339
Eye patches, 338–339
Eye rings, 338, 361
Eye spots, 339, 361
Eyebrows, 22, 39, 65, 82, 176, 186, 200, 204, 227, 239, 252, 297–298, 302, 306–307, 311, 324, 327, 338–339,

344–346, 361, 425, 465–467. (*See also* Eyebrow flash.)
Eyebrow flash, 17, 53–54, 84, 239, 297, 339, 424, 427, 465. (*See also* Eyebrows.)
Eyes, 176, 184, 186, 295, 300, 302, 307, 311, 325, 338–362, 354, 360, 411, 458, 467. (*See also* other Eye entries, Pupil size.)

Face, side of 327
Face-ism, 327, 455
Facial Action Coding System (FACS), 34, 306–311, 316, 329, 467
Facial emblems, 227, 297–298, 328
Facial expressions, 9–10, 13, 16, 18, 20, 24, 32–35, 37–39, 41, 45, 47, 51, 53–57, 65–67, 69–70, 72, 76, 78–85, 89, 144, 229, 250, 252, 268, 295–329, 350, 371, 386, 389, 391, 411–412, 415, 417, 428, 433, 436, 452–453, 456, 458, 460, 465, 467. (*See also* Affect displays, Display rules, Expressiveness, Facial emblems, Facial gestures, Micromomentary expressions.)
Facial features, 171, 183–187, 193, 295–296, 328
Facial feedback. (*See* Feedback.)
Facial gestures, 239. (*See also* Facial emblems, Facial expressions.)
Facial hair, 43, 179, 198–202, 428, 456. (*See also* Body hair.)
Facial primacy, 295
Facial recognition, 64, 86
Facilitated communication, 283–284
Fame, 278–280, 324
Familiarity, 106–107, 114, 129, 144, 147, 182, 269, 314–315, 375, 391, 417, 425–426, 434, 464
Family environment, 85
Family Expressiveness Questionnaire (FEQ), 85
Fear, 10, 32, 34, 39, 45–46, 48, 51, 54–57, 72, 297, 307, 310–312, 315–316, 320, 323–324, 329, 338, 345–346, 354, 384, 386–388, 395, 398, 433, 436–437, 456, 458, 469
Fear grimace, 47, 458
Feedback, 65–66, 85, 90, 286, 295, 300, 311, 323–325, 327–329, 341–343, 353, 360–361, 392, 395, 419, 427, 438, 460–461
Feet, 18, 43, 280, 287, 426, 428, 436
Feminine/femininity, 184, 192, 378
Fidgeting, 437, 460
Filled pauses, 387, 392–395, 422, 426
Film, 23
Fingerprints, 377
Fingers, 40, 43, 65, 413, 426, 429. (*See also* Emblems, Gestures.)
Fixed feature, 114
Flatus/flatulence, 198
Flirting/flirtacious, 53, 297, 346, 412–414
Forehead, 184, 186, 198, 295–296, 302, 306–307
Foreign service officers, 79
Formality, 105–107, 122–123, 129, 142, 274, 375, 413, 426